Guide to
THE BEST
BUSINESS SCHOOLS

EIGHTH EDITION

Guide to
THE BEST
BUSINESS SCHOOLS

EIGHTH EDITION

Jennifer Merritt

Management Education Editor, *BusinessWeek*

with

Elizabeth Garone
Kathryn Beaumont
Mica Schneider

McGraw-Hill

New York   Chicago   San Francisco
Lisbon   London   Madrid   Mexico City
Milan   New Delhi   San Juan   Seoul
Singapore   Sydney   Toronto

The **McGraw·Hill** Companies

2 3 4 5 6 7 8 9 0   DOC/DOC   0 9 8 7 6 5 4

ISBN 0-07-141521-1 (PBK)

McGraw-Hill books are available at special quantity discounts to use as premiums and sales promotions, or for use in corporate training programs. For more information, please write to the Director of Special Sales, McGraw-Hill, Professional Publishing, Two Penn Plaza, New York, NY 10121-2298. Or contact your local bookstore.

This book is printed on recycled, acid-free paper containing a minimum of 50% recycled, de-inked fiber.

Library of Congress Cataloging-in-Publication Data

BusinessWeek guide to the best business schools.—8th ed. / by Jennifer Merritt with Elizabeth Garone, Kathryn Beaumont, Mica Schneider.
        p. cm.
Rev. ed. of: BusinessWeek guide to the best business schools / Betsy Gruber, Margaret Littman, Jennifer Merritt.
ISBN 0-07-141521-1 (alk. paper)
    1. Business schools—United States—Evaluation.   2. College choice—United States—Handbooks, manuals, etc.   3. Master of business administration degree—United States—Handbooks, manuals, etc.
I. Title: BusinessWeek guide to the best business schools.   II. Merritt, Jennifer.
III. Gruber, Betsy. BusinessWeek guide to the best business schools.
    HF1131.B95 2003
    650'.071'173—dc21   2003007869

BusinessWeek

CONTENTS

PREFACE

Scratching your head trying to figure out whether or not to get an MBA—and where to get one if the answer sounds like a yes? You've come to the right place. You are now reading the eighth and most comprehensive edition of a book that is considered the bible for all students and observers of graduate schools of business. Hundreds of thousands of applicants have relied on earlier versions of this book for its wealth of unvarnished, tell-it-like-it-is information and analysis of the top MBA programs. Deans and recruiters also use this guide as a benchmark of how well they've put their ideas and strategies into place.

For this guide, *BusinessWeek* magazine used as primary research material the thousands of surveys of graduates and corporate recruiters collected for its most recent ranking of business schools. That was just the beginning: next, the staff interviewed hundreds of students, alumni, recruiters, faculty members, and deans to gain an even better understanding of the strengths and weaknesses of the top schools. The result is this book—a product that reveals far more information and intelligence on the best B-schools than exists anywhere else.

This guidebook is an outgrowth of *BusinessWeek*'s biennial ranking of the best business schools, a project first tackled in 1988. Since then, the magazine has carved out management education as an important and critical area of coverage. It's a mission that extends far beyond the pages of the magazine. *BusinessWeek* online, for example, has an extensive site devoted to the best business schools, including lengthy profiles of the more than 90 schools surveyed in 2002. Featured are helpful statistics, links to schools' Web sites, and dozens of student comments from the surveys. This year, there are even more profiles on nonranked schools—more than 300 total B-schools, divided by geographic region. There's a return-on-investment calculator that helps you determine the true costs of any one program and a host of transcripts of chats with students at the top schools. And there are dozens of video interviews with B-school deans, admissions officers, and placement directors. You can download the transcripts of online conferences with admissions and placement professionals, read the journals of current and recently graduated MBA students, and post a question on a variety of message boards to be answered by *BusinessWeek* staffers or other visitors to the site. You can access the site at www.businessweek.com/bschools or by going to keyword BW on America Online.

The authors for this eighth edition are *BusinessWeek* management education editor Jennifer Merritt; Elizabeth Garone, a freelance writer in Silicon Valley; Kathryn Beaumont, a freelance writer in Princeton, New Jersey; and Mica Schneider, a former *BusinessWeek* online reporter. Merritt, who is based in New York, is responsible for *BusinessWeek*'s coverage of management education and directed the 2000 and 2002 rankings projects. The format for this book follows that used by *BusinessWeek* senior writer John A. Byrne, who authored the first five editions and created the *BusinessWeek* ranking of the top schools back in 1988.

Making significant contributions to this book were *BusinessWeek* online reporter Brian Hindo, who assisted in the research; and Geoffrey Gloeckler and Ana Mantica, former *BusinessWeek* interns on the rankings project, who combined wrote more than a dozen of the school profiles. *BusinessWeek* intern Rebecca Weber also helped put together statistics and tables for the book. Both Gloeckler and Mantica assisted in research and survey response gathering for the rankings project. Frederick Jespersen served as our number-crunching guru and provided invaluable survey analysis. Cambria Consulting created and managed the online portion of the survey. Hindo; producer Jessica Loudon; and technical gurus Joshua Tanzer, Arthur Eves, and Matthew Kopit managed the flow of information to the Web site. Managing Editor Mark Morrison and Assistant Managing Editor Frank Comes supervised the project.

WHY GO FOR THE MBA?

A soaring stock market. Plentiful venture capital. An economy—and job base—growing at unprecedented rates. Six-figure salaries and jobs aplenty. Those used to be some of the deciding factors for getting an MBA. And why not? The sky was the limit and the MBA paraded as the ticket to anywhere; managing on the upswing was more than just appealing, it was the way of business, and the MBA was the tool to have to figure it all out and bring blessings to the bottom line. The choices were limitless, as grads in 1999 and 2000 were showered with half a dozen or more job offers months before donning cap and gown. But that was the 1990s. This is a new decade, and the world faces a different economic reality where 30 percent of the class of 2002 at the top 30 schools found themselves without a job offer at graduation.

Given the new reality, it might seem that the MBA has lost its luster, and some might question whether or not it's even worth it to forgo two years of salary and ante up tuitions upward of $70,000, especially when doing so might not bring you the immediate success it did just three years ago. But, in today's climate, the MBA might be one of the most worthwhile degrees in the marketplace. In fact, down to almost the last jobless graduate in 2002, newly minted MBAs will tell you that it's the best investment they've ever made—instant job or not.

And that's just what the MBA has always been—a long-term investment in career and future successes as a manager. In the heady days of the boom, the MBA was touted as an instant entrée to success and riches, but it still remains what it was well before the boom—a degree that will pack your brain full of the skills and terms and knowledge that you'll need to be a successful manager. "Smart, idealistic students still go to law schools despite the endless flow of lawyer jokes because a law degree gives them the tools to make a positive difference in the world," says Richard Schmalensee, dean of MIT's Sloan School of Management. "Smart, idealistic students are going to management schools for the same reason."

It's a combination of technical and practical skills, a sometimes brutal two-year boot camp in which you learn to deconstruct a balance sheet, negotiate a raise, and make buddies and

> The MBA is a worthwhile investment for the long term.

1

business contacts everywhere on the planet. Says Donald P. Jacobs, former dean of Northwestern University's Kellogg School of Management: "Twenty-five years ago, the degree was something that mimicked best practices. Since then, it has become a research-based curriculum that is really at the frontier."

But more than that, "the MBA provides both a door opener for career opportunities and, more importantly, the knowledge to be a better manager," says Bruce Willison, dean of UCLA's Anderson School. Indeed, despite a spate of scandals in the business world, and a soft economy, the MBA—particularly from an elite school—is still one of the hottest degrees you can hold. The stats prove it: at virtually all of the best schools, GMAT scores and starting pay packages are setting records. Applications are, too, and not just from out-of-work investment bankers or dot-com dropouts. Domestic applications had been relatively flat, in part because so many Americans didn't want to miss out on the thriving economy, but that application pool has picked up. The 88 U.S., Canadian, Latin American, and European schools surveyed by *BusinessWeek* for its 2002 rankings waded through some 170,000 applications for the class of 2002, and the average GMAT score was 679 for those attending the top 30 schools, up from 672 just two years earlier. And applications were up by double digits for the class entering fall of 2002.

This isn't terribly surprising, because in past decades MBA education has been a countercyclical phenomenon—something you did when the job market was shaky and you wanted to stand out when people were hiring again. But, bad economy or good, more and more twentysomethings are considering earning an MBA. Today, the MBA is on its way to becoming a requirement for anyone who hopes to build a career in corporate America—and, indeed, much of the world. "A capitalist society needs well-trained business school graduates who can apply cross-disciplinary principles that create value," says William Christie, dean of Vanderbilt University's Owen School. Indeed, some deans say the biggest social contribution a business school makes is to churn out leaders who can manage through good times and bad.

Certainly, even in an economic slump, corporate recruiters continue to hire MBAs these days, and those that have cut hiring consistently say they'll be back when the economy—and business—picks up. The 247 recruiters who participated in *Business-Week*'s 2000 survey of the best business schools hired 15,558 MBAs

MBA's are always in demand in the corporate world.

in total, while in 2002, the 219 companies that participated hired 11,199—more in line with the number of MBAs hired in 1998 (about 11,000). The median pay package (salary, bonus, and extras such as stock options or moving expenses) at the top 30 schools is still quite respectable—$110,970, down 12.6 percent from the heady days of the boom the class of 2000 experienced—but salary alone did not decline. Much of the decline came in the form of signing bonuses, which had regularly topped $25,000 but have since fallen to more earthly amounts, averaging $15,000. Another telling figure: median pay topped $100,000 at 25 of our top 30 schools, versus 5 only a half-dozen years ago.

Those numbers come from the top of the heap. Grads of the very best B-schools weren't as able to hold all the cards in the recruiting game in 2002, but there were jobs to be found—and a lot of soul-searching on the parts of grads trying to discern what it was they wanted to do. With jobs not falling from trees as they were in 2000—when grads usually had half a dozen offers—the class of 2002 went back to the basics with one or two carefully researched and well-interviewed choices. One thing the down economy has done is create a wider gap between the upper-echelon schools and the second tier, and between the second tier and other schools. What that means is that you should try to attend the best school possible, as recruiters with fewer slots to fill drop the middle-of-the-road schools from their rosters and target only the very best.

The main reason for the MBA's current success is that the degree has changed significantly over the last decade or so. B-schools have listened to their customers—their students and the recruiters who hire them—and reinvented themselves as learning laboratories where students gain the ability to immediately add value to their place of work. The first and most radical change is the injection of real-world experience into the degree program itself. Although you may imagine B-school as a quiet, contemplative experience full of staid, sweater-clad, pipe-smoking profs, think again: B-school is fast-moving, exciting, in many cases collegial, and more relevant than it's ever been.

Start with your physical surroundings, which are likely to be a lot more comfortable and more high-tech than you probably imagine. Almost all of *BusinessWeek*'s top 30 schools have opened brand-new facilities or significant additions since the mid-1990s

Try to attend the best school possible.

or are planning to break ground within the next few years. Deans now spend a large part of their time on the road, raising millions so that they can offer their students glistening new buildings (some including everything from showers to a concierge desk to a burrito joint), comfortable placement facilities, and the best in technology. Indeed, you might think of B-school as a way to catch up with the real world rather than to check out of it. At Cornell's Johnson Graduate School of Management, for example, the Parker Center offers a simulated trading floor with the same analyst software used by the most tech-savvy professionals. And the University of Texas's McCombs School has an even more sophisticated trading floor and learning lab.

WHAT WILL YOU LEARN?

It's not simply the physical plant that has changed. Today, not only do professors spend much of their time consulting with companies, but students do too. At more and more schools, tackling a real-time project for a real-life company—in which a student may have to present his or her findings to the senior management team—is part of the degree. At Washington University's Olin School of Business, for example, four-student teams spend a full semester working with client companies, and the companies pay the school for the services of its "consultants," who also can make some money, depending on performance. And, with executive education booming on the same campuses that offer the full-time programs, both students and faculty are interacting on a regular basis with working executives. Schools are also grasping the fact that leadership skills and teamwork, ignored in the past by academic institutions and companies alike, make as much of a difference to a company's ultimate success or failure as a sound financial strategy does.

Another trend that companies are applauding is the slow but gradual move to change the way students learn. Although you are still likely to take a finance course, an accounting course, and a marketing course at different times and with different professors, most schools are putting pressure on their faculties to break down the professional silos and recognize that the real world has very few subject-specific problems. At the University of Virginia's Darden Graduate School of Business Administration, the whole faculty works together to create a truly integrated group of courses.

You may spend two weeks learning finance before you stop to integrate a section on commodity trading in different parts of the world. Then you might return to finance to work on both the micro and macro levels of a metals company's capital-raising options, with both professors guiding you. This breakdown of standard procedure means that more and more students are able to tailor their own programs to personal career goals and interests. It also means, however, that companies play a greater role in this academic arena than ever before—for better and for worse. One somewhat disturbing example is the growing tendency of schools to allow students to take electives earlier and earlier, sometimes before they've had the chance to comprehend the basics relevant to that subject. This is done primarily so that students can show some level of specialization before they leave for their summer internships. The intended result? The student outshines his or her colleagues and gets the final job offer. The responsiveness to customers is a good thing, but some worry that the pendulum is swinging too far away from academic pursuits. "I've always felt that professional schools of business must not allow themselves to become simply a farm system for industries," says Rex D. Adams, former dean of the Fuqua School of Business at Duke University. "I think we should have the courage of our convictions."

Cynicism aside, it's hard to find a graduate from one of the top schools who doesn't now think his or her investment was worth it—even those who were still pounding the pavement after graduation, still looking for work in a tough MBA job market. They describe their two years of graduate study as one of the high points of their lives: meeting bright new friends, sharing new experiences, discovering horizons and careers they never knew existed. The skills and knowledge you accumulate in a good MBA program teach you to think and analyze complicated business problems. They open doors to some of the world's great organizations, including the highest-paying public and private corporations, consulting firms, and investment banks. Yet, because some prospective students fail to do their homework, they end up wasting a lot of time and money. They don't find out what an MBA can and can't do for them. They fail to properly evaluate a particular school or program to discover what it can deliver. The upshot: some people find the rewards of their degree elusive. Much to their chagrin, it fails to deliver a better job, a bigger salary, and a quick

You might be able to tailor your program to your interests.

climb up the corporate ladder. But that's not the purpose of the MBA—it's an education, after all.

SELECT A
SCHOOL THAT
MATCHES
YOUR
INTERESTS

You can avoid that disappointment if you take the MBA quest seriously. You are now holding the best possible guide to help take the guesswork out of one of the most important career decisions you'll ever make. Not merely an uninformed ranking or a series of flimsy profiles written by public relations folks employed by the schools, this guide is a tell-it-like-it-is scouting report on the best of the bunch. You'll get the inside scoop on the curriculum, the vision the administration has for each school, and the less academic elements, like housing availability and social life. You'll also learn a lot about the culture of the school and get a feel for which schools might best fit—or might not fit—your personality.

For years, as many as 50 schools claimed they were among the top 30, and well over 100 institutions told prospective applicants that they were in the top 50. We chose the 88 schools we felt were the best in the United States, Canada, Latin America, and Europe, surveyed nearly 17,000 of their grads (of whom more than 11,500 responded), and then got feedback from 219 important corporate recruiters. The result: the top 50 U.S. B-schools and 10 international schools profiled in this book. You can get information about some 250 other schools, too, by going to our Web site (www. businessweek.com/bschools). You can also create your own ranking based on the criteria that are important to you, using our MBA comparator, and you can assess how long it will take to earn a monetary payback on your degree with our return on investment calculator. You can also read tips from admissions directors at the top 50 schools and some international schools.

In the 1990s, business school emerged as the top draw for the best and the brightest young people—those who in other eras might have become teachers, politicians, or doctors but have chosen business because of its influence and relevance. In this decade and this new millennium, that has not changed. Indeed, there's more need for qualified business leaders today than ever before, as corporate America looks for strong leadership and companies across the globe pick up the pace in the worldwide marketplace. We are living in an era when, for better or worse, everyone seems to have come down with the capitalism bug. What that means is that there's no longer much stereotyping when it comes to the typical MBA student. Of course, you can still find a group of narrow-minded, competitive folks uninterested in much beyond the almighty dollar. But there are fewer and fewer of them these days, and, indeed, admissions officers aren't very interested in that stereotype.

What the admissions folks prefer—and what those at the best schools have the luxury to choose—are true all-arounders, diverse and fascinating members of society who want an MBA for a multitude of reasons, whether it be to start a lightbulb company or to find a way to make charities more efficient. Although many have known exactly what they wanted to do since they were six, just as many others are career changers who never really planned a career in business and grew unhappy with what they were doing for a living. That doesn't mean they're shiftless, however. You can expect to find some of the most focused individuals you've ever met.

More and more, MBA students are not likely to be corporate drones (although you won't see many pierced tongues, either) and they may be planning to start their own businesses—if not immediately after school, then a few years later, after they've paid off some of that hefty debt. Schools have responded to the calls of these students for entrepreneurial training with a bevy of courses, majors, and, occasionally, complete programs in the subject. If you go to a top 50 school, you should be able to count on offerings dealing with how to assemble a business plan; raise money from venture capitalists and other investors; incorporate your business; and produce, market, and sell a product. There should be plenty of outside speakers and potential money sources brought in to network with you on a regular basis.

Your fellow students are also likely to be social types who like to let their hair down occasionally. Remember that B-school, unlike other academic experiences you may have had, places nearly as much emphasis on socializing and building teamwork and communication skills as it does on your classroom performance. At many schools, such as Kellogg, you won't be admitted unless you show that you can handle a social situation as well as an intricate analytical problem.

There is an upside, however—more fun than you probably ever expected to have at B-school. Charity events, salsa parties, international political meetings, hockey or Frisbee games, and formal balls are part of the MBA experience, and some say that the most tiring thing is making a choice about which gatherings to

> You should have opportunities to meet with alumni and outside speakers from the corporate world.

attend. Despite the reputation of MBAs as being overly concerned with money and not much else, a large part of the socializing is done to support nonprofit charities or other good works. One case in point is University of Michigan, which requires its incoming class to participate in a one-day community service project. Nearly 70 percent end up devoting many more days to their charity during their two-year MBA program. At Notre Dame, the incredible popularity of the university's football team provides opportunities for students to get to know recruiters out of the sterile cocktail party setting. Before every game, the school's MBA association gets a prominent company to sponsor a tailgate party in the courtyard of the building.

NOT ALL MBAs ARE CREATED EQUAL

The increased value placed on the MBA by corporate America has led to an explosion of full-time, part-time, and evening MBA programs for executives. Many schools are relying on these programs to subsidize a slew of other degrees that are losing funding or are not able to support themselves. Indeed, there are now more than 800 MBA programs in the United States that require the GMAT, and dozens more around the world. Some 55,000 to 65,000 students started full-time or part-time programs in the fall of 2002. Yet, although the MBA has become the graduate degree of choice among the corporate elite, emblazoning those initials on your resume doesn't guarantee you stardom in the business world. Although many MBA programs appear similar at first glance, they're not. The quality of the faculty, the fellow students, the buildings, and the level of technology all have a dramatic impact on your education. Also important is how that degree is perceived by the outside world. If your dream company doesn't even know that your program exists, you'll have a really tough time getting a job there. (You can get a glimpse of what companies hire at which schools in the individual profiles or at www.businessweek.com/bschools, where there's a much more detailed listing.) It's not impossible, of course, but you'll have to get hired on your own, rather than using the connections and the historic relationship developed by other schools' placement offices.

The upshot: little-known institutions with small MBA programs that lack accreditation aren't likely to give you either a quality business education or a hefty starting salary. It's tougher to get those from some part-time evening MBA programs, where the dropout rates are high and you don't get to move through the classes with a cohort of bright students. Certainly many part-time programs are exceptional, but to succeed in them, you need to be incredibly self-disciplined—even more so than those embarking on a full-time MBA plan.

If you want a worthwhile MBA, you need to get it from a school with prestige and a reputation for quality—whether it's known worldwide, throughout the United States, or regionally, depending upon your career goals. Says Meyer Feldberg, dean of Columbia Business School: "The top-ranked MBA programs all share something in common—an outstanding research-based faculty that is not only creating knowledge but able to carry that into the classroom." It's also the students, he says. "You're going to learn a great deal from the faculty, but you'll learn the same amount or more from each other. My advice would be always to go for the quality. You want to be surrounded by people who are going to be as successful as you, if not more successful than you, because it creates the network you will need for so many years."

BusinessWeek's customer satisfaction surveys of graduates have found that the greater the reputation of the school, the more likely you are to be happy with your results. Still, you might consider ignoring the big national schools if your goal is to take over the family business or simply to gain basic business know-how. In some cases, a degree from a local school could be more valuable than one from Harvard or Kellogg, because the relevant business and government contacts to help you in your career would be nearby. It's likely to cost a lot less, too.

When should you think about business school, and where should you go? As flip as it sounds, the answer to the first question is: when you've got enough experience under your belt to get into a school that's good enough to have a real impact on you and your career. Although years ago most applicants applied to a huge range of schools, from "safeties" to the truly elite, today a common strategy is to focus only on the very best. If you don't make it the first time, simply reapply. Many schools will meet with rejected students to explain why they didn't make the cut and what they might do differently next time. At Wharton, for example, admissions staffers conduct about 1000 why-deny meetings every year.

There is no perfect time for B-school, although applicants average about 26 or 27 years of age when they start, according to the Graduate Management Admission Council (GMAC). That's

---

Think about your goals as you select schools.

partly due to career changers, who've long seen a pot of gold at the end of the MBA rainbow. But it's also because, until the last year or two, companies have preferred to hire MBAs who already have some work experience and will be able to jump right into a management position as soon as they get out of school. Although it's becoming a little easier to get into business school with only a year or so of experience, you'll have to be truly brilliant or have some outstanding experiences to make the cut—only about 1 percent of the incoming class of 2004 could make that claim. At the elite schools, admissions officers, while asking for at least two and often three years of work experience, will make exceptions for truly outstanding candidates with two years or less of experience. Because so much of your education comes from other students with different backgrounds, it's nice to be able to contribute to the discussion with an example from the workplace. If all of your examples are straight out of your undergrad economics class, your classmates may not be too pleased. That said, you'll get more out of the program if you've already tried to tackle an organizational behavior problem or financial conundrum before going to school. Many MBAs who went directly to B-school from undergrad say they regret not having waited a few years first. But, on the other hand, straight-from-undergrad MBAs who started a business while in college may have more than ample experience with real-world business issues to hold their own and get something out of the MBA program.

WHAT ARE MBA STUDENTS LIKE?

The profile of people getting their MBAs has changed some over the years, although it still tends to skew toward white males in their twenties. According to the GMAC, nearly 50 percent of people taking the GMAT (the standardized test required for most B-schools, usually taken one to two years before entering school), were between the ages of 22 and 25 in 2001–2002 (June to July), in sharp contrast to 1996–1997, when 57 percent of U.S. test takers were between the ages of 24 and 27. (The biggest segment of international test takers are between the ages of 26 and 30, though the 24- to 25-year-old group is growing quickly.) The 20- to 21-year-old test-taker sector is growing: in 1997–1998, only about 6,000 20- and 21-year-olds took the GMAT, whereas some 11,000 sat for the exam in 2001–2002. Some 75,000 test takers were U.S. men, while 50,000 were U.S. women. Another 72,000 international men and 38,000 international women also took the test between June 2001 and July 2002.

Like most things valued and coveted by many people, the MBA degree isn't cheap and probably won't ever be. Other than buying a house, going to graduate school is probably the single largest investment a twenty- or thirtysomething will make. In addition to spending more than $60,000 for two years of tuition and another $25,000 in room and board at many top schools, you're likely to give up twice as much in lost earnings from the job you would have held. Indeed, you could practically start a business on what it costs to get through business school today. The average total investment (two years of tuition plus two years of forgone earnings) for graduates of *BusinessWeek*'s 88 surveyed schools was $122,300, with the costliest total investment the incredible $185,800 spent by members of Stanford Business School's class of 2002. That helps put into context the fact that those graduates were able to snag the highest average total pay package of all B-schools surveyed by *BusinessWeek* when they finished— $136,800, including salary, bonus, and such extra perks as moving expenses, stock options, and computers.

That's quite a pretty penny for a business education and a piece of parchment, isn't it? The exorbitant cost of the MBA helps explain why so many grads flock to the best-paid sectors—management consulting and investment banking. Of the 2002 graduates from the top 30 B-schools, about 60 percent chose one of those two areas, even if they had plans to strike out on their own later on. The entrepreneurship craze now has died down a bit: whereas previously about 8 percent of grads headed for start-ups or their own new ventures, fewer than 4 percent of the class of 2002 chose to work in a start-up straight out of school. Perhaps they thought they'd do better if they got a few years of more general experience and paid off some of their debt first—the average 2002 grad owed more than $44,000 coming out of school.

Yet all of that expense seems to pay off, both in the long run and—until recently, at least—the short run. According to an analysis done for *BusinessWeek* by Jens Stephan, associate professor of accounting at the University of Cincinnati, the class of 2002 will take between four and seven years (including the two years of school) to pay back its investment. That class got a running start on the payback this year, with 2002 grads of the top 50 schools earning an average of $102,300 in total compensation. Offering

> The MBA is expensive, so make sure your finances are in good shape.

the fastest return was Brigham Young University's Marriott School of Business, thanks to affordable tuition and an impressive 97.8 percent salary increase over pre-MBA levels. At Marriott, you'll pay back the $71,100 total investment in 4.1 years, compared with an average of 5.6 years for the 88 B-schools surveyed by *Business-Week*. The slowest return? The University of Southern California's Marshall School. With a total investment of $163,100 and an average salary increase of 56.7 percent, it will take more than seven years for students to break even.

Some top B-schools are now offering, in addition to their two-year flagship degree, the compressed MBA, in which students with lots of prior business experience can finish the program in one year or less. Now available in some form at a few of the top 30 B-schools, it's often half the price and gets you out into the workplace quicker. The downside: less opportunity to network, and no summer internship opportunity for those who aren't 100 percent certain of their career goals.

There are other ways to limit the degree's cost. If you're an entrepreneur, Cornell's Johnson and Virginia's Darden now offer fellowships that help pay off debt incurred in school. And although many public B-schools are moving to boost their tuition to private school rates so that they can be self-sufficient and break free of many of their parent universities' restrictions, there are still deals to be had. If you're a California resident, for example, you can get a two-year MBA at the University of California at Berkeley or UCLA for about $11,700 per year. Even if you're not a resident, you can get a better deal than you would at a place like Columbia, where the annual tuition (not to mention New York City living expenses) will run you over $40,000.

Although that's a pretty compelling argument in favor of the public university, keep in mind that one reason people agree to pay inflated tuitions is that they sometimes lead to inflated salaries. Those 2002 Columbia grads, for example, took home a median pay package of $123,600, while grads at the University of Illinois (where tuition and expenses average about $27,000 for an out-of-state student) earned about $74,000. Not included in the return on investment calculations are intangibles such as the added confidence and psychological comfort you get from having the MBA under your belt, or the all-important alumni network—cited by many students at schools such as Harvard or Dartmouth's Tuck School of Business as the best reason for going there. Good con-

Public universities can be less expensive, but just as good.

nections can help you get your first job, but they can also help you make the transition to a better gig years down the road. Cost, then, is certainly one criterion in deciding whether you should go for an MBA and where you should go. But it shouldn't be the only consideration.

As tempting as it is to choose a school on the basis of the *BusinessWeek* rankings alone, you should resist doing so. The rankings are a wonderful tool, perhaps the best one available, for those considering a top 50 program. But not every school is right for every person, and you should study the culture and strengths of each school to determine what best fits your needs. That means that a school ranked number 18 may be a better choice for you than number 7.

Not every school is right for every person.

Are you the type of person who needs the buzz and bustle of the big city to be happy? You'd probably do better at Columbia, NYU's Stern, the University of Chicago, or UCLA than in a wooded, secluded setting like that of Tuck in Hanover, New Hampshire or Cornell's tranquil and out-of-the-way Ithaca, New York. By contrast, if you like an intimate, close-knit community with access to the great outdoors, Tuck's the place for you. If you're a type A person who thrives on a pressured, individualized, highly competitive atmosphere, Harvard may be your choice. On the other hand, if you want to spend most of your time working in small groups, you might prefer a Kellogg or a Duke, both of whose grads gave their schools stellar marks in the teamwork department. (See Chapter 3 for *BusinessWeek*'s survey of top graduates and what they say about their schools.)

Certainly, most B-schools offer the same basic curriculum—a group of core requirements with the option to choose your own electives—but there are plenty of variations to pick from. At the University of Chicago, for example, there are no mandatory classes except for a special orientation and quasi-core program. Students are encouraged to branch out on their own, pursuing advanced topics in finance or accounting if they already know the basics. But the flexible curriculum is fairly unconventional these days at B-school; many schools require first-year students to move in lockstep through their core courses. The rationale? The CPA in the class will learn more about management and teamwork from helping his classmates to grasp basic concepts than he loses by repeating material he already knows cold. That's the idea at North Carolina's Kenan-Flagler Business School, where students must work with a single team for the entire first year, and everyone must take the requirements—no substitutions allowed.

Areas of specialty are another important consideration in your decision-making process. Some schools, such as Harvard or Darden, are focused on teaching general management and tend to send forth graduates who work well in areas of general expertise such as consulting rather than narrow technical specialties. Other schools pride themselves on their niche programs, attracting students who know exactly what they want. Wisconsin has risk management/insurance and real estate and urban land economics; Babson is world-famous for entrepreneurship; Michigan State emphasizes its supply chain management training. Cornell has put into place a unique immersion course in manufacturing and six other subjects, offered in the second semester of the first year. It's the only course of the semester, and you spend much of your time out of the classroom, visiting manufacturing plants, studying live cases, and working on your final presentation.

Before applying to any school, do your homework. Go beyond the slick brochures, Web sites, and promises made by the marketing staffs. Read the extended profiles in this book, and check out the MBA journals, student survey comments, links to hundreds of school profiles, and everything else that's available on *Business-Week*'s B-school Web site (www.businessweek.com/bschools). Treat it the way an MBA would in a typical case study. Be sure to speak with students and faculty, and take special note of how they react to your inquiries. Are professors gregarious and open or stern and dismissive? Do students seem enthused about their school or not? Trust your senses. If you get a bad feeling, it's most likely going to be worse when you show up in the fall," says Brian Sowinski, a 2002 grad at Washington University. Attend a class or two; talk to the students; grab a recruiter during a coffee break to find out what he or she thinks the place is like. Then look at yourself in the mirror and see if you really match up with the school.

It's not a bad idea to speak with recent graduates of the programs that you're interested in—keeping in mind, of course, that things are changing so quickly in the B-school world that the experience they've had may be radically different from the journey you're about to embark on. If you already have your heart set on becoming a consultant at McKinsey & Co., it would be wise to find a McKinsey staffer who is an alumnus of the school you want to attend. Most alumni and/or admissions departments will help you

Do your homework before applying.

find recent grads, and Wharton goes so far as to send all applicants a directory of alumni who have volunteered to share their first-hand knowledge of Wharton by telephone. What's more, once students are admitted to Wharton, they gain access to a system that lets incoming students get to know one another online even before they arrive on campus. While Wharton was one of the first to introduce the handy chat mechanism, many other schools have followed suit: it allows incoming students to bond before classes, figure out housing shares, and arrange in-person meetings.

In general, you're not likely to find too many terribly disappointed people. MBAs from top schools generally give positive endorsements of the experience, whether they are recent graduates or not. Most have little doubt that the time and expense of getting the degree were well worth it. They say they forged friendships and contacts that will endure for a lifetime, and they linked up with new jobs that paid better and offered greater opportunities for advancement than the positions they left. Some consider it the most important and formative decision they've made in their lifetimes. Raves one Kellogg grad from 2002: "I have truly enjoyed my experience here at Kellogg and consider my time here to have been very well spent. The faculty, administration, and staff go out of their way to help students wherever possible. It truly feels as if they are here to do whatever they can to help us. It's like a family."

The MBA will give you skills that will last a lifetime.

HOW TO GET INTO ONE OF THE BEST B-SCHOOLS

If you've got your sights set on business school, expect plenty of company. Although the opening of the decade has seen a cooling off in the MBA job market, applications for business schools are still on the rise. Most schools in the top 30 saw increases upward of 20 percent for the class of 2004, on top of application surges of 30 to 40 percent for the two previous classes. It's too early to tell if the robust application pool will grow for the class of 2005, but most schools have more applicants than they have spots to be filled, no matter the situation.

Indeed, at most schools in the top 30, fewer than 20 percent of applicants make the cut. At Stanford University's Graduate School of Business, only 8 percent of applicants get a call from the admissions office welcoming them to the next MBA class. At the number 1 school, Northwestern University's Kellogg School of Management, 13 percent of those who apply get a thumbs-up to join the nearly-600-person class. Harvard Business School receives almost 10,000 applications for a class of just under 1,000 MBAs, a 10 percent admittance rate. As a whole, California schools are the toughest tickets: besides Stanford's high selectivity, UC Berkeley's Haas School of Business admits only 11 percent of applicants, UCLA's Anderson School admits only 15 percent, and USC—one of the handful of schools turning away fewer than 80 percent of applicants—admits about 21 percent of its applicants.

The upshot: getting into B-school is more competitive than ever. And the economic downturn has only slowed the frenzied pace minimally, especially since B-school applications tend to rise when there's not much happening on the job front.

GETTING TO KNOW YOU

So what does an MBA wannabe have to do to get inside the hallowed halls of a good B-school? First and foremost, don't rush. Give yourself enough time to become an informed consumer. Some admissions directors suggest starting the process a full year before actually applying to carefully gauge your fit with a program. That may be a touch unrealistic, but you should give yourself at least a full year to do your homework before enrolling in B-school. Read the school profiles in this book. Check out the admission director Q&As on the *BusinessWeek* business schools Web site (www.businessweek.com/bschools). Surf the Web sites of the schools you're interested in. Send away for literature. Swap stories and advice with fellow applicants on various online message boards—*BusinessWeek*'s have more than 40,000 registered users, and school admissions directors and admissions counselors unaffiliated with the schools often host forums on the site. You can also banter with other prospective MBAs and current students at the online message board. And attend an MBA Forum, a GMAC-sponsored event that connects prospective students with over 100 school admissions officers. Held worldwide in dozens of cities internationally and in the United States, the forums provide an informal venue for applicants to converse one-on-one with school officials. They are held at different times in different cities between September and January. You can check the GMAT Web site (www.gmat.org) for a calendar of events.

THE "IT" FACTORS

The major factors B-schools consider when evaluating applications are your undergraduate grades, GMAT score, and work experience—called the Big Three by many admissions folks. The GMAT is important—although some admissions directors will tell you it's not the deciding factor, that doesn't mean you won't need a respectable score. Many applicants admitted to top schools score over 650 on the GMAT, even though schools are known to take strong applicants with lower scores. Above all, work hard to score high on the quant section—a good GMAT score with a low quant is a disadvantage. You may need to take the GMAT twice, or even sign up for a prep course, depending on your test-taking strengths.

You may not be able to do too much about your undergraduate grades. But, if your marks were less than stellar in finance, economics, or math, you'd be smart to take some continuing education classes to show that you're capable of higher marks and that you can handle the quant work in B-school.

In recent years, work experience has fluctuated in importance. It used to be that, to secure admission, you'd need upward of four years of work experience. However, in the late 1980s and booming 1990s, corporate recruiters demanded workers already familiar with the business world and corporate ways, and B-schools responded by upping their average work experience requirements to about 4.5 years. Lately, companies have backtracked a bit—they still want experienced MBAs, but they're more interested in smart grads who can learn quickly even if they have a little less experience—and, frankly, who aren't already set in their management ways from laboring four or five years at another company. To that end, a number of schools—including Harvard, Stanford, and the University of Pennsylvania's Wharton School—have begun looking at and even actively recruiting students with one or two years of work experience (and, in rare cases, no formal work experience). That doesn't mean anyone with two years of post-college work is a shoo-in. These schools are looking for the cream of the crop of young, high-potential applicants. If you fit in that category, and are certain you want to pursue an MBA, you'll have a better shot now than ever before.

There are, of course, other factors besides the Big Three on which admissions committees base their decisions, including leadership ability, special talents, background characteristics, motivation, and career interest. Although these factors are less tangible, and it's harder to predict how they'll be weighed, they do help admissions directors determine whether you can add to the diversity they're trying to create. "There isn't one piece of the application process that we care about any more than the others—we care about them all. There is no magic formula that we use to determine admissibility. It is a holistic view of the candidate, from GMAT scores to undergraduate record, to essays, recommendations, and the interview," says Elizabeth Riley, admissions director at Duke University's Fuqua School of Business. Part of that look increasingly includes an interview, which can be a make-or-break factor if you're a borderline applicant. Ace the interview and you might get accepted; bomb, and you'll likely be rejected.

Above all, hedge your bets by applying to a minimum of three schools, and up to half a dozen or so—the norm for today's applicants. Don't apply randomly: schools get data on which other schools you've applied to, and if the types of schools you apply to are all over the board, you may appear unfocused to the admissions committee. Make sure each school fits your goals and isn't just a nameplate. And try to apply as early as possible. Although most schools list their final deadlines for applications between March 1 and June 1 (some even later, depending on their rolling admissions process), ignore them; the later your application arrives, the more you put yourself at a disadvantage. True, the class

Schools consider more than test scores and years of experience when reviewing applications.

isn't filled in the first round, but there are generally fewer spots to offer in later rounds, so the competition is even stiffer. In general, it's best to apply by the first two rounds. "We always recommend early, the first deadline. When we're just starting to read applications, we tend to be aggressive. We don't know what the class looks like yet. So in the first round, we're filling the class. The reason it gets competitive in the second round is because we know what the applicant pool looks like, and how the class is starting to take shape. You're just looking to round out the class in this round," says Rod Garcia, admissions director at MIT's Sloan School. Most programs now have their first deadline scheduled for as early as November. Ideally, you should get your application in no later than early January for fall admission. And although the earlier applicants tend to have higher credentials, an application that doesn't make it in the first round will usually be dropped into the next round for further consideration. Check with the admissions committees to see if this is the case or not. If it's a one-shot deal, you might want to take an extra few weeks to spiff up your application for the second round or even the third, if it will make a difference in the strength of your application. "The bottom line is that if you're a good candidate, you'll be admitted no matter the round. If you're a weak candidate, it doesn't matter what round you apply," says Garcia.

GET ORGANIZED

It might help you to organize your plan of attack by creating a calendar. That will put you on a defined schedule and make it easier for you to meet critical deadlines. Here's a loose outline:

- *Spring or early summer:* Narrow down schools, check out Web sites, request program literature and applications, chat with other aspirants on message boards, and set up on-campus visits for the early fall.
- *August:* Enroll in a six-week GMAT prep course or set aside two months to practice the test at home.
- *September:* Begin to visit campuses, attend classes, and chat with current students and faculty. Attend an MBA Forum, if there is one in a nearby city. Do an admissions interview, if allowed before you file an official application.

- *October:* Take the GMAT. Begin the application process by filling out the forms, requesting undergraduate transcripts, creating a personal marketing plan for yourself, crafting answers to essay questions, and choosing recommenders. If you want a recommendation from your boss, inform your employer that you're considering business school.
- *November:* Visit more campuses if needed. Retake the GMAT if dissatisfied with your score (anything less than a 600 will put you at a big disadvantage for the best schools). Schedule the bulk of your personal interviews. Begin to file your applications with schools. First complete the applications for schools that are not at the very top of your list. Save the best for last, when you can approach them having had more practice. In almost all cases, it's better to file early, never in the last round.
- *December:* Finish up the rest of your applications. Ask for personal interviews at schools that refused to do an interview before an application was filed. Cross your fingers!

THE APPLICATION

As you might expect, one of the most time-consuming tasks in the entire B-school process is the application itself. Although technology has shortened the time it takes to complete each mind-numbing, head-scratching, 15-page application, the typical MBA candidate still can expect to spend a good 40 hours slogging away at it. Fortunately, that slogging can be focused on the truly difficult parts, since a host of products has made filling in your demographic information (i.e., name, birthplace, Social Security number, job history, etc.) a relatively painless process.

For example, there's multiple application software, which allows you to enter those pesky vitals each school demands in one fell swoop, for as many schools as you like. If you want to cut even more toil and cost out of your life, apply online. Many schools now only accept online or electronic applications, and a growing number don't even send out paper applications anymore. You'll be allowed to save partly finished applications through any computer that has access to the Internet and send everything but recommendations and academic transcripts electronically. That means your forms reach admissions offices almost immediately, cutting out Federal

Express charges. It's particularly helpful for international applicants, many of whom must contend with inefficient postal systems.

Two online application services are relative old-timer CollegeEdge and Embark, the product of a partnership between GMAC, ETS, and *The Princeton Review* that hit the scene in August 1998. Similar in many ways, the two services are inexpensive—costing $10 and $12 per application, respectively—and are rapidly expanding their networks of participating schools. As of December 2002, CollegeEdge, now part of *The Princeton Review* (you can access the applications directly from that site) has 105 applications online. Most of the schools currently online are part of *BusinessWeek*'s top 50. Once you've filled out the basic information (name, address, test scores, etc.), which takes about 45 minutes, the software neatly distributes the information to each application you've selected. When you open each application online, you'll find that core info already entered. Next, you'll have to tackle the school-specific questions on the application, including the dreaded essays. Here, you'll have an attractive but dangerous option: with a keystroke, you can copy an essay written for one school to any application. You'll then have to customize the essay manually for each school. This can be tempting, but, at a time when most B-schools hear from far more qualified applicants than they can accept, it's a better idea to tailor your essays to each individual school to which you're applying.

To apply online, you'll first have to create secure user IDs and passwords. (If you forget your password, you'll have to answer a personalized question or two correctly before it is e-mailed to you again.) CollegeEdge then prompts you to enter your personal information into two quick forms—taking 5 to 10 minutes total—that are then filtered into all of your chosen applications, much like MULTI-App. CollegeEdge creates replicas of school applications but allows you to fill out standard information that the program loads in for you. Both CollegeEdge and Embark provide ample space for school-specific questions, particularly the essays, which can be written entirely online in one or several sittings (although there is no spell checker). You can also cut and paste your essays if you prefer to use a desktop word-processing program. Be sure to save early and often: these services are vulnerable to abrupt Internet connection failure. As a reminder, the programs have save buttons prominently displayed on their browsers, and CollegeEdge requires its users to save their work at the end of each application page before continuing.

> Online applications have made the process less cumbersome.

Embark does a good job of helping users keep track of the progress of their applications. On reentry to the site, users receive an overall view of the applications they've submitted and the ones they're still working on. CollegeEdge, meanwhile, offers a checklist function that essentially reminds you what remains to be done, and tells you where other applicants also apply—i.e., if you apply to Purdue, the program will tell you (much like Amazon.com) where others applying to Purdue have also applied. Once you've finished up an application, your work will be inspected to make sure all of the proper fields have been filled out, providing a direct link to the area in question if there's not enough information in that section. Finally, you enter a credit card number, and with a click of a button, your application flies cyberstyle to the school of choice (although you can print it out and mail it in if you prefer). Indeed, admissions directors at the elite B-schools expect online applications to make up between 50 and 60 percent of their overall applicant pools, with several likely to require online applications within the next five years.

TAKING THE GMAT

No matter how you slice it, your chances of getting into a good school depend in large part on how well you score on the Graduate Management Admissions Test (GMAT), long viewed by admissions officers as one of the best predictors of academic success. The exam judges an applicant's quantitative, problem-solving, and verbal and written English skills, and spins out a number as high as 800 that can make or break your chances of getting into top programs. The Test of English as a Foreign Language (TOEFL) measures the English of people whose native language is not English. Scores on the test are required by more than 4300 colleges and universities, professional schools, and sponsoring institutions. To get a good idea of what you'll face and how to prepare, you can start with the comprehensive overview at www.businessweek.com/bschools/gmat, where you will find practice questions, prep strategies, minitests, and more.

Since October 1997, the GMAT has been administered only via computer, forever altering the landscape for the 265,000 people who sign up for it each year. For one thing, scheduling the test, called the computer-adaptive test (CAT), is definitely a lot easier than it was in the paper-based days, when the GMAT was offered only four times a year at 970 different locations. Now test takers can choose to take the exam any one of 250 days of the year (during the first three weeks of every month) as long as they schedule in advance.

The CAT is similar in content to the old test, with verbal and math sections and two essays. But the computerized test has different ground rules, the most important of which is that it is adaptive. Unlike the paper version, how well you do on early questions determines how hard the questions that follow will be. What's more, the difficulty of the questions, not just the number you get right, affects your final score. The more difficult questions you answer, the higher the score you receive. By the CAT's end, you come to a point where you are consistently getting the same level of questions correct, and your score reflects that, says Fred McHale, a vice president at GMAC and the lead developer of the CAT. What this means is that questions must be answered in order; you can't jump to the no-brainers and save the puzzlers for later, as you could with the paper-based version. You're also penalized for not finishing all the sections. So guessing and knowing how to eliminate incorrect answers is more important than ever. Adding to the pressure of taking the test, the CAT requires that you decide before you leave the test center whether you want to cancel your score. Otherwise, you get the multiple-choice results immediately, tattooing an official score on your academic file for the next five years. On the old paper test, a test taker had one week to cancel and didn't find out the grade for more than a month.

While you do still have to wait for your essay grades, they don't contribute to the main score. Every accredited B-school requires the GMAT, and admissions officers typically give a weight of anywhere from 20 to 40 percent to the score alone. If you manage to eke out only the average score of about 540 (that's within a range from 200 to 800), your chances of making it into a top school are pretty slim. You really need to score above 600 to seriously entertain the idea of making it into a top 30 school, where students entering in the fall of 2002 averaged a score of over 670. And you probably need to score no less than 600 to walk through the door of one of *BusinessWeek*'s runners-up; their members of the class of 2000 averaged a score of more than 630. Certainly, there are exceptions, but the GMAT average at the number 1 school, Kellogg, is 700, and the highest average score can be found at Columbia University Business School—a whopping 711 average. Overall, the

Aim to score above 600 on the GMAT.

average GMAT score for a top 30 applicant has increased by some 50 to 70 points over the last half-decade.

Although you want to score as well as you can, admissions directors do say there's a lot more to getting into a top school than the GMAT alone. "The GMAT is just one component of your application," says Julia Min, assistant dean for MBA admissions at NYU's Stern School. "While it's important to put your best foot forward, my suggestion is to not overemphasize one area, but to create a strong profile in all areas, including essays." If your test score doesn't quite measure up, don't surrender just yet. It's possible that you could be rejected from one school based on your GMAT score and be accepted by another top 30 school with the same score. Why? Some schools, feverishly working to boost their reputations by appearing selective, will simply toss you out of their admit pool for a subpar score. They are using GMAT averages as a marketing tool to attract better candidates. Other schools, already confident of their quality reputation, might pay more attention to other parts of your application: work experience, essays, personal interviews, and undergraduate grades.

If you feel your score is too low, however, then retaking the test might be your best plan of action. But that doesn't mean you should retake it half a dozen times just to raise your score a few points. While admissions directors will take only your highest score into consideration, they might question the goal of someone who has taken the test three or four times, only to boost his or her score by a tiny amount each time. The CAT's average change in score from one test to the next is about 30 points, and most admissions directors won't attach much value to your second go-round if you fall within that range.

Before taking the CAT, it's imperative to gain familiarity with its structure. There is one verbal and one quantitative section, as well as two essay questions. The verbal section has 41 questions, the quant 37, and you are given 75 minutes for each—nearly twice the average amount of time per question as in the previous test—with 30 minutes for each of the two essays. The verbal questions measure your ability to understand and evaluate what you read, while the quant questions test basic math skills (tougher than your old SATs) as well as your ability to solve quantitative problems and interpret data in graphs, charts, and tables. It's a good idea to brush up on algebra and geometry.

Familiarize yourself with the GMAT CAT.

Since 1994, GMAC has also required two essays to measure how well you present logical arguments and express ideas that are "correct, concise, and persuasive." Called the Analytical Writing Assessment (AWA), the section is also an easy way to expose applicants with weak English skills. You can cut and paste your essays on the screen, but there's no spell checker, so be careful. The first question asks you to analyze a given issue by presenting a statement followed by a series of questions. Here's an example:

> Ask most older people to identify the key to success, and they are likely to reply "hard work." Yet I would tell people starting off in a career that work in itself is not the key. In fact, you have to approach work cautiously—too much or too little can be self-defeating.

After reading the statement, you'll be asked the following:

> To what extent do you agree or disagree with this view of work? Develop your position by using reasons and/or examples from your reading, experience, or observations.

The second essay question requires you to analyze an argument, also using a statement followed by several questions. For example:

> In a recent citywide poll, 15 percent more residents said that they watch television programs about the visual arts than was the case in a poll conducted five years ago. During these past five years, the number of people visiting our city's art museums has increased by a similar percentage. Since the corporate funding that supports public television, where most of the visual arts programs appear, is now being threatened with severe cuts, we can expect that attendance at our city's art museums will also start to decrease. Thus, some of the city's funds for supporting the arts should be reallocated to public television.

After reading and digesting this bit of esotericism, you'll be asked to assess the validity of this argument. You'll want to analyze the line of reasoning and the use of evidence and suggest ways to

Essay questions on the GMAT add context.

strengthen or refute the argument using examples. If you'd like to practice answering a few of the AWA questions, you can download for free a complete listing of actual writing topics used in the CAT at GMAC's Web site (www.gmac.com or www.mba.com). You'll need Acrobat Reader software to view this listing (which you can also download). Or, if you want to shell out a few bucks, you'll also find the topics included in the latest *Official Guide for GMAT Review*. The essay section is graded separately from the others, with scores ranging from zero (unscorable because the test taker failed to write on the assigned topic) to six (outstanding). Two people score each essay, and you'll get an average of their scores.

Note, however, that going to take the GMAT is a bare-bones experience. Test-takers are not allowed to bring anything in to the exam with them—not water, not a pencil, not a scrap of paper. At the test center, you'll be given some scratch paper, pencils, and instructions, usually typed. You'll have to turn in the scratch paper you've got if you end up needing more. Kaplan Test Prep says GMAT takers have reported abbreviated tutorials on how to take the CAT, and in some cases there has been no tutorial at all. That means you better be ready to start the test after you read the simple instructions. Still feeling nervous about the CAT? GMAC has a customer service line (609-771-7330) as well as an e-mail address (gmat@ets.org) to field questions about anything from a test score to a situation at a test center.

SHOULD YOU TAKE A PREP COURSE?

The GMAT CAT is likely to be the first time many generation Xers (and late-blooming baby boomers, for that matter) have to take an exam on a PC. So it's not surprising that applicants are clamoring for help from test preparation services. Indeed, enrollment in the test prep classes run by *The Princeton Review* and Kaplan Educational Centers has skyrocketed in the year since the GMAT went digital. One thing you can expect from a prep course is plenty of practice GMAT tests (at least three, plus as many as you like on your own). You'll begin by taking a paper-based GMAT to diagnose your strengths and weaknesses. Instructors will then analyze which mistakes tend to be made frequently, and then work those areas to death. If you're weak in algebra, expect to get drilled in the subject. If it's reading comprehension that throws you off, get ready for a customized lesson. After the first diagnostic test, the rest

If you lack self-discipline, consider a prep course.

of the exams will be administered on the computer to make you more comfortable with the medium of the CAT.

Some B-schoolers will tell you that plain hard studying is about enough to do well on the GMAT. And if you're disciplined and feel comfortable with the types of questions asked on the GMAT, that's probably true. A Kaplan or Princeton course may be right for some applicants, however, especially those lacking self-discipline. If you want to review specific subject matter or discuss test-taking strategy, the classes can be valuable. If you're worried about taking the test on a computer, you will gain familiarity with the format. And if nothing else, paying the steep fee ($1200) inspires applicants to prepare more rigorously. Moreover, going to a classroom on a regular basis with other MBA hopefuls helps to keep you motivated.

Kaplan offers several options, the priciest of which is a 15-session private tutorial for $1999 (up to 35 hours of private lessons for $3999) that allows you to prepare one-on-one with a Kaplan teacher with schedules and locations set by you. You and your tutor will work through a customized curriculum geared specifically to your test strengths and weaknesses. The more traditional group option might be more affordable: your payment of $1199 includes computer practice tests at Kaplan and GMAT practice software to take home, along with a home study book and take-home diagnostic tests and 25 to 40 hours of class time. There's also an online option—you access the course from your own personalized student homepage where you can start, pause, and rewind lessons at your convenience, take practice tests and quizzes, and view supplemental workshops—for $499. *The Princeton Review* offers one-to-one tutoring as well as group classes and a new online service. Prices are similar to those of Kaplan, and Princeton also offers *The Princeton Review's Manual for the GMAT Exam* and the *Official Guide for GMAT Review,* the publication from the creators of the GMAT, as part of the fee. Both services provide financial aid to offset the cost, although you must fill out a financial aid form in order to be eligible. Kaplan offers tuition assistance covering up to 50 percent of the cost for those earning less than $18,000 a year, while *The Princeton Review* discounts its classes up to $350 for those who prove financial hardship.

So which course should you take? It's a tough call, since so much depends on the individual instructor and how well he or she motivates you. The best strategy overall is to compare both services to see which curriculum better meets your needs. Princeton, for example, caps its classes at 15 students, compared with 25 at Kaplan. Princeton also wins kudos for requiring the teacher to schedule one-on-one sessions as often as students request. Kaplan offers extra help sessions, but not always with the same person, though it does offer its own computer labs in which to practice the CAT. To get more information on the *Review*'s courses, call 800-2-REVIEW or check on the Web at www.review.com. To obtain more information on the Kaplan courses, call 800-KAP-TEST or check www.kaplan.com.

There's another, less expensive option: simply buy a workbook for around $20 and use the sample tests in it for practice. To gain a true sense for how the CAT works, pick up GMAC's review guide ($30) and POWERPREP software—downloadable for free from the company's Web site at www.gmac.org—which includes two complete tests. There's also a new essay product called Essay Insight ($20). You can order the package from www.mba.org, where you can also download a list of essay topics for free. *The Princeton Review*'s site offers a book and CD-ROM with four practice tests for $40, and Kaplan sells software review packages for $37.

If you do decide to enroll in one of the prep courses, do so no more than two months before you sit down for the real deal. Preparing for the GMAT is the equivalent of training for a race: you don't stop two months before the starting gun is set to go off. It also helps to start preparing for the test before classes begin. Get Kaplan or *The Princeton Review* to give you the study materials a few weeks before you start so you have the time to familiarize yourself with them. There are usually so many books and tests that it's virtually impossible to get through all of them during the course.

MARKET YOURSELF

As you've probably figured out by now, you've really got to make yourself stand out in order to successfully clear the admissions hurdles at the top business schools. Don't expect to be a shoo-in if all you've got are a solid GMAT score and a 4.0 grade point average. Whether you have those qualifications or not, the one thing you need in this incredibly competitive environment is a strategy with which to market yourself; it's a concept they'll soon be teaching you at B-school. It will help guide you through your admissions interview and your application, particularly your answers to essay questions and your choice of recommenders. More importantly, though, it will convey a clear picture of who you are to the admissions committee.

Consider the strategy of Phil Carpenter, a Stanford MBA graduate: "When I was applying to business school, I developed a positioning strategy based on what I thought made me unique. I was a liberal arts major, yet had plunged into the fray of Silicon Valley and over the course of three years had become fairly technical. I therefore positioned myself as the liberal arts guy with a technical twist, and provided evidence to show just how my combination of strong written and verbal skills, plus a solid technology background, made me not only a unique candidate but one who had been very successful in my chosen field of high-tech marketing."

Carpenter, who has gone on to coauthor the superb *Marketing Yourself to the Top Business Schools,* reinforced this image of himself through his selection of recommenders. One was the chief executive of the start-up company he worked for before business school; another was an art history professor whom he got to know during his undergraduate studies; yet another was a Stanford Law School professor who had known him since he was a child. Together, they helped to position him as a "liberal arts guy with a technical twist."

The bottom line is that admissions officers are looking for diverse and interesting people who will contribute something to the general educational process, not just a group of successful analysts who know how to pick a stock. That's why a typical elite B-school class these days might include such varied types as an Olympic fencer, a venture capitalist, a navy SEAL, and an artist. Put yourself in the admissions director's shoes and envision the type of person to whom you would want to give the nod. "Candidates with atypical backgrounds that are successful in our process tend to have a good story, a good rationale for why business school and Kellogg make sense for them," says Michele Rogers, Kellogg's admissions director. "We aren't looking for just one type of student." Temper your accomplishments at work, which are important but often tend to look like those of many aspirants with similar employment backgrounds, with anecdotes that display your unique characteristics. That means discussing the confidence and conviction you learned as editor of a newspaper you started in college, your failed attempt to start an online business, the maturity and language skills you developed while working in the Peace Corps, or how your passion for rock climbing has changed your

Covey a clear picture of who you are.

management style and your approach to life. Don't sell yourself short—let admissions folks know how special you really are, even if it seems unconventional.

THE PERFECTLY CRAFTED ESSAY

The B-school essay questions are your single best opportunity to make yourself really shine for an admissions staff. Start with a little navel gazing. Ask yourself, "Who am I, and how can I convey my essence in writing?" In doing so, you should be bold and incisive, explaining through relevant, colorful examples why you want to earn an MBA and what you'd like to accomplish with it. Draw from unique personal experiences: the more detail, the better. Most B-school applications will hit you with about four mandatory essay questions, with an optional fifth that invites you to explain any potential shortfall in your application. That's not an absolute, however. The University of Texas Graduate School of Business has only two mandatory essays with an optional third, while Harvard Business School requires its applicants to answer seven. You should use the optional essay if there's something you haven't yet explained, or if you feel that the admissions officers might see a problem with your application. It's the perfect place to explain, for example, that your low GPA is partly the result of taking on a 50-hour-per-week job to help support your family or to deal with a medical situation that at one point hurt your professional performance.

What will the essays ask? Many schools pose the same question, phrased slightly differently: if accepted, how would you add to this class? MBA programs are trying to understand what makes you tick and which leadership positions, jobs, and responsibilities make you a winner. Look at a few of Harvard Business School's previous essay questions: "While recognizing that no day is typical, please describe a representative work day"; "What specifically have you done to help a group or organization change?"; "Describe your three most substantial accomplishments and explain why you view them as such"; and "What are your career aspirations and why? How will you get there?" Or consider UC Berkeley's Haas School question: "If you could have dinner with one individual, past or present, who would it be? What would you order?" ("I think the applicant who wanted to have "bloomin' onions" with Jesus was one of the more novel ones I have seen this year! In terms of what we do look for in the "dinner" answer, the most important thing is who you select and what it says about you and your goals, motivation, and personality," says Pete Johnson, codirector of admissions at Haas.) These queries are pretty straightforward, broad, and potentially dangerous to the applicant because they are so similar to essay questions on other schools' applications. Don't surrender to the temptation of writing a one-size-fits-all essay. It may come off as unfeeling and vapid, and, more important, it will miss the subtle nuances a school uses to figure out whether you're really the right fit. (Plus you risk accidentally writing the wrong school name on the form.) And more than that, admissions directors are quite savvy and can often detect nonindividualized, cut-and-paste essay answers. "No school wants to see that their competitor is the only school for you. I see this mistake in more than three dozen applications each year. Right there, the credibility is shot," says Natalie Grinblatt, director of admissions at Cornell University's Johnson School. Don't risk it.

That's not to say that all essay questions conform to a specific formula. Some schools seem to delight in thinking up unusual questions. One recently asked potential students to write a succinct description of how they handled real-life ethical challenges—a big deal these days, and a question sure to find its way into the regular question category. Another asked applicants to describe the details behind the failures in their careers. As part of their applications, candidates to Northwestern's Kellogg face the unusual task of responding in short answers to three of six questions or statements. The novel ones include: "Outside of work I enjoy . . ."; "Describe a situation that forced you to re-evaluate a personal belief"; "I wish the Admissions Committee had asked me. . . ."

Remember, when answering the essay questions, be sure to emphasize how different you are, not only how great you are. To stand apart from the all-quite-capable masses, write about how you have tutored underprivileged children. Discuss the influence your father or other family members have had on you, or your role as a neighborhood activist working to combat crime, or what it's like to play lead guitar in a budding rock band. Speaking of essays, many unsuccessful applicants trip up on the most basic question: why do you want an MBA from this school? If your essay spouts off a laundry list of reasons that make you a good candidate, dressed up by a few taken from the school's own literature, chances are your application will be viewed with skepticism. Try focusing on one or two things that are important to you and link them to

> Do not cut and paste essays from one application to another.

the characteristics of the MBA program. Says Rosemaria Martinelli, director of admissions at Wharton: "We're interested in the life lessons you've learned."

Keep in mind that schools also use the essays to assess your personal goals and values so that they can create a class of interesting people. Try to blend those goals and values in your essays by discussing an accomplishment in terms of the obstacles you overcame to achieve it. It's not enough to write about leading a project team or managing people of diverse backgrounds; you also need to discuss how you dealt with someone who didn't accept or respect you. Use personal experiences that reveal strength of character, leadership qualities, and integrity. Too frequent use of the word *I* and too rare use of the word *we* in recording your accomplishments can put off some B-school admissions officers. Sensitive to criticisms that MBAs are too self-centered, many schools today emphasize teamwork and read essays with an eye toward ferreting out the egomaniacs.

Of course, crafting well-thought-out, creative essays that articulate your vision can't be accomplished overnight. Expect to spend between 20 and 40 hours thinking, organizing, drafting, and polishing each set. For each individual essay, be sure that you stick to the point you want to make and that your point addresses the question being posed. Besides typos and grammatical errors, not answering the question asked is the single greatest mistake admissions directors say they come across. Also, be succinct. Most schools ask for responses of about 500 to 750 words (which works out to be about two printed double-spaced pages), and admissions staff, weary from reading through thousands of applications, favor quality over quantity. Although a few schools have a minimum required length for essays, that's not an open invitation to submit a 20-page tome. A good rule of thumb is to stay within 10 percent of the suggested upper word limit.

If you're having trouble putting pen to paper—or, more aptly, saving type to disk—you may consider contacting a B-school consultant for help with the application process. For a few hundred to several thousand dollars, consultants offer you inside connections from their previous jobs at B-schools, tips on interviewing, and, sometimes, essay critiques. MBA Strategies (www.mbastrategies. com) is one of the largest domestic consulting firms, with over 1000 clients. At $150 an hour, President Sally Lannin, a former

Craft essays from your personal experiences.

placement officer at Stanford University, says her company some-times helps clients brainstorm on essay topics, although for ethical reasons it doesn't edit essays. The drill is similar at Kaplan Educational Centers, which opened an admissions consulting arm in 1996. If you're looking for help that runs a lot cheaper, $50 to $65 will buy you a package of about 40 essays written by applicants who have been accepted by your preferred school from an online service named IvyEssays (www.ivyessays.com). Needless to say, the essays should be used as examples only. IvyEssays also offers editing for about $75 per three-page essay.

Yet such services could backfire. "If the school feels any part of the application is not the student's own work, they are immediately disqualified," says Robert Alig, Wharton's former director of admissions and financial aid. Alig's comment underscores a simple and very important point: above all, honesty is vital. Certainly emphasize everything you've done, but don't cross the line by lying or padding your accomplishments. Admissions staff aren't likely to check your facts, but they've read through so many applications that they can sense when something doesn't quite add up. And each year, top schools kick out a small number of MBA students when they discover lies on applications—often when recruiters do background checks for summer internships and alert the school to something amiss.

If you know a graduate of the school, ask him or her to read over your essays before you turn them in. As far as gimmicks go, don't get too carried away. Writing your responses in crayon, or submitting videotapes or CD-ROMs to accompany your essays, can be both clever and cute, helping to differentiate you from the crowd, but can also flop. Don't go overboard unless you've got a lot of substance to begin with.

PREPARING FOR THE PERSONAL INTERVIEW

With selectivity on the rise, the personal interview has gone from being simply an extra to an integral part of the application process. Kellogg was the first B-school to interview every applicant to its full-time program. "The interview is important for two reasons," says Michele Rogers, Kellogg's director of admissions. "First, it answers the question: can the candidate effectively present himself or herself to another person? But it's also a chance for the student to learn about our programs from someone who knows what we really offer." Kellogg officials don't think you can assess a person's composure, ability to articulate ideas, or leadership qualities from test scores or past grades alone. And many observers believe that one reason Kellogg's corporate recruiters continually rank the school high—placing its 2002 grads in the top 5 for general management, marketing, global scope, and teamwork skills—is because it prescreens its candidates so well.

Today, the interview is required or encouraged at many top MBA programs. A growing number of schools, including NYU, Chicago, Harvard, Virginia, Stanford, and MIT, say that most of the applicants who ended up being accepted did have an interview. In order to speak with more potential students, schools are asking current students to conduct campus interviews and alumni to file interview reports on candidates living in remote parts of the world. There's also an increasing emphasis on telephone interviews—which are required for international applicants at Washington University's Olin School, for example—and on using other events such as the MBA Forums as a place for admissions officers to set up sessions.

| It's in your best interest to have a personal interview. |

What all of this means is that it's probably in your best interest to try to arrange an interview, especially if you're articulate and think you can demonstrate some leadership skills. It's always helpful for admissions officers to put a face to an application, and it's another opportunity for you to fill in some of the gray areas that might be putting your acceptance at risk. If you feel you're not likely to do well in an interview, however, especially if your English skills aren't up to snuff, you might consider trying to gracefully avoid it, since a lousy showing can torpedo your chances. That won't be easy to do, however, since so many schools are paying more attention to the interview than ever before. Some may interpret declining the interview as a lack of interest. Your best bet: practice what you'd like to say in advance, and stay calm.

If you can, visit the campus. Sit in on classes and meet with anyone you can. "These visits are key to determining the quality of teaching," says Dawna Clarke, admissions director at the Darden Graduate School of Business at the University of Virginia. Be sure to speak with students, faculty, and alumni who are doing the kind of work you plan to seek. (You can usually get names from the admissions and alumni offices.) Don't fret if you can't spend the money on an on-campus interview; schools say that alumni and student interviews are just as worthwhile. But there is a reason to spend the cash if you can—it gives you a chance to interview the school as well and make sure that the flavor and culture of the place are right for you. Those direct experiences with the schools will also make for better essays, according to Linda Baldwin, director of admissions at the Anderson School of Business at the University of California at Los Angeles. Applicants who've visited the schools "can express much more insightfully why they belong there," she says. If you do have a face-to-face, sit-down meeting, treat it like a job interview: be punctual, dress professionally (no sandals, jeans, T-shirts, or sweats), and remember to write a thank-you note afterward.

What is a personal interview like? In general, interviewers want to evaluate leadership and communication skills. For nonnative English speakers, it's also a way to assess English proficiency. Interviews are conversations, but they are also geared toward getting information. "We're going to ask them about their careers, their goals, and how our program fits into those goals. Why have they made some of the decisions they've made? We'll explore how the applicant analyzes, but I can't tell you how. That would ruin it. We'll explore leadership, because it's a key aspect of the program, as are team skills," says Cornell's Grinblatt. "We may ask questions regarding current business events. We are also going assess their interpersonal skills. Remember—strong handshake, eye contact, and good energy." Grinblatt's tips prove a good point. Most interviews are behavioral; the questions asked have no right or wrong answers. They usually begin with broad questions and then home in on the individual's particular interests and characteristics. For instance, at Washington University, the interview starts with why applicants are interested in an MBA program and in Olin in particular. Then it moves on to what they think they can add both in and out of the classroom, and what type of community involvement they've had. At the end, they're asked if there's anything they'd like to say that wasn't brought up earlier. Sometimes interviews will be conducted in groups. MIT, for example, does this with its foreign applicants to get a sense of how much a candidate will participate in a discussion. No matter what the setting, however, the keys to success are the same: try to relax; don't be afraid to talk or ask questions; be sure to answer a question directly without waffling; and, above all, be yourself.

Interviews tell a lot about who you are and what you can add to a classroom.

MANAGING YOUR RECOM- MENDERS

Choosing the right people to recommend you is one of the most important parts of the application process, and most applicants don't spend enough time doing it. If possible, start with successful alums of your target school, but ask them only if they really know you and can write eloquently on your behalf. "A recommendation is the other way we find out about someone's personal characteristics and potential. It's so important for applicants to choose recommenders who know them well and have worked with them, not someone they think is going to impress us. We want to know what kind of person this is, how motivated, what's their leadership potential." says Linda Meehan, director of admissions at Columbia Business School. Don't choose a big-name CEO, government official, or celebrity to write about you unless they really know who you are. Big names do not impress admissions officers, nor do they improve your chances of acceptance if they refer to you in broad platitudes.

Most schools require two to three recommendations, usually from people whose experience with you has been professional. Approaching a professor who knows you well is also appropriate. Do not, however, ask a family member to extol your virtues unless you work in a family-run business. Admissions directors will assume bias and probably not attach any weight to such a recommendation. Although this may seem obvious, make sure you pick someone on whom you can rely to write you a good recommendation, and who won't forget to send it in on time. Remember, writing recommendations can be hard work. At Harvard, for example, recommenders must rate you on a scale from outstanding (top 5 percent) to below average (bottom third) on such characteristics as integrity, sensitivity to others, personal and professional maturity, intellectual ability, and imagination. Be sure to prepare recommenders for their assignment by providing them with background material on you, including your resume. Consider sharing completed parts of your application, and, at the very least, put together a quick memo outlining why you want to pursue the MBA and what it will do to help further your goals.

PAYING YOUR WAY

Getting accepted to B-school is a great achievement. Now you've got a new challenge: finding a way to pay for the two years of education. That's no small feat if you're aiming for one of *Business-Week*'s top 30 programs, where the annual tuition is up to a whopping $36,770 (at Harvard) and not much less than that at most of the other schools. That works out to roughly $70,000 over two years, not including the salary and benefits you're forgoing by going to school rather than working. The MBA programs at Harvard, Stanford, Wharton, and Dartmouth now clear the $33,000 tuition barrier, with most other schools in the top 15 not far behind. It's not surprising, then, that the average loan taken out by a 2002 graduate of one of *BusinessWeek*'s top 30 was a stunning $44,000.

"The main way students pay the MBA is through loans and personal funds," says Don Martin, associate dean of admissions at the University of Chicago Graduate School of Business, where 75 percent of students get some financial aid from the school. Martin says some students still receive funding from their employers, but, because of the economy and students' reluctance to be bound to their companies, he estimates corporate sponsorship has fallen 20 to 30 percent in the past 10 years. At Chicago, like other B-schools, the loan process starts at the federal level. Prospective students fill out the Free Application for Federal Student Aid (FAFSA), available on the Web at www.fafsa.ed.gov. Based on savings, investments, and income statements, the government determines students' eligibility for Stafford Loans, which go as high as $18,500 per academic year. Students who demonstrate greater need can qualify for the federal Perkins Loan as well. Fixed at 5 percent interest, that loan may be as large as $6000 per year. Interest starts after graduation. On top of federal aid, most B-schools offer institution-specific loans through banking partners, such as the CitiAssist loan at nearly every school. The loan terms and rates vary by school. Be aware, however, that CitiAssist can be all too eager to loan money and you can get in over your head—be sure to take a loan for only what you really need.

Some schools, such as Stanford University, require students to submit separate financial aid forms directly to the school. Be aware of these deadlines as well. MBAs need not be saddled with loans. With a little digging, resourceful students can supplement financial aid packages with grants, either from private groups or the

B-schools themselves. A good place to start is *BusinessWeek* online. First, go to www.businessweek.com, then click on the B-schools tab. Scroll down to the link for financial aid. There you'll find Q&As with the financial aid directors of 29 B-schools and links to helpful financial aid Web sites.

Scholarships and financial aid can help you cope with the staggering costs of an MBA degree, but that money doesn't exactly grow on trees. You'll have to do your homework. That means searching for both public and private scholarships, applying for need-based and merit-based financial aid, and playing up the different aspects of your background if they can help you qualify for a special deal. The best way to get financial help is to ask for it, and ask early. That means your aid application should arrive at the admissions office on the first day possible. Ask the admissions staff and student aid office what's available. Most schools offer merit scholarships that cover part of the cost of tuition and set specific early deadlines for consideration. Also, find out whether work-study or graduate research and/or teaching assistantships are available. Although assistantships aren't used as much by business schools as they are by other types of graduate programs, they are an option at some schools and are growing in popularity. At Purdue's Krannert School of Management, for instance, B-school students can put a dent in their already cheap tuition with graduate assistantships or jobs as residential advisers for the 30,000 Purdue undergraduates. Southern Methodist University in Dallas will begin offering assistantships as part of aid packages this fall. At SMU, like most B-schools, a TA can expect a per-semester stipend of about $1500 for 10 hours of work a week, usually papers and leading discussion sections. That's time you won't get to spend on your own work, though. You can also try for private scholarships. A good source is www.fastweb.com, a free site that lists hundreds of available scholarships and has a searchable database.

Many scholarships are based on either merit or need, so you have to prove one or the other, and it's nice if you can prove both. Consider, too, that a top applicant may be offered better financial aid packages from a second-tier school than a brand-name one; only a handful of top 30 schools offer full rides to more than a few students. At Vanderbilt University's Owen School, the 25 most desired students are brought to Nashville for the weekend and wooed with full-ride scholarships in an attempt to get them to commit to Owen and not another top school where they might

> Get your
> financial aid
> applications
> in early.

already have been admitted. Another innovative plan, the Park Leadership Fellows Program, comes from Cornell's Johnson School. Funded by a foundation named after the late media entrepreneur Roy Park, the program brings 30 top MBA applicants with identifiable leadership potential to Cornell by awarding them two full years of tuition plus living expenses. The idea behind the fellowship is to allow Cornell to compete more aggressively for the best students.

Most schools offer merit-based financial assistance to 20 to 35 percent of their students. At Northwestern's Kellogg School, 20 to 25 percent of the class gets scholarship money, while Indiana's Kelley School says 35 percent of its MBAs get a boost. That's pretty slim pickings overall—slimmer if you're not a member of a minority group, whose students tend to get the few full scholarships available. There is, however, no shortage of companies willing to loan money to MBA wannabes, who are considered good credit risks by most banks. One option: the MBA Loans program run by the Graduate Management Admission Council (GMAC). The program ties together federal need-based loans and private loans in a one-stop-shopping approach. Students who apply for help under this program are simultaneously considered for all federal loan programs as well as private loans, eliminating the need to fill out numerous applications. (For more information on the program, call 1-888-440-4MBA or visit www.gmac.org.) It's also a good move to surf the Web for ideas and resources. One notable site is FinAid (www.finaid.org), which provides a slew of links to Web sites containing scholarship information for all students, not just B-schoolers. It's broken down by special qualifications (i.e., minority, female, disabled), offers tools such as a calculator projecting loan payback, and provides text of the latest government legislation on financial aid. And the creator of the site, Mark Kantrowitz, knows a thing or two about paying for a graduate education. He financed a degree and has completed all but his dissertation in computer science at Carnegie Mellon University. For graduate students, the maximum under the Stafford Loan is $18,500 a year. And there's a cumulative limit of $138,500 for graduate and undergraduate combined. "Private loans have limits set by lenders, and they vary considerably. It's important to minimize the amount of money you borrow. A good rule of thumb is: live like a student now so that you don't have to live like a student after you graduate," says Kantrowitz.

Most MBA students will need loans.

Minority students looking for help have another resource: the Consortium for Graduate Study in Management (CGSM), an alliance of 14 schools, 13 of which are top 30. The CGSM's goal is to propel people of African American, Hispanic, and Native American descent into managerial positions, and it offers 250 students per year fellowships covering full tuition and fees at 1 of the 14 schools. Those odds aren't too shabby, since only about 1000 individuals apply for admission to the schools directly through the CGSM and are eligible for the aid. Applicants rank their desired schools in order of preference, and the CGSM uses the ranking to determine how to extend its fellowships—although admission to B-school through the CGSM doesn't guarantee a fellowship. To learn more, visit the organization's Web page (www.cgsm.org).

The financial aid situation is far grimmer for international students, who must rely primarily on merit-based aid because virtually no federal aid is available to them. Adding to the problem is the dearth of loans offered by U.S. banks, which fear a higher rate of default from students returning to home countries where they can't be as easily tracked or the economic situation is relatively unstable. Although they can apply through the GMAC MBA Loans program, international students must have a U.S. citizen cosigner. "Generally speaking, there aren't loans without cosigners for most international students. And there are very few grants," says Krantowitz. He recommends contacting the country's ministry of education for information on home country loans or visiting www.edupass.org.

Financial aid is more scarce for international students.

RANKING THE B-SCHOOLS

Rankings. The word alone makes some people break into a sweat. Controversial by definition, rankings are loved by those that top the charts and dismissed as biased and irrelevant by those that don't. This is true of beauty pageants, consumer products such as cars, and stockbrokers. And it's very true of business schools, many of which believe that their reputations rest entirely on how they do in the four most widely followed rankings, two done by magazines (the biennial *BusinessWeek* list and the *U.S. News and World Report* project) and two done by newspapers (the *Financial Times* and *The Wall Street Journal*).

Although the rankings presented by all these publications are taken seriously, the approaches they use are entirely different, as are the results. *BusinessWeek* uses extensive surveys of graduates and corporate recruiters to come up with its ranking. By contrast, *U.S. News* determines much of its list through admissions and placement data, including average GMAT scores and starting salaries of MBAs. Most of this data comes directly from the schools, whereas *BusinessWeek*'s ranking data comes only from the schools' customers—the graduates, and the recruiters who hire those graduates.

This attention to customer satisfaction may seem somewhat obvious at a time when everyone's favorite mantra is "The customer is always right." But that was not always the case, especially at B-schools. In fact, until *BusinessWeek* began to rate the schools on customer satisfaction in 1988, most rankings were based on the reputation of the schools' professors and their published papers in academic journals. B-school deans and/or faculty were usually asked to list their top schools in order of personal preference. That meant that a school's academic prestige and reputation for academic research usually had a great impact on its rating. Although it is clear that research is vital both to schools and to American business (and we've added a component to try to measure the impact of that research on the practicing manager), those surveys didn't take into account how this knowledge was conveyed to the students. They ignored such key attributes of a B-school as teaching excellence, the quality of the curriculum, and the value of a school's graduates to the world's business leaders.

BUSINESS-WEEK'S TOP 30 BUSINESS SCHOOLS

We think that the people in the best position to call it as they see it are the graduates, who pay a small fortune to go to B-school, and the recruiters, who must live with the results once they've hired the grads to work at their companies. So those are the folks whose input we use to compile the *BusinessWeek* rankings. The 2002 graduate poll, consisting of 45 questions, was e-mailed to 16,906 graduates of 88 schools in North America, Latin America, and Europe, and we heard back from 11,518 (68 percent). We then added the views of the class of 2002 to those we gathered in 1998 and 2000 to create our graduate ranking, for a total of 27,577 responses. The corporate poll was mailed to 420 companies that actively recruit MBAs from the campuses of the best B-schools. Our surveys were filled out by 219 companies, who together hired 11,199 MBAs in 2002, for a response rate of 52 percent. Table 3.1 shows the results.

The *BusinessWeek* results are very different from the 2002 rankings posted by *U.S. News and World Report,* which listed the top 30 schools as follows: (1) Stanford; (2) Harvard; (3) Penn; (4) MIT; (5) Northwestern; (6) Duke, Chicago (tied); (8) Columbia; (9) Dartmouth; (10) UC Berkeley, University of Michigan, Virginia (tied); (13) NYU, Yale (tied); (15) UCLA; (16) Cornell; (17) UNC-Chapel Hill; (18) Carnegie Mellon, Texas (tied); (20) USC; (21) Indiana; (22) Emory; (23) Rochester; (24) Georgetown, Michigan State, Ohio State, University of Minnesota (tied); (28) Purdue; (29) BYU, Vanderbilt (tied).

Why such a discrepancy? It's all about methodologies. The *U.S. News* ranking relies mostly on numerical data, and changes its formula from year to year. In 2002, peer assessments by schools counted for 25 percent, recruiter assessments counted for 15 percent (they used to count for 40 percent), starting salary and bonus counted for 14 percent, placement success counted for 21 percent (it used to count for about 35 percent), GMAT scores counted for 16.25 percent, GPA counted for 7.5 percent, and selectivity counted for 1.25 percent. Students weren't surveyed, and some 60 percent of the ranking is a product of shuffling numbers and another 25 percent is a sort of beauty contest among peer institutions, leaving only 15 percent for an assessment by a customer.

The newest entrant to the marketplace, *The Wall Street Journal,* bases its ranking solely on recruiter responses—and anyone a school submits as a recruiter can be surveyed. That means some companies could submit dozens of responses, and, because most first-level, on-campus recruiters are alumni of the B-school where

Table 3.1   *BusinessWeek*'s TOP 30 BUSINESS SCHOOLS

OVERALL RANKING	2000 RANKING	CORPORATE RANKING	GRADUATE RANKING	INTELLECTUAL CAPITAL RANKING	% OF GRADS WITH OFFER BY GRADUATION
1. Northwestern (Kellogg)	2	2	1	18	83
2. Chicago	10	5	3	16	75
3. Harvard	3	1	14	6	81
4. Stanford	11	7	5	1	81
5. Pennsylvania (Wharton)	1	3	12	8	76
6. MIT (Sloan)	4	8	11	2	82
7. Columbia	7	4	17	7	73
8. Michigan	6	6	13	13	66
9. Duke (Fuqua)	5	9	9	4	76
10. Dartmouth (Tuck)	16	12	4	11	74
11. Cornell (Johnson)	8	13	2	12	67
12. Virginia (Darden)	9	11	6	14	79
13. UC Berkeley (Haas)	18	16	10	3	72
14. Yale	19	20	8	9	69
15. NYU (Stern)	13	10	20	32	72
16. UCLA (Anderson)	12	23	7	10	58
17. USC (Marshall)	24	14	16	33	60
18. UNC-Chapel Hill (Kenan-Flagler)	15	15	18	27	68
19. Carnegie Mellon	14	18	22	15	70
20. Indiana (Kelley)	20	19	23	39	70
21. Texas-Austin (McCombs)	17	22	25	24	64
22. Emory (Goizueta)	28	30	19	19	60
23. Michigan State (Broad)	29	17	28	29	69
24. Washington (Olin)	23	33	21	20	58
25. Maryland (Smith)	27	42	15	21	64
26. Purdue (Krannert)	25	33	26	22	73
27. Rochester (Simon)	21	39	24	25	59
28. Vanderbilt (Owen)	22	35	27	17	53
29. Notre Dame (Mendoza)	na	24	35	23	66
30. Georgetown (McDonough)	26	28	32	41	50

they recruit, many who do respond may be pledging more alumni loyalty than anything. Indeed, *WSJ* admits that schools that topped the list had a large number of alumni recruiters answering the survey. The *WSJ* rankings for 2002 were as follows: (1) Dartmouth; (2) University of Michigan; (3) Carnegie Mellon; (4) Northwestern; (5) Penn; (6) Chicago; (7) Texas; (8); Yale; (9) Harvard; (10) Columbia; (11) Purdue; (12) UNC-Chapel Hill; (13) Michigan State; (14) Indiana; (15) UC Berkeley; (16) Maryland; (17) Emory; (18) Ohio State; (19) Cornell; (20) Virginia; (21) IMD; (22) Rochester; (23) Wake Forest; (24) NYU; (25) Duke; (26) Vanderbilt; (27) ITESM; (28) IPADE; (29) SMU; (30) MIT. (Wondering Where Stanford is? Number 35.)

At the end of the day, most rankings help a potential student to identify the superior business programs in the country. *BusinessWeek*'s rankings have far more detailed information on the strengths and weaknesses of one program over another. If you're the type of person who favors teamwork and cooperation, you'd probably do best at Dartmouth or Kellogg. On the other hand, if you thrive on competing with your teammates, you might consider Harvard or Rice. Need a school where technology flows through the classroom? Try Carnegie Mellon or Iowa. Prefer an environment in which faculty members are at the leading edge of their research areas? Think about Chicago, Cornell, or Rochester. None of these tidbits are captured in other rankings. But this information and lots more can be found on the following pages, which give a question-by-question breakdown of the student survey along with a list of the top and bottom schools for each question out of the top 50 schools we surveyed. If you're interested in a school that doesn't appear, you can assume that the school got average marks—neither excellent nor poor.

THE SURVEY QUESTIONS

1. To what extent did your MBA experience meet your expectations of what a good program should be?

In this less-than-appealing job market and down economy, many 2002 grads voiced disappointment and frustration, but hardly any of this ill will was directed at the MBA programs themselves. In fact, many grads felt their schools went above and beyond the call of duty in preparing them for the future. Which schools did the best of meeting students' expectations? Chicago, Northwestern (Kellogg), Dartmouth (Tuck), Virginia (Darden), Stanford, Yale, Duke (Fuqua), Cornell (Johnson), Berkeley (Haas), and Pennsylvania (Wharton). At the bottom: Fordham, Tennessee, Texas A&M, Connecticut, South Carolina (Darla Moore), Syracuse, and Clark Atlanta.

2. Do you believe your MBA was worth its cost in time, tuition, and lost earnings?

For most potential MBA students, the amount of money they plunk down for B-school may be the largest purchase they have ever made—not to mention the decent salary given up to do so. A good number of grads were able to find jobs that paid considerably more than what they earned before the MBA, but many were forced to settle for a position that paid nearly the same, leaving grads to question whether the costs were worth it. Which students reported feeling they got the best return? BYU (Marriott), Chicago, Northwestern (Kellogg), Stanford, Maryland (Smith), Berkeley (Haas), Virginia (Darden), Dartmouth (Tuck), Florida and UCLA (Anderson). The worst: Northeastern, American, Texas A&M, Miami, George Washington, Thunderbird, Boston College (Carroll), South Carolina, Pepperdine, Clark Atlanta, Fordham, and Syracuse.

3. Would you urge your friends or colleagues to enroll in the same MBA program at the school?

It's the ultimate recommendation: would you wish your experience on your best buddy or your spouse? Would you do it all over again? In a year like 2002, many students were hesitant to answer positively. Those who would do it again in a heartbeat went to Chicago, Northwestern (Kellogg), Stanford, Duke (Fuqua), Dartmouth, Harvard, Virginia (Darden), Pennsylvania (Wharton), UC Berkeley (Haas), and Yale. Less enthusiastic were grads from Arizona State, George Washington, Illinois, Penn State (Smeal), Tennessee, Texas A&M (Mays), Clark Atlanta, Syracuse, and South Carolina.

4. How would you rate the quality of the teaching in core courses?

Virtually everyone at B-school takes a version of the following fundamentals: accounting, finance, marketing, statistics, organizational behavior, and economics. But not every school does a good job of getting the basics across in a quality way. The best: Virginia (Darden), Chicago, Indiana (Kelley), William & Mary, Dartmouth, Northwestern (Kellogg), Cornell (Johnson), Maryland (Smith), Yale, and Ohio State (Fisher). The worst: Penn State (Smeal), SUNY-Buffalo, Rutgers, Fordham, Arizona State, Tennessee, Notre Dame (Mendoza), South Carolina (Darla Moore), Syracuse, and Clark Atlanta.

5. How would you rate the quality of teaching in elective courses?

Once you've covered the common territory, it's time to specialize in an area that you can tailor to your own specific career goals, be they in the fast-paced world of investment banking or in starting your own com-

> It's a good sign when grads say they'd recommend their alma mater to friends.

pany. Here's the class of 2002's perspective on the best and worst schools for elective teaching and quality. Best: Chicago, Stanford, Dartmouth, Northwestern (Kellogg), Yale, Maryland (Smith), Virginia (Darden), Cornell (Johnson), Columbia, and Pennsylvania (Wharton). Worst: Northeastern, Pepperdine, Fordham, Syracuse, Arizona State, Connecticut, Wake Forest (Babcock), Texas A&M (Mays), and Clark Atlanta.

> Don't under-estimate the value of good teaching when choosing a school.

6. Overall, how did the quality of the teachers compare with others you have had in the past?

Going to an elite B-school should be an eye-popping intellectual experience, one that surpasses those overcrowded, boring, lecture courses in college taught by teaching assistants barely out of school. But B-school profs are under tremendous pressure these days to teach not only in MBA programs, but also in executive education classes and outside consulting gigs—not to mention their research commitments. Leading the pack here are: Chicago, Virginia (Darden), Northwestern (Kellogg), Dartmouth (Tuck), Yale, Cornell (Johnson), Harvard, Maryland (Smith), MIT (Sloan), and Stanford. The laggards: Rutgers, Tennessee, Connecticut, George Washington, SUNY-Buffalo, Arizona State, South Carolina, Syracuse, and Clark Atlanta.

7. Were your teachers at the leading edge of knowledge in their fields?

Although students are thrilled to have full-time corporate warriors in the classroom telling them what things are really like, it's also important for schools to give their students teachers who are at the cutting edge of thinking in such subjects as marketing, finance, and entrepreneurship. Students said that most advanced thinkers were found at Chicago, MIT (Sloan), Stanford, Yale, Maryland (Smith), Cornell (Johnson), Northwestern (Kellogg), UC Berkeley (Haas), Harvard, and Pennsylvania (Wharton). Those least likely to lead the way: Penn State (Smeal), Rutgers, Notre Dame, South Carolina, SUNY-Buffalo, Wake Forest (Babcock), Connecticut, Fordham, Syracuse, and Clark Atlanta.

8. Were faculty members available for informal discussion when classes were not in session?

Learning is never confined to the classroom, and students know it. But many professors, constrained by consulting deals, research, and other requirements, can't seem to make extra time to help students through a challenging assignment. Others, however, go out of their way to be around at any time of the day or night. Most available: Dartmouth (Tuck), Virginia (Darden), Cornell, Yale, Stanford, Wake Forest, Northwestern (Kellogg), Emory (Goizueta), Maryland (Smith), and Washington-St. Louis (Olin). Least available: Tennessee, SUNY-Buffalo, Fordham, Connecticut, Northeastern, Syracuse, Rutgers, South Carolina, and Clark Atlanta.

9. To what extent were faculty members aware of the material other faculty members would cover?

Although faculty members specialize in one discipline, they should certainly have an understanding of what their counterparts are teaching. It's frustrating for students to begin to cover a concept in one class and then find out that another professor thinks they know it cold (and assigns work based on that assumption) or rehashes it. Which schools' faculties do the best job of communicating between faculty members? Chicago, Rochester (Simon), Virginia (Darden), Northwestern (Kellogg), Babson (Olin), Stanford, Cornell (Johnson), Yale, Dartmouth (Tuck), and Emory (Goizueta). Worst: SUNY-Buffalo, Arizona State, Fordham, Tennessee, Syracuse, Notre Dame (Mendoza), South Carolina (Darla Moore), Rutgers, Connecticut, and Clark Atlanta.

10. To what extent was coursework integrated as opposed to being taught as a cluster of loosely related topics?

In the real world, you don't have an accounting problem or a finance problem. Usually it's a combination of both. That's why many schools are trying to better integrate their curricula and to redesign programs to combine these topics rather than keep them in separate silos. The most integrated: Babson (Olin), Virginia (Darden), Rochester (Simon), Indiana (Kelley), Dartmouth (Tuck), Yale, Chicago, Stanford, Maryland (Smith), and Northwestern (Kellogg). The least integrated: Wisconsin-Madison, Texas A&M, UC Davis, Arizona (Eller), Fordham, Notre Dame (Mendoza), South Carolina (Darla Moore), Connecticut, Rutgers, and Clark Atlanta.

11. Were the school's most prominent academics actively involved in teaching in the MBA program?

B-schoolers are paying big bucks to get the best education, and they expect some of that to be provided by the marquee names the schools tout in their view books and marketing material. Which schools have the big names in the classroom? Virginia (Darden), Chicago, Dartmouth (Tuck), Yale, Rochester (Simon), NYU (Stern), Pennsylvania (Wharton), Cornell (Johnson), Indiana (Kelley), and Maryland (Smith). Those that don't? Connecticut, Arizona (Eller), Penn State (Smeal), SUNY-Buffalo, Michigan, South Carolina (Darla Moore), Rutgers, Syracuse, Texas A&M (Mays), and Clark Atlanta.

12. Do you believe faculty members compromised teaching in order to pursue their own research or consulting?

The balance between teaching and research is a tough one for professors. On the one hand, many tenure decisions are made strictly on the basis of publication of scholarly journals. On the other hand, students expect their professors to be prepared for every class and able to com-

> More schools are trying to better integrate the curriculum.

municate their ideas. Grads say the schools that get this right are Virginia (Darden), Northwestern (Kellogg), Dartmouth (Tuck), Stanford, Washington, BYU (Marriott), Indiana (Kelley), Washington-St. Louis (Olin), Duke (Fuqua), and William & Mary. Those that struggle: Connecticut, Texas-Austin (McCombs), Rochester (Simon), Case Western (Weatherhead), Thunderbird, American, Wisconsin-Madison, Illinois, and SUNY-Buffalo.

13. How often was the material/research presented in class for discussion and review current?

With the business world changing faster than anyone could ever have anticipated, it's important that professors be able to place their research in a contemporary context. Students who must learn from out-of-date material often feel they're not as well prepared as their colleagues at other schools. Most current: Chicago, Northwestern (Kellogg), Cornell (Johnson), Maryland (Smith), Yale, Dartmouth (Tuck), UC Berkeley (Haas), Stanford, Ohio State (Fisher), and Harvard. Least current: Connecticut, UC Davis, SUNY-Buffalo, Rutgers, Arizona State, Syracuse, Penn State (Smeal), South Carolina (Darla Moore), and Clark Atlanta.

14. Did you receive information during the program that will be useful on the job?

B-school, unlike other academic disciplines, is as much about the real world as it is about theory. So the job of a professor is to get esoteric ideas across but also to make sure students have some street smarts. Best in this category: Chicago, Northwestern (Kellogg), Cornell (Johnson), Dartmouth (Tuck), Maryland (Smith), Yale, MIT (Sloan), UC Berkeley (Haas), Virginia (Darden), and Columbia. Bringing up the rear: Penn State (Smeal), Fordham, George Washington, Connecticut, Northeastern, SUNY-Buffalo, Rutgers, Syracuse, South Carolina (Darla Moore), and Clark Atlanta.

15. Was the amount of assigned reading either too little or so excessive that it impeded learning?

B-schoolers expect to work their collective tails off. But if the workload is too intense, they're unable to absorb everything. Conversely, if it's too much of a party atmosphere, they've gotten a piece of paper but little they can use when they enter the workforce. Schools with the best balance were: Fordham, Miami, Northwestern (Kellogg), Maryland (Smith), UC Davis, Emory (Goizueta), Duke (Fuqua), UCLA (Anderson), Yale, and Florida. Those that are struggling: Purdue (Krannert), Clark Atlanta, Carnegie Mellon, Penn State (Smeal), Georgetown (McDonough), Rice, Indiana (Kelley), William & Mary, and Babson (Olin).

Real-world application of classroom material should be clear.

16. To what extent did your school weave e-business topics throughout the curriculum?

E-business is all the rage, and despite the downward spiral of the market, even the most traditional of Old Economy companies have e-commerce efforts under way or around the bend. MBAs need to know how to manage these ventures and their specific challenges. Which schools do the best without going overboard or underplaying? Northwestern (Kellogg), Pennsylvania (Wharton), Babson (Olin), Emory (Goizueta), Yale, Virginia (Darden), Chicago, Dartmouth (Tuck), Stanford, and Michigan. Those still looking for the right recipe? Washington, George Washington, American, Syracuse, South Carolina (Darla Moore), Tulane, Pepperdine, Connecticut, Clark Atlanta, and UC Irvine.

17. To what extent were interpersonal skills stressed in the curriculum?

Touchy-feely things may not get respect from the number crunchers, but it's a fact that those who can't communicate or manage well won't go far, no matter how smart they are. Which schools do the best job in this category? Stanford, UC Berkeley (Haas), Chicago, Virginia (Darden), Yale, Dartmouth (Tuck), Northwestern (Kellogg), Washington, and Maryland (Smith). Those that miss? George Washington, Penn State (Smeal), Illinois, Clark Atlanta, Thunderbird, Connecticut, Pepperdine, Case Western (Weatherhead), Syracuse.

> Many MBAs hope to have their own business one day.

18. Did your school provide you with enough information to make you feel confident starting your own business?

If you ask a class of first-year MBA students to raise their hands if they ever hope to start their own businesses sometime down the road, you can be sure that about half the students will extend their arms. Even though that dream isn't always realized, skills learned in B-school can give an MBA the confidence to take that hope and turn it into reality. So which schools provide the necessary tools? Babson (Olin), Stanford, Chicago, UCLA (Anderson), Virginia (Darden), UC Berkeley (Haas), Dartmouth (Tuck), Northwestern (Kellogg), Southern Methodist, and Maryland (Smith). Those that leave grads jelly-legged? Tennessee, SUNY-Buffalo, Fordham, Texas A&M (Mays), Syracuse, Michigan State (Broad), Clark Atlanta, Arizona State, South Carolina, and Connecticut.

19. How useful do you think the computer skills and analytical tools taught at your school will be in your job as a manager?

More and more, technical knowledge and analytical models are key to getting an edge in the workplace—especially now, say recruiters, who find many grads lacking in even Excel basics. Many B-schools have gotten on the ball, teaching more relevant and up-to-date computer and analytical models. Those that have done the best: Carnegie Mellon,

Dartmouth (Tuck), Northwestern (Kellogg), Chicago, Duke (Fuqua), Indiana (Kelley), Maryland (Smith), Virginia (Darden), Cornell (Johnson), and MIT (Sloan). Those that trail: Michigan State (Broad), Harvard, George Washington, Notre Dame (Mendoza), Boston, Fordham, Texas A&M (Mays), Syracuse, South Carolina, and Clark Atlanta.

20. To what extent was the learning environment enhanced by the use of technology?

In this category, students say that Carnegie Mellon, Virginia (Darden), UC Irvine, Northwestern (Kellogg), Dartmouth (Tuck), Vanderbilt, Cornell (Johnson), UCLA (Anderson), Texas-Austin (McCombs), and MIT (Sloan) are the best. Less tech-savvy are Arizona (Eller), Boston, Syracuse, George Washington, Washington, Fordham, Texas A&M (Mays), Notre Dame (Mendoza), South Carolina (Darla Moore), and Clark Atlanta.

21. To what extent did technological tools become a part of the curriculum?

Face it, technology is evolutionizing the workplace, and the more experience B-school students have with tech tools, the better prepared they'll be at managing them and using them in their jobs. So who's getting it right? Carnegie Mellon, UC Irvine, Dartmouth (Tuck), Northwestern (Kellogg), Maryland (Smith), Virginia (Darden), Iowa (Tippie), Illinois, and Georgia (Terry). And who's playing catch-up? Southern Methodist, Rice (Jones), Syracuse, Boston College (Carroll), Washington, Fordham, Notre Dame (Mendoza), Texas A&M (Mays), South Carolina (Darla Moore), and Clark Atlanta.

22. To what extent were analytical skills stressed in the curriculum?

Some schools are famous for their quantitative offerings, while others don't get much beyond the basics and spend much more time focusing on softer skills. Who does the analytics right? Dartmouth (Tuck), UC Berkeley (Haas), Stanford, Virginia (Darden), Pittsburgh (Katz), Georgia (Terry), UNC Chapel Hill (Kenan-Flagler), Northwestern (Kellogg), South Carolina (Darla Moore), and Minnesota (Carlson). Those that stress it too much or not enough: MIT (Sloan), Syracuse, Rochester (Simon), Penn State (Smeal), Connecticut, Clark Atlanta, Illinois, Purdue (Krannert), and Carnegie Mellon.

23. How would you judge the school's performance in providing you with numerous ways of thinking and approaching problems that will serve you well over the long haul?

It's not just what you learn, it's how well you can apply it—and that's just another part of the B-school education. Whose students feel like they've gotten it? Chicago, Northwestern (Kellogg), Virginia (Darden), Stanford, Dartmouth (Tuck), Yale, Harvard, UC Berkeley (Haas), MIT

> The use of technology on the job is critical, so it's even more important in the classroom.

(Sloan), and Cornell (Johnson). Those who feel a little shaky? SUNY-Buffalo, Penn State (Smeal), Rutgers, Connecticut, Arizona State, Fordham, Tennessee, Syracuse, South Carolina (Darla Moore), and Clark Atlanta.

24. Do you feel your classmates emphasized individual achievement at the expense of teamwork?

B-school is not the cutthroat place it once was; many schools eschew grades altogether (or at least avoid releasing them to recruiters). Yet there are still some places where being top dog really means something and other places where classmates would happily give others the shirts off their backs—or at least their notes. Increasingly, the workplace has moved to a team-style management approach that MBAs need to be well versed in. The best at teamwork: Stanford, Dartmouth (Tuck), Northwestern (Kellogg), UC Berkeley (Haas), UCLA (Anderson), Yale, UC Davis, Virginia (Darden), Michigan, and UNC Chapel Hill (Kenan-Flagler). The most competitive: Tennessee, Rochester (Simon), Northeastern, American, Illinois, Syracuse, SUNY-Buffalo, Connecticut, and Clark Atlanta.

25. Did the caliber of your classmates impede or advance the learning process?

Having smart colleagues often raises the bar in the classroom. Conversely, if you're the only one to grasp a concept, there may be many frustrating hours in your future. Because MBAs spend so much time in teams, they learn as much from one another as they do from teachers. Those with the most stellar classmates: Stanford, Northwestern (Kellogg), Chicago, Dartmouth (Tuck), Harvard, Yale, Virginia (Darden), MIT (Sloan), Pennsylvania (Wharton), and Columbia. The least: Wake Forest (Babcock), American, Fordham, Syracuse, Tennessee, Clark Atlanta, Miami, SUNY-Buffalo, and South Carolina (Darla Moore).

> Responsive faculty and administrators are key to a good B-school experience.

26. How would you judge the responsiveness of the faculty and administration to students' concerns and questions?

Some schools bend over backward to listen and respond (if not grant their wishes, which isn't a requirement of listening and responding) to their students—most of whom have definite ideas on things that might be improved on and off campus. Others still ignore them, preferring to rule by fiat instead. The most responsive teachers and staffers are found at Cornell (Johnson), Northwestern (Kellogg), Chicago, Dartmouth (Tuck), Duke (Fuqua), Emory (Goizueta), Washington-St. Louis (Olin), UC Berkeley (Haas), Indiana (Kelley), and BYU (Marriott). The least: Illinois, Syracuse, Tennessee, Texas-Austin (McCombs), Penn State (Smeal), South Carolina (Darla Moore), Thunderbird, Texas A&M (Mays), and Clark Atlanta.

27. How would you assess the responsiveness of the school in meeting the demand for popular electives?

If you've spent an entire year waiting for the opportunity to get into that Nobel prizewinner's corporate finance course and it ends up being over-subscribed every time, you may not feel you got your money's worth. That wasn't the case at some schools, which worked to create new sections and tried to meet the needs of every student. The most responsive: Dartmouth (Tuck), Washington-St. Louis (Olin), Cornell (Johnson), Northwestern (Kellogg), Chicago, Maryland (Smith), Duke (Fuqua), Minnesota (Carlson), Ohio State (Fisher), and Yale. The least: North-eastern, Pepperdine, Fordham, Thunderbird, South Carolina (Darla Moore), Syracuse, Texas A&M (Mays), Connecticut, and Clark Atlanta.

28. How would you judge the school's efforts—either in class or in extracurricular activities—to nurture your skills in leading others?

B-schools are, it is said, the incubators for the future leaders of corporate America and the entire world. But not every school takes that statement as seriously as it might by teaching leadership skills. The best, say the students, are Northwestern (Kellogg), Cornell (Johnson), Chicago, Dartmouth (Tuck), Stanford, Yale, Emory (Goizueta), UCLA (Anderson), Virginia (Darden), and Maryland (Smith). Surprisingly, Harvard is not mentioned: students there complained that some of the leadership talk was just that—talk. The worst: Texas-Austin (McCombs), SUNY-Buffalo, Syracuse, Arizona State, Northeastern, Connecticut, Fordham, Clark Atlanta, Texas A&M, and South Carolina (Darla Moore).

29. To what extent did your school foster interaction between various ethnic groups?

It's not enough to have a class full of diverse students from all sorts of backgrounds and countries. A B-school has to make strides to get folks together—much like the real world of multinational corporations and deals. Do it too much and it'll feel forced. Those doing a good job, say students, are Stanford, Chicago, MIT (Sloan), Emory (Goizueta), Clark Atlanta, BYU (Marriott), Northwestern (Kellogg), UCLA (Anderson), Columbia, and UC Davis. Those that aren't there yet: South Carolina (Darla Moore), Iowa (Tippie), SUNY-Buffalo, Miami, Syracuse, American, Illinois, Northeastern, and Thunderbird.

30. How would you appraise your school's efforts to bring you in contact with practicing professionals in the business community?

Hard as it may be to admit, a large part of B-school has to do with schmoozing for a job. Some schools have excellent connections with real-world professionals and exploit them, while others are happy to

---

Leadership skills are prized by recruiters.

remain ivory tower bastions and rarely bring in big shots. Still others bring in so many professionals that education falls by the wayside. The schools best able to balance this: Stanford, Northwestern (Kellogg), Dartmouth (Tuck), Duke (Fuqua), UC Berkeley (Haas), NYU (Stern), Yale, Cornell (Johnson), UNC Chapel Hill (Kenan-Flagler), and Harvard. The least: Wake Forest (Babcock), Clark Atlanta, American, Rutgers, Fordham, Texas A&M (Mays), George Washington, Northeastern, South Carolina (Darla Moore), and Syracuse.

31. How would you judge the school's network and connections that can help you throughout your career?

A school's network can prove critical to your job search.

As suggested by the previous question, networking can make a world of difference for a student hoping for start-up financing for a backpack company or one who needs an extra helping hand before a job interview. Having a strong alumni base works to the advantage of schools like Harvard, Dartmouth (Tuck), Stanford, Chicago, Columbia, USC (Marshall), Virginia (Darden), Notre Dame (Mendoza), Northwestern (Kellogg), and Cornell (Johnson). Others don't offer such a strong base, like Arizona (Eller), Wake Forest (Babcock), Pittsburgh (Katz), Connecticut, Northeastern, Fordham, Syracuse, George Washington, and South Carolina (Darla Moore).

32. How would you judge the aggressiveness of the school in helping you with summer job placement in an internship?

Getting a summer job after your first year is more important than it's ever been, because recruiters are focusing their efforts on first-years in hopes of building company loyalty early on. The schools putting forward the most outstanding summer placement efforts were Chicago, Northwestern (Kellogg), Cornell (Johnson), Virginia (Darden), Michigan State (Broad), Duke (Fuqua), Dartmouth (Tuck), Yale, Columbia, and UCLA (Anderson). Those that need to step up: Wake Forest (Babcock), Babson (Olin), William & Mary, Texas A&M (Mays), Rutgers, George Washington, Pepperdine, Syracuse, Fordham, and South Carolina (Darla Moore).

33. How would you characterize the school's performance in helping you find a job before graduation?

Students know from their own marketing coursework that you still need to sell a product, no matter how good it is. Some schools have brought in human resources executives from major companies as placement officers and have completely revamped their offices after benchmarking companies as well as other schools. The schools getting kudos from students for their efforts are Chicago, Cornell (Johnson), Northwestern (Kellogg), Virginia (Darden), Duke (Fuqua), Michigan State (Broad), Dartmouth (Tuck), UC Berkeley (Haas), Yale, and Stanford. Those getting panned: Arizona (Eller), Babson (Olin), Wake Forest (Babcock), Connecticut, South Carolina (Darla Moore), Pepperdine, Syracuse, George Washington, Fordham, and Northeastern.

34. How would you characterize the quantity, diversity, and quality of firm recruiting on your campus with the career placement office?

The on-campus interview experience can leave much to be desired if all the interviewers are from the same industry or the firms aren't desirable places to work. Moreover, if there aren't many recruiters coming to campus, finding a job can be frustrating. Which schools have plenty of quality recruiters from all sorts of industries? Chicago, Northwestern (Kellogg), Duke (Fuqua), Michigan, Columbia, Cornell (Johnson), Dartmouth (Tuck), Pennsylvania (Wharton), Virginia (Darden), and Yale. Which leave something to be desired? Syracuse, Pittsburgh (Katz), Northeastern, George Washington, Babson (Olin), Fordham, Connecticut, South Carolina (Darla Moore), Wake Forest (Babcock), and Pepperdine.

> Independent job searches are more and more common.

35. If the organizations you targeted for employment did not recruit on your campus, how would you characterize the school's assistance in supporting your independent search for a job?

While on-campus recruiting remains a core of most MBA job searches, with the volatile market, many students have had to look elsewhere. The schools that are best at supporting these searches, say students, are Chicago, Northwestern (Kellogg), Cornell (Johnson), Stanford, Minnesota (Carlson), UC Berkeley (Haas), Duke (Fuqua), Virginia (Darden), Dartmouth (Tuck), and UCLA (Anderson). Those that leave students hanging: William & Mary, Syracuse, Northeastern, Texas A&M (Mays), South Carolina (Darla Moore), Wake Forest (Babcock), George Washington, Connecticut, Clark Atlanta, and Fordham.

36. How would you characterize your school's assistance in connecting you with nontraditional or smaller recruiters?

MBAs want to make a difference, and that can sometimes be hard in a big company. B-schools that realize this are helping their students find that niche where they'll fit best. Those that lend a hand: Chicago, UC Berkeley (Haas), Cornell (Johnson), Stanford, Northwestern (Kellogg), Yale, Dartmouth (Tuck), Virginia (Darden), Duke (Fuqua), and Maryland (Smith). Those that don't do as much: South Carolina (Darla Moore), Pepperdine, Syracuse, Connecticut, Clark Atlanta, Wake Forest (Babcock), Texas A&M (Mays), William & Mary, Northeastern, and Fordham.

37. How would you appraise the placement office's help with matters such as interviews, training negotiation, resumes, etc.?

The placement office must make connections and market the students as the cream of the crop. But once an interview begins, it's the student who's completely in control of his or her own destiny. Schools can help make sure that students are polished and well-spoken and don't throw away a chance at a better salary then they asked for. Best at helping to prep students: Chicago, Michigan State (Broad), Northwestern (Kellogg), UC Berkeley (Haas), Cornell (Johnson), Virginia (Darden), Michigan, Duke (Fuqua), Minnesota (Carlson), and UCLA (Anderson). Those that aren't: Wake Forest (Babcock), Northeastern, Pepperdine, Rutgers, George Washington, Fordham, Babson (Olin), Connecticut, Syracuse, and Clark Atlanta.

38. Based on your level of satisfaction, please appraise your school's efforts to include international business in the MBA program.

Globalization has become so overused as to appear clichéd these days, even in B-school. Yet there are some schools that students think do a great job of exposing them to other cultures and management styles. Topping the list: Chicago, Georgetown (McDonough), South Carolina (Darla Moore), Pennsylvania (Wharton), Yale, Columbia, UC Berkeley (Haas), USC (Marshall), and George Washington. Schools that haven't quite gotten it yet: Iowa (Tippie), UC Irvine, UC Davis, SUNY-Buffalo, Penn State (Smeal), Connecticut, Tennessee, Arizona State, Arizona (Eller), and Clark Atlanta.

39. Based on your level of satisfaction, please appraise your school's efforts to include ethics in the MBA program.

Although only a handful of schools require a business ethics course in order to graduate, the debate continues about how to best teach ethical behavior in an industry plagued with violations. The schools singled out by grads as the best in the area: Virginia (Darden), Notre Dame (Mendoza), BYU (Marriott), Dartmouth (Tuck), Pepperdine, Maryland (Smith), Northwestern (Kellogg), Chicago, Pennsylvania (Wharton), and Michigan. The laggards: Clark Atlanta, Illinois, Texas A&M (Mays), Babson (Olin), Wisconsin-Madison, SUNY-Buffalo, Boston College (Carroll), Arizona (Eller), UC Irvine, and Connecticut.

40. Based on your level of satisfaction, please appraise your school's efforts to include leadership in the MBA program.

Weaving leadership skills throughout the curriculum is not an easy thing to do, and making them stick until graduates get an opportunity to put them into action is even tougher. Best in this category: Harvard, Stanford, Northwestern (Kellogg), Cornell (Johnson), Virginia (Dar-

Ethics is a hot topic at B-schools these days.

den), Chicago, Dartmouth (Tuck), Michigan, Yale, and UCLA (Anderson). Falling behind: Iowa (Tippie), Northeastern, Syracuse, Arizona (Eller), Connecticut, Arizona (Eller), Texas A&M (Mays), South Carolina (Darla Moore), UC Irvine, and Clark Atlanta.

41. Based on your level of satisfaction, please appraise your school's efforts to include teamwork in the MBA program.

A skill more immediately relevant to recent grads than leadership is teamwork. Without it, you'll be a disaster in the workplace, since few projects are undertaken by a solo flier. Schools that lead the teamwork pack are Northwestern (Kellogg), Duke (Fuqua), Dartmouth (Tuck), Stanford, Yale, UC Davis, Virginia (Darden), Michigan, UNC Chapel Hill (Kenan-Flagler), and Cornell (Johnson). Those that need to focus more on teamwork: UC Irvine, Northeastern, SUNY-Buffalo, Fordham, Arizona State, Syracuse, Harvard, South Carolina (Darla Moore), Connecticut, and Clark Atlanta.

42. Based on your level of satisfaction, please appraise your school's efforts to include entrepreneurship in the MBA program.

The level of interest in entrepreneurship has been heightened in past years, and nearly every school now offers a variety of courses or a concentration in the area. But there's a big difference between lip service and the kind of training that really helps launch a start-up or expand on an established company's repetoire, and the grads at the following schools say they got the latter: Stanford, Babson (Olin), MIT (Sloan), UCLA (Anderson), Texas-Austin (McCombs), UC Berkeley (Haas), Chicago, USC (Marshall), Case Western (Weatherhead), and Northwestern (Kellogg). Grads were most disappointed by the entrepreneurship offerings at these schools: Iowa (Tippie), SUNY-Buffalo, South Carolina (Darla Moore), Tennessee, William & Mary, Michigan State (Broad), Texas A&M (Mays), Arizona State, Connecticut, and Clark Atlanta.

43. Based on your level of satisfaction, please appraise your school's efforts to include diversity in the MBA program.

Nearly all B-schools have made a big push to include a large proportion of students from other countries in their programs. Not all have done the same with women and domestic minorities, who remain largely underrepresented in B-school. Overall, however, diversity isn't just a matter of the faces in the crowd looking a lot more varied that they have in the past; it's also about diversity of ideas and incorporating of all types of people and ideas into a program. Some do a good job, especially Thunderbird, Pennsylvania (Wharton), Northwestern (Kellogg), Columbia, American, Duke (Fuqua), Maryland (Smith), Georgetown (McDonough), Miami, and Rochester (Simon). Getting the lowest marks in this area: Vanderbilt, William & Mary, Clark Atlanta, UC

Teamwork skills are critical to success after B-school.

Davis, Wake Forest (Babcock), Notre Dame (Mendoza), Arizona State, Texas A&M (Mays), BYU (Marriott), and Tennessee.

44. Based on your level of satisfaction, please appraise your school's efforts to include information technology in the MBA program.

Depending on your career objectives, you may happily wear the quant geek label or reject it. But at B-school, having access to and superior training in info tech can make all the difference in your career, whether or not you choose to work at a tech firm. Grads were happiest with the info tech offerings at MIT (Sloan), UC Irvine, Carnegie Mellon, Maryland (Smith), Stanford, Minnesota (Carlson), Texas-Austin (McCombs), UC Berkeley (Haas), Georgia Tech (DuPree), and UCLA (Anderson). They were unimpressed at William & Mary, Rice (Jones), Pepperdine, Texas A&M (Mays), Georgetown (McDonough), Fordham, George Washington, Notre Dame (Mendoza), South Carolina (Mendoza), and Clark Atlanta.

45. Based on your level of satisfaction, please appraise your school's efforts to include e-business in the MBA program.

Despite the dot-com bust, even Old Economy stalwarts have e-commerce efforts. And B-schools are following suit. Those that do a good job are MIT (Sloan), Maryland (Smith), Carnegie Mellon, Stanford, UC Irvine, UC Berkeley (Haas), Georgia Tech (DuPree), American, Northwestern (Kellogg), and Vanderbilt. Those that don't: Tulane (Freeman), Fordham, Notre Dame (Mendoza), Georgetown (McDonough), William & Mary, Tennessee, Iowa (Tippie), Pepperdine, South Carolina (Darla Moore), and Clark Atlanta.

E-commerce is here to stay, even at traditional companies.

B-SCHOOLS BY THE NUMBERS

There are many ways to select a business school, and just as many ways to look at one. Here, we use numbers and statistics to provide a snapshot of the best 50 schools. Some of this data—enrollments and GMAT scores—was provided by the schools themselves. They routinely publish oodles of information. But you won't find a lot of what's available on the following pages elsewhere; it was gathered specifically for this project by *BusinessWeek* from the latest crop of MBA grads—the class of 2002. What really makes these figures and statistics valuable is that they allow you to make direct comparisons among the best schools, focusing on what is most important to you. Rather than looking at, say, GMAT numbers or selectivity in isolation, you'll see exactly how a school compares with its peers. And you can compare your own stats with a school's averages.

You'll find a wealth of information in these pages. You'll discover which of the top schools are the most selective and therefore the toughest to get into. You'll get a bird's-eye view of which schools enroll the most (and the fewest) minorities and women. Through international student enrollment statistics, you'll get a feel for which schools are truly going global. And you'll find out which schools boast the highest enrollments and which offer a cozier class size. You'll also find out how much an MBA graduate from each of these schools is likely to command in the job market. And you'll discover which schools' graduates leave campus with the largest debt burdens hanging over their heads.

None of this information constitutes a ranking, nor is any of this data used by *BusinessWeek* to compile its own ranking of the top schools. But it may help you put the schools you're thinking about in a broader context.

> Make your own direct comparisons with these numbers.

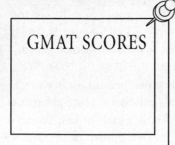

GMAT SCORES

One of the most nerve-wracking parts of the admissions process is the Graduate Management Admissions Test, taken by more than 210,000 people each year. Now computerized, it's required by some 850 business schools worldwide, including the 50 schools listed here. Although it's hardly perfect, the test is one of the only consistent yardsticks used to measure student quality, and it usually counts for some 20 to 40 percent of an application's overall weight. Scores continue to climb, with the largest jumps over the past two years occurring at UC Berkeley and Penn State, where average scores rose 29 points to 703 and 645, respectively. Table 4.1 shows the numbers for the class of 2004.

Table 4.1 GMAT SCORES

TOP 30 SCHOOLS	AVERAGE GMAT	RUNNER-UP SCHOOLS	AVERAGE GMAT
Columbia	711	UC Irvine	682
MIT	707	Washington	673
Harvard	705	Southern Methodist	660
Pennsylvania	703	Boston College	658
UC Berkeley	703	Ohio State	655
Duke	701	Arizona State	654
Northwestern	700	Brigham Young	650
NYU	700	Penn State	645
UCLA	700	Minnesota	645
Yale	698	Georgia Tech	645
Dartmouth	695	Babson	643
Chicago	687	Illinois	640
USC	684	Wake Forest	639
Virginia	683	Iowa	638
Michigan	681	Wisconsin	632
Texas-Austin	678	Rice	630
UNC	676	Pittsburgh	613
Emory	675	Case Western	610
Cornell	673	William & Mary	607
Carnegie Mellon	672	Thunderbird	600
Notre Dame	668		
Georgetown	663		
Maryland	656		
Indiana	651		
Washington U	651		
Purdue	651		
Rochester	649		
Vanderbilt	648		
Michigan State	639		
Stanford	NA		

B-SCHOOL SELECTIVITY

Another critical indicator of a business school's quality is the number of applicants it accepts and rejects. As it has for the past several years, Stanford remains the most selective school, rejecting an amazing 92 percent of applicants for the class of 2004. With MBAs more in demand than ever, it has gotten even tougher to get into a top 50 school. Although top-ranked Kellogg accepted some 22 percent of its applicants in 1994, today it allows in just 13 percent. Of the top 10 schools, only 2 (Dartmouth and Duke) accepted the same percentage of applicants in 2000 and 2002. For the other 8 schools, the percentage of applicants accepted dropped from anywhere between 1 and 10 percent. Table 4.2 shows the numbers for the class of 2004.

Table 4.2 B-SCHOOL SELECTIVITY

TOP 30 SCHOOLS	APPLICANTS ACCEPTED (%)	RUNNER-UP SCHOOLS	APPLICANTS ACCEPTED (%)
Stanford	8	Boston College	14
Harvard	10	Penn State	24
Columbia	11	Wisconsin	27
UC Berkeley	11	Ohio State	29
Northwestern	13	Arizona State	29
Pennsylvania	13	Southern Methodist	30
MIT	13	UC Irvine	31
Dartmouth	14	Illinois	31
Chicago	15	Washington	32
Yale	15	Iowa	33
NYU	15	Babson	39
UCLA	15	Georgia Tech	39
Virginia	18	Rice	39
Michigan	19	Minnesota	40
Duke	19	Brigham Young	44
USC	21	Wake Forest	47
Cornell	22	Case Western	48
Indiana	22	Pittsburgh	54
Michigan State	22	William & Mary	73
Maryland	23	Thunderbird	80
Notre Dame	23		
Georgetown	23		
Emory	24		
Carnegie Mellon	26		
Purdue	26		
Rochester	26		
Texas-Austin	29		
UNC	30		
Washington U	35		
Vanderbilt	47		

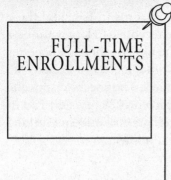

FULL-TIME ENROLLMENTS

The size of an MBA program is an important attribute of a school's culture and a key element in choosing your ideal school. Do you like the energy of a big city and the chance to meet more than 1000 students? You might do well at Harvard, Pennsylvania, or Columbia. Do you prefer a more secluded, intimate environment? Dartmouth or Purdue might make a better fit. Enrollments have remained more or less steady, fluctuating by no more than 60 students in the larger schools and 20 in the smaller schools. (Virginia, which added 86 students to its medium-sized roster, is one exception.) Table 4.3 shows the total full-time enrollments for the combined classes of 2001 and 2002.

Table 4.3 FULL-TIME ENROLLMENTS

TOP 30 SCHOOLS	FULL-TIME ENROLLMENT	RUNNER-UP SCHOOLS	FULL-TIME ENROLLMENT
Harvard	1805	Thunderbird	1100
Pennsylvania	1604	Illinois	387
Northwestern	1250	Wisconsin	355
Columbia	1172	Rice	353
Chicago	992	Babson	350
Michigan	869	Case Western	320
NYU	817	Ohio State	288
Texas-Austin	805	Arizona State	287
Stanford	752	Brigham Young	268
MIT	744	Washington	258
Duke	696	Minnesota	240
UCLA	671	Wake Forest	235
USC	581	UC Irvine	232
Virginia	574	Southern Methodist	230
Cornell	562	Boston College	223
UNC	554	Georgia Tech	210
Indiana	546	Penn State	197
Georgetown	530	William & Mary	185
Maryland	516	Pittsburgh	154
UC Berkeley	497	Iowa	152
Yale	480		
Carnegie Mellon	469		
Dartmouth	464		
Rochester	429		
Vanderbilt	422		
Emory	388		
Notre Dame	325		
Washington U	313		
Purdue	295		
Michigan State	209		

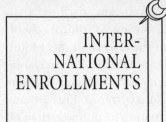

INTER-
NATIONAL
ENROLLMENTS

Global is one of the most overused buzzwords in B-school these days, yet some schools have been more receptive to large numbers of non-U.S. students than others. In the top 30 schools, Rochester leads the pack with almost half of its student body (45 percent) coming from outside of the United States. Thunderbird tops the runners-up list with a whopping 64 percent. The greatest rise in MBA applications has come from international students seeking an American MBA. Table 4.4 gives the rundown.

Table 4.4 INTERNATIONAL ENROLLMENTS

TOP 30 SCHOOLS	INTERNATIONAL STUDENTS (%)	RUNNER-UP SCHOOLS	INTERNATIONAL STUDENTS (%)
Rochester	45	Thunderbird	64
Pennsylvania	39	Case Western	47
Yale	39	Illinois	47
Carnegie Mellon	38	Iowa	44
Maryland	38	Pittsburgh	42
Washington U	36	William & Mary	39
Purdue	36	Wisconsin	37
Georgetown	35	Penn State	36
MIT	35	Babson	34
Michigan State	35	Ohio State	34
Chicago	34	Wake Forest	31
Harvard	34	Minnesota	29
Duke	34	Georgia Tech	29
UC Berkeley	34	Washington	28
NYU	34	Boston College	28
Emory	34	UC Irvine	24
Notre Dame	33	Rice	24
Northwestern	32	Southern Methodist	22
Indiana	31	Arizona State	22
Michigan	30	Brigham Young	12
Dartmouth	30		
UNC	30		
Stanford	28		
Cornell	28		
Virginia	28		
Columbia	27		
UCLA	26		
USC	26		
Texas-Austin	26		
Vanderbilt	25		

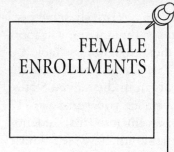

FEMALE ENROLLMENTS

Although women now make up a good half of all medical and law school students, you won't see the same statistics for the top 50 business schools, where women made up just 28 percent of the total for the graduating class of 2000—virtually unchanged from 1988. The percentage of women varies widely in the top 30, from a high of 38 percent at Stanford and NYU to a low of 20 percent at Washington University. Boston College heads the runners-up with 41 percent—more women than at any of the top 30 schools. Table 4.5 shows the figures for the combined classes of 2001 and 2002.

Table 4.5 FEMALE ENROLLMENTS

TOP 30 SCHOOLS	WOMEN STUDENTS (%)	RUNNER-UP SCHOOLS	WOMEN STUDENTS (%)
Stanford	38	Boston College	41
NYU	38	Rice	36
Harvard	35	Ohio State	35
Columbia	35	Case Western	34
Pennsylvania	33	William & Mary	34
Duke	32	Washington	33
USC	32	Pittsburgh	29
Northwestern	31	Wisconsin	29
Maryland	31	Thunderbird	29
UC Berkeley	30	UC Irvine	29
Yale	30	Illinois	29
UNC	30	Southern Methodist	28
UCLA	29	Babson	28
Georgetown	29	Minnesota	27
Michigan	28	Georgia Tech	27
Dartmouth	28	Penn State	26
Virginia	28	Wake Forest	25
Chicago	27	Iowa	22
Cornell	27	Arizona State	22
Carnegie Mellon	26	Brigham Young	15
MIT	25		
Texas-Austin	25		
Indiana	24		
Michigan State	24		
Vanderbilt	24		
Notre Dame	24		
Rochester	23		
Emory	22		
Purdue	22		
Washington U	20		

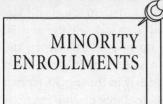

MINORITY ENROLLMENTS

Underrepresented minorities still make up a relatively small percentage of business school enrollments, although some schools have been more successful at wooing them than others. Table 4.6 shows percentages from the class of 2004 for African American, Hispanic, and Native American students from the United States. Rochester, which had the highest percentage two years ago (17 percent) still leads the pack with 25 percent minority students. Other schools, such as Harvard and Dartmouth, have seen similar 8 to 9 percent increases. UC Berkeley, Vanderbilt, Michigan State, and Chicago, by contrast, have just 5 to 6 percent. Case Western heads the runners-up with 13 percent.

Table 4.6 MINORITY ENROLLMENTS

TOP 30 SCHOOLS	MINORITY STUDENTS (%)	RUNNER-UP SCHOOLS	MINORITY STUDENTS (%)
Rochester	25	Case Western	13
Harvard	22	Ohio State	12
Northwestern	19	Wisconsin	11
Dartmouth	18	Georgia Tech	11
Duke	17	Rice	11
Maryland	15	Southern Methodist	10
Notre Dame	15	Arizona State	9
Carnegie Mellon	14	Penn State	8
Georgetown	13	Wake Forest	8
Stanford	12	Pittsburgh	7
Columbia	11	Babson	7
Michigan	11	William & Mary	7
NYU	11	Illinois	7
UNC	11	Brigham Young	5
USC	10	Minnesota	4
Washington U	10	Thunderbird	4
Pennsylvania	9	Iowa	3
Cornell	9	UC Irvine	3
Indiana	9	Boston College	3
Purdue	9	Washington	2
Virginia	8		
Yale	8		
MIT	7		
UCLA	7		
Texas-Austin	7		
Emory	7		
Chicago	6		
Michigan State	6		
Vanderbilt	6		
UC Berkeley	5		

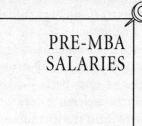

Schools tend to focus on GMAT scores and essays as indicators of applicant quality. But another important measure is the salaries applicants earn before deciding to go back to school. The larger the salary, the more likely it is that the candidate left a meaningful job in a demanding environment. In 2000, with the market booming, many students left jobs that paid more than ever to attend B-school. In 1998, students entered Stanford after earning a median pre-MBA salary of $65,000. Two years later, students entering Stanford left jobs earning them $80,000—a $15,000 increase in median pre-MBA salary. Table 4.7 shows the figures for median salaries for the members of the class of 2002 before they got their degrees.

Table 4.7 PRE-MBA SALARIES

TOP 30 SCHOOLS	PRE-MBA SALARY	RUNNER-UP SCHOOLS	PRE-MBA SALARY
Stanford	$80,000	UC Irvine	$53,000
Harvard	75,000	Penn State	50,000
Pennsylvania	65,000	Pittsburgh	50,000
MIT	65,000	Babson	50,000
Northwestern	60,000	Rice	50,000
Chicago	60,000	Minnesota	47,000
Columbia	60,000	Southern Methodist	45,500
Dartmouth	60,000	Georgia Tech	45,000
UC Berkeley	60,000	Boston College	45,000
UCLA	60,000	Arizona State	45,000
Michigan	58,000	Case Western	45,000
NYU	57,000	Washington	44,000
Cornell	55,000	Wisconsin	41,500
USC	52,000	Thunderbird	40,000
Texas-Austin	51,000	Illinois	40,000
Emory	51,000	Wake Forest	40,000
Duke	50,000	Ohio State	40,000
Virginia	50,000	William & Mary	40,000
Yale	50,000	Iowa	35,000
UNC	50,000	Brigham Young	31,000
Carnegie Mellon	50,000		
Vanderbilt	48,000		
Indiana	45,000		
Washington U	45,000		
Maryland	45,000		
Purdue	45,000		
Georgetown	45,000		
Rochester	42,000		
Notre Dame	40,000		
Michigan State	37,000		

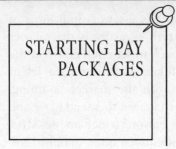

STARTING PAY PACKAGES

The technology bust and the sluggish economy resulted in considerably lower starting pay packages for graduates of the class of 2002. Still, these mostly six-figure numbers are nothing to scoff at. And, despite the poor economy, newly minted MBAs still earned hefty sign-on bonuses, along with benefits and perks—all of which *BusinessWeek* includes in the total pay package. That's why the figures in Table 4.8, which come directly from student surveys, tend to be higher than those reported by the schools.

Table 4.8 STARTING PAY PACKAGES

TOP 30 SCHOOLS	TOTAL PAY	RUNNER-UP SCHOOLS	TOTAL PAY
Stanford	$138,100	Rice	$103,000
Harvard	134,600	Ohio State	102,500
Pennsylvania	124,500	Boston College	100,000
Columbia	123,600	Penn State	96,900
Dartmouth	122,100	Wisconsin	95,000
MIT	121,800	Minnesota	94,500
Northwestern	119,800	Wake Forest	94,000
Chicago	119,400	Babson	91,250
Virginia	119,100	Arizona State	91,000
Cornell	116,400	Southern Methodist	90,000
Michigan	115,200	Pittsburgh	88,000
UC Berkeley	115,000	UC Irvine	86,987
Duke	113,600	Thunderbird	85,500
NYU	113,300	Iowa	85,000
UCLA	111,100	Brigham Young	83,000
Yale	110,200	William & Mary	80,000
Carnegie Mellon	108,000	Washington	80,000
Washington U	106,100	Illinois	79,750
Georgetown	105,000	Georgia Tech	78,000
Texas-Austin	104,000	Case Western	76,000
UNC	103,800		
Indiana	102,700		
Emory	101,400		
USC	100,900		
Vanderbilt	100,200		
Purdue	99,900		
Maryland	98,300		
Notre Dame	97,100		
Rochester	96,800		
Michigan State	90,300		

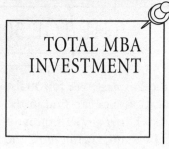

TOTAL MBA INVESTMENT

Sure, you're likely to boost your standard of living significantly by getting an MBA from a good school. But more likely than not this will come with a hefty price tag, which most people finance by borrowing money. The numbers in Table 4.9 reflect the average outstanding loans and lost wages for the graduates of the class of 2002—and the debt load can be staggering. At public universities, the pressure isn't quite as great as at private institutions, where debt can total $60,000 or more.

Table 4.9 TOTAL MBA INVESTMENT

TOP 30 SCHOOLS	MEDIAN TOTAL INVESTMENT	RUNNER-UP SCHOOLS	MEDIAN TOTAL INVESTMENT
Stanford	$186,200	Babson	$149,500
Harvard	185,800	Southern Methodist	147,600
MIT	181,000	Thunderbird	142,700
Columbia	179,900	Rice	142,000
Chicago	179,600	Case Western	140,900
Northwestern	177,300	Boston College	132,600
Dartmouth	177,000	Wake Forest	130,600
Pennsylvania	173,300	Minnesota	114,900
NYU	172,500	UC Irvine	112,800
Duke	167,700	Illinois	105,400
Cornell	165,100	Penn State	98,300
USC	163,100	Wisconsin	93,700
Yale	162,900	Arizona State	92,400
Carnegie Mellon	159,800	Ohio State	91,200
Washington U	159,000	Washington	89,200
Michigan	157,800	William & Mary	86,000
Emory	157,300	Georgia Tech	79,900
Vanderbilt	154,400	Iowa	75,900
Georgetown	154,000	Pittsburgh	73,300
Rochester	150,300	Brigham Young	71,100
Notre Dame	140,100		
Virginia	137,700		
UC Berkeley	123,000		
UCLA	122,600		
Maryland	107,900		
Texas-Austin	106,500		
Indiana	103,600		
UNC	100,600		
Michigan State	98,800		
Purdue	97,200		

THE TOP 30

The business schools that make up the *BusinessWeek* top 30 list offer the highest-quality MBA education you can find in the United States, and perhaps in the world. While many schools have moved toward similar styles of teaching and curriculum, the schools on this list all have their own distinct personalities, environments, and cultures. Each has strengths and weaknesses, differing curriculum styles, experiential learning opportunities, and more. And each offers a different education and experience.

So which school is the best fit for you? Read through the following profiles and you'll be well on your way to figuring that out. Each profile starts with a snapshot view providing information about a school's size, diversity, costs, selectivity, standing with corporate recruiters, graduates, and intellectual capital—and the big question for many prospective MBA students, the tally of grads with jobs by commencement and their starting pay packages. Near the end of each profile, we identify the companies that hire the most graduates of each school; the most outstanding faculty, as identified by the class of 2002; tips for applicants straight from the admission directors' mouths; and candid comments on the schools from graduates of the class of 2002.

There are other interesting tidbits in each profile, too. For example, did you know that more than 600 students gather each Thanksgiving for dinner at Northwestern University's Kellogg Graduate School of Management—a tradition started by the dean more than 20 years ago? Or, did you know that you can sign up for more than a half dozen double majors at schools like the University of Michigan Business School and the University of Pennsylvania's Wharton School?

Virtually all of the figures in these profiles apply to the class that entered in the fall of 2002—or, in the case of enrollment figures, the combined class currently enrolled at each school (class of 2003 and class of 2004). An asterisk next to any number indicates that the figure is a *BusinessWeek* estimate. The lists of each school's outstanding professors are based on the results of *BusinessWeek*'s graduate survey. Information about GMAT scores, selectivity, and diversity are provided by the schools, while salary figures are provided by the graduates of the class of 2002 who answered the *BusinessWeek* survey.

> Which of the top schools is right for you? Read these profiles and find out.

1. NORTHWESTERN UNIVERSITY

NORTHWESTERN UNIVERSITY

Kellogg School of Management
Donald P. Jacobs Center
2001 Sheridan Road
Evanston, Illinois 60208-2001
E-mail address: MBAadmissions@kellogg.northestern.edu
Web site address: www.kellogg.nwu.edu

Enrollment: 1250	Annual tuition and fees: $32,800
Women: 31%	Estimated annual budget: $55,200
Non-U.S.: 32%	Average GMAT score: 700
Minority: 19%	Average months of work experience: 54
Part-time: 1350	Accepted applicants enrolled: 64%
Average age: 27	Corporate ranking: 2
Applicants accepted: 13%	Graduate ranking: 1
Median starting pay: $85,000	Intellectual capital rank: 18

Teaching methods: lecture 30%, case study 30%, experiential learning 5%, simulations 5%, team projects 30%

The "Kellogg Spirit" isn't a myth. There's a reason students continuously rave about the tight-knit Kellogg Family. When push comes to shove, members of the school pull together to work as a family, and in 2002, when finding a job became an even greater challenge, administrators and staff alike pulled together to help the students. "We asked the assistant and associate deans to let us know who would be willing to reach out to students still looking for jobs," says Roxanne Hori, assistant dean and director of career management. "We divvied up the list of students, brainstormed with them, and came up with new alumni connections." That's just one example of the new things that Northwestern University's Kellogg School of Management tried out recently. But it's what meant the most to the students, adds Hori—that and newly minted dean Dipak Jain's trips around the world to drum up support from recruiters. On those trips, the soft-spoken dean, whose efforts to improve the king of B-schools are following in the school's strong general management tradition, went beyond meeting with recruiting companies: he also made small talk with airplane seatmates on his trips. Don't laugh—some half dozen students found their full-time jobs owing to Jain's plane talks.

Despite Kellogg's being a larger school in the B-school spectrum (about 600 MBAs), students continuously praise the school's nurturing, close-knit environment. With all of the top MBA programs offering the same standard courses and electives these days, B-schools are constantly searching for a way to set themselves apart. Kellogg came through this year, living up to its team-oriented nature, helping it pull ahead of the pack. It wasn't rare to walk into an office and find deans on the phone with personal address files in hand making phone calls to recruiters, alums, and friends. Their teamwork-based style played a major role in creating a near flawless performance in a harrowing job market for graduates this year. Teamwork is simply a standard at Kellogg, and not just when it comes to students. For newly installed dean Dipak C. Jain, "strength attracts strength," meaning that Kellogg creates an environment to attract and retain top faculty members and also gives them ample resources for research, funding, the latest technology, and the freedom they need to perform their best. The school has succeeded in maintaining collegiality and cooperative culture among the faculty, which in turn translates into a stronger and more integrated curriculum. "The more you help [faculty members] grow," Jain says, "the more they'll help the institution grow."

Longtime dean Donald P. Jacobs stepped down from his post at the end of the 2001 school year, leaving behind a legacy built on teamwork and team learning, the cornerstones of this MBA powerhouse. In his wake, he left behind not only a new high-tech three-building complex that bears his name but a sturdy program, which finds itself sitting atop *Business-Week*'s rankings once more after a six-year run as number 2. Jacobs took the reins at Kellogg back in 1975 and outlasted the deans of every top 30 school. As Kellogg's dean for over 25 years, he established the model of the modern business school in the early 1980s by turning toward building a culture founded on cooperative learning and student empowerment. He also helped build Kellogg's superb reputation in marketing. Tag words like teamwork, customer-serviced administration, and well-rounded student body can be found throughout all top B-schools' promotional literature.

With the end of Jacobs's long reign, what's in store for Kellogg in the future? It begins with Dean Jain, who took the helm in the summer of 2001 and plans on continuing to build upon Jacobs's solid foundation. Jain, who previously served as an associate dean and has been at Kellogg for 16 years, has some pretty big shoes to fill. He's off to a good start, however, pushing initiatives encapsulating the areas of leadership, scholarship, and partnership. Jain is continuing to build on leadership, a hallmark at Kellogg, beginning in his own office. To better meet the needs of students and faculty alike, Jain reorganized the senior administrative points, splitting his former role of associate dean into two branches: faculty/research and academic affairs/curriculum. When it comes to scholarship, Jain's catchphrase is "rigor to relevance." According to Jain, research must not exist in a vacuum, and Kellogg puts that belief into action on a daily basis. Research, and incorporating research into the curriculum, is key among professors at the school, and the administration readily encourages collaboration across disciplines to develop new ideas further. A case in point: over 50 new courses have been added since 1995, most within months of inception, not years as is the case at many schools.

Also high on Jain's agenda is strengthening partnerships. For the past year Jain has traveled around the globe meeting with recruiters and alums to work toward his goal of building a stronger and more closely knit network. At nearly every stop, Jain has met with alumni clubs, recruiters, and corporate friends in an effort to add value for the school's grads and partners within the business community and to just simply introduce himself.

Kellogg will immerse you in its team-oriented nature from day one during orientation week—or Conceptual Issues in Management (CIM) week, as it is known there. For starters, you'll meet the 60 students with whom you'll take your core courses. The week-long orientation program, organized by second-year students, includes a business simulation game, sessions on cultural diversity and academic advising, community service, a beach party, and a trip to Wrigley Field for a Cubs game. Plus, students also take the opportunity to participate in the Kellogg Outdoor Adventures (KOA), one of the most popular activities on campus. The weeklong KOA, which precedes CIM Week, takes you off campus and into nature, where you'll take part in a handful of exercises designed to put you in the teamwork state of mind. In the past, students have ventured through Alaska, Hawaii, the Caribbean, the Colorado Rockies, and even Iceland.

After the fun and games, you'll test your teamwork skills in a rigorous curriculum. At Kellogg, you'll follow an 11-week-quarter schedule, which is a bit different than other schools' semester or modular systems. Most students follow the traditional six-quarter schedule, with fall, winter, and spring classes followed by a summer internship and three more quarters during the second year. However, students with an undergraduate business degree can finish up in a more condensed consecutive four-quarter schedule starting in June and going straight through to graduation.

If you follow the regular full-time MBA track, you're required to take 23 classes to graduate (9 core courses and 14 from a long list of electives), but you can waive the basic core classes and replace them with an upper-level elective, as do about 50 percent of the students. Kellogg's program is one of the most flexible, and gives a lot of recognition to what you already know (e.g., not forcing a Wall Street whiz to sit through a finance core class). In your first year, you'll dive right into the core and take Accounting for Decision Making, Mathematical Methods for Management Decision, Statistical Methods for Management Decisions, Business Strategy, Strategies for Leading and Managing Organizations, Finance I, Microeconomic Analysis, Marketing Management, and Operations Management. Once you're done with the core, you're free to design your MBA and navigate through one, two, or even three majors.

Kellogg is split into six departments: Accounting and Information Management, Finance, Management and Organizations, Management and Strategy, Managerial Economics and Decision Sciences, and Marketing. The departments further offer over 20 major tracks including Finance, Biotechnology, Marketing, Health Industry Management, Human Resources Management, and International Business and Markets. You can also opt for 1 of 10 professional program offerings including media management, public and nonprofit, transportation and logistics, and real estate management. Though Kellogg built its reputation in marketing, these days you'll find more and more students heading down the finance route as well, or pursuing a dual degree in medicine, education, or public policy. The well-balanced curriculum you'll get from Kellogg is one thing grads continuously laud the school for. As a 2002 grad with a heavy technical background in engineering said, "The MBA at Kellogg made me a more well-rounded individual with incredible financial, strategic, managerial, and leadership skills." It's not rare to hear grads, faculty, and recruiters alike praise Kellogg as a place where you'll get a well-rounded MBA.

Kellogg maintains its balance, remaining on top of the game. In the past few years, new courses include Model and Technology, Entertainment Management, and Creating an Innovation Mind-Set. Keeping the curriculum current and flexible is key at B-schools today, and Kellogg's new programs have students talking. To complement its ongoing ethics curriculum, Kellogg revised its curriculum in the fall of 2002, placing ethics at the front and center of the core. Nearly all students are required to take Management and Organizations (MORS): Strategies for Leading and Managing Organizations. In that course, faculty members present a common ethics case taken from current events, and students have the opportunity to explore things such as corporate codes of ethics and how they actually guide executive behavior. The course provides students with the social science tools they need to solve organizational problems and influence the actions of individuals, groups, and organizations. It also prepares managers to understand how best to organize and motivate human capital, manage social networks, and execute strategic change—all vital qualities and skills to possess when facing today's market.

Kellogg also introduced a new major in the fall of 2002: business and its social environment (BASE). The initiative comes as a result of a collaborative effort between faculty, students, and the administration attempting to address the evolving business community. The BASE major allows students to pursue an in-depth study of the role of the private corporation in its broader social environment. Students tap into Kellogg's many resources, such as the Ford Motor Company Center for Global Citizenship, the Center for Nonprofit Management, the Center for Biotechnology, and the Center for Healthy Industry Management, and take courses including Crisis Management, Environmental Management, and Nonprofit Leadership.

As dean, Jacobs pushed to internationalize Kellogg, and Jain hopes to continue doing the same. Already international students hail from over 60 countries and make up a third of the class. Kellogg operates three international executive MBA programs in France, Israel, and Hong Kong, which not only expand and globalize the alumni network, but also help familiarize potential MBA students from overseas with the program. And, you can also create your own international independent study called Global Initiatives in Management (GIM), focusing on a country of your choice. Under the guidance of a faculty advisor, you'll take 10 weeks of classes, followed by a two-week research trip to the chosen country where you'll meet with top executives and government officials. In the past, students have gone to China, Brazil, the Czech Republic, Ghana, South Africa, Russia, and Singapore, to name a few. For each of the geographic regions, students as a group arrange a syllabus, book guest speakers, determine research topics, and identify key issues facing local industries, under the guidance of a faculty sponsor. After completing their coursework during the winter quarter, students travel to their selected country of study over spring break for a two-week group consulting project, and on their return they present their results to faculty and visiting executives in the spring.

Kellogg also organizes an international speaker series that has brought to campus the likes of Ion Diaconescu, president of the Romanian parliament; Asda Jayanama, Thai ambassador to the United States; and Omar Carneiro, president of AT&T in Brazil. On the heels of GIM's success, the school launched a similar program, Tech Ventures, in 1999. Instead of studying across the world, though, students study companies just halfway across the country in Silicon Valley.

Innovative research lies at the heart of the curriculum. With over 20 research centers, you'll have a diverse pool of resources to tap into. Recently Kellogg added a few more centers, including some in areas that are making the business community talk these days. With a student body that is 30 percent female, it's no wonder that the topic of women in business is an issue at the forefront. Through the Center for Executive Women, established in 2001, professors and students alike address the issue of why there aren't more women achieving top positions in the business realm. Also in 2001, Kellogg opened its doors to the Center for Research in Technology, Innovation, and E-commerce. With a mission of seeking to understand the impact of technology on improving business performance, driving innovation, promoting organizational effectiveness, and creating competitive advantage, the center supports faculty members and MBAs by funding research projects, case studies, seminars, and conferences. In 2002, Kellogg introduced the Motorola Research Scholars Program. The Tech Center and the Motorola partnership will award two students

$40,000 toward tuition, along with a summer internship at Motorola.

Kellogg also offers an array of other programs, which brings the "family" to over 2500. It houses a part-time evening MBA program, which meets in downtown Chicago; an executive MBA program, which meets on weekends at the Allen Center, a few blocks away from the B-school's main Evanston campus complex; and an active executive education effort, which brings some 5000 top executives to campus each year for short-term courses. When students voiced complaints about the cramped quarters, Kellogg responded by starting construction of a $25 million, 75,000-square-foot addition to the Evanston campus center to alleviate space concerns. This comes after a $14 million renovation and expansion of the facilities in 1995 that included 15 new classrooms wired for network access, 20 group study rooms, a quiet study room, a 20-terminal computer training facility, an expanded computer lab, a student lounge and lockers, and a skylit atrium. In 2000, the Leverone Hall and Andersen Hall complex was named the Donald P. Jacobs Center, in honor of Jacobs's longstanding service.

It's hard for a B-school to reach the top on its own, though. Jain is working double time to reach out to faculty, alumni, and recruiters to ensure the network grows and strengthens. For the past year, Jain has met with leaders in the business community to help spread the word on Kellogg's successes. Ask the students, faculty, and administrators alike, and they'll tell you that it's the culture that sets the school apart from all other B-schools. And it's what makes students want to give back. A case in point: Fran Langewich, assistant dean and director of student life, graduated from the program in 1995, and she's been working for Kellogg ever since. She says it's the people that made her come back and make her want to stay. That's no surprise. Students at Kellogg tend be a collaborative bunch who know how to strike a balance between work and play. MBAs regularly take time to give back to

the school through their own student-run plans. For example, student initiatives brought the Learning Through Experience in Action Program (LEAP) to Kellogg. Chicago Tours, a series of student-organized trips to Chicago businesses for observation and networking, also developed from student initiatives. Students even designed the school's Web site. They also put out the Kellogg Serial, the student Web page for course bidding and student evaluations of the faculty and courses. The Graduate Management Association—the student government—has traditionally involved itself in school policy making. Sports are also big at this Big 10 school. You'll find MBAs actively involved in intramural hockey, soccer, and rugby teams, as well as in the over 100 clubs on campus, such as the Finance Club and Consulting Club, the Culture Connection Club and European Culture Club, and the performance-driven Kelloggrhythms and Special K. It's not rare to find students giving a helping hand to their community. The spirit of teamwork woven through the curriculum permeates beyond the student culture within the B-school's walls and out into the surrounding community. You'll find students working on Business With a Heart, raising money for charitable causes. Or you'll find them with hammer in hand building homes for low-income families through the Kellogg Service Initiative and Habitat for Humanity, collecting and distributing clothing, or just helping out a homeless shelter.

Students' spouses are made to feel at home and are commonly an integral part of the equation. You'll find a handful of them filling the post as deans' assistants. Through the Joint Ventures program, many spouses say they made more friends at Kellogg than the students. About a third of the students are chosen by lottery for dorm apartments in the McManus Living-Learning Center on the southern periphery of campus. Everyone else lives off campus, but luckily there are plenty of options in apartment complexes like upscale Park Evanston and Evanston Place, or numerous more affordable apartments that are just a five-minute walk from the campus.

Located on the banks of Lake Michigan, the tree-lined Evanston campus has a lot to offer, and Chicago is just a short elevated train ride away. Students tap a keg every Friday at 4:45 P.M. in Kellogg's atrium for the weekly TGIF pow-wow. You'll also find plenty of hot spots to head out to for a night of fun with your friends. Evanston is home to a handful of great bars, delicious restaurants, live venues, and even a hookah bar; and downtown Chicago is just a 40-minute elevated train ride away. MBAs frequent the cozy 1800, Tommy Nevins, and the Keg to throw back a beer with friends; the more upscale Prairie Moon and Bar Louie for a glass of wine or two; and Nevins Live for some good tunes. And you won't be disappointed with the good fare—there's Flat Top for stir-fry, Stained Glass to impress, and Tapas for fun Spanish-style food and sangria. Winter's cold chills will keep students indoors, but the spring's inviting afternoon breezes will find students out on Deering Meadow, directly in front of the Jacobs Center, where Frisbee and soccer are the sports of choice. You'll even run into faculty, administrators, and the dean joining in on the games.

PLACEMENT DETAILS

Both Director Hori and Dean Jain have focused their efforts on reaching out to employers. The pair traveled around the country and the world and met with employers to ask for feedback, get updates on hiring expectations, and introduce the new dean and his agenda. Hori and Jain also took these travel opportunities to meet with alumni in the different cities to reinforce connections with them, which came into play in the placement process.

For starters, they had an executive in residence program, where three alumni from different backgrounds came in to spend three days each and offer their career counseling services. "At some point during your job search, it's nice to get some insights from the people out there," Hori says, adding that they've worked on developing the topic of networking. Last school year they hosted four schoolwide networking workshops and events with over 300 students from across the school's programs and alumni. Through workshops, she's trying to further drive home the importance of the off-campus job search.

Plus, Hori says, she's aiming to do more functional and industry treks with students. For instance, there is a trip to Los Angeles and New York specifically focusing on media and entertainment companies, and one to the East Coast for those pursuing a marketing track, as well as the New York Wall Street trip. Plus, there's a pharmaceutical and biotech trek in the works.

International students are getting a little extra help as well. With the help of an immigration attorney, international students learn the ins and outs of finding employment both in their own country and in the United States by reviewing changes in the laws, issues with visas, and hurdles for employers.

Kellogg MBAs graduating in 2002 were the most employed of all B-school grads, with 83 percent having a job offer by commencement and 91 percent with offers three months after that. Most garnered only one or two offers this year, typical of the down economy. Average pay packages were nothing to sneeze at: 2002 grads earned $119,800. While consulting firms and banks cut back their hiring overall, Kellogg grads managed to snag quite a few offers in the fields. Still, Kellogg caters to a wide range of companies, from banks to automakers to consumer goods companies to tech firms, so there's no shortage of opportunity.

TOP HIRES

McKinsey & Company (24); Bain & Company (12); Merrill Lynch (12); A.T. Kearney (10); Deloitte Consulting (9); The Boston Consulting

Group (7); Goldman Sachs (7); JPMorgan Chase (7); Quaker Foods & Beverages (7).

OUTSTANDING FACULTY

David Besanko (strategy); Steven Rogers (finance); Scott Shaefer (management); Karl Schmedders (decision science); Daniel Diermeier (management); Mitchel Petersen (finance); Julie Hennessey (marketing); Sergio Rebelo (finance); Scott McKeon (decision science).

APPLICANT TIPS

So you want to get into the number 1 B-school? There are a few things you can do to get on the right track. According to Kellogg's admissions director, Michele Rogers, the best time to apply is when your application is the strongest, meaning data is complete, it's well put together, and it gives a good sense of the type of person you are. Rogers is looking for an applicant who will add to the class and develop through the program. When she's reading your application, she wants to understand your interests, goals, and motivations to determine whether there's an overall good fit with the program.

Your score on the GMAT will matter in terms of indicating whether you'll be able to handle the analytical coursework; however, it's not the be-all and end-all of the application. Rogers also pays close attention to other indicators, such as your undergraduate coursework, letters of recommendation, essays, and interview. All admitted applicants are interviewed. The initial hurdle is to demonstrate whether you can handle the work; the next big step is how you compare with the rest of the applicant pool.

It's not important whether you majored in economics or in English as an undergraduate.

Rogers says she seeks candidates from all backgrounds and majors; the important part is whether you've done well in your chosen track. The ability to learn is what's most important, rather than the particular area. However, Rogers adds, it's important to complete at least one or two quantitative courses, such as calculus and statistics, to provide you with the basic skills needed for analytical coursework.

If you prepared for the GMAT and gave it your best shot, but your score is still on the lower end of the scale, Rogers advises focusing on areas of the application where you have more control, such as the essay portion. In the essays, she's hoping to get a clearer picture of what you've already accomplished and what you hope to accomplish in the future. Her advice: just write what you want her to know. The more she knows about you, the easier it will be to determine whether you and the program are a good match. Don't discount the importance of your letters of recommendation—or Career Progress Surveys, as Kellogg likes to call them. The most effective surveys, Rogers explains, not only provide feedback on the candidate's performance and personal attributes, but also discuss some particular experience that demonstrates them.

Finally, interviews are not your ticket in just yet, Rogers says. In the interview process, she homes in on your personal attributes to get a clearer understanding of your goals and motivations. Candidates are required to request an interview, and all admitted are interviewed by a staff member, student, or alumnus. Rogers adds: "At Kellogg, we try to interview candidates before reviewing the application to provide an additional point of view without the anchor or balloon of the essays and recommendation."

KELLOGG MBAs SOUND OFF

This has been such an outstanding experience for me—so much more than I ever could have expected, and definitely not an experience that I would have had if attending another business school. Even though this is one of the more difficult times to be graduating with an MBA, I would not hesitate in a second to make the same decision to get my MBA and to attend Kellogg if I had to do it all again. I have grown so much as a person and learned so much from my peers and professors. From classroom discussions to late-night group sessions to late-night evenings out with friends, Kellogg provides the total package—a perfect mix of intellectual stimulation and learning, combined with an abundance of leadership opportunities and extracurricular activities (clubs, conferences, sports, and socializing). I truly feel that this has been the most intense, stressful, fun, energizing, crazy, hectic, fulfilling, challenging, rewarding, and worthwhile experience of my life. I leave Kellogg completely satisfied and, in my opinion, prepared and ready to tackle the challenges that lie ahead of me in my future career.

The Kellogg experience was exceptional. It is without doubt the best MBA program in the world when measured on all relevant metrics. The culture is unique, the training is the best, the student body is brilliant, and the leadership is sensational. As a doctor who has been through much higher-level education, the business school experience at Kellogg was the best learning experience I have ever had!

I honestly believe that Kellogg is far and away the top business school in the country. Its unique culture is major point of difference, and is something that cannot be replicated at other schools (no matter how hard they have tried to do just that).

Kellogg is a school that does an amazing job in updating the curriculum to the needs and requests of students, in involving the students in shaping the future of the school. The Kel-

logg culture is truly outstanding. The new dean is also doing a great job in enhancing the international brand awareness and presence of the school. Kellogg is not only a marketing school; most students major in finance and we have truly outstanding teachers in the major.

In my applications to business schools, I consciously selected schools with a strong teamwork profile and an experience reaching beyond the academics. Kellogg clearly exceeded my expectations as teamwork is synonymous with the school. The involvement of students in running the school and the diverse extracurricular activities was key to complement my personal development. As I leave Evanston, I feel properly equipped with the tools needed to succeed in the next step of my career and as an individual in the community. I am truly grateful to my co-students, our faculty and administration staff for their personal approach to the enrichment of my person.

Since the arrival of Dean Jain, the school's commitment to international education and building the international alumni network and reputation of the school has increased tenfold, which I think is excellent and a great investment in the school's future. Kellogg has long been characterized as a marketing school. The marketing department is very strong, but the strategy, finance and entrepreneurship programs for example that I focused on were all exceptional, with great faculty and a great mix of academics and practitioners.

Kellogg is even more geared towards teamwork and towards serving the student body than I had realized when applying. They truly turn this place over to the students in a lot of ways. While this leads to some whining by those students who would like everything handed to them on a silver platter, it has made for a great deal of responsibility and a great learning environment. I am excited for the future of the school. I think Dean Jain is the right leader at the right time. Dean Jacobs did a great job of building Kellogg, and Dean Jain will take it to the next level. Already he has done a great deal in terms of stressing teaching as well as research, and is going to great strides to improve the strength of the Kellogg alumni network. As a career-changer without a traditional business background, I was very impressed with the help I got over the two years from the Career Management Center (CMC). I found many of my classmates expected jobs to be handed to them, but I found that as long as you put forth effort, the CMC and its counselors were there to match you every step of the way.

Besides the solid academic formation that Kellogg (or other top business schools) can provide, Kellogg differentiates from other business schools through its unique environment of teamwork, cooperation, leadership and fair competitiveness. For me and my family, these two years at Kellogg have been the best of our lives.

Kellogg is an outstanding school. It excels not only in delivering top quality MBA education but most importantly it affords every student a multitude of choices on how to structure his or her MBA experience based on personal needs and career interests. I sincerely believe the abundance of electives and areas of concentration that Kellogg offers cannot be matched by most schools. The strengths and teaching qualities of every academic department ensure that top notch education is delivered across the board. Kellogg does not only excel in the classroom but also outside. The rigorous selection of the student body ensures a healthy social life for all and thriving non-academic activities through clubs, student organizations etc. All in all, my two years here at Kellogg have been a life-changing experience.

2.
UNIVERSITY OF CHICAGO

UNIVERSITY OF CHICAGO

Graduate School of Business
1101 East 58th Street
Chicago, Illinois 60637
E-mail address: admissions@gsb.uchicago.edu
Web site address: gsb.uchicago.edu

Enrollment: 992	Annual tuition and fees: $32,956
Women: 27%	Estimated annual budget: $57,730
Non-U.S.: 34%	Average GMAT score: 687
Minority: 6%	Average months of work experience: 53
Part-time: 1399	Accepted applicants enrolled: 67%
Average age: 28	Corporate ranking: 5
Applicants accepted: 15%	Graduate ranking: 3
Median starting pay: $85,000	Intellectual capital rank: 16

Teaching methods: Case study, experiential learning, other

During the search process for a new dean at the University of Chicago's School of Business, Robert S. Hamada, the dean at the time, said the GSB needed "a younger person infused with fresh energy" for its top position. What Chicago got in the summer of 2001 was Edward Snyder, 16 years younger than Hamada, and a Chicago alum. "Of all the schools where I have been, this is the place where people talk and they push ideas more than anywhere else," says Snyder. Before coming to Chicago, he held the top post at the Darden Graduate School of Business Administration at the University of Virginia, a school that prides itself on a high level of community.

Impressive credentials aside, it is really that sense of community that Dean Snyder will have to grow if he wants to please the students. In the past, Chicago MBAs complained loudly about the lack of community on the campus. Snyder and his team have taken it all to heart, and the changes are palpable. Shortly after taking office in the summer of 2001, the dean and his staff packed their bags and moved their offices a few blocks away from the B-school campus. How does moving farther away build community?

Where the administrative offices once stood, there is now a student lounge—something students never had before—complete with a giant screen TV, comfy couches, and a microwave. Avtar Bhatoey, a 2002 GSB graduate, loved the hang-out space. "My peers and I used this new space to relax, chat, read, or just watch TV. I made many new acquaintances through hanging out in the new space." Doug Baker, a 2002 graduate, agrees. "The amount of resources put toward creating common areas for the students is truly amazing." Indeed, the pluck the dean, Deputy

Dean Ann McGill, and the class of 2002 supplied the school are a big part of the reason Chicago bolted to number 2 in the 2002 ranking. However, the momentum will have to be fueled by someone other than McGill in 2003: she'll be returning to teaching when the class of 2005 arrives on campus in September 2003.

Administrators knew, of course, that one study lounge does not a community make. In March of 2002, ground was broken on a new 415,000-square-foot, state-of-the-art campus, which will replace the school's four buildings on the Hyde Park campus. "The new integrative campus pulls everything together," says McGill. The infrastructure will include technologically advanced classrooms, a study room with a giant stone fireplace, informal gathering space, a massive winter garden, and an outdoor courtyard. In addition, career services, admissions, and other administrative offices will all be under one roof. This can be a really big deal in winter—they don't call it the Windy City for nothing. If fall 2004—when the new campus debuts—feels too far away, you can always check out the live construction cam the school has set up on its Web site at gsbwww.uchicago.edu/campaign/webcam.htm.

In the meantime, the administrative staff is making an effort to reach out to students. Snyder says he isn't as worried about building community as he is about making students feel good about being at a professional school. "The number one thing business schools need to do is support their students in their job search and their careers. Even if you're doing everything else right and you're not doing that, the students don't feel good," says Snyder. Particularly in 2002, with one of the worst MBA job markets ever, that extra effort wasn't just important, it was critical.

Doug Baker remembers how he first met the new dean. Snyder noticed Baker's GSB T-shirt while working out at the campus workout center. "We spent the next few hours bouncing ideas off of each other as he particularly was interested in the hot topics among the student body—most of which he already knew about. He had obviously done his homework," remembers Baker. Snyder does what he can to interact with the students as much as possible, holding weekly breakfasts and regular forums with them. "What I really like about MBA students is that they're in that zone of their life where they've got some real experience behind them but they're still thinking about where they're going to go and what their life is going to be about," says Snyder.

The dean's staff's hard work is paying off. After a number of years of inconsistent showings in student satisfaction, Chicago jumped to number 3 in student ratings. Much of that can be attributed to the accessibility of the dean and his staff, say a number of students. In an unprecedented move, the class of 2002 invited Ann McGill, the school's deputy dean, to be the faculty speaker at graduation.

What Chicago may have lacked in community in the past, it has made up for in its innovative curriculum, which has not wavered through the years from its rigor and depth. *Core* is a misnomer at the school where students' only required course is Leadership Effectiveness and Development (LEAD). Three weeks before classes start in the fall, as part of LEAD, entering students are placed in 1 of 10 cohorts with 55 to 65 other students. Eight second-year students who went through an intensive 12-week training their first spring at the school lead each cohort out of the city for three days at an outdoor leadership resort in Lake Geneva, Wisconsin. Just when you begin to question what you're doing 40 feet above the ground attached by ropes to a dozen equally confused people you just met, you are whisked back to Hyde Park for 10 days of career planning workshops, executive coaching sessions, team dynamics sessions, and presentation skills training interspersed with social hours, cohort dinners, and a semiformal at a downtown Chicago hotel.

LEAD doesn't end with the start of other classes in the fall. You attend two three-hour

LEAD classes weekly, one focusing solely on career development. Other LEAD activities include numerous challenges throughout the fall: the Squad Challenge, in which you demonstrate your knowledge of LEAD principles by role-playing a day in the life of a business leader; the LEAD All-Star Challenge, in which you compete in simulations of leadership challenges faced by executives; and LEAD Olympics, an opportunity to strengthen friendships in a congenial and cooperative setting.

If you think the students in your LEAD cohort will accompany you the rest of your two years at Chicago, think again. After completing LEAD, you are free to choose from a number of choices for the school's nine required classes and 12 electives, half of which can be courses outside the confines of the business school. You can also choose from 13 different concentrations, ranging from the expected accounting and finance to international business and human resources management. The breadth reflects Chicago's commitment to broadening its reputation. "The myth about the GSB is that to come here you can only be interested in econ or finance," says Deputy Dean Ann McGill.

If you're hoping to spend your MBA education abroad, Chicago may be the place to look. Each year, about 60 students enroll in the two-year international MBA program, which combines traditional MBA courses with special courses on global business. In addition to the regular MBA course load, students in this program must take four international business courses and spend at least three months working or studying outside their home country. Opportunities for this abound, as GSB has affiliations with 33 different management schools in Europe, Asia, Australia, and Central and South America. International MBA students must also become fluent in at least one nonnative language before graduation. The program also includes a summer global study tour. Students who went on the 2002 trip visited London, where they met with corporate executives, attended corporate receptions, and went sightseeing. The GSB has campuses in Singapore and Barcelona.

The GSB reviews its curriculum every five years. The most recent review was scheduled for 2001, but didn't take place because of the many changes in the administration. Instead, it is taking place this academic year. Regardless of whether it is review time, changes happen frequently, says McGill. "By having such a flexible curriculum, the school is able to make curriculum changes almost instantly." For example, after speaking with recruiters about what changes they would like to see, McGill and her staff added seven new classes for fall 2002, among them courses in channels of distribution, a hot item these days for recruiters.

McGill is a strong proponent of the individualized curriculum Chicago offers. "It is meant to be extra-value-added. We start from what you know and move from there, and take you in the direction you want to go." This flexibility allowed one second-year student to take seven finance classes and another student to take six in marketing. "We respect your own goals and experience and the different jobs that you have held," says McGill, who stands behind the school's marketing phrase: "Ideas compete and people collaborate." For Steve Pattison, class of 2002, the flexible curriculum sold the school for him. "Having been a business major in college and having spent several years in public accounting and investment banking, I didn't want to be forced into taking entry-level accounting and finance courses. The curriculum at the GSB allowed me to focus on courses that would help me with my intended career field. I was able to secure a position in the private equity field upon graduation."

The weak economy has helped the GSB become more attractive to a wider variety of students, says McGill. "In 1997, when the economy was flying and interviews consisted of nothing more than proving that you had a pulse, being a serious school didn't matter.

When the economy tanked, all of a sudden the University of Chicago got to be hip."

In her first year as deputy dean, McGill made a decision to break the myths about Chicago, which often paint the school as all about economics and finance, the "chess club" of B-schools. Another area she pushed for was an increase in female enrollment. In the past year, the school saw female enrollment jump from 23 percent to 31 percent. McGill credits current students and alumni for helping attract a more diverse student body. For example, if you apply and you're female, you can now expect at least 10 e-mails from the 200-member Chicago Women in Business, one of the most popular clubs on campus, only to be outdone by the GSB Bowling Club, which bills itself as the premier social organization at the school. It boasts 400 members who occasionally bowl but more often host charity events and play "beer pong," a game of ping-pong involving a ball, a paddle, two glasses of beer, and two opponents.

One drawback to the new campus will be its location—no longer on the Midway, a field that cuts through the center of the school and down to the lake. On nice days, GSB students can be found tossing Frisbees or kicking back on the Midway, trying to catch a little sunshine, or, better yet, rollerblading at the new Midway Plaisance. In winter, you can ice-skate your way around at the new rink. Or, take a stroll down to Promontory Point, a grassy peninsula just east of campus that juts out into Lake Michigan. It's perfect for a picnic. If you're a jogger, you'll love to pound the paved path along the lake.

There's easy and quick access to downtown via the el (elevated train). Once there, you'll find the Art Institute, a world-class symphony orchestra, the United Center (home of the Chicago Bulls), and nightlife galore along Rush Street. Travel a little farther north from Rush Street and you'll find yourself in Lincoln Park, home to blues bars, restaurants, and lots of students, as housing in Hyde Park is limited. About 20 percent of GSB students live in university housing.

Choices include a new graduate residence hall (complete with private baths, exercise room, TV lounge, and community kitchen), International House, or university apartments (aka Neighborhood Student Apartments or NSA). Competition for the NSA is fierce, so apply early.

If downtown seems a little dicey for solo travel, you won't want to miss the unofficial but very regular and well-attended Thursday Night Drinking Club (TNDC), in which packs of GSB students roam the city's bars.

PLACEMENT DETAILS

Students who graduated from the GSB in 2000 were sitting pretty, with 96 percent landing jobs by the end of the summer. For the class of 2002, the numbers were very different. Some 25 percent of the graduating class was still trolling the want ads for jobs at the end of September. Julie Morton, associate dean for MBA Career Services, was amazed how positive students stayed despite the dismal market. "My hope is that it has permeated the class of 2003." Morton isn't expecting this year to be a cakewalk, either. Still, she's hopeful. In 2000, career services added a fifth position to the account management side of the department: associate director of employer development. The result: 21 new companies will be coming to campus this fall.

Morton takes a three-pronged approach to helping students find jobs: (1) increase the number of opportunities you have; (2) open your eyes to other opportunities, possibly outside of your chosen field; and (3) make sure you are top of your game. Her philosophy is simple: "Students can't afford to not get an offer for things within their control."

To make sure that students are at the top of their game for interviews in such a tight market, Morton and her staff increased their programming by 60 percent from fall 2001 to 2002. In the fall, first-years can attend Industry Immersion, with featured speakers spanning a variety of careers. In January, Winterview, a daylong opportunity to brush up on interview skills, is held. Students volunteer to sit in front of an audience of 25 to 30 people and be interviewed by alumni, who then critique the performance. First-years are also videotaped during mock interviews with second-year students.

One of Morton's first goals in the current market is to get students to focus. The tendency is to try and do a little bit of everything and appeal to the greatest number of employers. But that will only hurt you, says Morton. Right now, recruiters have tons of applicants to choose from, so they can be picky and look for those students with the right specialty rather than generalists without any area of expertise.

Among 2002 grads, only 75 percent had one offer by graduation. However, three months after graduation, 82 percent had offers, a number that compared favorably to those of other top 10 B-schools. The average pay package for the class of 2002 was $119,400. About 83 percent of the graduating class took jobs in the U.S., the majority in the Midwest and Northeast (61 percent). Western Europe (8 percent) and Asia (6 percent) were also top choices.

TOP HIRES

Merrill Lynch (22); McKinsey & Company (14); Goldman Sachs (12); A.T. Kearney (11); Credit Suisse First Boston (11); JPMorgan Chase (11); Citigroup/Salomon Smith Barney (10); Bear Stearns (9); Lehman Brothers (9); Morgan Stanley (9).

OUTSTANDING FACULTY

James Schrager (entrepreneurship); Nicholas Barbaris (finance); Steve Kaplan (finance/entrepreneurship); Kevin Murphy (economics); Raghuram Rajan (finance); Scott Meadow (entrepreneurship); Harry Davis (strategy); Robert Vishny (finance); Pradeep Chintagunta (marketing); Ann McGill (marketing).

APPLICANT TIPS

Six long-stemmed roses delivered on Valentine's Day didn't hurt one applicant's chances for getting in—she's now a member of the class of 2003—but Dean of Admissions Don Martin suggests a less novel approach for applicants. The single most important piece of advice, according to Martin: "Keep the school's instruction sheet very close to you at all times." In one year alone, Martin and his trained staff of 25 readers saw a handful of applicants who didn't follow the directions: one who wrote a 10-page essay when the application called for 300 words or fewer, and another who supplied seven references rather than the required two.

While Martin wouldn't say whether direction following was one of the eight criteria his department uses to screen applicants, he would say attention to detail couldn't hurt. The GSB's eight tightly guarded criteria give the admissions department a three-dimensional view of candidates: their academic achievements, professional development, and personal qualifications. Complete applications are looked at by a minimum of three people. For the first read, there is a good chance that it will be a first-year B-school student: more than 300 volunteer each year to read applications. Applications are given a scorecard, and each reader votes to accept, deny, or waitlist an applicant.

The average work experience for entering students is four to five years. While Chicago rarely admits students straight out of undergraduate school, a few made it into the class of 2004. The exceptions tend to be applicants with stellar qualifications: straight As in undergrad, exceptional scores on the GMATs, business experience (for example, starting their own business during undergrad and taking advantage of summer internships).

Interviews are all but required at Chicago, with 90 percent of applicants completing them either during a campus visit or with one of the school's alumni who have volunteered to meet with applicants living in their cities. Martin strongly recommends interviews—along with a visit to the campus. "You should not take the word of someone else. Visit the campus, so you can form your own opinion."

It's easy to identify those people who shouldn't apply to business school. Any of the following should make you think twice before applying, says Martin: you have no interest in business; you're not excited about the MBA process or this program in particular; or you already have an advanced degree.

CHICAGO MBAs SOUND OFF

Chicago GSB allowed me to take control of what I wanted to do with my MBA education. I was able to take PhD-level classes critical for my future job, go on an exchange program to gain a broader international perspective and help form a student club. Career Services has done a fantastic job at placing students, even in the current economic environment. New programs by Career Services constantly come up to make the on-campus and off-campus job search easier. They have been doing this consistently and with fervor over the whole year.

I had an incredibly valuable experience at the University of Chicago for the following reasons: passionate and outgoing student body, intelligent and thought-provoking faculty members, excellent career placement office, and flexibility of its curriculum.

The GSB is a truly remarkable place. I was initially concerned about social activities (quickly put to bed after the first few days of orientation) and teamwork. These concerns were assuaged almost immediately after arriving on campus. People at the GSB are smart. It is an environment where ideas are freely challenged (our own and those of the professors) in a friendly and collegial debate. GSBers are also good at balancing academic pursuits with fun and extra-curriculars.

This program by far exceeded my expectations. The professors were amazing and genuinely cared about each student's experience. The caliber of my colleagues was humbling. Their intelligence and experience added to my experience immensely. The school prepared me well for a job search and interviews. Despite the terrible economy, I was able to land a job with a top investment bank doing exactly what I wanted. The alumni, career services, and Chicago's brand name really came through for many of us during this tough recruiting season. I think this feeling explains our 90+ percent participation in our class gift. People feel they have gotten so much from this school that they owe something back.

I came from a science background with little business knowledge. I now feel very comfortable in discussing issues dealing in finance, tax strategies, marketing strategies, even human resources with any person within any organization. The value I received at the University of Chicago GSB far outweighed the tuition cost and opportunity cost of forgoing a salary.

I was concerned when I came to Chicago that it would be a cut-throat experience. I was pleasantly surprised to find my classmates very friendly and very helpful. While everyone wants to do well, there is no atmosphere of competition. What a great place. Maybe I'll come back and get another MBA in a few more years.

Outsiders seem to have the misperception that the GSB is only good for finance and that our students are all super-competitive quant-jocks bent on becoming investment bankers at any cost. Nothing could be further from the truth. As a graduating student, I can tell you that the school has fantastic courses and fac-ulty in all disciplines and that the community is alive and well. The students are amazing and diverse. They are some of the most impressive people I've ever met.

HARVARD UNIVERSITY

3.
HARVARD UNIVERSITY

HARVARD UNIVERSITY

Harvard Business School
Soldiers Field
Boston, Massachusetts 02163
E-mail address: admissions@hbs.edu
Web site address: www.hbs.edu

Enrollment: 1805
Women: 35%
Non-U.S.: 34%
Minority: 22%
Part-time: n/a
Average age: 27
Applicants accepted: 10%
Median starting pay: $93,050

Annual tuition and fees: $36,770
Estimated annual budget: $58,400
Average GMAT score: 705
Average months of work experience: 52
Accepted applicants enrolled: 89%
Corporate ranking: 1
Graduate ranking: 14
Intellectual capital rank: 6

Teaching methods: lecture 15%, case study 80%, other 5%

If you can make it through the rigorous selection process and then go on to survive your two years at Harvard Business School, you will join an elite but sizable club with worldwide recognition. Your fellow alums will include a former United States president, a New York mayor and the founder of Bloomberg Financial Markets, the chairman and CEO of Staples, the CEO of Handspring, the president and CEO of Merck & Company, the founder of Intuit, and the chairman and CEO of Goldman Sachs & Company, to mention a few.

Companies outside the school aren't the only ones fighting for HBS grads. "We actively recruit on campus," says Dean Kim Clark. The school's administration is awash in former students, from the director of admissions and the director of MBA career services all the way up to Dean Clark, a former HBS student and professor. "We have had a long-term policy of trying to hire our own graduates into key positions in the school," says Clark. "It has worked and is really wonderful for the school. The people we bring back are just extraordinary. Because they've been through the program, they have a real empathy with the students who are here, they really understand how things work, and they bring a level of commitment and a level of expertise and quality that is just fantastic,"

Fantastic as it may be, the administration still gets a number of complaints from students in the areas of career services, the availability of faculty outside of class, and the quality of teaching in the core courses. This, along with a number of other important factors, has kept HBS within the top five but always chasing that elusive number 1 spot in the rankings. There is something that an HBS degree does guarantee, however: international recognition and rewards. As one 2002 graduate put it simply, "The brand value is enormous." But it isn't enough to rest on your laurels, says 2002 graduate Kyle Barnett. "There are good things and bad things associated with an MBA and in particular one from Harvard. You still have to make it a point to set yourself apart. It's a mistake just to rely on the school you graduated from." Relying on it or not, recruiters still rank HBS graduates among their favorites. Despite the giant class size—some 900 students—HBS remains among the most selective of B-schools, with only 10 percent of 10,382 applicants getting the coveted acceptance letter. Those accepted rarely refuse, with 89 percent showing up come September.

Recent graduates give loads of credit to Clark for opening up communication channels between the administration and the students, an area in which there has been criticism in the past. Clark can be found four or five times a week in Shad Hall, a private workout center just for the HBS community, peddling on an exercise bike or pounding the treadmill. Students have been known to sit on an exercise bike next to him, introduce themselves, and give him an assessment of HBS and the job he's doing running it. "I'm happy to see students when they want to see me. Everybody knows that if you want to see the dean, it's actually pretty simple. You just send me an e-mail, and you can get in to see me," says Clark. That's a lot different than deans with open door policies or regular lunch dates with students. And it's led to some grads complaining that Clark has ruled the school from afar. A case in point: last spring, a student e-mailed Clark, informing him that the second-years missed seeing him and were hoping for more opportunities like the ones they had in their first year. So Clark organized a Town Hall, and a few hundred students showed up. "It was great. They asked good questions about all sorts of things," says Clark. In addition, he holds lunch sessions with all the first-year sections during the first few months (even treating for their lunches). The more formal lunch dates end after the first few months, but about once a month, Clark heads over to Spangler Center, the school's hub, and sits down for lunch with any interested students. "You do things that try to get you connected," he says.

Luddites, take note: HBS is not the school for you. From the day you apply (online applications are required) to when you start scheduling your courses, you'll find yourself online all the time. Syllabi, schedules, and class assignments are all accessed through the school's intranet. More than 90 percent of professors at HBS administer their exams via computer. "We really want to get our students, our potential applicants, fully engaged online right from the very beginning," says Clark. "We have tried to make information technology, particularly the software environment and Web-based applications, really ubiquitous in the school. We have tried to put as much of the administrative process and the academic process as we could on the Web, or at least link it to the Web."

Work starts long before the first day of classes, and HBS will test your computer savvy and your business skills before you even step foot on campus. You will be given a list of Internet-based courses in six areas (accounting and finance, quantitative methods, business writing, class participation skills, computer and calculator skills, and general business knowledge), and these need to be completed before you arrive. Once you do get in the door, you won't have much time to settle in. During your first three weeks, you will be immersed in Foundations, a program of lectures, workshops, problem set reviews, case study discussions, and team projects. These are divided into five topic areas: applied personal skills; business simulation; creating modern capitalism; leadership, values, and decision making; and career development. You will get to experience all of them. No need to start stressing over grades yet; Foundations courses aren't graded, but you still need to show up.

For the duration of your first year, you will be assigned to a section of 80 students with whom you take all of your required classes. These sections function both academically and socially, with planned section pub nights and meetings with the dean. After Foundations, your first year at HBS is divided into two terms, each with five or six required classes. Term 1 courses home in on what HBS calls "the internal functional operations of business enterprise." Similar to the core at most B-schools, these classes include finance, financial reporting and control, leadership and organizational behavior, marketing, and technology and operations management. Term 2 builds on the first term's curriculum and looks at the broader picture of the relationship of the organizations to larger economic, governmental, and social environments. The six courses in term 2 cover it all: business government and the international economy, strategy, the entrepreneurial manager, negotiation, social enterprise, and a second round of finance.

Now you can start stressing about your grades, which are calculated on a forced curve. They come in high pass (top 10 percent of students), pass (middle 70 to 80 percent), and the dreaded low pass (bottom 10 percent). Because of this system, the school often gets a reputation as cutthroat. But that is not really true, says a 2002 graduate. "Before getting to school, I was a little nervous about that reputation," he says. "But it turned out not to be as cutthroat as I was expecting it to be. I learned a lot from my fellow classmates and was pleasantly surprised." Class participation counts for a whopping 50 percent of your grade, so by all means speak up. No matter how much they dislike it, former students say it is great experience for the real world. "Face-to-face interaction with the other students was vital to the learning experience, as was the opportunity to practice speaking in front of a group of 80 students every day," says one.

Now you can take a deep breath. Your second year should seem like a cakewalk, with all of your remaining classes electives of your own choosing. The one requirement is that you take at least five courses each term for a total of 30 credits for the year (unless you choose to participate in field service). You can also cross-register and take some classes outside of HBS and in other departments on campus as well as at nearby institutions. But it's hard to imagine that you will want to stray too far, what with the sheer number (79 at last count) and breadth of the HBS electives roster. Even in these electronic times, HBS still publishes a 100-page printed roster of the elective curriculum, which is divided into 10 subject areas: accounting and control; business, government, and the international economy; entrepreneurial management; finance; general management; marketing; negotiation, organizations and markets; organizational behavior; strategy; and technology and operations management. The bulk of the courses are in entrepreneurial management, finance, and general management.

If you do decide to cross-register, one option, in addition to taking courses in other graduate departments at Harvard, is signing up for courses at the Sloan School of Business at the Massachusetts Institute of Technology (MIT) or the Fletcher School of Law and Diplomacy at Tufts University. You are allowed to cross-register once per semester during your second year, for a total of up to two courses. The courses you choose need to be graduate-level and must contribute to your expertise in management. (HBS administrators will tell you whether a course fits the bill.) If a course is already offered at HBS, you can't sign up for it elsewhere. HBS also gives you the option of auditing classes in other Harvard departments or at surrounding campuses. After reviewing your workload and realizing that you will have mastered some 500 cases by the time you graduate, it's easy to see why this option isn't chosen too often among students.

As the result of new internationally based facilities in Hong Kong, Buenos Aires, and

Europe and increased demand from other B-schools, the number of cases—both print and electronic—HBS publishes is on the rise. The centers are used for faculty research and development of cases, which form the basis of the HBS curriculum (80 percent). Cases also come from the Global Research Group, located on the Boston side of the Charles River. The GRG is the latest addition to Harvard's ever expanding research empire. HBS graduates have been known to stay on at Harvard as research associates, helping to write cases. "It gives you some additional time to think about what you want to do," says one 2002 graduate who did just that.

One popular option for second-year HBS students is field study in 1 of 11 areas. More than half the class chooses to participate in these outside-the-classroom experiences. HBS field studies are typically conducted in teams of three or more students who work closely with a sponsoring organization and a faculty advisor. Projects can involve the launch of a new product, development of a new business and a plan for it, or finding a solution to a real-world problem. Recent project sponsors have included Disneyland, Cybersmith, BMW, Nike, Massachusetts Children's Hospital, the African Communications Group, and the New England Conservatory of Music.

Students who choose to develop their own business plans in field studies or elsewhere often decide to enter them in the school's annual business plan contest, the capstone of HBC's myriad entrepreneurial offerings. The contest, started in 1996, awards $10,000 in cash and $10,000 in professional services to the top winners in two categories: traditional business and social enterprise. In 2002, FishLogic, a designer of semiconductor technology, won top honors in the traditional business category, and BEST Educational Partners, Inc., a for-profit educational services provider, took the social enterprise award.

Those students interested in careers in the nonprofit sector have a new opportunity at the end of two years. In 2002, the school started a Service Leadership Fellows Program. Graduates in the one-year program work for a participating nonprofit and receive a salary that compares favorably with offers they might receive from for-profit businesses. The fellowship is part of the Initiative on Social Enterprise, the umbrella for all social enterprise activities at HBS. As part of the required curriculum, all HBS students now take a social enterprise course their first year. There are also a handful of social enterprise electives available to second-years. Alumni and HBS also sponsor a number of loan forgiveness programs for graduates who commit to working in nonprofits and the government.

In contrast to the average B-school, HBS is its own residential, self-contained campus. It sits on 35 acres of red brick buildings, tree-lined walkways, and open courtyards. Located across the Charles River from Harvard University's main campus in Harvard Square, the HBS campus gives students easy access to other departments and to Boston, but also allows them to get away when they need quiet time to spend the evening cramming. More than 60 percent of HBS students choose to live on campus. Housing is available for singles (by lottery) in Mellon Hall, which was completely renovated in January of 2001, or in one of five other residential halls. Couples and families have Harvard-affiliated off-campus options, like Soldiers Field Park and Peabody Terrace. Deciding to venture into nearby Cambridge and the surrounding residential areas will mean paying top price for private apartments.

When they're not cramming for exams or dissecting the latest case studies, HBS students are active in any one of the more than 75 clubs and associations, or you can find them at Shad Hall, the workout center exclusively reserved for the HBS community. This is when the public school/private school distinction is most apparent (and where some of all that $31,800 in tuition goes). Not many other B-schools can boast of a team of personal trainers and a staff of professionals who offer counseling on nutrition, fitness, and stress management. To get students ready for their potential future days and evenings as CEOs, Shad offers golf swing clinics and ballroom dance lessons. There's even a café with made-to-order sandwiches located on the second floor.

If students want nightlife, they don't need to venture very far. It's a quick trip across the Charles River to grab a beer or two at Grendel's or Shey's. Harvard Square is packed with cafés, bookstores, restaurants, and street performers. Close by in Chinatown is Pho Pasteur with gargantuan bowls of cheap, tasty Vietnamese noodle soup. Regina Pizzeria on Thatcher Street is rumored to serve the best thin-crust pizza in all of Boston. On the weekends, students often head into downtown Boston to trendy Newbury Street for dining and shopping. Nightlife doesn't just happen off campus. Every December, the HBS Student Association puts on the Hollidazzle Ball, attended by 1500 people, and there are enough events to keep your calendar filled every weekend of the year. One fall favorite not to be missed is the Australia–New Zealand Club's Priscilla Ball, which features 500 of the best and brightest dressed in drag.

PLACEMENT DETAILS

The nice thing about a Harvard MBA is that graduates immediately become part of a large and influential network of 37,979 alums who are easily accessed and identified by industry or location through an online database. Graduates know this; they give the school the highest marks of any for networks and connections that will last a lifetime.

With close to 40 percent of graduates of the class of 2002 choosing to stay in the Northeast after graduation, Director of MBA Career Services Matthew Merrick has decided to tap into that vast resource around him to help current students find jobs. "We really try to impress the value of networking," says Merrick. "You don't just do it to get a job. You do it to the level that forms a relationship that will last a lifetime."

To help facilitate networking, Merrick and his staff have set up a mentor program between local Boston alums and HBS students. In addition, second-year students now meet monthly one on one with first-years to help identify what the first-years want to do with their lives.

In the current market, Harvard graduates are learning how to humble themselves a little more than they are used to doing. Those 2002 graduates expecting to cash in on their Harvard MBAs had to lower their expectations a little. Still higher than a lot of other schools, the average median starting salary for HBS graduates went from a whopping $160,000 in 2000 to an even $100,000 in 2002. "We're definitely seeing more anxiety about jobs," says Merrick. "We want to impress on students that the experiences they get here are for their lifetime—not just the first job out of school."

In 2002, grads faced a tough market. Even Dean Clark admits that the school did not act quickly enough to head off the recruiting slump, and the Harvard name didn't get the job done on its own. The result? Some 81 percent of grads had a job offer before graduating in June, a number that climbed to 88 percent three months later. When you add in signing bonuses, starting pay packages average $134,600—not too shabby, if work can be found. Of those who found work, 18 percent found jobs outside the U.S., with 38 percent staying in the Northeast.

TOP HIRES

Harvard declined to release this information.

OUTSTANDING FACULTY

Andre Perold (finance); Francis Frei (technology); Jan Rivkin (strategy); Clayton Christensen (strategy); Das Narayandas (marketing); Brian Hall (organization behavior); Mihir Desai (finance); Stuart Gilson (finance); Richard Tedlow (management).

APPLICANT TIPS

For the entering class of 2002, HBS received its highest number of applicants on record—10,382. Already one of the toughest schools to get in, HBS became even more selective, allowing admission to only 10 percent of the 2002 applicant pool. Once admitted, most applicants do pick HBS; in 2002, 86 percent took the plunge and matriculated.

So, what does it take? "It is not a black box," says Brit Dewey, the managing director of admissions and financial aid. "The mission of this school is to educate leaders who will contribute to the well-being of society, so these are the people we want to find." Some of the winning characteristics for acceptance to the school are excellent academic ability, strong leadership experience, and intellectual curiosity. "You have to be willing to play, to speak up, to take risks," says Dewey. She should know; Dewey graduated from HBS in 1995.

One of the biggest mistakes Dewey sees time and time again is applicants whose essays are too generic and don't offer any concrete examples of leadership experience. "Too many applicants don't make a case for leadership," she says. "Show specific examples of leadership. We want to see insights, thoughtful self-awareness with regards to leadership." Dewey recommends taking enough time to apply and do a thorough job; in other words, applicants shouldn't rush their applications. Dewey spent two months getting her own application ready for submission. There are three application deadlines, all of which are given equal consideration. However, applicants interested in on-campus housing should apply by the January deadline in order to secure a spot in the housing lottery.

Every application to HBS gets at least two reviews. With 10,000-plus applications to weed through, the school has a full-time professional staff dedicated to doing just that. "It's their day-in-day-out job," says Dewey. That job has been made a little easier now that applicants

are required to apply online. "Doing the application online is just a natural evolution of this fundamental strategy of getting our students immersed into the technology world," says Dean Clark, a strong proponent of the requirement.

Interviews are by invitation only and are conducted by either admissions staff or a network of 80 to 100 alums around the globe. The goal is for all admitted applicants to be interviewed. (If you get called for an interview, it means you're very close.) Dewey encourages anyone considering applying to the school to visit first. "In order to understand HBS, you must come to campus," she says. "Sit in on a class. Hear the voices, the different perspectives in the classrooms. We want for you to come see us."

HARVARD MBAs SOUND OFF

The HBS experience I believe is unique in that it gives you three things: the confidence that you are capable to rise to the top of whatever endeavor you choose to follow, be it a large or small company, non-profit, etc.; The belief that you are born to lead others and improve society; the ability to identify opportunities in situations where others might not. It is truly a transformational experience.

I honestly feel that Harvard Business School is the best school out there. Perhaps the only negative is that when people meet you, they sometimes have the preconceived notion that you're arrogant. In many circles, you definitely have to downplay the fact that you go to Harvard Business School as it sometimes causes resentment.

My experience at HBS has far exceeded my expectations. I was surprised to see how responsive the faculty and administration were to changing and challenging market conditions, and to whatever current needs the student population may have. The professors are top notch, and the quality people I have met really made the experience a positive one.

I believe that HBS really delivers one of the very best MBA programs in the world. That said, I think it's really important to understand that an MBA program only offers as much as the student is willing to put in, so a great student can extract a lot of value from a bad program, and a poor student would not gain much from going to HBS. I think one of the things I was able to do at HBS was reflect on my real career goals and accept the right job for me. Many courses and cases emphasize the value of this reflection.

Harvard is an incredible institution. The faculty and students are excellent. Unlike what many people say, HBS is not a place where people are very aggressive.

HBS helped me get to the next level of my career path. And while the school is not perfect (too large a student body would be my biggest complaint), it does deliver on all of the reasons I went to business school in the first place. It was a great learning experience and one that I will continue to leverage throughout my career.

Much attention is paid to Harvard's brand name and its network of alumni. Both are incredibly powerful and have already helped me in a number of ways. (I am still shocked by how many business executives, including CEOs, returned my calls when I was looking for help completing class assignments!) But to focus only on these two aspects of the Harvard MBA would be to neglect the powerful learning that takes place here. The education is truly outstanding.

Perhaps the best, and most surprising (to me), part of my HBS experience was the consistent emphasis on finding a career path that works for you. This was stressed throughout the curriculum from day one, and, although it is not clear the extent to which this learning was digested by all students, HBS did an excellent job in pushing people, as much as is possible in the context of a top business school, to find a job/career that suited them, rather than simply following the herd of the most recent trend.

I think that the first-year curriculum at HBS is a bit more difficult than the second-year curriculum. The courses are integrated extremely well and the faculty coordinates case selection timing so that related topics can be discussed in parallel. However, the reading load is a bit heavy and there is little free time to internalize all of the learning. On the other hand, the second-year curriculum is more enjoyable and leaves more time for a job search and other extracurricular activities.

STANFORD UNIVERSITY

4.
STANFORD
UNIVERSITY

STANFORD UNIVERSITY

Stanford Graduate School of Business
518 Memorial Way
Stanford, California 94087
E-mail address: mba@gsb.stanford.edu
Web site address: www.gsb.stanford.edu

Enrollment: 752
Women: 38%
Non-U.S.: 28%
Minority: 12%
Part-time: 0
Average age: 28
Applicants accepted: 8%
Median starting pay: $95,000

Annual tuition and fees: $33,300
Estimated annual budget: $57,756
Average GMAT score: n/a
Average months of work experience: 56
Accepted applicants enrolled: n/a
Corporate ranking: 7
Graduate ranking: 5
Intellectual capital rank: 1

Teaching methods: lecture 10%, case study 50%, experiential learning 5%, simulations 5%, team projects 15%, other 15%

If the old adage, "Put your money where your mouth is," holds any weight, then graduates from the class of 2002 at Stanford University's Graduate School of Business have spoken loudly. They gave a record-breaking gift of $311,000 to the school, with 91 percent of the class contributing.

The school must be doing something right if its graduates are that thankful after already having spent plenty of money ($33,000 for tuition alone in 2002–2003) for the privilege of attending the school. After slipping out of the hallowed top 10 in 2000, Stanford has returned with a vengeance to the number 4 spot in 2002. The buzz around campus is good; students seem genuinely happier with the school and the administration. "Never before have I been part of such a talented and supportive community. I learned a tremendous amount both inside and outside the classroom, especially how to serve as a leader when working with such capable peers. The location, teaching, and activities of Stanford spur innovation and rank it as the top program," says one 2002 graduate.

Okay, so it's not the top program yet, but the school's location and setting are hard to beat. Smack-dab in the middle of the hustle and bustle of Silicon Valley (although the Valley's a little quieter these days), the campus is expansive, with massive palm trees that gently sway in the afternoon breezes. There are views of San Francisco Bay, but the ocean is just far enough away that the school rarely gets enveloped in pea soup fog as its neighbors to the north do. Students have acres and acres of what is still sometimes affectionately called "the farm" to explore.

Stanford has no part-time or evening MBAs and only a small executive education program. That's both an advantage and a disadvantage for the MBA program—more attention for MBAs, but fewer opportunities to connect with execs who might be roaming around during exec ed courses. Since the B-school opened its doors in 1925, the focus of the school has been and remains its full-time, two-year residential MBA program. It has done an excellent job of fulfilling a mission set out by Herbert Hoover to create a graduate school that would stop the flood of bright students heading back east for school and careers. Once students move to Northern California, it's hard to get them to move anywhere else. That's not always great if you're looking for East Coast recruiters to hire you away, but for many who fall in love with the area, it may be a moot point. Sixty-one percent of the class of 2002 chose to stay on the West Coast. "Before coming here, I was a lifelong New Yorker, but I have no plans to leave," says 2002 graduate Jason Gastwirth, who now lives in San Francisco. Gastwirth says he rarely misses the school—not because of any bad experiences during his time there, but quite the opposite. "At times, it feels like I never left," he says. "I bump into my old classmates all the time. It's great."

It is a truly select group of students who get to be a part of the Stanford B-school family. Of the 5864 applicants who applied in 2002, only 8 percent were accepted. The class size is smaller, at least among the top schools: 370 for the entering class in 2002. Not many other schools can boast of a 6:1 faculty-to-student ratio. "We're fortunate that we have a tremendous opportunity here to have what I think is the best scale for this sort of thing," says Dean Robert Joss, a Stanford alum and former Wells Fargo executive. "It's a smaller scale where the learning can be a different experience than when you're at a place that is three time the size. Yet, we're big enough to cover all the bases, get all the top faculty to be available throughout the disciplines, but still small enough to have that interactive learning process that I think is intense and in-depth and really gives you a much more lasting educational experience, that really serves you 35 years later. I

can testify to that, because I was here 37 years ago, so I still use it."

Joss makes his presence known around campus. But that's something he wasn't keen on when he first arrived in 1999. Since then, Joss has worked to soften his aloof manner. Students now often see him in the B-school cafeteria; he goes there twice a day to get his coffee and eats lunch there whenever he's on campus. He'll sit at a table, welcoming students to join him—but whether they do or not, he stays. Joss holds monthly town halls that are open to both first- and second-year students. "Any student has the right to talk to the dean by e-mail or in person," he says. Some of the goals he has set (and is well on the way to achieving) are to communicate better, be more open, and, as he puts it, "make the whole place more transparent." It's all gone a long way toward creating some sense of belonging to a bigger community that Joss admits was lacking when he arrived.

Joss believes that a combination of winning factors makes Stanford Graduate School of Business stand out and keeps the degree in such high demand. "What is unique about Stanford is that we're smaller than most, we're in the middle of Stanford University, which has got this incredible breadth and diversity of top-notch schools. No one else has quite that aggregation," he says. "And, we're in the middle of Silicon Valley. So you've got this sort of laboratory of entrepreneurship. Our students have this incredible opportunity to meet these people, to work there in the summertime, to engage in small projects there which are part of their coursework."

Despite the tech downturn, Stanford students still take advantage of internship and career opportunities in the surrounding area. Entrepreneurial studies are still big at the school, with more than 90 percent of students taking at least one class in entrepreneurship over their two years. "We really never got carried away with looking at the dot-coms," says Irv Grousbeck, professor and codirector of the school's Center for Entrepreneurial Studies. "Either way, management practice hasn't changed. Good human resources practice is still good human resources practice." Whereas a few years ago more students might have jumped straight in to start their own businesses, they are now getting experience at established companies first. "Instead of rushing over to start something with a napkin idea, graduates are going to small to medium-sized companies to get operations experience," says Grousbeck.

Students rate Stanford higher than any school surveyed by *BusinessWeek* for the opportunity to interact with various ethnic groups. Thirty-two percent of the class is international, and 11 percent are minorities. Plus, the school has one of the highest percentages of female students among the top schools—37 percent. Joss says he is happy with the diversity of the students on campus but wants to see more diversity in their experiences before coming to B-school. "I'm really very satisfied in terms of the mix of gender and ethnicity and international diversity. I'm not completely satisfied with the diversity of experience. There are too many coming from a similar academic, similar work, similar lifestyle experience. Few of them have had real operating experience." That's a good thing if you're not one of these "similar" candidates.

When Joss talks about operating experience, he is talking about all levels and in all industries. Thought you would take that job as a manager at a fast food chain off your resume before submitting it to Stanford? You might want to think twice before doing that. "The fact that you might have run the McDonald's store for a couple of years can be unbelievable experience," says Joss. "The typical McDonald's store has 100 people on the staff. You've got to juggle them all, you've got customers in queues, you've got problems, complaints. Even if you did that in high school, that might be a tremendous experience for some person as opposed to two years at some Wall Street firm." Joss is often surprised by the number of applicants who have yet

to make and live with any major decisions. On more than one occasion, he has received calls from parents asking when their son or daughter should apply, what it takes to get in, when the deadline is, and some who even write their own recommendations for their children. "It boggles my mind," says Joss. "We look for people who think for themselves."

Like every school in California, Stanford was struck by the tech wave, beefing up its entrepreneurial and e-commerce offerings. But, at its core, it remains a school of general management. Speaking of core, Stanford has the usual smattering of core courses (finance, marketing, management, and operations). If you have a strong background in a particular area, you can exempt out of classes by exam. Students are encouraged to do this, according to Sharon Hoffman, associate dean and director of the MBA program. With some core classes, there is an option to take a "turbo" version of the class, or you can fill your schedule with any number of electives. As Stanford prides itself on being a general management school, there's no need to declare a major or concentration during your two years, but the options are there for dual degrees. These include the MBA/AM (education), the MBA/MSE (engineering), and the JD/MBA (law).

All students at Stanford start off with pre-term, two weeks of refresher courses and an introduction to some new areas as well as to your classmates. Pre-term coursework includes Managing Through Mutual Agreement, Ethics, an introduction to the Career Management Center, and an optional class in Excel. From there, you will delve right into your core coursework, which is divided into three quarters. In the fall, you will focus on foundations of management such as quantitative methods (including data analysis), microeconomics, social psychology, and sociology. In the winter, you move on to management's functions, including the general business disciplines of finance, management, operations, and strategy. Spring is considered the capstone, integrating what you have learned in the previous two quarters with a general management perspective.

During your second year at Stanford, you're free to choose from more than 100 electives. Since the school is on a quarter system, you can take up to 18 electives your second year; most students sign up for about 14. The school prides itself on refreshing its electives every year, and every five years at least 50 percent are changed. You also have the option of taking up to 16 units (out of a total of 100) outside of the B-school. You might want to consider passing on that option; in 2002, out of all of the schools surveyed by *BusinessWeek,* students rated Stanford second only to the University of Chicago in the quality of teaching in electives.

One program students are encouraged to sign up for is the 28-year-old public management program, a Stanford institution. MBAs who complete a series of courses in this area receive a certificate. Even those students not pursuing the certificate can choose to take part in study trips and case studies that are part of the program. Interested in public service but worried about mounting college loans? The Stanford Management Internship Fund offers financial support to students who spend their summer in a low-paying nonprofit or public sector position.

It would be hard to complete your two years at Stanford without taking at least one management communications class. These noncredit courses cover everything from media skills to improving your interview skills. There's even one in effective listening.

The students at Stanford are a congenial group and balk at any mention of cutthroat competition. "No one would step on someone else to get ahead," says a current second-year student. "You check your ego at the door. You have to do that in everything you do, so everyone can learn from each other." Students are quick to admit that the workload can be tough at times. "Don't plan to come here if you just want to get your ticket punched, and don't plan to sit on your laurels while you're here," says one student.

During the first year, students live on campus. Most popular among singles are the 200 rooms in the Schwab Residential Center, a five-minute walk from the B-school. Looking more like a Miami hotel than a student residence hall, Schwab boasts hues of bright blues and oranges. It has a reflecting pool, open courtyards ready for barbecuing, lounges with pool tables and a big screen TV, a computer lab, study rooms, and a weight room donated by Nike's Phil Knight. Each student has a private room and bath and shares a kitchen with a classmate. Couples and families live just down the street in Escondido Village. By the second year, almost all students choose to move off campus. Pricey apartments can be found in Palo Alto and surrounding towns, but a number of students usually decide they would rather pool their housing funds and share houses in surrounding hill towns like Woodside and Atherton.

On weekends, students take off for San Francisco, an hour north. The beaches of Santa Cruz are an easy drive, as are Carmel and the Wine Country. With no classes on Wednesdays, Tuesday nights' FOAM—visiting a different bar each week—is popular. During the winter, FOAM participants head all the way to Las Vegas for one night. "Our students work hard, and they play hard," says Courtney Gwyn Payne, director of student life.

PLACEMENT DETAILS

Here's one clear indication that the job market has softened. In 2000, 270 companies recruited second-year Stanford students for full-time jobs and internships on campus; in 2002, that number dropped to 121. Not a recruiter favorite in terms of effectiveness, the MBA Career Management Center has taken a number of steps to win them back. The first thing Andy Chan, the director of the CMC, did when he took the position in 2001 was to hire more staff. The department went from 9 to 13 staff members. One person is fully dedicated to corporate outreach, "rebuilding old relationships and establishing new ones," says Chan. Recruiters now have direct access to students' e-mails and can post jobs to the school's intranet site. And they're starting to come around: a number of recruiters noted the improvements in 2002.

There are eight student advisors in the CMC, with one designated as the go-to person for international students. This is important at a school where nearly one-third of the class is from overseas. "We are now able to give the students a lot more attention," says Chan, a 1988 graduate of the B-school. Students can schedule appointments with advisors or talk to them during drop-in office hours. For quick questions, students are given the option of e-mailing anyone on the staff.

Students first get an introduction to the CMC during pre-term, the three weeks before the official start of classes. Throughout the year, Chan and his staff schedule dozens of workshops and panels for students. With 25 percent of the class still heading into careers in consulting, one that always proves popular is "Cracking the Case: Consulting Interviews." Students hear what is expected and how to effectively handle the consulting case interviews. Firms that have participated in the workshop include Booz Allen & Hamilton, The Boston Consulting Group, Bain & Company, McKinsey & Company, and Andersen Consulting.

In October of each year, the CMC puts on its daylong Career Conference, with industry and function panels covering everything from entertainment to venture capital. Co-sponsored by the school's alumni office, the conference also gives students an opportunity for networking with alumni in a number of career areas. At the 2002 conference, students had their choice of the following 10 panels: banking/private client services/sales & trading, consulting, entertainment/communications, hedge funds/investment management, Internet/e-commerce, private equity/LBO, retail/consumer marketing, social enterprise, strategic planning/business development, and technology.

Stanford grads in 2002 had as much trouble as any finding jobs: some 19 percent were without an offer by graduation. A full 88 percent of 2002 grads found work by three months after commencement. Those with jobs became the highest paid of all MBAs, with starting pay packages of $138,100.

TOP HIRES

McKinsey & Company; The Boston Consulting Group; Bain & Company; Goldman Sachs; Siebel Systems; Microsoft; Morgan Stanley; Lucent; Capital Group; General Mills

OUTSTANDING FACULTY

Irving Grousbeck (entrepreneurship); James Van Horne (finance); Joel Peterson (strategy and entrepreneurship); Edward Lazear (economics); Ming Huang (finance); Garth Saloner (management); Jennifer Aaker (marketing); Jim Patell (operations); Andy Grove (strategy).

APPLICANT TIPS

You know you're going to a small school when the phone rings and it's the admissions director congratulating you on your acceptance. Of the 370 students entering Stanford's B-school in 2002, Director of Admissions Bolton Derrick was able to contact all but three, and they were in China. "It's a very, very Stanford thing to do," Derrick says. Of course, it also causes a tremendous amount of angst for those waiting for the call—and a lot of speculation and commiseration as some folks get calls on one coast while others wait and watch the phone. It might be a nice touch, but it can also be frustrating for applicants.

While the number of applicants being interviewed has always been high, Joss and Derrick only recently instituted a policy aiming to interview every applicant that the school admits. "You want to know the real person. You like to validate what you see on paper," says Joss. "No one that's recruiting at our school would ever hire anyone on paper without an interview. It's the same principle for school." Those interviews are often done by alums of the school, if not admissions officers. Even if you live in Silicon Valley, you may find yourself meeting with an alum and not an admissions staff member. No matter, the school also hires alums to read applications for selection.

Stanford looks at GMATs, but Derrick says there isn't a minimum cutoff, and the range of scores can be quite broad. In the class that just entered, GMAT scores ranged from 550 to 800. Students also come to Stanford at all ages. "Our oldest student could have fathered our youngest student," says Derrick. There is no requirement for number of years of work experience; what matters, says Derrick, is that an applicant can demonstrate leadership potential. Indeed, Stanford, along with a few others, has begun targeting younger students—even a year or two out of college.

The biggest problem the admissions department sees is essays in which applicants say what they think the school wants to hear. "We can end up with 6000 essays saying the same thing," says Derrick. "If they've done it right, each essay is very different." In the essays, the admissions committee wants to see a commitment to making a difference and to what unique qualities an applicant can bring to the school. "Due to our small size, we rely on every person to contribute much more than at any other school," says Derrick

While Derrick doesn't want applicants to rush their applications, he does encourage applying in the first or second round. One misconception a lot of applicants have is that the school has a quota to fill, and once it's filled, the doors close. Derrick says there's nothing further from the truth. "We look at person versus person, not banker versus consultant."

STANFORD MBAs SOUND OFF

I have been incredibly impressed by the many dimensions on which the Stanford MBA experience has exceeded my expectations—from the well-roundedness of the student body (intelligent, collaborative, professionally exceptional, athletic, genuinely nice people) to the responsiveness of the faculty and administration to requested improvements/changes, to the focus on leadership and interpersonal interactions. All in all, it provides an excellent forum for learning, while allowing the students to personally develop as well. I cannot imagine having had a better experience than the one I had at the Stanford GSB.

Stanford was truly a life-changing experience for me. I was introduced to a network of incredibly talented and approachable people and received rock-solid general management education. My eyes were opened to several new possible directions and I was able to leverage the degree to get a marketing role at a leading company that I never would have gotten without the Stanford MBA. The community is one that encourages dissent and challenging the status quo, yet is a more cohesive group than any I have ever been a part of. It's truly inclusive. Friendships cross throughout the entire class, rather than forming cliques based on ethnicity, nationality, career pre-business school, or even which section you start out in. It has played a very developmental, positive role in both my career and my personal growth and friendships.

The Stanford MBA exceeded even my highest expectations. The program has a very nice balance of case study and lecture. This balance allows students to develop good business judgment rooted in solid and rigorous analytical thinking. In addition, I found that professors were highly concerned with the development of the students and went to great extents to make sure that we all had an outstanding experience. More importantly, I found mentors in the faculty that clearly transmitted the importance of conducting business with utmost honesty and commitment to excellence. The Stanford MBA is a life transforming experience.

Before coming here I had a very narrow focus and just fell into my career. Now I feel like I have the resources and knowledge to make a career switch, and I know better what I want to do and what I don't want to do. The alumni at Stanford have been really helpful, especially in this rough economy. Alumni have taken time out of their day to take me to lunch, to give me advice on how to get a job, opened up their Rolodexes to hook me up with colleagues. These are people who have never met me, who I have cold called out of the alumni database. Financing the program wasn't as bad as I thought. For those who qualify, there are fellowships (grants) available.

Stanford's greatest strength is in developing individuals who want to make a difference through people. Stanford does this by first selecting well-rounded, ethical students many of whom have endured some hardship and understand the value of perserverance, hard work, and respect for others. Next, the GSB is exceptional at developing the nuanced interpersonal skills needed to become self-aware, intuitive managers—people who can sense what people need to succeed and provide that to them. Stanford's courses in high performance leadership and interpersonal dynamics are outstanding and cited by alumni as containing some of the most valuable lessons for their careers. Stanford also stresses the technical skills business leaders need in order to deliver hardline results and judge performance. The school achieves that through a balanced, top-notch core curriculum and a variety of exceptional electives.

As an international student, I felt more and more initiatives were taken to meet my specific needs: it is now part of the mission of our career center to deal with international students.

Dean Joss and his administrative team were incredibly responsive to student needs, and they were always there to listen and provide guidance. Dean Joss made himself available not only through student lunches, dinners, and cocktail events, but also through teaching—I was fortunate enough to take a seminar with him on leadership. In all of my contact with him he has been very open to student concerns and willing to try new programs in order to make Stanford a better place. Stanford has been very supportive of women MBAs, which I have really appreciated over my two years here.

One of the things that I was surprised about when I enrolled in Stanford was the seriousness of the academics. Usually, the seats are full at class and most students are prepared and ready and willing to contribute. During the core, my classmates and I worked very hard—much harder than I thought. Throughout, the one thing that I have been most impressed with is the Stanford community. Students are very active and caring and helpful and I have relied on my peers many times for help, advice and contacts.

5.
UNIVERSITY OF PENNSYLVANIA

UNIVERSITY OF PENNSYLVANIA

The Wharton School
Suite 420 Jon M. Huntsman Hall
3730 Walnut Street
Philadelphia, Pennsylvania 19104-6340
E-mail address: mba.admissions@wharton.upenn.edu
Web site address: www.wharton.upenn.edu

Enrollment: 1604
Women: 33%
Non-U.S.: 39%
Minority: 9%
Part-time: 0
Average age: 28
Applicants accepted: 13%
Median starting pay: $85,000

Annual tuition and fees: $34,946
Estimated annual budget: $58,681
Average GMAT score: 703
Average months of work experience: 77
Accepted applicants enrolled: 74%
Corporate ranking: 3
Graduate ranking: 12
Intellectual capital rank: 8

Teaching methods: lecture 35%, case study 35%, experiential learning 20%, team projects 10%

The University of Pennsylvania's Wharton School has undergone a very noticeable face-lift—a brand new $139.9 million facility, Huntsman Hall, opened for the Class of 2004 with great fanfare. The building is more than 10 times as large as the venerable B-school's former home, where MBAs were commonly found studying in cramped hallways and in snaked-around lines waiting for computer lab privileges. The new facility is just one of the changes Wharton administrators have put in place to help the one-time king of B-schools—number 1 in *Business-Week*'s ranking since 1996—pull back from its disappointing fall to number 5, its lowest showing since *BusinessWeek* began rating MBA programs in 1988. Faced with a dismal job market, students—like those in every other MBA program—complained of a complacent career service office, which was without a director for more than three months leading up to graduation. Technology woes continued to plague the school, leaving students even more frustrated. To top it off, recruiters (largely banks and consulting firms) reeling from cutbacks were less enamored with Wharton grads, while, at the same time, the school had trouble attracting alternative companies to its grads, pulling Wharton from its number 1 spot with recruiters.

But, at a school that is in a constant state of transformation and self-improvement, change is already afoot. The newest Wharton MBAs have been met with improvements to many elements of the program that even the class of 2002 complained about. On top of the new state-of-the-art building, which addressed the facilities issue, the school has stocked up on the best of technology, including interactive classrooms, study spaces equipped with the latest network hookups, and more. To answer the woeful year career services had in 2002, a new placement director, Peter Degnan, came aboard in August, in plenty of time to help the class of 2003 with their pursuits. Already Degnan has made changes, including a heavy set of meetings with the school's primary recruiters. And he's already been very active with recruiters, making trips to major cities to meet with corporations and figure out how to get them—and keep them—coming for Wharton MBAs.

Wharton's commanding presence has been edged out by longtime top-of-the-mountain rival Northwestern's Kellogg School, and in 2002, with lagging student satisfaction, the school found itself behind stalwarts like Harvard Business School, the University of Chicago Graduate School of Business, and Stanford University's Graduate School of Business. Still, despite the slip, and despite a poorer recruiter showing—only 76 percent of Wharton grads had jobs by graduation—recruiters still say the Wharton MBA is a dynamic program that produces the highest-quality graduates, something that has been a staple of Wharton's program.

New dean Patrick T. Harker is demanding that the Wharton MBA program maintain its reputation as a leader and an innovator in the B-school arena. Harker, who took over in 1998, is himself a leader, and he's certainly no stranger to the University of Pennsylvania. He received a bachelor's and master's degree in civil and urban engineering there in 1981. In 1983, he earned a University of Pennsylvania master's degree in economics and a PhD in civil engineering. In 1984, he joined the Wharton faculty as the Stephen M. Peck Term Assistant Professor of Decision Sciences, which was followed by a promotion to associate professor in 1987. By 1991, he secured a spot as the UPS Transportation Professor for the Private Sector. "I loved teaching," Harker says. "I still view myself first and foremost as a professor." For many students, it is that connection to the faculty that gives Harker an extra bit of appeal. And perhaps a bit unlike many of his colleagues, Harker was named a White House fellow in the early nineties.

Nowadays, Harker can be thankful for the school's long-lasting tradition of success—something that should help the school implement its improvements. Before the economic downturn of 2001–2002, a Wharton MBA practically guaranteed an array of job offers from the world's most prestigious investment banks, accounting firms, and consulting companies. And with more than 26,000 alumni, and alumni clubs in more than 50 countries, students can find an ally in almost any company—something no prospective MBA can dismiss. The Wharton network so far has served its alumni just so-so. That's something Harker plans to change, and quickly. With such a vast number of alums, the school will work harder to tap into the wealth of knowledge—and career advisors, too—that should be the hallmark of a school like Wharton.

Success can be sweet, but even the most well oiled of machines has a few squeaks. Though the job offers have stopped flowing temporarily, and recruiters applaud students, the career services office made a less than stellar showing in the 2000 rankings and an even worse showing in 2002, a big part of the reason the school slipped in the student satisfaction poll. Indeed, while recruiters gave the school better marks than in 2000, grads in 2002 were deeply unsatisfied by the school's efforts to help them find a job and to reach out to less traditional recruiters as staple consulting firms and financial services companies slashed hiring. Students questioned the school's aggressiveness when it came to job searches, some worrying that the placement office may have been resting on its laurels. Indeed, one 2002 grad said, "The placement office thought it could just hang out a shingle and recruiters would come rushing in. When it didn't happen, it took them months to even consider changing their strategy." Perhaps the worst aspect of the placement office: when the placement director left in March of 2000, the spot was left vacant in one of the worst MBA job markets ever. The complaints haven't fallen on deaf ears—placement officials say they've moved quickly to assuage some of the problems, and future alumni may very well benefit from a more aggressive and knowledgeable placement staff led by the real-world-experienced Degnan.

Wharton students are an exacting bunch who, while appreciative of what is overwhelmingly right with the school (an extremely talented faculty, a cohesive student body, and a much anticipated new building coming online, to name just a few of the highlights), aren't shy about pointing out things that need fixing. At the top of the students' list: academics. Wharton was the only school in the top five to score less than an A for curriculum. The school earned a meager B—better than the C received in 2000, but a less than perfect mark on the otherwise pristine report card of one of the oldest B-schools. Not everyone agreed that the curriculum was suffering, but students who expressed concern pointed to a scattered teaching of courses, without a lot of integration, and graduates complained that the first-year curriculum tended to be repetitive. Harker has at least a partial answer. He plans to leverage the praise the school received for its global scope by emphasizing international initiatives and thinking of new approaches to teaching. Globalization is on the top of Harker's priority list. "Globalization isn't only a nice thing to do, it's reality," he says. Partnerships, like a technology-enhanced joint program with INSEAD, are an example of Harker's vision. He believes B-schools must look at distance learning and other types of technology and find ways for students to learn 24/7. This is the future—and it's a future that is quickly coming to Wharton, with 2002 graduates noting the wealth of new courses, and some new changes that have improved the curriculum already.

"At Wharton, we have an ongoing process of curriculum enhancement and change," says Anjani Jain, vice dean and director of the MBA program. The desire for more flexibility in the first year led Jain to reduce the total number of courses required in that year, although the total number of units required to graduate has not changed. "This change was largely driven by students wanting more flexibility in their first year. It also offers a greater opportunity for students to take electives in their first year," says Jain. In addition, Wharton professors tend to be liberal in their allowances for students to waive courses, even those in the core. Many first-year students have substantial business experience and don't need some of the core courses. "If you're one of these experienced students, consider yourself lucky—the administration decided to make a number of required courses electives instead—if you can waive out, that is," explains Jain. One example: the course called Field Application Project (FAP) focuses on giving students a practical business problem to work on. The half-unit course used to be required of all first-year students. Under the new curriculum, it is now an elective. Another change: the bracket core courses introduced 10 years ago, Risk and Crisis Management, Geopolitics, Innovation, Change & Entrepreneurship, Information: Industry Structure and Competitive Strategy, The Environment and the Firm, and Technology for Managers, were always intended to be phased out. As of this year, they're still around, but while in the past, first-year students were required to take one or more of these courses, they're all electives for the class of 2003.

Of course, Wharton students do have access to some of the top thinkers in the business world, practically a who's who with names like leadership expert Michael Useem and markets guru Jeremy Siegel. Siegel's classes remain standing room only as he does the morning markets report. Indeed, Wharton professors published more journal works and books than any other faculty—and while those minds might not be as accessible as students would like, their thinking undoubtedly translates into classroom knowledge. For certain, it's an experience of a caliber you won't likely experience at too many other schools.

As for the present, students had other gripes with the academic realm at Wharton. Some students criticize a nondisclosure grading policy instituted in 1999. It could be a catch-22 for the school, with some saying the secretive grading allows students to concentrate more on things that interest them, but some arguing that in a teamwork environment, students can end up not pulling their weight in some classes in favor of others.

Students at Wharton are full partners in the constant massaging of the MBA program—what Wharton dubs its coproduction learning model. Courses and teaching styles are continuously retooled during each term according to student feedback gathered through frequent stakeholder surveys and quality circle meetings with individual professors. Students formed a group to come up with ways to make the first-year curriculum more relevant. And a panel of students even directs an annual reinvention of the school's intranet.

Despite the facilities update—and it's a big one—the class of 2002 still criticized Wharton's poor facilities—and that included few places to hook up a laptop, and poor computer labs. The impressive Jon M. Huntsman Hall, a 300,000-square-foot academic building, goes more than a long way toward answering the criticism, even if the class of 2002 didn't get to enjoy the new digs. After gathering extensive input from faculty and students, Kohn Pedersen Fox Associates PC designed the building, which opened in fall of 2002. Huntsman Hall fills the void along 38th Street from Walnut Street to Locust Walk, where the old University Bookstore was once located. More than 50 group study rooms, equipped with the latest technology in audio and video conferencing and video production and editing, are intended to serve as mini-labs for student research. The Colloquium, which is located at the top of the building, serves as a conference area. The main presentation room includes 200 seats and can be used for laid-back luncheons or spiffy evening affairs. Huntsman Hall houses both Wharton undergraduates and MBAs. The MBA Café is on the second floor, alongside an outdoor plaza that can be used for Wharton events and club gatherings.

The new facilities serve as a nice complement to the administration's promise of an innovative and modern MBA education supported by a highly developed information technology infrastructure. Known affectionately as "Spike," the school's electronic communications suite isn't just a tool but has become an important part of the culture here. Even before you get to campus, you may already be well acquainted with some of your classmates through E-talk, an on-line forum that allows accepted applicants to communicate with one another, and with current students, as soon as they find out they've been admitted. An idea generated by the Wharton Graduate Association, E-talk provides bulletin board forums for those who want to trade tips on what type of computer to purchase, for others seeking roommates, and for still others who want inside tips on Philly's nightlife.

Wharton intends for its IT to impact you from your first contact with the school until long after you've left campus. After exploring the school's smartly designed online catalog and asking questions of current students through the Student2Student chat line, you can submit your application via computer (Wharton was the first B-school to offer that option, although almost all top-ranked schools do so these days). Databases, notes, and syllabi for every MBA course are posted electronically—as well as bulletin boards for all 125 or so student clubs, the student directory, individual Web pages set up by most students, and continuously updated broadcasts of school news and announcements. As for bidding for courses and setting up interviews with job recruiters, both are done online. After graduation, you'll have access to WAVE, a huge, searchable database of the school's 26,000-strong alumni network.

Incoming students arrive in early August, a full four weeks before the start of the fall term, to ensure that students from diverse backgrounds begin on equal footing. Courses in basic accounting, microeconomics, and statistics bring liberal arts majors up to speed while preparing those with a business background for exams to waive out of several core courses. Classes in communications, computer skills, nine different languages, and a two-day leadership retreat, as well as tours of companies in Philadelphia, New York, and Washington, DC, and plenty of barbecues, parties, and other social gatherings all get you ready to hit the ground running when the school year actually begins.

Your first year at Wharton is divided into four six-week quarters. You'll move through your core courses as part of a 60-student cohort, with groups of three cohorts forming a "cluster," a kind of class within a class. Each cluster shares the same team of core professors who work together to integrate the coursework and coordinate student workload, which helps to keep you from feeling too much at sea amid the enormous class size. (With some 1550 full-time students per year, Wharton is one of the biggest of the top-tier MBA programs; add to that 2400 undergraduate business majors; several hundred evening, executive MBA, and doctoral students; and about 8600 executive education participants moving through campus each year, and you can see how you might feel a bit lost in the shuffle.) In the first-semester leadership course, you will work alone and in a five-person team on such soft skills as ethics, communications, managing diversity, and career development. In the second semester, your team will be assigned a 12-week-long field application project in which your analysis of a real-world problem will be presented to executives actively involved in the case. You'll also get to choose from a set of six-week elective courses in such topics as information, entrepreneurship, geopolitics, crisis management, technology, or the environment.

Another option for first-year students is the Global Immersion Program—six weeks of introductory lectures on a country or region critical to the world economy, with a four-week overseas experience following final exams in which students meet corporate and government officials, tour, and attend cultural events in Southeast Asia, China, South America, or Eastern Europe. You'll be expected to submit a written assignment the next fall, and you'll have to pony up an additional $5000 or so beyond your already hefty tuition to pay for the trip. The global practicum is just one of a number of Wharton's international programs. The school's famous Lauder Institute, which offers an MBA/MA in international studies, is among the very best global management experiences anywhere, besting a degree from a top European B-school or any U.S. school claiming to offer a truly international MBA. A joint venture between the B-school and the university's School of Arts and Sciences, this 24-month program allows students to specialize in a global region such as East Asia, Europe, Latin America, or North America (for non-U.S. natives). Students spend about 25 percent of their time abroad, including a cultural immersion program before the start of their Wharton classes and a summer internship with a multinational company that requires extensive use of a foreign language. There's also a joint MBA/MA program in international relations, in which Wharton joins forces with Johns Hopkins University's Nitze School of Advanced International Studies. Students spend about half the three-year program at the Wharton campus in Philadelphia and the other half at the Nitze School campus in Washington, DC.

Even when pursuing a regular MBA degree, students can opt to spend a full semester abroad in 1 of 14 exchange programs with non-U.S. business schools in Italy, France, Spain, Japan, Hong Kong, Brazil, England, the Netherlands, Sweden, Australia, the Philippines, or Thailand. Or you can participate in the Multinational

Marketing and Management Program, which partners Wharton with B-schools in Israel, Canada, and other locations to form multi-school MBA teams that design marketing strategies for companies hoping to enter the North American market.

On top of the many international offerings, you'll find a dizzying selection of courses to choose from in your second year. Employers rank Wharton at or near the top in every bread-and-butter business discipline across the board, from finance to general management, marketing, and technology. The breadth of offerings beyond the basics is equally impressive: More than 140 electives and two dozen majors in everything from actuarial science to public and nonprofit management, including new concentrations in technological innovation and information and strategy. Don't find a major to your liking? Create your own, with faculty approval. Or join the three or four dozen Wharton students each year who pursue dual degree programs with some of the Ivy League university's other world-class schools, including communication, law, medical sciences, nursing and health-care management, social work, and engineering. "We are known for the depth and breadth of our elective offerings," says Jain. Wharton offers more than 200 electives. A number of these, according to Jain, are "off the beaten track." One example is Employee Benefits Planning, which is taught by Olivia Mitchell, considered the country's foremost expert on benefit plans. Students can major in real estate. "A small but dedicated group of students choose to major in it," says Jain. Other examples include legal studies and risk and insurance management. The school boasts 200 standing faculty members and a number of affiliated faculty members. About one-third of Wharton students pursue more than one major. To major in a certain area, students need to take five units (or courses) in that area. The second-year curriculum is much more driven by the individual department and the faculty members who cre-

ate new courses. "The second-year curriculum is not delivered in a lockstep method by the school," says Jain.

Outside of class, students tend to scatter from this decidedly urban campus. Wharton has set aside a dozen floors of Grad Tower B for MBAs, and about 350 students, especially those among the international contingent, reside in the on-campus dormitory. Many MBAs opt to live in center city, a 10-minute bike or bus ride from campus, because desirable housing is scarce in West Philadelphia, a rundown neighborhood that is gradually being swallowed by the ever encroaching expansion of the university. Crime is an issue as well, with several highly publicized incidents taking place on campus in recent years. The most noteworthy incident was the injury of a graduate student working in an office, who was struck by a stray bullet that came from a fatal sidewalk shooting between two spectators at a sporting event at Penn's Palestra arena. The university has beefed up security, and administrators say safety hasn't been as much of an issue for the B-school as it has been for the undergraduate college; MBA students tend to be older and more savvy about the attentiveness needed when attending any urban institution.

For a school of this size and scope, Wharton does a surprisingly good job of holding down nasty competition among its highly ambitious and demanding students. Make no mistake: You won't find the cozy, cooperative atmosphere here that you'd find at Dartmouth, Virginia, or Northwestern, but it's no Harvard, either, according to Business Week's surveys. Students gravitate toward the serious-minded and business-oriented extracurricular activities, like the "It Adds Up" program, which has student volunteers helping low-income families file their income tax returns. There's also the annual Christmas in April program that renovates housing for disadvantaged Philadelphians.

But there are ways to blow off steam, too. Philadelphia may not be New York, but it's a beautiful city with plenty to see and do—from the high culture of the world-class art museum and orchestra to historic sites such as the Liberty Bell and Independence Hall. The lower-brow bar scenes along South Street and the shores of the Delaware River give students a chance to unwind after a hard week's work. And no self-respecting Wharton student would miss the once-a-semester ritual known as "Walnut Walk"; after midterms, MBAs don a combination of formal attire and shorts and begin a bar crawl through as many as 20 local pubs, ending with a sobering 3 A.M. breakfast.

PLACEMENT DETAILS

Employment is a much bigger worry for Wharton grads these days; in fact, second-year students who used to find themselves with an embarrassment of riches in the job search barely scraped by in 2002, and many went jobless. After a dramatic drop in 2000, the number of companies recruiting on campus and via Internet job posting fell again in 2002. And with financial services firms (investment banks and the like) slashing MBA recruiting, Wharton's mainstay of employers practically vanished. Add to the problem a dearth of consulting firm recruiting, and the destination of over 70 percent of Wharton grads was collectively absent. Now the school is trying to bounce back, again by responding to the needs of consumers—both recruiters and students. Harker says the problems revolve around the mechanics of the career services office, a problem that will be alleviated when staff finds a roomier home in Huntsman Hall and as Degnan gets situated in the job. And the administration is investing in Web-based technology that will link recruiters and students regardless of whether the company can actually step foot on campus. Clearly, the Wharton brand name still brings in a number of employers who give glowing reports about grads. But the head honcho of B-schools does have some work to do in this area.

Some 24 percent of grads were without a job at graduation, and 13 percent were still pounding the pavement three months later. But those that found jobs raked in a healthy starting pay package of $124,500. That's down about $22,000 from 2000, but still among the top for MBAs in the class of 2002, behind Stanford and Harvard grads.

TOP HIRES

McKinsey & Company (24); Bain & Company (20); Deloitte Consulting (19); Johnson & Johnson (18); Boston Consulting Group (15); Goldman Sachs (14); UBS Warburg (13); Deutsche Bank AG (12); Merrill Lynch (12); Morgan Stanley (11).

OUTSTANDING FACULTY

Philip Berger (accounting); Ian MacMillan (entrepreneurship); Jeremy Siegel (finance); Franklin Allen (finance); Andrew Metrick (finance); Robert Inman (finance); Richard Shell (legal affairs); William Tyson (legal affairs); Nicolaj Siggelkow (management); Michael Useem (management); George Day (marketing); Karl Ulrich (operations and information management).

APPLICANT TIPS

If your heart is set on attending Wharton, be sure to get your application in early—at least if you are applying for the class of 2005. The school had operated on a rolling admissions basis, with applications starting to arrive as early as September for the following fall. Those who waited until March to apply put themselves in a predicament: only 1 out of 50 who applied in April were accepted, compared with 1 out of 10 who applied by February. The administration retooled its admissions process at the end of 2001, when the school shifted to three deadlines and ended the rolling admissions process. So keep an eye on the Web site for the exact deadlines.

The admissions office is also scheduling interviews by invitation only. All admitted applicants are interviewed each year, but not all who are interviewed are admitted. Still, it's yet another venue in which you can attempt to distinguish yourself from the crowd. Rosemaria Martinelli, director of MBA admissions and financial aid, warns that students should highlight personal contributions and be honest on the application. She also says that they should not settle for less-than-stellar GMAT scores or GPAs. "Take the GMAT again," Martinelli says. "Do it right." Applications are available through the school's Web site or by calling the admissions department, and can be submitted either electronically or by mail. Financial aid has also shifted to a more merit-based model.

Who should and should not apply? "I think the MBA is relevant for every field, even if it just helps a person to understand how effectively to lead and manage people. I think, however, that people should save money if they haven't spent the time doing the preparation work in advance of the application. Otherwise, it's like throwing money away, since the application process for all schools has become so competitive," says Martinelli. As for applications, Martinelli says the committee looks for "personal awareness" in essays and in interviews. "Someone who has done a thorough self-assessment can effectively write about their experiences and how those experiences have shaped them and impacted their future choices. Most people write about accomplishments, but fail to articulate the take-aways," she warns.

Despite the new admissions system, Martinelli says students should still apply early in round one or two. But, she advises, hold off until your application is the best it can be. "Wharton is looking for students who will be the next generation of leaders, whether in busi-

ness, government, or nonprofit sectors," says Martinelli. "That means we look for students who have a desire to make a positive impact beyond their own personal/professional aspirations. People who tend to be successful have a history of accomplishment, but also an awareness of what that means to them and how that has shaped them as an individual."

WHARTON MBAs SOUND OFF

In my two years at Wharton, the school has made great strides in integrating leadership training as part of the curriculum, and really brought home the notion that Wharton is not only a place to gain technical skills, but also a place to learn and practice leadership skills. I firmly believe many of my classmates will emerge as business leaders in the future.

I strongly believe that Wharton has the best MBA program. However, Wharton has to solve two major issues if it wants to maintain its leadership: Career Management Center and strengthening the ties with the alumni network.

I think that the faculty and the education at Wharton are phenomenal. I feel that I truly learned a great deal at this school. My only criticisms are: the career placement is lacking at Wharton and the debt is staggering to the point that it may close more doors than the education opens.

My Wharton experience exceeded my expectation by far. I learned a lot both in the classroom and outside the classroom. I worked with very talented and very nice people and I made friends that will last for life. I believe that Wharton deserves great credit for selecting such a diverse student body and for fostering teamwork and sense of community among students.

Wharton is an amazing place in many ways. But one area where the school needs to work hard is Career Management. It's all fine and good to learn for oneself and enhance one's potential, but if this does not translate into a decent job, it means nothing. Students pay extremely expensive tuition, and get substandard service when trying to find a job. Apart from banking, consulting, and U.S.-based jobs in general, the variety of companies recruiting here is lacking. European companies for example are very much underrepresented.

I recommend Wharton very highly. The average age is 28–29, students are more mature, have had more work experience, and thus the relationships and friendships formed are much more deep and long-lasting. There is a great depth and breadth in work experience and students are incredibly willing to share and help each other. Teamwork and a community spirit characterize this school. As evidenced by the record-setting 2002 class gift campaign, Wharton students are willing to give back and support their school. The school also not only has tremendous diversity (almost half of the student body is international), but it cherishes it and promotes it in the International Cultural Show and the Rainbow Party.

The students, faculty, and community are amazing—in every sense of the word. My one complaint when I started was that the facilities were shabby and overcrowded. Fortunately for the upcoming classes, they have the state-of-the-art Huntsman building (but unfortunately we did not). Finally, Philly does not deserve the ugly stepchild rap it gets. It's the fifth largest U.S. city and therefore offers a little bit of everything from culture to entertainment to history to sports, etc. Rittenhouse Square, where most Penn students live, offers restaurants, bars, shops, entertainment, workout facilities, a park—convenient, young, active area to spend two years. In addition, Penn's campus has some very nice areas—and in my opinion Wharton and the surrounding is a safe, fun, and lively place to go to school.

For a liberal arts major (English and art history) a quant program like Wharton is a challenge. But there are plenty of classmates to help, as is the faculty, and the academic safeguards are there to help you learn. Wharton does an incredible job of personalizing the MBA experience, from academic counseling to recruiting, and the best part is that they are so receptive to feedback and student participation in even the highest level of decision making.

Wharton is an amazing place. Not only does it attract the best and brightest students from all over the world, it attracts students with very diverse backgrounds and experiences, which contributes greatly to the learning environment. Wharton is also fantastic at constantly reinventing itself, continually innovating and changing even when it would be easy to rest on past laurels. This leads to an incredibly dynamic and creative environment, which benefits everyone here—student, faculty, administration, and alumni as well. Finally, Wharton is almost entirely student run, which still amazes me to this day. Students do not sit back and complain to the administration, they go out and create/fix/do things that they think should be done.

MASSACHUSETTS INSTITUTE OF TECHNOLOGY

6.
MASSACHUSETTS
INSTITUTE OF
TECHNOLOGY

MASSACHUSETTS INSTITUTE OF TECHNOLOGY

Sloan School of Management
50 Memorial Drive
Cambridge, Massachusetts 02142
E-mail address: mbaadmissions@sloan.mit.edu
Web site address: http://mitsloan.mit.edu

Enrollment: 744
Women: 25%
Non-U.S.: 35%
Minority: 7%
Part-time: 0
Average age: 28
Applicants accepted: 13%
Median starting pay: $85,000

Annual tuition and fees: $32,470
Estimated annual budget: $56,470
Average GMAT score: 707
Average months of work experience: 60
Accepted applicants enrolled: 68%
Corporate ranking: 8
Graduate ranking: 11
Intellectual capital rank: 2

Teaching methods: lecture 30%, case study 30%, experiential learning 15%, team projects 25%

In a sense, Sloan is a school of conundrums. Is it overrun with the MIT stereotype of geeky engineers and computer whizzes, or is it a school where even an English major can go for an MBA? Is the quant-heavy workload competitive and crushing, or can students actually bond and have fun? Is the physical space a bit long in the tooth, and do students stare wistfully over the river at the gleaming cafés and classrooms at Harvard Business School, or do they accept its cramped classrooms? Most important, perhaps, is the B-school overshadowed by MIT's heady technology-centered reputation in a waning national tech renaissance, or can Sloan carve a niche for itself in today's global business world?

The answer seems to be yes to all of the above. "There's an MIT halo. An idea of 'If it's MIT, it must be quantitative,'" says Dean Richard Schmalensee. "I think if we taught only organization studies, people would still come here assuming it was quantitative. We are rigorous, we do have good quantitative stuff. MIT is a very powerful brand. We are hip-deep in MIT. But we're a management school."

So despite—or perhaps because of—these polarities, Sloan holds fast in the top 10, not falling behind like other schools mired—rightfully or not—in the tech world. It's a testament to the fact that Sloan is a lot more than an engineering–quant jock school. How to take the experimental nature of MIT's legacy and give it a business-oriented twist is something Sloan seems to have mastered, and the school has focused on the word *innovation* to articulate this particular priority. As Sloan celebrated its 50th anniversary in 2002, it underwent a curriculum review to figure out how to implement this idea of innovation throughout its academic program. "Experimentation and innovation are part of our heritage and culture at MIT Sloan," says Margaret Andrews, executive director of the MBA program. "In addition to developing new theories and frameworks, we also experiment with the educational process."

This often occurs through ambitious new courses that challenge conventional classroom paradigms. For example, in 2002 a new course was introduced to train students to be leaders in communications and ethics, taught by a former actor who conducted the course as a play. "Some classes work and become great, and some don't work, and we learn why," says Deputy Dean Gabriel Bitran. The Global Entrepreneurship lab (or "Global E-lab") is one example of an experiment that worked. Second-year students spend the last six weeks of the fall semester learning about international entrepreneurship, then spend January in a start-up in South America, Europe, or Asia. When you return for the spring semester, you'll spend another six weeks sharing your experiences and coalescing all you've learned into a final report. When the idea was initially proposed by the faculty, the administration thought the class couldn't possibly take off on such a global scale, and first time the course was offered, there were just 20 to 40 students. Now, enrollment is capped at 100, with students competing to win a spot in this popular elective, and companies all over the world request the input of student teams.

Another idea that worked embraces innovation quite literally. In 2002, Sloan students began taking part in a course known as the Medical Innovations Lab, which had already existed as a joint project between MIT's department of electrical engineering and Massachusetts General Hospital. Medical doctors from Mass General's unit for minimally invasive therapy come to class to describe problems they are facing in their practices and ask students to come up with solutions. For example, one doctor asked students how he might avoid the problem of torsion in the leg after hip replacement surgery. Sloan students add value not only by coming up with solutions themselves, but by coming up with economically viable ones at that. The Sloan students who solved the hip replacement problem went on to use their MBAs to start a company to put their idea to work.

And the idea of innovation expands to student life, where students are constantly creating new clubs and programs to try to make the school a better place, despite limitations such as a severe lack of study space. Be it in the classroom or through extracurricular activities, Sloan students learn that theory is all well and good, but it's putting theory into practice that gets results.

Two weeks before classes start at MIT, you'll head up to campus for orientation week. You'll go through team-building and leadership activities while getting a sense of MIT culture. If you need some brush-up work on your accounting, economic, calculus, or statistics skills, you'll head to school even before orientation for pre-term courses.

The core curriculum at MIT lasts only through the fall semester of the first year. You'll take Strategic Management, Financial Accounting, Organizational Processes, Managerial Communications, Data Models and Decisions, and Microeconomics. You'll also be introduced to some career development issues in Organizational Processes—Sloan tries to streamline your requirements as much as possible. Within the core, you'll be divided into sections called "cohorts" of about 60 students, and you'll also be divided up into teams of four to six students for all of your core group work assignments. These teams are arranged to foster diversity in terms of backgrounds and skills.

After the fall semester, you'll be able to choose from a series of electives that include things like the economics of the health care industry, the software business, power and culture in organizations, mergers and acquisitions, and quantitative investment management. The core is compacted into the first semester so that you'll have a chance to start choosing the path that will fit your particular interests. You will have certain divisional requirements to satisfy before you graduate, but you can choose the sequence you want to take. "Students are not forced into a box for 12 months," explains Bitran.

Breaking up the first and second semesters is January's Independent Activities Period (IAP), during which you can have some fun and experiment with your coursework. There's a huge course catalog of credit and not-for-credit classes offered by MIT faculty and employees that sometimes reflect their niche interests. For example, you can take a five-day leadership intensive—or a class on how to taste port wines. Investment banks and consulting firms show up on campus the third week in January to start interviewing first-years, so most students find themselves at Sloan for some or all of IAP, but you can also opt to spend those six weeks away from campus as pure vacation time.

In your second year you'll take all elective courses, and you can enroll in one of seven management tracks: digital business strategy, financial engineering, financial management, information technology and business transformation, new project and venture development, operations and manufacturing, strategic and management consulting, and a self-managed track. These tracks are not majors, but consist of about 8 to 10 courses—half the elective requirement for graduation—that help you focus on a specific career path. A professional seminar (ProSem) for each track brings outside practitioners (often Sloan alums) into the class to lead discussion groups and field projects in their specialties. There seems to be almost an inordinate number of electives given the size of the student body, and they can range from topics as broad as strategic management to as focused as competition in the telecommunications industry.

"Personally I went after the best professors in their field, regardless of topic, so I got a very broad, top-notch education, and creating this kind of schedule was easy. I didn't have time to take all the courses I would have liked to," says 2002 grad Amanda Whalen. "I also had friends who wanted to do nothing but complex financial derivatives, and that opportunity was open to them as well. It prepared them incredibly well to become technical analysts on Wall Street, while my broader array helped me a great deal in general management training appropriate for my current job as a consultant."

You can also take classes at Harvard Business School through an exchange agreement, and students often take language classes through MIT. Sloan's classes are a mixture of casework and theory, but Sloan does pride itself on giving students a solid analytical background. And while this type of coursework is challenging, it's not all seriousness and drudgery. For example, Roberto Rigobon, a popular professor of economics, finance, and accounting, is known for starting his classes with stunts and then relating them to the topic. "This year I got an Elvis costume," he says, "and now I'm trying to find the case where (I can) use it." He's been known to scream and drop to the floor in class to make his point, or to give out his daughter's stuffed pig for the class period to people he feels have been sucking up in class.

Histrionics aside, Sloan students rank the school's faculty among the best at all business schools, praising their teaching and their availability and expertise. And, in a research-driven faculty, students have lots of opportunities not only to be exposed to the professors' current research in class, but to participate in studies with professors themselves. "Most of my research is in the area of international economics and monetary policy. Both are quite relevant for the students, and therefore I talk about it in class," says the ever humorous Professor Rigobon, adding, "Usually making jokes about how irrelevant it is, and how that is why I'm still poor."

Students looking for some more real-life experience can enter the annual $50K Entrepreneurship Contest, which swings into gear in the spring and has become one of the school year's most anticipated events. Undergrads and graduate students from all five schools at MIT— Sloan, Engineering, Science, Humanities, and Architecture—craft business plans to try to win $50,000 in seed money. If you win, you're required to use the money to turn your plan into a corporation, but you don't have to win to see your dream come to life. Since the contest was started in 1990, it has spawned over 60 companies. The contest (most teams in it have at least one Sloan student on them) shows the potential that comes from Sloan's affiliation with a great research institution like MIT. "If you're thinking about starting a business, you're going to need engineers, so hanging out with them at the $50K competition is a good idea," says one Sloan grad.

Another joint opportunity with the engineering school is Sloan's elite Leaders for Manufacturing Program, which you might want to consider if you've been heavily into science since your undergraduate years. Each year 48 students enroll in an even more intense 24-month experience than the typical MBA but come out with dual degrees in business and engineering. You have to have an undergraduate degree in science or engineering, two full years of work experience in manufacturing or a related field, acceptance by special application (note that the application deadline of January 3 is more than a month earlier than that for the regular MBA program), and a sense of humor about giving over two full years of your life to work and study. LFM currently gives scholarships—basically full tuition.

In the less infotech- and e-business-focused slower economy, Sloan seems to have reemphasized a broader reach with its commitment to entrepreneurship and specialized programs like manufacturing as well as its global economy perspective. Along with the Global Entrepreneur Lab, Sloan students fan out across the globe on spring break trips not only to Europe, but to places well off the beaten MBA trip path such as China, Cuba, and West Africa. A degree from MIT has cachet all over the world, so students from more than 60 countries attend Sloan. Recruiters rank Sloan grads tops in technology, but Sloan grads also top the list when it comes to being prepared to compete on a global scale.

The concept of innovation reaches into student life at Sloan to the extent that many of the school's out-of-class activities—for better or for worse—are run by students. Students say that there's not a ton of administrative support services to help them get things done on campus, but it's a testament to Sloan students that they're ambitious enough to make things happen on their own. For example, when some students began to sense that their professional image with recruiters could use a little polishing, two first-year students went to the school's Entrepreneurship Center to get help with starting and running a "charm school," through which other students could get feedback from professors on what recruiters were seeing in their interviews. "There's not a resistance to doing things differently or starting up new things," says a 2002 grad. "There's not a whole lot of road blocks that are placed in people's way." Another prime example: traditionally, Sloan has not made a big deal out of admit weekend—that weekend in the spring where business schools typically woo admits. It took the initiative of a student to start putting together activities in a professional, fun, three-day weekend where admits are exposed to the "real Sloan."

Indeed, many current students will tell you that to get a sense of the school beyond the geeky, intense MIT stereotype, you really should visit. "I do think there's a real drive among the students," says Christina Cragholm, a member of the class of 2003. "There's a drive that this is a top school—so there's no reason that we shouldn't be breaking down stereotypes and getting more attention." If you're motivated and willing to take initiative to make Sloan a better place, the administration will nearly give you carte blanche.

This sense of collaboration also helps students put a good spin on some of the school's shortcomings, most notably the lack of study space. If a study group needs to meet to work on an assignment, there's a degree of hunting and pecking among classrooms to find a free spot. Students will admit to some wistful glances at the facilities at nearby Harvard Business School, but, when pressed, will say that their space issues make them resourceful, strategic, and organized. "If you're trying to find a place for your group to meet, someone will say, 'OK, you nail the room and call me on my cell phone as soon as you have it,' " recalls one recent grad. "It adds to the sense of community because you do end up seeing people all the time."

The availability of graduate student housing at MIT is relatively slim, though a new student dorm has been in Sloan's plans for awhile (Schmalensee is shooting for a 2006–2007 completion date). In the meantime, Sloan students disperse throughout Boston, mostly congregating up and down the Red Line of the T, which runs past the school. Many students wind up living in charming Beacon Hill and take a scenic 20-minute walk across the Charles River to get to class. Students gather for drinks at the Beacon Hill Pub, Sevens, Miracle of Science, or the on-campus cheap beer joint called Muddy Charles.

The most formal—and the most famous—organized social event at Sloan is the Thursday night C-functions (short for consumption functions, Cultural Functions, or both) that occur either on campus or at a local bar. Often, C-functions have a cultural theme and are organized by foreign student groups (who make up 40 percent of Sloan's population.) These events can get pretty rowdy—the Brazilian C-function is downright infamous.

Sloan has active cross-country, hockey, and competitive soccer clubs, and the Vintners Club does five wine tastings a semester, which brings out a mix of students, spouses, and significant others. Significant others and spouses have their own club called SOS, and they're included in team dinners and part of orientation as well.

There are literally dozens of other clubs, both social and career related. One of the largest student clubs, Media Tech, does "tech treks" where you'll spend an extended weekend in various locations visiting with executives. The marquee event is the week-long trek to Silicon Valley over IAP in January. In 2002, 80 students took part in the excursion, which included a wine-tasting tour through California wine country.

PLACEMENT DETAILS

In 2000, Sloan scored high marks in terms of placement numbers, as recruiters started to flock to the technically savvy grads. In 2002, however, the tech downturn left Sloan in a slight lurch. However, the school managed to pick up the slack, stacking up well compared to its peers.

Sloan makes sure that its students get plenty of career counseling both in and out of the classroom. In 2002, one day of the orientation week was given the touchy-feely label "Reflections," and students focused on self-assessment and their professional presence. You'll now also get some career placement work done in two of your core classes, Organizational Processes and Communication for Managers, where you'll work on resume writing, career decision making, negotiations, and developing a career marketing strategy. Out of the classroom, you can take one of many seminars offered by the Career Development Office on topics like hiring theory and practice and conducting market research.

In January, the Career Development Office holds its Interview Blitz Weekend for first-years. You'll get a chance to experience all the different MBA recruiting interviews (the case interview, the behavioral interview) and to practice with other students and Sloan alums.

When corporate recruiting slowed somewhat in 2001–2002, Sloan, like many B-schools, reached out to its alumni network to help get students jobs and internships. The school recruited alums to be a part of the newly developed Industry Advisors program, where professionals in different industries meet with Sloan students on an individual basis to discuss their job search strategies and long-term career plans. An impressive 83 percent of grads had jobs by 2002 graduation—second only to Kellogg, which placed 83 percent of its grads by graduation. Three months after commencement, 90 percent of 2002 grads who were looking for jobs had offers. And Sloan grads' pay packages were among the highest—an average of $121,800. A full 23 percent of grads found employment outside of the U.S., and those that stayed in the States mostly stuck to the Northeast.

TOP HIRES

IBM (11); Goldman Sachs (9); Merrill Lynch (9); Boston Consulting Group (8); McKinsey & Company (8); Siebel Systems (8); Citigroup (6); Banc of America Securities (5); Johnson & Johnson (5); Bain & Company (4); Putnam Investments (4).

OUTSTANDING FACULTY

Paul Asquith (finance); Rebecca Henderson (management); Robert Pindyck (economics); Kevin Rock (finance); Roberto Rigobon (economics); J. Sterman (business dynamics); Rudi Dornbusch (economics and international management); Duncan Simester (marketing).

APPLICANT TIPS

As chair of the student admissions committee, 2003 grad Christina Cragholm says that the committee just needs to get more people to visit campus. "One of the things that we find is that people are much more pumped up about Sloan after they've met with someone or have gotten to interact," Cragholm says. To that extent, the Sloan Ambassador's Program, which shepherds prospective students around campus for an afternoon or to Thursday night C-functions—in combination with the aforementioned reinvigorated admit weekend—have been successful in giving a sense of a vibrant, cohesive school. "People see that it's a social place and that breaks down a lot of stereotypes," Cragholm says.

You will need to have analytical ability to succeed at Sloan, but that ability need not be strictly numbers-based; rather, the admissions committee will want to see that you're open to new experiences—for example, joining the $50K contest or starting a new student club. Still, you will need a certain numerical aptitude in order to express sometimes complicated classroom concepts. If your quantitative background is meager, the admissions office might ask you to take calculus or a microeconomics course before you arrive so that Sloan's pace won't overwhelm you.

You'll be evaluated not only on your GMAT scores and transcripts, but, most important, on your essays and your interview. The weight of your GMAT score depends on the rest of your application. If a low GMAT score is just one part of a strong application with compelling essays and a great interview, you shouldn't be deterred from applying.

"Keep in mind, though, that each applicant is in a pool where a lot of people are doing everything very well," says Rod Garcia, director of admissions, "so it pays to make everything as strong as he or she can reasonably make it."

Sloan prides itself on having a straightforward application, so answer the essay questions directly. Interviews are required for admission, but are by invitation only. Because they're really the final stage of the evaluation process, they'll be weighted heavily. The core of the interview is your responses to behavioral questions, where you'll be asked what you did in certain situations, and you'll be evaluated on your ability to communicate effectively, your professional presence, and whether or not you have some insights into your own professional growth process. But, above all, says Garcia, "Be yourself, be yourself, be yourself."

In general, successful Sloan applicants can find a way to set themselves apart from the crowd. "They don't just say, 'I was a negotiator on a $10 million project,'" says Garcia, "they outline how they established a rapport with the other companies' teams, convinced their own team to separate what was necessary to fight over and what could be used to establish credibility, and did enough research that they were more informed than anyone." So you'll want to make sure you've done some self-analysis before you apply to Sloan, and have given some real thought to why it might be the place for you.

Sloan requires you to complete your application online. You can also sign up online for a variety of admissions events around the globe. International students are urged to apply in the first round of applications to ensure that any visa issues will get sorted out.

SLOAN MBAs SOUND OFF

MIT Sloan is an excellent MBA program, with very bright students and dedicated professors, many of whom are the best in their fields. Admissions does a great job in finding an intelligent and very diverse student body. The curriculum is academically rigorous, which is refreshing for a business school.

I really enjoyed the fact that Sloan was 40 percent international. The first-semester teams were set up so that each team had some foreign students. As a result, my experience felt a lot more diverse than if there had only been Americans on the team. Sloan is a great example of how diversity of background can benefit the MBA experience.

The Sloan administration works very closely with students and is highly responsive to students' interests and initiatives. It also promotes the active participation of students into important decisions or tasks of the MBA program.

My MIT experience was enhanced by access to resources throughout MIT. Ability to cross register and access resources in any department at MIT really added to my learning experience. Even the electives had students from all over MIT enhancing the class learning experience. The class was very diverse both in terms of nationality and previous backgrounds thus adding to the learning experience.

MIT Sloan is an incredible MBA program, focused on developing innovative and collaborative leaders. It is a fantastic place for anyone who wants to develop his or her ability to think critically about the toughest problems in business. The administration really gives free reign to the students and empowers the students to mold the program to best suit their individual needs and interests.

Sloan has its roots in quantitative work, and it is demanding in that sense, but it has done a great deal to expand its coverage of other topics and skills. I was concerned before attending, but came away glad I had acquired the analytics I did. I do not feel I lost out on other skills for having come to Sloan. If anything, I feel confident in my ability to understand and assess most any business problem. From what I hear from friends at other schools, I believe Sloan has prepared us well with analytic and general business skills.

MIT Sloan's MBA is an outstanding program with the right balance of "hard" quantitative skills and "softer" social skills. As an institution MIT Sloan is at the forefront of research, which benefits the MBA program greatly. The small size of the school ensures an extremely strong community. People at MIT Sloan, whether students or faculty, are very "down to earth" and are always eager to help each other out. The network of alumni is also very strong.

The return on my experience is orders of magnitude above the investment. The quality of the experience has been driven by the caliber of both the students and professors, and the attention the administration has placed on continuous improvement. Improvements are needed—especially in areas such as leadership and career advisement, but the school has already made great strides in improving those areas.

COLUMBIA UNIVERSITY
Columbia Business School
216 Uris Hall
3022 Broadway
New York, NY 10027
E-mail address: apply@claven.gsb.columbia.edu
Web site address: www.gsb.columbia.edu

7.
COLUMBIA
UNIVERSITY

Enrollment: 1172	Annual tuition and fees: $32,154
Women: 35%	Estimated annual budget: $54,960
Non-U.S.: 27%	Average GMAT score: 711
Minority: 11%	Average months of work experience: 53
Part-time: 0	Accepted applicants enrolled: 72%
Average age: 27	Corporate ranking: 4
Applicants accepted: 11%	Graduate ranking: 17
Median starting pay: $90,000	Intellectual capital rank: 7

Teaching methods: lecture 40%, case study 40%, team projects 20%

What's Columbia Business School got going for it? A lot more then just the Big Apple. "Columbia Business School practices what it preaches," says one very satisfied 2002 grad. "It understands that like any other organization, it has customers and in order to keep attracting the best customers it can, it must continually strive to improve itself and be forward thinking, anticipating customers' needs." Just like any successful business, Columbia has tweaked its machinery in the last two years, adding new programs and revamping existing ones all with the end goal of "preserving excellence" in every dimension, as one administrator puts it. It's not just empty talk. 2002 grads praise the school's administrators for their responsiveness in addressing student concerns and meeting student expectations.

So it's no wonder applications have increased by 150 percent in the past 10 years. Columbia is a hot ticket on the MBA market not only because of its first-rate academic programs and distinguished reputation, but also for its prestigious alumni network and prime location. The school has become increasingly selective, accepting just 10 percent of applicants for the class of 2004, compared to 10 years ago, when the acceptance rate was a hefty 47 percent.

The school prides itself on its "New York Advantage," a signature slogan you'll find emblazoned across every brochure. With the center of the business world a quick subway ride away, you'll have the opportunity to participate firsthand in the global marketplace both on and off campus. "One of the most significant elements in my MBA experience, if not the most significant, was the access I had to top executives," says one satisfied 2002 grad. Cohesive efforts from the 131 full-time faculty, 80 adjuncts, and numerous administrators have succeeded in exposing students to international business leaders and prominent industry leaders who come to campus each year. The 2001–2002 school year roster of speakers boasted the likes of Goldman Sachs CEO and chairman Hank Paulson, Estee Lauder president and CEO Fred Langhammer, and eBay CEO Meg Whitman.

The main drawback to the urban locale is space—or rather, the lack of it. Some students complain that study space is inadequate—you try studying in a cramped New York apartment or a bustling coffee shop when the meeting rooms are booked. To alleviate this tight squeeze, Columbia recently acquired new spaces in midtown Manhattan and moved many of its administrative offices there in order to free up study space for students and office space for faculty in Uris Hall (the B-school's main building). The school also opened up Warren Hall in 1999, just a five-minute walk from Uris, which provides some breakout rooms for students.

Though space may be scarce, one area that Columbia doesn't lack in is technology. In the classroom, students are met with an array of resources from high-resolution video document cameras and dual LCD projectors to videoconferencing capabilities. The virtual financial markets laboratory, frequented by finance students, makes data programs like BridgeFeed and Nexis available to keep up with every industry and market movement. Students can also access these programs from their own notebook computers, a requirement for all MBAs here.

Columbia's MBA program heavily emphasizes a global perspective. When you graduate, you're expected to have the capacity to function in a heterogeneous environment and to speak multiple languages and work across cultural and geographical boundaries, says Dean Meyer Feldberg. Administrators' efforts to maintain a diverse student body allow ample opportunity to learn not only from professionals on campus but also from the cultural, geographical, and professional background of your classmates. Says Admissions Director Kathy Swan: "It isn't just a matter of ethnicity, it's where you've been and where you're going. We work hard to get a class full of people with different experiences." These efforts have kept Columbia at the top of the charts in enrollment of minorities and international students, with numbers at 20 percent and 28 percent, respectively, for the class of 2004. And while MBA enrollment for women has been stagnant at most schools, Columbia has a 35 percent female class. The Columbia Women in Business Conference, which in 2002 drew a record 600 students, prospective students, alumnae, faculty, and business women may be one reason why. The school fosters diversity. "Perhaps the best aspect of the school is the strong sense of community that unites students who bring unique experiences and offer very different perspectives to the learning process," cites one 2002 grad. You might actually find yourself in a statistics class sitting between a former football player and a horse farmer.

When you arrive, you're assigned to a cluster of about 60 students on the first day of a weeklong orientation, which grads adequately describe as a "mini–boot camp" in bonding. These clusters go through core courses together through the two terms of their first year, and you'll be further divided into project groups of six to work on team assignments. The program is designed to encourage teamwork and collaboration while leaving plenty of room to sharpen students' competitive edges. This may not be what you might expect in the competition-driven finance capital of the world. Although originally skeptical about Columbia's competitive reputation, 2002 grad Craig Swanson describes the school's atmosphere as collaborative rather than competitive. The teams help mitigate the effects of a strict grading curve that could otherwise lead to a more cutthroat atmosphere. Says Swanson: "Our cluster had social events a couple times weekly and we were very collaborative with school work."

Most grads agree that teaching at the school is top-notch; however, some complain that teaching quality is inconsistent and runs hot and cold. That may be largely due to the high number of adjuncts—around 80 for 2002. Most gripes, though, are voiced about the core curriculum, with grads ranking the quality of core teaching way below that of electives instruction. Administrators hope to see a drop-off in the number of complaints with the opening of the Arthur J. Samberg Institute for Teaching Excellence in the fall of 2002. Hiring, which has averaged 7 to 10 faculty members a year, is one area—along with faculty training—where Columbia has launched a full-on assault. "We felt it was extremely important to put more muscle behind faculty development, specifically for new faculty," says Vice Dean and Samberg Institute Director Safwan Masri. "The idea is to help socialize new faculty into the culture." As part of the program, new faculty members, who do not teach their first semester, are paired with current faculty for mentoring, training, and all-around support. The Institute will also include a component for curriculum and case development to keep all faculty members informed of the latest developments in teaching skills and technology, a program students will benefit from in the classroom. That's a boon for you future MBA students. What better way to improve your academic experience than to have your professors go through a bit of training to ensure you're getting the best and latest information? The center is just one example of Columbia's commitment to excellence in the classroom.

So who should apply to this fast-paced school? The numbers of applicants bent on manufacturing and entrepreneurial management have risen as of late, but about a third of applicants still say finance is the only game in town. Historically known as a factory for pumping out finance grads, Columbia has shown con-

sistent strength in this field, with more than half of its 2002 graduates landing jobs in finance. However, if number crunching isn't your forte, Columbia offers preterm, noncredit courses—also known as math and computer camp—at no extra cost. Most classes are offered online. Seminars on presentation skills, team building, and writing proficiency are also offered to all students in the first year, but they aren't required, so it's up to you to take advantage of them. And, with 12 areas of concentration, over 150 electives, and nearly 90 on-campus clubs and organizations such as the Columbia Entrepreneur Association, Media Management Association, Social Enterprise Club, Gourmet Club, and Micro-Brew Society, you'll find a number of avenues to satiate your appetite for a unique outlet. The electives offered and the professors who teach them are what really set Columbia apart from the rest of the B-schools, says Todd Combs. Among electives offered for 2002–2003 are Consulting in the Non-Profit Sector, Social Entrepreneurship, and Search of a Perfect Prince, a course on leadership that uses Shakespeare's works—an unlikely source for a B-school. Some of the most popular electives include Launching New Ventures, Managerial Negotiations, and Retailing. Swanson, who was involved in various clubs, says the Small Business Consulting Program club, in groups of four to five students, worked on a consulting project with the business manager of small businesses in the area that was the highlight of his two years. "It was an excellent entry into the world of consulting as well as a great way to put recently learned academic knowledge to use in a real-world application," Swanson adds. It's not something other schools can easily copy, simply because of the vast resources of New York City.

The 13 required first-year core courses and half-courses, which include broad areas such as economics, corporate finance, management, marketing, and accounting, will keep you busy because the school has restructured the core courses so that no requirements are taken in the second year. Columbia has a knack for keeping up with business trends, updating the curriculum as necessary. That's easily reflected in new courses offered each year, such as an ethics elective to be added to the fall 2002 course list. You can exempt yourself from core courses by exam, and although you'll need to replace them with electives, you don't have to stick to the same subject areas. Beware, though—because of the large MBA class (over 490), you'll choose your courses through a bidding system where points are used to indicate preferred classes.

If you want to couple your MBA with another degree, Columbia encourages students to take advantage of the other top-quality departments at the Ivy League university through any of the 12 dual degree programs including architecture, engineering, international affairs, journalism, law, nursing, public health, social work, education, medicine, and dentistry. Even if you choose not to steer down the dual degree road, you can still take up to two courses in some of these schools. Or, if you have an adventurous streak, you can venture outside the comforts of Columbia's walled campus, as do about 50 students a year, and participate in one of 22 exchange programs offered in 20 different centers including Brazil, Mexico, West and South Africa, Central and Eastern Europe, China, and Japan—at B-schools like The Chinese University of Hong Kong, The Rotterdam School of Management in The Netherlands, and the Getulio Vargas School of Business Administration in São Paulo. And the school is looking to forge more alliances with schools in Asia, Feldberg adds.

The class of 2004 will break in a number of newly strengthened programs. In early 2002, the real estate program found a permanent home in the Paul Milstein Center for Real Estate. Through a $5 million grant from the Milstein family, the Center will further solidify the program's mission by providing students with stronger links to industry leaders, a focused curriculum, and a broad business background with a finance emphasis. The program couples theory and prac-

tice with its well-known case study curriculum that looks at everything from asset management and restructuring to ethics in real estate. Cases are developed annually by professionals working in real estate finance and investment management in New York. Participating firms include Citicorp Real Estate, Prudential Real Estate Investors, and Merrill Lynch. "Being in New York allows us to get professionals in the classroom and get them involved in the curriculum integrating theory and practice," says Professor and Milstein Center Director Lynne Sagalyn. The top-notch value of the program can be seen in the laundry list of industry leaders, including Vornado Realty Trust president Michael Fascitelli and Morgan Stanley Dean Witter vice president Brent Elkins. Real estate is hot now, and Sagalyn plans to take advantage of it. Sagalyn adds: "It's a hard asset, and when the bubble bursts people are looking for what's real."

Another area seeing increased interest is the Social Enterprise Program (formerly the Public Non-Profit Management Program), which expanded its mission in 2002 to include a broader scope and perspective seeking to expand students' comprehension of the role of the private, nonprofit, and governmental sectors in solving societal problems. In addition to non-profit management courses, the program offers a menu of courses, activities, and lectures covering various areas including social venture, social entrepreneurship, ethics, international development, and corporate social and environmental responsibility. New courses for 2002 include Social Entrepreneurship, Managerial Ethics, Consulting in the Nonprofit Sector, Business Strategies for Emerging Markets, and Transnational Business and Human Rights. You can participate in the program by taking courses, joining the student-run Social Enterprise Club, participating in an independent study, or opting to work on pro bono consulting. Another option, the Small Business Consulting Program, is a student-led organization that provides services from creating business plans to conducting market research for small businesses and nonprofits. The "New York Advantage" comes into play here too: as a huge center for government and nonprofit activities, the city is a relative treasure chest of opportunity. "It used to be more straight, academic, and in the classroom," says Ray Horton, program director and management professor. "Now it's much more real world." Columbia is getting more students out into the field to better learn about and develop networking relationships. "We've always been pretty good at bringing people into the university, and now we're exporting students," Horton says. The program also offers help to subsidize students working in nonprofit and government settings in both summer internships and full-time jobs. The CORPS fellowship program, for example, subsidizes students' summer internships, and is funded by donations from students, faculty, and alumni. In the past, students have worked for organizations such as the National Parks Conservation Association, Teach for America, and the Lower Manhattan Development Corporation.

Maintaining Columbia's global perspective, the Jerome A. Chazen Institute of International Business will launch a new addition this fall—a Web journal. The student-run journal is designed to provide information on issues in international business. The first edition of the journal will explore entrepreneurship in Africa, inspired by a student trip to Africa in January 2002 by Managers in International Development Initiative (MIDI), a student organization established soon before the trip that explores the interplay between business and international development and provides opportunities for students to consult with small business ventures in developing countries. The Web journal, which anyone can access, will feature such items as video interviews with leading figures in international business. Besides the journal, the Chazen Institute continues to weave an international thread through the school and daily student life in other ways. For $300, you can take

eight weeks of intensive three-hour classes in any of 12 languages. And the international zeal carries over after graduation, as all grads have the opportunity to participate in the annual Pan-European Alumni Reunion, which draws more than 500 alumni from over 25 countries.

Another area turning heads off 116th and Broadway is the Eugene M. Lang Center for Entrepreneurship. New courses in the fall of 2002 focused on Private Equity and Entrepreneurship in Emerging Markets and Social Entrepreneurship. You can opt to take courses at the center in one of four specialized career paths, including entrepreneurship in new ventures, entrepreneurship in large organizations, private equity financing, and social entrepreneurship. The Entrepreneurial Greenhouse Program, an incubator of sorts, provides a lucky few students with funding for new business ventures, including prelaunch expenses, and provides access to experts and investors in the field. Another option is the Launching New Ventures course, in which you'll be taught to develop a comprehensive and effective presentation of a business concept. MBAs address product or service design, in-depth market analysis, developing marketing campaigns, assessing human resource requirements, and building realistic financial forecasts. In keeping with Columbia's hands-on approach, you can also apply for funding from the Lang Fund, a unique business school investment fund that doles out $250,000 annually in seed capital to selected student businesses. In 2002, more than 82 students participated in the Lang Fund. One key factor that sets the Fund apart from similar ventures at other B-schools is its extensive mentoring process. Students are matched with experienced, industry-appropriate financiers and other professionals who provide guidance and help students develop and shape high-quality business proposals. The 2002 grads' crop of new businesses vary from The Folklore Company, a multimedia company that focuses on children's educational entertainment, to Schneider Vineyards, a Long Island–based vineyard that produces handcrafted wines. It doesn't stop there: in 2001, Columbia partnered with UC Berkeley's Haas School of Business and the Goldman Sachs Foundation to host the National Social Venture Competition, which began at Haas in 1999. In 2002, the competition yielded 77 applications from 32 schools around the country, and winners from the various categories received a total of $100,000 in prize money. The partnership intends to provide a national stage to bring together the academic and financial worlds to support social ventures. That's not something you might expect from a city where greed and riches can seem to rule the day. As if these efforts weren't enough, the Heilbrunn Graham and Dodd Center for Value Investing, led by finance and economics professor Bruce Greenwald, opened in fall 2002, continuing Columbia's pioneering role in the value investing arena. The Center will help develop materials for students in core courses and sponsor research initiatives in value-investing.

Beyond the walls of Uris Hall, building networks with alumni can play an invaluable role in your job-hunting efforts, especially if you're looking to stay in New York (as more than half the graduates in many classes have done). An extensive alumni database (BANC), managed by the career services office, keeps track of more than 26,000 graduates who can be easily accessed online by field or locations. If you're looking into smaller companies that haven't traditionally recruited Columbia MBAs, career counselors at the school are a good resource, and some programs and clubs host their own events that provide prime networking opportunities. "The network is unbelievable, particularly in New York," says 2002 graduate Combs. "I never had anyone who's a Columbia alum say no. There's a sense that you want to help your colleagues be successful."

Though the market was tight for the class of 2002 in general, Columbia grads praise the placement office when it comes to preparing them to land a job on graduation. "Our major

mission is to provide long-term career education and career development so that people will have skill sets now and later," says Regina Resnick, assistant dean and director of career services. "It's not our job to give them the job but to give them the skills to be the most competitive possible."

In 2002, more than ever, the individual initiative to network was even more important. Resnick responded to this sense of urgency and redoubled her efforts to ensure students were well equipped for the job hunt. As an example, Columbia career services beefed up the workshops offered and adapted topics to coincide with the market at hand. "Whereas in the past I would have done a workshop on valuing options," Resnick says, "now we have one on uncovering the hidden job market." What a difference two years makes. Students and alums also played a major role in terms of networking and placement. Through the Job Opportunities Exchanges (JOE) program, students met to-gether in small groups to discuss things like how to prepare for interviews, making the initial call, and preparing elevator pitches. Though normally these forums don't usually get under way until later in the second year, in 2002 they started in February to give students the chance to support one another in a tough market. Such changes are the hallmark of a school that can shift on the fly to meet students' needs. Alums also played a larger role in 2002. Alums, and especially the Young Alumni Council, made sure opportunities were brought to students' attention.

There is life outside Uris Hall and the job search when you're not just hitting the books. Students can take advantage of the fact that New York City is home not only to top corporations but to top entertainment spots as well. No classes are scheduled on Fridays, which are reserved for study sessions, work on group projects, interviews, and, for some students, resting up from the previous night's festivities. But that also means the weekend starts a day early. After Thursday night happy hours at Uris Deli, you can head in any direction to different Manhattan neighborhoods like the posh Upper East Side, trendy Greenwich Village, and the gritty Lower East Side to grab a drink or a bite to eat and listen to some good jazz. Students regularly venture off campus to experience the various and diverse cultural offerings New York is known for, such as museums, operas, ballets, restaurants, and Broadway shows. Bars, restaurants, open-air fruit markets, shops, and outdoor cafes overfill Broadway and Amsterdam Avenues, the two main commercial streets in the B-school's Morningside Heights neighborhood. One grad adds, "There was never a shortage of things to do, just a shortage of money."

That's a big consideration if you're looking to go to school in one of the world's most expensive locales. For housing, students can apply to live on campus in one of the university's 143 apartment buildings, though just about 60 percent will get the scarce housing, with preference given to those coming from farthest away. However, most MBAs dig deep into their pockets and team up with other students to live in sometimes small apartments on the Upper West Side. Whichever option you take, bring a fat checkbook along. With so much to see and do, you're bound to find something that fits your interest in housing and in social setting. The urban locale isn't for everyone, though. "Those looking for a nice quiet campus in a rural community would probably not be comfortable at Columbia," warns 2002 graduate Swanson.

PLACEMENT DETAILS

In any market, you've got to have clear career goals, but for the class of 2002 there was a different sense of urgency and redoubling of efforts to make sure students understood they needed a clear plan along with key skills to help them snag a job, explains Career Services Director Regina Resnick. That's why the placement office offered a series of workshops on things like net-working skills and how to uncover the hidden job market. They also bumped up their Job Opportunity Exchanges (JOE) meetings to earlier in the year to help students give each other a boost in core skills like interviewing, cold calling, elevator pitches, and resume writing.

Their major mission is to provide long-term career education and career development. "It's not our job to give them a job, but to give them the skills to be the most competitive possible," Resnick adds. Though she says she recognizes it's important to facilitate as many opportunities to meet with companies as possible, especially in a tight market, she says (holding an MBA herself) that it's even more crucial to make sure students leave with a strong skill set that will propel them into a future jobs.

Resnick is also quick to laud Columbia's alumni network. Though alumni have always been a reliable source for placement information, says Resnick, this time around the individual initiative to network was ever more important. Alums provided strong connections, she adds, as did the Young Alumni Council, which provided additional forums to aid students in their job search. Students also have access to the alumni BANC database, which provides information on alums by location and industry, for example.

International students also receive a helping hand. The school offers special workshops aimed at international skills, like workshops for nonnative English speakers, activities with alums, and sessions on a range of issues like work requirements, internationalizing your resume, and even etiquette to prepare you for different cultural norms. Plus, the Chazen Institute hosts an annual International Career Services Conference, with 100 peers from around the world gathering to discuss key issues and develop strategies for international students and international placement.

In 2002, about 73 percent of Columbia grads had job offers by graduation, and 84 percent had offers by three months after commencement. Columbia grads earned average starting pay packages of about $123,600, and nearly all grads who stayed in the U.S. took jobs in the Northeast—but a full 20 percent of Columbia grads took work overseas.

TOP HIRES

Citigroup/Citibank (36); Deutsche Bank (22); Goldman Sachs (18); Lehman Brothers (16); Merrill Lynch (14); Bear Stearns (13); JPMorgan Chase (13); McKinsey & Company (12); Morgan Stanley (12); Credit Suisse First Boston (11).

OUTSTANDING FACULTY

Bruce Greenwald (finance and economics); Raymond Horton (economics); Laurie Hodrick (finance); Ralph Biggadike (management); Michael Feiner (management); Amar Bhide (management); David Juran (statistics).

APPLICANT TIPS

Like most B-schools, Columbia is looking for students who can show a strong academic record, professional promise, and a well-rounded background. But, with a 10 percent acceptance rate for the class of 2004, this B-school keeps getting increasingly selective, and with its rolling admissions process, the earlier you get your application in, the better. While your GPA and GMAT scores are important, admissions officers aren't just looking at the numbers. Admissions Director Kathy Swan says she's looking at the kind of undergraduate institution you went to, the subjects you studied, and the activities you participated in. She adds that if your GMAT score isn't up to par with most Columbia students' average numbers, showing that you've taken every step possible to get that score is key. "I admire tenacity. If people are taking the steps to improve their score, that's a plus for us," Swan adds. Successful applicants demonstrate leadership skills, initiative, entrepreneurial instincts, the ability to work with a team, and contribution to the community. And although three to four years is the average amount of experience for most applicants, it's not always a deal breaker if you're coming in with just a year of experience under your belt or applying straight out of college.

Perhaps the most important quality the admissions committee considers is a student's professional promise. Swan says she's looking for students who have demonstrated leadership and initiative on the job or in school, a resume that illustrates growth, and, most important, someone with a clear idea of what he or she wants to do post-MBA. The common denominator, says Swan, is the ability to take tools of the MBA and achieve post-MBA goals with those tools. One major problem that will put your application at the bottom of the pile is a lack of focus. Swan says unsuccessful candidates aren't sure why they want to get an MBA and, thus, aren't able to fully articulate their reasons for applying to graduate school. "It comes across on the application if you don't have a personal commitment to [an MBA]," she warns.

Though interviews are by invitation only, based on an initial review of application, they are not required. However, if invited, be sure to take advantage of the offer. Only about 20 percent of the class of 2004 was admitted without an interview. "We use it as a way to get to know an attractive candidate better and figure out somebody who isn't clear off the paper," Swan notes. Alumni and current students do the majority of the interviews.

COLUMBIA MBAs SOUND OFF

The alumni network can't be beat. I wanted a job in finance—career services had a whole

Rolodex of people for me to call and they all invited me down to their offices. I was so lucky to go to school in NYC because it made interviewing that much easier. Plus it meant that recruiters knew my name and face, which helped a lot.

The sense of community at Columbia is tremendous. Our entire cluster of 60 people all participated in social events, charity events, and fund-raising. Never in my life have I seen that level of willingness to get to know and help other people. So while Columbia classes teach us lessons to guide our decision making and career choices, the Columbia social network teaches us how to build communities and teams that will last a lifetime.

Columbia's reputation is a great foot in the door in this respect. What I didn't expect at Columbia was the caring community. Not being a native New Yorker, I had no trouble making friends early, and they're still the foundation of my social circle two years later. Columbia turned out to be a collaborative, constructive environment, not at all the "back-stabbing" environment it was purported to be. My loans don't worry me in the slightest, as I feel that Columbia has put me in a position to benefit financially and strategically throughout my career.

Great program, great city, great diversity of background, highly intelligent classmates, and excellent professors—would not have gone anywhere else.

I would recommend my MBA experience at Columbia to anyone who likes intellectual challenge, living in a big and exciting city and never losing contact with the real world. Finally, I believe that Columbia's most interesting assets are its people, who always have great stories to tell about their past in the most exotic parts of the world.

I'm thoroughly happy that I attended Columbia for my MBA. Despite the difficult job market, I felt the school coped admirably. More importantly, my MBA was greatly enhanced by the caliber of students and faculty with whom I interacted on a daily basis.

8.
UNIVERSITY OF MICHIGAN

UNIVERSITY OF MICHIGAN

University of Michigan Business School
701 Tappan
Ann Arbor, Michigan 48109
E-mail address: umbsmba@umich.edu
Web site address: www.bus.umich.edu

Enrollment: 869	Annual tuition and fees: $32,686
Women: 28%	Estimated annual budget: $47,932
Non-U.S.: 30%	Average GMAT score: 681
Minority: 11%	Average months of work experience: 66
Part-time: 944	Accepted applicants enrolled: 57%
Average age: 28	Corporate ranking: 6
Applicants accepted: 19%	Graduate ranking: 13
Median starting pay: $85,000	Intellectual capital rank: 13

Teaching methods: lecture 25%, case study 30%, experiential learning 15%, team projects 20%, simulations 10%

In the spring of 2001, as his first year as dean of the Graduate School of Business at the University of Michigan was winding down, Robert Dolan met with a group of second-year MBA students to discuss their concerns. One student began to voice a litany of complaints to the new dean, but quickly was confronted by another student, who said, "You know why you're making those complaints? You're complaining because you thought it would be a puppet show. This is not a place where you sit back and get entertained." Indeed, the sheer size of the school and the number of possible paths a Michigan student can take might be daunting for someone who thrives in a more regulated, streamlined atmosphere. But for those with an "inner compass," as Dolan puts it, who are willing to immerse themselves in Michigan's hands-on curriculum—which combines a strong set of core courses with a seemingly endless number of electives—Michigan's continued place in the top 10 list of business schools makes it an attractive choice for the engaged, focused MBA candidate.

Dolan, who spent 21 years at Harvard Business School before taking over at Michigan, intends to strengthen the B-school's ties to Michigan's other top-notch research facilities. "I came here from a university where the business school is on one side of the river and the rest of the university is on the other side, so there really is not a lot of crossover," Dolan says. "Here, it is exactly the opposite." Dolan is also trying to boost Michigan's already well-established reputation for being committed to social issues in the business world. Issues such as hunger, education, environment, ethics, and medicine "don't fit neatly within the traditional business school bucket," Dolan says. "We can put together a program based in the business school, but we can reach out to other schools around."

For example, you can apply to the Corporate Environmental Management Program, a three-year joint degree in conjunction with the School of Natural Resources and the Environment, in which you'll take classes in environmental management, energy, corporate social responsibility, organizational learning, and human rights. The class of 2002 had some 40 students take part in CEMP, and the number grows every year. Another popular option is a MBA/Master's in engineering or MBA/Master's in manufacturing through the Tauber Manufacturing Institute, which integrates the B-school with the university's top-ranked college of engineering. These are but 3 of 20 dual degrees offered. The school's ability to focus and support diverse areas of concentration attracts students with diverse pre-MBA backgrounds—you won't find Michigan a program of just wannabe investment bankers.

With the philosophy of "Define a problem, make a plan, execute it" running through the school from the application process through the recruiting season, if you know what you want, Michigan will give you the resources to go after it. It is most definitely a school for those who plan to be active participants in creating their educational experience because of the number of experiential opportunities, the first of which comes at the end of the first year and is part of the core curriculum: the Multi-disciplinary Action Project (MAP). In its eleventh year as of 2002–2003, this program is unique both for the depth of integration of different subjects and for its use of real-time, real-world situations and teaching. In this shorter, business school version of a medical school residency—a requirement during the last seven weeks of the first year—students bid to work on projects in industries that interest them, from financial services to information technology. Then, under the guid-

ance of a cross-functional teaching team of Michigan faculty, groups of about six or seven MBAs work hand in hand on special projects with senior corporate managers from companies such as Apple Computer, Bank One, General Motors, Focus: HOPE, Kenya-based Ecosandals, and Daimler Chrysler. In 2001–2002, the program was expanded to include international companies through the International Multi-Disciplinary Action Project (IMAP), and in EMAP, which formalizes the entrepreneurial options, students work with start-ups.

After a few weeks of instruction on the company and the project you're assigned, you'll spend three to four weeks on-site. You could be just across campus at the University of Michigan Cancer Center, working on a financial model, or as far away as Peru, targeting niche markets for an ecotourism company. Indeed, the wide array of projects allows students to tailor their MAP experience to their interests. Students consistently rave about the experience, saying the trial-by-fire management exercise essentially provides them with a second internship and an opportunity to apply their skills. Inevitably, some students are not happy with their assignment or their group; however, as one 2002 grad puts it in perspective, "It's part of the challenge of the program." You'll learn about leadership and team dynamics and, "after that, team projects in the second year were a piece of cake."

MAP is part of a first-year schedule known as "The Core," which accounts for a little more than half of the 60 credit hours you'll need to graduate and encompasses a broad range of general management–focused areas: financial accounting, microeconomics, marketing management, finance, corporate strategy, the world economy, management accounting, human behavior and organization, operations management, and business statistics. Students move through the core in six sections of 70 students. Each section is assigned its own team of professors, which helps make the large aggregate of MBA faces seem a little more familiar. While a few core courses (Financial Accounting, Applied Microeconomics, and Marketing Management) last 14 weeks, most are just 7 weeks in length, forcing professors to pare their material to the essentials. Though the majority of your first year is spent in The Core, you'll still have room for at least one elective before your summer internship. Michigan's philosophy is that it wants to give you a really solid grounding in GM essentials before throwing you into the wide world of internships and electives.

With cold calls and a heavy workload, The Core may be overwhelming, but first-years find themselves doing a large number of group projects that foster cooperation, not competition. As one 2002 grad who came to Michigan with a nonprofit background explains, "In my finance group there was a friend who was always willing to spend extra time during our meetings or on the phone to help me out. This sentiment was everywhere at the school."

During the second year, MBAs are required to take courses in either ethics or business law. They also must fulfill a managerial writing requirement if they haven't passed a test to waive out. However, the rest of a second-year's schedule is left open for electives—more than 100 course offerings in more specialized business areas. Because electives are competitive—only those with consistent enrollment survive year to year—they are necessarily reactive to the topics and business issues in which students are interested. Those who haven't had their fill of business skills in their regular classes can sign up several times a semester for optional executive skills seminars. The daylong courses, held on Fridays, provide exec ed training for MBAs on workplace topics such as managing diversity and negotiations.

Moreover, students are able to take classes on relevant topics at the larger university. The school prides itself on its close connection with "Big Blue"—some 30 percent of the faculty have joint appointments with other university departments. Not interested in a joint degree? You can also take up to 10 credits outside the B-school, allowing you to take relevant courses without having to pursue a dual degree.

The school has no majors, but, again, you're encouraged to pursue a track of courses that revolves around your individual career goals. Along with the dual degree programs, Michigan also has a number of specialized programs. The Tauber Manufacturing Institute offers not only its joint manufacturing degrees but a range of courses that complement the core's operations management course. All entrepreneurship-related electives are overseen by the Samuel Zell and Robert H. Lurie Institute for Entrepreneurial Studies, begun in 1999 with a $10 million gift from the two real estate moguls. Want to sit on the other side of the VC table? The Zell-Lurie Institute also oversees the Wolverine Venture Fund, where you'll help manage a $3 million early-stage venture capital fund. The William Davidson Institute serves as the umbrella for international assignments, including a 14-week Global Project Course elective.

Michigan's international outreach—which includes the Global Project Course and IMAP—is one of its distinguishing features, but it's really part of a larger philosophy that aims to get B-school students out of the classroom. The push starts as soon as you show up for the Leadership Development Program, a weeklong orientation before classes begin. First-years are led by second-years through a week of exercises designed to help them work in teams, so you may find yourself getting your entire team to balance on a beam without crushing tomatoes placed underneath. "Michigan has pulled a lot of the touchy-feely stuff out of the curriculum and put it into the leadership program," says one former team leader. But students also hear high-profile speakers, do labs that assess their managerial skills, and spend one day of the week working on a volunteer project in nearby inner-city areas.

This particular day introduces students to Michigan's subtle effort to sow seeds of social consciousness throughout the MBA experience. You'll be encouraged to sign up for seminars in executive skills such as providing transformational leadership, managing workforce diversity, and balancing work and family. Last year, a group of students got the administration to include environmental cases in the core if the professor agreed, and many of the school's extracurricular activities tend to have a socially conscious bent. Not only does the school have the largest chapter of Net Impact in the country, but the student-run Global Citizenship raises money for Focus: Hope in Detroit, and students founded and run the Business School Food Fight, a competition among 25 top B-schools to raise food and money for a national charity.

"There *is* a sense of morals that runs through the student body," says a 2002 grad. "It can be found in all types of students, not just those in CEMP and Net Impact. It comes out in class discussions and clubs."

Students give the school high marks for the diversity of its students. And Michigan continues to demonstrate its support for women in business. The Michigan Business Women students' organization has been around for some 30 years, and in 1998 the school, along with the Center for the Education of Women and Catalyst, Inc., launched a study called "Women in the MBA: Gateway to Opportunity," which looked at graduates of leading MBA programs and their experiences with business school, careers, and why more women are not pursuing MBAs. To foster this study, published in 2000, the school created the Women in Business Initiative, which has become the umbrella organization for a Women's Leadership Council, launched in 2000, which brings together business leaders and advises the school on programs that support women in business. The Women in Leadership Steering Committee, composed of students, faculty, and staff, tries to foster a larger network of women throughout the B-school.

Though the school now provides wireless/LAN connections throughout the campus, students still gripe pretty consistently about Michigan's facilities and their technological capacity. The school's organic growth over the years does not accommodate the large number students who use the facilities: classrooms are small, computer clusters are crammed to capacity, and breakout rooms are at times full. While the schoolwide wireless network does come in handy during group meetings, there is a severe shortage of outlets into which students can plug laptops. This can become a real problem when final exams require laptops on which to draft case analysis. "Imagine 200+ laptops competing for perhaps 10 power outlets during a four-hour long exam," recalls one student. Dean Dolan admits that such complaints are valid. Perhaps the school's new capital campaign will start to address such facilities-related complaints.

Frigid winters aside, Ann Arbor deserves its reputation as one of the nation's most livable college towns. There are art festivals all summer long, you can boat and fish in the Huron River, and "The Arb"—a local arboretum—has an abundance of hiking and nature trails. Closer to campus, there's a myriad of bars and restaurants that serve the 40,000 or so students who attend the University of Michigan. B-schoolers head to bars like Connor O'Neills for Monday night trivia, shoot pool on Thursdays at the Full Moon Brewery after class, or just chill outside at Dominic's, a popular spot adjacent to the B-school and the law school. A little farther from campus you'll find some quiet places for drinks and dinner, and when you want to feel like an adult, you can head to The Earle, a trendy place with a jazz trio.

Sports fans will find themselves in heaven at Michigan, with the Detroit Lions, Tigers, Pistons, and Red Wings nearby and Michigan football games and tailgate parties dominating the fall social scene. "What could be better than spending a crisp fall afternoon with 110,000 screaming maniacs at the Big House watching the Wolverines trounce an opponent?" asks one 2002 grad.

"UMBS students are very social creatures who rarely pass up an opportunity to get together and network," says another recent graduate. The B-school's student association sponsors weekly happy hours, and individual sections often meet up to go bowling, have potluck dinners, or play Whirly Ball, an Ann Arbor favorite.

There's a club for every interest, ranging from the typical career clubs like the marketing, finance, and high-tech clubs to socially conscious clubs such as Net Impact and Global Citizenship. The Wine Club holds tastings for the entire school. Many students write for the *Monroe Street Journal,* the B-school's weekly paper. Don't see a club that strikes your fancy? Every year students start their own, from the women's ice hockey club to the energy club.

M-trek, an Outward Bound–type program, was started by students and offers two-week trips for incoming students before the school year, returning in time for the Leadership Development Program. Second-year MBA students are the leaders, and the treks vary in difficulty—the cushier ones feature van-supported biking, while more rugged trips feature some serious backpacking. In 2001, over 200 students took part in 19 treks to places like Hawaii, South Africa, and Macchu Picchu in Peru.

The Significant Others and Spouses club (SOS) also has a large membership at the school. Its yearly highlight is the "Baby MBA" Halloween parade, where UMBS students' offspring parade through the halls in their costumes.

PLACEMENT DETAILS

The guidance offered by the career placement office at Michigan starts with some serious self-assessment: you need to know where you want to go and where you can make a difference. Then you need to network, using connections—including a huge University of Michigan alumni base—to help you find the right job. These two steps, says Al Cotrone, director of career development, are the more difficult backbone of what he considers the "easy" part of the job hunt: the resume and interview.

While Michigan's size ensures a large cadre of on-campus recruiters, the school also promotes the off-campus side of the job-hunt, bolstering its commitment to self-assessment and networking through Career Strategy Groups. These voluntary groups of 8 to 10 students meet in four-week cycles to talk about the job search process ("to keep each others' spirits up," explains Cotrone). Each week students must come back with job leads not only for themselves but for the rest of their group, bolstering their networking skills.

Second-years compete to be trained as career counselors to help first-years with resumes and interviews. Students also play a role in recruiting events on the East and West Coasts, and student clubs are encouraged to come up with lists of companies they want to see recruit on campus, which the career office will then actively pursue. Placement was a sticking point in 2002, though, with only 66 percent of grads securing job offers before graduation. By three months after graduation, only 74 percent had offers—a far cry from the 80 percent-plus 90-day-out placement rates at many top schools. Still, those who did have jobs earned respectable pay packages, averaging $115,200. Most grads stayed in the Midwest or moved to the East or West Coasts. Only about 10 percent found employment outside the United States.

TOP HIRES

Deloitte Consulting (10); A.T. Kearney (9); Johnson & Johnson (9); Siebel Systems (8); Eli Lily (7); McKinsey & Company (7); Citigroup Saloman Smith Barney (6); Goldman Sachs (6); Kraft Foods (6).

OUTSTANDING FACULTY

Aneel Karnani (corporate strategy); M. P. Narayanan (finance); Keith Crocker (economics); Tom Kinnear (marketing); Gautam Ahuja (corporate strategy); Sugato Bhattacharaya (finance); Allan Afuah (corporate strategy); Anjen Thakor (finance); James Desimpelare (accounting).

APPLICANT TIPS

Michigan likes to think there is a flow between admissions and career services: just as career services wants you to have a vision and a plan with which to execute your job hunt, the admissions office wants to see the same initiative in your application, even before you get to the school. Of course, they'll look to see whether your GMAT, GPA scores, and undergraduate education show that you can handle the rigor of the program, but equally important is the progression of your full-time work experience, your demonstrated leadership skills, and the clarity of your goals: why do you want an MBA and why do you want it at Michigan?

"The whole application process is introspective," says Kris Nebel, Michigan's director of admissions. Let the admissions staff know that you have really thought about Michigan and its particular offerings. Make an effort to talk to admissions staffers when they're on the road at receptions and forums, or reach out to an alum in your company or in your area. "Demonstrate that you've done more research than reading the viewbook," Nebel says. She points out that the unsuccessful applicant, while he or she may have good experience, will have an application that could be sent to any top B-school and doesn't distinguish itself as having been written solely for Michigan.

Because Michigan has such a large and diverse candidate pool—not only Wall Street bankers but ex-teachers and Peace Corps workers—keep in mind that your work experience need not be as quant-heavy as it might for other schools. Michigan just wants to know that you've made the most of your experiences, and,

again, that you have a vision for your future and can be an active participant in the school.

"It really comes down to essays, interviews, and recommendations," says Nebel, Michigan's essays ask you to not just tell a story, but to tell the hows and whys in your background. "If you write, 'I passed the CPA exam,'" says Knebel, "I can already tell that from your resume. Instead, tell me something you've done now that you're a CPA."

Interviews are strongly encouraged at Michigan, and you're required to do them before you submit your application, so that they become a part of the application. However, the admissions staff won't look at your interview until after they've considered the rest of your application. "It gives us that gut check of, 'Is this the right person?'" Nebel explains. Think of the Michigan interview as a job interview. You'll be walked through your resume, and you'll be asked questions about teamwork and decision-making experiences.

International students are also encouraged to apply in the first two decision rounds (November 1 and January 7) because of international scholarship decisions; all admitted international students are guaranteed funding. International alums do some of the overseas interviewing, but you can interview by phone as well.

MICHIGAN MBAs SOUND OFF

Michigan's secret is in the system of incentives and deliberate program design choices. The combination of admitting by interview more than application, not ranking class members, and not calculating GPAs on the transcripts allows an environment of creativity and collaboration that is hard to achieve with 400+ type A personalities. The people in a program of this caliber are self-motivated, and don't need false incentives or competitive frameworks to be driven. By having the flexibility to design their own curriculum and being encouraged to focus less on grades and step outside of their expertise areas, they graduate as much stronger managers with much broader knowledge than most MBAs that I encounter in the business world.

The spirit of camaraderie here is amazing. There is so much cooperation among the students. I really feel like I am part of a big family here. With the economy the way it is today it was fascinating to see how the students came together to help one another land jobs, when it would have been much easier for them to become ultracompetitive.

UMBS has an exceptionally intelligent student body. Having worked as a surgeon I thought I knew some very bright people; then I came to UMBS and realized what I was missing out on. The faculty and students are very supportive. The dean is making great efforts. School admissions officers look beyond just numbers when selecting students—rather, the emphasis is placed on management potential and achievements in previous careers. This created an amazing student body.

The environment at UMBS is perfect for MBA learning. This learning includes critical core MBA skills such as finance, marketing, accounting, economics, strategy and entrepreneurship. But it also includes cultural and interpersonal learning. The classes and extracurricular programs/speakers are designed in such a way as to allow each individual MBA student to select the optimal learning environment for him- or herself. The key to UMBS's success is its people, which are the most diverse, incredible, inspiring people I have ever met. This includes faculty, guest speakers, students, etc.

UMBS is an excellent school with a great mixture of academia, teamwork, cases and exams. I would recommend it to anyone. Needless to say, the sport opportunities are awesome and fun, from football to hockey. Also sports facilities are excellent. You can really find the right balance here at Michigan.

I found the congenial atmosphere and teamwork at Michigan to be the hallmarks of the program. Courses like MAP were innovative but programs can be replicated. True teamwork and leadership cannot be so easily replicated. I feel that Michigan spent as much time developing and emphasizing my emotional intelligence as they did business acumen. I also had the pleasure of working with two different faculty members on independent studies. These experiences highlighted how invested and engaged the faculty are with the learning process.

Michigan provided a great experience not only inside the MBA program but also through what the entire university has to offer such as other excellent academic programs which offer talks and seminars and an excellent athletic program which makes the time outside the classroom very enjoyable. In addition to that the city of Ann Arbor offers up a variety of activities and is close enough to other major cities.

I have had a great time at the University of Michigan Business School. It has met my expectations and surpassed them in many ways. I feel now I have a very solid grasp of the fundamentals of business and general management, and, through my participation in extracurricular activities, have gained immensely (professionally, socially, and culturally). The out-of-class experiences were the real value added at the school.

9.
DUKE UNIVERSITY

DUKE UNIVERSITY

Fuqua School of Business
1 Towerview Drive
Durham, North Carolina 27708
E-mail address: admissions-info@fuqua.duke.edu
Web site address: www.fuqua.duke.edu

Enrollment: 696
Women: 32%
Non-U.S.: 34%
Minority: 17%
Part-time: 0
Average age: 28
Applicants accepted: 19%
Median starting pay: $85,250

Annual tuition and fees: $31,350
Estimated annual budget: $46,778
Average GMAT score: 701
Average months of work experience: 64
Accepted applicants enrolled: 57%
Corporate ranking: 9
Graduate ranking: 9
Intellectual capital rank: 4

Teaching methods: lecture 30%, case study 30%, experiential learning 10%, team projects 20%, simulations 10%

Talk to anyone at Fuqua about the school, and within minutes they'll mention the concept of Team Fuqua. It sounds hokey to an outsider, but everyone at the school, from top administrators to professors to students, buys into it. What is it? It's a kind of school spirit derived from the team-based learning that goes on in just about all of Fuqua's classes and from students' involvement in almost every aspect of running the school (they sit on the curriculum committee, for example, and have a say in which companies recruit on campus). It affects not only students' study habits but their social lives as well.

"You realize that your classmates are like your family and any success they have is a success for you," says one 2002 grad. "Team Fuqua means helping your fellow students in any way you can. It means automatically wishing someone you see in an interview suit good luck, and meaning it." It seems to be symbolic of everything from collaboration to just plain niceness. Don't be fooled; it can get a little overwhelming and the collegial nature can sometimes be corny. But overall, Team Fuqua rules the B-school.

Duke's dean, Douglas T. Breeden, who took over from the legendary Rex Adams in 2001, inherits this spirit of cooperation and is poised to make Fuqua's name recognizable once and for all in the realm of top B-schools. He also inherits a strong recruiting program—overseen by Dan Nagy, associate dean for admissions, recruiting and business development, and run by Sheryle Dirks, director of the Career Management Center—which has continued to shine despite a tough economic year. Breeden's priority for the next few years: faculty recruitment. In the past two years, Fuqua hired PhDs to increase its faculty from 68 to 86, and the dean's goal is to have a total of 100 faculty members two years from now to accommodate what he hopes will be an increase in the student body to 400 first-years in August 2003. That's a tall order, since PhDs are constantly in demand, but the school has already done well.

Why are faculty attracted to this midsize campus, nestled in the North Carolina Research Triangle? It's not the basketball, even though Coach K. will sometimes let a faculty recruit watch a practice. Basketball still comes in second to the sense of community that even professors say they feel at the school. "We have a tradition of engaging in joint research and providing help to each other in the form of constructive feedback," says Professor Bill Boudling.

In addition to luring faculty, Breeden logged thousands of miles during his first year traveling to Europe and Asia to recruit more international students (whose numbers in the student body have risen slightly from 31 to 34 percent) and to bolster the Global Executive and Cross-Continent MBA programs, which were begun to help top- and mid-level executives, respectively, achieve degrees through a combination of face-to-face classes and online learning. The school also touts the concept of lifelong learning for Fuqua grads by providing faculty-taught seminars to alums when they visit campus or over the Internet. The idea is for alums to create a recruiting network as strong as those of older B-schools, as Fuqua 2002 grads give the school only average marks for its alumni network and connections. This could be a drawback for students who are looking for alumni to help them in areas other than banking and consulting—i.e., industries with a heavy on-campus presence.

As it is, students give the school praise for smart, accessible faculty and relevant, team-oriented coursework. The program strives for balance: a middle-of-the-road general management approach that doesn't emphasize one spe-cialty over another (the school offers only one formal concentration, in health sector management). The school also shows a strong commitment to building leadership skills. In fact, Team Building and Leadership Development is the name of the first of two required, graded Integrative Learning Experiences (ILEs) that begin each year of classes. After a week of orientation (run, in Fuqua style, by the returning second-year students), the incoming class is divided into five sections that rotate through five days of the ILE's team-building exercises, including a day on a high ropes course in the woods outside Durham, a Myers-Briggs personality test, a class on ethics, and other activities designed to assess communication and leadership skills with the aim of getting you to think deeply about what you want to achieve—not just at Fuqua, but in your career and your life.

The schedule of classes for both first-year and second-year students is intense and highly compacted into terms that last just seven weeks—two terms per semester. This model makes each course a mini-immersion into a topic, and mirrors the experiences many students may have had in investment banking or consulting jobs where you focus on one project intensely for a few weeks and then move on. In your first year, you'll take four classes per term—except for the third term, when you'll take three, to leave more time for summer internship interviewing—which allows you to complete the core curriculum and save some room for electives. Electives at Fuqua fall into several different categories: the mainstays are accounting, economics, finance, marketing, and operations, and there are also opportunities for global travel with the GATE program, management communications, and health sector management courses.

Your first year may be all about Team Fuqua, but that doesn't mean the school lacks competitive spirit. The second year begins with yet another ILE, Competitive Business Strategy. A one-week computer simulation pits eight teams of 40 students against one another in a competition to formulate and implement strategy for a global business. The exercise is designed to give students the opportunity to apply in a cross-disciplinary, practical way what they learned during their first-year core sequence. Having spent your first year working with the same teams, breaking into groups of students you have not worked with before creates a challenging environment for the exercise. After this ILE, you'll take three classes per term—all electives. That will allow ample time to focus on the job hunt.

Almost every class is divided, at the beginning of the term, into groups of four to eight students. These teams remain the same for the entire term. In the first year, these smaller teams remain the same for all classes. The teams are purposely diversified in terms of ethnicity, previous employment, and age. "You really get a chance—and are essentially forced—to work out all the kinks in your team because you have to figure out a way to work together," says Krissie Ames, a 2002 grad. The "forced" teams personify the workplace, or at least that's the idea. In the second year you pick your own teams for each class. Professors will encourage you to pick teams with similar diversity, and while the tendency might be to team with friends, Ames says that things tend to stay fairly diverse. "Even if you wanted to form a team of your close friends, you probably wouldn't find them all in one class."

The professors see the team-based learning as a unique attribute of Fuqua and incorporate it into class by having written projects handled by teams or cold-calling on teams rather than individual students. "If I think about what we stand for, it's innovation through collaboration," explains marketing professor John Lynch. You might not like it here if you find group-based work frustrating; people who are willing to share their knowledge and exhibit patience while working within a group fit in best at Fuqua.

While professors do create some team-based competitions within their classes, Fuqua students emphasize the noncompetitive atmosphere of collaboration that pervades their studies. Students organize study groups, create study guides, and share their notes with everyone. "You don't compete against your classmates," one grad says, "you compete with yourself to raise yourself to the high standards that you see your fellow students embodying." Some students, however, do find that this team-based atmosphere can stifle what might otherwise be considered healthy competition. And though this learning system may be relatively stress free, it is not necessarily an accurate reflection of the business environment you'll encounter after school. "You're unlikely to find a lot of conflict at Fuqua, both the healthy and the unhealthy kind," says one recent grad. "This makes the learning experience outstanding for those looking to switch careers or try new disciplines, but may make things a bit dull for former bankers looking to stamp their resumes as they head back to Wall Street." Dean Breeden is aware of such criticisms, but says the idea is for students to work within the team-based culture while still having their own ambitions and personal goals. Thus, the school looks favorably on applicants who can demonstrate these sorts of personal traits.

Not all learning takes place on the Fuqua campus. An ever popular option is the Global Academic Travel Experience (GATE), with courses taught by Fuqua faculty in the region of your choice—Asia, Latin America, Russia, South Africa, the Middle East, or Australia. Six weeks of classes—in which you'll study cultural differences, business practices, and various manufacturing operations—culminate with two weeks of travel to companies in the area. Students can also choose to spend a term or an entire semester abroad at one of many universities with which Fuqua has an exchange arrangement in Australia, Europe, Africa, and Asia. Two new additions to this exchange program will be with Seoul National University in South Korea and with the University of Peking in China.

The big buzz on campus this year surrounds the completion of the new $27.5 million

Lafe P. and Rita D. Fox Student Center, considered by faculty and students alike to be Fuqua's "living room." Previously, student activity centered around a student-run kiosk and the "mallway" outside the classrooms; for hot meals students had to trek across the bridge to the R. David Thomas (that's right, "Dave," the Wendy's founder) executive education center for a pricier meal. Along with a student lounge, and showers and changing rooms for students who want to go for a jog in the afternoon before evening study sessions or presentations, the Fox Student Center boasts several different eateries, including a café (complete with espresso bar) and a restaurant with student budget–friendly entrees. With a large open space and outdoor seating areas, the Fox Student Center is the perfect home for Fuqua Fridays. These Friday night get-togethers are a solid school tradition attended by faculty and students alike. Students regroup on campus with friends and families around 5:30 every Friday for free beer and food to celebrate making it through another week of classes. The informal party sometimes centers around a theme—International Night, featuring food from many students' home countries, is a popular evening, for example.

Fuqua Fridays often serve as a jumping-off point for the night's social activities. Groups of students may head into Durham to hang out at the bars and restaurants on 9th Street or in Brightleaf Square, or they may make the 15-minute drive to Chapel Hill to sample the nightlife on Franklin Street. Raleigh, the third point on the Research Triangle, is a 25-minute drive away. Students make this drive when they want a little variety: theaters, art museums, the Carolina Hurricanes hockey team. "Between Durham, Raleigh, and Chapel Hill," says Brian Bolten, a 2002 grad, "you have everything you could ever need." Like California's Silicon Valley and Massachusetts's Route 128, the Triangle has leveraged its nearby academic resources to woo businesses. You'll never confuse the area for New York or Chicago, but you won't feel like you're in the middle of nowhere either. Indeed, Durham is a nice compromise between the access a big city provides and the serenity that a tucked-away college town offers.

The relaxed intellectual atmosphere and the beauty of the Gothic Duke campus keep many Fuqua students close to home. Most spare time is spent on Team Fuqua activities—students play an active role in running the school and participate in the plethora of clubs focusing on everything from marketing to soccer to wine. Many of the clubs' activities serve as fundraisers for the pinnacle of the annual social season—the Fuqua MBA Games, a series of wacky competitions held each spring to raise money for the Special Olympics of North Carolina. In the past 10 years, the MBA Games have raised over $1 million for the Special Olympics of North Carolina. Another fund-raiser, the International Business School Rugby Tournament, hosted by Fuqua every April, pits student teams from 20 B-schools in the United States, Canada, Great Britain, and Australia against each other to benefit Habitat for Humanity.

When they're not out raising money, Fuqua students attend the school's other big social events, such as the annual Christmas Formal and Beach Week (the week between finals and graduation, when both first-year and second-year students migrate to Nag's Head, on the Outer Banks, to spend the week relaxing and partying in the sun). Once every quarter, students gather in Geneen Auditorium to drink beer and laugh at each other during FuquaVision—student-produced skits and spoofs. Athletes can hone their competitive edge in the soccer club, which travels all over the country to tournaments. Singers can participate in an a cappella group or get on the stage for Fuqua Unplugged, an open mike night event that has morphed into an annual CD recorded and sold to help raise money for the MBA Games.

No one will deny that Durham has a mild, outdoor-friendly climate. Many students take advantage of the proximity of beaches and hiking trails. And because the Washington Duke golf course is almost adjacent to the business school, golf is a huge after-class activity. (With reduced rates for students on weekdays, Wednesdays, for second-years, are known as "Golf Day.") However popular the sport of golf, nothing quite beats Duke basketball frenzy. During the season, the social life revolves around watching the games at Cameron Indoor Stadium (for those lucky enough to score tickets) or crowding around TVs with friends. Basketball proves yet another bonding experience for students who embark on Camp Out Weekend—when students rent RVs and U-Hauls to camp out for the chance to be entered into a ticket lottery. Whether or not they end up with tickets, many students say it's a social highlight of the year.

Almost all students live off campus with other students. With the downturn in the tech market affecting the Triangle, Durham offers apartments in complexes with tennis courts, pools, and lots of outdoor space for reasonable rents—especially if you're relocating from a big city. One such complex, Pinnacle Ridge, usually houses so many Fuqua students that it's almost like a dorm, but with much nicer accommodations.

This quality of life is a plus for those students who come to campus with significant others, spouses, or families. And, because the average age of the Fuqua students is 28, family life isn't necessarily an exception to the norm. Spouses are welcomed, encouraged, and even expected to attend all social functions. The "Fuqua Partners Association," run by spouses or boyfriends/girlfriends of Duke students, organizes dinners and job networking events throughout the year. "My wife would often comment that she did not feel as if she was competing against Fuqua for my attention," says Steven Miller. "She felt like a member of the community as well." Miller also says that the Fuqua environment was also a wonderful one in which to welcome his daughter, born in January of his first year. "Friends would be concerned or would give me a hard time if we didn't bring our daughter to Fuqua Friday," he says.

PLACEMENT DETAILS

In a year where many recruiters cut back on campus interviews, 2002 Fuqua grads say the Career Management Center came through for them, even though Fuqua is a small school with fewer students for recruiters to interview. But the Fuqua-wide ideals of balance and teamwork come into play here as well. Students are as much a part of the job-hunting process as the Career Management Center. Through the Career Fellows Program, second-year students counsel first-years on interview skills and job-hunting techniques. Career-oriented clubs, such as the marketing club or the finance club, arrange symposiums each fall to which they invite companies to give presentations and workshops. Student clubs also have a mentoring system whereby a second-year student who had completed an internship in, say, operations, might help a first-year considering a career change to that field. Clubs organize weekend trips to different cities to meet with companies; the Finance Club, for example, organizes an annual Weekend on Wall Street.

The Career Management Center starts its formal involvement during first-year orientation, and corporate presentations begin in early September. On-campus interviewing for second-years begins in late October and runs through early December, while on-campus interviewing for first-year summer internships runs from January through March. Sheryle Dirks, the director of the Career Management Center, said that in 2001–2002, her office made an effort to do even more for the students, not only teaching them the basics of resume writing and interviewing but also proactively marketing students to companies and uncovering job opportunities in new areas—something her office had not had to do in the past. The result?

2002 grads ranked Fuqua among the top five for the number, diversity, and quality of the firms recruiting on campus.

"Second year, as the economy tanked, things got a bit more stressful for sure," says 2002 grad Ames. "Companies canceled their recruiting schedules and jobs were extremely scarce. Career services went above and beyond to reach out to alums to see if anyone could hire Fuqua students for internships or full time."

Though Fuqua's placement rates—only 76 percent of grads had jobs by graduation—show that recruiting did not deliver as much as in past years, the schoolwide commitment to a balanced, generalized MBA program equalized the influence of the dot-com boom in the late 1990s, and Fuqua never really neglected stalwarts such as Ford, GE, or IBM in the face of the sexier start-ups. Indeed, 89 percent of grads did land jobs by three months after graduation, and 2002 grads earned about $113,600 in starting pay packages.

The Career Management Center offers a number of workshops and special programs to support international students. In addition to online resume books, there's a day of mock interviews for international students prior to the regular session, and Fuqua hosts an international career event for networking and interviews in conjunction with the business schools at the University of Virginia and the University of North Carolina. It's more than some schools offer, but with international students the fastest-growing population at many business schools, it's not as comprehensive a boast as it could be for international students, who can have a tough time job hunting.

TOP HIRES

Johnson & Johnson (11); Merrill Lynch (8); Lehman Brothers (6); Procter & Gamble (6); IBM (5); American Airlines (5); Dell (5); Capital One (5).

OUTSTANDING FACULTY

Jennifer Francis (accounting); John Graham (finance); Bill Boulding (marketing); Campbell Harvey (finance); Debu Purohit (marketing); John Lynch (marketing); Robert Whaley (finance); Laura Kornish (decision science).

APPLICANT TIPS

"We definitely want students who want to go to school here," says Associate Dean for Admissions Dan Nagy. He and Admissions Director Liz Riley want creative leaders who demonstrate a desire to truly make a change in their post-MBA world. "We're looking for a little bit of that pizzazz and motivation," says Nagy. And, perhaps most important, the willingness to be a part of Team Fuqua.

"Fuqua has had a team-based culture for as long as anyone here can remember," Nagy says. This means the school is looking for people who can relate and work well with others. But, as admissions have become ever more selective, so you'll also need high GMAT scores to get in, and they will be weighed heavily. The average score now tops 700, but Nagy does point out that the school rejects a fair number of applicants with those scores if they don't have the team player qualities in their professional and extracurricular activities to back them up; at the same time, they might take a chance on a candidate with GMAT scores in the low 600s with an impressive work and extracurricular background. In any event, you'll want to use an interview and your essay to highlight these qualities through specific examples.

Interviews, while not required, are completed by almost 90 percent of applicants. Get interviewed. It will give you a chance to show you've got the qualities Fuqua is looking for. "Do your homework" and "give examples" are two tips for interviewees. "There's obviously something that draws you to the schools on your short list," Riley says. "You want your interviewer to know why you're here. Are you interested in seeing the new student center? Then ask a pointed question about it. Let the interviewer know you know more about the school than its ranking." Similarly, come armed with examples of how you're a team player, and most importantly, why Fuqua is the school for you.

Fuqua chooses its essay questions carefully. Riley points out that many times candidates try to anticipate the answers they think the admission office is looking for. "Be specific to Fuqua," Riley says. "We know you have to write six different essays for two different schools, but don't cut and paste another school's essay into ours. We know!" Instead, she suggests, the successful essay is creative as well as informative, with a certain spin on the story to grab her attention.

Get your application in as early as possible without sacrificing quality. International students and those who live too far away to make it to campus for a visit should plan to attend an alumni or admissions informational forum in their area and try to set up an interview there.

FUQUA MBAs SOUND OFF

Fuqua truly surpassed my expectations. I went to a very good undergraduate program, but found that the teachers here were more impressive and more dedicated. The students at Fuqua form a very important part of the experience. As I was relatively new to the high profile finance world, I needed help from students to absorb the lingo, attitudes, and expectations. Without exception, I found students were ready and willing to help, even when I was interviewing for the same positions. I picked Fuqua for its hardworking but collaborative atmosphere, and the students and faculty have been better than I hoped.

I had a great experience at Fuqua and have nothing but positive things to say about my classmates, the faculty, administration, coursework, the facilities, etc. Having only lived in Southern California and Washington, DC, I admittedly had initial reservations about Durham, NC. But I think being in a smaller town helped to create such an amazing tight-knit community at Fuqua.

I am very satisfied with the education that I received from Fuqua. I met a lot of people from all over the world, and I will definitely stay in touch with them. I was able to establish contacts with a lot of the world-leading firms in my area of interest, and this will make my life over the next few years much easier. A lot of faculty members are not only professors to me, but also good friends.

I think Fuqua is a wonderful school and community. This year is a tough year with the job market, but Fuqua career services has risen to the challenge, working with independent job-searchers, soliciting job postings from alumni, smaller companies, and companies who do not normally recruit on campus. Another outstanding part of Fuqua is the student involvement. It seems that nearly everybody is involved in the running of at least one club or event—makes for a strong school culture.

Fuqua has come a long way in a short period of time and is working hard to improve information technology, recruiting, and the hiring of additional professors. The school is very community oriented and focuses on both business and social issues, which makes for well rounded students.

Duke places heavy emphasis on interpersonal skills and the ability to build and maintain relationships. They screen applicants for these qualities and corporate recruiters seem to appreciate this. During my interviews for summer and full-time employment, I became more aware of Duke's reputation as a business school that turns out a well-rounded product—people you want on your team. That is, I think most recruiting companies view Fuqua students as smart people with excellent technical training who can also handle themselves socially.

Fuqua has been a great experience for me and my family. Durham provides an excellent atmosphere for students with children, including excellent schools and family neighborhoods close to campus. The new student center (which is huge and unbelievably luxurious) will certainly boost Fuqua's attractiveness to new students. I have been repeatedly impressed with the approachability and responsiveness of the faculty and administration, as well as the accessibility of the Career Services Office. There is no question in my mind that my decision to attend Fuqua served me and my family best.

DARTMOUTH COLLEGE

Tuck School of Business
100 Tuck Hall
Hanover, New Hampshire 03755
E-mail address: tuck.school@dartmouth.edu
Web site address: www.tuck.dartmouth.edu

10. DARTMOUTH COLLEGE

Enrollment: 464	Annual tuition and fees: $33,577
Women: 28%	Estimated annual budget: $55,290
Non-U.S.: 30%	Average GMAT score: 695
Minority: 18%	Average months of work experience: 57
Part-time: 0	Accepted applicants enrolled: 51%
Average age: 28	Corporate ranking: 12
Applicants accepted: 14%	Graduate ranking: 4
Median starting pay: $87,000	Intellectual capital rank: 11

Teaching methods: lecture 25%, case study 40%, experiential learning 5%, team projects 20%, distance learning 5%, simulations 5%

At no other business school, perhaps, will a study group break up at 10:30 P.M.—every night—for ice hockey practice. And at no other school, perhaps, will you be quite so surrounded by your fellow students: almost all Tuck first-years live in dorms on campus. Such close-knit intimacy and the charming, rural town of Hanover, New Hampshire, combined with more than 100 years of history, only grounds the Tuck School of Business at Dartmouth College further in tradition, in terms of both academics and student life. Still, Tuck's drop from number 10 in the 1998 *BusinessWeek* rankings to number 16 in 2000 showed that the school couldn't rest on its laurels or its legacy. Nor did it: it climbed back up to its number 10 spot in 2002.

Curriculum changes launched in the fall of 2000—which added some flexibility to a once rigid core curriculum—combined with better marks for the recruiting office have put Tuck back on track in 2002. The administration gets high marks from students for being more receptive to their concerns as they tried out the new curriculum. Case in point: the class of 2002 complained that the fall workload was too heavy. Now faculty members meet regularly to make sure that large assignments and projects for different classes are not due at the same time. The Tuck Leadership Forum—initially called the Tuck General Management Forum—is the cornerstone of the first-year curriculum redesign, and, as the administration works out the kinks, it gets good reviews from students. For example, when the group project portion of the Leadership Forum initially stretched out over both winter and spring semesters, students complained that the prolonged time frame caused them to procrastinate. Now the project is completed in the shorter winter term, allowing students the chance to really focus on the experience without the distraction of two semesters of other coursework.

In addition to the Leadership Forum, the first-year core now includes classes in technology and entrepreneurship. Perhaps even more important, students can take two electives in the spring semester (previously, there were no electives in the first year), helping them prep for summer internships. This breadth of scope, as well as the flexibility in the first year and the responsiveness of the administration to student concerns, seems to strike a balance that is working for Tuck.

Make no mistake: Tuck is an intense place. "This is not a place where you go home at night and you're across town," says Dean Paul Danos. With the school's small size (the class size recently expanded from 180 to 240 students, but Tuck is still one of the smallest MBA programs), faculty and administrators really get to know you: don't expect to walk across campus without someone calling out to say hello. And for those without a lot of experience in quantitative fields such as banking or consulting, the first-year workload can be particularly draining. But all of this, according to Danos, is what makes Tuck unique. "It's the epitome of total immersion," he says. "In one sense it's a throwback to a different era—a sincere education effort—and people crave that. But it's also something for the future." Of course, the school's remote location only adds to the immersion. There's really nowhere to go, even if you wanted to hop off to the nearest city.

The curriculum at Tuck is geared initially to get you thinking about your immediate future: your summer internship and the job you'll land after graduation. To that extent, your first year will give you the tools and techniques to make a contribution at these places, so expect to learn the basics of general management largely through lectures and homework problems. "We

want our students to be ready as possible, given the limited amount of time we have, to walk into a company and say, 'You've got a production planning problem or an inventory problem,'" says Professor David Pyke, associate dean for the MBA program.

The academic year is broken up into four parts: fall A (8 weeks) and fall B (6 weeks), winter term (9 weeks), and spring term (9 weeks). Fall A and B are the most substantive for first-years. You'll take Financial Measurement, Analysis and Reporting, Statistics, Leading Organizations, Decision Science, Global Economics for Managers, and Capital Markets. In winter term you'll take Corporate Finance, Marketing, and Strategic Analysis of Technology. Spring term includes Global and Competitive Strategy, Operations Management, and two elective courses. Two major changes to this core curriculum are the addition of the Strategic Analysis of Technology course—which will help you understand technological changes in general and how to think about them as they relate to your business—and the two electives, with which you can tee yourself up for your summer internship.

To help you through this heavy course load, the administration breaks the first-year class up into study groups of five or six students within sections of about 60 students. You'll prepare homework assignments on your own, but you'll meet each night to help each other out. Groups are chosen for diversity, so you might find yourself working not only with people from different ethnic and gender backgrounds, but with an experienced marketer, a quant-focused banker, and a nonprofit-oriented people person.

In addition to the core courses and the two electives, running through the entire first year is the aforementioned Tuck Leadership Forum, a series of events including half-term academic classes, team experiential projects, and a speaker series. The idea behind the forum is to give students a sense of the current market and factors affecting it without sacrificing the skills taught in the core curriculum. Therefore, the first class you'll take as part of the forum is Analysis for General Managers, one of the half-term courses, which is right at the front of fall A. You'll focus on the meanings of leadership and the role of a general manager in a corporation, giving you a broad view of what you're going to learn at Tuck over the next two years. The theory is that, before you start piecing together business theories on your own in your different classes and electives, you'll have an overview from the perspective of a general manager from the very beginning.

Next, in fall B, you'll take Management Communications, where you'll implement the leadership vision you got in Analysis for General Managers by learning how to communicate on both a corporate level and a personal level. You'll use the writing and oral presentation skills you learn in this class throughout your time at Tuck. This course gets rave reviews from students, who say it helped them immeasurably not only at Tuck but once they got out into the business world. "It teaches you to literally put thought around every thing you write—letters, business plans, presentations, even e-mails—because it really matters," says one 2002 grad.

The third classroom piece of the Leadership Forum comprises two ungraded sessions on entrepreneurial management during fall B, taught by Professor Michael Hovarth, an academic with an entrepreneurial background himself. In these sessions Hovarth discusses the fundamentals of what business plans are all about, which will whet your appetite for the next big piece of the Leadership Forum: the project.

Students start thinking up project ideas and forming groups of five or six during fall B so they're ready to hit the ground running at the start of winter term. Whereas the administration sets up your fall study groups, for this project you'll be allowed to gravitate toward people who might have ideas that interest you while being strongly encouraged to maintain diversity (if a group is too homogenous, the administra-tion will get involved). How do people get their project ideas? Some students will hatch their own business plan ideas—things they may have been thinking about before even coming to Tuck. Some will make contacts with professors in the Thayer School of Engineering or with medical students to find ideas that might need development or marketing. In 2000–2001, with entrepreneurship a hot B-school buzzword, all student groups were encouraged to go the start-up/entrepreneurial route with their projects. But now that the economy has cooled some-what, Steve Lubrano, assistant dean and director of the MBA program, culls 20 to 30 project ideas from companies like Nike, Stride Rite, and Ben & Jerry's, on which student groups who'd rather do a more consulting- than entrepreneurial-based project can bid.

At the end of the term, students present their project results not just to professors, but also to professional audiences. Consulting teams report to their clients and to professional consultants, and entrepreneurial teams are expected to pitch their businesses to venture capitalists who'll give them feedback.

The final component of the Leadership Forum is a two-part speaker series: the Leadership Speaker Series and Sector Smarts. The Leadership Speaker Series brings to campus top executives such as Orit Gadiesh, chair of Bain & Company, or ex-GE CEO Jack Welch, and runs through all three terms. The Sector Smarts series happens in the fall term only and is designed to educate students on the issues they'll face when they start their jobs. For example, if you're learning about valuation techniques in one of your core classes, the school will bring in a sell-side analyst who'll offer one opinion, and then the next day a buy-side analyst who'll offer yet another. To top it off, you'll hear a CFO talk about his or her opinions on valuation issues from yet another viewpoint. "In short," says Lubrano, "the Leadership Forum is a way to package and brand the aspect of the first-year curriculum that in itself is entrepreneurial."

In your second year, you'll be exposed to the next level of Tuck's course strategy, in which you'll consider the more strategic side of business, and to this end you'll do a lot more case analysis. Students praise the school's top-notch operations electives, as well as its international opportunities, including the popular Field Study in International Business, in which some 40 percent of the second-year class participates. In this class, you'll again be working in teams, assigned to projects in developing countries such as Nepal, India, Poland, or Peru. You'll spend a few weeks working on the project in the classroom, and then three to four weeks in the country itself, putting your project in place. "I'd have to rank this as my most outstanding experience at Tuck," says one 2002 grad. "It sounds dorky to say this, but the Field Study was quintessential in applying what you learned, and we really gelled as a team and felt like we added value to the client."

Tuck now also has five research centers with teaching faculty and courses linked to them. The Glassmeyer/McNamee Center for Digital Strategies, for example, concentrates research on the theory and practice of how corporations can be more effective digitally. The center, like the four others, often hosts events for students, where leaders in the field come in to discuss things like the future of wireless technology. The William F. Achtmeyer Center for Global Leadership is cosponsor of the Leadership Forum's Leadership Speaker Series. The Center for Asia and the Emerging Economies includes partnerships with universities in China, India, Japan, the Philippines, Vietnam, and Argentina. The Center for Corporate Governance brings together Tuck's resources in corporate governance as a center of knowledge for the faculty. The John H. Foster Center for Private Equity brings venture capitalists into the school.

In addition to its much-touted research and entrepreneurial aspects, Tuck is also committed to social awareness and nonprofit ventures. The Initiative for Corporate Citizenship, an alumni-funded office with its own director and staff, brings together all Tuck's efforts in volunteerism, creating days of service, working with not-for-profit clubs, and sponsoring activities such as the Tuck Gives Auction. This student-run auction, one of the school's major social events, raised over $66,000 in 2002—not bad for such a small school. The proceeds from the auction go to a fund established to help subsidize student summer internships in the nonprofit arena. As the fund grows, the school hopes to also be able to subsidize even nonprofit full-time jobs taken by graduates.

The closeness of a community that is happy to shell out money for a school cause is something that Danos has worked hard to keep even as he expanded the class size. Before bringing the class size up to 240, he increased the number of full-time faculty members from 34 to 50, making sure there was still a high faculty-to-student ratio. Danos says the increase in class size has also helped him to increase the diversity of the school. And indeed, with 60 more students per class, a Tuck class now reflects the typical B-school demographic of one-third women, one-third international, and 20 percent minority students. Danos acknowledges that in the past, Tuck's reputation for diversity has not been stellar, but, he says, "We've really changed the demographics."

That being said, Tuck students are a self-selecting bunch. If you're a die-hard city person or a Southern California native, you might want to think hard about spending two years in snowy, rural Hanover. Yet, if you want to escape to an outdoor-focused life for two years—accentuated by the close ties you'll develop with your classmates as you tackle the tough curriculum—this is the place for you. "You're probably going to spend the rest of your life living in a city, so why not come spend two years with us?" is the standard pitch of Associate Director of Admissions Gretchen Boehm.

Once you get to Hanover, you'll find that Tuck students are able to pack an enormous amount of activity around their studying. Indeed, many people choose Tuck for the ability to take long hikes on weekends, ski all winter, and be a part of the ice hockey craze: there are at least three ice hockey teams each for men and women. Never been on skates? You're still welcome on the "Tri-pods" team. Hockey, it seems, is as much a stress reliever and social activity as it is an athletic pursuit. While the A teams do compete against other B-schools, the B, C, and Tri-pods teams simply play for fun. "I can't believe I own a full set of hockey equipment," says Gretchen Moore, a 2002 graduate. "It's such a great bonding activity. You always have horrible ice time, but it's a great way to end the day. It gives you a goal in your study groups to wind things up in time for hockey practice."

Even if you don't want to get out on the ice, there are plenty of other clubs and social events to get you through the long Hanover winters. Every other Thursday, people congregate on campus for Tucktails, a family-friendly event where kids can do art projects together while their parents sip drinks and mingle with classmates and faculty. Though not quite as debaucherous as the famous Dartmouth College Winter Carnival, Tuck Winter Carnival is still the highlight of the social season. A Friday night B-school Battle of the Bands is followed by a Saturday ski race and hockey tournament with other B-schools, culminating in a huge party.

In your first year, the living situation tends to be a bit collegiate, with the vast majority of students living in one of two student dorms. Though you can opt out, most students say that the dorms are part of the Tuck experience, and they revel in this chance to bond with classmates. Buchanan, the "old dorm," was built in the 1960s, and its lounge is the site of late-night parties. The ski-lodge-like Whittemore opened in 2001 and is rather luxurious, with private bathrooms and refrigerators, air-conditioning, big desks, and queen-size beds—not your typical dorm-room amenities. Married student housing is in Sachem—small, adequate houses, about two

miles from the school—but some married couples prefer to live in condos near the medical center.

Second-years live off campus within a 10-mile radius of the school. Many students group together to rent houses, some of which are classic New England farmhouses with colorful names like End Zone, Sky Box, Canoe Club, Penalty Box, Caddyshack, and the Monastery. The houses get handed down year to year—the landlords agree to keep the leases in the Tuck family. Where first-years congregate at Hanover bars like Murphy's and Five Olde, second-years—who have spent a year in kitchen-less dorms—become veritable gourmets ("I never thought I'd learn to cook at business school!" says one grad) and throw dinner parties for each other at different houses. Though Hanover is a college town, it's a small one, without a great deal of variety in terms of restaurants and bars. But this is not necessarily a bad thing. "The flip side is that if I am studying late on a Thursday night, and I decide to go out," says 2003 grad Bill Madden, "I know exactly where my friends will be. There's no need to take a cab or try to find the group by cell phone. You just show up where you know they are."

The bonds that form at Tuck show up again in its alumni relations, which, for the school's small size, are one of its assets. Over 62 percent of alums contribute to the school, and many are frequent visitors to campus, something students say is a boon when it comes to the job hunt. Matt Fates, a 2002 grad who currently works for a venture capital firm, says his ability to call on alums for advice significantly helped his job search while a student, and he still networks with Tuck alums in the VC world now that he's part of it. "They're responsive and helpful," he says. "I don't think any of them fail to return my calls."

PLACEMENT DETAILS

Tuck's willingness to adapt its curriculum to current MBA needs is also mirrored in its career services office, which acknowledges that the era when 75 percent of the student body would have job offers even before their second year is long gone. "Now, some of the greatest places to work do not know they need MBA talent until weeks before they want those students to start," says Steve Lubrano, who, in addition to running the MBA program, oversees the career services office as well. In this latter role, he tries to help students understand what they are looking for, how they should pitch themselves to these places, and how to network effectively to make a first call of introduction.

Along with heading up the MBA program office and directing the Tuck Leadership Forum, Lubrano also spearheads Tuck's new efforts to integrate career services with the overall MBA program. He hopes to create more of an intertwining relationship between the often distinct business school worlds of academics and the job hunt. For example, he tries to eliminate scheduling conflicts that might arise when recruiting season is in full swing, and he keeps an eye out for students for whom a frustrating career search might be affecting their academics—and vice versa.

"This is a small community, so we get to know the students and better understand who they are and what they are seeking," Lubrano says. "We become their advocates, their champions—to support their learning and to assist as they manage their career searches and their pursuit of an MBA."

While this individual attention can perhaps only happen at a school as small as Tuck, the school's size and location do affect the numbers of companies who put out-of-the-way Hanover on their recruiting schedule. It shows: more than 25 percent of 2002 students did not have a job offer at graduation. To overcome its geographical isolation (the local airport in West Lebanon, six miles to the south, can handle prop planes only, and Boston, the closest major city, is a two-hour drive away) the career services office will send its students out to interested companies and to career fairs. Students can also go on networking trips with various career clubs. Still, in 2002, grads earned an average starting pay package of $122,100. And size doesn't really seem to matter to the students. "You might not get as many companies to come to Tuck, but the big firms do," says Matt Fates, a 2002 grad. "And they're all looking to hire 10 people. So if Goldman Sachs, Morgan Stanley, and Merrill Lynch come, and there are only 40 or so people interested in investment banking to begin with, you'll get interviews. Even if you don't necessarily graduate with one of these jobs, you'll still graduate having done several interviews."

TOP HIRES

Goldman Sachs (6); Bain & Company (5); The Parthenon Group (5); Booz Allen Hamilton (3); Cambridge Associates (3); IBM Strategy & Change (3); Investor Group Services (3); J.M. Huber (3).

OUTSTANDING FACULTY

Clyde Stickney (accounting); John Shank (finance); David Pyke (operations); Scott Neslin (marketing); Vijay Govindarajan (strategy); Ken French (finance); Robert Howell (accounting).

APPLICANT TIPS

To spend two years at an intense, small school such as Tuck, you've got to have a passion for what you want to do both while you're at the school and with your MBA degree once you finish. And you've got to show the admissions office this passion. "When reading an application, I get really excited about a candidate when someone can articulate clearly why they want to do this," says Dean Sally Jaeger. "They can talk about their professional career, and they can tie it to getting an MBA, and then they can tie it to where they want to go from there, and then they can tie that to why they want to do it at Tuck."

Ideal Tuck applicants will have done their research on business schools and will be able to convince the admissions committee that they'll be a good fit with the Tuck culture of community, civility, and teamwork. The admissions committee at Tuck will evaluate your application in the following areas: your academic background, your work experience, your interpersonal experiences, and your leadership skills. Your college grades and your GMAT scores will be testaments to your academic readiness for Tuck's difficult curriculum. If you don't have much quantitative experience in your background, you might want to think about taking a course or two in something like financial accounting before applying. The average GMAT score at Tuck is 698—only one or two students a year are admitted with a score below 600. But if your score is lower than the average, your work experience, leadership qualities, and undergraduate record can still make up for it.

Your interviews and essays will play the biggest role in helping the school decide whether you'll fit in with a close-knit community. You'll need to request an interview, and you should check the Tuck Web site for the dates when interviews should be completed for each application round. If you can't make it to campus, an interview with a traveling admissions staff member or an alum is sufficient.

Tuck's application contains one longer case-type essay question, and four short-answer questions. In the case essay, you'll be evaluated on the way your argument is structured (and whether you do in fact have a point to your argument). The admissions committee would rather you go slightly over the allotted word limit than sacrifice the content or structure of the essay. Also, it goes without saying to find a proofreader other than your spell-checker.

Tuck's admissions deadlines used to be later than those of other business schools, but the school has bumped up the deadlines and added an early action round of admissions. A PDF version of the application is available on the Tuck Web site. You'll also be self-reporting your college grades and courses, along with your GMAT scores, to speed up the admissions process. Because of the increased scrutiny over obtaining foreign visas, international students must apply in the early decision round or the November or January round.

TUCK MBAs SOUND OFF

Tuck is a special place that taught me invaluable lessons about business and life. Sometimes the isolation combined with the intensity was difficult, but where else can you live on 5 acres, ski after class and leave your computer unattended? I'm not foolish enough to think that I could not have gotten a quality business education at any of the other top 10 schools but the quality of life would have been very difficult to replicate.

Tuck is a fantastic school that provided me with an incredible business education. Beyond the educational experience, Tuck was fantastic because of its small size and outgoing culture. I would not trade my experiences over the last two years for anything.

Tuck has been an outstanding experience for me. I significantly strengthened my analytical skills, my presentation abilities, and most importantly the way I view and solve problems strategically. The Tuck community is very diverse and collaborative, so I have learned as much from my fellow U.S., minority, and international students as from my professors. I have made many lifelong friends among students, administrators, professors and alumni. Looking forward, I am really enthusiastic about my career and plan to contribute to Tuck financially, as an admissions volunteer, and by organizing alumni events.

Tuck's culture really is unique. It fosters teamwork, a solid work ethic, a sense of social responsibility and the social skills to succeed. Its alumni network is also amazing. The speakers that are brought to campus are incredible and the interactions with them were a highlight. Tuck's real genius is that it pulls off being world class in its career placement and education while succeeding as an intimate, community-based school at the same time.

Tuck is more than what I expected in every area—and I already had very high expectations based on the extremely positive word of the alumni. The education is extraordinary—professors and students are outstanding. For my summer internship, Career Services helped me get a unique opportunity that integrated all my interests and they even supported me with money—I am sure you don't see that anywhere else.

Tuck gives you a first-rate education with first-rate facilities in a beautiful Northern New England environment without sacrificing access to great employers.

I can't imagine a better place (students, faculty, career opportunities, beautiful surroundings, social life, etc.) to earn an MBA.

11. CORNELL UNIVERSITY

CORNELL UNIVERSITY

Johnson Graduate School of Management
Sage Hall
Cornell University
Ithaca, New York 14853
E-mail address: mba@cornell.edu
Web site address: www.johnson.cornell.edu

Enrollment: 703
Women: 27%
Non-U.S.: 28%
Minority: 9%
Part-time: 0
Average age: 28
Applicants accepted: 22%
Median starting pay: $85,000

Annual tuition and fees: $30,975
Estimated annual budget: $45,821
Average GMAT score: 673
Average months of work experience: 61
Accepted applicants enrolled: 57%
Corporate ranking: 13
Graduate ranking: 2
Intellectual capital rank: 12

Teaching methods: lecture 28%, case study 35%, experiential learning 10%, team projects 20%, distance learning 3%, simulations 4%

Dean Robert J. Swieringa will tell you that walking through the doors of the Johnson School's atrium is "magical." The soaring, three-story glass-roofed atrium, also referred to as the "town square," is a popular meeting spot for Johnson's MBAs. The glass-enclosed roof and glass-brick floor allow natural light to permeate throughout the building, even to the lower classrooms. It seems fitting for a B-school that sits at the heart of the 745-acre Cornell campus, overlooking Cayuga Lake. Streams, wineries, hiking trails, Gothic buildings, and tree-lined walkways offer something for everyone, and are bright spots in the usually dreary winters, when the "town square" becomes the meeting place of choice for the close-knit bunch of MBA students at the Johnson School.

Not only do these students have the luxury of their building, they leave satisfied with their education and enamored with the community they've stumbled into. Graduates laud the Johnson school for meeting and exceeding their expectations. In fact, Cornell saw the biggest jump in student satisfaction this year, taking a giant leap to number 2 in the poll. "Cornell far exceeded my expectations in almost every area," says one pleased grad. "The program is large enough to have a true international flavor and to expose you to the expansive world of business, yet small enough to remain a true community of friends where people do not fall through the cracks."

Why are students so happy? It all goes back to the quality of the experience they have at Johnson, Swieringa says. He attributes it to the community—the caliber of the student body coupled with the quality and accessibility of the faculty and staff. Plus, he adds, students here are seen as the school's partners. "We get significant changes to happen here," Swieringa adds. "We try to engage the important players in the environment and have them come on board."

While core courses will occupy much of your first year, there's still room in your schedule to take two or more electives. The core is small by design, giving you some room to personalize your degree. The first semester is split into two halves, and you'll take the first six core courses—Microeconomics for Management, Financial Accounting, Managing and Leading Organizations, Statistics for Management, Managerial Finance, and Marketing Management. Your second semester, you'll take the remaining two—Strategy and Managing Operations. You'll also either take classes in one of the six immersion areas, or customize your own program.

Johnson's unique immersion learning semester is a boon for students. Swieringa describes it as "reality-based education" that combines theory with hands-on practice. About 90 percent of students participate each year, taking advanced courses in manufacturing; managerial finance; investment banking; brand management; entrepreneurship and private equity; and research, sales, and trading (new in fall 2002). Though e-business immersion wasn't offered formally in the fall of 2002, classes on the subject were offered. (The e-business immersion is being revamped and will be offered again in the future.) In class, you'll work in teams to analyze live cases submitted by Procter & Gamble, American Express, and JPMorgan Chase, among other firms. You'll also have the opportunity to visit related work sites, allowing you to meet prospective employers early on and learn from among the best practitioners in the field. All of this takes place right before the crucial summer internship, which gives you an edge over other MBAs.

Beyond the core, the Johnson School offers a varied menu of more than 80 electives in 10 areas including entrepreneurship, management information systems, and international management. You can also pursue a joint degree in engineering, human resources, Asian studies, or law, as about 12 percent of students do. Up to 25 percent of the curriculum can be taken in other Cornell schools, and most students end up taking at least one course offered in another school. The B-school takes that one step further, and consistently invites professors from the other schools to speak at the Johnson School. The Johnson School also offers experiential, for-credit minicourses on leadership skills that are led by trainers from such corporations as General Electric, McKinsey & Company, and Sprint, as well as from professional training firms. With a program as flexible as Johnson's, the design of your MBA is in your hands—it's all about what you make of it.

What more could you ask from an MBA program? Perhaps the opportunity to go for free. The Johnson School offers the Park Leadership Fellows Program, awarding about 30 entering students each year a full tuition grant plus a stipend. Students are selected through a highly competitive process that seeks demonstrated leadership qualities, professional and personal life accomplishment, past academic achievement, and demonstrated commitment to community service and/or socially responsible business. In return, students are expected to work on a service leadership project that leaves something behind for the business school, Cornell University, or the Ithaca community.

The Johnson School is big on leadership. From day one, you'll be immersed in leadership training. Orientation, which starts in mid-August, kicks off with a 3½-day workshop, Leadership Assessment for Managers, which includes experiential team exercises, self-assessment, feedback, business simulations, and completion of a personal development plan. Students rave about the gained insight and push in the right direction to focus on a specific path. Orientation culminates in another intense leadership experience—the Johnson Outdoor Experience (JOE), a weekend event held at nearby Lake Owasco. Leadership training doesn't stop with the two-week orientation; you can also participate in the Leadership Skills Program. Courses cover topics such as leadership, team building, project planning, negotiation, international protocol, communication skills, and effective use of the Internet. The program helps you home in on crucial management skills to enable you to gain a competitive edge with employers.

Building on the fundamental business skills developed in the core MBA curriculum, students interested in start-ups get many opportunities to create business plans, meet venture capitalists and business owners, and get a vivid sense for the process and pitfalls of growing a new business. Entrepreneurship is popular on this campus, with about two-thirds of all Johnson School students taking Professor Ben Daniel's Entrepreneurship and Enterprise class, which focuses on a series of live cases. Special modules on mergers and acquisitions, venture capital, leveraged buyouts, and valuation of businesses make it applicable to a large group of students. One of the latest vehicles for start-ups is the Big Red Venture Fund, begun by Park Fellows Alex Ivanov and John Kyles and three other classmates from the class of 2002 with some advice from Daniel. Its first project was Gene Network Sciences, a start-up founded by a Cornell alum. Big Red's consulting arm, the Big Red Incubator, is also taking promising ventures from the business planning stage up through the initial funding phase.

Despite the demanding curricular schedule, Johnson School students still find a way to wet their feet in a plethora of activities. Students are a special bunch here. They have an "energizing, positive can-do attitude," Swieringa says. Professor Charles M. C. Lee, who's been at the Johnson School for six years, praises the sense of community. "There's a tradition of caring for people," he says. MBAs channel their energy into the various clubs they participate in. You'll find Johnson School students taking part in one of the 40-plus clubs like Leading Edge or Old Ezra, the investment banking group. A popular tradition is the annual ice hockey game between the Frozen Assets, the women's ice hockey club, and faculty members.

The Johnson School knows how to capitalize on its small size. "It allows us to be more focused on our students and more agile in the sense that we can be quicker in doing things," Swieringa says. Teachers also make themselves available at all times and operate under an open door policy for both each other and the students. Students ranked their faculty third overall in accessibility. And faculty members try to stay up to speed on each other's research. All core faculty members have lunch once a week throughout the semester to discuss how to integrate topics across the core. This really helps drive points home, adds Professor Kathleen M. O'Connor. These efforts haven't gone unnoticed: students rank the faculty eighth in this area.

Resources aren't scarce at this small B-school. The school, which sits in the middle of Cornell's 745-acre campus, opened up a renovated $38 million home, Sage Hall, in 1998. The 120-year-old Venetian Gothic structure's outside was reconstructed and rewired with the latest technology. Inside, you'll find eight amphitheater classrooms where each seat is equipped with laptop connections. And you can tap into the 100,000-volume management library and a multimedia computer lab with 56 well-equipped workstations, work in one of 32 team project rooms, or make use of tech resources and conduct videoconferences.

Sage Hall also houses faculty offices, admissions and career services, student lounges, a dining area, and the executive education center. On the second floor, you'll find the Parker Center for Investment Research, where students take in the "Wall Street Wakeup Call," a weekly interactive broadcast from the New York Stock Exchange exclusively to the Johnson School. Finance students especially make use of the full-scale trading room and research studio, which has $2 million worth of hardware and software and a back wall electronic display of market happenings that's nearly identical to those at the stock exchange. Plus, 20 lucky students can flex their fund management skills through the Cayuga MBA Fund, launched by the class of 1998. Guided by Professor Charles M. C. Lee, students learn how to use a valuation model and real-time data to unearth stock values. The competitively chosen MBAs conduct research, perform portfolio risk management and financial analysis, and make stock selection based on a two-thirds majority vote. Students manage real money, thanks in part to the class of 1998 and alumni investments, and the fund, which consistently outperforms the S&P 500, now has over $2 million invested.

One source of contention in the past has been the lack of diversity on campus. To combat this, the Office for Minorities and Women in Business opened up in 1999, headed by Angela Noble-Grange, a 1994 Johnson School grad. Since the office's inception, the number of minorities on campus has doubled from just 5 percent a few years ago to 10 percent. And women's enrollment is up to about 28 percent. Noble-Grange says that though it's a start, she's still not completely satisfied with these numbers, so she's stepping up her efforts. For example, since 2001, she's been hosting Johnson Means Business, a minority weekend sponsored by Citigroup in which 30 students are invited from a pool of applicants to stay at the B-school and participate in activities like Homecoming. Another new initiative, Camp $tart-up, brings high school girls to campus for a summer business experience. Noble hopes to reach out not only to prospective students but to current students, faculty and staff, and alums to help create awareness of the B-school among underrepresented minorities and women.

The B-school also has been extending its reach and going global. There are several options to venture outside of the Johnson school. Each year, students and faculty pack up and take a trip focusing on another region's business and cultural practices. In 2002, for example, students traveled to Belgium and Brazil. You can also study abroad in 1 of 20 business schools in 15 different countries, such as SDA Bocconi (Italy), London Business School, or the School of Business and Management, Hong Kong University of Science and Technology. There's also the annual European Alumni Symposium, which MBA students interested in working in Europe attend for a little networking. Or you can stay on campus and take 1 of the 20-plus international courses, such as Global Management Structures or International Finance.

The Walk Down Wall Street gives you the chance to meet firms like JPMorgan Chase, Lehman Brothers, and UBS Warburg. Similarly, some 50 students make it out to California for the High-Tech Club's Weeks in Silicon Valley. There's also a 12-month option for those with graduate degrees in engineering, mathematics, or a physical or natural science. You'll follow an accelerated version of the core curriculum during an intensive summer program beginning in May, and then you'll join the second-year class in August and earn your MBA along with them.

Ithaca has lots to offer. It's not rare to find students out on the slopes maximizing their beautiful surroundings. There are plenty of cozy bars and delicious restaurants, such as the classy Moosewood Restaurant, the New Orleans Cajun-style Maxie's Supper Club, and Thai Cuisine, which defines Thai food. Go to Nines in Collegetown for some deep-dish pizza, stop by The Chapter House, a traditional pub, for a beer, and hit up the Royal Palm Taverns (a.k.a. The Palms) for some good music and drinks. In a town where it's hard to find yourself more than 10 minutes away from campus, it's easy to find affordable and conveniently located housing. MBA housing for singles and families, including children, is available through the school. However, a popular MBA spot is Westview Apartments, where a large majority of residents are twenty- and thirty-something Johnson students. Second-year students often take over the lakefront homes rented out by previous students.

PLACEMENT DETAILS

The Johnson School's collaborative nature extends into the Career Services office. "Everyone is on board and working together, from the dean on down," says Karin Ash, the new Career Management Center director. For example, in 2002, the office created the SWAT team—four Johnson School grads who had their offers delayed who worked full-time to develop new job-hunting initiatives. They developed pitch books that marketed students to various companies by presenting their resumes in groups targeting specific industries. The career service office also developed job treks to places such as New York, Boston, Seattle, and South Florida, covering all areas from energy to investment banking.

The school also added new things, like Industry Days for the first-years led by second-years coming back from internships. The industry workshops covered everything from consulting and investment banking to marketing and entertainment—giving first-years a real-world view of the career paths they might be interested in. The SWAT team even developed an entire curriculum—the Career Management Program—a two-day orientation session focused just on the career services office. Though the SWAT team is hanging up its reins, a career action group is stepping in to develop more programs, job treks, and job searches.

In 2002, only 67 percent of Cornell grads had job offers by graduation, with many companies avoiding the trek to Ithaca, thus getting less exposure to Cornell students despite the school's stellar efforts. Only 77 percent of grads had offers by three months after graduation, one of the lowest placement rates among the top 30 schools, even after considering the 4 percent of students who were company sponsored and returned to their pre-MBA employers. But administrators expected that all or most grads would find work by the end of 2002. And those who did have jobs earned respectable starting pay packages of about $116,400.

Despite the somewhat poor showing, the amazing efforts of the placement office did not go unnoticed by grads in the class of 2002. Indeed, the placement center was awarded the "Johnsonite of the Year" award by the graduating class, many of whom were grateful to see the staff in the office do everything possible to help them launch their post-MBA careers. Grads gave career services mostly high marks in the 2002 *BusinessWeek* survey.

TOP HIRES

Johnson & Johnson (17); Deutsche Bank (7); Standard & Poor's (7); CIGNA (5); Deloitte Consulting (5); JPMorgan Chase (5); Lehman Brothers (5); Ansell (4); General Electric (4).

OUTSTANDING FACULTY

Mark Nelson (accounting); Bhaskaran Swaminathan (finance); Jan Suwinski (management); Maureen O'Hara (finance); Robert Libby (accounting); Sanjeev Bhojraj (accounting).

APPLICANT TIPS

Director of Admissions Natalie Grinblatt is looking for "bright, articulate, passionate, and positive" students to add to the Johnson School MBA family. It's essential, she says, for applicants to know themselves, know what they want, and know how to go after it. That's why one of the most important things Grinblatt wants to see is an achievements oriented resume. She adds that on the application she can look at your work history, so on other parts of your application—resume, essays, and recommendations—focus on demonstrating your leadership and quantifying your achievements by describing how your accomplishments added value to the job.

Though GPA and GMAT scores are important, Grinblatt is more concerned with reviewing your overall academic record, including the caliber of institution you went to, the courses you took, and how well you did. There's also no work experience minimum here; the average is about five years. The key here is to demonstrate leadership. Grinblatt notes that this year she accepted a student with no work experience, but the work he'd accomplished on summer internships gave her the confidence to believe he'd make a good leader. Interviews aren't a required part of the application; rather they're invitation based. However, no successful applicants are admitted without one, so if you're invited, don't pass up on it. You'll meet with an admissions officer, alum, faculty member, or current student.

If you feel you're lagging in an area of your application, counteract it by being proactive and demonstrating your drive and initiative. If, for example, you're weak on your quant skills and need some brushing up, take a refresher course before applying. Grinblatt says she favors the proactive applicant over the students "in a bubble" waiting to be told what to do.

Successful applicants—and Johnson students—tend to be positive and proactive. They don't just complain; they suggest ways for improvements and then follow through. A big part of this B-school is the community—interactions with B-school students and faculty and also with the university at large. Many students venture out of the Johnson School confines, taking classes in other departments. "To put it simply, if you're not a team player you probably won't fit in around here," Grinblatt adds.

Admissions at the Johnson School are on a batched basis, with a designated number of spots available for each batch. However, if you're looking to be considered for a scholarship or fellowship—such as the Park Fellows Scholarship—apply within the first two rounds. It's to your advantage to apply early, especially if you want to go Destination Johnson, the B-school's welcome weekend held in April.

JOHNSON MBAs SOUND OFF

Attending the Johnson School was one of the best choices I have ever made. Even in a terrible job market I was able to get the position of my dreams. The immersions do a great job of preparing students for summer internships and the curriculum as a whole is very flexible. With a small school size, students are able to know all of their classmates. Overall it was a fantastic educational experience.

Attending Cornell-Johnson was the best career decision I've made to date. I'd do it all over again if given the chance. The intellectual stimulation, the personal relationships and the career advice I've received here are second to none.

The dismal job market was an overshadowing factor in my MBA experience; however, I would praise the Johnson School Career Services and faculty in doing everything they could to assist the students. The Career Services office started early in the fall preparing us for a difficult market. The open door policy among faculty, which is great academically, was also very helpful in the job search. Faculty were readily available for career advice and helpful expanding our network of contacts and job opportunities.

I enjoyed every aspect of MBA experience. The skill set that I acquired at Cornell's Johnson School and the network that I have established will be invaluable in my career. I can't say enough good things about this school and my MBA experience.

Cornell far exceeded my expectations in almost every area. The program is large enough to have a true international flavor and to expose you to the expansive world of business, yet small enough to remain a true community of friends where people do not fall through the cracks. The one area that impressed me most about Cornell was the responsiveness of the faculty and administration. During the first semester, after hearing some complaints about the curriculum, the administration surveyed the entire class. The very next day, changes to the curriculum were announced, effective immediately. This set the tone for my experience. We were always being asked for input, and I was able to see the results of the input.

My experience at the Johnson School was fantastic. The open door policy of the faculty is great. They are available at all times to talk about class, the economy, jobs, etc. The most special thing about the school is the intimate learning environment. This is fostered by a small class size and the school's location in Ithaca. I am leaving the school with almost 10 sure-to-be-lifelong friends.

The Johnson School workload was more rigorous than I anticipated. The facilities are without peer. The people in the program are team oriented, very friendly, and active in how the program is run. There are a large number of students with kids and an active support network. The winters in Ithaca are very long and cold. There isn't much to do in Ithaca except hike and drink. The teaching overall was excellent but there were cases in the core where new professors weren't very good. The school has been effective in immediately responding to the students' complaints. When the students talk the school listens and makes changes.

The professors here are truly very dedicated. I have had dinner at several professors' houses, and have also seen a few of them walking through the Atrium late at night to make sure that everyone was okay with projects due early the next morning.

12.
UNIVERSITY OF VIRGINIA

UNIVERSITY OF VIRGINIA

Darden Graduate School of Business Administration
P.O. Box 6550
100 Darden Boulevard
Charlottesville, Virginia 22906
E-mail address: darden@virginia.edu
Web site address: www.darden.virginia.edu

Enrollment: 574	Annual tuition and fees: $30,844
Women: 28%	Estimated annual budget: $44,844
Non-U.S.: 28%	Average GMAT score: 683
Minority: 8%	Average months of work experience: 65
Part-time: 0	Accepted applicants enrolled: 53%
Average age: 27	Corporate ranking: 11
Applicants accepted: 18%	Graduate ranking: 6
Median starting pay: $85,000	Intellectual capital rank: 14

Teaching methods: lecture 6%, case study 70%, distance learning 4%, experiential learning 8%, simulations 3%, team projects 6%, other 3%

Mornings at Darden start with a healthy dose of fear. The "cold call" begins every class of every day, as each professor chooses a student who will be stuck answering the dreaded first question. Everyone's turn comes soon enough (Darden's small class sizes guarantee it); yet this initially terrifying experience sums up all that is unique about Darden's case study method, its emphasis on participation, its rigorous style of management education, and the quality of its teaching. "The first few months people are frantic, not looking the professor in the eye and e-mailing each other spreadsheets before class," says one recent grad, "but by your second year you're like, 'Bring it on!'"

Steeped in the honor-bound traditions of the University of Virginia, Darden is not a school for the faint of heart when it comes to intensity and workload. Still, this intensity and the small size of the student body create a close-knit community. Mornings may begin with the dreaded cold call—often after very late nights of reviewing cases with your learning teams—but they are soon broken up by the congenial tradition of "First Coffee," held in the gracious rotunda since the school's founding in 1954, where students can relax, revive themselves with free caffeine, and mix with friends and faculty alike.

Dean Robert Harris, who assumed the helm of Darden in October 2001 after popular dean Edward Snyder unexpectedly left to take the helm of his alma mater, the University of Chicago Graduate School of Business, has the challenge of balancing this sense of intimacy with the 2002 expansion from 240 to 300 students per class, and the need to put

Darden—tucked away in rural Charlottesville, Virginia—on the radar screens of more recruiters. More than that, he's had to work quickly to solidify the community after Snyder's departure. But Harris, a former professor at the school, has lots of raw material to work with: a top-notch faculty, a newly renovated campus, an entrepreneurial incubator, and a well-established center for ethics in business. He hopes to use these to make Darden more of an international player in the world of business education. "An increasing number of businesses are competing in global markets, so we are increasing our exchange programs and the number of visiting faculty," Harris says. He hopes to encourage faculty members to expand their reputations globally as well. "Writing an editorial for the publications like *The Washington Post* is something I'd like to see Darden's faculty do more of," Harris says. It's too early to tell whether Harris's efforts will pay off, but if perception is any indication, they may be working so far: 2002 grads lauded faculty members for being at the leading edge of their fields.

In order to meet the needs of the larger student body, Harris expanded the size of the faculty by six professors for the 2002–2003 year. And students agree that the quality of the faculty is what drives their experience. "It's amazing to watch a professor shape a class," says one graduate. "They are people who choose Darden not because they want to lecture, but because they want to ask the first question and watch the students take off—perhaps never speaking for the rest of class."

If you're headed to Darden, don't delude yourself into thinking it'll be anything less than a two-year intensive intellectual experience. Sure, the school is just five miles from The Barracks, a horse stable that will provide you with entry into the Blue Ridge Mountains and Shenandoah Valley. But students rarely have time to take off like that. Darden's boot camp reputation isn't based on fiction: its program is designed to be rigorous. The rigorous nature of the Darden MBA lies

in its heart—and in its strength: the case study method. Semesters are broken up into two quarters of about seven weeks each. In the first year, when you'll take five core classes a quarter, the week is divided up into two-case or three-case days, meaning you will have to have prepared either two cases or three cases (one per class) for that particular day. And each case requires at least two hours of modeling and analysis as homework—not to mention that, although many B-schools finish their week on Thursdays, Darden students still have at least two cases to prepare for Friday classes.

But this heavy workload is tempered by the fact that it's not a lonely, nose-in-the-book pursuit. Darden's emphasis on the case study method requires MBAs to work in "learning teams." In the first year, these study groups are carefully selected by the administration to reflect the diversity of the class in terms of not only ethnicity and gender but also professional background. And, unique to most business schools where learning teams or study groups are created within academic sections, Darden's learning teams are composed of one student from each section. This means that though you'll be doing homework problems with your team, the next morning your accounting class might meet a period before that of your learning teammates. Students say that this arrangement is not so much confusing as it is helpful in eliminating a sense of competition among students: there's no reason not to help your teammates as much as possible in a study session if you know that the professor won't be comparing you to them in class. Moreover, you get to know students beyond the boundaries of your particular section.

In theory, you are supposed to prepare cases on your own and meet up each night with your learning team to take your analysis to a new level. There are 60 dedicated study rooms at the school, set aside from 8 to 11 P.M. each night, where students can hook up their laptops and get to work. Many students stick with their learning groups for the whole first year, though there are a few cases each year where students unhappy with their assigned groups go it alone. This happens when the rare student doesn't want the group experience he or she has been assigned, and the drawback is that he or she then has to tackle the mounds of casework alone. Many Darden first-years say not only that their learning team experiences were some of their best at Darden, but that there's no way they could have handled the workload without help.

Because the curriculum is integrated, all 300 first-year students move in lockstep through the 10 core courses, which include B-school standards such as Economics, Finance, Organizational Behavior, Marketing, Operations, and Accounting. Also required for first-years are an ethics course and a management communications course. The highly integrated first-year course load is a well-oiled machine in which you'll often see the same case in more than one class. The planning involved makes it difficult to react quickly to changes in the marketplace (a case on, say, Enron actually has to be written before it can be discussed in class), although professors will often assign supplemental articles to reflect hot topics in the world of business. Instead of seeming stiff, students say that the careful planning and integration of the first-year's work—which ensures that if something like the theory of waiting in lines is taught in operations, probability is being concurrently taught in quantitative analysis—seems smart.

By their second year, students are free to take electives in areas that range from corporate finance to managing teams. Darden has no majors, but you must take one of five offered leadership electives, such as Leading in the New Economy or Leadership and Diversity through Literature, taught by Professor Alec Horniman. Another series of electives, the Darden Business Projects, allows students to work with an existing business in the areas of consulting, venture, or case development, in which you can work with a faculty member to write a case, which might then even be incorporated into the curriculum.

One of the more unique electives is a reading course called Business Ethics through Literature, taught by the popular Ed Freeman, in which students discuss books and short stories. Freeman thinks that by studying and discussing literature, his students learn people skills that they take with them into the business world. The class also has come to be known as "Dinners with Ed," because its other component is the mandatory weekly dinners that students cook for each other, culminating with a dinner cooked by Professor Freeman himself at his home, during which students can read from short stories they themselves have written for the class.

In your second year, the case study method still rules the classroom, but, due to the varied nature of schedules, learning teams are not formalized. Instead, you'll work on group projects or meet at classmates' apartments to review cases.

An emphasis on teamwork and respect for others are aspects of a larger focus on ethics that has been long established at Darden. While many schools have been grappling with how to incorporate ethics into the classroom, the Olsson Center for Applied Ethics, founded way back in 1969, creates teaching materials, tracks scholarship in business ethics, and sponsors seminars on the subject for executives. Every year Darden sells about 10,000 copies of its ethics cases to faculty at other business schools. The school's commitment to entrepreneurship is also growing. The Batten Institute, founded in 1996 with a $60 million endowment, assists start-ups in central and northern Virginia and provides a resource for a burgeoning segment of MBA students and faculty who are interested in studying entrepreneurship, not only through networking opportunities, but through the Darden Progressive Incubator. Other UVA professors and students from the law, medicine, engineering, and arts and sciences schools team with Darden students in this incubator to start their own ventures. The Batten Fellows Program brings researchers and business people to Darden for three- to five-day stays to teach classes and to present seminars and workshops.

As Dean Harris also tries to expand Darden's global horizon, the Global Business Experience program is now offered to first-year and second-year students. During a week of spring break in April, students travel to meet with business leaders in countries such as Slovenia, Spain, Belgium, Bahrain, and Mexico. For example, a weeklong Entrepreneurship in Developing Countries trip to Bled, in Slovenia, included not only time in a classroom being taught macroeconomic dynamics by Slovenian business professors, but time spent with local entrepreneurs, such as one of the world's best designers of racing sailboats. In addition, Darden has an exchange program with 10 international business schools, including schools in Japan, Buenos Aires, Barcelona, Stockholm, Hong Kong, Melbourne, and Brussels. Students can choose to spend either a quarter or a semester of their second year abroad—such an exchange isn't really an option for first-years, who have such a regimented course load. Even so, many more second-years opt for the week-long Global Business Exchange rather than an exchange program. "It seems more of an option for people who wanted to study abroad in college and never did it," says one graduate. "You miss out on a lot by not being on campus."

Your learning experience will be enhanced by major renovations, including a 500-space parking garage, more rooms for learning teams, a new dining hall, new classrooms and faculty offices, and a 470-seat auditorium (with half the seats equipped with Internet and electricity hook-ups).

Students' reactions to the workload at Darden run the gamut from "It's flippin' hard!" to "I wouldn't describe it as brutal. . . ." Even professors know it—"and revel in it," says one student. Professor Alec Horniman puts it this way:

"There's an engagement process at Darden. If you come and you're uncomfortable learning in class and working with a study group, it's a terrible place. People get stomachaches and can't sleep. You've got to want to learn this way." But students will agree that the work pays off when it comes to putting skills to use in summer internships and jobs. Professors will make allowances during recruiting season if you're not completely on the ball during a cold call, and if you do start to bomb one, "the professors aren't going to try to embarrass you," says Peter Harrison, a member of the 2003 class.

In any case, Darden's attempts to create a real community atmosphere through student clubs, parties, and a myriad of activities surrounding UVA make the pain of the workload bearable. Students find camaraderie within their sections, some of which have their own traditions. Section B, for example, has its own mascot—a stuffed bird that is awarded (with a special song) every Friday to someone who said something particularly amusing in class that week. Some graduates have expressed concern that with the school's expansion, this feeling of community might be lost. Dean Harris understands these concerns, but feels they can be addressed not only by the realities of the recruiting market—"The growth in class size will benefit in our relationships to companies," he says—but with new facilities that offer more room for the school to get together, be it more learning team rooms or a new auditorium that will hold the entire class.

A typical Darden day begins around 8 A.M. and ends around 11 P.M. Many students agree with Erin Kennedy, a 2002 grad, who says, "The first semester of the first year was tough, but that didn't keep me from getting a good night's sleep and exercising daily." Learning how to manage the stress is part of the experience. To that end, you can get involved with clubs devoted not only to career groups, but to volunteer and athletic opportunities. A gorgeous UVA golf course allows almost year-round play at student rates. Hiking and fly-fishing opportunities abound in the mountains and streams just outside Charlottesville. UVA offers Division I sports with the requisite tailgate parties, and spring and fall bring the Foxfield Races to the rolling country around Charlottesville. On weekends, students often head to The Corner, a strip of main street with restaurants and music venues. There's no on-campus housing for Darden students, but Charlottesville, while not cheap, is certainly more affordable than New York, San Francisco, or Boston. First-years tend to live in nearby apartment complexes like Ivy Gardens, which is just a short traipse over a footbridge to the Darden campus. Second-years get together to rent houses that tend to be handed down from previous Darden students, either in town or out a little way in the gorgeous countryside.

Darden has several big social events during the year, including the chili cook-off, the international students' food festival, and the formal Graduate Women in Business Christmas in April auction. "Cold Call" is an informal beer-drinking happy hour on campus every few weeks, and the Thursday Night Drinking Club gives first- and second-year students a chance to bond at a bar downtown. First-years look forward to the infamous 100 Case Party after they have finished reviewing their 100th case study in class.

Charlottesville has a mellow, intimate, comfortable feel. "It's self-selective," says Erin Kennedy. "You have people who have chosen Charlottesville for a reason and are not expecting an extremely sophisticated—trendy bars and fancy parties—social life. People are very down-to-earth and don't have an attitude about where they go to school."

PLACEMENT DETAILS

The rural, small-town attractions of Charlottesville can sometimes work against you in the recruiting process when economic times are tough, as they were for the class of 2001 and 2002. The school's out-of-the-way location, coupled with a small class size, just doesn't attract as many recruiters in a slow economy as a school of similar caliber in a big city might: it's not like there are lots of business schools concentrated in this rural area, as there are in, say, Chicago or Boston, where recruiters can increase their cost-benefit ratio. Recruiters may be hesitant to spend a day of travel and money for such a small class size. At the same time, the school does provide a myriad of opportunities, both structured into the curriculum—such as the Professional Development series—and extracurricular—such as the Financial Club trip to Wall Street—to negate these gripes somewhat. The expansion of the class by some 65 students was done in large part to lure more companies to the campus. "We want to make sure companies get the most bang for buck," says John Worth, the school's interim director of career development. And one of Darden's strengths (as demonstrated by the 37 percent of alumni who contribute to its endowment—the second highest percentage after the Tuck Graduate School of Business at Dartmouth), especially in a tough economic year, is the loyalty of its alumni base, into which Worth has encouraged students to tap now more than ever. Indeed, despite its locale, grads rank Darden among the top 10 for its alumni network and its connections—and more important, their helpfulness.

The 85-minute Professional Development class, dropped into the curriculum 11 times during your first year at Darden, is timed to provide information as it arises in the job search. For example, the very first session in September, entitled "Planning and Conducting a Job Search Strategy," is followed by "Networking and Communicating with Employers," "Cover Letter Review," and the series culminates in April with "Preparing for the Internship: Maximizing Your Success." Worth acknowledges that with the students' busy schedules, the built-in job-hunting classes are almost a necessity.

In addition to the Professional Development series, you'll have the ability to work one on one with an advisor in the career development office. Student-run clubs also play a large part in the career exposure at Darden. The industry-focused clubs ("clubs that are solely devoted to helping you get a job," as one student put it), such as the Finance Club or Marketing Club, regularly host speakers and organize treks to other cities to network with Darden alums, such as the annual Week on Wall Street. These trips allow you to meet informally with company representatives who might not otherwise come to campus.

Worth is now trying to steer students' focus and club activities toward smaller companies. Indeed, grads also praise the school's ability to help them get in touch with smaller and nontraditional employers—a key in a waning MBA job market. Reaching out to smaller companies in a tough job market is also where Darden's strong alumni base steps in. "We have an amazingly loyal base of Darden alums that browbeat their companies to come," says Director Worth. Out of its approximately 7000 alumni, some 1600 volunteer to be "alumni partners," who will talk with students about contacts and referrals in their industries. And almost 90 percent of speakers tapped for career alumni programs in the banking and consulting industry are alums.

Though Worth himself admits, "The bad news about Darden is that it's a small school," its growing reputation as a school with a strong base in ethics will be an asset to companies taking a closer look at who will be joining their ranks. "Darden is a school where if a company does things correctly in recruiting, word—through the alumni network—spreads like wildfire," Worth says. And, as one grad notes, "People have been complaining about Darden's size and location forever. With all the alumni networking and recruiting, if you work within the bounds you'll do as well as you will anywhere else." Indeed, about 79 percent of grads had jobs by graduation in 2002. A total of 87 percent had offers by three months after commencement, and average pay packages were $119,100 for grads at Darden. Grads still sing the praises of the placement office, but a downturn in consulting firm recruiting hit the school harder than most.

TOP HIRES

Citigroup (8); Lehman Brothers (7); Merrill Lynch (7); United Technologies (6); JPMorgan (5); Colfax (4); Conoco (4).

OUTSTANDING FACULTY

Yiorgos Allayannis (finance); Robert Bruner (finance); Sherwood Frey (quantitative analysis); Edward Freeman (ethics); Robert Conroy (finance); Ken Eades (finance); Richard Brownlee (accounting).

APPLICANT TIPS

"I think of Darden as a liberal arts business school," says Dawna Clarke, director of admissions. "Applicants should keep in mind that it's a general management program. So going into specifics about one project at work isn't helpful. Keeping in mind the big picture is." Darden's ideal applicant is individually motivated enough to handle the rigorous course load, but will also be team-oriented and willing to share experiences in groups in order to fit in with learning-team-based, case study method of work. "You're expected to articulate your opinion and to promote classroom discussion," Clarke says. "It's a little daunting, but some people know they need to work on this and they know that this experience will stretch them."

And, because the Darden case study method relies so heavily on student participation—indeed, as much as 50 percent of a grade in a class can be based on participation—you should highlight your ability to communicate. To this end, sign up early and spend some time thinking about your mandatory interview. Between August 1 and February 11, interviews are available on a first-come, first-served basis, but after February 11 they're by invitation only.

In your interview, keep in mind the overarching theme of why you want an MBA at Darden, but be sure to prepare beforehand with specific anecdotes and vignettes to demonstrate team and interpersonal skills. "You have 45 minutes and a lifetime of experiences," Clarke says. "Prioritize two or three facets that you really want to get across no matter what. Have a strong story that the admissions office will remember." In addition, don't use the interview time to dwell on weaknesses such as why you're concerned about a low GMAT score, but rather to accentuate strong points in your background.

Convincing the admissions office that there's a strong fit between your background and Darden's case study culture should be a priority not only for interviews, but also for the essays. Darden requires four essays, along with one optional essay (which it behooves you to write) on the question, "Is there anything else about your background that you'd like the admissions committee to know?" Use this essay to explain extenuating circumstances that might be reflected in your transcript, or even how you went skydiving in Ethiopia. One of Darden's required questions, "Pose and address your own essay question," is unique to the school, and Clarke says she does know when people cut and paste in from other business school applications. "Spend a few hours posing your own question," she says.

Also keep in mind that Darden is trying to become more global. Have you ever lived, traveled, or studied abroad? Use any of these experiences to try to stand out from the crowd. Along with interviews and essays, your two letters of recommendation are essential to the admissions process. The admissions office strongly prefers that these letters be professional rather than academic. "We want a credible source who has observed the candidate in a professional environment," Clarke says. The questions on the letters of recommendation are geared toward the Darden culture—can this person work in a team and articulate thoughts in a meeting? Think about who might best be able to answer those questions.

Darden's average GMAT score in 2001 was 683: 5 percent of applicants fell in the 500 to 590 range and would certainly need to compensate those scores with grades or professional experience, as the rigorous case study method does require that applicants have at least two years of full-time work experience. Likewise, you should have a certain comfort with numbers, having taken at least an introductory accounting or statistics class. Darden does have a conditional offer program for people with more of a liberal arts background who have high MBA potential but are a bit lacking in quantitative skills such as accounting, finance, and statistics. You'll have to take an accredited course in one or all of these areas and receive a B or higher before starting school in the fall.

Applications are now only available online, and applying as early as possible makes it easier for you stand out in the process. When you head to Darden for an interview, you can also spend the day sitting in on classes and lunching with second-year students; Director Clarke herself hosts informational sessions on many days.

For international students who can't make it to campus for interviews or campus tours, Darden will come to you during recruiting trips to Latin America, Europe, and Asia in the fall and follow-up trips to London, Paris, and Asia in the winter. Foreign students should also seek out alumni interviewers in their area, and Darden will also set you up with a current student who might be returning for Christmas break. The online admissions process should make applying easier for international students, but again, earlier is better, especially if you want to apply for one of the scholarships reserved for internationals. In any event, apply by the February 11 deadline to qualify for merit-based scholarships of any kind.

DARDEN MBAs SOUND OFF

Darden was a truly transforming experience for me. The outstanding faculty dedicated to teaching, the highly motivated and collaborative peers, and the school's superior supporting systems and staffs made it possible.

Darden has taught me how to hold a high ethical standard in my future career. After seeing what happened to Enron and Anderson, I am so proud that I went through one of the best educations in ethics in the entire MBA world.

Darden is most distinguished by its tight community. In particular, the access to and openness of the professors make this a very special institution. I have built many, many sincere and what I hope will be lasting relationships with faculty members as well as classmates. Other top schools have bigger networks (i.e., more alumni), but it is hard to imagine a more loyal group than our alumni and faculty.

Coming from a liberal arts background and having worked in nonprofits before, I never thought I would feel at home in any MBA program. But this place really helped me flourish, professionally and personally.

Darden is a very special community of people, centered around students, but not limited to students. I honestly believe we have the greatest collection of faculty members assembled anywhere—not only in terms of talent, but more importantly in their passion for facilitating the learning experience for their students. The small class sizes and case study approach make this a very interpersonal experience—it's not a place for those who want to sit back or work independently most of the time.

Darden has an image of boot camp and that is accurate. However, I believe that is a good point, since it helps us a lot in the workplace in the future. Among other things, the school makes you get more efficient in time management and teamwork because of the workload. In addition, certainly, we are among the students who learn the most because of the constant flow of information.

Darden is always improving, and it is not a perfect place. But I wouldn't trade my two years here for anything. Darden has changed the way I approach the world, and has helped me expand my view of myself and others. It is truly transformational.

UNIVERSITY OF CALIFORNIA AT BERKELEY

13.
UNIVERSITY OF CALIFORNIA AT BERKELEY

Haas School of Business
S430 Student Services Bldg. #1902
Berkeley, California 94720-1902
E-mail address: mbaadms@haas.berkeley.edu
Web site address: www.haas.berkeley.edu

Enrollment: 497
Women: 30%
Non-U.S.: 34%
Minority: 5%
Part-time: 385
Average age: 28
Applicants accepted: 11%
Median starting pay: $85,000
Annual tuition and fees:
    resident—$11,700
    nonresident—$22,153

Estimated annual budget: $39,206
Average GMAT score: 703
Average months of work
    experience: 66
Accepted applicants enrolled: 48%
Corporate ranking: 16
Graduate ranking: 10
Intellectual capital rank: 3

Teaching methods: case study 50%, distance learning 1%, experiential learning 3%, lecture 25%, simulations 1%, team projects 20%

Just a few years ago, a statistics professor at the Haas School of Business told his students they could bring whatever notes they could fit on a 4 × 5-inch index card to the final exam. Imagine the professor's surprise when all the students had the same card: one of the students had squeezed all of her semester notes on a card and then e-mailed her "cheat sheet" to the rest of the class. What the professor thought would be a little help on the final exam turned out to be a lesson in the cooperative spirit that has epitomized the Haas School of Business since it opened its doors to students in 1898. This spirit is echoed all over the Haas campus, by administration, faculty, students, and graduates alike. "If you're looking to be a loner, this is probably not the best place for you," says Haas accounting professor Brett Trueman.

Nothing could be more true. Those who choose the Haas community experience are a diverse crowd, with more than half of the class of 2004 composed of minorities and international students. Work experience runs the gamut, with consulting, high technology, and computer-related positions the top three. And the professions students dive into after Haas are as varied as the work experiences they had before entering the school: a manager from a dot-com could very well become a marketing consultant, and former marketing types have been swayed toward nonprofit careers on leaving Haas.

Also as wide-ranging are the 40 student clubs at Haas, which offer something for everyone's taste. You'll find everything from the Wine Industry Club to the Redwoods@Haas and the ever-popular Real Estate Club. One quirk: Haas is the smallest top 30 B-school with a weekly newspaper, the *HaasWeek*. The school's small size sets it apart and allows it to offer individualized attention and quality customer service despite a public school facade, says David Downes, MBA program director. Downes likens most students' experiences with public schools—prior to coming to Haas—to that of being treated like road-kill. "The advantage of having a small size is that we get to know [everyone], and we employ innovative ways to insulate them from the campus bureaucracy," Downes says. From day one, the Berkeley campus, with its more than 30,000 students, fades into the backdrop for Haas students. At the forefront is a mini-campus with just 240 students per class year. The change from the main campus to Haas is dramatic. The B-school's layout forces your eyes up (or down, depending on where you enter) a meandering outdoor walkway and staircase, stretching three stories. Stationed along the way are stone benches and walls where students and professors mingle and discuss class assignments and the latest business news.

While the emphasis on teamwork is as strong as ever at Haas, change is in the air for the school. Fall 2002 brings with it a new dean and a new vision, along with a major redesign for first-year students' core curriculum. Former Republican Congressman Tom Campbell has assumed the post of dean. He's got a tough act to follow, replacing the popular Laura D'Andrea Tyson, a former Clinton White House economic advisor, who left to take the reigns at the London Business School. "It is the most important time in my lifetime for business education," says Campbell, who compares the B-school experience to his own law school education during Watergate 30 years ago. "There were questions then, there are questions now," he says.

For the past eight years, Campbell has been a law professor at Stanford University, researching and teaching antitrust law, public policy, international law, and international business. Fewer than 50 miles separate Stanford and Berkeley, but the schools feel worlds apart. An early reminder of the change from private to public school for Campbell was reporting to work his first day and finding out there wasn't even a parking space reserved for him. For now, he's staying at a local Berkeley institution, the Durant Hotel, which has complimentary parking. Eventually, he hopes to commute to campus with his wife, who also works for the university, from their home near San Jose, about 90 minutes away.

During the nineties, Campbell served five terms as a U.S. representative for Silicon Valley and had a two-year stint as state senator. By choosing him for the post, Haas hopes to tap into Campbell's long-standing relationships in the Bay Area. That would be a boon for the school, which can feel isolated in its Berkeley confines, far from the hustle and bustle of Silicon Valley—and even far from the lights of San Francisco, just 15 miles away. Just how easy is it for Campbell to tap into those high-tech resources? In his first week of official duty as dean, Campbell made a call to a friend whose Silicon Valley company used to recruit at Haas but had decided not to visit the school this year. Campbell asked the friend to reconsider. Connections like that one are what Haas hopes to leverage with Campbell in place. Campbell has big plans for Haas, the biggest of which includes moving the school into the top 5. He plans on doing this by increasing the number, quality, and pay of the faculty members and the number of electives. "We are the smallest of the top-rated schools, and we need to grow," he says. Campbell has a five-year contract at Haas and has received the go-ahead from the university to grow the number of faculty by 20 from its current 64. Faculty salaries are also being raised to match others in the area. "The key is to pay them what the market says they are worth, so as to retain the best and attract the best," Campbell says. To do this, he will have to battle a trend; in the past few years, the school has lost a number of its top faculty members, including accounting guru Baruch Lev, who left for New York University's Stern School of Business. The shift is important for prospective Haas students, because the Bay Area, and the university's vast intellectual resources, may be a draw for top-notch faculty from other well-known schools. Keep your eyes open for new additions as you go through the application process.

The make-up of the Haas student body has also gone through some radical changes. Starting in 1998, due partly to a change in California law that forbids public schools from using race to help determine admission, the number of underrepresented minority students started to slide, landing at a low of just 4 percent. Recently, due in part to efforts by the school, that number has jumped. This year, the admissions department saw a 41 percent increase in the number of all minority applicants. Minority recruiting efforts have included the formation of the Diversity Alliance, a joint effort with business schools at Duke, Yale, NYU, and Cornell. The schools travel around the country conducting workshops aimed at underrepresented minorities. Haas has also started conducting its own day-long Minority MBA workshop. Nearly 150 people attended the first one, held in 2001.

Change isn't coming just in the form of a new dean and student body. In response to student demand to design their own course schedules and a need for better preparation for the spring recruiting season, the school's core curriculum has been completely revamped. Semesters at Haas are 15 weeks long. In the past, first-year students would take six of their core classes in the fall and another six in the spring, allowing little time for any electives during the first year. This setup proved disastrous when it came time for interviews for summer internships. When company representatives come trolling for potential summer internship candidates in the early spring, they expect students to have a good knowledge of all of the core disciplines. Instead, Haas students were familiar with some of them but had to feign knowledge of others or explain sheepishly that those classes weren't offered until late spring or during their second year. In a market that fluctuates as wildly as today's, Program Director Downes is trying to provide Haas students with any advantage he can give them. The upshot: starting with the fall of 2002, students' first semester at Haas will be broken down into two phases, each lasting seven weeks, with one week between. That middle week will focus on career and professional development workshops. The newly designed curriculum will allow more time to take elective courses. Under the old curriculum, core courses made up 57 percent of the course load at Haas. Under the revised plan, that shifts to 40 percent. Even with this change, Downes and his staff have been able to squeeze in an additional core course in ethics, something Dean Campbell and others find necessary. "What with Enron and the like, the timing couldn't be better," quips one former student.

Most students supported the curriculum change, and many helped bring it to fruition by getting involved in discussions regarding the proposed changes, says Director Downes. Still, there was some argument that core courses should continue the way they had all along. "The full core courses are an 'eating your broccoli' kind of experience. You have to do it," says Jay Badenhope, a 2002 Haas graduate. But even Badenhope would have to admit the new core is a boon for summer internship seekers.

The myriad electives Haas has to offer will make it easy for you to fill your newly opened schedules in the spring and during your second year. "The biggest challenge for me was prioritizing and choosing what I wanted to take. It's a fantastic problem to have," says Badenhope. Popular electives include Competitive and Corporate Strategy, Corporate Financial Reporting (a hot ticket these days), and Marketing

Research. Some of the newer electives include Telecommunications Economics, Strategic Corporate Responsibility, and Introduction to the Healthcare System. You're not required to declare a major or concentration during your two years at Haas, but you will be encouraged to earn a certificate in one of the school's four certificate programs: entrepreneurship and innovation, global management, management of technology, and the newest offering, business and financial engineering.

Haas recently expanded the Management of Technology (MOT) program, which integrates business and technology education with courses that bring MBA students together with engineering PhD students for semester-long projects. MOT is a joint program with Berkeley's College of Engineering and School of Information Management Systems. Highlights include a lecture series with speakers from Silicon Valley, close to 50 MOT courses, consulting projects with 40 Silicon Valley firms, and three different fellowships (Mayfield, Lucent, and Hitachi) that offer paid summer internships. Mayfield Fellows enjoyed a summer trip to Shanghai to investigate entrepreneurship Chinese-style. Hitachi Fellows spent the summer conducting market research for Hitachi's Mu chip, the smallest semiconductor device in development.

The newer MFE/MBA degree might be up your alley if you have superior quantitative skills. If you're considering a career in risk management, investment banking, asset management, derivative trading, or specialized securities, this program could be for you. MFE students take a one-year intensive program from April of their first year through March of the second. Applicants who are admitted to both the MFE and MBA programs can complete a two-year concurrent degree, essentially ending up with two degrees for the same tuition. Not a bad deal, especially if you're an in-state student: tuition is $11,700 per year. Even out-of-state students will find this MBA program a bargain at about $23,000 for the first year—and you'll be eligible to become a California resident after the first year, at which point you can take advantage of the lower tuition for the second year. Establish your residency a little earlier than the start of your first year to reap the full benefits of the in-state status your second year.

If you're considering technology consulting careers, you would do well to check out the two-year-old Haas/Darden/Michigan Partnership program. A professor at one of the schools conducts live classes that are also offered via a videoconferencing system for students at all three schools. This year's program includes a new Darden-taught consulting course in which you form teams with members from each school and use project management software designed for remote teams to develop consulting proposals, much as in the real world of consulting. As part of the program, Haas professor Terrance Odean will teach a behavioral finance course, focusing on how systematic departures from rationality affect financial markets and investors' welfare. Odean made national headlines a few years back when he demonstrated how investors make decisions based on their emotions rather than a rational thought process.

High-tech delivery of courses is not the only evidence of up-to-date technology at Haas. An invisible but important innovation is coming to campus this year: Haas is part of a pilot project to bring wireless access to the school. You'll be able to take advantage of the Bay Area's balmy weather and roam cable-free anywhere within the boundaries of the Haas campus both indoors and outdoors while staying connected to the school's intranet and the Web. You will be able to sit under one of the many giant redwoods and e-mail your fellow students or a professor about tomorrow's assignment. Have a question for a certain professor? Don't fret. Haas architects purposely designed the campus layout to increase student-professor interaction; a professor can't get to his/her office without passing through the student forum and courtyard after teaching a class. "We hope it encourages discussion," says a campus administrator.

If wireless e-mail isn't your bag and you still want the tethered experience, you can choose from one of 450 laptop docking stations around the Haas campus. In addition, the school's three interconnected buildings offer 55 videoconferencing locations and 30 broadcast origination sites. There's also a computer center and a financial engineering lab for MFE/MBA students. The business economics library is stocked with 130,000 bound volumes, more than 300 network ports, and the B-school research essentials: Dow Jones Interactive, Lexis-Nexis Universe, and Datastream.

Like the city that surrounds it, Haas and its MBAs are known for having a social conscience. To show just how serious the school is about social responsibility, it has combined a number of projects under the umbrella of the Socially Responsible Business Leadership (SRBL) initiative. The initiative has received $1 million in funding to get it rolling. Kellie McElhaney, the former managing director of the Corporate Environmental Management Program at the University of Michigan Business School, is the executive director of the new initiative. McElhaney is teaching a new student-initiated course called Introduction to Corporate Social Responsibility. On the first day of class, students were treated to a guest lecture by the school's new dean. Says Shannon Graham, a second-year student in the class, "He certainly has a vision for the school."

You could easily argue the SRBL initiative is representative of the Haas philosophy. "I want every MBA who graduates from here to be infused with a sense of social responsibility," says program director Downes. The new dean also has plans to raise the ethical standards of Haas MBAs. To that end, in addition to the new ethics requirement, Campbell is encouraging professors to share their own real-world experiences dealing with ethical dilemmas within the context of their courses. One innovative step

Campbell is taking—which he learned from the University of Maryland—is having Haas students visit white-collar criminals serving time in California jails. "It's very easy to separate, demonize, and say, 'that can never be me.' Well, wait till you see who's in jail with the kind of education you had and the background you had and how they got there," says Campbell, who has already received the okay from California's Attorney General Bill Lockyear for the visits.

Another way Haas students give back—to each other this time—is through a program called Students for Students. Those students not working in for-profits during their summer internships donate one day's salary to the S4S Fund. Those students working at nonprofits can then apply for money from the fund. During the summer of 2001, students raised and distributed in the neighborhood of $17,000.

Each year, students with an entrepreneurial bent get to show off their do-good spirit in the Haas Social Venture Competition, which recently was renamed the National Social Venture Competition. The school has teamed up with Columbia Business School and the Goldman Sachs Foundation to expand the competition. In the April 2002 contest, held at Haas, participation was up 141 percent from the previous year. The 2003 contest will be held at Columbia Business School in New York.

When you want to batten down the hatches and get studying, you can break out from the cocoon of Haas's mini-campus and head across the street to the Law Library at Boalt Hall. "Haas's library tends to get pretty loud, what with all the group projects. You can always find a quiet corner at Boalt," says one recent grad. Another place you'll often find B-school students deep in their textbooks with a latte in hand is Café Roma on the north side of campus.

The main building at Haas anchors the B-school, which is located on the eastern edge of the Berkeley campus near the California Memorial Stadium. Opened in 1995, the expanded Haas campus still feels new to a first-time visitor. The school's gray and turquoise modern exterior stands out from the rest of the more eclectic, decades-old buildings on campus. The main building is connected by a bridge with the two other buildings and surrounds the courtyard where students gather by day and every other Friday night for the "Consumption Function." The club-sponsored event started out as a simple keg party but has since become a bigger and more refined affair, with each club trying to outdo the next one with elaborate food and drink offerings. After the party ends, students are known to fan out to one of the city's dozens of bars and ethnic restaurants or students' apartments. Wednesday offers Bar of the Week night. Each week, students choose a different bar, either in Berkeley or in one of the surrounding cities. Favorite Berkeley spots include Henry's, with more than 30 beers on tap; Beckett's Irish Pub; and Jupiter for beer and pizza.

First-year students tend to live within a few miles of campus, in either Berkeley, Albany, or North Oakland. One popular Oakland neighborhood is Rockridge, which has easy access to BART and shopping and restaurants, including perpetually packed Zachary's Chicago Pizza, where Haas students can often be found congregating. Second-year students, whose schedules are more flexible, tend to branch out, with about half of them living across the Bay in San Francisco. Bay Area rents are steep, but lower than they have been in the past few years. In a 2001 student survey, the average rent for a studio was $900 to $1500, and one-bedrooms were $1100 to $1800. A few students choose to live on campus. You can't get much closer than International House, some 50 yards from Haas. There is also subsidized housing for families and a very limited number of graduate apartments.

If you want to see the other city by the bay, that's easy. San Francisco is only a 20-minute ride away on BART—the Bay Area's answer to subways—or an easy drive over the Bay Bridge.

Once there, the nightlife is endless. Haas students tend to gravitate toward the Italian section of North Beach and South of Market (SOMA), the city's high-tech hub. If crowds aren't your thing, look no further than the Golden Gate Bridge, the gateway to countless hiking trails through Muir Woods and beaches in Marin County. Golden Gate Park can keep you entertained and relaxed for most of the day. Beyond that, there's Napa Valley, the place for wine enthusiasts. Your best bet: swing by the Niebaum-Coppola Winery, owned by Francis Ford Coppola, grab a bottle of Merlot, and head west to Sonoma for a mud bath to get you back in the mood for classes Monday morning.

PLACEMENT DETAILS

In response to the Bay Area's especially weak economy, the career center at Haas has stepped up its efforts to help students land jobs. Students are now assigned to an individual account manager or staff member. These days, the center is offering so many workshops and guest speakers that administrators felt the need to install an electronic sign over the center's doorway, which constantly scrolls a rundown of center activities. "This way, students can come by and browse a list of the day's events and decide what they want to attend," says Abby Scott, Director of MBA Career Services. During the 2001–2002 school year, students had 95 panels and workshops from which to choose. Career Services also holds daily drop-in hours, and students can always schedule an appointment with one of the account managers (one of whom specializes in international careers) or career advisors.

With 65 to 70 percent of Haas graduates staying in the Bay Area, Director Scott takes full advantage of alumni as a resource for current students. Every year, she holds networking events with each of the three local alumni chapters. Scott also taps into this strong local alumni network for student internships and guest speakers. This can help, but, in a tough year for the MBA job market, Haas saw only 72 percent of its grads garner job offers by graduation. That number rose to 80 percent three months later, and those that had jobs had pay packages of about $115,000. A full 16 percent of the class of 2002 found jobs outside the U.S. Of the rest, only about 16 percent left the West Coast.

Students rate Haas very high on customer service. Scott tries hard to satisfy, with the motto: "You can never tell an MBA no. Instead, tell them what you can give them." What the career center offers is a nine-person staff made up of three account managers, three career advisors, and three people in operations. Career Services doesn't wait long to get the ball rolling; the first two weeks of school include daily brown bag lunch sessions where local members of the business community come in and tell you what it's really like to work in their profession. Career Services also hires 27 second-year students (one for every 10 first-years) part-time to work in the office. They help with resumes and stage mock interviews with the first-years, grilling them as if it were the real thing. "It benefits them both," says Scott. "First-years get experience, and second-years hone their skills."

TOP HIRES

Siebel Systems (8); Wells Fargo (5); Boston Consulting Group (3); Citigroup (3); Clorox (3); Deloitte Consulting (3); Johnson & Johnson (3); Lehman Brothers (3).

OUTSTANDING FACULTY

Severin Borenstein (economics); Rashi Glazer (marketing); Sara Tasker (accounting); Richard Lyons (finance); Paul Tiffany (strategy); Janet Yellen (economics); Hayne Leland (finance); Andrew Rose (economics).

APPLICANT TIPS

There is really no one ideal candidate for the Haas School of Business, at least not according to Jeff Pihakis, Haas's director of domestic admissions. "We try to get a diverse a group as possible, with all different backgrounds and from different areas of the world," Pihakis says. The class of 2004 is no exception: 37 countries are represented, and 34 percent of the class is international.

The Haas application is unique among B-schools in that it includes, in addition to the typical required long essay and an optional long one, a series of short, personal essay questions. The application committee at Haas doesn't just want to know with what one individual you would choose to dine, but what you would order. "We want to get to know the applicants as individuals, what makes then tick. The short essay questions add an element of richness to the application and a glimpse into their soul," says Pihakis, who adds that the single biggest mistake an applicant can make is to be too conscious of the audience reading the essays and how the answers will be interpreted. Nothing is more obvious and disappointing than mechanical answers. Pihakis' advice to prospective MBAs: "Fix yourself some hot tea or some warm milk, or grab yourself a glass of red wine, and let the admissions committee know what it is you're passionate about."

A no-no that Haas sees time and again is fact fudging on an application, especially when it comes to resumes, the scope of your responsibilities, or the amount of time you spent in a particular position. Tell the truth, warns Pihakis. "As soon as we doubt their ethics, they're gone. It's just not worth the risk." While the committee isn't able to screen all of the

3000-plus applications it receives, random spot checks do take place and have resulted in expulsion.

With the stagnating economy, it doesn't come as a surprise that Haas saw a 37 percent increase in the number of applications for the class of 2004, with the biggest gain in the domestic applicant pool. Competition is steep for the 241 spots. For the class of 2003, the percent of applicants accepted was 14.5. For class of 2004, this number dropped to an even more competive 11 percent. The average GMAT score for the school is up, hitting 700 for the first time. (703, to be exact.)

Interviews at Haas are the exception rather than the rule, and the school is the one to request them, not the applicant. Such a request should be looked on as something to be happy about, says Pihakis. It means the committee is having a hard time deciding whether to admit you and a strong interview can put you over the top. Of those applicants who do interview, more than half are admitted. If you are waitlisted, Pihakis encourages you to contact the school and let the staff know whether you are still interested.

Applicants are asked to submit two letters of recommendation, with at least one being from a current employer. Supervisors and major clients are the best categories. Pihakis doesn't recommend following the example of one prospective student a few years back, who submitted a letter from his father. Needless to say, that student didn't make it to the final round.

HAAS MBAs SOUND OFF

I believe that the location of Haas allows it to provide a unique experience relative to other schools. Renowned venture capitalists were regular guest speakers, high-tech CEOs spoke routinely, and faculty all had direct consulting experience with local high-tech companies such as Sun, Cisco, Oracle, etc. and could speak intimately about it.

What has impressed me with my classmates and experience at Berkeley is collaborative atmosphere and the diversity of the students. More than the usual number of people truly are independent thinkers who go their own ways. Personally, I have also found the dynamic, sometimes radical and a bit "crazy" environment of the Berkeley campus stimulating.

Haas is as great as I heard it was. I feel the most important thing is that my MBA experience at Haas opened my eyes to new possibilities. After Haas, my career approach took the quantum leap from that of an "accountant" mentality (calculating debits and credits all day long) to that of a strategist.

No other institution offers such a diverse, well-spoken, intelligent student body and a curriculum that is open to letting students explore any interests that they so desire. From the unique student-created courses to the cross-graduate-school certificate programs, Haas has created a program that has far exceeded my expectations.

Easily the best two years of my life: I learned a lot in the classroom and personally, traveled a lot, got my feet wet in a start-up environment, helped write a winning business plan, and landed a job with one of the best consulting firms. The people at this school are amazing and I look forward to working with them in the real world. I wanted to study in California and it was fantastic. Now I am prepared to work in an international position in Europe.

The first semester had so many assignments that it was overwhelming. I know this is typical of many business schools but it would be more helpful if the workload were more easily spread throughout the first year. With core reform, options available to students for classes should improve further. The second year is as busy and interesting as you want it to be.

Haas has shown that it has the flexibility to change with the market. It was at the forefront of IT and e-business, and as the economy adjusts, so too does the coursework and teaching at my school. The faculty is dynamic and will always be leaders in their fields.

Great people and culture, awesome location, excellent faculty, supportive administrative services . . . what else could one ask for in an MBA? I'm leaving this place forever indebted for two years of great learning and great fun. I have no doubt that these will serve as two of the most instrumental years of my career.

14.
YALE
UNIVERSITY

YALE UNIVERSITY

Yale School of Management
135 Prospect Street
Box 208200
New Haven, Connecticut 06520-8200
E-mail address: mba.admissions@yale.edu
Web site address: http://mba.yale.edu

Enrollment: 480	Annual tuition and fees: $30,365
Women: 30%	Estimated annual budget: $47,637
Non-U.S.: 39%	Average GMAT score: 698
Minority: 8%	Average months of work experience: 59
Part-time: 0	Accepted applicants enrolled: 63%
Average age: 28	Corporate ranking: 20
Applicants accepted: 15%	Graduate ranking: 8
Median starting pay: $85,000	Intellectual capital rank: 9

Teaching methods: case study 25%, experiential learning 10%, lecture 45%, simulations 10%, team projects 10%

Innovation has defined Yale's School of Management (SOM) as of late. From new initiatives to unique programs to an increased faculty, the B-school has constructed an intricate map toward continuous improvement aimed at fulfilling its mission—"to educate leaders for business and society." How do you create the best learning environment? Ask Dean Jeffrey Garten, and he'll tell you the key is to become enmeshed within the university at large. A key component to his latest initiatives centers around just this strategy of interacting with the Ivy League school. And it's working—SOM moved up five notches on *BusinessWeek*'s ranking to the number 14 spot. It doesn't stop there; SOM also topped the charts when it comes to meeting students' needs.

SOM's efforts have come to fruition. For starters, the school received a grant from the Pew Charitable Trusts and Goldman Sachs to head up a nonprofit venture. The school also took full advantage of its affiliation with Yale and started the International Center for Finance and the International Institute for Corporate Governance. Not only are there key programs responding to students' needs, but soon students will also have a significantly larger faculty to better serve them, as Dean Garten aims to increase the faculty size by 60 percent.

Since taking over the deanship in 1995, Garten, a former investment banker who served in the Clinton Administration, has gradually been moving this young B-school (established in 1976) in a more mainstream direction—forging stronger ties with corporate America and directing the bulk of the school's resources toward training for private-sector careers, where most grads end up taking jobs. But the school hasn't lost sight of its roots as an institution geared at preparing students for both private and public America. A case in point is the newly minted partnership with the Pew Charitable Trusts and Goldman Sachs. The collaborative effort has SOM abuzz with fervor. In the fall of 2001, SOM received a pair of grants totaling $4.5 million to put toward studying nonprofits. The Pew Charitable Trusts and the Goldman Sachs Foundation partnered with SOM to create The Partnership on Non-Profit Ventures. The main goal is to help nonprofits develop satellite for-profit operations that can generate new sources of revenue for the parent organization. Sound a bit off the mark for a B-school? It's not so far-fetched for SOM. Yale's youngest professional school also houses the national Business Plan Competition for Nonprofit Organizations, which conducts research projects in social entrepreneurship and operates an online resource center to share nonprofit enterprise information. The partnership grew out of a concern that nonprofits are increasingly turning toward the marketplace to generate revenue, so the idea was hatched to provide targeted guidance and resource to nonprofits most capable of launching operation revenue–generated business ventures. The competition offers consulting input at every stage of business plan development. Four grand prizes of $100,000 and four semifinalist prizes of $25,000 are awarded to the winning business ventures.

At the center of SOM's mission lies the effort to take full advantage of the wealth of resources that Yale has to offer. In the spotlight is a university-wide international center from which SOM and its MBAs are reaping the benefits. Yale launched an interdisciplinary campus think tank, the International Center for Finance (ICF), in 1999. The center, which has garnered attention as of late, taps into the larger university, bringing together prominent scholars from the law school and the economics and mathematics departments. At the MBA level, the center offers a financial analysis workshop and

provides data and technology support to its members. One of the center's major components of research is the study of the history of the world's financial markets. For example, the New York Stock Exchange Research Projects is an ongoing collection effort that assembles data chronicling the history of the NYSE. And, at your fingertips, you'll have access to the center's state-of-the-art research facilities, a financial library, and a meeting room specifically for research interaction and working seminars. The center also presents conferences and seminars throughout the school year on current topics in the world of finance. Some recent meetings have included discussions on the theory of financial institutions and corporations, behavioral finance, and advances in asset pricing. The ICF has been instrumental in luring top faculty to the school as well, and it's also brought some visibility to the SOM program thanks to the "Smart Investor" National Public Radio talk show, a monthly program featuring several ICF fellows who discuss financial issues and dish out investment advice. Also recently launched: The International Institute for Corporate Governance (IICG). The IICG is a new research and teaching center for corporate governance worldwide, examining the relationship between legal regulatory frameworks and the global economy. The center poises itself on a mission to build capacity in the private and public sector through teaching and advising on corporate governance, disseminating best practices internationally, and interacting with academic institutions throughout the world.

Another program that has students and CEOs alike talking is the Chief Executive Leadership Institute (CELI). The program initially began at Emory University's Goizueta Business School, but three years ago it moved to SOM, where it's now the first university-based peer-driven leadership education program for top executives. It attracts not only CEOs from a multitude of industries, but also distinguished scholars from the top B-schools and from across disciplines, says Jeffrey Sonnenfeld, director of the program. Some past participants include the likes of James P. Kelly, chairman and CEO of United Parcel Service, and Gordon Binder, chairman and CEO of Amgen. Sonnenfeld notes that SOM's MBAs are also invited to the conferences to participate in discussions with executives and professors and also to network a bit. Branching out from this initiative is the Leadership Exchange and Analysis Program (LEAP), a concentrated weeklong exchange with top management officials. In 2002, for example, the series focused on the global economy. Entitled "Global Commerce Will Never Be the Same: Risks, Retreat, and Resilience," the program was held in New York City.

Other initiatives garnering attention include Sachem Ventures, LLC, a $1.5 million MBA-managed independent venture capital fund with investors such as Zilkha Venture Partners, the New Haven savings Bank, and Yale. Led by adjunct professor and former CEO of JPMorgan Capital Corporation David M. Cromwell, the fund offers portfolio companies expertise, consulting services, and human capital needed to build up budding businesses, while at the same time offering MBAs hands-on experience in venture capital. SOM also created a faculty lecture series and instituted two schoolwide meetings to air out pertinent current issues. Lecturers have included the president and CFO of PepsiCo, Indra Nooyi (an SOM 1980 grad); the vice-chairman and CEO of Nestlé, Peter Brabeck-Letmathe; and the chairman and CEO of Ogilvy & Mather Worldwide, Shelly Lazarus. If you're interested in pursuing a summer internship in the public or nonprofit sector, the Internship Fund is there to provide you with financial support. Throughout the academic year, the Fund coordinates fundraising activities, raising $140,000. Since its inception, approximately 20 percent of each class has received funding. There's also the Summer Internship Program in Entrepreneurship, which enables students to work on local entrepreneurial ventures.

Besides bulking up SOM's programming, Dean Garten is also pushing forth to change the face of the school. More important, Garten wants to see the percentage of women enrolled at SOM increase. (In the past, the number has remained stagnant at 27 percent.) An initiative started by some of the already enrolled women MBAs garnered responses from numerous prospective students. Via e-mail and over the phone, the female MBAs began serving as mentors to women who were considering applying to the B-school. Garten also plans to continue building on the initiatives already launched. "We want students to come here and feel at the end of their two years that their minds were opened beyond anything they ever thought possible," he adds. SOM is also working on establishing strong favor with underrepresented minorities. The school still remains at the lower end of the spectrum in that department, but it's going up the improvement ramp. In 2002, applications for underrepresented minorities, including African Americans, Hispanics, and Native Americans, increased by 62 percent from previous years.

One of several things SOM is offering to attract a greater number of students is special merit scholarships designated just for these students. The new Megunticook Scholars Program selects two first-year MBA candidates each year who demonstrate a core intent to give back to their communities. The award covers full tuition and fees for your two-year stay at SOM. SOM is also active in the Management Leadership for Tomorrow mentoring program, which is cosponsored by several minority student interest groups and offers advising to minority undergraduates on business school. Plus, for those students interested in pursuing an MBA, SOM launched a pre-MBA prep program in the summer and fall of 2002. SOM, along with Management Leadership for Tomorrow, presents to minority students the elements of a successful MBA application, from reviewing essays to mock interviews.

The school's innovative nature also spills into the very flexible curriculum, whose direction is up to you to personally craft. The curriculum emphasizes strengthening the fundamentals of business while at the same time focusing on the softer side of business. During your first year at SOM, you will take 10 required courses, 5 in each 13-week-long semester. Among the requirements are Financial Accounting, Data Analysis, Economic Analysis, Decision Analysis and Game Theory, the Strategic Environment of Management, Leadership, Marketing Management, Operations Management, and Valuation and Investment. You can exempt yourselves from any of these core classes, though you must replace it with an elective. Expect to take most of your core courses with a cohort of 50 to 60 students. Teamwork is the norm at SOM, as assigned and student-generated groups tackle projects and study together for almost every class. You can opt to concentrate in one of seven areas—finance, strategy, marketing, leadership, operations management, public management, or nonprofit management. During your second year, you'll have the chance to choose an area of interest for either a two-course in-depth training sequence in any of a broad range of advanced management topics such as international finance, corporate finance, policy analysis, or consumer behavior, or a three-course concentration in finance, marketing, strategy, operations management, public management, or nonprofit management. From then on, you're free to choose from among the menu of over 70 electives that span the spectrum from finance courses to nonprofit courses. When a curriculum is this flexible, the MBA becomes everything you put into it. It will allow you to home in on those skills you think you'll need most to achieve your goals in your post-MBA career track.

An international focus is a common thread throughout most of SOM's newest initiatives. It's one of the areas the B-school is aiming to beef up. Already, the school draws about a third of its students from across the world. These students can give you firsthand knowledge on their experiences outside of the United States. But, if you need to brush up on some background in international finance, the B-school offers an array of courses including Business, Government and Globalization; International Strategy and Competition; and Analysis of Finance Policy for Emerging Market Nations. You can take what you learn in the classroom and apply it to your work outside of the classroom either through one of the research centers or abroad. In the past, students have organized spring break educational trips to explore other cultures. For example, in 2002, 15 MBA students visited Japan for a weeklong study trip during their spring break. They visited an array of Japanese firms and multinational corporations as part of their studies in current strategy, operations and financial institutions, and general management in Japan.

A big bonus of being a part of an Ivy League powerhouse is the numerous strong schools that make up the university. You're allowed to take up to one-quarter of your courses outside of the B-school. You can take classes in other schools at Yale, such as Engineering, Forestry, Environmental Studies, or the Center for International and Area Studies, for example. Or you can pursue a dual degree in law, public health, medicine, architecture, drama, divinity, nursing, or the school of arts and sciences.

SOM students tend to be very passionate and competitive, but with a humanistic element mixed in and an honorable set of values, Dean Garten says. "You want to be around them when the chips are down and you need a strong team effort, and also when you're having a beer and socializing," he adds. Indeed, students also continuously praise the small, close-knit, highly involved atmosphere at the school. Despite the expansion throughout the school, the classes still remain small, further magnifying the extra attention and added benefits you'll get from the intimate culture at SOM. Garten won't soon be getting rid of that; it's his favorite part of the school. Although the grading system shifted in 1996 from a pass/fail system to a system resembling the A through F structure—Distinction, Proficient, Pass, and Fail—there are still no grading curves or class ranks. And students still describe the atmosphere as collaborative and noncompetitive. "What we hope makes a difference is that it's all about learning, it's small, it's very intimate . . . there's a lot of interaction between students and faculty," Garten notes. When students leave, they carry this collaborative nature with them. They remain very involved in the SOM community, especially in doling out funds to better the program. The SOM alumni base (4500 alums) is small in comparison to other top B-schools. But the giving isn't small. At over 50 percent, SOM alums are tops in giving back to their MBA program. And when students leave, they tend to give back to the SOM community.

Though SOM has developed substantially since Garten's arrival, there's still room for improvement. Garten has a plan to help SOM excel. Topping the agenda for the upcoming two years is the ultimate expansion of the faculty by over 60 percent across all disciplines. "We're trying to achieve a great mix of hard and soft skills," Garten explains. When it comes to recruiting faculty, Garten says he's looking for the right combination of research and teaching skills. He has his sights set on recruiting faculty members who are on the cutting edge of research and who can bring their work into the classroom. However, they're not planning on increasing the class size any time soon. Talk about responding to students' needs—SOM is aiming for a very intimate 5:1 student-teacher ratio.

Despite SOM's push for integration across Yale's schools, the actual B-school is set apart from the rest of the campus. SOM sits atop Hillhouse Avenue and is housed in four historic mansions—Horchow Hall, Evans Hall, Steinbach Hall, and the International Center for Finance. In the first three halls, you'll find classrooms, study halls, and faculty offices. If you're looking for some extra study space, check out Yale's extensive library system. Most MBAs make use of the Social Science Library right across the street from the SOM complex. You'll run into the undergrads and other graduate students at Donaldson Commons, the SOM dining facility. You can also expel your extra energy at Payne Whitney Gymnasium, the athletic facilities that house an ice rink, tennis courts, a yacht club, and one of the best-rated golf courses in the country, which is open to students for just $18. Students are active in athletics at SOM. Each year, the school's United Soccer Club hosts a tournament attracting hundreds of players from the other top B-schools. They also compete against the Ivy Leaguers in the Harvard Business School's Graduate School Rowing Championships and the Wharton Business School Sprints. Plus, SOM's MBAs take part in a yearly ice-hockey competition—the Stanley Garstka Cup—named after the school's deputy dean. In the traditional friendly competition, the first-year class goes up against the second-years to battle it out for the title. Students are also very active in MBA Student Interest Groups. From the more standard Marketing Club, Entrepreneurship Club, and Consulting Club, to the more civic-minded groups involved with nonprofits and community service, to the high-culture clubs like the Wine Club, SOM students find a way to expand their leadership skills in a multitude of arenas.

There are no classes on Fridays, so every Thursday night the keg party kicks off the three-day weekend. Students frequent the likes of Bar and Archie Mores, which is not too far from where the students tend to live. You don't have to venture very far for good entertainment: the Yale campus offers a variety of cultural activities to satisfy just about any taste. From the Yale School of Music's plethora of performances to the art galleries right on campus, including the Yale Center for British Art and the Peabody

Museum of Natural History, there's fun for everyone. The B-school offers limited housing to a small percentage of incoming students; however, most students live in the Grad Student Ghetto—a yuppified sector of New Haven's residential neighborhoods that consists of gracious Victorians that have been split up into student apartments—or along the Connecticut shoreline. Luckily there are good options for housing, because on-campus housing is pretty scarce. Along the neighborhood streets, you'll find grocery stories and cafes all within a 15-minute walk of campus.

PLACEMENT DETAILS

SOM's Career Development Office is bulking up its programming. One of the major new initiatives, which began in 2002, is the Alumni Job Squad, a group of alums who have been successful in unearthing job opportunities for SOM's MBAs. The group of seven alums opened new doors for students to companies like Cigna, Honeywell, and the American Red Cross, says Director of Career Development Coleen Singer.

Also new is a workshop on transitioning your skills from one industry to another. "We're focused on creating new doors to different industries like gaming, nonprofit, and defense," Singer adds. A lecture series is being launched in which practitioners from various industry backgrounds fill students in on the variety of industries and job capacities out there.

The career office also threw its efforts into helping out international students. Singer says a cross-cultural series has been started to further educate international students in things like adapting to a culture during an interview. One of the alums on the job squad also specifically worked with international students and their placement needs.

In 2002, only 69 percent of grads had job offers by graduation, though that number climbed to 80 percent by three months later. Those with jobs earned respectable starting pay packages of $110,200, with most grads remaining in the Northeast after graduation.

TOP HIRES

Standard & Poor's (7); American Express (6); Goldman Sachs (6); IBM (5); Booz Allen Hamilton (5); Credit Suisse First Boston (5); Deutsche Bank; (5); McKinsey & Company (5); General Electric (3); PricewaterhouseCoopers (3).

OUTSTANDING FACULTY

Sharon Oster (economics); David Cromwell (finance); Arturo Bris (finance); Meghan Busse (economics); Art Swersey (operations).

APPLICANT TIPS

Admissions Director James Stevens says he's especially interested in applicants who have a broader appreciation for social, political, and economic issues. "We're looking for people who have made an impact on their organizations—work, school, community—who have really made a difference. Stevens remembers that one recently admitted student was passionate about environmental issues and that as an undergraduate she had started an organization focused on environmental responsibility. She took it one step further and demonstrated through her application how an SOM MBA would allow her to more effectively pursue her goals. That's key when applying to SOM. "Some of our most successful students know what they want to do and how they want to use an MBA for that next step," Stevens adds. Likewise, he notes, applicants who come across as unfocused and uninterested in the broader issues don't make the most ideal candidates.

With applications reaching a record high and the admittance rate reaching a record low of 15 percent, SOM is getting increasingly more selective. So how do you make your application stand out from the bunch? When filling out your application, let the school's mission—educating leaders for business and society—guide you. Director Stevens says he particularly seeks applicants who really believe in the mission and who can demonstrate an understanding of and appreciation for it.

When looking at the GMAT and GPA numbers, Stevens says he doesn't just look at your final score, but he assesses your individual component scores as well. For example, he says, he'll look to see if a sociologist has quantitative aptitude as well. When reviewing your GPA, Stevens places emphasis on your undergraduate record, the strength of your school, and evidence that you challenged yourself through your courses.

Interviews aren't required, but all admitted applicants are invited for one. During the interview, Stevens says he assesses your communication skills and also tries to get a sense for how everything fits together and how you'll fit in with the SOM culture. Stevens also says not to be afraid to indicate you have interest in an area that may not coincide with the school's stereotype. He's always interested by those students who demonstrate an interest in a unique area. It just increases the diversity of the program, he adds.

Stevens suggests one area that applicants can really improve in is their recommendations. "The ones that are most effective are those that reinforce other parts of the application," he adds. "Have a good conversation with your recommender and give them a copy of your resume to help them get a better sense of who you are."

YALE MBAs SOUND OFF

I believe that the caliber of the faculty and students at the Yale School of Management is unmatched by any other business school in the world, including those with ostensibly higher rankings. I couldn't be more pleased with my experience over the two years. The cooperative learning environment at Yale cannot be exaggerated. For the first time in my educational life, I was truly learning for the sake of learning, and loving every minute of it.

The Yale MBA Program is all about access! The program's small size means students are on a first name basis with top faculty. It also means great access to recruiters. Students are encouraged to take classes at other parts of the university—many of my friends took classes at the Law School and the Drama School. The alumni network of the School of Management includes alumni from the entire university, so despite the relative youth of the program, the alumni base is very broad, diverse and influential. Students are also encouraged to take on leadership positions, which, for me, resulted in contact with many big players in the business world. It's pretty exciting to have an e-mail exchange with the CFO or CEO of a large company, escort him/her around campus, have lunch, and introduce him/her to a large audience.

If I had to do my MBA again I would only apply to Yale SOM. The school has it right. If the MBA is about networking, Yale's small class size allows us to know all our classmates. If it is about competition, we compete with other business school graduates not with our classmates. If it's about leadership, we are trained to be socially responsible leaders. If it's about fun, you cannot escape the parties and celebrations at Yale.

My only complaint is that SOM does not have enough marketing elective programs, and not enough consumer products companies which recruit for marketers on campus. These are areas in need of improvement for the program.

The Yale MBA is different from any other program I have seen or heard about. They take smart kids that have spent their last two years in the Navy, the Peace Corps, the NHL, or a Himalayan expedition and put them together under a rigorous program of business and economics. The dynamic is amazing.

There are huge benefits to being in a smaller school: easier to stand out in front of recruiters, faculty get involved with school life, easy to get involved in faculty research if you want, and you get to know everyone.

While I expected business school to be stimulating and challenging, what I experienced at Yale has been most rewarding and of highest quality. For me, the choice of business school could not have been better: the diversity of professional backgrounds of my classmates, the rigor of the academic training, and the welcoming, collaborative environment of the school made my experience at Yale extremely positive.

NEW YORK UNIVERSITY

15.
NEW YORK
UNIVERSITY

NEW YORK UNIVERSITY

Leonard N. Stern School of Business
44 West Fourth Street
New York, New York 10012
E-mail address: sternmba@stern.nyu.edu
Web site address: www.stern.nyu.edu

Enrollment: 817
Women: 38%
Non-U.S.: 34%
Minority: 11%
Part-time: 1834
Average age: 27
Applicants accepted: 15%
Median starting pay: $85,000

Annual tuition and fees: $30,365
Estimated annual budget: $55,876
Average GMAT score: 700
Average months of work experience: 56
Accepted applicants enrolled: 52%
Corporate ranking: 10
Graduate ranking: 20
Intellectual capital rank: 32

Teaching methods: case study 35%, distance learning 7%, experiential learning 6%, lecture 25%, simulations 7%, team projects 20%

Ed Altman's office is bursting at the seams with information. Books, papers, and file folders litter the desk and floor. In his 35 years at the Leonard N. Stern School of Business, Altman has pretty much written the book on bankruptcy, and from the looks of it, every piece of paper that has come across his desk in those three and a half decades is piled or filed somewhere in his small corner office on the ninth floor. Shelves are lined with books bearing titles such as *Crashes and Panics, Universal Banking, Case Problems in Finance,* and so on. There are filing shelves overflowing with papers; on the tops of those shelves there are more books that climb to the ceiling.

Then there is a piece of newsprint taped to the desk, hanging down for all to see: a black-and-white photo of the New York City skyline from the water at the southern edge of Manhattan, near the bottom of which, large white letters shout, "THIS IS OUR CAMPUS." A fitting description.

Ask anyone at Stern why he or she chose the school, and the answer is the same: location. It is true that Stern does not reside on a traditional college campus with lush green landscapes and tailgating before the big game on Saturday mornings, but that doesn't matter. "I already went to college," says Jeb Armstrong, a 2002 graduate. "I don't need to do that again."

Students like to say that the city itself is the campus, and in many ways that's true. At Stern, the students like to talk about all the things they are able to take advantage of outside of the classroom, experiences that are impossible for other schools to mimic simply because they are not in New York. Hop on a train at a moment's notice, and be on Wall Street or at a conference or hearing in no time flat. It's one thing to read about something in the paper or in textbooks, but something else altogether to say that you were actually there.

Just one example: in the fall of 2001, Stern MBAs experienced a part of New York that few get to see, courtesy of the Metropolitan Opera. Students enrolled in the Managing Operations course were asked to analyze a case study focusing on the organization and complexity that are involved in staging an opera, in this case, "A Celebration of Giuseppe Verdi." To better understand how the Met was run, students went to the Lincoln Center to meet with general manager Joseph Volpe, received a backstage tour of the facility, and attended a dress rehearsal of the final act of Verdi's *Rigoletto*. The case study was ultimately used to introduce students to central theories in management so they could apply them later on when dealing with real managerial problems.

Being in the heart of the business world also brings renowned personalities such as Alan Greenspan (a Stern alum), Harvey Golub, Richard Grasso, and Jack Welch to campus to lecture on current issues and to provide words of wisdom to students. "Being in New York, we are in a position to really define what business education is all about," explains newly appointed dean Thomas Cooley. "We really are located in the 'belly of the beast,' which gives us the ability to incorporate the city into our MBA program." That turns out to be a big advantage for Stern, says Cooley.

Cooley took over as dean of Stern in August 2002, after George Daly vacated the position after nine years of service. Prior to being named dean, Cooley had been on the faculty of the economics department at Stern since 1999. Cooley was also the president of the Society for Economic Dynamics and a fellow of the Econometric Society. As dean of Stern, Cooley says he'll remain active in the everyday life of the school,

as well as make sure it continues to build on the foundations of academic achievement and grow even stronger.

"I want to be very involved internally with both the faculty and students," Cooley says. "I think choosing someone like me to be dean was motivated by the idea that it takes an academic leader to continue to develop academic excellence. I feel like my goals are the same as those of the institution itself in striving toward this excellence. My game plan is to initiate discussions about what business education is about and to raise the intellectual standards at Stern." That's a tall order, but if the past few years are any indication of what's to come, Stern is on the right track, with average GMAT scores rising and the quality of students getting stronger by the year. "There has definitely been a significant increase in the quality of students in the last five or so years," Altman says.

As an institution for higher learning, Stern has made a name for itself in finance, and is widely regarded as one of a handful of standout schools in the field. Because of the school's proximity to Wall Street, students can network with financial specialists and strategists and get firsthand experience via top-notch speakers and visiting professors. One other plus: the wide range of internships that are available right in Stern's backyard. The big selling point to current students might be the high-caliber faculty that incorporates real-world examples in the classroom setting. Take Aswath Damodaran, associate professor of courses such as Corporate Finance and Financial Markets, whom students overwhelmingly pick as a favorite professor. Damodaran's classes are so popular, in fact, that they have to be taught in a 400-seat theater instead of a normal classroom.

What's his secret? "There are three things that human beings are always interested in: salvation, sex, and stocks," Damodaran explains. "I can't do much about the first two, though there are some who claim to find salvation in a large portfolio, but I do talk about stocks. People are fascinated by markets and how they work and don't work, and I try to build on that fascination. Using real-world examples as they occur is much more interesting and informative than talking about cases set 10 or 15 years ago."

In fields other than finance, students don't always feel as confident, saying they'd be hesitant to recommend Stern to friends who were going to focus on specialties like marketing or management. In the eyes of marketing professor John Czepiel, the issue is more a misconception than a problem. "A lot of the time, students are unaware as to what marketing is," Czepiel explains. "I think part of the onus is on us to be able to demonstrate the applicability of these ideas at the front end of the course. Many of the people who transfer into marketing do so as a result of taking the first marketing course and saying, 'Hey, this is interesting stuff, this is fun. I like this.' " However, according to Czepiel, there is no problem in the strength of the faculty. "We are definitely moving upward."

One advantage Stern students have is the school's 60,000-plus alumni working all over the world. This is a wonderful resource for students to take advantage of, and many do. The alumni base is so large because of the swarms of part-time students who take over the classrooms and corridors in the evenings. But part-timers are a touchy subject for some full-time students. "I feel like too much emphasis is put on the part-time program at Stern," says one 2002 graduate. "Many classes I wanted to take were only offered in the evening." This feeling is widespread among full-timers, mainly because the part-time program is built partially of students who were denied admittance to the full-time program. It makes the school's priorities seem backward. There is not much chance for full-timers and part-timers to intermingle, and when they do, the feeling is one of ill will. This has to do with the amount of time that part-timers are able to give to projects and other group-related activities. Some students, how-

ever, use the opportunity for night classes to their advantage, taking electives they wanted during the day and getting the core courses at night. That's a level of flexibility you won't find at most schools, but there are trade-offs. Take a core course with part-timers and you can count on having their help only part of the time. Where full-timers are able to work throughout the day on long-term projects, part-timers have little free time in their schedules due to work and classes, so their contributions are less than what is expected.

You begin your two years at Stern before you even make it to campus, with a computer e-group to which only admitted students have access. The e-group is a chat room of sorts that gives you a chance to interact with classmates to discuss goals and reservations, share tips on finding housing, and begin to get to know the people with whom you will be spending a good majority of the next two years.

Two weeks before second-year students return, they take part in pre-term, an orientation period used as a way to make sure everyone is prepared in areas such as computer proficiency, ethics, management communication, case analysis techniques, and diversity. During this period, you will be strategically divided into blocks consisting of 60 or so students from all walks of life and experience levels. Don't be surprised to find a wide array of individuals in your block. The purpose is to remove your comfort zone and introduce you to a group of people that are not like you. Once the regular term begins, you attend core classes with your block, giving you a group of peers you will see and interact with on a regular basis, whether you like it or not. One of the things that Stern prides itself on is the tremendous sense of community that students feel, which is mostly attributed to the block structure.

"You are able to build a bond and a sense of camaraderie in the group," Jeb Armstrong says. "After the first year, you all branch out, but because in the first semester you spend so much time with that group, those become your close friends, the people you do things with."

The core curriculum is made up of cross-disciplinary courses such as Corporate Strategy Analysis, foundation courses such as Statistics and Data Analysis, and breadth courses such as Marketing. Incoming MBAs can choose among eight majors and two co-majors, as well as a number of program initiatives, innovative concentrations in nontraditional areas. Many of these initiatives take advantage of the resources New York has to offer. A prime example of this is the Entertainment, Media and Technology Initiative (EMT), in which students interested in getting involved in the entertainment industry in any facet, from music to television to sports, are able to get a feel for the field by experiencing the industries at first hand. And where better to do it? New York is home to some of the world's largest and best-known media corporations, such as ABC, CBS, NBC, HBO, Nickelodeon, Condé Nast, Reuters, Bertelsmann, Disney, Miramax, and Universal Music, as well as the NBA, NHL, and NFL. No other city in the world can offer the exposure to the entertainment industry that New York has, and being right at the center of the city gives students what they like to call the New York edge.

To major in a traditional field, students must take at least 12 of the 61 course units required for graduation in that area. They can also combine these majors with further concentrations in such areas as EMT, digital economy, or law and business. In an effort to give students a multitude of choices and a wide range of knowledge, the administration offers formal joint degree programs as well. Students can opt for joint degrees in law, French studies, creative arts, politics, and statistics and operations research.

The facilities at Stern are comfortable, yet at the same time professional. It isn't spacious by any means—nothing in New York is—but every resource you'll need is readily available. With major renovations of some classrooms, student lounges, study areas, and the career development office, you'll be made to feel like you're walking the halls of a company, complete with plush leather chairs and couches and tiled floors decorated in soft tones and colors. Study areas are plentiful and conference rooms are available for discussion groups or meetings, complete with large whiteboards and tables, which appear to have been ordered from the same company that provided the undergrads' top-of-the-line dorm room furnishings.

While many students choose to live off campus, finding a place to call home in New York is about as easy as getting out of the subway without being solicited for loose change. For students who would rather not have to deal with the stresses of apartment hunting, Stern offers a residence hall just north of campus on 14th Street near Union Square. On the site of the old Palladium night club, the Palladium Residence Hall offers all the amenities of an apartment complex and then some. Four floors of the Palladium are set aside exclusively for MBA students, who have the option of choosing a single studio or a two-bedroom suite. Each apartment comes fully furnished and includes telephones, cable, and computer access as well as small kitchens. The Palladium also boasts a sports center with an Olympic-size swimming pool, 24-hour security, and a dining facility. The rest of the floors of the Palladium are reserved for rowdy undergrads, which could be a curse or a blessing, depending on what you're looking for. Yes, the amenities are plentiful, and it's not cheap, but compared to the price of a regular apartment in the city, it's reasonable. The only problem with the Palladium is that students miss out on the rodents, nut-case roommates, and crackpot landlords that make living in New York so special.

The lifestyle at Stern is fast-paced and strenuous. What with classwork and the many activities students take part in, there is little time left to socialize. One student says his schedule consists of eating, going to class, and working his backside off, with a few hours of sleep thrown in here and there when necessary. Students know how to have a good time, however, and Stern's Greenwich Village locale makes bar hopping, clubbing, and getting home extremely easy. Even better, the prices in the area aren't as steep as in other parts of the city. "A lot of social events revolve around the many bars around Stern," says Alice Luong, a 2002 grad. The school itself also goes out of its way to make sure students aren't too bogged down in work to enjoy themselves. For example, each Thursday evening in the first-floor lounge of Stern, the school hosts Beer Blast, where students come to unwind, socialize, listen to music, and drink their cares away.

Another popular annual event at Stern is International Passport Day, where international students are given the opportunity to introduce their peers to the traditions and culture of their homelands. On the exotic brick of the Gould Plaza concourse just outside the doors of Stern, international students set up booths showcasing the best their countries have to offer. You can sample the cuisine, some prepared by the students themselves, some catered in from local restaurants; you can groove to the music, some performed by classmates, some played on CD players; and you can learn more about the lifestyles that your colleagues and friends call their own.

Stern students can work off some aggression by joining the Stern rugby team or representing NYU against other local B-schools in the Stern Challenge flag football tournament in Central Park, which benefits the Make-a-Wish Foundation.

Volunteerism is an important aspect of the Stern community. Mentoring programs in city schools are popular, as well as various outreach programs to help better the area. Alice Luong volunteered with Junior Achievement, for ex-

ample. "The purpose of the program is to bring real-life business experience into the classroom of New York schools," she says.

Stern students are known to pitch in for a worthy cause. In the aftermath of September 11, students started a program called Stern Rebuilds, an ad hoc group set up to aid adversely affected local businesses. Students set up consulting teams made up of students and alumni to provide practical and personal solutions pro bono to businesses that needed help. Teams provided businesses with short- and long-term business plans as well as help in marketing planning, financial strategy, and loan applications. Over 60 businesses, ranging from retail shops to restaurants to professional service firms, were helped by Stern rebuilds.

For the most part, 2002 grads are satisfied with their experience at Stern. The networking opportunities and connections through alumni are considered be outstanding, and most grads say the caliber of their classmates greatly enhances the experience. Grads also applaud the job the career counseling department does in job placement, an impressive feat considering the depressed market in 2001–2002.

Grads are less than thrilled in a few areas. Many found classwork to be excessive. Others say excessive focus was put on e-business, as well as the school's extreme efforts to foster interaction between various ethnic and national groups. At Stern it is important and necessary to foster such interaction, the reason being that over a third of its students are international.

Stern helped pioneer the study of international business, and the school continues to excel in the field through top faculty research and exchange opportunities. The International Management Program (IMP), in which students are offered the option to study overseas for a semester at a top international business school, is just one example. In partnership with 35 schools, Stern students can choose to travel to various European locations or to Australia, South Africa, or Hong Kong. Ed Altman was one of the founders of the program 30 years ago. While some question the need for such a program when Stern already boasts the top international business faculty and more than a third of its students coming from foreign lands, its value is obvious: "There really is no substitute for being there," says Altman, as he glances over the stacks of paper on his windowsill toward the Empire State Building 30 blocks uptown. The same might be said about getting an MBA in the Big Apple.

PLACEMENT DETAILS

With the economy on the downswing, job offers and starting salaries for the class of 2002 dropped considerably from 2000, with averages of just over one offer and $113,300, compared to 2.8 offers and a starting package of $140,000 two years earlier. Only 69 percent of grads had job offers by graduation.

To deal with the unstable nature of the job market, the Office of Career Development, led by Assistant Dean Gary Fraser, made some changes to the curriculum at Stern. In the past, optional career planning workshops had been available to any student who wanted to participate, but with the job market not as plentiful as it has been in years past, the workshops have been revamped and made mandatory for every student. After completing the workshops, which include lessons on resume building and interview skills, students can better examine exactly what it is they want when they begin looking for jobs.

"We felt like we needed to redevelop the career development series so that we really give students a complete array of tools in the two years they are here," Fraser says. The goal was to have students do a self-assessment and to be able to clearly tell their story. "The job finding process is not a natural one, and there is some training that has to be done. As much as we can prepare them, it is a question of how well they can communicate their skill set to that employer. We want to take everyone through the same process and allow them to do that," explains Fraser.

Another change that has taken place: a frantic search for a wider array of recruiters. In the past, two-thirds of Stern grads would be hired by large consulting or investment banking companies. That number decreased considerably in 2002. To deal with this drop, Fraser and his staff began identifying new industries and emerging opportunities. According to Fraser, nearly 400 companies were identified and visited the campus. "Granted, these are not companies that are going to hire 10 MBAs, but they might hire 1," he says.

TOP HIRES

Citigroup (including Salomon Smith Barney) (16); American Express (14); JPMorgan Chase (14); Lehman Brothers (13); Merrill Lynch (11); Deutsche Bank (9); Pfizer (9); Goldman Sachs (8); Unilever (8).

OUTSTANDING FACULTY

Aswath Damodaran (finance); David Yermack (finance); William Silber (finance); Dan Gode (accounting); Aaron Tenebein (statistics); Nouriel Roubini (economics).

APPLICANT TIPS

Over the last few years, each incoming class at Stern has been more and more impressive, touting impeccable undergraduate records and high GMAT scores. But that's not all the admissions office looks for. Work experience, application essays, and involvement in the community are also of the utmost importance to the admissions board.

According to Director of Admissions Julia Min, "There really is no ideal candidate. We are looking for work experience—not work experience in certain industries or functions, but someone who has shown progression and has made an impact in their organization. We also like to see people who have really taken on a leadership role and demonstrated teamwork. In addition, we look at their extracurricular activities and how they have given back to the community, because that is a clear indicator to us about how active they will be at Stern. Not one thing is exclusive. We look at the whole picture."

Stern is looking for students who are unique and really understand who they are. A way of doing this is a question on the application that asks for applicants to creatively describe themselves. It is here that you can step outside of the box and let your creativity run wild. In the past, applicants have done all sorts of things, from baking pies to taking photographs to writing poetry to creating Web sites. The sky is the limit here, and prospective students who take advantage of the question and show creativity can boost their chances.

Also, be sure to take the time to polish your essays. "You can always tell when someone put their application together in five minutes," Min warns. "Especially in the essays, we can tell where someone just filled in Stern for the school name and really does not know what the program is about. Maybe they read through our brochure. But we wrote it; we kind of know what it says. We recognize that students are applying to more than one school, and they should be, but again, if you don't do the research ahead of time, I think you do a great disservice to yourself, because it is an arduous process and it's also an expensive process."

So what does that mean for you? Says Min, "Applicants should really sit down and think about what they want. If you come here as a prospective student and get a chance to see Stern firsthand, I think eventually it will build a level of enthusiasm, and that comes through loud and clear in the essays. When we ask them 'Why Stern?' or 'Why an MBA at Stern?,' that level of enthusiasm really comes out in people who have done their research."

STERN MBAs SOUND OFF

Stern probably has the best finance program in the world. I think the program is underrated—there are a lot of very talented professors besides the more well-known faculty members. There are a lot of in-depth courses and lectures that may not be appreciated. However, a finance professional who wants to be at the frontier of the industry can expect to learn and advance his knowledge virtually in all aspects of finance.

An MBA is as good as you make it, at least to some extent. Stern is in a great location, which matters more than I had originally thought it would when it comes down to finding a job. The people are terrific—very supportive and they work hard.

NYU is in the center of the financial world. In good times and most importantly in bad times, the firms I want to work for are easy to contact and it is easy for them to reach me. This is a huge advantage over most any other program. I find my counterparts from other top programs—ones ranked higher than NYU—finding it very difficult to reach firms, whereas my experience is dramatically more positive. Further, the caliber of guest speakers and faculty is extremely high. And from a personal angle, living in NYC provides NYU students with numerous outlets to relax and take in some culture and just get out and enjoy the city.

Stern is fantastic for finance. It has several professors in key areas that surpassed anything I had expected. However, if you're interested in other areas, you may be a bit disappointed.

I do have complaints about our school: class size too big. The value of our full-time program is diluted by part-timers. But finance courses are incomparable. Those who are interested in finance won't regret if they choose Stern.

While Stern is a great school in many academic areas (especially finance and entrepreneurship), more effort could be made to increase the number of management and marketing offerings as well as the quality of teaching in the marketing department. Teamwork, students' great personalities, and the opportunity to lead inter- and intraschool activities are the strongest qualities of the school, besides straight academics.

Overall, my academic experience was good. However, the marketing program has a lot of room for improvement. I believe the school needs to strengthen its position with the recruiters. In a tight job market like this year's, the school has not been able to stand for its students' interests. The alumni network is not working to its full potential. This to a big extent is the reason why Stern has not been able to establish strong positions with recruiters. However, the school does put some effort into developing the network: hopefully, results will follow.

I have had some of the most amazing teachers I have ever encountered at Stern, but have also had a few professors who couldn't teach someone how to escape from a paper bag. My experience in business school has been incredibly positive, mostly because of the people that I went to school with. Having met numerous people from other schools through my summer internship and rugby tournaments, I know that I would have been much less happy at any other school.

UNIVERSITY OF CALIFORNIA AT LOS ANGELES

16.
UNIVERSITY OF CALIFORNIA AT LOS ANGELES

The Anderson School
110 Westwood Plaza
Gold Hall, Suite B201
Los Angeles, California 90095-1481
E-mail address: mba.admissions@anderson.ucla.edu
Web site address: www.anderson.ucla.edu

Enrollment: 671
Women: 29%
Non-U.S.: 26%
Minority: 7%
Part-time: 585
Average age: 28
Applicants accepted: 15%
Median starting pay: $85,000
Annual tuition and fees:
    resident—$11,820
    nonresident—$22,592

Estimated annual budget: $32,071
Average GMAT score: 700
Average months of work
    experience: 57
Accepted applicants enrolled: 52%
Corporate ranking: 23
Graduate ranking: 7
Intellectual capital rank: 10

Teaching methods: case study 30%, lecture 50%, other 20%

The Anderson School at UCLA is using its proximity to Hollywood to break into the other business, the one that attracts countless numbers of young starlets and aspiring thespians with caviar dreams and champagne wishes. "Being so close to the entertainment industry, as well as the budding field of digital media, we have an advantage that other schools don't," says Dean Bruce Willison. "We thought it was about time that we capitalized on that." Anderson has been involved in the entertainment industry for nearly 20 years through its Entertainment Program. Now, to put more focus on the area, the program has become the Center for Communication Policy and Entertainment/Media. The program focuses on the three pillars of UCLA—research, teaching, and community service—to look at the forces of change on the management of enterprises in entertainment and media, including the impacts of technology, consolidation, and globalization on entertainment and media in terms of content and distribution. Over 800 Anderson alumni are active managers and executives in entertainment and media, which not only helps in bringing in a high caliber of speakers, but also greatly aids students in networking and getting internships and jobs in the entertainment industry. According to placement records, a good number of students come to Anderson just for that reason (approximately 10 percent of first-year MBAs choose to intern in the entertainment and media industries). The EMP program focuses on entertainment and media content and distribution, including film and television production, postproduction, and distribution; cable television, magazine, book, and newspaper publishing; radio and television station management and programming; music creation and distribution; theatrical exhibition; games and gaming; Internet content and distribution; sports; live theater and concerts; advertising; and theme and amusement parks.

Willison is the seventh dean at Anderson, and the first to come from the rat race—he spent 26 years in the banking industry at places like Home Savings of America, H.F. Ahmanson & Co., and, most recently, Bank of America and First Interstate Bancorp. Willison has been at Anderson for nearly four years now, and though he is the first to point out the differences between the business world and the world of academia, he is also quick to discuss the similarities. "The management process is the same," he says. "The most successful businesspeople are not the ones who dictate or command and control, but the ones who build teams and empower teams. That's what I am doing here."

Besides the EMP program, there are a number of other changes at Anderson. First, the program is going "back to basics," says Eric Mokover, director of MBA programming. "We had our nose in the high-tech stuff that disappeared, so back to basics means getting back to our rigorous MBA program, learning accounting, finance, marketing, operations, and learning them well from the start, and then developing a program that meets your need. We learned our lesson." From the looks of things, this change in focus might be a good idea. After peaking as the number 9 MBA program in the 1994 rankings, Anderson leveled out at number 12 for the next three periods, then dropped to 16 this time around.

This back-to-basics approach begins with the review and alteration of the Anderson curriculum. We aren't talking about a few nips and tucks; this is an all-out revamping of everything from the core, and how it is designed, down to

something as simple as the calendars. Many times, when a school makes the kinds of changes that get down to the heart of the program, things begin to return to the old way as time goes by. Director Mokover is hoping this doesn't happen at Anderson. "This is a 'nothing is sacred' type of review. When I look at curricular reviews at other schools, I have seen a lot of hard work go in, then the same exact thing just repackaged over and over again. We are trying very hard not to fall into that trap. I am cautiously optimistic." This marks the first major curriculum change at Anderson in nearly 10 years.

For the most part, 2002 grads are pleased with the experience and knowledge base they are taking from Anderson. They rank the overall program near the top, and feel the positives much outweigh the negatives. One major problem is that, with such large class sizes (nearly 335 per class), it is very hard for students to get into the electives they want. There is also a problem when it comes to responding to students' needs. In addition, the teaching in core courses leaves something to be desired.

A good number of students complain about their peers and the feeling that many of them are only interested in their own personal gain at the expense of teamwork. Students also question the integration of coursework, which seems almost nonexistent. According to Mokover, the school is working to remedy the issue, but such a change isn't as straightforward as it may seem. "One of our chief challenges right now is to improve the integration efforts within the core," he says. "There are ways to do it, but it's easier said than done."

Anderson is able to attract many of the most well-known speakers in the business world and elsewhere to campus due to its location in Los Angeles. Recently, Lou Dobbs hosted *Moneyline* live from the Alumni Plaza, and guests such as James A. Baker III, Tom Peters, Ehud Barak, and Earvin "Magic" Johnson were on hand for the West Coast Business Leadership Conference, which was cosponsored by Anderson, Impact

Education, and American Express. It is not uncommon to see the school's namesake, John Anderson, around campus, meeting with students, giving them advice, and bringing in some of the most notable speakers in the area, such as Sherry Lansing, president of Paramount Studios.

The alumni network is quite large at Anderson, and, according to Dean Willison, the school does a good deal in trying to utilize the network. This would seem to be a huge advantage to students; however, that doesn't seem to be the case. Says one 2002 grad, "Not only are alumni unhelpful in finding jobs, they often don't even bother to respond to e-mails, calls and letters from students. It has nothing to do with the bad economy: many students have fallen back on alumni networks from undergrad institutions and found those more helpful."

An issue that students have historically had about the Anderson program is the lack of diversity. In 2000, grads asked that the school look into the fact that the female, international, and minority populations were far below the numbers posted by other top MBA programs. However, if any efforts have been made in the past two years to remedy the problem, they have not worked; the percentages for all three of the aforementioned groups have dropped. According to grads of the class of 2002, Anderson is more reactive than proactive when it comes to diversity. Says one grad, "Every time any special interest group perceives any kind of slight at Anderson, a huge hubbub is raised, and the administration is called on to baby-sit, which they are all too eager to do. It's like the playground at elementary school."

But don't let all this criticism give you the wrong idea: by and large, members of the class of 2002 had nothing but positive things to say about the program. Students rank the program at the top in entrepreneurship and near the top in e-business, IT, networking, and career placement. They have only good things to say about the school's facilities, and they laud the quality of professors that Anderson offers, many mention-

ing the likes of Bill Cockrum and Al Osborne by name for their unique brands of teaching. Osborne, who serves as director of the Price Center in addition to his teaching duties, feels that the reason he is successful in getting theories and practices across to students is because he is able to relate them to current issues in both the news and his own life. "Because I am the director of several corporations, I have credibility," he says. "When I bring the issues I am dealing with in the boardroom into the classroom and relate them to the issues we are talking about, students seem more receptive."

Students at Anderson can be assured that they will get an interesting course load. The current curriculum requires students to take eight core courses, allowing time in the first year to enroll in some of its 140-plus elective courses. The last time the core was changed was in 1998. It consists of classes in human resources, statistics, financial accounting, managerial economics and finance, operations and technology management, and marketing. The classes are tackled in 65-student sections, which are reshuffled after each of the three 10-week quarters that make up the first year. Students who pass exams can waive core courses, but the credits must be replaced with more advanced classes. Teamwork is the mantra at Anderson. And most graduates also add that without their classmates, Anderson wouldn't be Anderson. Says one 2002 grad, "Anderson students are a great source of learning; people come from all sorts of different backgrounds and have invaluable knowledge and experiences to share. You won't find cutthroat competition here, but a cooperative team-oriented atmosphere."

And the teamwork doesn't stop after the first year. A 37-year-old required capstone field study spans the last one or two quarters, depending on the scope of the project. Teams of three to five students put on their consulting hats with a sponsoring client company and its managers, working on substantive issues and problems in real time. Ultimately, students take the analytical and theoretical lessons learned in the classroom to the highway for a test drive. Sure, a lot of B-schools consider such projects a staple these days, but Anderson MBAs have a chance to work with the many illustrious clients that call the Los Angeles area home, such as Microsoft, Dream-Works Studios, and the Los Angeles Center for Community and Family Services. Maybe the most exciting perk for students approaching the end of their two-year stint at Anderson and dreading the loan payments on the horizon is that the two best field studies are each awarded cash prizes of $4000—thanks to a Deloitte & Touche sponsorship—to be split among team members. Anderson requires 14 additional courses for graduation, 11 of which are chosen from among the school's large assortment of electives. Students may concentrate in 1 of 12 traditional functional areas, ranging from entertainment management and high-technology management to information systems and marketing, or they can craft their own.

But as many enterpreneurs say, you can only learn so much in the classroom. The Harold Price Center; the student-run Enterpreneur Association (EA), with the largest number of students of any club at Anderson (over 500); and the High-Tech Business Association (HTBA), with nearly 275 members, tap into the local venture capital, high-tech, and entertainment communities for assistance often. And if the expertise of local business leaders does not provide enough practice, the school has a student investment fund of over $2 million to be managed. Another program matches local entrepreneurs with students, and over 75 speakers visit campus to share war stories from the front lines. The Wolfen Fund helps students trying to start their own businesses by providing them with cash to live on as they're writing their business plans, and doesn't even ask for anything in return . . . at least not for a few years.

Before your first quarter at Anderson begins, you will take part in a five-day, two-unit course in which you will be immersed in the program's learning culture and get acclimated to the Anderson curriculum. In the course, called Management Foundations, you begin to develop conceptual frameworks that will help you organize and integrate your experiences in core courses, and you will also get to know your classmates and faculty members. Near the end of the course, you will be presented with a live case that focuses on an existing company. You will research and prepare a case analysis, then present it to company executives.

No matter what you choose, you'll have to have the school's required laptop computers. Every seat in every classroom, office, study room, and library is wired for access to the computer network—over 2900 ports in all. Of course, materials are posted on the school's intranet, along with faculty and student directories, student Web pages and resumes, course bidding and registration, and job search resources. Multimedia presentation equipment, videoconferencing capabilities, laser printers, and other high-tech gadgetry are at your disposal as well.

Although global management isn't one of Anderson's strengths, the school is making strides to get students more accustomed to world business. Students participate in the International Management Fellows Program, a two-year program sponsored by the Center for International Business Education & Research. The program begins in June and runs concurrently with a regular MBA program, offering MBAs in-depth exposure to international business practices, culture, and language. In the summer before the beginning of the program, participants take intensive classes in language and culture. One year later, they head off to a foreign country for nine months of internship, work at a local company, and study everything from political economy to history and, of course, business at a local university before returning to finish up their last two quarters. If you would rather not make such a commitment, there are various other opportunities. For instance, 50 to 60 second-year students enroll each year in exchange partnerships with one of the 40-plus institutions that Anderson partners with in countries all over the globe, from Brazil to Japan to Israel. Back at home, the core curriculum allows students to take up to three courses in the larger university's extensive offerings; joint degrees can be taken in law, computer science, Latin American studies, library and information science, nursing, urban planning, public health, and medicine.

Anderson may not be number 1 in terms of B-schools, but it does rank at the top for best tans. And why not? You'd be hard pressed to find a more beautiful B-school, where the sun shines 334 days out of the year. With the beach less than 10 miles from campus, it doesn't take much coercion to get students to the sandy shores of the Pacific. The lifestyle at Anderson is one of the school's biggest draws. One downside of this is the fact that some of this warm-weather, anything-goes mentality may have rubbed off on the faculty and administration at Anderson. Says one 2002 grad, "The school suffers from the attitude that every answer is a good answer, and generally has a soft and fuzzy demeanor that discourages the skepticism and hard-nosed decision-making skills that a good manager must possess."

Most students choose to rent apartments in Brentwood, Santa Monica, West Los Angeles, and Westwood. The Community Housing Office provides information and current listings of all kinds of available housing, from subleases to house-shares and rentals. Pricing all depends on the lifestyle you want to lead. If you want to live in the lap of luxury, expect to pay a pretty penny. There are, of course, more reasonable options, but nothing's going to come cheap in the area.

You need a car to survive in L.A., but remember that patience is a virtue in trying to find parking on campus. Even prospective MBAs quip that if you're driving to your interview at Anderson, give yourself an extra hour and bring your parking angel to find a spot. You can purchase a parking permit to park on campus, but even the permit does not guarantee a spot. Public transportation is a more viable option for many students. On campus, many end up taking the bus. But once students are settled into life at Anderson, they can't help but relax. They've got an on-site café, souped-up lecture halls to study in, venture capital competitions to test their business plans, and plenty of MBA nights to enjoy.

PLACEMENT DETAILS

2002 grads are not too pleased with the state of the Career Management Center at Anderson. They understand that they have graduated in the midst of one of the worst job markets ever, but many do not feel that they were given the attention and time they needed. One grad went so far as to call it the "Resume Proofreading Office." With so many students to work with, it is understandable that there may not be enough personnel to go around, but it also may be an issue of misunderstanding the role of the office in the students' job-finding process. "Our philosophy is not that we perform placement for them," says Mary Albright Smith, director of the Career Management Center. "We do everything we can to bring in opportunities for them, but we see ourselves more as partners in the career development process and less as a placement process. At the end of the day it is their job search and their career."

While it may not be the office's job to hold the hands of MBAs, something isn't right in the City of Angels. With only 58 percent of the class of 2002 having jobs by graduation, Anderson was way below the top 30 average, and even after three months, the number was still only 68 percent. One positive, however, is that students who do not find employment can choose to be part of what are known as success groups. In these groups, 8 to 10 students discuss the work they are doing to find employment and what they plan to do in the weeks to come. According to Albright Smith, the groups work on two fronts. "One, when folks make a public statement about what they are going to do, they tend to do it," she says. "Two, 10 heads are better than 1. When you have 10 people in a room, the networking power is amazing."

A good majority of the class of 2002 stayed on the West Coast after graduating (65 percent), while 85 percent stayed in the United States. According to grads, the average first-year compensation was around $125,000, a $10,000 drop from two years earlier.

TOP HIRES

Deloitte Consulting (8); Morgan Stanley (7); Lehman Brothers (6); McKinsey & Company (6); General Mills (4); Merrill Lynch (4); Toyota (4); BEA Systems (3); Deutsche Bank (3); DiamondCluster (3); Guidant (3).

OUTSTANDING FACULTY

Bill Cockrum (finance and entrepreneurship); Eric Sussman (accounting); Al Osborne (entrepreneurship); Bart Bronnenberg (marketing).

APPLICANT TIPS

Getting into Anderson is not impossible, but it's not easy. For the class of 2004, nearly 4700 prospective students applied for 330 seats. The admissions process is much like that at other top schools. There is no set formula, but students who stand out with high test scores, undergrad GPA, and experience are going to get first consideration. However, if your GMAT score doesn't fit into the range of those accepted at Anderson, don't count yourself out: though the low end of the average is 630, students with scores as low as a 490 have been admitted. Of course, you will have to have a lot of things going for you.

Interviews are not required at Anderson, but the majority of students do visit and interview. Also, if a part of your application is weak, Albright Smith says that the interview is a good opportunity to explain yourself. However, don't expect the usual question-and-answer interview. "Our interviews tend to be more of a dialogue than anything else," Albright Smith says. "We want to see that a student has made a commitment to self-development and is going to be very proactive for the school." Also, if you have an interesting background, or something that sets you apart from the typical applicant, play it up—it can only help.

ANDERSON MBAs SOUND OFF

Overall, it was a great experience. With only a couple of minor exceptions, I was very impressed with the professors. However, a better job could have been done to integrate the coursework. Also, the classes in entrepreneurship were great, but it would have been nice if the department facilitated networking with other schools on campus or professionals in the community. I also would have valued additional informal (one-on-one) interaction with local mentor-type professionals along with the very valuable speaking engagements.

Anderson has been a great experience: great classmates, classes, and a great city! Coming to Anderson has been the best professional decision I have made. There have been more opportunities to get involved and network with the business community than I had imagined prior to getting here. The diversity of students (both in terms of professional backgrounds and geographical background) is a boon to this school. These attributes have lent themselves to providing richness in classroom discussions.

Anderson has got the perfect mix between hard work and hard play. Anderson is for well-rounded individuals intent on making a difference in the business world—these are the skills that allow you to rise to CEO. Don't come to Anderson if you plan on a career in middle management.

I ended up choosing between three very good MBA programs and chose the Anderson School for its entrepreneurial track. I don't regret my decision to come here for one second and would highly recommend it to all interested students. Dean Willison is starting to make some great changes and he really cares what the students and faculty think. The student body is diverse, impressive and very collaborative and fraternal. The faculty is world-class, approachable, and incredibly helpful. At the Anderson School, students have every opportunity to make their experience great—which is what I did.

The flexibility of the curriculum at The Anderson School at UCLA is an extremely attractive aspect of this institution. As a liberal arts concentrator during my undergrad-

uate days, I gained a solid understanding of valuable business skills that will help me tremendously as I progress through my career. At Anderson, I have made lasting friendships with people of many different backgrounds, have become well-versed in the areas of accounting, finance, and marketing (to name just few), and I have become much more aware of how I can contribute to society. All in all, my decision to attend graduate business school—and Anderson specifically—is one of the best decisions I have ever made.

Anderson is an exciting and dynamic program. There are many great teachers and students. The weather is gorgeous and the social activities cannot be beat. Some of the improvements at Anderson could occur in alumni participation for the job search and an improved information technology program.

I feel as if Anderson is a well-kept secret. The school offers a terrific and relevant education with a low quotient of egos.

The Anderson experience has been one of the most enriching of my life. Not only have I created lifelong relationships and enhanced my business knowledge, but I have been able to pursue my dream. I have created a start-up, which would not have been possible without the full support of the school.

17.
UNIVERSITY OF SOUTHERN CALIFORNIA

UNIVERSITY OF SOUTHERN CALIFORNIA

Marshall School of Business
USC Marshall MBA Program
611 Exposition Blvd, JKP 200
Los Angeles, California 90089-2631
E-mail address: marshallmba@marshall.usc.edu
Web site address: www.marshall.usc.edu

Enrollment: 581	Annual tuition and fees: $31,680
Women: 32%	Estimated annual budget: $47,267
Non-U.S.: 26%	Average GMAT score: 684
Minority: 10%	Average months of work experience: 55
Part-time: 819	Accepted applicants enrolled: 51%
Average age: 28	Corporate ranking: 14
Applicants accepted: 21%	Graduate ranking: 16
Median starting pay: $79,000	Intellectual capital rank: 33

Teaching methods: case study 30%, distance learning 1% experiential learning 2%, lecture 45%, simulations 3%, team projects 15%, other 4%

Much like the man and the company the school is named for, the University of Southern California's Marshall School of Business has built itself up from small and seemingly inconsequential to a top-rate competitor. No longer is it in the shadows of its crosstown rival, UCLA's Anderson School. Today, Marshall has shed its safety school persona and rivals some of the best schools in the business. Even its hub, the three-year-old, $25 million Popovich Hall, reflects its newly found success, with the school's Web site touting it as the "the most technologically advanced business school building in the United States."

Much of the school's success can be attributed to Dean Randolph W. Westerfield, a former chair of Wharton's finance department. Westerfield will step down in 2003 after having completed two five-year terms. He isn't leaving the school, just planning a transition back from administrator to faculty member. A new dean has yet to be named.

Under Westerfield's tutelage, Marshall built up its reputation as a management education leader for the Pacific Rim and beyond. Much of this reputation came from a requirement that every student have an overseas experience while enrolled at Marshall. This requirement holds true for students no matter which of the school's four MBA programs they are enrolled in: full-time (PRIME); part-time MBA (PM.GLOBE); executive MBA (ExPORT); and, for multinational MBA students, the International Business Education and Research (IBEAR) Program.

The PRIME program, whose initials stand for Pacific Rim Education, was launched in 1997 and has been growing ever since. Students travel to China, Japan, Singapore, and Thailand. Today, PRIME is probably due for a name change, because students are also going to Mexico, Chile, and Cuba as part of the program. Marshall was the first B-school to set up such a program in Cuba. In 2001, Cuba's foreign investment ministry recognized Dean Westerfield and 50 Marshall students as the first official U.S. business school delegation to be invited to Havana to study Cuba's business practices.

Of the top 30 schools, Marshall is the only one to require students to complete an overseas study trip in order to graduate. A five-week classroom module (Business Practices in the Pacific Rim) followed by 10 days overseas is built into students' first-year core scheduling. Students don't seem to be complaining about the added expense or requirement; if anything, they can't get enough of the experience. A number of second-year students have recently chosen research trips abroad as part of their elective curriculum and have received Vice Dean of Graduate Programs Dennis Draper's okay for the trips. "We think it's critically important that students create the culture here, and we enable them to do that," says Draper. Many graduates consider PRIME the most memorable aspect of their time as students at Marshall. "My international trip to Santiago, Chile, was the highlight of my MBA career and opened my eyes to a whole new area of business . . . definitely an experience that could not have been comparable in a classroom," says a 2002 graduate.

In addition to PRIME and second-year elective opportunities, you will have plenty of other opportunities to go global while at Marshall. The school has exchange agreements with 24 schools around the world, and you can choose to spend a full semester at any one of them as part of the MBA International Exchange Program. If you're looking to commit to something longer-term than PRIME but not a full semester, you can always spend your summer abroad. Three- to four-week sessions are available during the summer months in Brazil, France, Germany, and Austria.

First, though, you will have to get through the school's rigorous two semesters of required core courses. Marshall takes a different approach to the first year than many of its competitors; the opportunity for electives is nonexistent. But times are changing, and the school wants to allow students some flexibility in their first year, says Vice Dean Draper. Starting with the fall of 2003, you can expect to see room for at least a few electives your first year. The school's required courses are divided up over two semesters, each consisting of two terms. The first term takes in Accounting Concepts and Financial Reporting, Communication for Management, Contemporary Issues in Competitive Strategy, and Managerial Economics. The second term covers Applied Managerial Statistics, Corporate Finance, and Issues in Electronic Commerce. The third term includes Current Trends in Business, Management Accounting, Marketing Management, and Operations Management. The fourth and final term looks at Behavior and Organizations, Contemporary Issues in Global Economic Strategy, The Firm in the National Economy, and the beloved PRIME. It is rare for students to waive out of core courses, says Draper. But when they do, they aren't off the hook. A course like Accounting Concepts and Financial Reporting could seem remedial for a CPA; a school-sanctioned alternative might be replacing it with an advanced finance or accounting course.

Second-year students are encouraged but not required to pick a concentration. With more than 20 to choose from, it shouldn't be too hard to find one to your liking. Electives can be structured around these concentrations, which range from information systems to the geographically apropos and tremendously popular business of entertainment. "If you're looking to stay in Southern California or hoping for a career in marketing or entertainment or to start your own company, Marshall is the place for you," gushes a 2002 graduate. Class sizes for electives are kept small, averaging only 30 students. Still, many students choose to venture outside the B-school for electives their second year.

If you're interested in an investment management career, then you might want to check out the school's Center for Investment Studies (CIS). In 2002, the center opened a state-of-the-art Capital Markets Training Room with both historical and real-time data on trading and security analyses. Students have access to a Bloomberg terminal, Barra (Portfolio Optimization and Performance Attribution), and FactSet analytics. Getting into the CIS seminars is competitive; second-years vie for 1 of only 12 student manager spots. In addition to an application, there are two rounds of interviews. If you make it in, you will be part of a team responsible for managing $1.5 million in endowment funds and generating returns as part of the Student Investment Fund (SIF). You'll produce and present an annual report. Too bad you don't get to keep your winnings to help pay off the hefty $31,680 you'll be paying in tuition each year. On the flip side, you don't have to pay up on your losses, either.

In addition to an MBA, Marshall also offers students a master's in medical management, business taxation, or accounting. Dual degrees from outside the B-school are also plentiful; students have a dozen from which to choose. If all of these PRIME experiences get you motivated for a Pacific Rim–focused career, you might want to consider the dual MBA/MA in East Asian Studies. There's also a full-time, 12-month International Business Education and Research program (IBEAR) specifically designed for experienced midlevel managers. A select group of 48 students are given the opportunity to participate in an intensive, hands-on international management.

Not that you will be limited to international studies while at USC. Everything from the requisite JD to the more unusual MD or nursing or engineering degree is available, and many students find themselves making radical career changes. "The USC program gave me the tools to convert from biochemical engineer to private equity associate," says one satisfied 2002 grad. "I

have the tools and experience to move forward with no ceiling. What more could I ask for?"

Teamwork is paramount at USC, and you will see the drive toward it immediately when you arrive on campus and participate in a two-day team-building exercise. Throughout your first year, you will be teamed with four to six classmates each term. All students participate in a number of team-based case competitions throughout the first year. "There is no replacement for the group interactions in an MBA program. The mixing of six individuals with diverse backgrounds to attack a business problem is where the value is added," says a 2002 graduate. Even PRIME sends you in teams of six or seven to your overseas destination.

Competition exists at Marshall, but not to the extent it does at some other schools, says Vice Dean Draper. "At Marshall, there isn't this notion that to get ahead I have to destroy you. We like the idea of fierce competition in a cooperative manner." The students seem to agree. "My peers were so helpful in sharing information and encouraging each other. The environment did not feel at all competitive but rather very supportive and one in which it seemed that everyone could experience success," says a satisfied 2002 graduate.

Beautiful campus, awful location. It is a description you will hear time and time again about USC. Despite the amazing weather, you won't see many students walking off campus, as the surrounding neighborhood can get a little rough after dark. Still, administrators insist that the surrounding area is getting better, and claim they'd walk around outside the campus gates. But of course this is Los Angeles, the city of cars. A 20-minute drive (not during rush hour, which in L.A. can be most of the day), and you're at the beach. A two-hour drive south, and you're in San Diego, then over the border and into Mexico. Students are known for spending time at USC's crosstown rival, UCLA, which offers easy access to first-rate art and sporting events.

Marshall students fan out around the city for housing, and many choose the beach communities of Santa Monica, Venice, Redondo, or Brentwood (near UCLA). A small but growing number are choosing to stay close to campus to beat the commute and the high rents in the trendier areas.

PLACEMENT DETAILS

One area that Marshall often gets criticized for is a dearth of on-campus recruiters. But this so-called problem has helped the school weather the bad economy, says Tom Kozicki, the executive director of the MBA Career Resource Center (CRC). Long before the economy went sour, Marshall began building students' job searches into the academic program. "We're ahead of the curve by a few years," says Kozicki. On day one of orientation, students start by accessing the Career Leader assessment tool. This is followed throughout the year by workshops on resumes, cover letters, strategic marketing plans for students' careers, and everything up to inking the deal with a firm.

Of the center's 16 employees, 15 are dedicated solely to MBA students. Until recently, the CRC had designated one person in the office as the international careers contact for students. But Kozicki saw a problem with that, as the majority of Marshall's international students want to stay in the United States. Now, they are free to see any counselor they want. All first-years are assigned a particular person for the duration of their core courses; during the second year, they are also free to choose the person who best matches their concentration.

One of Kozicki's goals has been to increase the number of international firms that recruit on campus. Not an easy task for any school, let alone one far from the plethora of top schools on the East Coast. Rather than wait for something that might never happen, Kozicki says he has taken a more proactive approach. As part of PRIME, Kozicki now sends a member of his staff along as a staff liaison with the students on their overseas trips. That person then visits compa-

nies in the area (currently, the Pacific Rim, Chile, and Cuba) and provides them with student information and resumes.

USC has a number of offices in strategic locations around Asia and will soon be opening one in Latin America. The CRC has also taken advantage of these by linking B-school students with alumni in those areas. "USC has always had a very strong reputation for alumni. We've always partnered with alumni in assisting people in the Trojan family," says Kozicki. Currently, alumni number some 50,000 in 44 countries. In addition to helping on the international front, Marshall alumni are willing participants in mock interviews with the students and regularly forward any job openings they hear about to the school.

No matter how much the Career Resource Center's staff bends over backward for Marshall students, "the ultimate customer" is still the employer, says Kozicki. "We do everything we can to make it easiest for them. Where some schools say, 'It's our way or no way,' we prefer to say, 'Well, how do you want it?'" The Career Resource Center does this through a variety of methods, the most recent addition being a module that allows employers to manage their activities on the Web without needing to go through the office. Employers can now see a list of interested students, modify their schedules, send invitations, and add and update job postings.

For a number of years, the CRC has been offering an on-campus distinguished speakers series. Each year it tries to outdo itself with impressive guests. Recent speakers have included Jack Welch of GE, Michael Eskew of UPS, Ronald Dollens of Guidant, and Carl Yankowski of Palm. Off campus, students have gotten to mingle with such CEO luminaries as Gerald Levin of AOL Time Warner, Michael Dell of Dell Computers, and James Copeland of Deloitte & Touche through the school's Town Hall Los Angeles lecture series.

Kozicki says it's important that as a prospective student, you think about what it is you might want to do after you graduate from B-school before that first day of classes—even before you apply. He highly recommends taking the time now to go on as many informational interviews as you can in the career areas that interest you. "Clarify your career goals. Get out there and talk to people who are doing it," he suggests.

TOP HIRES

Mattel (9); Wells Fargo (6); Agilent Technologies (4); Lehman Brothers (4); Merrill Lynch (3); Bank of America (3); Bear Stearns (3); Deloitte Consulting (3); Toyota (3); Barclays (3); Honeywell (3).

OUTSTANDING FACULTY

Nandini Rajagopalan (management); Harry DeAngelo (finance); Carl Voigt (strategy); Mark DeFond (accounting); Linda DeAngelo (finance); Delores Conway (operations).

APPLICANT TIPS

It comes as no surprise that as the average GMAT score has continued to rise at Marshall, the percentage of admitted students has decreased. In 2000, 27 percent of applicants were admitted. Today, it's a competitive 21.

Keith Vaughn, Marshall's director of admissions, says that before applying, you should ask yourself a straightforward question: "Why an MBA?" Also ask yourself how you can add value to the team environment at Marshall. Once you have done that and you feel good about your answers, it's time to apply, says Vaughn.

Like its competitors, Marshall is also looking for applicants with leadership potential, says Vaughn. You want to include any experiences that show your ability to be successful in the future and that you are management material. Your ability to be a team player is also analyzed carefully in the application review process. Ask yourself the following question, says Vaughn: "Where can you add value in a team environment?"

Every Marshall application is viewed by at least two individuals, and the admissions committee reviews all applications. Interviews are by invitation only. If you are asked for one, assume it's a good sign, as 99 percent of accepted applicants get interviewed. Remember that it's a chance for you to ask questions, too, says Vaughn. "Applicants should look at the interview as a two-way street." A tip for out-of-state and overseas applicants: during the months of September through April, Marshall's admissions department staff are often on the road and are willing to conduct off-site interviews. In these cases, it is okay to request an interview, and it will save you a trip to Los Angeles if it isn't on your radar screen over the coming months. But call early as schedules fill up quickly.

Almost all applicants choose to apply online. While applying online is not a requirement yet, Vaughn does recommend it. "It's the preferred method, because it keeps everything in one area," he says. Applicants have four rounds in which to apply: early December, mid-January, mid-February, and early April. Vaughn recommends getting your application in by round three because not many positions remain by round four. Scholarship and fellowship applicants should get their applications submitted in round one. International applicants are encouraged to apply by round two.

The average Marshall student has five years of work experience. While the admissions committee is willing to consider applicants with little time on the job, Vaughn says these candidates are definitely the exception. "Anyone with less than two years work experience should really think about whether now's the right time for business school," he says.

Attention to detail is an important part of the application, says Vaughn. "You need to do a little more than spell-check," he says. "I encourage applicants to always follow the directions. Don't assume that every school asks the same questions. Make sure you're answering the questions asked."

Female applicants, take note: Marshall wants you. The entering class of 2002 was 34 percent female, and Vaughn and his staff would like to see that number rise with future classes.

MARSHALL MBAs SOUND OFF

My experience at Marshall has been outstanding. I learned a lot about myself, met some great friends, and established a great network. Marshall isn't perfect, and there is definitely room for improvement, but all things that are being done are steps in the right direction. The administration has really listened to student concerns and made dramatic efforts to address them. I would definitely recommend Marshall to anyone.

The international experience was exceptional. I had subsidized language courses (Spanish). The PRIME program at USC requires all students to study a country and company within the Pacific Rim (now has expanded to Cuba) and then visit that company along with several other companies which other students have done projects with. I was also able to study abroad in Barcelona. While this option is available from most (all) top schools I noticed some important differences. At USC this was not just a vacation.

In general, the students at Marshall were incredibly selfless and friendly. My classmates were noncompetitive and helpful when it came to academics and the job search. Marshall alumni I've communicated with on the telephone, via e-mail or in person have given me the time, generosity and insight I would expect from a close friend.

I found USC to be a top-notch program. The administration was proactive in addressing student concerns; the caliber of my classmates exceeded my expectations; and the first-rate faculty displayed a rare combination of excellence in the academic arena and enthusiasm in the classroom. And the weather's not too bad either.

I am grateful to have attended Marshall. I was able to receive a top-tier education, travel the globe with my classmates through the PRIME program, and build a lasting network. I was also able to secure the jobs that I wanted, both for my summer internship and full-time position. The uniqueness of the program lies in the underlying momentum in the school. There is a great sense of pride and a cooperative attitude by the administration and students. Teamwork is essential. We all try to help each other.

The abilities and knowledge of the professors were beyond anything I had experienced previously in my academic career. I leave this school with a confidence in my own abilities to manage that I would have never expected. In addition, the closeness of the community here and the selflessness of the people here blew me away.

Faculty at USC really do make an effort to interact offline as well as in class and are always open to helping students pursue their goals. In fact one faculty member highly encourages interaction and has aided many students in finding jobs.

I am very satisfied with my experience at USC. I met some of the smartest fellow students that I could ever have hoped to meet. I met professors with great reputations in their field who went out of their way to bring relevant current events and discussions into the classroom when appropriate. I developed contacts with alumni who were more helpful than I ever could have expected in my search for an internship and full-time job.

18. UNIVERSITY OF NORTH CAROLINA AT CHAPEL HILL

UNIVERSITY OF NORTH CAROLINA AT CHAPEL HILL

Kenan-Flagler Business School
CB 3490, McColl Building
University of North Carolina at Chapel Hill
Chapel Hill, North Carolina 27599-3490
E-mail address: mba_info@unc.edu
Web site address: www.kenan-flagler.unc.edu

Enrollment: 554
Women: 30%
Non-U.S.: 30%
Minority: 11%
Part-time: 0
Average age: 28
Applicants accepted: 30%
Median starting pay: $81,763
Annual tuition and fees:
   resident—$14,975
   nonresident—$28,930

Estimated annual budget: $45,982
Average GMAT score: 676
Average months of work
   experience: 62
Accepted applicants enrolled: 46%
Corporate ranking: 15
Graduate ranking: 18
Intellectual capital rank: 27

Teaching methods: case study 40%, lecture 30%, simulations 10%, team projects 20%

When the University of North Carolina's Kenan-Flagler Business School revamped its curriculum in 2000, faculty and administrators took the opportunity to ask themselves the question on every B-school leader's mind these days: what does the school embody? The answer: five core values—excellence, leadership, integrity, community, and teamwork. Excellence is the capstone of everything the B-school strives for, Dean Robert S. Sullivan proudly notes. "The bar has been raised for us and it's something we're always working on," he adds. That's not all talk. The school took these core values to heart and celebrated community with a schoolwide service day in 2000–2001. Then, in 2002, Kenan-Flagler showed it was on top of its game—and not just in basketball—when students chose integrity as their core value of focus and participated in events like Integrity Week. Noted ethics author Rushworth M. Kidder spoke to the school during its 11-day celebration of integrity, highlighting honesty, fairness, responsibility, respect, compassion, and courage as integral universal ethical values.

Kenan-Flagler's strong character is a quality administrators are prompt to note. Ask newly appointed Associate Dean of the MBA program Robert Adler, and he'll quickly say the school holds a set of long-lasting ideals—community, integrity, and dedication—that go beyond just making a buck. Adler points out that the school's financial success isn't the be-all and end-all; instead, he says, the focus is on instilling the general life skills, such as strong leadership, that can be applied to just about anything. It's only one example of the type of atmosphere you'll find at this B-school, where students rave about the sense of community. 2002 grad Chris Widmayer describes the atmosphere as supportive, friendly, and family-like. "It's competitive to the point where people push you to work, but not the point where people don't help you," Widmayer notes. And Kenan-Flagler MBAs don't hold back when it comes to giving back to the community either. Over a third of students are involved in some sort of community service, whether through their community service day, working on houses for Habitat for Humanity, or raising money for the Children's Hospital by participating in a 5K run. Faculty and staff roll up their sleeves too; you'll even find them painting walls right along side the students. "I'm out there with the students and staff," Dean Sullivan adds. "You have to lead by example."

MBAs consistently recognize Kenan-Flagler's faculty and administration as top-notch. Former MBA program Associate Dean Jim Dean attributes some of this to the medium-sized aspect of the school. "The relationship between faculty and students is unique at Kenan-Flagler," he notes. "It's one of our highest-rated items when we speak with students." Albert Segars, a professor of information technology and e-commerce, agrees. He says he makes himself as accessible to students as possible and always tries to get to know students on an individual basis. Even years after graduation, Segars has students calling him for help on the job. According to Jim Dean, it's all about hiring the right people. "If you hire the right kind of people, they will understand that the effort goes beyond just their specific areas," Dean says. And at Kenan-Flagler the right kind of person has strong leadership skills. "We have one of the strongest leadership teams. They're strong, self-confident leaders that have transformed the

quality of the staff we have," Dean notes. And that isn't just tooting their own horn: Kenan-Flagler developed a scorecard as a method of measuring how the school's efforts have influenced overall performance.

Yet another example of this close community is the stellar alumni network. The unrelenting help of alumni and the career services office's hard work led to 100 percent of the first-years landing summer internships in 2002. Dean adds that in the last few years Kenan-Flagler has also made efforts to develop strong corporate bonds, making them a more integral part of school's community. Kenan-Flagler has not always done the best job of managing corporate partnerships and relationships with various firms across all programs, Dean says. But it's something they're working on. "It's important to speak with one voice with our corporate sponsors," he adds. These efforts kicked in for the 2003 crop, if not the class of 2002. All first-year MBAs secured summer internships, but only 68 percent of the 2002 class had jobs by graduation.

The school seems to have found a system with which it is comfortable. Adler says his task now is to take what's been handed to him and make certain that things are implemented properly—that is, of course, with a few tweaks here and there. Any school that isn't constantly fixing its curriculum will fall behind, he warns. That's why this detail-oriented associate dean says he's going to be paying close attention to the program's progress to fix the necessary kinks. Adds Dean Sullivan: "A notion of chance and continuous improvement is very important to us, and as we look to the future we will not rest on our laurels."

Teamwork plays an integral role at Kenan-Flagler. From day one you'll be immersed in teamwork. On the first day of orientation, you'll meet your study group of four to five students and get a head start on learning about the classmates with whom you'll be pulling all-nighters. You'll be assigned to your "nonnegotiable" study group and participate in management skills workshops and team-building exercises. You'll stick with this group throughout the first year's core courses in accounting, finance, strategy, operations, marketing, quantitative methods, international business, management skills, and ethics. There's no switching groups for any reason, despite personality conflicts, closely paralleling the real business world post B-school. The weeklong activities also entail a business statistics course the following week. There is also a Community Leadership Day where first-years, faculty, and staff form teams and visit sites within the community. In 2001–2002, teams went to the Ronald McDonald House, the Orange County Senior Center, and the YMCA, to name a few. If you need to brush up on your number-crunching skills, there is an optional three-week summer prep program, usually attended by more than half of the incoming class, with courses available in accounting, microeconomics, and statistics. There is also a separate international student orientation to help international students get better acclimated to the American academic scene. There are information sessions on things from the grading system to the university policies that will affect these students.

In 2000, Kenan-Flagler rolled out a new core curriculum based on a business process model covering four main themes—analyzing capabilities and resources, monitoring the marketplace and external environment, formulating strategy, and implementing strategy and assessing firm performance. The core was reorganized to achieve better integration among the courses, says Dean. He adds that recruiters were consistently enthusiastic about students learning how to integrate skills from cross-subject areas. The first-year program consists of 17 courses divided among four modules, or "mods," corresponding to the four previously mentioned themes. Each mod ends with an integrative exercise: in mod 1 you'll evaluate a company; in mods 2 and 3 you'll complete business plan exercises; and in mod 4

you'll experience a comprehensive business simulation. In 2002–2003, for example, at the end of mod 1 students worked on an analysis of a hospital to decide if it should remain not-for-profit or become a for-profit organization. All the while students are working within small teams. Though the curriculum is now more challenging and at times frustrates students, Dean notes the changes have received overall positive feedback and students are realizing that this format is in their best interest—especially since it is so closely tied to recruiters' interests. An added bonus with this format is the allowance for greater flexibility. There's an additional elective opportunity, for a total of two in the first year—a big plus when homing in on specific skills to help you land a summer internship. Along with the revamp came the addition of over 100 electives and the creation of one corporate advisory board for each concentration. Industry experts in specific areas such as consulting or corporate finance serve as board members and advise faculty on ways to modify the curriculum to more accurately reflect changes or movements in their fields. The board members can also be important resources for students eager to find related jobs.

Besides an innovative core, Kenan-Flagler offers seven career concentrations and three enrichment concentrations. You can even go so far as to design your own general management curriculum from the wide selection of electives. The career concentrations include corporate finance, customer and product management, investment management, global supply chain management, management consulting, real estate, entrepreneurship, venture development, sustainable enterprise, international business, and electronic business and digital commerce. Each is tied to a corporate advisory board, which keeps the B-school up to speed with what MBAs need to succeed in the job market. Since choosing a concentration isn't mandatory, it's up to you to take advantage and create yourself a customized path.

As if small groups and group exercises weren't enough to stir up your team spirit, students are also required to take a Leading and Managing course taught in two parts, at the beginning and at the end of the first year, to assess their progress on their self-development plans. Before starting the school year, you'll be required to have your bosses, peers, and subordinates at your former jobs fill out a 360° personal evaluation to help determine areas you can improve on to become a better leader. You will then create a personal leadership development plan to continuously work on throughout the year. Kenan-Flagler believes that effective leaders and successful managers develop from the inside out, making self-management a prerequisite for leading and managing others effectively. In the first module of the course, you'll focus most on self-management skills. At the end of the year, in your fourth module, you'll work on how effective leaders create a vision, empower others, expand influence, and engineer organizational change. The course also emphasizes hiring and developing people—two processes that are important but have not received enough attention in past leadership courses.

You can also couple your MBA with a joint degree from the university at large. UNC offers degrees in public health, information sciences, law, and regional planning. If you want to venture outside of the curriculum, you can gain specialized business experience through an independent study or a practicum project. Recent team-based, faculty-led practicum projects for national and international companies have included developing a commercialization strategy for a steel company, designing a capital structure and dividend policy for a pharmaceutical firm, and creating a marketing strategy for a symphony orchestra.

In recent years, the B-school has focused on developing a greater diverse scope. Jim Dean, who's been at the school for five years, says the school has more of an international feeling these days. One noticeable change, he adds, is the incorporation of a strong faculty with an international background, along with an increase in international students and the countries from where they come. In 2002–2003, professors from countries including Italy, Turkey, and Ireland came aboard, and the number of international students went up to 32 percent. In 2002, the executive MBA program rolled out One MBA, a unique joint MBA venture between Kenan-Flagler, Monterrey Tech in Mexico, Getulio Vargas in Brazil, Rotterdam in The Netherlands, and the Chinese University of Hong Kong, allowing students to achieve one degree from all five top institutions. The concentration in international business focuses on cross-border management and regional studies through a combination of courses in international business management, experiential learning activities, language, and cross-cultural studies. Within the concentration, you are required to take a minimum of six credit hours in international business, area studies, or language courses. Classes include Global Context of Business, International Competitive Strategy, and International Business Analysis. Also, you have the opportunity to obtain a graduate certificate focused on one of seven areas: cultural studies, international development and social change, Latin American studies, Russian/Eastern European studies, or international and area studies. Or, you can complete an international practicum, tackle an international summer internship, or take part in the international student exchange program. The Office of International Programs has contacts at over 40 business schools worldwide and sometimes offers internships as part of an exchange. Need a refresher course in a language before you take off? Classes in Spanish, French, and German are available to brush up on your foreign language skills, or you can take advantage of the 22 languages offered by the university at large. Kenan-Flagler has also placed great efforts into cultivating the female community on campus. In the fall of 2002, the B-school hosted two major events featuring women in business: the national conference of Graduate Women in Business and Springboard, a venture forum for women.

Kenan-Flagler has also witnessed a growing interest in nonprofits and social corporate responsibility. One area turning heads lately is the Center for Sustainable Enterprise, which offers education programs, research, and outreach to help companies and nonprofit organizations grow and profit in nontraditional and emerging markets with economically, environmentally, and socially sustainable strategies. The sustainable enterprise concentration will equip you with the skills and tools to create a competitive advantage for firms and nonprofits via strategic approaches to matters such as stakeholder issues, value creation in untapped markets, and entrepreneurial solutions for urban renewal. You can also join Net Impact and the Nonprofit Club, which have witnessed a recent rise in membership, or check out the Carolina/Kauffman Social Entrepreneur Internship Program launched in 1998 to provide students with an experience-based learning opportunity in new and emerging social enterprises. Students are matched up with companies based on shared interests, and the B-school subsidizes summer stipends up to $2000. Another outlet, the MBA Enterprise Corps, is a nonprofit volunteer organization modeled after the Peace Corps providing technical and managerial assistance to private enterprises in emerging and transforming markets. The program sends MBAs from Kenan-Flagler and other top B-schools on one- to two-year assignments assisting newly privatized businesses and start-ups in the emerging markets of Eastern Europe, Asia, and Africa. Possible locales for 2002–2003 include Thailand, Croatia, and Kyrgyztan.

Similar to other schools, this B-school's entrepreneurship program has also turned heads as of late. The Center for Entrepreneurship and Technology Venturing is a resource sector students are tapping into. Many of the 20 courses you'll take are taught by practicing entrepreneurs, venture capitalists, and venture lawyers, and you can concentrate in entrepreneurship and venture development. The B-school encourages students to take advantage of the practicum program, in which teams of three to five students work on a consulting project for a business or nonprofit. Some companies that have hosted practicum teams in the past include Ericsson, Micell Technologies, and LIPSinc. Or, check out one of the B-school's clubs, such as the MBA Entrepreneurship Club or the MBA Venture Capital Club. Another outlet for students is the Venture Capital Investment Competition, founded in 1998, which attracts MBAs from top schools around the country. Teams play the role of venture capital firms and decide among various investment opportunities, re-viewing business plans, listening to company presentations, engaging in question-and-answer sessions with company management teams, and preparing term sheets for investments that are presented to a panel of judges—real venture capitalists. Even the entrepreneurship program has a civic-minded dynamic. The Urban Enterprise Corps, which took off in 1998, takes recently graduated MBA grads from Kenan-Flagler and other top B-schools to work in inner cities in North Carolina to help create seed capital and businesses run largely by minorities and women. Through the Kenan Institute, the Durham Scholars Program organizes Kenan-Flagler MBAs to tutor inner-city Durham students in grades six through nine.

The Real Estate program is also booming. If you choose this track, you'll take courses in the B-school, planning school, and law school. The program culminates in an intensive, hands-on project in which you'll have the opportunity to produce a presentation for potential investors. 2002 grad Chris Widmayer, who works for Regency Centers, says he's pleased with his experience. What makes this program unique, he adds, is the development component. He notes that although other B-schools have strong real estate programs, Kenan-Flagler was the one he felt focused on the development aspect, which sparked his interest. In February 2002, Kenan-Flagler launched the Center for Real Estate Development to focus on education, research, and outreach initiatives. Already, the Center has raised more than $3.5 million to endow two professorships and an MBA fellowship. The Center is unique in its focus on real estate from the broad context of development, reflecting the growing importance of a developer's ability to manage financial, legal, and design issues, as well as the public approval process and community concerns for smart growth and sustainability. In 2002, the Center for Real Estate Development also had a hand in the redesign of the MBA real estate concentration. The Center also partnered with the Real Estate Department at Cambridge University in England, with Center faculty developing and teaching courses in real estate development for Cambridge's master's program. In the spring of 2002, Cambridge faculty and students visited Kenan-Flagler to participate in the final presentations of students in Kenan-Flagler's real estate development course. The B-school's MBAs plan to travel to England for site visits and meetings in London and Cambridge.

Most students, says Dean Sullivan, become "intoxicated" with the B-school thanks in part to its picturesque location in Chapel Hill. With great weather year round, a beautiful campus, and a tight-knit community, it's not hard to see why. One 2002 grad, Ty Stober, describes a charm that surrounds the school with the historic brick buildings on campus. The B-school's facilities, which are now separate from the main Chapel Hill campus, were built to match the same historic flavor. "The brick buildings, stone walkways, and gorgeous trees, make for a very welcoming campus," says Debbie Clarke, director of the MBA program. "The town-gown feeling is endearing. People who live here are passionate about this place, and they really do fall in love with it." The McColl building, which is home to the MBA program, houses 19 classrooms, 2800 Internet connections, a large auditorium, study rooms, and a dining hall—all with the most up-to-date video-conferencing and multimedia presentation capabilities. The Paul J. Rizzo Center at Meadowmont, a cyber-community for executive education, corporate board meetings, and retreat planning, opened in 2000. The Rizzo Center's McLean Hall residence building boasts 56 guest rooms, six study rooms, and two multipurpose seminar rooms. Loudermilk Hall, the brain center of the conference facility, is equipped with high-speed Internet access and advanced instructional technologies among its two 65-seat tiered classrooms and 14 breakout rooms. Additionally, the 15,800-square-foot DuBose House, a 1933 Georgian Revival home, was renovated to become a social and dining center. Kenan-Flagler expects to break ground in late 2003 on a new Global Knowledge Center, a 60,000-square-foot addition to the business school complex. The building, designed to accommodate evolving technologies enhancing the study of global business education, will be the hub of MBA student life in the community and will house various global programs, a digital library, and expanded investment trading room and behavioral labs. The school is also completely wireless, so students and faculty have network access anytime, anywhere, without being tied to cables and network ports.

The B-school's geographic location has also come into play. The past e-business emphasis brought greater attention to the school because of its proximity to the highly regarded Research Triangle Park, well known as one of the world's top high-tech hubs. With UNC, North Carolina State, and Duke University making up the three points of the triangle, the zone is an effective spot for generating high-tech business ideas and obtaining funding and sources to back them. The Triangle encompasses more than 130 organizations, including about 20 biotech and biopharmaceutical companies, 22 software companies, and a handful of others, such as Cisco and Nortel. All MBAs take a first-year required core course in information technology; during your second year, you can choose from electives in IT strategy, data mining, intellectual property, global supply chain management, designing an online customer experience, and technology commercialization.

Despite the demands of the curriculum, Kenan-Flagler students find time to participate in one of over 30 clubs, committees, and advisory boards that govern the school; relax and have some fun; and catch a basketball game or two. On the weekends, you're bound to run into these MBAs on Franklin Street, lined with popular bars and restaurants. As a class, students also rent out facilities for special events such as Halloween parties and other theme-based parties. And of course they get together to head to McColl to the "Dean Dome," the UNC basketball arena, to see the top-rated Tar Heels fearlessly take on their opponents. Housing is a bit tight on campus, so check out apartment complexes near the school, such as Poplar Place, Sterling Brook, Autumn Woods, and Alta Springs, where a lot of MBAs tend to live. One of the biggest draws is the pleasant year-round mild climate, making this a great town for families and singles alike.

PLACEMENT DETAILS

In 2002, Kenan-Flagler's career services office added to its menu of workshops and training. Students needed to think in terms beyond just writing a cover letter, says Director Mindy Storrie: it was a matter of learning how to convince a recruiter to create an opportunity for you. "It shifted to having to sell yourself, and helping students market themselves," she adds.

Storrie views herself as having two customers—students and recruiters. Her objective is to make sure students understand they've got to be her partner as well. "I can't do the interview for them; I can't decide for them what's a desirable employer," she adds. "I'll help them, but they've ultimately got to do that." Which is why she stresses the importance of polishing up on research and presentation skills.

The other part of the job is matching students to recruiters. The center had to get creative, Storrie adds, so instead of sending companies a huge resume book, they sent select resumes of students who would really fit the companies' needs. This is something recruiters appreciated, she added, because it made things easier. Recruitment in turn became "more personalized and customer oriented."

Storrie says the center also tried to help students understand that it's a multitiered search. It's important to conduct a search with resources on campus at the same time you're conducting a search of off campus offerings, she adds. There's an alumni database and current students who are willing to help, she adds, plus all the office's resources. It's just a matter of taking these and then reaching out.

A few new workshops available to students in 2002 include how to market yourself through correspondence, such as e-mail, and how to conduct company research. "It's not just about clicking on the Web site," Storrie adds. "Now it's about finding out if the company is stable."

These efforts saw results, with 100 percent placement of 2002 first-year students in internships. But, for the class of 2002, full-time jobs were not as easy to come by—only 68 percent of grads had job offers by graduation and 24 percent of grads were still searching three months after commencement. Those with jobs reported starting pay packages of about $103,800.

TOP HIRES

IBM (8); Progress Energy (7); Johnson & Johnson (6); Goldman Sachs (5); Lehman Brothers (5); Bellsouth (4); Citigroup (4); Deloitte Consulting (4); Kraft Foods (4).

OUTSTANDING FACULTY

Peter Brews (strategy); Neil Morgan (marketing); Robert Bushman (accounting); John

Pringle (finance); Stuart Hart (strategy); Joseph Bylinski (accounting); David Hartzell (finance); Jennifer Conrad (finance).

APPLICANT TIPS

Admissions Director Sherry Wallace is looking for a level of leadership that is "distinctive." For starters, there's a two-year post-undergraduate work experience requirement, and the average student has over five years of experience. On top of that, Wallace says she's looking for indicators that demonstrate your levels of leadership and ability to manage and motivate people. Specifically, she homes in on your track record of results. Letters of recommendation also come into play here, as they can point out specific examples of how you stepped up to the plate. Choose people who are really familiar with your work, advises Wallace. She adds that she really likes to see letters of recommendation that can point to specific projects you worked on that exemplify how you were able to deliver.

Interviews are also key at this B-school. Since the fall of 2002, interviews are being conducted using a hybrid system of sorts. From September to December, interviews run on a "stop in if you're in town" basis. Once January hits, interviews are by invitation only. Director Wallace hopes this system will better help accommodate all applicants.

Don't discount those essays. Wallace says that's where you place your personal stamp on your application package. She adds that it's the one thing you can control most in your application. "This is your place to distinguish yourself and let your humanity shine through," she adds. Your essay is also where you can highlight your unique experiences and qualities that can make up for any deficiencies in your GMAT score or undergraduate GPA. Wallace's favorite aspect about the school is the all-for-one atmosphere. "There's a warmth and an appreciation for the time you spent on Chapel Hill," she

notes. So, she warns, if you're just looking to get the credentials and not make a significant effort to give back to the community, then Kenan-Flagler is probably not the best place for you.

KENAN-FLAGLER MBAs SOUND OFF

Kenan-Flagler was great! They helped me launch a company in my first year, so I went part-time during my second and finished in my third. I couldn't have afforded to go three years at most schools and I enjoyed every minute of it. Also, what a great learning experience. UNC's faculty and administration always bent over backward to listen to students and implement their suggestions. I really feel a part of a strong supportive community here that I do not think I would have found elsewhere.

The administration is very responsive to student needs, the learning atmosphere was very teamwork oriented and the faculty prepared us well for our careers. Also, Chapel Hill is a very nice place to live.

I think Kenan-Flagler is a great environment for learning. The curriculum is rigorous (both analytically and from a sheer workload volume perspective), but is balanced by the emphasis on teamwork and collaboration. I feel like having successfully finished this program has prepared me for just about anything that could get thrown my way, both at work and in personal challenges that arise. I say personal challenges because I think I've really improved my ability to prioritize, delegate, and negotiate. And I don't think all of the learning was done in the classroom. The high caliber of my classmates (for the most part) has really made the two-year commitment/opportunity cost worth it.

As with any program, it is what you make of it. Through my interaction with my professors and classmates, I was able to learn much more than if I had just attended classes and done only the required coursework. The UNC MBA program allows you the access to faculty, staff and classmates to develop the knowledge, networks and work habits to succeed in any business endeavor. Also, you know the commitment of the school and faculty to help you in the future is genuine. The alumni network is strong and always willing to help the students.

I feel very positive about my MBA experience at Kenan-Flagler. The teachers/program/people/location are exceptional and the administration is constantly listening to the students to evolve the program.

Kenan-Flagler offers a program where the students work alongside the administration to make a difference and to accept ownership of the program. The quality of the student body, in their commitment to teamwork, is unparalleled.

19.
CARNEGIE MELLON UNIVERSITY

CARNEGIE MELLON UNIVERSITY

Graduate School of Industrial Administration

5000 Forbes Avenue

GSIA

Pittsburgh, Pennsylvania 15212

E-mail address: mba-admissions@andrew.cmu.edu

Web site address: www.gsia.cmu.edu

Enrollment: 469

Women: 26%

Non-U.S.: 38%

Minority: 14%

Part-time: 284 (on-campus 163, distance 121)

Average age: 28

Applicants accepted: 26%

Median starting pay: $83,400

Annual tuition and fees: $30,700

Estimated annual budget: $46,200

Average GMAT score: 672

Average months of work experience: 66

Accepted applicants enrolled: 54%

Corporate ranking: 18

Graduate ranking: 22

Intellectual capital rank: 15

Teaching methods: case study 20%, distance learning 5%, lecture 50%, simulations 15%, team projects 10%

If anyone should have the math savvy to calculate the chances of two deans in a row with the same last name at a top business school, it would be the students at Carnegie Mellon's Graduate School of Industrial Association. In addition to their superior analytical skills, they have a more personal stake in it; the deans are from their school. In July of 2002, Kenneth B. Dunn took over the top post at the GSIA from Douglas M. Dunn (no relation). The new dean, a former finance and economics professor at the school, left 15 years ago to go into the private business sector and ended up as a managing director for Morgan Stanley. "There are a lot of new buildings, and we have a bigger and better faculty, but the culture is still the same. It's a comfortable and familiar place, and I'm glad to be back," says Dunn.

One area that the new dean is especially excited about is continuing and strengthening the GSIA's relationship with the School of Engineering. Starting in the fall of 2003, the two schools will offer students the opportunity to receive a bachelor's degree in engineering and an MBA in five years through a joint program. Up to 20 students a year will be allowed to enroll in the program. "Something like this can't be created elsewhere. It just doesn't happen at other universities," says Dunn.

While the GSIA is strengthening its ties to the school's more technical departments, it is also trying to shed its computer-geek-only image. Entering students are still required to have completed one semester of calculus and a second math course before enrolling. But even that requirement has been toned down; the school now asks for any advanced math class for the second course (it used to be you could only choose from statistics, calculus II, or linear algebra). Under a retooled curriculum, GSIA students can also take more electives during both years of their studies, and they are encouraged to take classes outside of the B-school. They even have access to a drama course, says Dunn. "We're trying to create as much flexibility as possible."

Still, it's analytical and technical skills that have given the school its reputation, and Dunn is well aware of that. "We believe in teaching management as a science, and we believe in teaching the fundamentals. If students understand the fundamentals, they can use them to solve problems they've never seen before," he says, in explaining the school's philosophy. "Technology is very much integrated into the overall curriculum. We leverage that, and it's what makes us distinctive. Our students hit the ground running, and they are able to have an immediate impact on the organizations they work for. This isn't possible at other universities."

It is that science and tech-based curriculum that still gets high scores with the students. "I found CMU's GSIA program to be an excellent fit for me. I really enjoyed the quantitative aspect of the program and saw the advantages over other schools during my summer internship," says one satisfied 2002 graduate. Students also seem to like being surrounded by other smart people. "In some respects, everyone is the best of the best. You look around at the GSIA and say to yourself, 'If I took everyone in my class to my next company, we would crush the competition,'" says another 2002 graduate. In other, less academic areas, the school does not rate so highly. While international enrollment is among the highest of the top 30, underrepresented minorities have the lowest percentage in the top 30, with only 5 percent making up the current enrollment. Those minorities who do choose to come don't necessarily find the GSIA

the most welcoming place. "The school is NOT the place for minority students," says one 2002 graduate. "The atmosphere is not hostile, but you can sense that a large number of your classmates are not excited about you being there."

The GSIA operates on a semester calendar, but that is somewhat misleading as almost all of the school's classes are seven-week-long minisemesters. One benefit of this short but intense system is that you will have plenty of opportunities to take electives, even during your first year. However, you will be taking your first midterms within three and a half weeks of arriving on campus and your first finals three and a half weeks after that. Students do complain about the amount of work in the core, but they also say that there isn't anything like it for honing their time management skills. They also like the edge it gives them on students from competing schools when it comes time to interview for summer internships.

The administration and faculty at the GSIA know the workload is one of the heaviest around and have instituted a number of measures to ensure that students don't fail out or simply give up. Second-years are teamed up with first-years on a one-on-one basis, explains Michael Kaplan, director of student services. In addition, all students have access to tutoring if they need it. Early on, Student Services sponsors panels (with pizza provided) at which second-years speak about their first-year experiences and tell the junior class members not to worry. For many reasons, students like the smaller size of the student body (currently, there are a total of 486 first- and second-years), but they also say it can have its downside when it comes to the competition. "The small size is what makes the school really good; but at the same time, it makes it hard to get respect in the sea of other schools," says a 2002 graduate.

The GSIA's core covers everything found at a general management B-school, with some extra quantitative analysis thrown in. So, in addition to taking financial accounting, managerial economics, and management communications your first minisemester, you will also take quantitative methods for management science. Following that are the typical finance and human behavior in organizations courses coupled with decision models and an entry into probability and statistics. Minisemester three encompasses marketing management, production/operations management, advanced probability and statistics, and room for at least one elective. By minisemester four, managerial accounting is all you have left in the core. There's room for at least two electives. Plus, the GSIA's capstone course, the Management Game, begins.

In addition to being the first B-school to offer a master's degree in e-commerce, Carnegie Mellon also pioneered the Management Game. The game starts in the fourth minisemester of your first year and continues over the summer and into the first mini-semester of your second year. It is an applied strategic management exercise in which five to seven students become members of a team and operate a computer-simulated company with the goal of marketing wristwatches across six countries. As a member of the team, your job is to act as senior management. Teams compete against each other and against students at B-schools around the world. Everyone is trying to add value to his or her company.

A unique feature of the game is that outside professionals are the primary judges of the teams' performances and act as the board of directors. Past board members have included senior executives from Pittsburgh's own leading corporations, like Alcoa, H. J. Heinz, and PNC Bank. Each team must defend its plans and outcomes to its board at meetings held in the companies' own boardrooms. The board then provides feedback and evaluates performances. Each team is asked to negotiate a labor agreement with real union representatives and present its marketing plans to real-world marketing executives. Teams call on third-year law students at nearby University of Pittsburgh Law

School for legal advice. "The game is very, very rigorous but well worth it. What's great about it is it's one of the closest things you can do without actually starting a company in the actual world," says 2002 graduate Christopher Gross. "The game is nice, because it compresses the time scale of companies in business from years to months."

A recent addition to the game was a simulated real-time stock market in which team members can act as individual and company investors, buying and selling shares of the simulated companies. "It has added some interesting perspectives," says John Mather, executive director of MBA programs. "Would you buy stock in your own company?"

Technically minded students who want more than an MBA have a number of options for dual degrees while studying at the GSIA. Depending on their qualifications, GSIA students can earn MBAs and master's degrees in computational finance, software engineering, civil engineering, or environmental engineering. The GSIA also offers a four-year JD/MBA dual degree in conjunction with neighboring University of Pittsburgh School of Law. Those students interested in the interface between the public and private business sectors might want to consider a collaborative program between the GSIA and Carnegie Mellon's H. John Heinz III School of Public Policy and Management. The program focuses on issues pertaining to regulation/deregulation, corporate-government relations, economic and industrial policymaking, economic revitalization, and urban redevelopment. Students indicate their interest in the collaborative program by mid-March of their first year. Rather than a second degree, the program earns them a minor from the other school.

Most students don't come to the GSIA for its international offerings, but the school has been developing a number of relationships with overseas schools. Students can choose to spend a semester abroad at one of seven exchange partner schools in Europe, Japan, or Mexico. In addition, the GSIA recently added a new offering: students can now apply for 1 of 28 spots in an exchange program that spans the last two minisemesters of the second year. The first seven weeks are spent on campus in a course offered by the Fine Arts department, which covers language, customs, and issues in Europe. For the second half of the program, students head off to Germany, where they become part of the student body at WHU-Koblenz, a leading European business school. In addition to four weeks at the university, students spend three weeks visiting established and emerging markets in Bratislava, Prague, and Berlin. The first year proved immensely popular, with more than 50 students vying for the 28 spots. "Our vision for this is to have two or three school partners in various parts of the globe," says John Mather, executive director of MBA programs.

If you don't decide to head overseas, you will be spending your two years in Pittsburgh. This city, once dubbed "Smoky City" because of its polluted, smokestack-filled steel-town flavor, has reinvented itself over the past few years. It now has several museums, including the ultra-hip Andy Warhol Museum, and numerous options for nightlife. Head to East Carson Street on the south side for R&B and funk. Favorites include Nick's Fat City and Lava Lounge. Sports fans should have no complaints; the Pirates, Steelers, and Penguins all play nearby. Both Carnegie Mellon and the University of Pittsburgh are located in hilly Oakland. Cheap eats catering to the growing student population can be found up and down Forbes Avenue. Also on Forbes is the Beehive Coffee House & Theater, known for live music on the weekends and plenty of caffeine. Dorm life is nonexistent at the GSIA, so students instead find $700 to $800 apartments in the nearby Shadyside and Squirrel Hill neighborhoods.

During the week, you'll find GSIA students hunkering down in Hunt Library, located right next to the B-school. The GSIA's Posner Hall is also a popular spot with a comfy student lounge and lots of room to spread out. The school recently added a number of computerized classrooms to the decade-old building. It's easy for students to move around freely with their required laptops; since 2000, the school has offered students wireless access anywhere on campus. When students need a study break, they tend to gravitate to the university's Student Center for a workout or swim. There's also a food court and several shops housed there. The GSIA borders on the 500-acre Schenley Park, with trails for jogging, a public golf course, a swimming pool, tennis courts, baseball diamonds, and a skating rink. Studying slows down a little at the beginning of the week as students head to a pub of the week for Tuesday Bar Crawl. The GSIA's 26 extracurricular clubs span everything from the Entrepreneurship Club to the *Robber Barrons,* the school's irreverent newspaper. Even with their seemingly unmanageable workloads, students find time to participate in the Monte Carlo Casino Night in the fall, the annual Halloween party, the International Festival in the spring, and an end-of-the-year student talent show.

PLACEMENT DETAILS

The Career Opportunities Center (COC) at the GSIA has always been big on offering workshops to students to help them in their job searches. The only difference now is the flavor of those workshops. Here's a sampling of titles from the past year: My Resume Is Not Getting Results; Optimizing My Internship; Drugs, Money & the Law; and Marketing Yourself Post Summer 2002.

Like everything else at the GSIA, the Career Opportunities Center takes full advantage of the school's technological advances in servicing its students. Students now have online access to the school's alumni database, which can be searched by a number of factors including class year, name, degree, and company name. "It's excellent for job searches," says Ken Keeley, the COC director and a big proponent of networking. "In good times and bad, networking is the name of the game."

Another way the COC takes advantage of the technology is through the use of Web-based on-campus interviews. Companies can now send a list of questions to COC staff, and professional actors and actresses are used to ask the students the questions via Web-based technology. Similarly, the COC conducts live mock interviews using alumni and corporate friends as the interviewers.

Keeley says that follow-up is a key component of the COC. When a number of students weren't able to find internships this summer, Keeley sent out an e-mail asking who among them would be willing to work without pay in the Pittsburgh area. Ten students responded, and Keeley was able to place all of them on projects with big names such as Alcoa, Heinz, and Eden Corporation. "One of them not only got paid, he ended up with a job," says Keeley. "They were pretty darn smart to say yes."

In 2002, about 70 percent of grads had a job offer by graduation, and 81 percent had found work by three months later. Another 9 percent were company sponsored and returned to work for their pre-MBA employer. Grads in 2002 earned starting pay packages of about $108,000.

TOP HIRES

M&T Bank (6); Deutsche Bank (5); IBM (5); Citigroup (4); United Technologies (4); Honeywell (4); Merck (4); Ford Motor Company (3).

OUTSTANDING FACULTY

Robert Dammon (finance); Duane Seppi (finance); Bryan Routledge (finance); Kathryn Shaw (economics) Sridhar Tayur (operations).

APPLICANT TIPS

Despite high numbers in the international student population at the GSIA, the school has made little headway in its recruitment of minorities. While the number of minority applicants is up, the number actually admitted is dismally low. Underrepresented minorities represent a dismal 5 percent of the current class. No one can blame the school for not trying. Every winter, it holds a Minority Challenge Weekend, which provides information about the GSIA to prospective minority students. In 2001, the school joined the Consortium for Graduate Study in Management (CGSM), an alliance of 14 schools with the express goal of recruiting more minority students through relaxed entrance requirements and scholarships. In 2002, nine students entered the GSIA through the CGSM program.

What all accepted GSIA students share is clear and solid reasons for wanting an MBA, says Director of Admissions Laurie Stewart. "They are well-rounded people with strong teamwork experience." While the average student at the GSIA has five years work experience before entering the school, don't assume that the admissions department isn't interested in speaking with you if you're straight out of undergraduate school. "We look at applications on a case-by-case basis," says Director Stewart. "We're seeking candidates of all experience levels." Stewart adds that there is no minimum standard for work experience for acceptance to the school.

It's no secret that the GSIA is interested in your quantitative aptitude, but that doesn't mean that the admissions department is only going to look at your GMAT score. "We have no cutoff for the GMAT or a student's GPA," says Stewart. "We dig quite a bit deeper than the GPA. We deconstruct the entire academic record to determine how successful an applicant would be in our program."

Interviews are not required, but they are recommended, and about 75 percent of applicants take the opportunity to have them. They are conducted by admissions officers on campus and at candidate forums held across the United States, Europe, Asia, and Latin America. Only those applicants who have submitted completed applications will be scheduled for interviews, which are conducted at the discretion of the admissions department. Stewart would like to see all applicants visit the school, sit in on a class, spend time with the students, go on a tour, and attend an information session. "The value of visiting is really, really high. It helps our candidates be stronger applicants for the school," she says. You can expect to be asked to come in for an interview if the admissions office has questions after reviewing your application.

You should apply as early as possible without rushing your application, suggests Stewart. While the school has room for more students in all four of its rounds, the longer you wait, the fewer the number of openings.

CARNEGIE MELLON MBAs SOUND OFF

This is the only school that doesn't use the cold call as a means of ensuring that students are well prepared for the class. Therefore, when the professor asked questions of the class, nobody really raised their hands to offer their insight. Still, I have made some tremendous friends and believe that the true value of my MBA is not only the quantitative analysis but also the relationships that I have built over the two years since being here.

I believe CMU truly has an outstanding finance program that is not properly reflected outside of the CMU community. We have excellent professors who prepare their students with a very rigorous curriculum.

The greatest inhibitor to the MBA program at Carnegie Mellon University is the fact that it's located in Pittsburgh, Pennsylvania. Even though the cost of living is lower in Pittsburgh (which makes it very attractive for students), the city lacks for good dining, efficient transportation, and population diversity. Most MBA students who are not from the local region are not satisfied with Pittsburgh living standards and cannot wait to move away from Pittsburgh. These factors make it more difficult to attract high-caliber MBA students to this program. Somehow, the administration and faculty need to offer more to students to increase the perceived value of Carnegie Mellon MBA degree.

This program is not for everyone. It is heavily analytical and quantitative. The curriculum forms a solid foundation for the development of a business mind, but ultimately it is up to the graduate to connect the principles to the "real" world. The ability to continue the development is the difference between the successful alum and those who cannot see the applicability of their education.

Even though I do not yet have a full-time job, I am extremely satisfied with the GSIA program. I feel that the skills I have learned and the friendships I have forged over the last two years give me a competitive advantage in the business world. I am also extremely confident in my ability to execute at a very high level in any situation that may arise in the future because of the rigor of the program.

The workload is very heavy during the first two semesters, but it helps build a truly team-oriented environment and a basis for tackling business problems. The faculty members are very supportive (extra classes or help sessions) and highly involved in student clubs and case competitions. One of the great things about a smaller MBA school environment is how easy it is to organize social events and business case competitions. Participating, organizing, or simply observing a case competition is the real catalyst for internalizing the course material.

This program is absolutely challenging and demanding. You'll be stretched beyond your limits, and in the end, you'll walk away from this experience with a solid training in the functional areas, a powerful set of tools to manage and lead, a heightened level of self-confidence, and a more well-rounded approach to dealing with problems at work and in life. You'll experience transformations beyond what you expect, and the end product, the new you, truly makes these two years worth all the sacrifices and sweat.

20.
INDIANA UNIVERSITY

INDIANA UNIVERSITY

Kelley School of Business
Graduate & Executive Education Center, Suite 2010
Kelley School of Business, 1275 East Tenth Street
Bloomington, Indiana 47045-1703
E-mail address: mbaoffice@indiana.edu
Web site address: www.bus.indiana.edu

Enrollment: 546
Women: 24%
Non-U.S.: 31%
Minority: 9%
Part-time: 843 (308 on campus, 535 distance)
Average age: 29
Applicants accepted: 22%
Median starting pay: $80,000
Annual tuition and fees:
    resident—$26,711
    nonresident—$23,450

Estimated annual budget: $34,754
Average GMAT score: 651
Average months of
    work experience: 64
Accepted applicants enrolled: 45%
Corporate ranking: 19
Graduate ranking: 23
Intellectual capital rank: 39

Teaching methods: case study 40%, distance learning 5%, experiential learning 15%, lecture 25%, simulations 5%, team projects 10%

Walk through the glass doors of the new Graduate and Executive Education Center at Indiana University's Kelley School of Business and the mood is one of excitement. If you didn't know better, you'd think these students had been awarded a new lease on life. In the past, Kelley students would gripe about outdated technology and lack of innovation. Now, though, it's a different story. Today's students' wants and needs have been answered, thanks to donations of over $35 million from the friends of Kelley. "It is a technological marvel," says Dean Dan Dalton, when asked about the new facility. "It's amazing."

Gone are the days of burning the midnight oil in a classmate's cramped apartment. Lack of space is no longer a complaint. Wasting time searching for a jack to plug in a laptop is a thing of the past. Now, students have everything they need at their fingertips, with 38 technologically enhanced breakout rooms for meetings, a trading room that some say puts Goldman Sachs to shame, and classrooms equipped with high-tech devices that seem to have come out of the Jetsons' living room. Students have access to the new facility 24 hours a day, seven days a week. "There is literally no place in the building where they can't do their business at any time," Dalton says. "We don't think our MBAs are studying 24/7, but if they wanted to, they could."

After four years of planning and construction, the classes of 2003 and 2004 are the first to use the new building, and the buzz among them is that the building will raise the value of their education. "There is no question that the hidden benefit that comes from the new building is that it makes students feel a greater sense of pride in the school and in the program," says Dan Smith, professor of marketing.

But the new building isn't the only thing attracting students to Kelley. As surprising as it may seem, one of the biggest draws is the city the school calls home. True, Bloomington, Indiana, is by no means a booming metropolis, but to students the city is ideal. On one hand, it is a small town so there aren't a lot of distractions and everything is a stone's throw away; but on the other hand, it is big enough that there's always something going on, whether it be a sporting event, a play, or a concert (maybe by John Mellencamp, a Bloomington local). The restaurant scene is diverse, and, with the rolling hills and spacious grassland on the 2000-acre campus, boredom is not an option. Also, because of the size of Bloomington, it is not rare to run into a professor at the gym or the grocery store. In fact, there are many occasions when students and professors find time to socialize—for instance, at a wine-tasting at the home of Professor Cooper Speaks, watching the Final Four at Dan Smith's place, or a Super Bowl party at Professor Wayne Winston's house.

As a public university, Indiana doesn't get the kind of monetary support that many of the private MBA programs are blessed with. But instead of using this as an excuse, Kelley has taken every opportunity to grow and mature into an even better center of learning—and in the eyes of Dean Dalton, it is succeeding. "We are a state institution and we compete against the very finest private institutions that, by and large, can outspend us," he says. "We are asked to succeed with a lot less investment, and we are proud that we have been able to do that. There

are only a handful of top notch public schools, and we are proud to maintain our membership in that group."

Though not centrally located in a large urban area, Kelley does a good job of attracting recruiters to Bloomington from many large companies nearby, such as Procter & Gamble, Ford, and PricewaterhouseCoopers. According to Dick McCracken, director of the Graduate Career Services Office, recruiters are attracted to Kelley students because they are willing to move around and because of their tremendous work ethic. "I am often told that our students have a very good perspective on work," he says. "Our students are taught early on that it is unlikely that they will be the CEO tomorrow, and that if you are going into a brand or associate brand, you are expected to make a contribution and go to it. Companies appreciate that."

Kelley students might be called the "blue-collar" MBAs. They are not going to sit back and let someone else do the dirty work. If you want to join their ranks, you'll need to have no fear of diving right into a problem and working tirelessly on it until a solution is reached. "They come in, roll up their sleeves the first day of the job, and they try to get it done," says Professor Smith. "I think they are very good at doing whatever it takes to get the job done. Our students also have a very strong work ethic. There aren't many prima donnas here."

One reason for the sense of ownership among the students is the way they are taught. Instead of regurgitating archaic textbook theories, discussions are focused on real-world examples. For instance, in Professor Winston's Operations and Decisions Technology class, you are brought right into some of the problems that Winston deals with when working with Microsoft or the U.S. Army as a consultant. Want to know how to set point spreads for NFL games? Winston will teach you. Want to know how Dallas Mavericks owner Mark Cuban, a former student of Winston's, rates basketball players and officials? The answer is, he doesn't: Winston does it for him. "I always like to use real-life applications," Winston says. "We do things that they are going to use in their jobs." Whatever Winston is doing is working; not only is he a favorite professor among students, but his class is always packed, and it doesn't even count toward any of the majors!

Your two years at Kelley begin with a two-week orientation where you will get a chance to get to know some of your classmates and better acclimate yourself to the campus. During this period, your leadership skills will be tested in a number of exercises that will be videotaped, then viewed again at the end of your two years at Kelley to see how much you have grown and accomplished as a leader. At orientation you will also get a chance to meet the dean and some other important members of the Kelley School; you will spend a day meeting with the career services staff; and one afternoon will be devoted to what are called Career Roundtables, where you will meet in groups and have the opportunity to converse with various corporate execs. Last, because most incoming MBAs have been out of the classroom for a while, blocks of time are set aside for what are called jump-start sessions, which serve as refresher courses in areas such as accounting and quantitative skills.

Your first year at Kelley is broken down into 14 modules of integrated core courses, ranging in length from 4 to 24 sessions. Dealing with such topics as critical thinking, leadership development, finance, and information systems and technology, the modules are set up to give you a comprehensive foundation of business problem-solving skills needed to understand the more complex situations and cases you will come across later on. But before you get to the modules, you will complete a leadership assessment exercise that makes you play the role of a newly appointed senior vice president the first day on the job. After observing your actions, the Leadership Development Institute will give you extensive feedback on various leadership skills and what you can work on.

About halfway through the fall semester, you will get an opportunity to apply the concepts you have learned in a case competition, where you and your four-person team will prepare an analysis of a new business opportunity. The remaining eight weeks of the first semester are devoted to electives, in which you can begin to branch out and get an idea as to what you will focus on in the next year.

After you come back from your summer internship, the second year at Kelley will be focused on developing the skills you picked up in the first year. You will select 1 of 11 majors, from finance or marketing to e-business or new venture and business development—or, if none of the majors fits into what you are looking for, you can create your own. In the second year, the emphasis is put on understanding such concepts as integrating across functional areas; making decisions despite conflicting information; and thinking inductively, creatively, and strategically.

Not holding classes on Fridays perpetuates the B-school tradition of Thursday nights out. But here, faculty will often join you at The Bluebird, Kilroy's, or Nick's, Bloomington's oldest bar and an IU institution.

If you want to live on campus, housing is available. Eigenmann Hall is the choice of MBAs for on-campus living. It's air-conditioned, and it's got high-speed Internet jacks in each room and a specialty food shop on the ground floor if you have the munchies. You can choose from a single or double room, or, if you are married, you can choose from an efficiency to a three-bedroom apartment.

IU also has a group of apartment complexes that are also available for MBAs. These are a healthy walk from Kelley, but if walking isn't your cup of tea, university buses can accommodate you for a minimal charge (you can purchase a full-year bus pass for $158). The complexes give you a variety of living arrangement choices. The buildings have cable TV jacks and Internet ports, and each building has laundry facilities.

Oh, and the sports. If you don't know anything about Hoosier basketball before coming to Kelley, take a crash course or you will be left out. Bloomington is a ghost town on Saturday afternoons and weeknights during the late fall and winter months. The place to be seen is in the stands at Assembly Hall, where the beloved Hoosiers hold court, candy-striped warm-ups and all. Says one 2002 grad, "This is Hoosier country. If you aren't a basketball fan coming in, you will be when you leave."

One thing that students and faculty alike applaud is the way the administration attends to their needs without getting in the way, a management philosophy that Dean Dalton installed on coming to Kelley in 1997. For instance, a group of Chinese students approached Director McCracken and explained to him that the Chinese economy was moving along agreeably, but the Kelley School was not well known in the principle markets of China so they were unable to get in touch with recruiters overseas. They asked McCracken what he could do for them. McCracken told them that if they were willing to help out, he would help underwrite a trip to Shanghai and host a reception for employers in the marketplace. "That was an idea the students came up with, and I did not have to go to the dean and ask for permission," he explains. "That would have slowed us down." Eventually, McCracken and a group of students, along with MBA director Terrill Cosgray, went to Shanghai and hosted a reception for nearly 40 employers.

There are a good number of clubs and organizations on campus, many of which (144, to be exact) have leadership positions available where students can put to use some of the managerial practices they learn in class. There are nine professional clubs at Kelley, including the Investment Club, the e-Business Club, and the Finance Guild. There are also several networking clubs, such as the Asian MBA Association, Graduate Women in Business, and the Gay-Straight Business Alliance.

A concern that students as well as faculty have about Kelley is the wide-ranging quality of students. The top students could go head to head with MBAs from any elite school, but the students near the bottom are questionable, leading many to call for interviews of all incoming students. (Currently, only about a third of accepted applicants are interviewed.) "I think what happens is that we get a lot more variance in our students," says Smith. "We have some who are truly phenomenal, a lot are very, very good, and there are several that you wonder, 'how did they get in?'"

PLACEMENT DETAILS

Kelley has been called a national program, and McCracken tends to agree with such a classification. "Our students come from all over the U.S. and return to all over the U.S.," he says. "Not many people stay in Bloomington, Indiana after they graduate, and I think recruiters like that." However, a good number of Kelley grads do tend to stay in the Midwest (62 percent of the class of 2002), much like their MBA counterparts at Purdue. Along with placement rates, median pay packages dropped considerably in 2002, to $102,700 from $114,000 two years earlier.

Though placement rates for the class of 2002 were not as low as at other schools, 30 percent of grads were still looking for work at graduation. About 80 percent had an offer after three months. Though grads were not pleased that so many of their peers were without work, they understood that the career services office was not to blame, and many went so far as to applaud the office for the work it did put in to help them in their searches. The school is able to bring in a good number of recruiters, and a large alumni base also helps the cause.

TOP HIRES

Eli Lilly (13); General Mills (5); Whirlpool (5); AEP Energy Services (4); Banc of America Securities (4); Bristol-Myers Squibb/Mead Johnson (4); Cinergy (4); General Electric (4); Guidant (4); Johnson & Johnson/Ethicon/Depuy (4); JPMorgan (4); Kraft Foods (4).

OUTSTANDING FACULTY

Dan Smith (marketing); Wayne Winston (decisions science); Richard Shickley (finance); Scott Smart (finance); Idalene Kesner (management).

APPLICANT TIPS

The Kelley School of Business is looking for team players. If you are not one who works well in groups, then Kelley probably isn't for you. The atmosphere at Kelley is one of collaboration and communication. "We are looking for the student who is willing to work in a team-based environment and who is willing to contribute to the learning of their classmates," says Jim Holmen, director of admissions and financial aid. "We want someone who wants to do more than just sit back and let things happen."

In terms of the weight of the GMAT, undergraduate GPA, essays, and recommendations, there is no set formula, but they are all looked at very carefully. According to Director Holmen, the GPA itself isn't as important as the grade trends. "We look at the nature of the academic work and we take it apart," he says. "We look at where they did well and where they struggled."

If you do have a deficiency in one part of your application, explain it. Holman understands that no one is going to be perfect, but at the same time, he says, "I don't want to set anyone up for failure." The ideal candidate at Kelley has a solid GMAT and a strong academic record, with four to five years of progressive experience in terms of increased responsibility and new opportunities, says Holman. "The people we want are motivated, and they are also focused," he explains. "The two years happen quickly and we want them to hit the ground running."

The best advice Holman can give is twofold. First, "Start early. There are always people who take the GMAT exam the day before the final due date, and I think they put a lot of pressure on themselves by doing that." Second, "Visit campus and interview, as a benefit to the school and to you. And while you're here, talk to some students; they really tell it like it is."

Compared to other schools, Kelley has a large number of international students as well as female students. This is due to increased recruiting on both fronts in order to create a diverse and balanced learning atmosphere for students. To target more female applicants, Kelley has tried more focused mailings as well as looking for female role models already at the school; judging from the numbers, it's working. With the class of 2004, female enrollment is up to 26 percent from 20 percent just two years ago.

KELLEY MBAs SOUND OFF

I feel Kelley has more than adequately prepared me. I cherish the tutelage that I have received while in Bloomington and will think fondly on my time spent here. As a testament to the sentiment felt by me and my class, we donated over $140,000 to the Alumni Association during our annual drive at a time when half of the class did not have job offers. Kelley graduates are extremely capable, quietly confident, fun to work with, and results oriented. Kelley alumni are always willing to speak to you concerning informational interviews or career advice. Alumni have stepped up their efforts in helping our class through this tough job market.

The career services office needs to improve. I am graduating at a time that the job market is terrible, but they have not adapted to the times and provide the resources and insight that I need to find permanent employment.

I cannot say enough about the collaborative learning environment at Kelley. Faculty feedback was immediate to any student concerns regarding the curriculum. With the downturn in the economy, the graduate career placement office has done a tremendous job conducting numerous seminars on self-directed searches, headhunter speakers, etc. I feel Kelley has more than prepared me with the tools and strategic focus to pursue my career goals.

In my entire educational career, I have never witnessed such an openness toward students' needs and aspirations. The MBA office and career services office do have a very positive attitude toward professional development and career placements. Although there is a lot more that can still be done, the school encourages student involvement and initiative. This is commendable and helps focus limited resources onto student-relevant programs.

The quality of the MBA Core was exceptional—the professors were outstanding and the curriculum was very well planned. The only thing that prevents me from rating my entire MBA experience in a similar manner as the core is the electives. While still very good, I did find a fair amount of redundancy (overlap) in the materials and a different-caliber professor. Most of the elective professors were still very good, but only a few were exceptional as in the core.

Getting an MBA at the Kelley School of Business at Indiana University has turned out to be the best decision I've ever made. The people in the program were truly team-oriented and diverse in their backgrounds. The faculty were approachable and flexible, as well as helpful in our challenging job search this year. Overall, the low cost combined with the high quality of education makes Kelley a real value.

The Kelley MBA program is a great MBA program. The professors are outstanding and are genuinely concerned about their students. The faculty and administration are very responsive to student concerns and opinions. There are great companies hiring on campus and the Graduate Career Services Office does a great job of preparing students for interviews and the job search. Also, Bloomington is a fun town to live in. Overall, I am extremely pleased with my experience at the Kelley School.

Kelley faces a challenge being located in the Midwest, south of Indianapolis, in terms of attracting recruiters and speakers to campus but it has taken deliberate actions to overcome this inherent obstacle. Kelley has a tremendous team culture and friendly environment that is most conducive to learning in a risk-free personal environment—thereby allowing us to take intellectual risks.

UNIVERSITY OF TEXAS AT AUSTIN

21.
UNIVERSITY OF TEXAS AT AUSTIN

McCombs School of Business
MBA Program Office, McCombs School of Business
University of Texas at Austin
1 University Station, B6004
Austin, Texas 78712
E-mail address: McCombsMBA@bus.utexas.edu
Web site address: www.bus.utexas.edu

Enrollment: 1922
Women: 25%
Non-U.S.: 26%
Minority: 7%
Part-time: 2000
Average age: 28
Applicants accepted: 29%
Median starting pay: $80,000
Annual tuition and fees:
  resident—$11,926
  nonresident—$25,006

Estimated annual budget: $35,000
Average GMAT score: 678
Average months of work
  experience: 62
Accepted applicants enrolled: 52%
Corporate ranking: 22
Graduate ranking: 25
Intellectual capital rank: 24

Teaching methods: case study 35%, experiential learning 10%, lecture 40%, team projects 15%

The University of Texas at Austin's McCombs Business School has a new leader at its helm: in June 2002, George Gau took hold of the reins. As the ninth dean in the B-school's 80-year history, Gau is no stranger to leadership. He hails from the school's finance department, where he was chair for 10 years. As chair, he concentrated on integrating student, faculty, and corporate interests and pioneered a series of research centers such as the Center for Real Estate. As dean, he's planning to repeat his stellar performance. This enthusiastic and amiable dean is big on communication. "What any good dean should do is develop good discussions and be a generator of ideas," Gau explains.

New ideas are pushing this newly installed dean and his administration along these days. Though the new administration stepped in during a controversial time for the school's entrepreneurial program, it has already gone through great lengths to get the school back on track. In the spring of 2002, the entrepreneurial program faced difficulty with tenure-track faculty, which resulted in several faculty members leaving and in students questioning the quality of the program. But, despite taking over the deanship during a downturn, Dean Gau is excited about pushing forward. Four areas he's looking to home in on are improving the MBA academic program, building strategic alliances with local companies, furthering research, and expanding McCombs' resource base. He also plans to add 30 new tenure-track faculty members (a 26 percent increase) to the whole school over the next five years, starting in the 2003–2004 academic year.

Management professor John Doggett, who's been a professor at McCombs for 13 years, says he has seen the B-school evolve into the more rigorous program it is today. "The program is designed entirely to respond to concerns of students, alums, and recruiters," he explains. "We're much more customer-focused now than we were in the past. We push students harder, have higher expectations, and make them really have to work." He adds he's also witnessed a huge change in students' attitude toward learning, noting that today McCombs MBAs are more hardworking and eager to learn. However, Doggett further adds, the dramatic change in students' attitude hasn't changed the overall close-knit community feeling at this school. Students like 2002 grad Windy Hodges gush about the people here. Hodges says a big part of the reason she came to McCombs was because of its "sense of community and collaborative atmosphere."

Perhaps creating the biggest buzz at the B-school is the Plus Program introduced in the fall of 2002. The program's aim is to create a "practical, experiential, and interactive" engagement. Faculty members hope the program will encourage students to take initiative and apply their academic training in concrete ways that create value while helping them better understand the complete picture of the business realm. "We want to make students feel more confident as leaders and decision makers," explains program director and economics professor Steven Tomlinson. With Plus added to the curriculum, classes are scheduled with a two-week break in the middle of each semester. During those two weeks, you'll participate in an intensive professional development seminar specifically designed to help you sharpen your ommunication and leadership skills. The four Plus units include Sales and Persuasion, Leading in Teams, Business Ethics,

and International Studies. Under each unit, you're assigned to one of six "Academies of Interest" based on your skills, interests, and preferences. Academies covered in the fall of 2002 included community development and social enterprise, new technology assessment, producing film and television, business across boundaries, small business consultancy, and the business of entertainment. In each academy, MBAs work in teams of six, with each team assigned a "client" that they'll work with to complete projects in the first year's Plus Program units. For example, each team in the community development academy will be assigned to a nonprofit organization and each team in the small business academy will be assigned to one small business. Your first year, you'll concentrate on communication skills and teamwork. In the first semester, you'll participate in Sales and Persuasion, where you'll learn to craft powerful methods of communication. Your main task will be to create your client's message, designed to sell the organization to potential partners. In the second semester, you'll focus on Leading in Teams: Collaboration and Coordination. As part of the team, you'll be expected to apply what you've learned in your courses to a problem that your client is facing. For example, students in the community development academy will work on executing a project for their client, like a fundraising campaign or reorganization of volunteer recruitment efforts. You'll also attend a 10-hour minicourse on writing for business and a workshop that teaches the techniques of improvisational theatre applied to managing meetings, office politics, and other challenges associated with getting things done in groups. The Plus Program isn't just all work and no play, however. The 2002 fall program included several opportunities for students and families to connect socially. Students organized an International Student Night showcasing food, arts, and music of the multitude of cultures represented in the MBA class. Students also hosted a family picnic complete with barbecue, organized sports activities, and even special events for the kids.

During your second year, you'll participate in the ethics and international portions of Plus. For Steve Salbu, who has been at McCombs for 12 years and is a business ethics professor, this is the most exciting change yet. Salbu notes that, although ethics has always been offered as an elective, this is the first time every student will be required to participate in intensive ethics training. In the final unit students can flex their business brawn in a number of countries. 2002 grad Jared Johnson says he wishes this program had been offered when he was there. Though he's wary of splitting the semester in two, he's sure it'll prove to be a boon for incoming students. During your third semester, you'll focus on ethics, community, and the environment, with a competitive simulation in which you'll play various members of an executive team trying to manage an evolving crisis that is threatening your company. And finally, in your fourth semester, you'll have the opportunity to learn about life and business in another country with two-week long trips to companies, meetings with government officials, and completing market research in different areas of the world including South America, Japan, China, and Souteast Asia.

Salbu's only concern is that the new changes will push students harder than ever. Despite adding the Plus component, the B-school isn't skimping on the core curriculum. In response to both student and alumni requests, McCombs will introduce a new curriculum come fall 2003. Though the old core was just one year old, starting in 2003 you'll take one more cohort class together in your third semester. The new core consists of 27 hours split into nine courses taken over the first three semesters. The core will include statistics; financial accounting; information technology; half of a semester of operations; and half of a semester of microeconomics, finance, marketing, and strategy, all in the first year. In the second year, you'll take half a semester of managerial accounting and half a semester of macroeconomics as well as one of three managing people electives in the first semester to complete the core require-

ments. To accommodate these changes, the required operations class will be reduced to a half course. You'll also be taking a managing people elective chosen from a selection of three classes: The Art and Science of Negotiation, Creating and Managing Human Capital, and Managing People and Organizations: The Consultant's Perspective. Salbu adds that the most common response from alumni was that the courses they found they needed most on the job were those on managing human interaction. Though 90 percent of students were already taking The Art and Science of Negotiation as an elective, these courses weren't required. "No matter what specialization you go into, you must be able to manage people, motivate, lead," Salbu adds. Other areas the core covers include statistics, financial accounting, information technology, finance, marketing, strategy, and microeconomics.

Although you can't exempt yourself from these core classes by exam or other means, there's still room left for electives starting in your second semester. At McCombs you're not required to choose a concentration, though most students do, leaving some room for customization in this otherwise rigorous curriculum. Dean Gau has his sights set on preparing students for the post-MBA world—and with the $50 million gift alumnus Red McCombs gave the B-school in 2000, there are plenty of resources with which to work here. Gau is looking to center the MBA curriculum based on job opportunities available and on correlating the program with the skills necessary to successfully fill jobs. One way you can take matters into your own hands is to choose the right electives to help you snag a summer internship. Electives run the spectrum from basics such as corporate and real estate finance to new areas such as entrepreneurship and human resources management. There's room to branch out, with five formal concentrations and 10 optional specialties. You can concentrate in accounting, finance, management, information technology, or marketing by taking at least 15 credit hours of electives in a chosen area. Or you can opt to specialize in an area by taking 12 to 24 credit hours of electives in that specialty. Salbu says he's also looking to add a specialization in social issues and management; such things as corporate governance will be covered. You can also pursue one of nine joint degrees in Asian studies; communications; Latin American studies; law; manufacturing systems engineering; Middle Eastern studies; nursing; public affairs; and Russian, Eastern, and Eurasian studies.

From day one of orientation, your class is divided into six cohorts of 70 students with whom you'll take your core classes. From the moment you arrive, McCombs aims to place you on the right track to landing your dream job. McCombs Connection, a new addition to the weeklong orientation, debuted in the fall of 2002. The three-day bonus program includes a day and a half of introducing you to the technology available at the school and a day and a half of career-focused training, including workshops on resume writing, networking, etiquette, and looking for jobs. The "Career Camp" culminates with a networking event and game with corporate recruiters, in which recruiters offer students tips and advice on what to do and say during networking receptions and career fairs.

Though the entrepreneurial program got people talking for the wrong reasons in 2002, Dean Gau went to great lengths to ensure students wouldn't feel a negative wave of effects. The entrepreneurial program still offers its regular five courses, four of the five instructors, and 90 percent of the same material, and MOOT Corp and the Austin Tech Incubator, two popular student programs, were integrated into the curriculum. And, if you're looking to start up a business, the Entrepreneur Society, with its wealth of resources, isn't a bad place to begin.

Other areas making heads turn these days are finance, consulting, and marketing. In fact, about 88 percent of students concentrate in one of these areas. Gau calls the finance department the "hidden jewel" of the school, no exaggeration given that 48 percent of the 2002 grads have been placed in finance positions. The marketing department, for example, teamed up with Procter & Gamble, 3M, and Motorola, providing five summer internships to students, who follow up their stint on the job with a symposium where executives from the three firms discuss cases in the field of customer business development. Student teams also have the chance to work on simulated cases and make analytical presentations to executives from sponsoring firms during annual corporate-sponsored academic challenges in accounting, consulting, entrepreneurship, finance, and marketing.

McCombs also has gone to great lengths to strengthen ties at top B-schools in Latin America. With an already particularly strong, extensive executive MBA program in Mexico City, Gau is looking to build similar relationships elsewhere. Currently you can take advantage of earning a double degree with a partner school like IESA in Caracas, Venezuela; ESAN in Lima, Peru; and Fundação Getulio Vargas in São Paulo, Brazil. Or you can participate in a semester exchange program at such schools as the Australian Graduate School of Management in Sydney or the Rotterdam School of Management in The Netherlands. In recent years, McCombs has turned its efforts toward minorities, women, and international students, changing its recruiting tactics to beef up enrollment. This year minorities make up 7 percent of the school. International enrollment was up 28 percent in 2002. Their efforts aren't going unrecognized: the National Society of Hispanic MBAs gave McCombs the Educational Institution Award in 2002. Plus, the Spanish language track is designed to provide students with the opportunity to gain Spanish language proficiency as part of the MBA track. Additionally, the program helps prepare students to participate in study-abroad or dual degree programs that require a language proficiency. There is no set number of required components to the Spanish language track, but students can choose from an array of courses, options, and activities that assist in achieving individual goals for Spanish proficiency. Through a sequence of courses and activities, you'll learn to communicate comfortably in normal business and academic situations and at the same time gain an understanding of the economic structures and business practices of Spanish-speaking countries.

Additionally, you can study halfway across the country in the nation's capital. The Washington Campus is a consortium of 17 nationally prominent business schools, including McCombs, in a nonpartisan, not-for-profit organization committed to educating business executives on the public policy process. The faculty includes members of Congress and their staff, senior administrative officials, lobbyists, journalists, scholars, and corporate executives. Each summer, students are selected to attend one of the four-week intensive summer programs. Students come away with valuable political insights and knowledge about the public policy process, complete with courses like The Formation of Economic Policy and Business Strategy and Comparative Political Studies and field trips to Capitol Hill and executive branch departments and agencies.

McCombs students are an active bunch—they're eager to learn and eager to dive right into the pool of activities. Administrators describe students as always actively looking to get involved within the B-school community, whether through clubs such as Central Charity Challenge, Grad Finance Association, or Graduate Business Women's Network or through starting their own clubs. 2002 grad Lauren Ward is one example: she participated in Net Impact, Graduate Business Women's Network, Marketing Network, Austin Power, Preview Weekend, and the Women in Business Leadership Conference. And this multitasking participation isn't rare.

One of the more popular extracurricular activities is the MBA Investment Fund, LLC, established in 1994 by Dean Gau. The fund offers MBAs a real-world experience in managing investment portfolios, running a business, and developing client relationships. Today, the fund

manages $12 million in its growth fund and an additional $1.9 million in a new value fund. Another outlet for students to wet their feet in is MOOT CORP, a worldwide business plan competition. Held in May, the competition draws entrepreneurs from all over the world. McCombs MBAs have the chance to pitch their business plans to venture capitalists, and, in 2002, the McCombs MBA team, Private Concepts, Inc., won the competition and the $100,000 prize to develop its product—the Pevlon Home Cervical Cancer Screen.

For the civic-minded, the Enterprise Corps is a private volunteer organization that provides MBA graduates the opportunity to assist private enterprises in transforming and emerging economies such as those in Eastern Europe, Asia, and Latin America. While on assignment, corps members serve as management consultants to their host companies and face an array of tasks from formulating new business plans and developing financial proposals to launching new products and negotiating joint ventures. A number of McCombs MBAs also participate in the Quality Management Consortium, a student-run business that arranges prestigious, paid work engagements for McCombs students with Austin-based businesses. Associate engagements are available in all areas of business, with both large and small companies. The consortium also has an unpaid program of undergrads called Brass Ring and hosts a bimonthly executive leadership seminar that is open to all consortium participants.

McCombs boasts a four-building, 350,000-square-foot complex that houses classrooms, offices, research centers, and computer laboratories. The B-school features a three-story atrium and cafeteria, a state-of-the-art multimedia service center, and the Frito-Lay Student Leadership Center, unveiled in 2000. The six-story, modern glass-and-concrete headquarters sits on the south end of the university's sprawling 350-acre campus. Renovations on MBA core course classrooms were recently completed for the fall of 2002, with rooms redesigned to include state-of-the-art technology such as laptop portals at every desk and Internet access. And the class of 2004 broke in the new Carpenter Lounge, an MBA-only student lounge in the main B-school building, which houses both the undergraduates and graduates. With student mailboxes, a conference room, space to meet with student organizations, and a coffee cart, you're bound to spend quality study time there.

Technological resources aren't scarce here either. There are more than 900 workstations in seven computer labs, 600 laptop ports, and access to the latest in corporate-standard software and networking. As part of a "laptop initiative," students must all come with the same portable computer so that they'll have access to the standardized technology. To obtain the latest information on classes, events, and recruiter schedules, and to access the school's vast alumni database, you'll be going through Texas Nexus, the school's intranet system.

With 1922 students, not only is McCombs one of the larger schools, students tend to be older and more experienced. The average age for the class of 2004 is 28, with an average work experience of five years. Maybe that's why students tend to be a bit more laid back. Administrators, faculty, and recruiters describe McCombs grads as hardworking and eager, yet as students who know how to take a step back and have a little fun. Students say there's a great sense of a tight-knit community. Students attend tailgate parties and sit as a bloc at the football games, kick back at weekly Think and Drinks on Thursday nights, and enjoy the nightlife in Austin.

Students say the community is a very close-knit and lively bunch. Located on the Colorado River at the edge of Central Texas hill country, students say Austin is a fulfilling place to spend two years. They rave about the many things Austin has to offer—good weather, great live music, and surplus restaurants and bars. And don't forget the plus of a large state school—athletics. Students love the collegiate feel, attending football, basketball, and baseball games. Some, like 2002 grad Jared Johnson, played on their own teams. There was always too much to do for fun in Austin, says Johnson. When he wasn't busy playing rugby or playing in his MBA rock band, his favorite thing to do was to go tubing down the Guadalupe River with friends. No matter where you end up setting up camp for two years, you'll be sure to find this laid-back bunch hanging out on 6th Street or at area hangouts like Crown & Anchor, Trudy's Texas House, and Mozart's Café.

Most students live in Hyde Park, conveniently located within walking distance just north of campus. Some students also live in the Riverside and Farwest neighborhoods. And a few chose to live on the loud and rambunctious West Campus, overrun with undergraduate Greeks. Students note the lack of parking on campus and advise new students to bring a bike or live on a bus line.

PLACEMENT DETAILS

It wasn't a huge surprise that the class of 2002 would have difficulty finding jobs, so the McCombs placement office did its homework to help prepare students for the worst-case scenario. Career Services Director Sharon Lutz says the office helps students learn other ways of identifying job opportunities, gets help from alumni networks, and reaches out to new employers. The office also had nine people dedicated to actively searching Web sites, newspapers, and journals for different job opportunities for students; their findings were sent to students on a weekly basis. The center also has career resource network groups—support groups for students that meet on a weekly basis and are also responsible for bringing in job leads. All of this kept the pipeline flowing with job opportunities.

Though there have always been a slew of workshops for students, this time around students gave them a bit more attention, Director Lutz says. Workshops on things like networking and launching a job search were well attended by students. "It's important to discipline yourself to do it [the job search]," she adds. "So you have to organize yourself to be consistent and follow up and follow through." Lutz also notes that alums were exceptionally important in 2002. They were also hit pretty hard, she adds, so it was a matter of give and take, ensuring a positive relationship with them so they could help each other out.

Career services also started a new program for first-years in 2002—Career Camp, sponsored by companies such as Microsoft and Motorola. It's a day and half of orientation to get you acclimated to what you'll be expecting come job search time. There's even an etiquette luncheon and opportunities to network. Employer sponsors set up a career fair and organize a game that will introduce you to the type of environment you'll find yourself in when you really begin your job search. The employer will also give you instant personal feedback on how to improve your techniques on things like introductions, holding conversations, and proper etiquette.

Lutz's number one piece of advice to MBAs out there is to have a focused career target within your first year. "Expectations are quite high for MBAs," she notes. "But it's a whole new ball game and you can't take it for granted."

Only 64 percent of Texas's 2002 grads had job offers by graduation, and 26 percent were still job hunting three months later. But grads who did manage to snag an offer earned average pay packages of $104,000. Some 60 percent remained in the Southwest, while 20 percent headed to the Midwest or Northeast and 9 percent went to the West Coast.

TOP HIRES

Dell (15); The Williams Company (10); Citibank (7); SABRE (6); Eli Lilly (6); Johnson & Johnson (5); General Mills (5); Frito-Lay (5); Reliant Energy (5); Barclay's Capital (5).

OUTSTANDING FACULTY

James Nolen (finance); John Doggett (management); Andres Almazan (finance); James Fredrickson (management); Steven Tomlinson (economics); Keith Brown (finance); Marylea Mcanally (accounting); Jeff Sandefer (entrepreneurship).

APPLICANT TIPS

If you're thinking of applying to McCombs, make sure you've got at least two years of work experience under your belt. The average applicant has 4.5 years of experience and the average admitted student has 5.2 years of experience.

Matt Turner's biggest word of advice is to seem genuinely enthusiastic about the McCombs program and show you've carefully researched the school. "We always want to feel like we're your top choice," he adds. He takes the answer to "Why McCombs?" very seriously, and he wants to see things like motivation, management skills, supervision skills, and personal skills that will contribute to the whole class and that recruiters will find attractive.

Turner looks to the baseline—GMAT (target is 686) and GPA—to measure quantitative ability and determine if you'll be able to handle the curriculum. He's looking for people with strong leadership, teamwork, presentation, and interpersonal skills. The McCombs environment is very community oriented, and Turner's looking to see how you'd get involved at the school and give back to the program.

So how do you set yourself apart from the rest? Point out what's stellar, unusual, or outstanding about you. Turner says successful applicants have demonstrated high levels of responsibilities, global interest, and initiative in their applications. With so many solid applicants, the best way to separate yourself from the "homogenous MBA pool," Turner adds, is to "add spice to your stew" with things like extensive living abroad, international exposure, a foreign language, or background in an unusual industry. He points to a student who mastered Chinese on her own and opened her own import-export company.

With over 2900 applicants a year, interviews remain optional. It's up to you to choose to do one. Both alums and current students conduct interviews for the admissions office, so, if you're good with face-to-face interviews, go ahead and schedule one; it can only help. About five years ago, McCombs started using a 100-person student committee that has become heavily involved in the admissions process. First-years are involved in first reads of the applications, while second-years give a hand with interviews. Though the staff makes final calls, Turner says he turns to the students whenever he's in doubt.

Recommendations are at the bottom of the list. Turner says that since most people seem able to get the required two good recommendations, he's looking more for those that point out caution or concern. The exceptional recommendations, he says, come from direct supervisors who are intimately familiar with your work. And throw out those pens; McCombs only accepts applications online.

McCOMBS MBAs SOUND OFF

I had a good experience here. I learned a great deal and felt very comfortable asking for assistance when necessary. My teachers were very knowledgeable and focused on teaching. I particularly liked the team-oriented environment, the emphasis on group projects, and the high standards the school expected from all students.

I came here to start a business. UT's entrepreneurial curriculum has wildly exceeded my expectations.

The Texas MBA program gave me unlimited opportunities to succeed. I was able to inter-

view with top investment banking and consulting firms, work for an investment bank in New York over the summer, and find permanent employment with my first-choice employer. The Texas MBA program gave me the opportunity to participate in unique, real-world projects as part of the course curriculum.

I'm not sure if all business schools are as diverse as McCombs, but the international students were extremely impressive and greatly added to the overall MBA experience. The world is definitely becoming a smaller place and UT's program helped me bridge gaps in my understanding of life and opportunities outside the United States.

My experience at the McCombs School of Business was extraordinary. The school has a strong faculty and attracts very diverse and active students. Additionally, the program offers numerous opportunities to engage in learning experiences outside of the classroom.

The school's major weakness is its career services. The school is relatively weak in reaching out to corporations outside of Texas. The efforts for international students are considerably less compared with Americans.

Texas was a great experience. It helped me learn what I was good at and has given me the confidence to pursue any goal I want to. Classes like Managing Complexity changed the way I think about the world and challenged many of the fundamental assumptions I held. The people at the school are phenomenal, and cooperation is encouraged. I wouldn't have gotten through accounting without the help of the CPAs in my class. That is just one example of the positive and team-oriented environment at the school. Also living in Austin is one of life's great pleasures. It's a small town with the opportunities of a large city.

22.
EMORY UNIVERSITY

EMORY UNIVERSITY

Goizueta Business School
1300 Clifton Road, Suite 402
Atlanta, Georgia 30322
E-mail address: admissions@bus.emory.edu
Web site address: www.bus.emory.edu

Enrollment: 388
Women: 22%
Non-U.S.: 34%
Minority: 7%
Part-time: 187 (168 on campus, 19 distance)
Average age: 28
Applicants accepted: 24%
Median starting pay: $78,000

Annual tuition and fees: $29,408
Estimated annual budget: $43,440
Average GMAT score: 675
Average months of work experience: 63
Accepted applicants enrolled: 46%
Corporate ranking: 30
Graduate ranking: 19
Intellectual capital rank: 19

Teaching methods: case study 50%, distance learning 1%, experiential learning 2%, lecture 20%, simulations 2%, team projects 20%, other 5%

It's a bird, it's a plane, it's a Goizueta MBA! Why are Goizueta students falling from the sky? No, the rigorous curriculum hasn't driven students that far just yet. In 2001, Goizueta started a new tradition—sky diving. As part of their orientation, first-years take a giant leap to represent courage—one of seven core values Goizueta strives to emphasize. Of course it's an optional activity, but the first time around in 2001, 100 students jumped; in 2002, 135 jumped, out of a class of 165. From day one, this small B-school's sense of community is readily apparent.

Students aren't the only ones taking the plunge: assistant dean and director of the full-time MBA program Kembrel Jones, also a Goizueta alum, was the first to take to the skies. It's not rare to find the faculty and staff in the thick of things. Grads consistently rate their teachers and administration as top-notch when it comes to their receptiveness to new ideas and their quick response to student suggestions. One way students get their say is through Student Action Groups, which work with the administration to voice student concerns. Dean Tom Robertson also makes himself available at monthly afternoon teas and town hall meetings twice a semester. Plus, he gets a taste of student life by switching places with a student who gets to be Dean for a Day. Robertson describes his and the administration's relationship with students as a partnership. "We welcome their involvement," he adds. "It's about leadership in action, it's about a community." It's just one of the benefits of a small school, Assistant Dean Jones adds.

Goizueta underwent a series of dramatic changes two years ago with the arrival of a new dean, the opening of a new building, and the overhaul of the curriculum and programming. Since his arrival in 2000, Jones has concentrated his efforts on maintaining and improving the new additions. One way he has done this is through a branding initiative. The B-school embarked on an extensive branding project in 2002 to better define what it was looking for in a Goizueta MBA. After a yearlong process of consulting with alums, students, and recruiters, the school came up with the umbrella slogan, "Ethical Leaders for Global Enterprise." The MBA program took it a step further and developed the tag line, "Leaders in Action." If that wasn't already enough to set the school in the right direction, student leaders, faculty, and staff spent four hours on a Sunday afternoon whittling a list of 70 values down to 7—community, team, diversity, rigor, accountability, integrity, and courage—all of which you'll find emblazoned across the wall as a daily reminder when you walk through the doors of the B-school building.

The changes Emory has made to the program in the past two years all stem from these recently established initiatives. Curriculum changes are also on the horizon for fall 2004. Though changes won't be made specifically to the core, new required courses and programs to be determined will be added. A unique quality of the core curriculum that won't soon be changing is its flexibility. You can waive a core class by taking an exam, but you have to replace it with an elective. And the Flex Core option allows you to request a flexible core sequence, enabling you to begin taking electives your first semester, which can prepare you for summer internship competition. Students are also pleased with the quality of teaching; they ranked their core classes 16th overall in the survey this year. Goizueta also gave the curriculum a facelift by adding new electives to the mix each year to respond to students' changing interests. In

2000, 14 new academic concentrations were introduced, and 16 electives were added to the roster in 2002, including New Venture Financing, Supply Chain Management, and Organizational Growth Management.

Emphasizing the MBA experience is vitally important to Jones. "The way we look at it, our students are taking two years out of their life and paying good money," Jones emphatically explains. "It goes beyond education." Changes made to the program in the last two years echo Jones's sentiments. Goizueta revamped its orientation after an overhaul just two years ago. The orientation week centers around the seven values, taking one day to represent each value. Students go skydiving to represent courage, meet their five-member team and work through team-building activities on community day, and are introduced to the academic program and their fall faculty on rigor day. The orientation week culminates in Winshape Wilderness, an overnight outward bound experience in the mountains of northern Georgia. Students work in their small teams to complete low ropes and high ropes courses as an introduction to trust, communication, and teamwork—all essential qualities for a team, as they'll be sticking with this small group the rest of their first year.

Before classes start, you'll have a chance to put your skills into motion. Each 12-week semester kicks off with Lead Week. In existence since 1997, the program underwent a revamp in 2002. In fall 2002, first-years worked in teams on structured problem solving and effective presentation. In four days they went through eight cases—one to represent each core course—each dealing with the viability and future of the airline industry. The exercise, supervised by Delta Airlines executives, ended with the top three teams presenting their research to Delta's CEO. Second-years participated in an innovation challenge where they took a look at already established companies, like Coca-Cola, and created new products and services. Whereas in the past the focus was on new ventures, says Jones, it is now on innovation. Again, the top three teams went on to pitch their ideas to company executives. Springtime Lead Week took global studies to another level. In January, students took three weeks to travel through China, Brazil, Chile, Peru, South Africa, Thailand, Singapore, Vietnam, and Mexico, meeting with company executives and immersing themselves in cultural studies as well. One satisfied grad, Justin Milrad, never expected to get as much real-world experience as he did. He was surprised by the various opportunities to work with companies and help them solve real-life problems.

Another added bonus is the yearlong Goizueta Plus Program. Introduced in 2000, Goizueta Plus offers first-years the opportunity to polish up on their leadership and communication skills. In the fall, you'll focus on leadership and ethics, and in the spring you'll tackle communication skills. "We really believe you won't be a strong leader if you're not a strong communicator," Jones adds. The courses include seminars on leading, working in teams, and finding a career focus, as well as a forum for practicing communication skills and receiving constructive feedback. One thing the B-school did to emphasize a lesson in ethics in 2002 was invite a panel of convicted white-collar criminals who hold MBAs to share their stories. Two years later, Jones says the feedback has been hugely positive from employers and from students, who initially had some complaints about the extra coursework. Faculty members have noticed a change in the students as well. In the last two years, says marketing professor Doug Bowman, the quality of students has increased tremendously. He attributes it to all of the "little things" that Goizueta offers, like the Plus Program.

One area in which Dean Tom Robertson, who's originally from Scotland, has stepped up his efforts is the international component of the MBA experience. About one-third of Goizueta MBAs come from outside of the United States— from over 30 different countries. Besides the spring Lead Week trips, the B-school offers summer and semester study abroad programs at over 30 exchange partner schools in Asia, Eastern and Western Europe, and Latin America, like the HEC Graduate School of Business in France, Hong Kong University of Science and Technology in China, and the Rotterdam School of Management in The Netherlands. Students also regularly obtain internships in Asia, Europe, Latin America, and the former Soviet Union at a wide variety of international offices like Beecham (Budapest), BMW (Munich), and Merrill Lynch (London). Don't have the travel itch? Area studies certificates in Russian and Eastern European, Latin American, and Caribbean studies are also available by taking four electives focused on the region and demonstrating foreign language proficiency. Goizueta makes learning another language easy. You can take advantage of short and inexpensive evening language courses taught through Emory's community education program and regular Emory language courses you can audit. You can also opt to spend a fifth semester at one of three business schools in France, Austria, or The Netherlands and earn a dual MBA/international studies degree.

Minority student enrollment has also blossomed as of late. Goizueta joined the Consortium for Graduate Study in Management in 2001. As a result, minority numbers inched up a bit from 5 percent in 2001 to 9 percent in 2002. "We're on the right path," says Admissions Director Julie Barefoot.

Though this school may be small in size (165 students per class), it steps up to the challenge and uses size to its advantage. For starters, the community—students, faculty, and staff—is close-knit and collaborative, students say. Professor Patrick Noonan, who's been at Goizueta for 10 years, describes a nice group of students who can strike a great balance between personal drive and ambition and team and community values. Plus, administrators add, it's much easier to tweak the program if it's small. Students also laud professors and administrators for their efforts in making themselves available and in responding to student suggestions. The 2002 grads ranked the school's responsiveness sixth overall in *BusinessWeek*'s 2002 survey. Graduate Justin Milrad adds, "They really cared about the students and put forth their best efforts to prepare for class and challenge the students."

And though the small size may keep some recruiters from making visits, there's no stopping Goizueta from helping its students. Starting in 2002, the career management office added treks to companies throughout the United States. In November, students take off three days from classes and are expected to participate in one of the treks to either an Atlanta office or an out-of-state office. Treks made in November 2002 include visits to Wall Street, Silicon Valley, consumer goods and pharmaceutical companies in New York and New Jersey, and media and entertainment outlets in L.A. and New York. "It's not the traditional way to do it," Jones adds. "But it's a great way to maintain our small size and still do everything." Though the school has made the decision to keep the class size down, it has beefed up its faculty size. The faculty doubled from 1998 to 2000, and in the last two years 22 new professors have been hired, with plans to hire six more in 2003. An added program that has helped attract these top-notch faculty is the PhD program, which kicked off in the fall of 2002. Robertson adds that this new program will be important to faculty research productivity, which will in turn improve the intellectual life of the B-school.

A high-tech building was added in 1997, and ground will be broken in the summer of 2003 on a new building set to house classrooms, social space for MBAs, admissions and career management, the doctoral program, and some research centers. Desks are all wired for laptops, and nearly every seat in the common areas within the B-school is also equipped for computers.

Students here are an active bunch. With over 60 student clubs, MBAs have plenty of opportunities to get involved and take on leadership positions. It's not rare to find them at the B-school's KO Café (named for Coca-Cola's stock ticker symbol) taking a break or creating a business plan—while sipping on a Coke, of course.

Don't discount this B-school's location. Atlanta may not be New York City, but it is home to such giants as Coca-Cola, Delta Airlines, and UPS. "The Atlanta business community is dynamic and growing," says 2002 grad Dan Murphy. Plus, it attracts big-name speakers such as former president Jimmy Carter, Warren Buffett, and DuPont Company CEO Chad Holliday to the Dean's Leadership Speaker Series. Most students tend to live within five miles of campus. The campus is just a few minutes away from Virginia-Highlands, a laid-back neighborhood peppered with casual restaurants and bars; Buckhead, one of the trendier areas of the city lined with clubs; and Midtown, a venue for plenty of live music. Students have the best of both worlds here—a beautiful tree-lined campus tucked away within a bustling city.

PLACEMENT DETAILS

Goizueta has a new face in the career management office. David Bergheim, who joined the B-school in the summer of 2002, hails from Yale's School of Management, where he spent five years working in the placement office. As a newcomer to Goizueta, Bergheim is not looking to make too many adjustments just yet. His goal is to wait a year before he starts to smooth out the bumps in the office. In any case, 2002 grads weren't displeased with their office's efforts in 2002.

At the career management office, the staff has a saying, "Vision without action is a daydream, action without vision is a nightmare." "Our goal is to help them understand their vision, bring opportunities to them, and teach them how to create their own opportunities,"

Bergheim adds. At this B-school they're concerned with making sure you walk away with the tools to help you succeed, and not just about landing a first internship or job. "Our focus is on the long term," says Bergheim.

One way to accomplish just that is take students on treks to companies in different sectors throughout the country. In the past, treks have visited hot spots like Wall Street; in 2002 the list was expanded to include visits to tech companies in Silicon Valley, along with the New Jersey and New York trips.

The career guide program will also help you get on the right track with a little help from the more seasoned second-years, as will the alumni mentoring program. You can get a little inside help from those who've been in your place before, and they can provide great contacts and tips to help you succeed. Bergheim adds that he warns his students to not think just about what's hot today, but rather to broaden their horizons a bit because "what's hot today may not be hot tomorrow."

Only 60 percent of the class of 2002 had secured a job offer by graduation, but a total of 81 percent had one three months later. About 13 percent of grads took jobs outside the U.S., but of those that sought employment in the States, some 82 percent got work in the Southeast or Northeast. Grads earned starting pay packages of about $101,400.

TOP HIRES

Coca-Cola (11); Delta Airlines (7); IBM Consulting (4); Bank of America (3); Honeywell International (3); JPMorgan Chase (3); Kimberly-Clark (3); UBS Warburg (3).

OUTSTANDING FACULTY

Patrick Noonan (decision science); Al Hartgraves (accounting); David Wessels (finance);
Robert Kazanjian (organizational behavior); Nicholas Valerio (finance).

APPLICANT TIPS

Though five years is the average amount of work experience students have when they get to Gouizueta, admissions director Julie Barefoot adds that work experience isn't just about the number. She goes to great lengths to assess an applicant's quality of work experience. One way is through the interview. Though interviews aren't required to complete your application, no applicant is accepted without one. After an initial review of applications, interviews are set up with applicants the school is interested in. Alums and second-years help out, but the admissions committee does 90 percent of interviews, whether on campus, on a recruiting trip, or on the phone.

Barefoot looks for several things in an applicant. She describes one recent admittee as having had great work experience; some analytical coursework, though she was a liberal arts major; a clear and realistic understanding of how hard she would have to work to accomplish her goals; and excellent letters of recommendation. There's no magic formula, but probably the most important component of the equation is the caliber of your work experience. "The bottom line is if they don't have good work experience they won't get a spot in the class," Barefoot says. Experience doesn't have to be from the corporate world, Barefoot adds. The school accepts an eclectic bunch—from Fulbright scholars to those who work with nonprofits. "We want people with meaningful things to contribute about the business world. Someone who understands organizations," Barefoot notes.

The Goizueta community is highly involved and very close knit. So, says Barefoot, she's looking for someone who shows potential for contributing to the overall community, whether it be having been involved in collegiate activities as an alum or having worked for a social or church organization. If you're looking for a super-competitive experience, this probably isn't the best place for you, Barefoot adds. She says that in this collegial environment, the best fits are those students looking to be highly involved in the program. "It's not just about coming to class and then leaving," she notes.

This year, the dean's office gave Barefoot and her staff extra scholarships to bring in a strong pool of applicants. Students and alums are all excited about the MBA program, Barefoot adds, which is why they're such a strong help when it comes to attracting new students. This, coupled with the extra money, helped attract a stronger group of applicants, indicated by the jump in average GMAT score from 650 in 2000 to 675 in 2002. The B-school also got a bit more selective this time around, accepting a total of 24 percent of applicants, as opposed to 32 percent just two years ago.

Though international numbers went down a bit in 2002, Barefoot notes that the number of minority students went up from 5 percent to 9 percent. She attributes the drop in international students from 37 percent to 31 percent mostly to the economy, but says she and the admissions committee will be stepping up their recruitment efforts and will continue visiting countries around the world to maintain their numbers. She's also looking to beef up the number of minority students in years to come, especially now with the school's membership in the consortium.

Barefoot adds two last bits of advice for those looking to apply to Goizueta: choose those who write your letters of recommendation carefully. She's looking for strong, passionate letters from those people who can really vouch for your work and for your ability to excel in and contribute to the MBA program. And do a little research beforehand about why you want an MBA and what you think it can do for you. Successful applicants knew what they were looking for and were really knowledgeable about what the MBA would do for them, Barefoot adds.

And of course, with rolling admissions in place, it's wise to apply early.

GOIZUETA MBAs SOUND OFF

Goizueta was absolutely the best school for me and I would select the same school having to make the decision over again. The caliber of the students is a perfect mix of intelligence, curiosity, initiative and kindness that made the two years fly by!

Emory was a great choice. I wouldn't trade the last two years for anything. Not only did I have numerous opportunities to travel on international business, but I also scored a great internship/job post graduation. Emory faculty and staff really treat the students like royalty.

The lowest points of the school are the career management center, which has gone through high staff turnover in the past two years. Also, the IT component is not very strong. Other than these two areas, the school is truly excellent and striving for greatness. If I had to make the decision all over again, I would choose to attend Goizueta all over again.

Goizueta's facilities are excellent and offer great technology throughout, including wired and wireless networks. There are lots of breakout rooms, a great commons area and comfortable, high-tech case classrooms. A key advantage of Goizueta, being a small school, is the accessibility of faculty and administrators. I've consistently found doors (and minds) open, whether I've stopped by to clarify or further discuss course material, make a recommendation for a class or ask for career-related advice.

Emory's business school program is a terrific alternative to the programs in the Northeast.

The school puts a tremendous amount of resources into the program and is truly interested in seeing each student succeed. Atlanta is also a great city to live in while attending business school. The students at school are extremely friendly and willing to help fellow students. It's a great learning experience. While the career management center was weak this year, steps are being taken to greatly improve this resource for next year. The current economy did not help either.

The experience was much more than just academics and future job placement. The past two years have been an important time to determine personal values, goals, and principles to be used in my life. This introspective look was not due to any course, but instead happened as a result of the environment of the MBA program.

The Goizueta Business School has developed and fostered an atmosphere where teamwork and team building are essential to a student's success in the program. The administration is very responsive to student issues and concerns and the faculty makes an extra effort to be accessible.

My experiences at Goizueta were tremendous. I would encourage others seeking an MBA to consider the program. The program is characterized by exceptional students and professors that enrich the learning process.

MICHIGAN STATE UNIVERSITY

MICHIGAN STATE UNIVERSITY

Eli Broad Graduate School of Management

215 Eppley Center

Michigan State University

East Lansing, Michigan 48824-1121

E-mail address: mba@msu.edu

Web site address: www.bus.msu.edu

23.
MICHIGAN
STATE
UNIVERSITY

Enrollment: 209

Women: 24%

Non-U.S.: 35%

Minority: 6%

Part-time: 186

Average age: 28

Applicants accepted: 22%

Median starting pay: $77,560

Annual tuition and fees:
   resident—$14,250
   nonresident—$20,250

Estimated annual budget: $32,810

Average GMAT score: 639

Average months of work
   experience: 60

Accepted applicants enrolled: 53%

Corporate ranking: 17

Graduate ranking: 28

Intellectual capital rank: 29

Teaching methods: case study 35%, lecture 25%, team projects 30%, other 10%

With new dean Robert Duncan eager to play up his students' teamwork, the Eli Broad School of Management at Michigan State University may hold its own within the fiercely competitive job market. It doesn't hurt that adapting is Duncan's area of expertise. Duncan, who started in January, was a leadership and change professor at Northwestern, where he also served as provost. Broad, known for its supply chain management concentration, also boasts a unique military-inspired Team Effectiveness Research Laboratory and a new financial trading room. "We're able to do these things because we're smaller," Dean Duncan explains. Students say they enjoy the intimate community, though it does limit the number of recruiters who visit. Duncan says he regularly meets with such recruiters for feedback on how to better prepare students. Top recruiters from the economy of yesteryear were Ford Motor Company, Intel, and General Motors. Since September 11, these firms are not hiring with the same gusto. Duncan and his team have worked together to find alternatives.

    Many students cite the career management center, and in particular, its director, Helen Dashney, as the best part of the Broad experience. "She's just outstanding," says one 2002 graduate. "She puts in way too many hours." Students also praise the practical skills gleaned from supply chain management and Broad's hidden jewel—finance. And the team lab forces students to deal with difficult personalities. While some say the school is a best buy, a few students complained about freeloading classmates. "Classes are dumbed down to the lowest level," says one alumnus. Overall, Michigan State's business school offers a good, inexpensive education—and recruiters have begun to take notice, placing the school at number 17 in the recruiter poll in 2002.

Broad's labs distinguish its curriculum from that of other schools. Partly in response to recruiters' concerns regarding Broad students' lack of teamwork skills, in the fall of 2000, the school introduced a new, six-week lab exercise that places every Broad student in a military situation similar to what the U.S. Navy uses. Led by Professor John Hollenback, the Eli Broad Professor of Management and a psychologist by training, participants arrive at decisions by working in multiperson teams in response to a computer simulation. Students are evaluated constantly throughout the simulation based on the consequences of their decisions.

The lab grew out of the question: "What can you do to improve leadership under stress?" says Hollenback. In stopping the simulations at points of chaos, Hollenback captures what he calls "teachable moments" for analyzing leadership. "We don't assume that it's common sense," he says. The Department of Defense funneled in more than $2 million for the program, which remains a project of the Office of Naval Research. Broad's other notable lab—the Financial Analysis Laboratory—lets MBAs manage portfolios and trade finances, commodities, and energy. At the same time, the school lacks the financial finesse of the more prestigious schools. "We're not Columbia or Wharton in the finance area," admits MBA Program Director John Delaney.

For almost 30 years, Broad's forte has been supply chain management, an area that combines manufacturing operations, purchasing, transportation, and distribution. Also strong is finance, amid a lineup of concentrations that includes business information systems, corporate accounting, hospitality business, human resources management, general management, and marketing and technology.

A new curriculum will greet students in 2003. In 2000, students harshly criticized classes as disorganized and full of fluff. That's still true, according to some. Director Delaney maintains that the school continuously monitors student feedback, reeducating the teachers when necessary. "Our objective is to have quality teaching," he says. A new curriculum would certainly help. "We're in the process of making some changes," Delaney says. "The last major revision was 4 years ago." Changes in the marketplace have filtered through to the curriculum. Since the school views internships as essentially interviews for permanent jobs, Broad will offer more electives before internship interviews. "Students will be able to interview for internships with a little more depth," says Delaney. It's a trend many top schools have been following in the last year or so.

The school's team-building practices begin with a weeklong August orientation that has incoming MBAs participating in outdoor team-building exercises at nearby Camp Highlands. Students also take in some resume development advice from the school's placement center before sectioning off into 35- to 40-person cohorts from their larger group of about 110 entering MBAs to tackle their fall semester's required courses. Your team will meet its corporate advisor, assigned through the Leadership Alliance Program. These execs, from companies like the Big Three carmakers, Ameritech, EDS, and Dow Chemical—many of them alumni of the B-school's executive MBA program—help identify a company issue or problem that will serve as the basis for a team project in the Global Organization course. Students meet regularly with their corporate advisor to apply academic and practical research methods in arriving at analysis.

Students are asked to choose at least one concentration, which requires four courses in a subject area, but many are able to fit in two majors or to combine one major area of interest with a three-course subconcentration in international business or leadership and change management. The school is feeding off 2002's accounting scandals. Professor Tom Linsmeier, chair of the accounting and information systems department, recently testified before congress on Enron. After Linsmeier, the former special consultant to the SEC, taught students to critically look at statements, they wrote letters to Kmart's investor relations department. This was before the company filed for bankruptcy and bad accounting allegations surfaced. "They got a non-answer answer," Linsmeier says.

Globally minded students have the option of partaking in a faculty-led international study trip during the brief time between the end of classes and the start of a summer internship. Most recently, a group visited Thailand. MBAs can also extend their international experience by spending a semester in an exchange program with either the International University of Japan in Yamoto-Machi, ITESM-Monterrey in Mexico, the International University in Germany in Bruschal, or the Norwegian School of Management B1 in Sandvika. The number of Michigan State 2002 students who are non-U.S. citizens comes out to 34 percent, an increase from the class of 2000's 29 percent. International topics have become more integrated in the curriculum, too, and the program offers some flexibility for students with more than business, or an extraordinary amount of business, on their minds. Through Michigan State's Broad School and the Detroit College of Law, students can complete a combination JD/MBA degree in four years of full-time study. There's also a dual degree program with Thunderbird—The American Graduate School of International Management, which awards graduates with both the Master of International Management from Thunderbird and the Master of Business Administration from Michigan State in four years.

As far as information technology is concerned, the Broad School is about on track— finally—after first establishing a campuswide computer lab as late as 1991. Not until 1993 was there an MBA-only computer space, which was made possible when the $21.5 million North Business Complex freed up space for renovation in the old Epply Center building. Today, all students are required to bring their own laptops to class, where they can plug in at every seat. A new MBA computer lab opened in fall 1999, and students can now find state-of-the-art electronic research tools and a substantial selection of team meeting rooms on campus. Students and faculty use MBA Class Link to connect online, converse in chat rooms, and transmit or receive homework assignments and course materials. The school's library also houses laptop outlets at every carrel and table, along with online resources such as ABI/Inform, LexisNexis, and Dow Jones Interactive. The new placement center (open to business major undergrads, too) was remodeled from what used to be a business library, and students can also find resources for identifying firms and potential employers there, plus video interviewing capability and interview rooms.

Aside from the latest developments in new facilities, one of the school's biggest assets is its small size. Fewer than 300 students are enrolled, and more than 50 faculty members are on board each year, creating an intimate environment where "cohorts become like a family, and classes naturally develop a sense of camaraderie," according to John Delaney. "The program isn't so big that anyone can get lost," Delaney continues, "but with the larger university, students have access to all types of events and resources and still have a chance to get to know the faculty well." The dynamic makes it easier to offer students a degree of attention not found at other peer schools.

The MSU campus boasts 5000 acres of tree-lined grounds and the Red Cedar River, which flows throughout. "The summer is all green. The winter is all white," gasped one international graduate. There are miles of bike paths, rollerblade trails and walkways, and a bus system, plus two golf courses and three intramural athletic facilities. Another entertainment option is the Wharton Center for Performing Arts. The heart of campus sits across the Red Cedar River from the university's more modern additions, which include the law school and Broad's North Business Complex, the 59,000-square foot building connected by a covered walkway to Eppley Center, the B-school's old brick-and-sandstone home. The tiny MBA program can feel greatly overshadowed by the mammoth undergraduate business program's 5005 students, which in turn seems dwarfed by the 40,000 bodies that converge on campus each academic year. But with management-program-only options, such as biweekly coffee hours in the MBA lounge, Broad students can always find a level of comfort. However, some minority students wish the program were more ethnically diverse.

Housing is plentiful in East Lansing. The majority of MBA students live in nearby apartments staring at about $550 per month for a one-bedroom, and the MBA office facilitates the housing process by maintaining a notebook that lists information on more than 70 apartment complexes. Students use a protected housing discussion Web site to find roommates and the best housing options. They'll publish student requests for roommates, too. Still, approximately 30 percent of the students live on the campus, and with a student population greater than 43,000, Michigan State does well in offering a variety of apartments and housing options to suit different needs. Many MBAs take spots in the Owen Graduate Center ($2156 per semester) or in University Apartments, where the one-bedroom units start at $470 per month. As long as you reserve early, these are readily available.

As a Big Ten school, Michigan State offers an all-encompassing campus lifestyle for those who want it, with key social events revolving around the Spartans football squad. For pregame tailgate parties, MBAs get together across the street from the B-school and then walk to Spartan Stadium, where they have a choice block of tickets. There's also the annual MBA picnic, and every Thursday afternoon business grads pick a local bar in which to quaff and chat; Harper's Restaurant, Brewpub, and Beggar's Banquet are some of the favorites. The MBA Association has been active in running a charity auction and participating in the MBA food fight. Last year, Broad MBAs won the food fight's pounds-per-student category for the third consecutive year, collecting 550 pounds per Spartan. Students call the community down-to-earth and not hypercompetitive. If MBAs tire of East Lansing, Chicago, Detroit, and Toronto are not too far away, and neither is canoeing in northern Michigan. There's fun for MBAs' spouses, too. Spartan Spouses and Significant Others (S^3, or S cubed), started by three spouses about two years ago, is very active in coordinating dinners, hayrides, and workshops. And Broad offers a two-week support program for international students, including a lunch etiquette seminar (also available to U.S. students).

PLACEMENT DETAILS

While Michigan State may not get the same mix of recruiters as bigger schools, the placement office compensates for the loss in personal attention. In addition, major companies target Broad specifically for its supply management expertise. Logistics Professor Dave Closs says IBM hires from fewer graduate schools these days but still taps Broad.

After completing renovations last year, the center is ready for whatever the economy brings. The placement center elicits awe from students. Career center director Helen Dashney had a backup plan for September 11's beating—an alumni e-mail newsletter, online company database, and contacts from Broad's executive education programs. One student described Dashney's challenge as "trying to swim upstream with a ruler as a paddle." She expects the equivalent from students. They create their own databases with contacts. "It's in essence like taking another class," Dashney says. In this class, every student gets personal attention.

Still, personal attention didn't help the 31 percent of grads who had no job offers by graduation—a familiar refrain at many B-schools. While 80 percent of Michigan State's 2002 grads did have jobs by three months after graduation, their salaries lagged some of the top 30 schools: starting pay packages for Michigan State grads were about $90,300. A full 28 percent of grads with offers headed for jobs in manufacturing and operations, while the rest were spread out in marketing, finance, consulting, technology, and other functions. About 59 percent of Michigan State grads found employment in the Midwest, while another 15 percent headed for the Northeast.

TOP HIRES

Ford Motor Company (5); Raytheon (4); Visteon (4); United Technologies (3); Guidant (3); Whirlpool (2); Standard & Poor's Corporate Value Consulting (2); Johnson & Johnson (2); General Electric (2); Applied Materials (2); Dow Chemical (2); Federal-Mogul (2).

OUTSTANDING FACULTY

Naveen Khanna (finance); Kathy Petroni (accounting); Ted Stank (supply chain); Glenn Omura (marketing).

APPLICANT TIPS

Michigan State is looking for people with motivation, character, integrity, and strong communication, according to Jennifer Chizuk, the director of the full-time academic program. There is a two-step screening process.

First, applicants must be able to handle the academic rigor of the program. Then, the school considers interviews, resumes, and letters of recommendation. Chizuk looks for applicants who have done their research in applying. She wants people whose goals match the program's goals and who can look 5, 10, and 15 years ahead. If applicants do not meet the program's academic demands, she will advise them on how to strengthen their skill sets. After that, they can reapply the next year.

As with most schools, be certain to carefully think out your answers to essay questions. These provide the best opportunity to show who you are and how your goals match the program's goals. Finally, visit the campus if you can, to make certain the smaller environment of the school fits what you're looking for.

BROAD MBAs SOUND OFF

The degree of dynamic, interactive learning, in conjunction with the informal, personal feel of the program, make the Broad School an ideal fit for someone looking for these characteristics in his/her MBA. Someone enrolling here must realize that a large part of the learning is based on team assignments and group work—a program characteristic which emulates real-world experience. To succeed in this program, a person must be willing and capable of working with others and must be a conscientious contributor. The personality of the Broad School must fit the student just as the personality of the student must fit the program.

The golden egg of Michigan State's MBA program is the career placement. The staff is accessible and works tirelessly to find employment for students during this difficult year.

Michigan State is a wonderful place to get an MBA. The program is small, the workload is manageable, and the faculty and staff really care about our success. I would encourage my friends to come to MSU to get an MBA because I know they'll have fun, they'll learn a lot, and the placement office will do everything humanly possible to get them a great job!

My MBA experience at Michigan State University was one of the great decisions of my life. I was given personalized attention in classes and with the placement and career center. The placement and career center went out of their way to make sure I was successful in finding a summer internship and a full-time job during the tough economic environment.

The cost-benefit of the program is not going to be better anywhere else. Very low cost combined with an excellent placement office make it a very good choice. The small number of students in the program provides added camaraderie.

The Broad School has its own personality, which must match that of each of its students. I would recommend the program to a student looking for a small, personal, informal program with the intent of finding work in one of the Broad School's well-regarded concentration areas. A prospective student looking for such a program would be quite pleased here.

The small size of the program is a double-edged sword. It is great for faculty interaction, small class size and knowing your classmates well. It is a negative because fewer industries and companies can be served by the school and job searching outside of those relationships can be difficult.

The program is good and the school is making a lot of improvement. Assuming that effort will be maintained in the future, this school is a good place to get an MBA at an affordable cost.

The Broad program offers an excellent opportunity to learn about business concepts in a relaxed atmosphere. There aren't so many students that you get lost in the crowd, and, as a result, not only do all of the professors know you by name but so does the staff. This comes in handy during the job search! Furthermore, the workload isn't so heavy that you can't enjoy a healthy social life while earning your degree. I've had a great time and learned a lot, too.

24.
WASHINGTON
UNIVERSITY-
ST. LOUIS

WASHINGTON UNIVERSITY-ST. LOUIS

John M. Olin School of Business
Campus Box 1133
1 Brookings Drive
St. Louis, Missouri 63105-4899
E-mail address: mba@olin.wustl.edu
Web site address: www.olin.wustl.edu

Enrollment: 313
Women: 20%
Non-U.S.: 36%
Minority: 10%
Part-time: 354
Average age: 29
Applicants accepted: 35%
Median starting pay: $80,000
Annual tuition and fees: $30,290

Estimated annual budget: $51,822
Average GMAT score: 651
Average months of work
    experience: 66
Accepted applicants enrolled: 44%
Corporate ranking: 33
Graduate ranking: 21
Intellectual capital rank: 20

Teaching methods: case study 50%, experiential learning 15%, lecture 20%, simulations 5%, team projects 10%

Sometimes you want to go where everybody knows your name, whether it be to the local watering hole, the barbershop, or, in this case, to B-school. To the folks at the Olin School of Business on the campus of Washington University in St. Louis, this personal focus is very important. It is an idea that Dean Stuart Greenbaum calls "high-touch." "There is a demand for the personal attention," says Greenbaum, "They don't want to be a number, they want to be an individual. They want to be a name, and they want people to know their name." This interest in students is Olin's biggest selling point for both students and faculty.

At Olin, faculty members know you and care about your advancement. It is not unusual to see a group of students and professors out together sharing stories over a meal of toasted ravioli and Budweiser, two St. Louis staples. "Because (Olin) is small, you see students in the hallway and you talk about what's going on in their lives," explains Jeroen Swinkles, professor of managerial economics and strategy. "You drink a certain amount of beer with them, partly because it's fun, and partly because it's a great way to get a sense of what is really going on."

Much of this progress can be attributed to the leadership of Dean Greenbaum. Before coming to Olin in 1995, Greenbaum spent 20 years at Kellogg, where he was part of the group of visionaries that turned the school into the elite institution it is today. It was at Kellogg that Greenbaum realized the importance of responding to students' needs and the effectiveness of the high-touch mentality. After seven years at Olin,

Greenbaum feels that the school is on the right track. "My job when I came here was to extract the fullest benefits from a school of this size," says Greenbaum. The question remains, however, how successful the high-touch mentality is. True, it may create a more compassionate and focused student and employee, but such endeavors do little in helping to bring recruiters to Olin and to place students. The school is on a noticeable skid, falling in the rankings in each of the last four surveys since peaking at number 16 in 1996. If these benefits that Greenbaum speaks of are not brought to fruition soon, who knows where the school will end up in the next few years?

When you think of St. Louis, you don't think booming metropolis, but, according to students, the city has a lot to offer: the frozen concretes at Ted Drewes, watching the city's beloved baseball Cardinals at Busch Stadium, taking a cruise on a gondola in Forest Park, or listening to hometown favorite Chuck Berry perform at Blueberry Hill on the city's famous Loop, just blocks from campus. St. Louis is also home to companies such as Anheuser-Busch, Monsanto, and Ralston-Purina, something that Stacy Jackson, assistant dean and head of the Center for Experiential Learning, sees as a huge advantage because of the opportunities students are afforded that cannot be offered in the nation's larger cities. For instance, whereas at other schools students are lucky to have CEOs and other top officials of the business world visit and give a lecture, students at Olin can call such dignitaries colleagues. "We like to call St. Louis the biggest small city in the country," Jackson says. "In Chicago it is very hard to get access to the senior-level people. Here, students get access to senior people in companies. It's probably the biggest buzz among students."

In the past few years, the Center for Experiential Learning has been revamped, and four sections of focus have been developed: entrepreneurial, international, corporate, and community. The reason for the development of the program was the realization that students needed to get as much experience as possible. Says Jackson, "The whole emphasis for us is in that two-year time frame; in most cases you get a one-case shot to add to your degree, and that's the internship. We have four programs that will help students get experience to add to their resume." Each of the four programs gives students a chance to get involved in their respective area of focus.

In the Skandalaris Entrepreneurship Program (named for Bob Skandalaris, CEO of Noble International Ltd., who donated $3 million for the project), you can take part in the Hatchery, where you and your team can create a business plan for an emerging company or one for your own company.

If international business is your thing, the Global Management Studies course combines coursework on the history, culture, and business practices of a specific country or region with a consulting project completed during a two-week field research trip. In 2002, a group of students in the program put together a proposal to travel to Cuba. The proposal was signed off, and, after some preparation that included puffing on the country's famous cigars as partaking in its fine rum, the group traveled to the island country. In the past few years, students have also traveled to Eastern and Western Europe as well as to Asia.

The corporate program includes the Investment Praxis, where you have the opportunity to invest $500,000 of the school's money. You can also get experience through the Management Center Practicum. In the practicum, you and your four-person team and faculty member work on a consulting project with a client company, such as PricewaterhouseCoopers or MasterCard, applying management insights from coursework.

If you want to focus more on the community aspect of business, you can enroll in the Taylor Community Consulting Project. In the course you have the chance to work with St. Louis area nonprofit agencies, providing them with expertise and professional assistance.

With the relatively small number of students, it is easy to take one or even two of the courses offered by the experimental learning department, and any elective for that matter, something that 2002 grads commended. But with the small number of students comes the dilemma that Olin faces. On one hand, the school prides itself on being a small, tight-knit community where hands-on learning is job one. On the other hand, because the school's population is small, large recruiters from the coasts rarely schedule visits to interview students. Michael Gordinier, senior lecturer of management at Olin, feels that both can be achieved. "Right now we have two or three hundred students; if we could raise that up to something a little bit bigger, I think we could still maintain that same cozy atmosphere and be big enough to attract those recruiters who aren't coming now." Also, with such a small program, there aren't the vast numbers of alums available to students as there are at larger school. Grads of the class of 2002 also complained that the school is very homogenous, another downside of the school's size.

To compensate for the lack of recruiters from the coasts, special roadshows have been introduced in the past few years. Developed by Greg Hutchings, director of the Weston Career Resources Center, roadshows give students the chance to travel to where the recruiters are. The idea was a product of something Hutchings had experienced in his 15 years as an investment banker. "Roadshows were part of my life for many years," he explains. "As an investment banker, in order to sell public offerings, we would take our clients on the road to meet with institutional and retail investors. We are applying that same concept here to the students." Each year, students have the opportunity to travel on as many of the 8 to 10 scheduled roadshows as they want. In the past, roadshows have visited New York, Chicago, and San Francisco, as well as Texas and what remains of Silicon Valley.

Olin also makes an effort to present students in the best light possible, marketing them as a company would a product. To do this, the school has set up a Web-based ePortfolio, a database showcasing the talents and background of each student. For the classes of 2002 and 2003, the ePortfolio was sent to over 4000 recruiters worldwide. Students are grouped together by career interests, including consulting, industry finance, investment banking, and marketing. In addition to the ePortfolio, recruiters were sent a paper ticker tape in a 6-inch tube directing them to the ePortfolio site.

The curriculum at Olin is unique in that you have a wide variety of options because all of your core courses, with the exception of a second-level accounting course and a final capstone course, will be completed in your first semester. So instead of having only two semesters to take elective courses, at Olin you have three. Included in the core courses are the basics such as statistics, strategy, accounting, and marketing. These are squeezed into two seven-week minisemesters. Because you are learning so many things in such a short period of time, faculty members meet to make sure no information is being repeated and to try to intertwine lessons as much as possible. "We make sure that when we teach a particular topic, it gets integrated at exactly the time when other classes need it," says Gordinier. This integration is something that 2002 grads felt was extremely beneficial.

With this schedule, you are able to take as many as seven electives before your summer internship, which many employers look on highly. Also, at Olin there are no majors offered, which makes it possible for you to specialize in the traditional disciplines or to create your own concentration in any interdisciplinary combination you can think of. When the minisemesters were introduced in 1997, students found it hard to prepare for exams every eight weeks. To get around this, Olin switched from a traditional grading scale to a pass/fail scale. This successfully lowered the pressure put on students and also minimized competition between classmates. But if you are one of those people who bask in the limelight of being at the head of the class, don't fret; you can still set yourself apart by earning a high pass for outstanding performance—a designation limited to the top 20 percent of each class.

Your time at Olin begins a few weeks before the start of classes with a preterm period where you can take optional minicourses in accounting, quantitative methods, and skill building to hone your skills in such programs as Microsoft Excel. The accounting and quantitative methods modules are taught by the core faculty members who will teach the actual courses, which brings some continuity between the two. After preterm, you take part in a weeklong orientation that includes an overview of the curriculum as well as some ice-breaker activities that help you to get acquainted with your classmates and the school itself. At the end of orientation, you will receive the first part of a semester-long project called the Integrating Case Experience (ICE) course.

Throughout the semester, you and a group of peers will work on cases, each preparing you for the end of semester and the ICE case competition. Without giving too much away about the competition, it asks you to take high-level business cases and analyze them under tight time constraints, much as in the real world. You are asked to develop an approach, an analysis, and a conclusion, and then present them before a group of core faculty members, second-year students, and alums and eventually a group of execs from the sponsor's company. "We have a competition among the teams to try to get high passes and win awards for best presentation and highest scores and so on," says Joe Fox, director of MBA programs. "But probably more compelling to them is that our corporate sponsors have their representatives in the room." Immediately after the ICE case competition, you will decompress at the Icebreaker Party, a schoolwide event celebrating the end of an intense semester.

In your second year, all of your courses are electives except for a high-level accounting course. Because all of your core courses are out of the way, you can start to home in on the skills and the courses that will be important for your internships. After your internship, "it is all elective all the time," Fox says. "They come back in the second year after their internships and have all electives with the exception of a capstone course in the final semester, kind of a wrap-up strategy, and that's it."

The social atmosphere thrives at Olin. On Friday afternoons you can take part in the Friday Afternoon Club. Explains Gordinier, "After we've had some speakers lecture, we go out into the courtyard and enjoy the 'lubricants of learning,' as our dean likes to call them. It gives us all a chance to get to know everyone better, as well as talk about what they want to do and about what the speaker had to say." There are a good number of restaurants at the nearby Loop, giving you all kinds of options from Italian to Thai to Lebanese to Japanese—or, if you are feeling wild, you can also get a hamburger or pizza. The Loop is also home to many bars where Olinites can regularly be found. If staying in shape is a priority, you can use Washington U's athletic complex at any time to work out, play tennis or racquetball, swim, or play basketball.

Many 2002 grads appreciated the time set aside to address the needs and questions they had, thanks to the open-door policy that many faculty members have. However, the availability of the faculty is something that leads to some unusual complaints. Says Gordinier, "People complain that I am not available enough because the line outside my office is so long!"

A concern that some students have is space, or the lack thereof. Says one 2002 grad, "With the Olin building designated as home for BSBAs, full-time MBAs, and part-time MBAs, many areas resemble zoos, especially the computer lab. At peak times, it is not unusual to see three or four students crowded around one computer." Along the same lines, there is a good deal of resentment, bordering on jealousy, felt by the MBAs toward executive MBAs. With the opening of the new Knight Center for Executive

Education, many 2002 grads said they felt like the administration focused too much time and energy on the EMBA program at the expense of the MBAs. "The EMBAs have a state-of-the-art new building with amazing facilities which weren't available to us, while not even all our classrooms had Internet access," says Mary Karen Majerus, a 2002 grad. "If the administration wants to improve the experience, they need to focus their attention more equitably between the different channels."

Another gripe is the lack of student housing and the absence of parking options for MBAs. Because there are no residence halls set aside for MBAs on campus, students usually live in the surrounding neighborhoods in apartments or shared homes.

Some 2002 grads voiced concerns over the way the administration dealt with criticism. When asked for ideas on how to improve the program, administrators would take a reactive, defensive position, say many grads. One example, says a member of the class of 2002, is Olin's reaction to the 2000 *BusinessWeek* rankings, in which the school dropped from 16 to 23. "They were quite defensive in their communication to the student body, questioning *BusinessWeek*'s polling techniques and statistical sampling," she says. "I thought it would have been much more appropriate and constructive if they had spent less time picking apart the poll and its possible faults and more time on tangible actions on how to improve the full-time program." That said, students are quick to applaud the program as a whole. 2002 grads were surprised and impressed by the high caliber of their classmates, as well as the close-knit community that they were able to be a part of.

St. Louis is not your typical big city, and Olin is not your typical B-school. Both are small enough for you to feel at home, but big enough for you not to get bored. At Olin you will know your classmates, you will know your professors, and you may even know your dean. That is what Olin is good at, the hands-on, high-touch state of mind. Ask Dean Greenbaum what he is proudest of about Olin, and he won't say the accolades, the awards, the rankings, or the recognition; the answer is much closer to home. "It is our sense of family and community that I am proudest of," he says.

Olin still has a way to go if it wants to measure up to the elite schools, but with the strong leadership sense of Greenbaum, combined with his proven track record, good things may be on the horizon for Washington University. If you want to be a part of the change, and the prospect of a smaller school in the heart of the Midwest tickles your fancy, Olin may be just what you are looking for.

PLACEMENT DETAILS

Students were mostly pleased with the efforts of the Weston Career Resources Center in helping them find positions, especially those who were looking for less traditional positions. The roadshows also helped many students find positions that they would not have found otherwise. However, keeping this in mind, only 58 percent of the class of 2002 had at least one job offer by graduation, one of the lower numbers in the top 30. Even in 2000, when the high times of hiring were still upon us, Olin struggled in placing grads in comparison to other schools that placed nearly everyone. Also, Olin grads tend to come from the Midwest and to stay there after graduating—most likely a direct effect of the lack of national recruiters coming to campus. While every school suffered in placement in 2002, and the blame should not be cast on career services, there are few schools that had as much trouble placing students as Olin, leaving the effectiveness of the office open for question.

Olin grads do tend to make a good deal more money in their starting pay packages than graduates of other schools ranked comparably. With a median of $106,100, you would have to go all the way up to UCLA, ranked at 16, to find a school whose grads made more right out of school. However, the pay package did drop nearly $3000 in the past two years.

TOP HIRES

Emerson (4); Guidant (4); 3M (3); Bank of America (3); Citibank (3); Noble International (3); Wells Fargo (3).

OUTSTANDING FACULTY

Jeroen Swinkels (economics); Todd Milbourn (finance); Michael Gordinier (management); Patrick Moreton (strategy); Glenn MacDonald (strategy).

APPLICANT TIPS

With the class of 2004, 85 percent of students were interviewed, and eventually, Brad Pearson, director of MBA admissions and financial aid, hopes to get the number to 100 percent. To do this, a group known as the Admissions and Recruiting Champions (ARCh) of Olin was created, made up of students who help in the admissions process through such things as conducting interviews with potential students and reading through applications. Students involved in ARCh also travel to every domestic recruiting event that Olin schedules throughout the year, and they get the opportunity to do international travel with the program as well. In its first year, 70 students were involved in ARCh, and the interest continues to rise.

A direct result of ARCh is the high yield and quality of students who accepted their admittance to Olin. Average GMAT scores are up, as well as work experience and GPA. "In just looking at our stats and comparing them to the last three years, [the incoming class of 2004] is stellar and I think the direct impact is the students connecting with the candidates," says Pearson. "I can talk until I am blue in the face, but applicants connect with the students and it has paid off 10-fold."

So what does it take to get into Olin? According to Pearson, Olin is not looking for a perfect 800 GMAT or a 4.0 GPA, but for someone who stands out. "We're looking for someone who has personality, who has the soft skills," he says. "We are looking for students who have had a track record of being involved. We want people who are going to get involved here and remain involved once they leave as a partner of the school."

A good way to get off on the right foot is to visit campus and take the time to schedule an interview. "The interview is very instrumental," says Pearson. "In meeting students that I hadn't interviewed, yeah, they look great on paper, but they are really missing those soft skills. They may be the smartest person in the world, but if they can't connect to the customer or client, you've lost them."

Pearson has a few tips for potential applicants: first, apply early. As the last deadline nears, the class is coming together and it gets extremely competitive. Second, explain any red flags. "Don't make excuses, explain and move on. We are all human; we understand that no one is perfect. If your GPA suffered for some reason, tell us why."

OLIN MBAs SOUND OFF

Olin was the perfect match for what I was looking for in a business school—faculty and staff who were genuinely dedicated to my progress. Moreover, the atmosphere evokes teamwork among classmates that I have not found elsewhere in my career. I could not have reasonably asked for more in a business school experience.

Wash U. has exceeded all of my expectations. Name recognition is our biggest challenge. Prior to Olin, I worked in Vermont and if it was not for one of my customers that took time to educate me about the school, I may not have even applied.

Olin lacks a lot externally (brand name, recognition among employers, active career development recruiters). In addition, Olin caters only toward the Midwestern companies and doesn't do enough to attract companies from both the East and West Coasts.

My only negative aspects to comment on are the career placement services that Olin offers. Much of the Career Resource Center's placement efficacy, however, is due to the current state of the economy, which is understandable. I still feel, however, that in spite of these external factors affecting the efficiency of the office, there is room for recruitment improvement.

My MBA experience has been fantastic. It has provided me with the necessary tools and knowledge to approach my career field with greater confidence and capabilities. The opportunity to interact and meet students from various ethnic, social and professional backgrounds has been the highlight of my experience. The Olin experience provided me more than I expected to gain in an MBA program.

The common theme here is that it's your program. I feel that I have put a great deal into this program and gotten a great deal out of it, not only in terms of raw skills but also in terms of leadership, accountability and experiential learning. I have learned a great deal about myself and I would highly urge a prospective student to look seriously at Olin.

There may be some pocket kinks that need to be ironed out, but with the school's quick, consistent, and decisive response, I am certain all will be fixed and constantly be improved upon. The Olin MBA surpassed all my expectations. I am completely satisfied and confident that I received the best education that I could have hoped for.

**25.
UNIVERSITY
OF MARYLAND**

UNIVERSITY OF MARYLAND

Robert H. Smith School of Business
2308 Van Munching Hall
University of Maryland
College Park, Maryland 20742
E-mail address: mba_info@rhsmith.umd.edu
Web site address: www.rhsmith.umd.edu

Enrollment: 516
Women: 31%
Non-U.S.: 38%
Minority: 15%
Part-time: 740
Average age: 28
Applicants accepted: 23%
Median starting pay: $75,000
Annual tuition and fees:
    resident—$14,960
    nonresident—$23,706

Estimated annual budget: $33,000
Average GMAT score: 656
Average months of work
    experience: 59
Accepted applicants enrolled: 52%
Corporate ranking: 42
Graduate ranking: 6
Intellectual capital rank: 21

Teaching methods: case study 30%, distance learning 5%, experiential learning 10%, lecture 30%, simulation 5%, team projects 20%

In 2001, the Maryland Terrapins clinched the NCAA basketball championship, bringing acclaim to the entire University of Maryland campus—including the Robert H. Smith School of Business. But basketball doesn't explain the B-school's growing stature. In the last five years, the school, under Dean Howard Frank, has steadily climbed the ranks, casting aside its public school mantle and instituting the technology, curriculum, and attitude of a top private B-school. The school has a working trading floor, a beefed-up faculty, and improved ties to the DC area.

Still, not everything at Smith is so impressive. The school, named in honor of a real estate developer who donated $15 million to his alma mater, scored low with grads once again in one major department: career services. And while corporate recruiters had been warming up to Smith grads, when the economy headed south, recruiters did, too. Only about 50 percent of the 250-person class of 2002 was employed at graduation, and Dean Frank has a few ideas about why—recruiters chose their favorite schools, and while many had tried Smith in 1999 and 2000, when 2001 rolled around, their experiences were limited and Smith fell off a shortened must-have list. Second, the career service center was out of sync with the changing economy. "That's the one hole that we need to fill," says the dean, once a businessman himself, who took the helm of Smith in 1997 and has just signed up for another five years. His wish to see the institution rank among the truly great business schools may follow the Terrapins' success if his complete overhaul of the curriculum, and now career services, takes hold. Still, Smith has hurdles to jump. Dean Frank has increased faculty size, revenues, and curriculum offerings—not to mention built a brand-new, 103,000-square-foot wing, doubling the size of the Smith School's Van Munching Hall. Now, Frank wants Smith to sit among the top B-schools.

That's a tall order, considering 2002 grads complained about the career center's poor alumni network and marketing effort. To repair career services, the career center, like the rest of the business world, was restructured. Last spring, Smith promoted Assistant Dean Cherie Scricca to the position of Associate Dean for Master's Programs and Career Services, bringing new energy and organization to the office. The department, containing both the Master's Program Office and the Career Management Center, will add four new positions. The center must also make a comeback from the loss of its assistant dean for career services, who resigned in June. It is clear that Smith must take a lesson from its own marketing curriculum in selling its culture and curriculum to students. "We don't have a powerful brand yet," says Dean Frank.

If placement catches up, the school's neighbors—government agencies in Washington, DC, and research firms in Maryland and Virginia—should take notice. In addition to expanding on campus, the school has extended its cyber-reach. Smith's rooms feature videoconferencing, wired data jacks attached to every seat, and computers that can communicate with rooms abroad and next door in Van Munching Hall. The hall is home to both undergrads and grad students, which is both an anomaly and a boon. Because today's undergrads are so tech savvy, Frank says they often know things about computers that MBAs don't. Frank, an information systems expert himself and entrepreneur, pushed hard

for this futuristic classroom. "We decided we would use technology instead of getting on a plane when we wanted to communicate with 20 or 30 people."

Now, Frank needs to deliver on jobs and monitor teaching. The part-time MBA program inconvenienced some of the class of 2002, who complained about trekking to off-campus sites for nighttime classes. Frank has tackled some pretty grand plans before. Prior to coming to College Park, he oversaw the world's largest information technology budget as director of the IT office at the Defense Advanced Research Projects Agency, the federal entity that played a large part in the development of both the stealth bomber and the computer mouse. And, back in the 1970s, a telecommunications consulting firm he co-founded contracted with the U.S. government to develop "a network that linked computers and human beings, and that allowed computers to interact with one another," Frank remembers. With apologies to Al Gore, that project is now known as the Internet.

Smith now offers 17 e-commerce courses and added concentrations in supply chain management, entrepreneurship, financial engineering, global business and knowledge, management, business telecommunications, and management in technology in addition to e-commerce. New courses include Venture Capital for Investors and Entrepreneurs, Decision Modeling with Spreadsheets, and E-business Strategy. Also keeping ahead of the times, the accounting department, on its own volition, last year renamed itself the Department of Accounting and Information Insurance.

Beyond a blossoming curriculum, Smith is sprouting in almost every other capacity. Most of the MBA classes will be held this fall in a brand-new building. In the last five years, Smith has expanded its full-time faculty from 75 to more than 120 members. Over the next few years, the full-time faculty is expected to grow to about 140. Established in 1993 with $250,000, the Mayer

Fund now offers MBAs $1 million in assets for hands-on experience in securities analysis and portfolio management. The fund outpaced the S&P 500 and the Dow Jones during the fourth quarter of 2001. A slow-growth area is tuition. Although tuition is increasing by roughly 9 percent per year—now about $13,500 for in-state students and $22,300 for out-of-state students plus mandatory fees—a Maryland MBA remains one of the best bargains around. On the horizon, a global consortium with multiple companies and schools is growing. For example, Smith teamed up with about 10 international schools, including Rotterdam, CERAM Sophia Antipolis, and the Korea Institute for Technology and Science, to share skills at the Global Consortium for Technology and Business in Nice, France, in the fall of 2002 and held a videoconference prior to that kickoff event.

Closer to campus, Smith students also have good reason to stay put. MBAs tout their school's cooperative environment, and they value Smith's location. The Maryland suburbs just outside of Washington, DC, are a big draw for many, as are small class sizes, a high level of student involvement in running the school, and a notably diverse student body (38 percent international and 15 percent minority). The admissions office sweats over that last accolade. By targeting Miami, Texas, and Atlanta—cities heavily populated by minorities—and tapping its alumni base, UMD achieved a 10 percent increase in applications for the class of 2004 from African Americans and Hispanics, in line with the overall application boom.

Ask Smith graduates what they remember most about the MBA program, and they're likely to mention the Experiential Learning Modules (ELMs). These are four required one-week minicourses scattered throughout the two years and designed to expose you to aspects of business that aren't easily taught in a classroom. You'll kick off your first semester at Smith with a Foundations of Business ELM. The Founda-

tions of Business module features a five-day Integrative Simulation Exercise (ISE) in which you'll be grouped into teams to form a company and then asked to develop a business plan to secure venture funding. You'll present your plans to a group of venture capitalists. The ISE aims to teach you the value of teams, diversity, and communication in addition to the critical business functions of finance, marketing, human resources, and strategy. MBA core faculty members serve as advisors to each team. In the second year, a fall semester case competition captures campus attention for a week as student teams are put to the test, analyzing complex strategic problems, writing persuasive reports, and honing their presentation skills before a panel of judges who play the role of the company's board of directors. Finally, just before graduation, the class is hauled off to prison. A business ethics module includes a visit with former executives turned inmates at Allenwood Federal Prison to discuss the serious consequences of ethical compromises, as well as such topics as environmental issues, product defects, workplace discrimination, whistle blowing, and "creative" accounting.

The prison module reveals just how progressive Smith is these days. Before Enron entered liability lingo, Smith was already confronting integrity issues. Professor Mike Peters, who teaches a required accounting course, was preaching balance sheet scrutiny in the 1990s. Today, his students regularly knock on his door for accounting rules translation and send him e-mails after they have graduated. That's a level of accessibility that gives Smith an advantage over some of its peers. "We were ahead of this," Frank says. In fact, Smith appointed an integrity officer about a year ago, after students raised concerns about cheating.

MBAs, of course, are ultimately responsible for ethics and the rest of their educations. In the first year, you will complete your entire MBA core coursework, with 50 to 55 students tracked to take all their required classes together for the first semester, then reconfigured into new tracks for the second semester. The first half of the year comprises two terms of two-credit courses. Two three-credit core courses (Data, Models, and Decisions and Finance) span both terms. Fall semester courses include Financial Accounting, Managerial Economics and Public Policy, Leadership and Teamwork, Marketing Management, and Financial Management. In the spring, you will take Global Economic Environment, Managing Human Capital, Managerial Accounting, Strategic Management, Strategic Information Systems, and Supply Chain and Operations Management, plus one elective and the case competition. New to the curriculum—and a perk for job recruiters—is the requirement that students study communications for three semesters in Communications Mastery, a one-credit core course. In this course, you will master public speaking, attract an audience, and write professionally over three semesters. Three components may seem extreme, but you will benefit by gaining an ability to ace interviews and win case competitions after receiving personalized coaching and feedback in self-directed, interactive workshops.

In the second year, you can focus on areas of study through chosen electives, plus take a semester-long consulting project that many grads say is a highlight of the program. Teams of four to six students, led by a faculty adviser, grapple with real-world work thrown at them by paying client companies such as Sun Microsystems, Lockheed Martin, PepsiCo, the U.S. Postal Service, and Lehman Brothers. The MBA Consulting Program is attracting more clients from companies transforming their operations for New Economy business practice. Past MBA projects include development of a desktop management strategy, analyzing current supply chain management processes and identifying e-supply chain improvements, developing an IT infrastructure blueprint, and researching the impact of interactive marketing in business-to-business e-commerce.

Smith's favorite new toy may be its financial trading software with the Reuters news agency. The school's Netcentric Financial Markets Laboratory, which came to life last year, boasts nearly $1 million of real-time data and analytical hardware and software provided by Reuters, plus Daktronics electronic display boards and a 20-foot electronic stock ticker. Smith is one of the beta sites for the software, as part of its new Netcentricity Laboratory. The new high-tech teaching, research, and corporate resource facility is devoted exclusively to studying the instantaneous flow of information via the Internet and digital networks. The Laboratory has Sun Microsystems servers, terminals, and software to create a miniature version of the company's Menlo Park supply chain/e-commerce laboratory. The lab is also equipped with applications for real-time supply chain optimization and planning, Oracle's ERP applications, high-speed networks, wireless computing, TIBCO's real-time e-business infrastructure software, a sophisticated multimedia environment, and state-of-the-art flat panel displays and user workstations. Finance, along with entrepreneurship, is a strength at Smith, but it doesn't have the Wharton's cachet or Columbia's proximity to Wall Street.

International offerings are skyrocketing as well. You can travel to China or Chile for a few days or fly off to France for a full semester, with both multiple-day seminars and full-semester programs. Interested in going global? You can also cross-register at the Johns Hopkins University's Nitze School of Advanced International Studies, which provides access to 125 additional courses. Exchange programs are available at eight overseas management schools in Hong Kong, India, Spain, Denmark, the United Kingdom, France, Italy, and Germany through the school's center for global business. Full-time MBAs can do a summer or fall semester second-year exchange. And future mini-trips include Marketing of Biotechnology Products in Edinburgh, Scotland, Doing Business in China in Shanghai, and International Technology Policy and Global Internet Economics in Dublin, Ireland.

Smith's 2002 grads gripe about the school's shriveled alumni network. Some MBA 2002 grads found jobs only by bypassing the career center. "I had no choice. They just didn't have the skills or the network," said one grad. Now, with Scricca at the top of her game and a new communications-oriented focus, that should change. The old career services system focused on developing students' business skills, while the new system will both strengthen students' communications skills and sell Smith to recruiters. Although September 11 and a weakening MBA job market vanquished the $120,000 consulting gigs, government agencies and nonprofit groups are ripe with opportunities, if students keep an open mind, says Scricca. In these hard economic times, Scricca warns, the government jobs are "never the sexy ones that students want, [but] if all you're going to do is look for a position at Goldman Sachs, you're going to be disappointed."

B-school life at Smith centers around Van Munching Hall, a handsome four-story facility built in 1993, with a huge, skylighted roof that floods the cherry wood interior with sunshine. It's also one of the most attractive buildings on this pretty 1580-acre campus, an incongruously secluded oasis of manicured lawns and trees amidst the suburban sprawl and dizzying network of highways outside Washington. Students are an integral part of the workings of the B-school: the dean breakfasts with 25 MBAs every other week, holds regular town meetings, and includes students on all committees involving curriculum change and facilities planning. A number of student interest clubs connect MBAs with career-focused activities, such as a Visiting Executive Series; a mentoring program to help incoming students with the transition into the

school; a Social Concerns Committee that coordinates charitable efforts such as food drives, literacy programs, home repairs for the needy, and management advice to nonprofit organizations; and a social committee that arranges regular happy hours, tailgate parties when the Terps sports teams are in town, student-faculty picnics, and an annual MBA formal.

The Maryland campus breathes life from Washington's museums, monuments, and Metro subway system without inhaling its congestion. Students describe the campus as beautiful and their classmates as bright and motivated. "There was no slacker in the whole class," says one graduate. In the fall of 2002, Maryland cohosted with local universities the National Net Impact conference, a network dedicated to responsible business leadership.

Although a small number of apartments for graduate students are available on campus, most students live in surrounding suburban towns that are all well served by metropolitan Washington's extensive bus and subway system. It's also a reasonable commute should you choose to live either in Baltimore or downtown Washington, as both are reachable in under an hour by public transportation.

PLACEMENT DETAILS

With the career management center so shaky in 2002, students and staff need to rethink the system. Students called the center understaffed and in need of more contacts. For its part, the school says it's aware of its weaknesses and has already made strides toward improvement. "There has been a total refocus and redirection," says Scricca. In addition, there will be at least four new positions dedicated to employer development and outreach. The center must also fill the position of Assistant Dean for Career Services.

Before the reorganization, career management was split between the undergraduate and graduate levels. Now, the MBA program and undergraduate career management have combined forces. And Greater Washington provides the backdrop for many promising internship opportunities. Scricca's advice to all: "There are opportunities to be more creative in this wounded economy," if you are willing to take a salary hit. She cites government agencies and nonprofit groups as examples. "There are so many opportunities out there," Scricca says.

Additionally, Scricca wants employers to find students. She says her staff will market the Smith experience locally and nationally—in cyberspace, over the phone, and on the road. She'll need to get working: in 2002, only 64 percent of grads had jobs by commencement. Dean Frank admits that companies that were just getting to know the school had to cut schedules—and in tough times, long histories outweigh new relationships. Still, by three months after graduation, more than 80 percent of the class of 2002 managed to secure offers. And the employed grads garnered respectable pay packages of about $98,300. Nearly 80 percent of grads with jobs stayed in the Mid-Atlantic or Northeast after graduation.

TOP HIRES

Citibank (6); PepsiCo (5); Honeywell International (3); Booz Allen Hamilton (2); Washington Gas (2); Campbell Soup (2); Capital One (2); Ernst & Young (2); Fannie Mae (2); Intel (2); McKinsey & Company (2); SAIC (2); UBS Warburg (2); UBS PaineWebber (2); World Bank (2).

OUTSTANDING FACULTY

Mary VanDeWeghe (finance); Shreevardhan Lele (information technology); Joyce Russell (management and organization); Michael Peters (accounting); Ritu Agarwal (decision information technology); Alex Triantis (finance).

APPLICANT TIPS

Smith takes a whole-person approach to admissions. There is no secret ingredient to a Smith MBA. Admissions Director Sabrina White wants solid undergraduate GPAs; qualitative contribution at work, at school, or in the community; reference letters from previous employers; essays; and test scores—in no particular order. Someone who wants to leave a place better than he or she found it should apply, whereas someone who just counts billable hours should not bother. The class of 2004 hailed from the private sector, nonprofit organizations, family businesses, and self-employment. And PricewaterhouseCoopers supplied the most successful candidates. If you do not work for PricewaterhouseCoopers, do not fret. There is one other common denominator among all 2004 first-years. Director White notes that every student made a contribution to his or her workplace and was able to articulate that success during the application process. Also be able to articulate why you want an MBA and why you want a Smith MBA. Interviews are by invitation only, since Smith does not have enough resources to interview 2500 applicants for 204 slots.

You can't be too careful with your application. "Definitely read through it twice," says White. "Spell-check is your friend." And she does not want to see a hasty cut-and-paste job from another school's application. A final word of advice: make sure you stay in touch with the admissions office.

SMITH MBAs SOUND OFF

Maryland was a great place to be for two years. I received a great education, interacted with professors that are among the best, created a strong network of future business leaders and had a great time socially. There is a tremendous amount of momentum at the Smith School. Maryland can only get better going forward. The new school building is state of the art, allowing students to benefit even more from the great teachers and top research going on here. New activities and alumni events have brought the student/professor/alumni interaction to a new level.

My MBA experience was great! Far more than I expected, The Robert H. Smith School of business offered me not only good resources but also a good environment. The school is very open to students' suggestions, the dean is very close to the school daily life, the flexible curriculum allowed me to tailor my degree to a business development career and the executive visitor series and consulting projects allowed me to keep in touch with the business world. One of the most important lessons I have learned in my MBA experience in my school is that you must be in charge of managing your MBA experience and making the best use of all available resources to help you revamp your career business plan.

I selected Maryland because of its top tier standing and the proximity to the DC area. Because of the strength of the core courses, I realized that my planned concentration was not what I really want to do. With the guidance of faculty, I selected a concentration that really interests me—one that takes advantage of the excellent technology department. The MBA program at Maryland is top notch, as indicated by the number of professors that have been adjunct at the top five MBA programs.

The MBA experience not only enhances your knowledge of business topics, but it also enhances your interpersonal and presentation skills. These skills will prove extremely valuable in preparing me for my future career. Maryland was an excellent program that provides a great education at a fraction of the cost of other programs.

This school would be second to none if the placement office gets better. The faculty and peer students are great. The living cost is relatively low.

I think that Maryland is a great school in many aspects. However, I would not recommend the school for people who are looking to work on Wall Street. Those firms are just beginning to recruit at the school and students who got Wall Street offers did a lot of legwork to get them.

This program definitely provides great value for the money, with very good faculty, collaborative, conducive atmosphere and great classmates.

PURDUE UNIVERSITY

26.
PURDUE
UNIVERSITY

Krannert School of Management
1310 Krannert Building, Room 160
Purdue University
West Lafayette, Indiana 47907-1310
E-mail address: krannert_ms@mgmt.purdue.edu
Web site address: www.mgmt.purdue.edu

Enrollment: 295	Estimated annual budget: $32,172
Women: 22%	Average GMAT score: 651
Non-U.S.: 36%	Average months of work
Minority: 9%	experience: 53
Part-time: 0	Accepted applicants enrolled: 41%
Average age: 27	Corporate ranking: 33
Applicants accepted: 26%	Graduate ranking: 26
Median starting pay: $80,000	Intellectual capital rank: 22
Annual tuition and fees:	
resident—$12,248	
nonresident—$23,032	

Teaching methods: case study 45%, distance learning 2%, experiential learning 15%, lecture 23%, simulations 5%, team projects 10%

High-tech and *state-of-the-art* are two phrases not often heard across the green pastures of Indiana, unless the topic is farm equipment. But venture to West Lafayette, home of Purdue University's Krannert Graduate School of Management, and folks are using these terms until the cows come home. Why, you ask? The answer stands in the form of a $35 million dollar architectural masterpiece known as Rawls Hall, the new home to MBAs at Krannert. It's taken nearly 10 years to come to fruition, but when it opens its doors in the fall of 2003, Krannert will be the envy of MBAs from coast to coast. "It's been a long time coming," says Logan Jordan, associate dean for administration. "This building is designed for the students to address their needs. It is built around the way people work and we just think it is going to add a lot of leverage to what we do here."

For the Krannert community, it comes not a moment too soon. "The old classrooms are kind of on the dingy side and the technology is dated," says John McConnell, professor of finance. "There is only so much you can do in an almost 40-year-old building. I think we are all extraordinarily excited about the new building." McConnell isn't the only one who feels that way. Before the building was even completed, it won an Architectural Portfolio award from *American School & University* magazine for its design.

Rawls Hall will provide students with the most up-to-date technologies on the market. Each classroom will be wired for the Internet and will also be videoconference enabled and linked to a high-end media production center, complete with studio lighting. This will enable classes to interact with students and managers all over the world. The large commons area will provide walk-up Web kiosks, as well as furnishings where students can take a load off. The building offers students breakout rooms to do group work, as well as a boardroom and a large computer lab for students. With the expansion of facilities, Dean Rick Cosier hopes to increase class size by 15 to 20 percent in the next few years and to augment the number of faculty as well. "Part of our planning is to move to a level of preeminence," Cosier says. "By adding faculty and students, hopefully we can get there." And Rawls Hall is not the only development in the works.

The $100 million Discovery Park, described as a complex for advanced interdisciplinary research and education, is another development that has Krannert energized. Initial plans for the 40-acre site on the west edge of campus call for centers to house research in nanotechnology, bioscience/engineering, and e-enterprises. The park also will include an entrepreneurship center to help transfer research into products and services. The first of the centers is scheduled to open in the fall of 2004. Though the park is not directly associated with Krannert, MBAs will be able to take advantage of the resources that Discovery Park has to offer in terms of understanding how to make business out of the work scientists are doing.

With such advancements and opportunities, the tuition must be through the roof, right? Wrong. In fact, out-of-state tuition is just over $23,000, making Krannert one of the best values in the top 30 and leading one 2002 grad to quip, "Krannert is an excellent brand name with a discount price." To cut the already low cost even more, many students take advantage of teaching assistant or residential advising positions that pay for a good part of tuition and fees. So, after graduation, when students from other schools are getting ready to start paying off their student loans, Krannert grads can breathe easier.

But the quality of education suffers due to the low tuition, right? Wrong again. The difficulty and thorough nature of the program are some of the things that attract students to Krannert in the first place. However, one gripe grads have is that the quality of students is not the highest, which can be frustrating considering the heavy workload at Krannert especially in the first year, leading grads to agree that if you can make it through the first year, you can make it through anything. One grad went as far as to say that going back to work would be a vacation in comparison to Krannert. Despite—or perhaps because of—the difficulty, grads say they come out of school as knowledgeable and prepared as any of their counterparts from other top schools.

In hiring a Krannert grad, recruiters say that they are getting a hardworking, level-headed, down-to-earth employee and that this is what keeps them coming back. Krannert's traditional operations management emphasis and natural foundation in quantitative methods and analytical techniques are a direct reflection of Purdue in many ways. So it makes sense that Krannert has traditionally attracted the same kind of student the university attracts: Midwesterners and technical types with undergraduate degrees in such fields as engineering, technology, or science. "There is no question that a high percentage of the students coming here have a technical background," says Allan Ferrell, director of graduate career services, "and in recent years it has been even higher; up to 50 or 60 percent will have a technical undergraduate degree and probably two-thirds of those are some sort of an engineering degree." Recruiters are aware of this and know Krannert students as some of the best in the manufacturing sectors. Even though it may not be a growing field, says Charlene Sullivan, professor of finance, it is a rock-solid part of the economy. "When [recruiters] come to Krannert looking for employees, Krannert is seen as a place where they can get good engineers with manufacturing backgrounds," Sullivan says.

A major difference between the university's student body and Krannert's, however, can be found in the number of international students that Krannert enrolls. With more than a third of the student body hailing from overseas, classes are very diverse. Many of the students coming to West Lafayette from abroad are drawn to Krannert's reputation as a strong quant program, and word spreads quickly throughout their homelands, mobilizing a new batch of international applicants for the following years. The significant number of faculty members from the larger university who are non-U.S. citizens also helps to enhance the diverse community. One issue that international grads have raised, however, is that there is little exposure to international companies, making it hard for them to build a list of contacts if their plans are to return home, as many do.

Because such a large number of Krannert's students are from overseas, administrators developed study abroad options for students. In 1999, Krannert started an exchange program with the German International Graduate School of Management and Administration (GISMA) Foundation in Hanover, Germany. Through the program, you have the opportunity to spend one eight-week session in Germany, taking the same core courses that are taught at Krannert. Another option is a two-week exchange with Group ISC in Paris. In this intensive course, you spend your time learning about doing business in the new Europe. Students take this class after their first year at Krannert, in the weeks before the summer internship.

At Krannert, you can earn your degree in one of three areas: management, human resources, or industrial administration. Each focus combines the scientific facets of management, such as facts and formulas, with more procedural skills such as

teamwork and leadership. Although there is some overlap in required courses among the three master's programs, the big difference is that those students getting their MBA can select 13 elective courses of the 86 offered during their two years, while those in the human resources sequence choose six and those in industrial administration take just seven in their accelerated study period of 11 months. You are not required to specialize in an "option," otherwise known as a major, but most do, choosing from accounting, finance, human resources management, management information systems, marketing, operations, or strategy. You can also choose from four additional interdisciplinary options of general management, international management, manufacturing and technology management, and e-business. In the past few years, a big focus has been put on integrating topics and cases across various courses, as well as bringing the best teachers into the core classes. According to Jerry Lynch, associate dean for programs and special services, "We have a centralized effort now. We have coordinated across the core more than we have in the past and we are paying more attention to what is taught where." This comes after grads in previous years complained about the quality of teaching in the core.

Krannert students are increasingly better able to understand their value in the marketplace, thanks to an improved educational process covering career-building skills. Seminars on such topics as the comprehensive job search process and salary negotiations take place regularly, and outside speakers often lead workshops in resume writing and other preparatory practices. A series targeted to international students includes insight on the hiring practices of U.S. firms and processes for securing proper visas and work permission. Even with the international series in place, a complaint from 2002 grads from overseas is that the location of Krannert leaves something to be desired, especially to those students looking to return to their native land, because they had little access to international recruiters. To deal with this issue, a new position in the Career Management Service office was created, specifically focusing on international recruiting, to help international students get the contacts and positions they're looking for. Besides that, Krannert students can post their resumes online and search through electronic listings to reach beyond the school's recruiters—an estimated 1.1 for every second-year student seeking a job. In March of 2002, because of the uncertain economy and the declining job market for 2002 grads, Krannert joined with Indiana University's Kelley School of Business in Indianapolis for what Ferrell describes as an "old oaken bucket job fair." "It was the first collaboration of the career service type between the schools," he says. "We attracted 23 companies to the fair, and I believe we will do that again because students seemed to like it and it was productive for all involved."

Your two years at Krannert begin with a brief orientation, after which you are thrown to the wolves. Luckily, before you start classes, you are assigned to a team that will help you through the first semester, or module, to facilitate learning as well as to balance the intimidating workload. You will also be assigned a second-year student who will serve as a mentor to guide you through the transition into life at Krannert. The first year is divided into four modules, in which you will take the bulk of your core classes. The first, third, and fourth modules each consist of four two-credit classes, and the second module consists of four two-credit courses and one one-credit class in managerial communication skills. At the beginning of the second module, you will break out into different teams, so that the teamwork skills you learned in the first module will spill over into other areas. Once finished with your first year, you will have built a strong knowledge base that will lead you into your internship, as well as into your second year at

Krannert, which is focused mostly on electives of your own choosing, with a few leftover core courses thrown in for good measure. The only difference in the second year is that the modules don't include as many classes, and therefore the second year is a bit less strenuous. It isn't easy, but compared to the first year, it is a break.

West Lafayette is across the Wabash River from Lafayette, Indiana—literally a stone's throw away. The Krannert community is small and tightly knit, which is a good thing, because West Lafayette isn't exactly a New York City or even a Lafayette, and without the companionship of your classmates, you'll be spending a lot of time alone watching reruns of *Green Acres*. But it isn't as bad as it sounds. According to Lynch, West Lafayette has the best of both worlds. "Even though it has the benefits of a small town where we don't have the traffic and you are not overwhelmed with people," he says, "because the university is here you still have the opportunity to see a lot of things, from blues groups to Broadway shows." And if you yearn for big city life, Chicago isn't more than a three-hour drive, with Indianapolis even closer.

Boilermaker football and basketball are popular events, and being in the Big Ten brings some of the best teams to town. Also, the city-famous 42nd Royal Highlanders, a local Scottish bagpipe group, are a popular draw. A large part of the social scene at Krannert revolves around community service projects such as clothing and food drives for a local homeless shelter, cleaning up a stretch of state highway, and working with Habitat for Humanity. Other activities are more career related, including the Preparing Leaders and Stewards program, in which students commit to 20 hours of leadership skills practice through additional coursework, self-assessment exercises, and self-directed team consulting with local companies.

Krannert prides itself on being a tough, meat-and-potatoes MBA with a down-home feel in small-town USA. At Krannert, what you see is what you get, and this is what attracts many to West Lafayette. There aren't many other schools that stop classes for an hourlong coffee break each day as a way for faculty and students to intermingle in a more social setting.

PLACEMENT DETAILS

Because Krannert students tend to focus more on technical positions in the more established, traditional companies, they did not have as much trouble as grads of other schools in finding jobs in the sour job market. Granted, grads did not receive quite as many offers, but by graduation 73 percent of the class of 2002 had at least one offer to chew on. Half of the class of 2002 chose to remain in the Midwest after graduation, where living expenses don't venture anywhere near those of either coast. The median starting pay package for the class of 2002 dropped a bit in comparison to 2000, from $101,500 to $99,900. Though the number fell, the package is comparable to those of schools ranked similarly—and the decrease is far less than what grads at other schools saw.

The placement office prepares students for interviews and other job-hunting skills during Forum Days, and these are augmented by student-initiated activities such as alumni mentoring matchups and an annual Career Assessment Conference in which professionals in various business functions are invited to campus to share information and advice with students.

TOP HIRES

Guidant (6); IBM (6); United Technologies (5); Whirlpool (4); Owens Corning (4); General Electric (4); Procter & Gamble (3); Air Products and Chemicals (3); Capital One Services (3).

OUTSTANDING FACULTY

John McConnell (finance); Jerry Lynch (economics); Mark Bagnoli (finance/accounting); Mark Shanley (strategy); Charlene Sullivan (finance); Wilfred Amaldoss (marketing).

APPLICANT TIPS

Krannert's quant-heavy program places a natural emphasis on undergraduate grades, work experience, and GMAT scores, which averaged 651 among the class of 2004 entrants. Krannert obviously wants the best students, but Director of Admissions Ward Snearly stresses the point that acceptance to Krannert is a matching process. "We want someone who is going to add value to the student body, someone who will come into the classroom and make the faculty's job more fun, and make everyone's experience more rewarding," Snearly says. "But we also want a student who is going to be able to get what they want from us."

Though interviews are not required, Snearly recommends that students come to West Lafayette and interview. But be aware that the interview at Krannert is a bit different than interviews at other schools. Instead of just sitting down with an admissions representative, you will meet with four different people: someone from admissions, someone from the director of MBA programs office, someone from the career services office, and a faculty member. Each one of those interviews takes 20 to 25 minutes. You can also opt to have a student host who will show you around and give you an unbiased account of life at Krannert. The reasoning behind the extensive interviews is simple. "It gives us the best chance to get to know them and for them to get to know us," says Director Snearly.

The bottom line is that Krannert wants students who know what they want, and who are going to excel in the fast-paced, sometimes intimidating course load and work well in the team-based environment.

KRANNERT MBAs SOUND OFF

Krannert pulls a wide variety of students from all over the world. This diversity is outstanding but I was amazed how well these various cultures were integrated into one large team. I believe the fact that Krannert is in a smaller town in the Midwest part of the U.S. helped promote this relationship between the students and the faculty.

I thought Krannert was great. The program has reshaped my perceptions and knowledge of business. Its strengths lie in the community and strong work ethic found in its students and staff. The level of competition is appropriate and not destructive. The graduates of this program are ready to put in the amount of work required to be successful, and they don't carry around an elitist attitude about their education. I feel this is the type of program that truly adds value to the businesses around the world.

Krannert exceeded most of my expectations for an MBA program. It provided an excellent opportunity to develop my business skills while increasing my knowledge base. Slight improvements in the quality of the student population coupled with more attention to entrepreneurship and business plan development will only further improve the quality of the program. Overall, I was pleased with my experiences at Krannert and will be encouraging my colleagues to go there in the future.

Krannert School of Management is definitely a place I'd recommend to someone thinking about B-school. It offers a well-rounded curriculum and a diverse student body and prepares you to become an analytical and strategic thinker. The professors are extremely knowledgeable, bringing great experiences to the table. If I could do it again, I would have made the same choices.

Krannert has top-rated faculty and an outstanding teaching methodology that can be tailored to an individual's needs. The team building is also a huge factor in my preference of Krannert. The students are sincerely promoted to work together. Another aspect of Krannert I did not expect but took full advantage of was the exposure to international culture and business practices. Although known for its excellence in operations and quantitative skills, Krannert has one of the best finance and strategy curriculums.

I fundamentally believe that most MBA programs teach the same materials. The only difference is the status of the faculty, the quality of the students and the reputation of the school. Krannert struggles with recognition on all those fronts but still delivers a top-notch education.

The program is great for someone with a technical background, especially the engineers and the scientists. The professors did a great job, the rigors of the program toughen you up and the tuition and living expenses are a lot more affordable than some other B-schools.

27.
UNIVERSITY
OF
ROCHESTER

UNIVERSITY OF ROCHESTER

William E. Simon Graduate School of Business Administration
305 Schlegel Hall
Rochester, New York 14627
E-mail address: mbaadm@simon.rochester.edu
Web site address: www.simon.rochester.edu

Enrollment: 429
Women: 23%
Non-U.S.: 45%
Minority: 25%
Part-time: 163
Average age: 29
Applicants accepted: 26%
Median starting pay: $79,000
Annual tuition and fees: $31,122

Estimated annual budget: n/a
Average GMAT score: 649
Average months of work
 experience: 73
Accepted applicants enrolled: 44%
Corporate ranking: 39
Graduate ranking: 24
Intellectual capital rank: 25

Teaching methods: case study 30%, lecture 50%, team projects 20%

Many business schools divide first-year students into study teams or learning teams; typically, this will be a group of five or six students of varying professional and personal backgrounds, and you'll be expected to meet with your team nightly to hash out homework assignments. Often, some significant part of your core coursework grades will be based on group projects. And, usually, there will be some teams where personalities will clash. Maybe someone doesn't pull his or her own weight. Maybe the finance person in the group feels like you're not using his or her expertise enough on problem sets. Or maybe you'll argue over whether or not to spend your three hours on the marketing case due the next day or to review some accounting problem sets. When these sorts of issues arise, as they inevitably do, both students and administrations tend to adopt a "that's the way things work in the business world" attitude, and you're left to duke things out yourselves.

At the Simon Graduate School of Business at the University of Rochester, however, student learning teams are not left to fend for themselves. Instead, in a unique twist on the team player idea, a second-year student called a coach is assigned to every team. The coaches are themselves selected through a competitive screening process, and their role is to not only help Simon students navigate the rigors of the core curriculum but help defuse meltdowns that can occur when a diverse group of students—who are balancing a full load of courses with the pressure of landing a summer internship—need to prioritize study plans every night. Instead of making an organizational behavior class a requirement, Simon lets its students learn about it themselves.

In the process, first-years learn to really work out their differences, and the coaches—who receive a meager $400 yearly stipend for their hours of effort—gain valuable management experience. These hands-on, experiential learning processes, along with a refocused professional development program, have helped Simon in bolstering its reputation as a solid academic MBA program with some needed professional polish and in putting the school's motto, "where thinkers become leaders," into practice. In 2002, Rochester grads were certainly happier than the recruiters that hired them: they cheered the integration of the coursework but complained about career placement services—a common refrain in 2002. Recruiters, largely from the tech and engineering sectors, weren't hiring many grads, and the placement office, say 2002 grads, was slow to bring in new strategies. All in all, much of Simon's growth and positive momentum came under the leadership of Dean Charles Plosser, who has announced that he will step down from his position in June 2003 at the completion of his second five-year term as dean. So the school will have to tackle these issues of placement and staying in touch with a broader range of recruiters under a new leader.

Simon's concerted push toward combining coursework and professional growth begins with the preterm program, which takes up the two weeks before your first-year classes start. Along with getting to know your cohort of some 60 students and receiving your Simon fleece jackets, you'll spend time assessing what you really want to get out of your two years in B-school by taking a Myers-Briggs test and by assessing your communications skills in order to pinpoint areas you'd like to work on. You'll also start thinking about your potential post-MBA career so that you can choose electives and concentrations accordingly.

Over the course of the first year, the core of the Simon curriculum shifts from a quant-heavy foundation in business basics to a more integrated system of core courses that revolve around areas such as e-commerce and technology or organizations and incentives. In the fall quarter, all four of your classes will be part of the required core, and they're geared toward business foundations. You'll take Corporate Financial Accounting, Managerial Economics, Capital Budgeting, and Applied Statistics and Data Analysis, along with the first of three one-credit management communications courses (as opposed to the regular four-credit classes). In the winter quarter, you'll take three core classes, all revolving around e-commerce and technology: Information Systems Management, Marketing Management, and Operations Management. You'll also take one elective, along with the second management communications course. In the spring quarter, you'll take your two remaining core classes—Economics Theory of Organizations and Accounting for Management Control—which are tightly wound around the theme of organizations and incentives. Simon considers this pairing its hallmark, as you'll get the big-picture perspective on the functioning infrastructure of a firm. In this third quarter you'll also take two more electives, as well as another one-credit management communications course.

Simon students say the integrated course load provided opportunities for interesting projects. "My first quarter we did a team project in managerial economics that involved valuating sports teams," says 2002 grad Jeff Sigel. "That involved finance, but it also involved economics as we tried to understand the consumer economics of how teams worked, and we did accounting as we were looking at the financial statements." But students also say the workload is demanding—"More than I ever could have imagined," says one recent graduate.

The time spent with your first-year learning team can help mitigate the workload somewhat. The dynamic of your team changes with the progression of the curriculum. In the first quarter, for example, when you are learning business basics, the assignments are pretty cut and dried, so you'll spend less time debating open-ended problems and more time getting to know each other and hammering out problem sets along with your studying priorities. In the second quarter, you'll have to start functioning as a cohesive group as you tackle more cases, and, by the third quarter, some 30 to 50 percent of your core class grades will be based on your group work. With the coach program in place to help smooth out some conflicts, students find value in the learning team concept. "Like any school, there are people who haven't seen a math class in 10 years," says one recent graduate. "And that's one of the places where the team stuff helps."

The management communications courses that you'll take each quarter are a direct result of Simon's desire to polish the professional skills of its students by overhauling its communications strategy. These courses, which began in the fall of 2002, aren't graded per se, but rather give you a chance to work in small groups and to spend at least five hours per quarter working one on one with faculty to enhance your skills in areas such as career placement communications (complete with mock interviews and critiques of videotaped presentations). By the end of the year you'll have a portfolio of projects, presentations, and videotapes, which will be evaluated on a pass/fail basis. By taking management communications out of the classroom, Simon hopes to avoid the historical problems of having students of different levels in the class—who need to focus on different areas—and a subjective grading system that confuses effort and ability. The course is pass/fail, but this doesn't mean you can slack off: if you do fail, you'll have to pay to make up the credit hours.

The second-year curriculum at Simon is much less structured than the first year's. You'll have the opportunity to choose your electives to satisfy 1 of 14 concentrations in areas such as business environment and public policy, corporate accounting, e-commerce, finance, entrepreneurship, international management, marketing, or operations management. Though you're not required to choose a concentration, the typical Simon student leaves with two. You'll need about five or six courses to satisfy a concentration, and many electives will meet more than one concentration's requirement.

Classes at Simon tend to be heavy on theory, but, as Stacy Kole, associate dean for the MBA program, explains, "We can do that because students really experience more than just theory." Many Simon professors are involved heavily in their own research, which makes its way into the classroom. In Cases in Finance, for example, you'll be put on a negotiation team to valuate certain companies—and your grade will depend on how much you end up paying for the companies you're buying. Companies with offices in Rochester, such as Procter & Gamble, will step into a brand management workshop to give students a new product for which they'll create a marketing plan. Budding entrepreneurs can rub elbows with professionals by playing host to participants in the Frederick Kalmbach Executive Speaker Series, as well as spending 10 hours per week shadowing them at work.

Simon also has expanded its joint degree programs, especially in the health care and biotech areas, and now offers an anesthesiology/MBA program for students already doing a residency or fellowship in anesthesiology, an MBA/MS in microbiology and immunology, an MBA/MPH, and an MD/MBA. Specialized degrees are offered in the areas of technology transfer and commercialization, manufacturing management and service management, information systems management, and finance.

While Simon has succeeded in integrating a sense of professionalism into its curriculum, it's still a bit behind the curve when it comes to catching up with the idea of the global MBA. While there is an international management concentration, the only opportunity to study abroad is an international exchange program with one of nine schools in places such as Argentina, Australia, Belgium, Finland, Hong

Kong, Israel, Germany, Japan, and Norway. While in the past few years the numbers of students going abroad have grown, the exchange program struggles to be more than a marketing tool: your international experience at Simon is largely gained from the international students on campus, who make up anywhere from 40 to 50 percent of the student body. The philosophy is that the trade-off of learning time you'd miss on campus is too great. "It's the amount of learning that can be accomplished in a week versus what you'd get through a trip abroad," says Dean Kole. But, some international students have complained of a too-weak support network to guide them through.

Outside of the classroom, your life at Simon will revolve around the intimacy that results from the small student body. Because Simon is committed to keeping its total number of students in both classes to less than 500, you'll get a chance to participate in (and to lead, if you are so inclined) the myriad of student activities that take place at the school. Indeed, many Simon students say that the opportunity to lead a club really helped round out their resume when they hit the job market their second year.

Clubs such as the marketing or finance club revolve around the more career-centered activities of career trips, case competitions, and speakers. Clubs also center around particular groups of students: the Pacific Basin Forum, the Latin American Students Organization, the Business Women's forum. These groups, however, also affect the school's social life: the Latin American club, for example, puts together dance parties. The Business Women's forum sponsors golf outings. Spring at Rochester brings the formal Black Jack Ball, and at the end of your second year there's a full week of school-sponsored fun, ranging from skydiving and rafting trips to excursions to Rochester's popular minor-league baseball games.

Rochester, a city best known, perhaps, for its ties to corporations such as Kodak and Bausch &

Lomb, provides an affordable lifestyle for the B-school student. While there is a limited amount of dorm housing for Simon students, including some university-owned housing for married students, most Simon students take advantage of Rochester's relatively cheap rents and live in apartment complexes within a few miles of school. Upstate New York, despite its winters, has natural highlights such as the wineries that dot the Finger Lakes region, downhill skiing, sailing, and lots of open land for golf courses (second-year students find themselves logging a lot of time on Rochester's many fairways). Rochester itself has such cultural stalwarts such as the world-famous Eastman School of Music, which draws a great deal of talent to the area. Simon students organize pub crawls and happy hours in downtown Rochester, or hang out at the affordable, comfortable restaurants near campus such as The Distillery or the Elmwood Inn.

"It's a very manageable city," says a 2002 grad. "It's not overwhelming. If you're used to Manhattan, you might look at it and wonder where you are. It's an almost more Midwestern pace." This more relaxed pace of life, and the smaller size of the school, bolster a sense of collegiality between students. Dinner parties with friends, for example, tend to be the social activity of choice for the large number of married Simon students. Dean Plosser himself invites all first-years over to a reception at his home in September, or he'll occasionally drop by on student pub nights.

Back on campus, Gleason Hall, completed in 2001, has increased the space for classrooms, admissions, and recruiting offices by over 50 percent, with dedicated interview rooms, study rooms, and classrooms.

PLACEMENT DETAILS

In the past, companies who had employed Rochester MBAs found that while Simon students were strong team players, they lacked a bit of professional polish. The school has reacted directly to this criticism by providing a more focused career counseling approach that emphasizes professionalism. In the first two weeks of school, during the preterm program—which itself is designed to get you thinking about your overall career—you'll even take a mandatory seminar called Dressed to Impress, with separate meetings for men and women.

"We teach students that in a business setting there are expectations and follow-through," says Lisa McGurn, assistant dean for career management. If you sign up for a corporate presentation, for example, you're expected to show up. If you don't, you'll be banned from future presentations. If you're late, you won't be allowed in. If you're not in business attire, you'll be turned away as well. Sound harsh?

"It's not a police state, but to help students be accountable for not only their job search but for holding up the image of the school and the expectations recruiters have of us," says McGurn. "If we're more committed to your success than you are, then this partnership doesn't work." So if you miss an on-campus interview, then your on-campus interview privileges will be revoked. And reneging on an offer is a huge no-no. Simon clearly wants recruiters to see the school's well-educated students in a more serious, professional light. But for now, the concentration will have to be on getting recruiters to notice and come to campus. Only 59 percent of Rochester MBAs had jobs by graduation, and three months later, the results weren't much better: 35 percent were still jobless. Those who did find jobs saw their pay packages decrease to about $96,800.

TOP HIRES

Johnson & Johnson (4); Citigroup (3); Bank of New York (3); Kraft Foods (3); Merck (3); Procter & Gamble (3).

OUTSTANDING FACULTY

Gregory Bauer (finance); Clifford Smith (finance); Charles Wasley (accounting); Greg Shaffer (marketing); Gregg Jarrell (finance); Robert Shumsky (operations); Erwan Morellec (finance).

APPLICANT TIPS

Prospective students have two choices for admittance: the mainstream 22-month program that begins each September and holds 190 students, or the 18-month accelerated MBA that 50 to 60 students enter in January. Those in the January program complete two quarters of core courses and then have three choices: taking a full schedule of coursework during the summer before joining the regular schedule of classes for the second year; taking a part-time load of summer classes in the evenings while working at an internship in the Rochester area, then taking one extra course during the second year; or pursuing a regular summer internship away from the school and then finishing up the first-year requirements on top of the regular second-year schedule, which means handling two extra courses.

Because you'll be spending lots of time working in groups—and because the school's small size gives you the opportunities to really interact with your fellow students and faculty—Simon wants applicants who are strong team players and who are really looking to develop their leadership skills. The admissions office will want to see that you've been involved in some sort of team-oriented organization, be it a sports team or a volunteer group.

Every year Simon will take a few applicants straight from their undergraduate work; there's also a special 3/2 program with the University of Rochester where students take the first year of the MBA program during their senior year. Most people, however, have some work experience, and Simon values diversity, accepting people with a gamut of experiences, from those with traditional finance backgrounds to teachers, nonprofit workers, and former naval officers. Your GMAT scores and transcripts will show the school that you can handle the rigorous core, but although the program is quantitative in nature, don't let that scare you—again, Simon is looking for a broad range of students.

There are three essays and one optional essay on the Simon application, and you'll be asked to write about your personal history, your personal goals, and what you can contribute to the school. The option essay is a seemingly open-ended, "Is there anything else we should know about you that's not on your resume?" You're advised to stick to the 350-word limit on this one. "Be brief and hard-hitting," recommends Pamela Colton-Black, assistant dean for MBA admissions and administration. "Like how you'd be in the business world." If you have a low GPA because you worked your way through college or because of a family health issue, here's your chance to explain how that's changed you.

And, of course, you'll want to proofread your essays carefully. "We don't want to know why you're dying to go to Sloan or Tuck," Colton-Black quips. You'll also be asked to submit two recommendations. Instead of choosing a reference who is impressive in name or title who doesn't know you—the CEO of your company, for example—pick someone who has worked with you and knows you as an individual.

Every candidate for admission is encouraged to interview, and while you're also encouraged to visit the Simon campus, you can schedule interviews with the admissions staff members when they're out visiting various cities. Look professional, and be prepared to sell yourself in the half-hour that you have. And when you're asked whether or not you have any questions about the school, make sure you can ask some that show you have given some thought to what you might want to get out of Simon. Indeed, you should give Simon's characteristics

careful thought before you even begin your application: keep in mind that it's a small school with a rigorous curriculum, but there are some things it doesn't offer—real estate, for example. Take a look at the catalog and see what is offered. Simon's application is online and downloadable. You can send it in through the mail or, with the click of a mouse, over the Internet.

SIMON MBAs SOUND OFF

My MBA experience at the Simon School far exceeded my expectations. Not only did I learn about business concepts, I also learned about different cultures and ways of thinking. One of the biggest surprises to me was how wide open the business world truly is. I came to school with a very narrow perspective of what I was capable of doing in my career and leave with a new and expansive horizon.

I really liked Simon because of its size. You get to know everyone in the first couple of weeks and form a strong bond. I do not think it is a typical MBA program since it has a good balance between teamwork and individual work.

I thought the level of quantitative analytical skills gained at Simon was unbelievable. These skills are highly transferable and are such that I will be using them the rest of my life. The faculty was outstanding and I am extremely happy with my decision to come to the Simon School.

At Simon, I found rewards through the various opportunities to take charge of parts of the school's organization as well as learning from top-tier faculty. Through a unique coach-leader program that actually gives second-years the responsibility of mentoring a first-year team, to a number of student steering committees, the leadership opportunities in clubs and the Graduate Business Council, I was able to be involved in making my B-school experience what I wanted it to be.

Simon is a small school, graduating about 200 students per year. This makes us less well known to recruiters as the body of alumni grows more slowly for Simon. However, those recruiters who know us appreciate the hard-working, well-prepared candidates at Simon. After returning from internships my peers and I realized how well prepared we really were for our jobs after interacting with other interns. Additionally, alumni are incredibly helpful in the job search process.

An often heard complaint about Simon is its location in Rochester. The winters can be a real drag, the nightlife is wanting, and the town desperately needs one good restaurant. However, the cost of living is incredibly cheap and you can get some of the best golf for your money than anywhere else I have ever seen.

I believe that Simon offers one of the best educations in finance and accounting in the country. The high international population added to my MBA experience and gave me insights and perspectives that I would not have been able to experience from other schools.

Overall a good experience and worth the money. The program, however, is not for everyone. If you are not strong in math you will have problems following the program. Also, all concepts taught here are based on microeconomic theory. If you have alternative ways of thinking about problems, you will be on your own. The workload is heavy but the quality of teaching is superb. If you want to master advanced finance come to the Simon School.

28. VANDERBILT UNIVERSITY

VANDERBILT UNIVERSITY

Owen Graduate School of Management
401 21st Avenue South
Nashville, Tennessee 37203
E-mail address: admissions@owen.vanderbilt.edu
Web site address: www.mba.vanderbilt.edu

Enrollment: 422
Women: 24%
Non-U.S.: 25%
Minority: 6%
Part-time: 0
Average age: 28
Applicants accepted: 47%
Median starting pay: $75,000
Annual tuition and fees: $29,160

Estimated annual budget: $47,074
Average GMAT score: 648
Average months of work
  experience: 56
Accepted applicants enrolled: 46%
Corporate ranking: 35
Graduate ranking: 27
Intellectual capital rank: 17

Teaching methods: case study 20%, distance learning 10%, experiential learning 5%, lecture 35%, simulations 5%, team projects 25%

Before the start of every semester, Owen Professor Nancy Lea Hyer makes dozens of flash cards—not inscribed with terms she'll be using in her class, but pasted with pictures of her students that she cuts from the face book. She spends 30 minutes a day memorizing the students' names and faces, so that she can recognize each and every one when they walk in the door to their first class. "It gives them accountability," she says. "I'm not going to forget something they say in class." Hyer's commitment, she hopes, will let her students know that they matter to her. It's a feeling that, with Owen's universal open-door policy between faculty and students, from the dean to the director of recruiting to the professors, seems to be pervasive through this small southern school with, as one recent grad puts it, an "exceptionally collegiate environment."

Since the last *BusinessWeek* rankings, when Dean Bill Christie had just assumed the helm at Owen in the tumultuous aftermath of the unexpected death of longtime dean Martin S. Geisel, Christie has cut his teaching load from four classes to one and has put his efforts into recruiting more faculty, overhauling the Career Management Center, and radically adding to areas of the curriculum such as entrepreneurship. With these tasks nearing completion, Christie also is looking to strengthen Owen's relationship with the rest of Vanderbilt University and with the city of Nashville itself. Owen now offers five joint degrees in medicine, law, engineering, nursing, and Latin American studies, and Christie has promoted partnerships with businesses in Nashville, relationships that give MBA students real-life experience in business management. Still, with all these changes, Christie is committed to keeping the school at its intimate size of some 215 students per class, which ensures that he—and professors like Nancy Lea Hyer—can continue to give the one-on-one attention to students on which Owen prides itself.

The curriculum at Owen is focused on a general management education, with a schedule that features courses in four seven-week modules per year. All required courses are completed before the end of the first year, with room for four electives before your summer internship. Core courses make up 40 percent of graduation requirements. Students start the program in August with an orientation that includes review classes in statistics (a review in math has been moved from the classroom to an online preterm venue). During the first semester, you'll be limited to lecture-heavy requirements, with the first seven weeks dedicated to accounting, macroeconomics, statistics, leading teams and organizations, and business writing. The second module covers some additional accounting, along with finance, operations, and marketing. After winter break, you'll take strategy in the third module and macroeconomics in the fourth; required courses in communications and human relations can be taken in either module. You'll fill out your first-year schedule with electives for a total of four courses per second-semester module. Be aware that you won't be able to get out of many classes you deem to be a rehash of what you think you already know: core exemptions have been reduced to a bare minimum, with waivers by examination allowed only in accounting, statistics, and economics. The module system ends up piling on a lot of work in these short seven-week periods, requiring you to orient yourself with the subject matter very quickly while finding your role within the teams to which you'll be assigned for group project work. "The pressure created simulates that found within most businesses," says 2002 grad Chris Ward.

The module system is designed to allow students to fit in more than one concentration (which typically requires six classes) or to combine a concentration with an "emphasis" (Owen's term for a minor, which requires about four courses). Concentrations include accounting, e-commerce, finance, human and organizational performance, information technology, marketing, operations, strategy, general management, and law and business, and a customized major in general management. Among the complementary emphases are international management, service, e-commerce, environmental management, entrepreneurship, and health care.

While the area of entrepreneurship was ill served at the time Dean Christie took over in 2000, it is here that the school has perhaps made the most progress. For starters, Christie hired Bruce Lynskey, a 1985 Owen grad and an experienced entrepreneur who had worked on successful start-ups in the software and telecommunications industries, such as Wellfleet Communications, but also on some not-so-successful ventures. This, says Christie, is just what he wanted—someone who could give students perspectives from every side of entrepreneurship. Lynskey has been responsible for new courses that include Launching the Venture, Managing Fast Growing Companies, Writing a Business Plan, Adventures in Entrepreneurship, and Advanced Entrepreneurship: Business Plan Development. Lynskey, who gets high marks from students not only for his teaching abilities but for his real-world knowledge, has also been integral in placing student teams in local (and a few not-so-local) businesses to get experience in creating business plans, marketing, strategic planning, and financial analysis. The companies range in size and scope from one that sells violins to a commercial real estate developer that asked groups of students to study different proposals on what to build on a tract of land south of Nashville. Lynskey stresses that the majority of these projects are not consulting deals, but, rather, projects with a firmly established goal and end. "We want students on-site if it's a local company or teleconferencing if it's not," he explains. "We want them immersed in the actual operations and not off on the side doing a study." Grading for these projects is, in fact, done by the companies, which Lynskey provides with grading objectives. "The company turns the grade in to me, and I record it," Lyskey says. The idea is to get you focused 100 percent on the company, and not on a faculty member looking over your shoulder.

Owen's small size helps it react to companies' needs and to set up these types of projects as they arise. For example, when Nashville music giant Gaylord Entertainment (the company that owns the Grand Ole Opry and the Opryland Hotel) approached Christie with an idea to get Owen students involved in a companywide reorganization in October of 2001, student teams were working with the company by November.

Along with giving you some real-world entrepreneur and management experience, Owen will encourage you to take advantage of Vanderbilt's other professional schools. The B-school has added an MBA/MD degree, and while it always has had a four-year joint MBA/JD degree, students who don't want to spend four years getting a JD on top of their MBA can now do a concentration in law and business that is co-taught by the law and business faculty. You'll take law classes with Vanderbilt law students, taught by law professors, including an introductory course taught by the law school's dean. As Christie points out, "You're going to have to work with lawyers for the rest of your life." Christie himself co-teaches a class called The Law and Finance of Equity Markets. And, though it's not yet a full

concentration, the Cal Turner Center for Moral Leadership program in moral leadership creates a relationship between Owen and the Vanderbilt law, divinity, and medical schools, bringing in speakers and sponsoring forums.

Owen may not be the place for you if you're looking for a broad range of choices when it comes to international studies. While the school does require one international business course before you graduate, the only option for overseas travel is the Seminar and Practicum in International Management. Each year, one country is picked to be studied—Argentina, for example, or the Czech republic—and students plan, manage, and arrange a group project that culminates in a weeklong fact-finding visit during spring break. Students who don't think this is enough international exposure can choose to spend a semester abroad at schools in places like Barcelona or Hong Kong. Karen Cherniss, a 2002 grad who spent her second semester at the Hong Kong University of Science and Technology, says that Owen was quite accommodating when it came to studying abroad. "It was easy to go, easy to get the credits, and easy to communicate with Owen faculty from abroad," she says.

Dean Christie contends that what Owen lacks in actual international study experiences is made up for in the number of international students, who constitute about a quarter of the student body. "We want to make sure domestic students will be working here with those whom they'll be working with after school." Christie admits that as a small school in the middle of the country, Owen has not embarked on many international partnerships, but it's something he's beginning to consider.

The communal atmosphere at Owen starts with the design of its main building, Management Hall, with study tables, classrooms, and faculty offices surrounding a two-story atrium. Faculty doors are almost always open, and walk-ins are welcome. Management Hall underwent a $2 million face-lift in 2001 to add a new student lounge (with breakout rooms, a food service area, a ticker tape, and a plasma TV), a renovated computer room and auditorium, and new library and office space.

The combination of openness and intimacy is essential to Christie's philosophy of running the school. He walks the halls looking for students to chat with and still hangs a sign outside his door from 5 to 6 P.M. on Mondays that reads, "The Dean Is In." Students are encouraged to come to him with questions and concerns. His wife, Kelly, who is in charge of curriculum and student services, makes sure that her office is staffed from 7 A.M. to 7 P.M., and, especially during add/drop period for courses, is often answering e-mails via her Blackberry until midnight.

Owen has the standard range of B-school clubs, such as the finance, strategy, marketing, and investment clubs, as well as various student associations for women, Latin American students, and minorities. With no classes on Fridays, the school hosts kegs at Thursday night socials, a casino night, bowling nights, an orientation week Tennessee barbeque, the formal Capitalist Ball in the spring, and the annual Owen Follies, where students can let off some steam by making fun of the school and professors in various skits and plays. There is no housing at Owen, although Vanderbilt does have some married student housing. Almost all Owen students, therefore, live in affordable apartments that are relatively close to the campus, including one complex that's just across the street—close enough so that students can receive the school's wireless signal. Another option is the historic Edgehill neighborhood within a half mile of campus; most students end up walking or riding bikes to and from school.

Though Nashville may not be as big a city as other top B-school hubs, neither is it a small, rural town. "People probably have a stereotype that it's a country town and hick town," says 2002 grad Ben Marks. "But it's a very progressive mid-upscale city with a lot of great things going on. There are only three cities in the country that are true homes of music—New York, L.A., and Nashville."

PLACEMENT DETAILS

Melinda Allen brought a much needed breath of fresh air to the Owen Career Management Center in the winter of 2002. The first thing she did was send out a survey to students to ask them their geographic, industry, and company preferences. With this information in hand, she made a huge marketing push within her own office, sending staff on city trips, organizing marketing events, and cold-calling companies with which Owen had no previous relationships.

"Basically, we said, 'Here's how things have been done, but let's react to the current marketplace,'" Allen explains. "Let's find ways to enhance and fine-tune. Everyone in my office does marketing." While the feeling at Owen was that Allen's mid-year arrival didn't help all that much when it came to overall job placement numbers, her efforts have not gone completely unnoticed by Owen grads. As one 2002 grad put it, "She could probably teach the new Change Management course next fall—or be a great guest speaker. This office has undergone a massive change in the past few months, with newsletters, greater student communication, student marketing trips, and they're in at 6 A.M., out at 8 P.M."

As a first-year, you'll take five mandatory Friday workshops to help with the job hunt that cover resume writing, cover letter writing, business research, interviewing, etiquette, and networking. Owen outsources its mock interviewing, and students go through the exercise in groups of three, so that you not only have a chance to do your own interview but can watch two others do them as well. In addition, you can attend seminars and brown bag lunches throughout the year that focus on specific industries or topics like corporate benefits or how to post your resume on a Web page.

Allen believes the size of the school lets her office adapt to the particular needs of a student or the economy in general. And she is committed to seeking out companies for which the southern city of Nashville may not be a regular recruiting stop. "We don't always do things traditionally," she says. "The top-tier schools have a traditional way to do recruiting with timelines for information sessions and campus visits. We recognize that companies have different needs, so we'll work with each company to see how we can meet them. We'd love to have companies on campus, but that may not be the best course of action. At the end of the day, I want to get a company our resumes. So I'll see if we can go to them or see them at a consortium."

Owen students certainly end up working in Nashville, Memphis, or nearby Huntsville, Alabama, but the B-school tries to market its students as being geographically mobile. And even though the school is a two-hour flight from New York, Washington, DC, and Atlanta, some students gripe that finding a job on the West Coast is difficult. "I feel there is a strong group of recruiting companies that come on campus from New York and the Southeast," says one 2002 grad. "However, if someone is looking to locate on the West Coast, I'm not sure Vanderbilt would be the best match." Despite this year's numbers, Allen and her staff's demonstrated willingness to react to student preferences may become more effective over time.

Owen's overall push to lure international students has carried over to the career office as well. The typical foreign student's CV needs to be translated into a corporate-America-friendly resume, and that work begins four weeks before school starts in the U.S. Business Communications and Culture class required for international students. The recruiting office also reacted quickly in 2001–2002 to the difficulties that international students were having finding jobs not only in the U.S., but back in their home countries. Christie St. John, director of international relations, worried the school's nine or so

Argentinean students would be unable to return home with jobs due to that country's financial crisis, did research to find out which U.S. companies were doing business in Argentina and which Argentinean companies had a presence in the U.S. After compiling a list of about 150 such companies, she sent them a resume book of about 25 students she had pulled together not only of Owen Argentineans, but of those who attended the B-schools at Northwestern, Indiana, MIT, and UT Austin as well.

Still, like many others, 2002 Owen grads had a tough time in the marketplace. Only 53 percent of grads had job offers by graduation. That number jumped to 74 percent three months after commencement, but by then most other top schools had placed 80 percent or more of their graduating classes. Owen grads earned pay packages of about $100,200.

TOP HIRES

Bank of America (4); Hewlett-Packard (3); CNA Financial (2); Gaylord Entertainment (2); GE Capital (2); General Motors (2); Harrah's (2); Jefferies & Company (2); Merrill Lynch (2); Union Planters Bank (2).

OUTSTANDING FACULTY

Debra Jeter (accounting); Michael Shor (economics); Piyush Kumar (marketing); Craig Lewis (finance); David Owens (leadership and organizational behavior); Nancy Lea Hyer (operations); Bruce Lynskey (entrepreneurship); Bill Christie (finance).

APPLICANT TIPS

While Owen looks at your test scores and undergraduate record as an indicator of your ability to handle the school's academics, your professional experiences and your personal qualities are equally important. Owen students average about five years of professional work, but there is no minimum work requirement because, as Director of Admissions Todd Reale points out, "some exceptional individuals can contribute earlier in their careers." About 90 percent of Owen students have at least two years of experience.

"We want people who are intelligent, critical, and intellectually curious," Reale says. In your application, essay, and interview, he'll assess whether or not you're a team player with strong leadership potential. Owen is also looking for cross-cultural experiences—not just in terms of whether or not you have worked, lived, or traveled abroad, but whether you have an appreciation for other cultures across socioeconomic or ethnic boundaries in your own country.

Because the school requires interviews of all candidates being considered for admission, you're encouraged to get the interview done even before you complete your application. Before you interview, make sure you have done your research on the school. Reale says that he looks at B-school interviews much as an employer might look at a hiring interview.

"We're essentially doing the first round of screening for the companies that hire our interns and full-time employees, so we're looking for the same qualities they are," he says, "someone's ability to clearly sell their strengths, interests, and vision. How are they going to contribute to the organization? Instead of what's in it for them, how are they going to help make Owen a better place?" You'll want to highlight your ability to work well in a team-oriented environment with specific examples, answering questions with a behavioral-style approach, such as, "Tell me about an original idea that you had, and how did you see it through from start to finish," or "Describe a time when you had to deal with dissension in a team." Be able to tell two- to-three minute anecdotes about experiences that motivated you to pursue an MBA.

Essays will ask you to describe an element of your past that led you to your current decision to apply to Owen, and will also ask you to focus on your future a bit. Owen is looking for a strong sense of self-awareness in your essays. Because Owen stresses a team-focused approach to learning, the folks who do best are competitive and driven, but not at the expense of others. Someone who is independent to the point of being hypercompetitive will probably not fit in quite as well. To be sure you'll thrive in the school's cooperative environment, Owen offers five weekends for prospective or admitted applicants to visit the school.

Prospective students can visit the school during November's preview weekend, January's diversity weekend, or February's community weekend—all three of which are open to anyone, regardless of where they are in the admissions process. You'll be able to attend panel discussions with current students and alums, sit in on presentations by faculty and the career management staff, and tour the Vanderbilt campus and the city of Nashville. Receptions on Friday and Saturday night let you mingle with the Owen community. Owen also has added a similar welcome weekend in mid-April for admitted students.

Perhaps the most sought-after weekend visit, however, is the invitation-only scholars' weekend, where 25 admitted applicants with the highest credentials are flown to Nashville and wooed with luncheons, dinners, and one-on-one meetings with faculty. Ten of these candidates will be selected as Dean's scholars, who receive a full scholarship plus a $10,000 stipend.

Foreign students may first need to get over preconceived notions that Nashville lacks a certain cosmopolitan sophistication; in the end, Owen's student enrollment ends up being between 30 and 35 percent international. The schools relies on its active international alumni base to help get the word out that Nashville is more than a small country music town. The admissions staff also takes four different international recruiting trips to meet and interview candidates in person. International students must take the TOEFL exam and are encouraged to apply early; their final deadline is March 15, earlier than that for U.S. candidates, because of the extra time needed for processing visas should the students be admitted.

Though Owen still accepts paper applications, you are strongly encouraged to apply online. In doing so, you'll be allowed to submit unofficial records of your GPA and GMAT scores to expedite the process from the Owen end; only after you are admitted will Owen ask you to submit the official transcripts.

OWEN MBAs SOUND OFF

I believe the Owen program is top-notch. As with most schools, Owen needs to improve in certain areas. However, I feel the school is taking steps to correct some of its problems. We have a new CMC director who is very hungry to make the Owen recruiting process better for students and companies. She has solicited advice and information from the students, and she is actually using the information she has received to make changes for the better.

Owen is a fantastic place because of its size. Having only 200 students in your class really makes it a big family. Almost everyone is willing to help one another. Competitiveness and drive still exist, but they do not overwhelm and consume students and rudeness is generally not tolerated. The downside to this is that students are not challenged as much as they should be. Owen could stand to benefit from more aggressive challenges from some professors, beginning with more cold calls.

I came to Owen looking to change directions and find a career that I would love for the next 20 years. I found a job and much more during my two years here. I would recommend Owen to anyone who wants a fun and challenging experience. There was not a better place that I could have gone.

Although the job market has been very difficult this year, the career center at Owen has played an active role in trying to place students. They have networked with hundreds of local businesses, coordinated student trips to targeted cities, conducted numerous workshops, and have been there as a means to support students in any way possible.

Owen continues to grow its abilities and bring in stronger professors. At the same time, the administration is willing to replace those professors that do not meet their or the students' expectations. While the career center struggled in the early part of my time here, the new director has quickly established her presence and is building the center's capabilities and reaches in the business community.

Owen has a lot of potential—it has some excellent and young professors and it attracts talented individuals that are easy to work with and learn from. Yet the new dean and his staff need to learn and grow very fast if they are going to convert this potential into tangible results. The program and its community need to be more aggressive and dissatisfied with the status quo.

I found the experience at Vanderbilt's MBA program to be exceptionally positive. My objectives for coming back to business school were easily surpassed. Not only did I fill in the gaps of business knowledge that I intended, but also I was able to do it with great people and have fun in the process. The program was rigorous yet I always felt that as a community of students we enjoyed our time together, even under the most stressful of situations. For me, this has been two very well spent years of my life.

UNIVERSITY OF NOTRE DAME

29.
UNIVERSITY OF NOTRE DAME

Mendoza College of Business
276 Mendoza College of Business
University of Notre Dame
Notre Dame, Indiana 46556
E-mail address: mba.1@nd.edu
Web site address: www.nd.edu/~cba

Enrollment: 325
Women: 24%
Non-U.S.: 33%
Minority: 15%
Part-time: 0
Average age: 26
Applicants accepted: 23%
Median starting pay: $75,000
Annual tuition and fees: $26,485

Estimated annual budget: $38,005
Average GMAT score: 668
Average months of work
  experience: 46
Accepted applicants enrolled: 52%
Corporate ranking: 24
Graduate ranking: 35
Intellectual capital rank: 23

Teaching methods: case study 22%, distance learning 2%, experiential learning 15%, lecture 26%, simulations 9%, team projects 17%, other 9%

The tides are turning in South Bend, Indiana. Tyrone Willingham resurrected Irish football; Mike Brey brought the basketball squad up from the basement of the Big East; and now, Carolyn Woo is waking up the echoes of the University of Notre Dame's Mendoza School of Business, guiding it into the realm of the top 30 for the first time in the school's brief history. Traditionally, Mendoza has been known for its strong focus on ethics, going along with the Catholic mission of the university. Now, as ethics has become an issue at the forefront of the business world, other top schools are trying to play catch-up to the Mendoza program. This shouldn't be surprising, because, as Woo explains, it's the Notre Dame way. "Succeeding is important, but how we succeed is also important," she says.

Founded in 1987, the Mendoza School is the youngest in the top 30, remaining true to the great tradition of the university whose name it bears. All of the decisions and actions that Mendoza takes are centered on the goals and values of the larger Notre Dame community. A prime example of this appears in the development of Mendoza's curriculum in the past few years. The curriculum focuses on four themes: values, balance, lifelong development, and community. While other schools are trying to edge out the competition by adding the newest state-of-the art facilities or technologies, Mendoza is developing the skills and traits that will help students become better individuals. "The people make the place," says Matt Bloom, professor of management. "It's not the buildings or anything like that. It's the people you surround yourself with that really make the difference." Students tend to agree. "The MBA program is about more than just classes, grades, starting salaries, and jobs," says one 2002 grad. "It's about friendship, community, a sense of belonging. Notre Dame offers excellence without sacrificing the attributes that make it special."

Notre Dame is one of the most recognized and revered universities in the United States, with alums, fans, and followers from all walks of life. If you were to ask most college-educated individuals to sing you their alma mater's fight song, they would probably be hard pressed to do so. But ask them to sing Notre Dame's, and that is a different story. It may be because there is so much exposure to Notre Dame (NBC has the television rights to every home football game in South Bend), or it may be movies like *Rudy* that feature the university as a backdrop, but, whatever the reason, there is a tremendous pride and tradition that goes along with the blue and gold. "There is a passion for this school that is hard to define," says Jerry Langley, professor of finance. "But I do know that it is something truly special to be a part of."

Before coming to Mendoza, Langley worked for McDonald's, doing international finance and capital markets. After accepting an early retirement package, Langley set up shop at Notre Dame. A Kellogg grad, Langley has been nothing but impressed by the quality of students that Mendoza brings in each year. "The test that I ask myself is, 'Would I hire them?'" he says. "Most of the time I say, 'I would hire them in a second.' I see a lot of students that I would love to have had working for me."

The downside of being known as an institution that stresses values and ethics is that many times, students' expectations are so high going in that it is hard not to be disappointed. For the most part, though, this is not the case—grads on the whole are happy with their experiences at Mendoza. Though it is the goal of Mendoza to have a student body composed of unselfish, humble leaders, there will always be a few that don't fit the mold, and these students tend to stick out like a Boston College fan in South Bend on a football Saturday. Some students complain that a number of their classmates were not willing to share possible job leads or contacts. "At a school where alumni are so valuable, you hate to see so many people in your class that care so little about their fellow classmates," says one student.

Mendoza is named for 1973 grad Tom Mendoza and his wife, Kathy, who donated $35 million to the school in 2000. He serves as president and she as director of Network Appliance, Inc., a California-based data storage firm. With the contribution, Woo has been able to take the school to the next level without having to change its mission or focus. None of the money has gone to the development of new buildings or centers; instead, improving the quality of students through scholarships and fellowships and recruiting top-notch junior faculty have been the top priority.

At Mendoza, you will find a fairly cut-and-dried program that comes in two different formats: the regular two-year program and a one-year version for students with undergraduate degrees in business. Students involved in that program are quick to recommend it. For the majority who do the two-year program, the first year will consist of the usual array of core courses and two electives. In the second year, students must choose an ethics elective and an international business elective.

It is common among the top business schools to hear career services officers describe students as being their customers. Woo believes this is a vast misnomer, at least at Mendoza. "Students are absolutely not our customers," she says. "It is not about transaction. Our job is not to make them happy, our job is to help them succeed." It is one thing to leave a B-school after two years with a new set of knowledge, but it is another to leave with a mature set of standards and values. Woo believes that, by and large, the education that students receive at any of the top schools is similar—it's the community and the values that a school holds that set it apart. Along these lines, it should be no surprise that Mendoza has moved into the upper echelon of schools, because the community it strives toward is one that few other schools can duplicate.

If you don't know the history and tradition that go along with the Notre Dame name, you might be better off applying elsewhere, because Mendoza is looking for students who display a strong desire be a part of the community. Says one 2002 grad, "I would not recommend the program to a friend who just wanted to attend an MBA program for the education and not expect to contribute to other aspects of the program." Virtually all MBAs participate in some form of volunteerism, thanks to the Community Service Committee, which organizes activities for three local charities. Students are aware of this focus from the moment they step on campus, since a community service event is part of the two-week-long orientation program.

The huge alumni base that Notre Dame possesses is a great benefit to students at Mendoza, and the career services office does everything within its power to use all the resources available to them. Unlike other schools, Notre Dame has a large group of what are known as "friends of the university"—that is, people who are not alumni but feel a strong connection to the school (a.k.a. Irish football fanatics). Being savvy businesspeople themselves, the career services staff is using football to their advantage by creating an MBA tailgate party of sorts, where students can mingle with alums and friends of the university for a few hours before kickoff. As can be expected, beer flows like water and charcoal and lighter fluid are used by the case, but at these gatherings an uncommon item is also shared among the assembled masses: business cards. For games in the fall of 2002, nearly 1000 people attended the events at each home football game and students routinely left with more contacts than they knew what to do with. Mendoza even brings in corporate sponsors such as IBM, Ford, and Procter & Gamble for the tailgates to help foot the bill for the large amount of food and drink consumed.

Located 90 miles east of Chicago, Notre Dame's hometown of South Bend has a population of just over 107,000. South Bend serves as the hub of the Michiana area—the term used to reflect the economy of Southwest Michigan and North Central Indiana. While it may not be the most interesting city in the world, or even the area, in the past few years South Bend has made strides to become more friendly, with the addition of such attractions as the College Football Hall of Fame. The campus is located on the northern edge of town, and students do not tend to stray too far from its friendly confines. There are a number of school-sponsored gatherings, ranging from the annual Halloween Costume Party to the Spring Formal, where students mix with faculty and administrators. The Senior Bar on campus is a hangout on Thursday nights. Popular spots include Coach's and The Linebacker, both just a few blocks off campus.

Student housing is available on campus within easy walking distance of Mendoza. All graduate housing is separate from the housing reserved for rowdy undergrads. Popular choices among MBAs are the Fisher or O'Hara-Grace townhouses, which are located across from the rec center. A good number of MBAs choose to live off campus in one of the many nearby apartment complexes. There is a lot of affordable housing available in South Bend, so you can be somewhat particular in the type of place you want and the amenities that you can't live without.

PLACEMENT DETAILS

Along with the tailgate parties, the career services office has developed a new initiative called ND NetWorks to help students find the jobs they are looking for. In a partnership between Mendoza, MBA Career Services, and the Notre Dame Career Center, ND NetWorks focuses on identifying career opportunities in small- to medium-size companies that do not do as much on-campus recruiting as some of the larger companies. According to Lee Svete, director of the Career Center, such initiatives will become more prevalent as companies begin to do less and less on-campus recruiting. "We need to be able to react to businesses and industries across the world that have opportunities, when they have opportunities," Svete says. "With ND NetWorks, we are going to be able to that."

In addition, the Career Center has developed what is known as the City Tour as part of ND NetWorks. The City Tour is a Web-based endeavor containing a diverse array of information about fast-growth companies, alumni club contacts, business and industry leaders, chamber of commerce data, and housing/relocation resources for 12 key job locations throughout the country. Svete describes the City Tour as a job search club where students can communicate with alums in a given city and share contacts, along with war stories. "There are alums living in that city, and there are students living in South Bend," he says. "We want to bring those two groups together and give them a platform to communicate and to share ideas and concepts and jobs." There are sites set up for cities such as New York, Chicago, San Francisco, Boston, and Washington, DC.

With the City Tour initiative up and running, grads have a number of options and resources that other schools cannot offer their students. Add that to the already mammoth number of alumni and friends of the university, and there should be no reason why Mendoza grads won't be turning recruiters away. That wasn't exactly the case for 2002 grads, of which only 66 percent had one offer by graduation. However, three months after graduation, 87 percent had offers, a number that compared very favorably even to the top 10 B-schools.

Unlike the case for most other schools in the top 30, the average pay package for the class of 2002 actually rose from $84,000 in 2000 to just under $100,000 for 2002. Nearly every member of the class of 2002 remained in the United States (99 percent), with the majority setting up shop in the Midwest (41 percent). Of the top hirers, the university itself ranked number two, hiring seven 2002 Mendoza grads. That is one way to boost hiring numbers.

TOP HIRES

IBM (8); University of Notre Dame (7); Honeywell (6); Kraft Foods (4); General Electric (3); Hewlett-Packard (3); Johnson & Johnson (3); Keane Consulting Group (3).

OUTSTANDING FACULTY

Jerry Langley (finance); Richard Mendenhall (finance); Frank Reilly (finance); Ram Ramanan (finance); William Wilkie (marketing).

APPLICANT TIPS

Mendoza has started to use current students more in the admissions process, because, as Hayden Estrada, director of admissions, explains, no one knows what kind of person excels at Mendoza better than a student. "It has been great because they can tell us whether or not a student is someone they would like to have work in a group, or if they could see the person at Notre Dame," he says. At the same time, it has worked the other way as well because no one can tell potential students what life at Mendoza is like better than current students.

Mendoza is looking for self-starters—students who are out to learn as much as they can—but also for students who value the community and the Notre Dame network. Adds Estrada, "People who are involved in a lot of activities here are also the most successful. Anyone can come here and just get an academic education, but really the goal of someone who comes to Notre Dame should be more than just academic, it should be of educating the whole person."

Mendoza is one of the few MBA programs that still has rolling admissions, but, of course, the sooner you can apply, the better. Expect to hear back two weeks after you apply, a time frame that Estrada has worked hard to achieve so that applicants will know if they are accepted soon after they apply.

MENDOZA MBAs SOUND OFF

Notre Dame is a great institution, from the community aspect of the school in general (more students live on campus than at any other school outside of the academies, including a high proportion of graduate students) to the friendships formed that will last a lifetime as we return for football games.

I actually think our program is as good as any other program out there. But being ND, I expected it to be more than any other program out there, in the non-academic dimensions, and what is disappointing is to find out that it is not.

As part of my education at Notre Dame I was able to work as an assistant rector in one of the undergraduate dorms serving nearly 300 residents. This enhanced my experience and education greatly and is something I will always cherish about my two years at Notre Dame. I was able to plug into the thriving ND community and enjoyed every minute of it.

Notre Dame represents the integrity and values that I wish to foster as a business leader. Everyone at this university is so nice and treats me as I treat them: like a loved family member. This is truly a special and unique place.

I know the Notre Dame MBA will become more valuable over time. I've made so many valuable relationships with alumni just from off-campus happenstance meetings and during the "homecoming style" football games. And those alumni are willing to go the distance for another Irish grad. I think many people forget that the MBA degree is a long-term investment. If you think of it in terms of a financial valuation model ND is probably about even with most top schools right at graduation, but the continuing value, driven mostly by opportunities from meeting ND alumni, is so much greater. The overall experience at the University of Notre Dame was great. I felt there was too much overlap between courses, and some of the elective courses were useless. The finance courses I took were, in general, excellent. The caliber of teaching was very good except for a few professors who I felt should not be teaching. Having a family, I would have liked to have seen more family-oriented get-togethers.

Although I appreciate having the University of Notre Dame brand on my resume, the program continues to have a long journey ahead of itself in terms of job placement services, diversity, and financial support for its students. The advice I typically received from job placement services tended to be suited for undergraduates. The advisors' comments and suggestion rarely met the center of my concerns (no matter how explicit I explained myself). The advisors were proficient in correcting typos on resumes, but as an MBA candidate I needed a far more sophisticated level of service.

GEORGETOWN UNIVERSITY

McDonough School of Business
P.O. Box 571148
Washington, DC 20057
E-mail address: MBA@georgetown.edu
Web site address: www.mgmt.purdue.edu

Enrollment: 530	Estimated annual budget: $50,720
Women: 29%	Average GMAT score: 663
Non-U.S.: 53%	Average months of work
Minority: 13%	experience: 64
Part-time: 0	Accepted applicants enrolled: 40%
Average age: 28	Corporate ranking: 28
Applicants accepted: 23%	Graduate ranking: 32
Median starting pay: $81,000	Intellectual capital rank: 41
Annual tuition and fees: $29,976	

Teaching methods: case study 40%, experiential learning 5%, lecture 40%, simulations 5%, team projects 10%

Paul Almeida, who teaches strategy at Georgetown University's Robert Emmett McDonough School of Business, does not baby his students. "My classes are very structured. I expect everyone to attend every time," Almeida says. "I end every class on time. Expectations are high." Almeida's expectations mirror the demands McDonough places on its students. The desire to create principled, autonomous leaders is buried deep within the school's Jesuit tradition. Almeida, a force to be reckoned with, doesn't hesitate to cold call, explaining that he doesn't care if students like him as long as they're learning. This tough love approach may prepare students for a brutal job market.

McDonough's career services isn't meeting all its students' needs. Georgetown's standout international program and legacy of high ethical standards cannot outshine a lackluster career placement center that managed to help place a meager 50 percent of grads by commencement—the worst of any top 30 school in 2002. Fortunately for future students, the school just hired a new director of MBA career management.

The career management director is one of many new faces around McDonough. The dean, MBA program director, and admissions director are all getting their feet wet. In August of 2002, after teaching economics for six years at Georgetown, John Mayo was appointed to a two-year term as dean. While he didn't schedule this move into his planner, Mayo says he thrives off the energy of McDonough's diverse student body. "My job is to get our faculty engaged," says Mayo, who's worked with some prominent figures before. In addition to serving at Washington University, the University of Tennessee, and Virginia Tech, Mayo was chief economist of the U.S. Senate Small Business Committee. Still, transitions are challenging, even as they can shed light on the strengths and weaknesses of a school. In that vein, Mayo hopes students partly take it on themselves to turn a McDonough education into a satisfying career, adding, "I don't want to be too paternalistic about this. Our job is to provide them with the core discipline skills. What we want to do is provide the baseline human capital." Mayo says it shouldn't matter which direction the economy takes. But don't tell that to MBA grads of 2002, who rated the school's placement office among the worst. Mayo's outlook is different than that of other top B-school deans, who see placement as a critical measure of the school's success—building relationships with recruiters and giving MBA students the skills and guidance they need to get recognized, and get jobs.

Marilyn Morgan, the dean and director of the MBA program, is also adjusting to a new environment. Having joined Georgetown in the fall of 2001 after leading the Global Executive MBA at the Fuqua School of Business at Duke University, she's well acquainted with the school's history. Morgan believes the McDonough curriculum is suited for the changing business world, "The ethics course is part of the Georgetown tradition." She adds, "It's not like teaching the principles of finance. It is part of the culture." Indeed, the school's powerful emphasis on ethics, bolstered by the university's Jesuit tradition, combined with new leadership, the school's previously established strengths in international and government business, the halo effect of being part of an excellent university, and an unbeatable location amid the hustle and bustle of the nation's capital make McDonough a B-school well worth consideration—if you don't mind putting up with what some would call lingering growing pains.

International business is the heart and soul of Georgetown's B-school, a tradition that's been around since the school's inception in 1981. It's a focus you might expect from a university whose Public Policy Institute and School of Foreign Service have long been considered among the finest of their kind in the world. The relatively new MBA curriculum for which students lobbied heavily and which went into effect in the 1998–1999 academic year aims to further enhance the program's already strong global perspective while injecting large doses of both hands-on experience and technology training.

As of fall 1998, first year is divided into four six-week modules consisting of four or five functional core courses, encompassing a traditional lineup of accounting, quantitative methods, organizational behavior, marketing, finance, strategy, communication, public policy, and ethics. These modules are interspersed with integrative experiences (IEs)—one-week team-based projects intended to bring together what you've learned in the different areas. IE1 kicks off year one in late August with a live case in which faculty and executives from an international company present students with a current problem or opportunity. In fall 2002, Federal Express provided the backdrop for this introduction to international business. IE2, which follows the first six-week module in October, emphasizes database decision making and provides instruction in quantitative methods, while IE3, which follows the third module, has students working in teams to analyze two international industries.

The second year starts with a third required integrative experience, New Business Trends, which examines the ways information and communication technologies affect business functions and operations. In addition, students must take a required course introducing them to advanced decision support models and systems in a functional area of their choice. Also required of all MBAs is a weeklong on-site team project outside of the United States, supported by 12 weeks of classroom work in the Global

Experience thread course during the last semester. So far, students have traveled to Hong Kong, London, Buenos Aires, New Delhi, São Paulo, and Prague.

Although the B-school doesn't have formal majors, students can follow school-designed career tracks in finance for those headed for investment banking or corporate finance, in marketing for those aiming to work for consumer products companies, or in strategy for wannabe consultants. The new curriculum leaves room for 20 electives, 3 in the first year before your summer internship and the rest in year two. Students can choose from the small menu of 45 electives available through the B-school or from the catalogs of other Georgetown schools and departments offering coursework in international affairs, government, or public policy and law. You can apply to pursue the highly competitive honors certificate in an area of study by passing a foreign language proficiency test and devoting 18 of your elective credits toward classes in the economy, history, language, culture, and governments of the Middle East, Europe, Latin America, or Eurasia, Eastern Europe, and Russia. There are also dual degrees available in law, public policy, foreign service, physics, and medicine, all nationally recognized schools of the larger university.

Georgetown's location in the nation's capital obviously provides MBAs with a window on the relationship between business and government, and the B-school capitalizes on the proximity with a vengeance. Its 24 full-time faculty members are supplemented by more than three dozen adjunct and visiting professors who spend most of their day working at places like the U.S. Treasury, the Federal Reserve Board, the Small Business Administration, and the U.S. Senate Banking Committee. Indeed, the DC location helps students develop a relationship with government. But it's not just politicos and Beltway insiders; don't write off Georgetown's business network either. Georgetown's strong relationship with the local business community is often overlooked, as is its dominant position

in tech employment, telecom, and biotech. Still, the school has had trouble capitalizing on the relationships in a tough MBA job market.

Being situated in Washington, as well as being part of the Georgetown franchise, helps the B-school draw a diverse student body, with a third of the students coming from some three dozen countries outside the United States. Still a relatively small program despite an enrollment expansion during the last couple of years to about 260 per class, Georgetown MBAs tend to be an outgoing bunch who take an active role in the running of the school. It was largely students who first prodded former dean Parker, then interim dean Kasra Ferdows, into initiating the curriculum revamp. And part of a $245,000 gift from the class of 1998 went toward development of a database on the Web to connect with the school's small but growing alumni network.

The B-school is in the middle of a $100 million capital campaign, part of which will go toward building a new headquarters. The goal is to raise $150 million in a fund-raising campaign scheduled to end in 2003. The effort began in 1998, and the school is more than halfway there. In the meantime, MBAs are housing the program in the Car Barn, a site made famous for the stairs that appeared in the movie *The Exorcist*. The interim state-of-the-art facility features four case-style classrooms, each with tiered seating for 65 students, Ethernet connections at every terminal, and overhead digital projectors. A laboratory and student lounge are also available for Georgetown MBAs as they wait.

The Car Barn also features long-distance videoconferencing, an example of how Georgetown is trying to enhance technology on campus. Back in 1998, students gave the school dramatically low marks for being technologically backward. The administrators are slowly climbing out of the dark ages. Full-time MBAs are using Blackboard, an online service that permits classmates and professors to chat with each other and to obtain and turn in assignments. The system gives students greater access to faculty and allows faculty to maintain longer office hours from home. Students are also logging on to Cyber Café, an intimate gathering at which a guest from the local technology sector stops by campus to chat with MBAs.

The section of Washington from which Georgetown University takes its name is itself a wonderful—albeit expensive—playground for young adults. Since there's no graduate housing on campus, most MBAs share townhouses in the cosmopolitan neighborhood filled with trendy bars, foreign restaurants, and tiny boutiques. There are cocktail parties in the MBA lounge at the Car Barn, and groups of students often head to The Tombs for thick, crusty pizza and beer after an exam. Some students take on additional jobs, like bartending, while others don't understand how anyone has time for fun. On campus, closer to classes, students can mingle in finance, consulting, marketing, and women's groups. Alternately, Baltimore and the Shenandoah Valley are nearby. McDonough graduates advise wannabe MBAs that the program is very group oriented and plenty of friendships result. "It's not a school where you go to network," says one 2002 graduate. "It's where you go to make friends." He adds that "those that are unfairly competitive do get ostracized," using a student who stole someone's work from a printer as an example.

PLACEMENT DETAILS

Reaction to career management was mixed, with students attacking or praising regardless of whether they found jobs through the system. One 2002 graduate complains, "All they did was to go on the Internet and look for job postings." Indeed, so many grads and recruiters complained about the placement office that it landed on the worst placement office list for 2002. Grads complained that the school barely showed up when it came to helping them find a job, helping them with independent job search issues, or even helping them prepare for interviews and negotiations. Indeed, Georgetown's placement office received the worst marks of any top 30 school. Recruiters increasingly say they've been dropping the school from their roster—though the problem has little to do with the quality of the graduates. Instead, they found the placement office hard to use and unresponsive—and in a time when recruiting is already being slashed, such hardships make Georgetown less desirable as a place to recruit.

Fresh blood should rejuvenate the placement center. Four-year Georgetown career services veteran Jim Dixey is the new assistant dean and director of MBA career management. Hailing from the airline industry, Dixey—who earned a master's degree in organizational development—is unhappy with the current operation. He says he will facilitate, rather than control, recruiter relations and wise up to current economic conditions. "There are jobs out there. The question is: where are the jobs?" Dixey cites one hypothetical situation from the old system as an example of how not to do things: Goldman Sachs—a company people trust with their life savings—had to ask for permission to look at the McDonough resume book. Dixey says that type of control signals mistrust and impedes the job search. In this cash-constrained environment, he will seek out new opportunities in defense, pharmaceuticals, and government, thank regular recruiters in person, and ask the oldies but goodies why they stopped showing up this year. And he's already knocked on some New York doors, asking the tough questions. Yet, Dixey wants students to know that ultimately the job search is their responsibility. "I never guarantee jobs. I don't give jobs. I give opportunities," Dixey says.

But, in 2002, only 50 percent of Georgetown grads had a job offer by graduation, the lowest of any school in the top 30. About 79 percent had work three months after graduation. And those that managed to find jobs earned respectable starting pay packages of about

$105,000. About 14 percent of Georgetown grads in 2002 found jobs outside the U.S., but those that stayed in the States congregated to the Northeast and Mid-Atlantic.

TOP HIRES

Citigroup (5); American Express (4); General Electric (4); Procter & Gamble (3); Barcap (3); KPMG (3); JPMorgan Chase (2); Merrill Lynch (2); Miller Brewing (2); Lehman Brothers (2); CSFB (2); EXIM Bank (2); RGS Associates (2); Community Wealth Ventures (2); Fannie Mae (2).

OUTSTANDING FACULTY

Ken Homa (marketing); Gary Blemaster (finance); Bardia Kamrad (decision science); Willis Emmons (management); Kastra Ferdows (operations).

APPLICANT TIPS

Monica Gray, the new director of MBA admissions, says there is no mathematical equation for the right stuff. McDonough students are anything but formulaic. "We're looking for students that are well rounded," says Gray, adding that diverse interests, second language proficiency, two years or more of work experience, and world travel are pluses. International students should understand that the program uses a lot of English.

Gray dissuades students from applying right out of college. "I don't think it benefits the applicant," Gray says. "I think that trend is largely a function of the economy." McDonough admissions personnel read essays very thoroughly, looking for people with strong interpersonal skills who are excited about learning and have a clear hold on what they want out of the curriculum and their careers. Students are encouraged to interview and sit in on classes. The school understands that GPAs vary by country and evaluates GMATs in the same manner. In 2002, McDonough saw an increase in women and minority enrollment, along with increased interest from the former Soviet Union and the Middle East.

McDONOUGH MBAs SOUND OFF

The professors are among the best I have ever been taught by. The career management office was by far the poorest excuse for a career management office that I have ever seen.

Georgetown is a rising star and you can see it all around. What is needed now is a clear vision for the future. With that, and a larger alumni body to tap for networking, I have no doubt the school will be among the very best in the world.

The Georgetown experience has been great. We all participated in an overseas residency program, all 247 of us, that was the capstone of our time here. It definitely separates the Georgetown MBA experience from the pack. Additionally, professors and the level of classroom instruction are also top notch. Like any emerging institution, we do suffer from growing pains, but it is nothing a large donation or some added monetary resources could not solve.

Except for the career management part of my school everything was like well-oiled machinery. Staff and faculty are exceptionally helpful. The international programs office is very helpful in dealing with problems of international students.

Georgetown has very dedicated professors who teach because they want to, certainly not for the money or prestige. The students are very diverse, which allows the classroom to explore numerous perspectives on every situation. The two major beefs I have with the school are the lack of experience and connections in the Career Management department and the lack of IT classes and facilities in the school.

The cooperative and supportive atmosphere at Georgetown was outstanding. I feel that I learned as much from peers as I did from the assigned curriculum. Georgetown's admissions staff did an excellent job of putting together an exceptionally talented, motivated and team-oriented group of students.

I valued the small class size and cohesive atmosphere at Georgetown. Furthermore, I cannot imagine studying in a remote town versus here in Washington, DC—I loved the international feel and the culture here.

As long as the student's focus is general management, the school offered enough high-quality electives. However, for those who wanted to focus on some specific area such as marketing or accounting, I think there were not enough high-quality electives. I was lucky because my focus was general management and I really enjoyed the learning experience at Georgetown.

THE RUNNERS-UP

Second-tier schools can still offer a lot of value.

If you're considering getting an MBA, no doubt you'll want a degree from one of the most prestigious and well-known business schools. There's no question that there are some big advantages to having an MBA from a brand-name school: beyond the superior educational benefits, starting pay packages tend to be higher at such schools, and many are known for their well-oiled alumni connection machines. But not everyone can pass the rigorous admissions standards set by the most elite schools—and, more than this, the most prestigious schools tend to get hundreds, even thousands, more applicants than they could ever admit. Besides, you may not want to spend two years in a location that boasts a top 30 school—perhaps you'd rather be in, say, Dallas. There, you could spend two excellent years at Southern Methodist University's Cox School of Business. Or maybe you're a fan of the Pacific Northwest, in which case University of Washington, a real up-and-comer in 2002, might be a choice prospect.

Some people mistakenly believe that if you can't manage to gain admission to a top 30 school, you shouldn't bother going for an MBA at all. That's simply not true. You don't have to go to a first-tier school to get a good graduate business education—or a good job, for that matter. The next group of 20 schools, dubbed the runners-up, generally deliver the same basic body of knowledge as the more prominent institutions. In some cases, these schools have floated in and out of the top tier of schools or have begun to catch the eye of top recruiters and students alike. Together, they round out *BusinessWeek*'s top 50 B-schools. In some cases, the quality of education at runner-up schools may even exceed that at some of the schools on the top list, especially in certain niche areas. Babson College is widely recognized to have the best business school in the world for entrepreneurship. UC Irvine has its hands wrapped around technology—especially the latest and most innovative types. Few schools can ever match the international offering of Thunderbird. And few can best the operations department at Penn State, the accounting department at the University of Illinois, or the tech savvy of Georgia Institute of Technology.

So what's the difference? Overall, these schools sometimes lack the breadth of quality offered at top 30 schools. Not only will you generally find a smaller percentage of superb teachers and scholars at these schools (many of them tend to stand out in a niche area, but it can be hit or miss on individual subject offerings), you'll also discover that these schools might lack some of the infrastructure needed to support demanding students—the high-tech bells and whistles; the deep-pocketed endowments; and the cohesive, high-powered alumni networks. Graduates of runner-up programs may find it just a little harder to connect with the job market, particularly the prestige employers. That said, these same challenges often present great opportunities for ambitious students to help lead the way in change.

Some of the runner-up schools are just as selective as their elite counterparts. Indeed, some boast even better records of placing their students. And some claim professors in niche areas that are so superior, they might put teachers in the top 30 to shame.

BusinessWeek lists this group alphabetically, without a numerical ranking.

> A runner-up school might be right for you.

ARIZONA STATE UNIVERSITY

College of Business
P.O. Box 874906
Tempe, Arizona 85287-4906
E-mail address: asu.mba@asu.edu
Web site address: www.cob.asu.edu/mba

Enrollment: 287
Women: 22%
Non-U.S.: 22%
Minority: 9%
Part-time: 720 (on-campus plus distance)
Average age: 28
Applicants accepted: 29%
Median starting pay: $75,000

Annual tuition and fees:
   resident—$11,585
   nonresident—$20,105
Estimated annual budget: $28,009
Average GMAT score: 654
Average months of work experience: 52
Accepted applicants enrolled: 52%

Teaching methods: case study 40%, lecture 40%, simulations 5%, team projects 15%

Most of the year, a climate like the one in Tempe, Arizona, is truly beneficial to B-school students. You won't see anyone trudging through snow to make it on time to a 9 A.M. managerial economics class in the middle of winter. In December, studying outside under palm trees can prove quite pleasant. But what about when the thermometer hits 105° and rearview mirrors in cars start melting and falling off? Under these conditions, it's pretty hard to dress up in a suit and tie first thing in the morning for a 2 P.M. interview with a consulting firm. So, Arizona State University's College of Business did what any smart school located in the middle of the desert would do. As part of a $6.9 million renovation, the school built student locker rooms with suit-length lockers, added spacious grooming areas with sinks, and installed full-length mirrors. Under the new setup, students can continue to come to school in the typical Arizona uniform of shorts and t-shirts and change into their interview clothes at the last minute. Much of the school was renovated, but a lot of it wasn't touched. Dean Larry E. Penley says he now would like to see the rest of the College of Business redone, but that it would take a significant fund-raising effort—something he plans to undertake over the next few years. For now, he says he is happy with the first-floor improvements.

Despite the myriad palm trees, golf courses, and swimming pools, your two years at Arizona State will be far from a vacation. Your time at the school will be spent deep in textbooks, analyzing cases and learning how to work in a team environment. You will choose from one of six niche markets for a required concentration: supply chain management, finance management and markets, services marketing and management, sports business, information management, and health services administration. Start thinking early about what area you want to specialize in: you'll be asked to pick one early in your first year, and some students even choose one as part of their application.

No matter when or what you choose, you will still need to take the school's 11 core courses your first year. Classes are broken into three trimesters, each 11 weeks long. Despite the school's claim that it isn't a general management school, the core resembles that of any other B-school, covering everything from financial and managerial accounting to global and managerial economics. Currently, waivers are not permitted for core courses. In the spring, you will also take one prerequisite for your chosen specialization, which can serve as good preparation for your summer internship.

During your second year, you will take courses required for your track. Students in the sports management track, for example, take five required courses: Sports Business Revenue Generation and Marketing, Sports Business Revenue and Financial Management, Customer Loyalty and Satisfaction Measurement, Negotiation, Relationship and Alliance Management, and Law and Politics of Sports Business. Students in this track are also required to take at least one elective and participate in the Rotation, a monthly seminar series with sports leaders in the community.

During the second year, all MBA students—no matter what their specialization—take part in a team-based consulting project that can span two or all three trimesters, depending on the chosen area of concentration.

One constant request Dennis Hoffman, associate dean for graduate programs, hears from students is the desire for more room for electives. In response, Hoffman decided not to compromise the core but to add more flexibility to the students' second-year curriculum. For example, students in the supply chain management track now take two-thirds the number of classes that they did before the change, which took place in the fall of 2002. "We still require students to have a strong major," says Hoffman. "So, we can still say to recruiters that our students have career focus and we don't have generalists here at ASU."

If one degree isn't enough for you, there's always the option of a dual degree. A handful of students choose to pursue dual degrees in information management, economics, health services administration, accounting and information systems, taxation, architecture, or law. There's also a joint program with the nearby American Graduate School of International Management (a.k.a. Thunderbird) for those students interested in combining the MBA with a master's in international management.

To help you stay as technologically advanced and up to date as possible, Arizona State now requires all students in the full-time MBA program to purchase a laptop computer. And we're not talking just any old laptop; it must be specifically licensed and configured for a wireless technology network. In order to meet the requirements, you are expected to purchase the already configured computer through the school. Once you've got your laptop, you'll be able to connect through the school's wireless network. With 300-plus days of sunshine a year, you'll want to take your laptop outside and work on school assignments near the fountain in the plaza or stretch out with it under a palm tree. Better yet, head to the student recreation center, where you can sit poolside while surfing the Web.

With more than 50,000 students on its three campuses, Arizona State is the fifth largest public university in the country. You'd be hard pressed to find much more of a college town than Tempe. The downtown area centers around Mill Avenue, a mélange of coffeehouses, bookstores, a movie theater, and cheap eats. Despite the heavy workload, you'll probably have time enough to participate in ASU MBA traditions like the Outdoor Adventure, the MBA Olympics, and the ASU MBA Roast and Toast. If you want to get away from it all, it doesn't take much; you can take the freeway in any direction, and within half an hour, you'll be smack dab in the middle of the desert surrounded by nothing but cacti and wide open spaces.

PLACEMENT DETAILS

When Career Services Director Kitty McGrath came to Arizona State in 2000, the Career Management Center had 10 people on its staff. Today, that number is 14, and students have the opportunity to see any one of the staff members to discuss their careers while at the school.

Students' first interaction with Career Management comes as soon as they are admitted to the MBA program. "They have already received information from us before they walk in the door," says McGrath. Incoming students receive welcome information about the department along with access to online career tests. When they do walk in the door, they are divided into three groups and are required to participate in a seminar series for the first three weeks, coinciding with their first classes.

Strategic Communication, a new course required of all first-years as of fall 2002, is designed to enhance students' presentation and interview skills. The course came about in direct response to feedback Associate Dean Hoffman was receiving from recruiters, who were telling him that the school's content was fine but students' presentation skills could use some help. "We want our students to be able to present themselves well, to be able to articulate concepts or ideas," says Hoffman. The course is led by two faculty members and two career services staff members. As part of it, students must submit their resumes for review and "revise and revise," says McGrath. In addition, all students are required to participate in a videotaped practice interview with a recruiter. "This is the single most powerful learning experience," says McGrath, who combed her recruiter files for volunteers. "The recruiters like doing it. It's a method of giving back." Maybe they're giving

back for the new recruiter lounge, built by the school as part of its renovation project, which features laptop links, phones, coffeemakers, and a refrigerator. The school also increased the number of interview rooms from 4 to 10.

In 2000, the Career Management Center decided to take advantage of some local opportunities. It started a new program capitalizing on the wealth of retired executives living in the Phoenix area. "The Executive Is In" pairs retired CEOs and other mid- to high-level executives living in the area with students for one-on-one consulting. "They are wonderful role models, and our students are the fortunate recipients of their knowledge," says McGrath.

TOP HIRES

Honeywell (9); Sprint (6); Intel (5); Raytheon (4); IBM (3); Chevron Texaco (3); Dell (3); Planar Systems (3).

OUTSTANDING FACULTY

Marianne Jennings (business law); Ajay Vinze (accounting); Frederico Nadari (finance); Stuart Low (economics); Julia Smith-David (accounting); Lisa Ellram (supply chain).

APPLICANT TIPS

One surefire way not to get into Arizona State's B-school is to apply without two years of work experience. "If you don't have it, don't waste your application fee," says Assistant Dean for Graduate Programs Carl Harris. "We have expectation of a type of skill set you can only acquire through professional experience."

If you make the decision to go ahead and apply anyway, at least the fee is relatively low: $45. What used to be a cumbersome, time-consuming, and expensive process has now been streamlined to a 30-minute online application (minus the essays, of course). No longer are MBA applicants required to submit two applications.

Interviews aren't required at Arizona State but are becoming increasingly popular. "For anybody who asks for an interview, we'll give them one," says Harris. The school might also request interviews from candidates who are right on the line. If you do get asked to interview, don't look it as the ultimate decision maker or the kiss of death, says Harris.

Most of the problems Harris sees are with applicants' essays. "Don't make the mistake of answering the question you want to be asked," he says. Essays should be looked at as a measure of communication. The admissions committee uses the essays to answer two questions about you: "If we let you in, will you survive?" and "If we let you graduate, will you make yourself and us look good?"

"There is nothing secret about the application process," says Harris. Each application goes through a triple review process. First, the student admissions committee takes a look. "They know what it's like to be sitting in the classroom," says Harris. "They can ask themselves, 'Is this the person I would want to be sitting next to?'" The second review is by the assistant director of admissions, who also makes a list of comments and a recommendation one way or the other. Finally, the application lands on the desk of the director of admissions, who has the final say in admitting or denying an applicant.

Arizona State operates on a modified rolling admissions basis. "The earlier you apply, the earlier your application will be reviewed," says Harris, who recommends getting your application in as soon as possible. While there are three suggested application deadlines, the admissions office does review applications until all spots are filled.

ARIZONA STATE MBAs SOUND OFF

I realize the job market affected all MBA programs this year and although I was disappointed in the assistance and the overall placement program for my specific concentration, I know that most of the other concentrations were solid and that ASU is in the process of changing the staff in career placement. As far as usefulness of classes, my specialization was excellent and I learned things from teachers that I have not learned anywhere else, including readings, real life business applications, etc. I was extremely pleased with the value and what a great education I received for such a comparatively small amount of tuition.

ASU is an excellent school, but unfortunately when the economy takes a dive, schools such as ASU are more affected, in terms of recruiting, than Ivy League schools. Consequently, my experience has been enriching, but the expected dividends upon graduation have not been met.

Overall a great experience but the B-school environment can be cutthroat at times. International students have a harder time since it is not always easy to integrate into the extracurricular groups where a lot of the networking is going on.

I found the workload to be manageable, the people to be (almost) always helpful and amicable, and that there are multiple, well-reasoned approaches to long-standing problems, but rarely any magic potions. Collectively, it was one of the best experiences of my life, and I would not have chosen to do anything differently.

The core courses are on par, content-wise, with most any other program in the country. The concentrations are what make this program special. The services marketing and management concentration provides an excellent course of study for management in the twenty-first century, especially given the tendency for businesses to move toward services as a means of competitive advantage.

BABSON COLLEGE

Franklin W. Olin Graduate School of Business
Babson Park, Massachusetts 02457
E-mail address: mbaadmission@babson.edu
Web site address: www.babson.edu/mba

Enrollment: 350
Women: 28%
Non-U.S.: 34%
Minority: 7%
Part-time: 30
Average age: 28
Applicants accepted: 39%

Median starting pay: $75,000
Annual tuition and fees: $27,800
Estimated annual budget: $44,946
Average GMAT score: 643
Average months of work
  experience: 63
Accepted applicants enrolled: 41%

Teaching methods: case study 75%, experiential learning 5%, lecture 5%, simulations 5%, team projects 10%

Talking with Babson College MBA students, faculty, and administrators on campus, there are two concepts you are bound to hear mentioned time and time again: innovation and entrepreneurship. It is with these two ideas in mind that the school has built its reputation—a reputation that the school's new dean, Mark Rice, would like to see grow. Rice, who has been at the school since the summer of 2001, wants to move Babson from hidden gem to well-known gem status. He's got a simple philosophy for leading the school: "Focus on a small number of strategic opportunities, and then engage Babson faculty, students, staff, alumni, and friends in excelling at pursuing those opportunities."

It sounds like a lofty—and maybe even impossible—idea, but at Babson, *can't* isn't really an option. Still, with the staggering economy, the school's entrepreneurial bent is being challenged, and Dean Rice has needed to find other areas on which to focus. One of these is the school's relationship with the newly opened Franklin W. Olin College of Engineering in nearby Needham, Massachusetts. "Babson thrives on innovation and entrepreneurship," says Rice, who came to the school from New York's Rensselaer Polytechnic Institute's Lally School of Management and Technology, his alma mater. At Rensselaer, he led an initiative to merge entrepreneurship and engineering. If Rice has his way, Babson will be headed on a similar path. Already, students from Babson and Olin take classes together, and the schools share faculty members, who work together on research proposals and curriculum development. If you do decide to participate in the Babson-Olin Partnership, Babson's goal is for you to come away with not just excellent entrepreneurship training but the technical skills to back it up. As part of the partnership, faculty members from both schools teach Babson's product design and development course, and the project teams for the course include both Olin and Babson students.

Babson and Olin have also developed a proposal for a shared "Innovation Gymnasium" in which innovation and entrepreneurship activities serve as a catalyst for bringing together the schools' business and technical communities. "Ultimately, the Babson-Olin partnership is a breakthrough innovation in higher education, defining novel ways for very different institutions to collaborate so that 1 + 1 = 10. It's the new math," says Rice.

When Rice wants student feedback on his new initiatives, he doesn't have to travel very far. He has been living in graduate student housing since he arrived at Babson in the summer of 2001 and will be living there alongside students for the 2002–2003 academic year. His youngest daughter is finishing up high school in Troy, New York, and Rice commutes there on weekends to be with her and his wife. "He is always willing to stop and talk for a moment when you run into him walking around or taking his trash out. When we barbeque on the lawn—which is circled by all the residence buildings—he'll come out and join us if he's home," says Denise Chew, a member of the class of 2003.

In addition to the new partnership with Olin, you'll find that the Babson curriculum—although heavily focused on case studies—is also unique. For many students, it is one of the main attractions of the school, ranking second only to the entrepreneurial emphasis. Says Andrea Godfrey, a 2002 grad: "Babson has a very innovative curriculum. This was another criterion in my B-school search, as I felt an innovative curriculum was a good proxy for a program that would be very current and in tune with the latest theories, concepts, and trends in the business world."

The emphasis is clearly on teamwork during the first year at Babson, and the coursework reflects this by giving students ample opportunities to work together and develop business plans. Babson has designed its second year to build on the first year's coursework, allowing students to focus their interests and customize their programs with elective courses. But that second year can prove to be a letdown after the fast-paced, in-and-out-of-the-classroom experience your first year.

Your Babson education begins in the fall with a monthlong module on creative management that is similar to other schools' teamwork exercises. Students work together in outdoor challenges and community service projects, all the time reviewing the basics: writing, math, accounting, economics, and computer skills. It's not all dry; there are also creative arts projects in drawing, sculpting, poetry, puppetry, movement, music, and improvisation.

You'll then spend the second half of the fall semester gaining real-world experience in the newly renamed Babson Consulting Alliance Program (BCAP). In BCAP, teams of six students work with a target company and a faculty mentor. In the past, these Boston area companies included giants in banking, high tech, communications, and consumer product industries, such as Microsoft and Reebok, as well as start-ups and nonprofits. Your assignment for the rest of the year: to conduct a comprehensive industry analysis for the company and manage a consulting project of the company's choosing. It's not that rare for a student to land a job—or at least a summer internship—through BCAP.

In the spring, in addition to working with your BCAP company, you'll split your time between module three, which focuses on operations and teaches you how to design and manage a business delivery system, and module four, which tries to integrate the whole first-year curriculum into a segment on how to deal with a changing global environment. Class guests include experts in economics, finance, and marketing.

In the second year of the program, you can participate in semester-long team consulting projects with a variety of companies, including Procter & Gamble, Timberland, Reebok, and

Staples. You also have the opportunity to gain management experience by leading undergraduate business students in team consulting projects. Electives are plentiful and fall into four categories: entrepreneurship, global business environment, strategy, and global strategy. You are required to take nine of these, six of which may be in one discipline.

To help you prepare for life after B-school, Babson has developed six career paths: consulting, entrepreneurship, finance, e-business, marketing, and (new for fall 2002) corporate growth and innovation. Picking a career path is optional, but many students choose to take advantage of the extra guidance it can provide. If you do choose to take advantage of the career paths, you will have access to a Web site with the various career paths (and subpaths, depending on your interests) along with recommended course schedules. If you're interested in starting your own business, you might want to consider the entrepreneurship intensity track, which allows you to simultaneously earn your MBA and launch a business.

As of a few years ago, all MBAs at Babson, with the exception of international students, are required to participate in one of a number of cross-cultural experiences. One option is an overseas summer internship, which can be arranged by the school in one of more than 35 countries. Another is spending a semester abroad at one of three European schools with which Babson has formal agreements: the University of St. Gallen (Switzerland), the European School of Management (France), or the Cranfield School of Management (England). If none of these options appeal to you, there are several international electives offered during the winter break and summer that will send you to Europe, Asia, or Latin America for three weeks of coursework, company visits, and meetings with executives.

Starting in the fall of 2002, Babson launched a fast track MBA program, modeled on the school's IntelMBA corporate degree, which will graduate its first class in 2003. One-half of the fast track program is online; the other half is face to face in the classroom. In 27 months, students earn an MBA and can continue to work full-time. It's designed for the working professional who doesn't want to (or can't) commit to weekly class visits, says MBA Program Director Wendy Baker. Many of the students in the program travel frequently as part of their jobs or don't live within commuting distance of the school. Others simply don't want to give up their current positions in such a tight job market.

No matter which program you choose at Babson, you'll be spending a lot of your time on the school's 370-acre campus, located 14 miles west of Boston, "the hub of the solar system," according to nineteenth-century poet and physician Oliver Wendell Holmes. The greater Boston area is home to 35 colleges and universities, so you'll never feel at a loss for peers. Boston is easily reached from Babson by commuter rail or car. Trendy restaurants are found in the North End of the city and along Newbury Street. Catch a Red Line train from the Park Street stop and you'll be in Cambridge in minutes. Get off at Harvard Square, which is filled with coffee shops, restaurants, bars, and students.

History buffs, rejoice! Living in New England, you'll be at the center of it all. In Boston, you can travel the two-and-a-half mile Freedom Trail with 16 colonial and revolutionary history sites along the way—such as the spot of the "shot heard 'round the world"; Old North Church, where Paul Revere saw the famous lanterns (remember "one if by land, two if by sea"?); and the USS Constitution, in Charlestown Harbor. In Lexington, just northwest of Boston, you can visit the site of the first battle of the Revolutionary War.

If you'd rather stay close to home, Babson's campus is only a few miles from Wellesley College and the town that gave the Seven Sisters school its name. On campus, MBA students tend to congregate at Olin Hall, the red brick and glass graduate center, which was built in 1996. The center boasts 1200 computer ports wired to the Babson intranet; a 200-seat auditorium; six interactive, class, team meeting, and study rooms; and administrative offices. MBA students gather for Thursday pub night at the campus pub just three minutes from Olin Hall. Most students choose to live off campus in pricey Wellesley or other neighboring towns. On campus, student housing is available for about 120 graduate students—and one dean—in Woodland Hill and Bryant Hall.

PLACEMENT DETAILS

In the current tight job market, entering Babson MBAs have a lot of homework to do on arriving at school, says Career Services Director Len Morrison. "Start early developing a network—classmates, former employers. Be a sponge and absorb what classmates, speakers, faculty, have done or are doing for work. Engage in thoughtful and realistic self-assessment of skills, interests, and abilities. Look to meet as many people as possible who can offer perspective or advice about a field of interest to you."

In response to today's tight job market, Career Services at Babson has become more cross-functional, with each professional now responsible for corporate outreach and employer relations activity in addition to career counseling/advising activities. Professional staff are now assigned "key accounts" representing prominent employer relationships. Additional outreach efforts are expected and conducted along functional/industry career paths. All staff have responsibility for completing call reports that capture outreach efforts and that assist in the dissemination of industry- or employer-specific information to students, staff, and faculty. "This has dramatically increased our top-of-mind awareness among employers and provided us with valuable insight into the employment market. It's also served to strengthen our alumni connections with employers and has resulted in increased job/internship opportunities for students," says Career Services Director Len Morrison.

New offerings at Babson include a fall internship program for second-year students who work part-time during the school year and build their resumes and contacts. These positions can lead to full-time positions with the firms by graduation. The school holds an alumni career panel to address challenges and opportunities to secure internships/full-time jobs. Babson offers partial subsidy of travel to consortiums to meet with employers; this increased participation by 33 percent. Students have access to phone lines in a private office during the day to assist in their job search efforts.

International students at Babson have a dedicated career counselor with whom they can make appointments. The school offers interview preparation, cover letter, and mock interview sessions for international students, along with workshops and small group sessions, which address U.S. employment expectations.

TOP HIRES

Fidelity Investments (10); Staples (3); Babson College (3); Citigroup (2); Ernst & Young (2); Global Market Access (2); Liberty Mutual (2); Merrill Lynch (2); PricewaterhouseCoopers (2).

OUTSTANDING FACULTY

John Shank (accounting); Anirudh Dhebar (marketing); William Lawler (accounting and strategy); John Marthinsen (finance); Anne Donnellon (management).

APPLICANT TIPS

"Babson is the leader in entrepreneurship education. We seek to enroll students who are creative, pragmatic, and energized by working with teams, yet comfortable with ambiguity," says Kate E. Klepper, director of MBA admissions. "We seek candidates with great potential for careers in management exhibited by strong academic preparation, intellectual ability, and a solid career path prior to enrolling in graduate school."

Still, there is no magic formula for getting into Babson, says Klepper. The school looks at a combination of applicants' past experiences, career plans, and academic preparation. Klepper doesn't want applicants who haven't researched Babson specifically. You need to demonstrate an understanding of how the Babson MBA will enhance your overall professional portfolio and how that in turn will lead to a successful career search. Klepper wants candidates who are "able to articulate how their unique characteristics will add value to the learning experience of others in the program."

It all comes down to demonstrating your ability to do the work, says Klepper. And not just classroom work. Your work begins the first day you think about applying to B-school. "In your application, let the admissions committee know the real you. Don't answer the essays with what you think the reader wants. Answer truthfully. If you've done your homework, the question of fit will be a nonissue." Applicants often get hung up on grades, says Klepper. "Your undergraduate record is an historic document and cannot be changed. Concentrate on those parts of the application that you can influence," she suggests.

Interviews are strongly encouraged at Babson. "We strive to interview 100 percent of our admitted candidates," Klepper says. "The interviews are designed to assess the candidate's fit with Babson's unique curriculum and learning style. Ours is a highly collaborative, team-based program. The interview helps determine a candidate's level of comfort and ability to function in this environment."

OLIN MBAs SOUND OFF

The first year of the program is very integrated and intense. This program shows the interactions of the different disciplines and covers a wide variety of material in a short amount of time. Students are expected to commit themselves to the program and in return the program prepares them for the business world.

The classes at Babson are great. We are very collaborative. We strive to help each other and have good class spirit. I strongly believe that this has a lot to do with the amount of group work that the program requires, and the small class size. I would not trade my time at Babson for anything, specifically because of the quality of friendships I have made. However, the institution itself still has some way to go. Professors are distant, and the passion for teaching is not always there. And bad professors survive poor student surveys and continue to teach.

Babson was a very good fit for me. I was looking for a small school that focused on thinking differently and being creative. Entrepreneurial thinking is embedded in all different areas of studies—not just in the entrepreneurship track.

Babson has the potential to be a great school, but it has quite a bit of work to do before it gets there. The type of students attracted to the school are very dynamic, high-caliber, and very impressive. Now, the faculty and administration need to catch up. For instance, the cases we use in classes are often outdated and not relevant to current business practices. Too many of the classes rely too heavily on the case method without teaching students the basic fundamentals of finance, operations, or marketing.

Although widely known internationally and in New England, Babson is not a recognized name throughout the U.S. Babson's intense focus on teamwork and entrepreneurship prepares students to contribute in any business situation by thinking critically, analyzing, and making solid data-driven recommendations. Babson also gets fairly close to teaching students to implement change, etc., which is very difficult to do.

The Babson two-year MBA program is a thorough and intensive MBA program. The workload is excessive—however, that challenges you to keep up with the workload and dedicate yourself to learning the material. I would recommend this program to anyone who wants a high-quality MBA. I learned a great deal and I was exposed to a wide range of topics.

BOSTON COLLEGE

Carroll School of Management
320 Fulton Hall
140 Commonwealth Avenue
Chestnut Hill, Massachusetts 02467-3808
E-mail address: bcmba@bc.edu
Web site address: http://bc.edu/mba

Enrollment: 223
Women: 41%
Non-U.S.: 28%
Minority: 3%
Part-time: 462
Average age: 28
Applicants accepted: 14%

Median starting pay: $75,000
Annual tuition and fees: $24,125
Estimated annual budget: $44,174
Average GMAT score: 658
Average months of work experience: 49
Accepted applicants enrolled: 53%

Teaching methods: case study 40%, experiential learning 5%, lecture 45%, team projects 10%

When Helen Frame Peters took over as dean of Boston College's Carroll School of Management in 2000, she had one thing on her mind: "I didn't want to ruin anything that was terrific," she says. "I asked everyone I encountered what it was they valued, and that grounded me about what it is that people really care about." Now, three years later, it looks like Dean Peters is on her way to achieving her goal—and then some. For a while, it appeared that Carroll was destined for mediocrity, finding itself in the third tier of B-schools since 1996. Now, however, BC jumps into the greener pastures of the second tier, and, if Peters has her way, the top 30 is the next step.

Since its founding in 1863, Boston College has been a school that has prided itself on the Jesuit morals of its founders. When Carroll was formed in 1965, it followed in the footsteps of the larger institution, stressing values of commitment to "integrating intellectual, personal, ethical, and religious formation; and to uniting high academic achievement with service to others." Recruiters are quick to mention the ethical views that are apparent in Carroll students, as well as the hardworking, get-down-to-business mentality that other MBAs sometimes lack. This isn't surprising, considering that teamwork is one of the main focuses of the program. Judging by the reaction of students, this philosophy is paying off not only during their time at Carroll, but also in internships and jobs.

Though not considered one of the most technologically up-to-date institutions, the school is making improvements in its networks and wiring after requests from students. In the past year, Carroll has added a wireless network to buildings and classrooms have been equipped with electronic video and multimedia equipment and laptop plug-in units. The MBA and MSF computer labs have also been expanded, and equipment has been upgraded.

The Carroll program is small and closely knit. With only about 115 students per class, students are able to get a great deal of personal support from faculty, as well as career services. While the goal is for the Carroll program to become more heterogeneous and diversified in terms of where students are coming from, currently the school is extremely regional, with upward of 80 percent of U.S. students coming from the Northeast. Diversity is one of the things that Carroll grads consistently ranked near the bottom. Something that BC is not lacking in is equality of the sexes: with female students making up 41 percent of the program, Carroll outranks top MBA programs in this respect. Because of this fact, campus organizations such as Women in MBA have very healthy numbers of members.

The first year at Carroll is what you would expect—mostly core courses with a few chances for electives in the second semester. Each semester is broken down into two modules of classes lasting different amounts of time depending on the semester. The first module in the first semester lasts only a week. Titled Management Intensive, it serves as an introduction of sorts. The second module lasts 13 weeks and is called Leadership & Business Development. Here you will take core courses in economics, marketing, and accounting. In this module you will also work on a business plan project, in which you and a team of peers conceptualize and develop proposals for new entrepreneurial ventures. Over the span of a few weeks, you create a business plan demonstrating the viability of the concept from all angles, financial to administrative. Each group has a student from the BC Law School assigned to it for aid in legal issues, and faculty members are always available for consultation. The project culminates with a formal presentation to faculty, classmates, and mem-

bers of the business community. While this is going on, you also begin formulating ideas for the consulting project that you will work on in the second semester. Besides these courses, you will take a six-credit management practice course that lasts the entire semester.

The second semester of the first year is very similar to the first, with the exception of the consulting project, which will require a good deal of your time and focus. In the consulting project— the hallmark of the Carroll program—you and your team will work with clients ranging from start-ups and small businesses to major multinational corporations, not-for-profits, and government agencies. Each team is responsible for improving the client organization through analyzing a significant challenge or opportunity and delivering practical solutions. In the past, teams have identified potential acquisition candidates, created and installed a new business process, evaluated large-scale operational practices, and developed a business plan for expanding overseas production capacity. As the projects progress, you and your team members contribute and assume leadership roles as required. You will meet with client representatives at key junctures and have regular meetings with a second-year consultant and faculty advisors to test your analyses and evolving solutions. Both you and your clients benefit from the vast reservoir of business acumen and experience resident in the Boston College community. You don't have to look very far to find such individuals, considering that Vincent O'Reilly, former vice chairman of Coopers & Lybrand, is the director of the project. The MBA consulting projects conclude in a series of formal presentations to the clients as well as to Boston College faculty. Clients for past groups have included companies such as MassMutual, Teradyne, and Boston Health Care for the Homeless. If you can't get enough of the project in your first year, you can apply to be a consultant to first-year teams. Ten students are selected to do this, and the time spent counts as an elective. It is a very prestigious and respected position, and only the top students are selected. "We have a great first-year program," says Dean Peters. "But the challenge is to make the second year just as strong." While aiming for that point, the second-year curriculum is a work in progress.

Year two at Carroll is broken into two 12-week modules. In each of the modules you will take three electives, as well as the third and fourth installments of the Management Practice courses you took in your first year. One of the changes in the second-year curriculum comes in the form of tracks—areas of specified focus depending on what your goals are. "One of those tracks is an investment management track," says Peters, "but we do not use a trading room, because we have no interest in generating a class full of day traders. That isn't the investment business, nor is it a stock market game, because then we are not teaching people about the investment industry if we reward me for my risky bet that wins and don't reward you for your risky bet that loses." There are a few different tracks, depending on what you want to do. If you want a functional or departmental focus, the 10 concentrations that Carroll recommends to students are the usual menu of selections, such as marketing, accounting, IT, and finance. If you would rather not specialize and instead want to get a taste of everything, Carroll recommends some industry or interdisciplinary concentrations, such as consulting, management of technology, development of new ventures, and entrepreneurship. Then there is a third grouping called "Techno-MBAs," where the recommended courses are technology strategies, IT venturing, and technology-based marketing, to name a few.

There are quite a few options at Carroll for study abroad, and many students take advantage of the electives that allow for some travel. For instance, in the International Management Experience (IME), you are given the opportunity to visit leading corporations and government agencies in Asia and Europe. Participants meet with business leaders and officials and observe the application of management principles and strategies in the global arena. You will study the economic, cultural, and social factors that affect the conduct of business in a variety of industries and contexts. In the past few years, Asia IME participants have traveled to such locales as Japan, Hong Kong, and Malaysia and have visited companies such as Nike, Samsung, Nissan, and Mitsubishi. In the Europe IME, students have traveled to France, Italy, Germany, and Switzerland and visited companies such as DaimlerChrysler Aerospace, BMW, and the International Committee of the Red Cross.

Another international option is the South-European Management Program, a partnership with the Bordeaux School of Business that is offered for students interested in traveling to France and Spain after the fall semester. Visits include the Chamber of Commerce and Industry of Bordeaux, Disneyland Paris, Aerospatiale, Volkswagen, and the Barcelona Chamber of Commerce.

Carroll grads were a bit more successful in getting job offers than some of the other schools in the second tier, but that isn't much of a consolation to those forty-odd students who were without work when they accepted their diplomas. One of the reasons Carroll is able to have some success in placing students is because of its large network of alumni who remain in close contact with students. Currently, students have access to a database of over 8000 BC alums who are willing to talk to students about what they do—and to network. Also, Carroll has a somewhat unique mentor program, in which each student is paired with a CEO or high-level person in a local Boston company to help them. This is one of the things that students are most excited about and appreciative of in the Carroll program, and it seems to be paying off. Says Jeanne Walter Garvey, director of career services, "I find that a 10-minute piece of advice from a senior-level executive in a company is worth two years of my advice. It just carries so much more weight. Students are using these people for reality checks, information about what their career path was, and skills on how to get to a senior-level position within a set time." Before being paired with a mentor, students are asked about their aspirations and goals to hopefully match them with a mentor who fits with where the student sees him- or herself going. And while it is not implied that these mentors will find students jobs, every once in a while it does happen.

Boston College's 116-acre main campus is located in an open suburban setting six miles from downtown Boston, with direct access to the city via trolley or subway. Boston is the seventh largest metropolitan area in the U.S. and serves as one of the nation's premier financial centers. Among the financial services giants headquartered in Boston are Fidelity Investments, the Liberty Mutual Group, John Hancock Mutual Life Insurance, the Fleet Financial Group, and State Street. Other corporate household names making their home in the Boston area include Raytheon, Gillette, and Reebok.

PLACEMENT DETAILS

Though only 63 percent of 2002 grads had job offers by graduation, 78 percent had offers three months out, and, considering the fact that only 80 percent were seeking employment, nearly everyone who wanted to be placed found a job. If you want to end up working in the greater Boston area, Carroll may be the school for you. Says one 2002 grad, "It may be the best school to attend for people looking to stay in the greater Boston area in terms of alumni connections." The figures support this statement: 90 percent of grads stay in the Northeast after graduation. Says Dean Peters, "The BC alums are one of the most dedicated groups of people out there. It fosters a type of environment that is very supportive and team based."

Though for the most part Carroll career services has a pretty good track record, there are a number of grads from the class of 2002 who did not feel the support they received was up to par. "The recruiting office needs to be demolished and rebuilt from the ground up," said one grad. This may just be a question of misunderstanding, however. "It is our job to help students in their job search, not to hand-feed them," says Jeanne Walter Garvey, director of career services. "I tell students that I am not their fairy job-mother. I would love nothing more than to be able to just give them all jobs, but unfortunately, it isn't that easy."

TOP HIRES

Liberty Mutual (6); Fidelity Investments (3); Fleet Boston Financial (3); Pricewaterhouse-Coopers (3); Analysis Group (2); Kean Consulting Group (2); McDermott, Will & Emery (2); Phillips Medical Systems (2); Standard & Poor's (2); Testa, Hurwitz & Thibeault (2).

OUTSTANDING FACULTY

G. Peter Wilson (accounting); Gerald Smith (marketing); John Gallaugher (information technology); Elliot Smith (finance).

APPLICANT TIPS

In the past few years, it has become increasingly difficult to be accepted to Carroll, with the rate of admittance dropping from 34 percent in 2000 to 14 percent in 2002. While interviews are not required, they are highly recommended, but don't wait until the last minute to schedule one, because after March 1, interviews are done at the school's request only.

Before applying, familiarize yourself with the intricacies of the program and make sure you have put a good deal of time and effort into the application. According to Shelley Conley, director of admissions, "We take a great deal of time and effort in evaluating candidates and not just reading applications, but getting to know them. While our admissions process serves a gatekeeper function, we also are the purveyor of resources, so we like to make sure they have everything they need to make an educated decision."

Carroll students typically have around four to five years of work experience, and come from a variety of backgrounds, so just because you are a zookeeper or a shop owner does not mean you don't have a chance at being admitted. Remember, diversity is very important at Carroll. "We want students who have a very clear understanding of their strengths and the areas that will challenge them in the program and who have identified a clear career goal orientation," says Conley.

CARROLL MBAs SOUND OFF

The whole MBA experience was very rewarding. The biggest take away from an MBA is the ability to think, think strategically keeping a whole picture/scenario in mind and not in isolation.

The education that I received at BC not only enhanced my previous doctoral training (in molecular biology), but it also provided me the opportunity to educate many of my fellow classmates (and professors) about the industry that I currently work in, health care and science. This is one of the truly unique qualities of the Carroll School, its emphasis on diversity and nontraditional backgrounds. It creates an open atmosphere of learning that inspires individuals to constantly question each other—igniting interests in each of us that we may not have realized that we had. I could not have asked for a better education.

The only thing that is holding Boston College back from climbing up the rankings is its career services department. Otherwise, the education and experience is excellent. I found the program very rewarding and I worked with many talented professors. I feel that I gained a great deal of practical skill as well as theory application.

BRIGHAM YOUNG UNIVERSITY

Marriott School of Management

640 TNB

BYU

Provo, Utah 84602

E-mail address: mba@byu.edu

Web site address: http://marriottschool.byu.edu

BRIGHAM
YOUNG
UNIVERSITY

Enrollment: 268

Women: 15%

Non-U.S.: 12%

Minority: 5%

Part-time: 0

Average age: 28

Applicants accepted: 44%

Median starting pay: $67,000

Annual tuition and fees:

   resident—$6,200

   nonresident—$9,270

Estimated annual budget: $18,840

Average GMAT score: 650

Average months of work

   experience: 36

Accepted applicants enrolled: 69%

Teaching methods: lecture 35%, case study 45%, experiential learning 10%, simulations 5%, team projects 5%

Brigham Young University's Marriott School of Business is back in the B-school rankings. And with the highest ROI in *BusinessWeek*'s survey, this hidden jewel, tucked away at the base of the Rocky Mountains, is basking in the spotlight. The school's mission is four-fold: education, research, outreach, and friendship. Founded on the principles of the Church of Jesus Christ of Latter Day Saints (the Mormons), the Marriott School aims to attract, develop, and place men and women of faith, character, and professional ability in leadership positions in professional organizations across the globe. The majority of students have gone on a two-year mission before attending, so most of your classmates will already speak several languages and come back with strong communication and interpersonal skills, says Career Services Director Maurice Stocks.

On the BYU campus, you won't find alcohol, drugs, or smoking. By the time even the undergraduates graduate, over 50 percent are already married, so there's no shortage of spouses and children around. Students here have very strong ethical and moral values, says Dean Ned C. Hill. But they're also very friendly and fun-loving, say grads. A case in point is the school's holiday card. Since taking up the deanship four years ago, Hill and the other deans send out a holiday card each year to alumni, donors, and recruiters. Last year, the three deans donned Santa Claus hats and posed in a bobsled. But, it's not all fun and games. In his four years as dean, Hill has worked on several initiatives to build up the program. For starters, the curriculum was overhauled and now offers specialized tracks, and the career services office was also revamped. Now, Hill is focusing on a new set of initiatives.

The B-school launched a major initiative in 2002 to improve minority representation among students and faculty, as well as to heighten cultural awareness and sensitivity to diversity issues. Specifically, the school is looking to recruit a greater number of women, African Americans, Hispanics, and Native Americans. With the support of seven sponsors (Ford Motor Company, Honeywell, Hewlett-Packard, Hollywood Video, Ernst & Young, Union Pacific, and PricewaterhouseCoopers), Marriott hopes to provide Extended Reach Scholarships to these incoming students. To heighten cultural awareness, all faculty are required to attend at least one school-sponsored diversity retreat. But Dean Hill can't do it all alone; he's also counting on strong alumni support. The dean has been on the road, reaching out to alumni for support in this initiative.

Hill also wants to further internationalize the school, including the student body, faculty, and curriculum. About 80 percent of students already speak a second language, and about 30 percent speak a third language, but only about 10 percent come from outside of the United States—on the lower end of the spectrum for top B-schools. So, Hill has proposed creating an international MBA program that would cater to international students who normally wouldn't qualify for admission to a regular MBA program because of language requirements. The program would bring these students in for special training in the summer before they would join the incoming MBA students in the fall.

At BYU, you might find yourself participating in a year-round MBA program. In response to the high demand for admittance, the B-school is working on developing a plan to hold class year-round with three different admittance pools. "It's a way to handle more students with a fixed faculty," Hill says. The program would entail students entering in different intervals—fall, winter,

and spring—and then following the regular curricular program. Hill says he's also looking to expand the faculty. With a full-time faculty of 139, and 50 part-time and visiting faculty, Marriott is aiming to increase the faculty for the year-round and international MBA programs. Moreover, Hill says he's working on the development of a center in New York City to provide students with a place to live in the city while they complete their summer internships there.

The program offers a curriculum that exposes students to the underlying disciplines, then reinforces those principles with practical field study projects—an interactive approach to management education that binds knowledge to experience. You'll gain a considerable amount from this intimate setting. At about 125 students per class, the Marriott School is on the smaller end of the top B-schools. The team emphasis starts right when you set foot on campus. Orientation includes a series of outdoor activities in the picturesque Wasatch Mountains that will get you acquainted with fellow students right off the bat.

Entering MBA students are divided into three clusters of about 40 students each, and each group is then further divided into smaller study teams of about five students. Your first semester you'll take Financial Accounting, Written and Oral Communications I, Business Finance, Operations Management, Marketing Management, Introduction to Strategy, and a management seminar. After resting up during winter break you'll take Managerial Accounting I, Human Resources Management, Introduction to Global Management, Strategy II, and a management seminar in your second semester. Your second year you'll finish up with required courses in Law, Ethics, Management Simulation, Strategy II, Strategic Implementation, and Leadership, plus you'll be able to choose from a comprehensive menu of electives. And you'll also have the option of following one of five specified tracks: finance, marketing, supply chain management, organizational behavior/human resources, and interdisciplinary product development. The special emphasis will help you home in on a special expertise in a designated field, providing you with the applicable skills needed to succeed in future internships and full-time employment. Furthermore, to support classroom activities, the Marriott School sponsors weekly management seminars where respected business leaders from around the world share their diverse experiences and expertise. Students are required to participate in these seminars each semester. The B-school also houses two research institutes to support the curriculum. The H. Taylor Peery Institute of Financial Services will complement the curriculum to help prepare you to enter the financial services industry. The Institute aims to foster research; attract and maintain leading faculty; develop new course material; and provide students with an arena for employment, internship, and field studies possibilities. The Institute of Marketing aims to support Marriott MBAs interested in the sales and retail industries in top organizations through programming in sales and retail management and through generating cutting-edge research.

Marriott offers several outlets for distinct hands-on experience through a handful of centers on campus including the Center for Entrepreneurship, the Global Management Center, and the e-Commerce Center. The Center for Entrepreneurship strives to educate, encourage, and support students in understanding how to successfully start and operate new business ventures domestically and internationally. The catchphrase is "Learn, Earn, Return." Entrepreneurship permeates the atmosphere at the Marriott School and at BYU, and it may be linked to the school's affiliation with the Church of Jesus Christ of Latter Day Saints. The school describes two main reasons for the students' interests in entrepreneurship: the high levels of entrepreneurial activity associated with the homes of church members coupled with the fact that the majority of students have taken their two-year break in schooling to serve as missionaries

throughout the world. The Center also houses the Student Entrepreneur of the Year contest and the Student Business Plan competition, giving students a platform for hands-on experience in developing entrepreneurial plans. Plus, with entrepreneur mentors, students have a successful contact to turn to for support along the way. Moreover, students who've counted on the Center for support participate post-MBA by attending Entrepreneur Founders Conferences to continue networking and mentoring students.

You can develop your international skills through the Global Management Center by pursuing extra courses or by going abroad and learning about the international experience hands on. The Center sponsors the Global Management Certificate, designed to further educate students in a foreign business language, expose students to the multiple layers of international business, and allow students to participate in an international experience. In step with Hill's initiative to internationalize the curriculum, you can now take classes in one of eight languages—Chinese, French, German, Japanese, Korean, Portuguese, Russian, and Spanish. Additionally, you have several options to go abroad—Europe, Mexico, and Asia. On these study abroad treks you'll be stopping by France, Cracow, Pforzheim, Cancun, Monterrey, Guadalajara, Tokyo, Vietnam, and Singapore, to name a few. In the summer of 2002, the school also launched an eight-week program in which students both studied and visited companies in Switzerland and Austria. And the B-school is working on raising funds to provide scholarships for more students to participate in these international excursions.

Marriott's e-Business Center will offer you the opportunity to get tech savvy through supporting curricular courses, a lecture series, and multiple research opportunities. Brush up on your e-skills with the likes of High-Tech Marketing, Internet Programming, and e-Business Consulting, to name a few courses. Or check out past lectures through the online collection of past professional and faculty lectures. Ultimately, the Center strives to encourage e-business development by supporting all facets of the curriculum. Additionally, Hill says he hopes to soon open a new Center for Economic Self-Reliance that would specifically look at researching the necessary policies companies need in order to effectively foster family independence in third-world countries.

The B-school is housed in the N. Eldon Tanner Building, a seven-story, 120,000-square-foot granite building in the middle of BYU. The Utah campus sits 45 miles south of Salt Lake City, right at the western base of the Wasatch Mountains, which are a part of the Rocky Mountain Range—not such a bad location especially if you're a fan of the outdoors. The Marriott School offers on-campus housing for both single students and families. Those apartments and dorms are conveniently located, but generally students live off campus in apartment complexes.

Students are highly involved both on and off campus. Their popular clubs include the MBA Association, Women in Management, and the International Student Association. Spouses get in on the action, too—they've got their MBA Spouse Association. Plus, once MBAs leave, they're good about giving back to their community. With over 37,500 alumni, the network is split up into over 60 chapters in locations across the United States and abroad. BYU alums not only donate cold cash—thanks to the high ROI—they also donate their time through the mentoring system. More than 700 alumni actively advise students through the volunteer mentor program, and more than 500 are involved with the school's advisory council.

PLACEMENT DETAILS

The Marriott School follows a multifaceted philosophy when it comes to career services and aiding students in their job hunt. The school has formed two-way relationships with recruiters under the Marriott Partners Program. "We want to have full-service connection with that company," Hill says. "They hire students, provide internships, provide scholarship money, and we do field studies for them, invite them to speak on campus, and have faculty do research for them." This has worked particularly well in the face of the not-so-hot economy. "When times are tough, they (recruiters) won't stop coming because they have strong connections here," Hill explains. As part of the Partners Program, the B-school also invites recruiters for a meeting at the beginning of the year to update them on changes in the program as well.

Four years ago, the placement office underwent a face-lift. For starters, a new career services center with 20 interview rooms was built, a new director and staff were hired, and an initiative to get students more involved was launched. Career Services Director Maurice Stocks says the placement office is no longer a place for students to just stop in to look for job openings. Students have been incorporated into the process. One way this has been done is by hiring student liaisons that represent the various clubs on campus. This way, all students have a conduit to career services, Stocks explains. The liaisons meet with Stocks once a week to review where each of the students is in the job-hunting process. And, for those second-year students who haven't secured a job by the end of the first semester, the career services office offers a second-semester course to help students further focus on the job search with industry experts and alumni support. Moreover, the career service staff's initiatives to entice recruiters have worked thus far, as Marriott has seen a marked increase in interest from corporate recruiters.

TOP HIRES

Ford (3); LexisNexis (3); Church of Jesus Christ of Latter Day Saints (2); Cigna (2); IBM (2);

Novell (2); Nutraceutical (2); Payless (2); Union Pacific (2); Yellow Freight (2).

OUTSTANDING FACULTY

Hal Heaton (finance); James Stice (Accounting); Grant McQueen (finance); David Whitlark (marketing).

APPLICANT TIPS

Because of Marriott's tie to the church, the school's mission is quite unique, says Admissions Director Debbie Ruse. Not only is Ruse on the lookout for applicants with a strong academic record and solid work experience, she's also looking for students who will represent the church and its mission as well. First and foremost, she says, she reviews an applicant's student record, including GMAT score and undergraduate work, along with essays and recommendations. From there she selects candidates for interviews. "This is where we make the final decision," Ruse says. "We try to make sure that the applicant and our program are going to be a good fit."

Successful candidates will not only have a proven school and work record, but will also know what they want to do post-MBA. If an applicant knows what direction he or she wants to pursue, it facilitates the process of determining whether the applicant and the program match up well. Plus, Ruse wants to see that you're enthusiastic about the program and wants to know how you'll help the program succeed, so do your homework on the Marriott School and what it has to offer before applying.

When it comes to preparing for the application process, Ruse advises students to take the GMAT while still in school. You'll do best if you take it when your skills are at your peak, she notes. Plus, if you're going to major in business, round it out with a minor in the humanities,

and conversely, if you're majoring in liberal arts, balance it with a business minor, she adds. And if your GMAT score isn't quite what you'd like it to be, take the test again and try using a different technique to study.

Ruse tells applicants not to be in a hurry when applying for graduate school. "We want students who have been out in the workforce and who know what a person with an MBA does," she notes. "We want someone who shares the same passion that we do." On the whole, Ruse advises potential applicants to "Visit schools, check out the schools on the Web site, talk to employers, and look at various regions of the United States." She adds that you should ask yourself what you want from an MBA and what your goals are; this will help you in finding the best fit.

MARRIOTT MBAs SOUND OFF

While I initially did not intend to return to BYU for a graduate degree, in hindsight, I am very glad I did. At BYU, the education is great and all of the professors and administrators are committed to making the student's experience a success. The opinion of the student body is taken very seriously and many changes were implemented as a direct result of student feedback and input. There are plenty of opportunities available for talented individuals who are interested in advancing their careers. The bonus is you don't have to sell yourself into slavery in order to pay off student loans when it is all over. I was pleasantly surprised to see a good amount of diversity in the type of companies that recruit at BYU and to see how geographically diverse these companies were.

I absolutely loved my experience here. Not only was it an incredible eye-opener for me, I made the best and strongest friendships I have ever had, outside my family. I believe that getting a BYU Marriott School MBA is about being well-rounded, not just being 150 percent focused on strictly schoolwork. Strong emphasis was made on service, ethics, religion, family, and creating social ties, not just the academic portion. The strong emphasis on teamwork during the first year also ingrained in me the importance of working together well on a team. I feel well prepared to head back out into the business world, work on a team, contribute to a company, and lead with confidence.

This experience has given me, more than anything, the ability and the tools to approach problems and situations with a rigor and work ethic that I had not previously possessed. The analytical skills that I learned in this relatively short time period dwarf the skills that I had coming out of my undergraduate program. Indeed, I believe that I am able to add value to any business in which I find myself employed. The confidence to say that is worth the investment of the time and money by itself.

BYU's MBA program, if such schools were a security trading on an exchange, would be the single most undervalued MBA school in the U.S. The fundamentals scream "undervalued" no matter how you look at it. It is a world-class program, particularly in finance. There is no more capable group of students in any program. Also, the program's leadership was one of its highlights. I always had an open door—all the way to the top. The faculty was incredibly professional, current, and well-versed in their trade. The student metrics place us at the very top. The Return on Investment is the very best.

CASE
WESTERN
RESERVE
UNIVERSITY

CASE WESTERN RESERVE UNIVERSITY

Weatherhead School of Management
Peter B. Lewis Building, Case Western Reserve University
10900 Euclid Avenue
Cleveland, Ohio 44106-7235
E-mail address: questions@exchange.cwru.edu
Web site address: www.weatherhead.cwru.edu

Enrollment: 320

Women: 34%

Non-U.S.: 47%

Minority: 13%

Part-time: 0

Average age: 27

Applicants accepted: 48%

Median starting pay: $66,000

Annual tuition and fees: $27,420

Estimated annual budget: $43,250

Average GMAT score: 610

Average months of work
 experience: 51

Accepted applicants enrolled: 51%

Teaching methods: case study 40%, experiential learning 20%, lecture 20%, simulations 5%, team projects 15%

Take some silver ribbon, ball it up in your hand, then multiply the size of the mass thousands of times. Throw in some bricks and glass for good measure and you can begin to understand exactly what has been erected at the Weatherhead School of Management on the campus of Case Western Reserve University. The structure, known as the Peter B. Lewis Building, is the new home of Weatherhead—a Frank Gehry–designed peculiarity that looks more like the discarded wrappings of a Christmas gift than a center for higher learning. The building is unique—different from any building at any other B-school in the world—and, if you ask Dean Moshen Anvari, it fits at the school, because he likes to think that the Weatherhead MBA is just as unique. "We wanted to have a structure whose architecture represented the mind-set of the school," Anvari says. "On top of that, we wanted to make sure that the building was technologically sound." To do this, the school partnered with Cisco and Sprint to see that the technology in the building was as up to date as the building that housed it. Multimedia and videoconferencing are available in all classrooms. Every seat in the building has power and data connections to the Internet and CWRUnet, the university's fiberoptic network. The building is chock-full of team meeting rooms, state-of-the-art offices, classrooms, and a café, each named for a corporate sponsor, such as the Jo-Ann Stores Graduate Lounge, the American Greetings Classroom, and the Key Bank Café.

Not surprisingly, the buzzword around Weatherhead is innovation, and if the Lewis building is any indication of what Anvari and his administration have in mind for the school, who knows what's to come? Weatherhead is currently in the midst of a five-year strategic plan, working toward becoming a stronger all-around program. The plan consists of several major areas of focus: strengthening programs by making them more market centered, increasing the research impact of professors in terms of the work they do and its effect on public policy, strengthening relationships with alumni and integrating them into the program, and revamping relationships with recruiters and getting them more involved in the school. To get off on the right foot, the school partnered with Accenture to figure out what the best practices were in dealing with recruiters and alumni. "These are areas where we have been weak," says Dean Anvari. "So we are putting a lot of effort in getting them involved in our program." Anvari took on the position of dean in August of 2001, and, since then, he has started to work toward the lofty goal of making his one of the top MBA programs in the country. After considering the scope of the plans Weatherhead has devised, it sounds as if the school is starting over and building from the ground up, but maybe that is what the school needs, if the past decade is any indication.

Weatherhead once was in *BusinessWeek*'s top 20, and first showed up in the second tier of top schools in 1996, 20 years after it was founded. In ensuing years, the school dropped into the third tier, where it remained. It appeared as if Weatherhead was just another flash in the pan. But now, in the first rankings since Anvari took over in 2001, some signs of new life are showing. Granted, to put all the credit on Anvari's shoulders would not be fair, but he does have a clear vision of where he would like to take the school and he is working hard to see it happen. "This is a school that has a tremendous amount of potential," Anvari says. "We know where we want to be; now we must get there."

One of these areas of potential is in the students themselves. It is assumed that students at a school like Weatherhead have the mind-set to be successful in a business setting, and intense core courses see to it that they are able to develop in areas where they may be lacking. But the interpersonal skills that distinguish successful managers from mediocre ones are something that the school feels can also be instilled in students. With the help of the Leadership Assessment Development program, or LEAD, students are taught to hone their emotional intelligence quotient (EQ), a principle developed by Case Western's organizational behavior faculty. "We have found that the students who are the most successful in business are the ones who are able to communicate and relate to people," says Christine Gill, director of admissions. "We have extreme success rates with students going into consulting, partly because they have the ability to work with a variety of people, and the academic curriculum that teaches them to look at the organization as a whole and not just one part or another." In the LEAD program, students do self-assessments, looking introspectively at who they are and what values they will be able to bring to a company. Says Denise Douglas, director of career services, "While it seems like a fluffy thing for an MBA to think about, it is actually a very useful tool, because when they come to meet with employers, employers get a sense that these students are really focused and understand where they can create value in an organization."

Weatherhead does have some things going for it, many of which have to do with being a part of the larger Case Western community. Case prides itself on being a top research institution, bringing in some of the best and brightest undergrads in the nation. Case awarded the first PhDs in organizational behavior and operations research, and was the first school with networks in place. With the current innovations in mind, Weatherhead is following in the university's footsteps. Says Dean Anvari, "We are introducing innovative programs which I think set us apart. We introduced an MBA concentration in bioscience that is one of a kind. The brand of research that goes on here is tremendous."

Weatherhead offers a functional core that integrates the management disciplines while also providing students with the tools necessary to identify and analyze issues. The eight required core courses (financial reporting and control, economics, financial management, human value in organizations, marketing, operations management, system design and management, statistics, and decision modeling) are integrated with the Strategic Issues and Applications course to form a solid foundation for management decision making.

The Weatherhead MBA comes in two forms: the traditional two-year program in which students take 63 credit hours, with each of the core courses worth three credit hours; or the accelerated one-year program (for undergraduate business degree holders) in which students take 47 credit hours, with each of the core courses being one-credit versions of the regular core. The accelerated program begins in May and lasts 11 months. Because of the integrated nature of both of the full-time core curricula, no core courses may be waived.

The first year at Weatherhead starts with a boot camp of sorts, getting you up to speed on statistics, finance, and accounting. These sessions are optional, but if you feel rusty in any of these areas, it may be a good idea to partake. The first semester at Weatherhead is a heart attack waiting to happen. You will take five of the eight core courses in the first semester, along with a course in leadership assessment and development and two brief courses in team building and career management. The second semester consists of the other three core courses, as well as two electives of your choice. While the first year at Weatherhead is strenuous, students like the idea of having all of their core courses out of the way before they leave for their summer internships. "It gives us a real advantage on students from other schools because we have covered all the bases, while they will still have some

core classes to finish when they return for their second year," says one 2002 grad.

The second year is composed solely of electives, with the exception of what is called an Action Learning Consulting Project, a real-life project with a set deadline and a loosely defined problem. In working with professional clients, you and your team will get the chance to put some of the concepts and ideas you have learned into practice. In the past, projects have included enterprise resource planning, supply chain management, and assessment and development of market entry strategies. At the end of the semester, your work is assessed on the quality of analysis, effective diagnosis of problems, and identification of opportunities for improvement.

Electives at Weatherhead are broken down into four categories, which makes it easy to know which ones to take based on what your interests and goals may be. Courses under the heading of "The Global Manager" include Global Perspectives, Managing in a Global Economy, and European Community Law. Under the grouping "Technology Issues and the Manager" are courses such as High-Tech Regions and Business Strategy, Principles of Biomedical Technology Development, and Managing Quality in Organizations. Courses such as Professional Responsibility, Conflict Management and Dispute Resolution, and Leadership and the Global Agenda fall under the grouping of "Leadership and Ethics in Management." And under the heading "The Manager and Society" you will find electives such as Issues in Health Care Management, History of Industrial Development, and Legal Environment for Managers.

In the past, Cleveland has received a bad rap for being dirty (rumor has it that Lake Erie caught on fire due to the great deal of waste it had collected) and uninteresting. In the past decade, the city has gone to great lengths to change the negative perception, and it appears to have worked. Millions of dollars were spent to bring the city's beloved Indians back from the graveyard of baseball; the Browns returned home to the Dawg Pound, the Rock and Roll Hall of Fame was erected on the banks of the Erie, and the result was a city with new life. Now, in the words of Drew Carey, "Cleveland Rocks!" There are a good number of pubs and brew houses in the Flats entertainment district on the banks of the Cuyahoga River, as well as parks and other recreational facilities either on or within walking distance from campus. Also, just two hours away in Sandusky is Cedar Point, named by *Amusement Today* as the best amusement park in the world for five years straight. Cedar Point is also home to the highest number of roller coasters in one amusement park in the world, with 15.

The Greater Cleveland area is home to dozens of Fortune 500 corporations, offices of all Big Five accounting firms, the fourth district Federal Reserve Bank, world-renowned health care organizations, and a growing number of high-tech firms and entrepreneurial businesses. This helps students in networking, as well as in bringing recruiters to campus, but outside of the companies located within close proximity of the school, very few other recruiters come to campus. This makes it hard for students to gain exposure to companies in the larger cities. Grads of the class of 2002 question the leadership in the B-school, especially the fact that in their two years in the program, two deans came and went.

With the completion of the new building, a buzz is stirring. With the buzz comes visibility, and, with that visibility, Dean Anvari hopes, will come the recruiters. There could be some truth to this line of thinking, or it could be that the administration at Weatherhead may have watched *Field of Dreams* one too many times: only time will tell. But either way, from now on, families getting their kicks on Route 66 by visiting such oddities as the world's largest ball of twine or the Museum of Questionable Medical Devices will have to veer north toward Cleveland, because no trip will be complete without visiting the world's most unique-looking B-school.

PLACEMENT DETAILS

Grads say that Weatherhead is perceived to be a regional school, which hurts in bringing in recruiters from outside of the Cleveland area. Says one grad, "There are limited opportunities for those not wanting to (work for) a regional bank like National City or Key." Weatherhead does make a number of recruiting trips to cities such as New York and Chicago available to students, but according to students, such trips are not the answer; they simply serve as a change of scenery.

The number of members of the class of 2002 with one job offer by graduation was dismal, and left many wondering about the career services office. Anvari understands that recruiting is a problem; hence the hiring of Accenture to come up with ways to remedy the situation. But if the solution were that easy, every B-school would have 100 percent placement rates at graduation.

The student life center at Weatherhead is unique in that it encompasses career planning, student life, alumni affairs, placement, and employer relations. "We look at our interactions with our students from the beginning to the end," says Director Douglas. "Our offices are responsible for everything from orientation to graduation and everywhere in between." This gives a feel of cohesion to students, and it helps make them feel like they are an integral part of something bigger, rather than just a placement office or admissions.

The location of Weatherhead, combined with the fact that the school is not widely known, hurts in bringing in recruiters. Cleveland isn't exactly the business center country. It isn't even the business center of Ohio. But with the initiatives and strategic plan the school now has in place, things should begin to turn around for the young school.

Grads from the class of 2002 reported first-year payment packages in excess of $115,000, which compares favorably to those of even the top B-schools. So while grads with jobs at graduation were few and far between, those who were working were doing quite well for themselves.

TOP HIRES

Samsung (4); Johnson & Johnson (4); American Electric Power (3); Capital One (3); Emerson Electric (3); National City (2); Johnson Controls (2); FBI (2); Progressive (2); TRW (2); KeyCorp (2).

OUTSTANDING FACULTY

Sam Thomas (finance); Richard Osborne (policy); Mohan Reddy (marketing); Jay Dial (policy); J. B. Silvers (finance); Thomas Bogart (economics).

APPLICANT TIPS

The admissions office at Weatherhead is looking for diversity, and it means a lot of different things. Of course, it means diversity in terms of race, sex, and country of origin, but it also means diversity in life experience and background. "We look for diversity when it comes to work experience," says Director Gill. "And for us, because we have the concentrations in some areas that are outside the norm for most schools, we tend to draw people with various backgrounds."

Case Western is also looking for people with strong interpersonal skills, or at least students who are willing to work on such skills. Says Gill. "If someone only wants to come in here and

work on the hard skills—the quant, so to speak—they might not be very happy here because from the moment they get there they are in teams and in groups. Folks who are not looking for diversity may not be as happy here, either."

Interviews are not required at Weatherhead, unless you want to be considered for a scholarship. However, Gill recommends visiting Cleveland, coming to campus, and spending some time talking to students and administrators. "You can only get so much from a brochure," she says. "It might look great on paper, but the atmosphere might not suit you."

WEATHERHEAD MBAs SOUND OFF

Weatherhead has gone through a great deal of change over the past year and much more is in the near future. Our graduating class was supposed to be in the new building, designed by Frank Gehry, but, unfortunately, the building was not completed on time. Next year's entering class will be in an entirely new environment, including one of the most advanced wireless networks in the world. Regardless, my experience at Weatherhead was rewarding and I achieved my goals.

Weatherhead is a diamond in the rough program. It has a fantastic faculty, world-class courses and an outstanding student body. Unfortunately it suffers because the school does a poor job communicating its strengths outside of the Cleveland area. This weakens the alumni base and hurts recruiting with some companies. The university has poor name recognition outside of Ohio.

Overall I was very satisfied with the program. In many respects my expectations were exceeded. I was particularly impressed with the breadth of elective courses offered, as well as the practical experience that many of these course instructors had. For example, I had instructors/professors that were either current or former CEOs, directors on boards, and even an owner of a venture capital fund.

The school has made very sincere efforts to enhance management education. A fantastic new building is opening, a new dean has been hired, and career placement is being reorganized. Students are very bright, professors are excellent, and the university is a well known and rigorous one. The international flavor of the program is strong with students from various countries and diverse body of exchange students as well. The career placement office needs to be improved as the school is not being represented commensurate with its strength and quality to an extraregional area.

COLLEGE OF
WILLIAM &
MARY

THE COLLEGE OF WILLIAM & MARY

School of Business
P.O. Box 8795
Williamsburg, Virginia 23187-8795
E-mail address: Admissions@business.wm.edu
Web site address: www.business.wm.edu

Enrollment: 185
Women: 34%
Non-U.S.: 39%
Minority: 7%
Part-time: 147
Average age: 28
Applicants accepted: 73%
Median starting pay: $70,000

Annual tuition and fees:
 resident—$11,878
 nonresident—$23,158
Estimated annual budget: $38,088
Average GMAT score: 607
Average months of work
 experience: 52
Accepted applicants enrolled: 54%

Teaching methods: case study 40%, experiential learning 10%, lecture 25%, simulations 5%, team projects 20%

Colonial Williamsburg, the educational vacation Mecca of the United States. You'd be hard pressed to find a place in the country with more history linked to it than the quaint Virginia town. When you think about Williamsburg, images of horse-drawn carriages, wicker furniture, powdered wigs, and palatial plantations come to mind, not a top MBA program. But, surprisingly, right in the middle of the eighteenth-century village stands The College of William & Mary and its Graduate School of Business. The school boasts alumni such as Thomas Jefferson and John Marshall, but how does such a rich historical tradition help a William & Mary MBA find a job?

"That is the question a lot of students ask us," says Kathy Pattison, director of admissions. "Students know that our reputation going back to the four original presidents has some standing in the world, but what is it going to do for their individual career?" While many prospective students will ask this, the answer can be found in the brand of students that graduate from the B-school each year and the high praise they heap upon the school year after year. True, the surroundings are old fashioned, and the buildings on campus are designed in the traditional colonial style, but inside the walls of Blow Memorial Hall, the atmosphere is all business. If you are looking for a dated, turn-of-the-nineteenth-century MBA, look elsewhere. You aren't going to find it here.

One of the advantages of William & Mary is its ability to afford its students a high-touch, personalized MBA. The class size is around 100, making it one of the smallest programs of the top 50 B-schools. "The fact that we are a small school makes it possible for us to use a very high-touch model of teaching, and students really seem to enjoy that," Dean Lawrence Pulley says. "They have access to their professors and administrators and we try to make sure their needs are heard." Students are quick to applaud the school for this personal attention and care. There is a schoolwide open-door policy, so that students have access to their professors and peers whenever they need them. This is something that the students find very helpful and was the deciding factor for a good number of current students, as well as grads, in where they'd attend an MBA program.

At many schools, it is hard to tell what is more important to faculty members, students or their research, but at William & Mary, it's clear that this is not an issue. However, with the small class size comes the dilemma that many smaller MBA programs experience: the challenge of bringing in top recruiters to see only a small number of students. This problem was exacerbated for the class of 2002 by the sour economy and lack of hiring, with only 62 percent receiving one offer by graduation, leading many to complain that the career services office was not doing a satisfactory job.

The faculty at William & Mary is strong, especially in the core curriculum—so strong, in fact, that the class of 2002 ranked it in the top 30 schools. Topics addressed in class are also current, something that students appreciate. The percentages of women and international students at William & Mary are high, but deceiving. In the past, while the number of international students was over one-third of the class, they were traditionally all from similar areas around Europe and Asia and rarely from elsewhere, so class demographics were surprisingly homogeneous. To remedy this, the school's traditional MBA tour is visiting countries such as Japan, Thailand, Korea, Taiwan, and the Philippines for the first time. "We have noticed a distinct change in the distribution of our Asian students," says Director Pattison. "It has always been predominantly China and India, and now we are getting other groups as well, and we have moved into Latin America." Bringing in a more diverse group of students is only a start, however.

As pointed out by the class of 2002, the bigger issue is interaction between the various groups of students, something that is currently lacking. To deal with this, career services has introduced the Senior Executive Resource Corps (SERC). Williamsburg has become a hot spot for people to retire to in the past few decades, and SERC was developed to capitalize on this. Through SERC, the school has called on recently retired execs from corporations across the country to teach and mentor MBAs on the topics and problems they will encounter in the business world. "We have a group of about 75 senior executives who, rather than be big names in the industry who come in and make a big splash and you never see them again, are around constantly for students," says Tony Somers, director of career services. "We have a number of them that work pretty much full time for our office. It really helps with the counseling side of things, the work that is in between that no one really sees." This is something that other schools cannot offer their students. Explains Dean Pulley, "The history here is hard to ignore, and the fact that in the executive program, these folks don't have the distractions that they would have in a New York or a Chicago means that they are able to devote 10, 15, or 20 hours a week just to working with students and seeing that they can learn from their experiences."

Because the class makeup is so diverse, there are many incoming students who do not have a background in business. To bring these students up to speed, there are two-week crash courses in accounting, information technology, quantitative analysis, team building, and writing, to better prepare you to start your MBA.

In your first year at William & Mary, the rigorous core courses help to provide the tools necessary to excel in an internship and second-year courses. The curriculum is integrated in a way that makes it easy to understand problems and solutions from many different angles, and the fact that your professors have firsthand experience with many of the topics you discuss makes the process much more interesting. It is not rare for class schedule to vary from week to week, to make room for various topic modules or for events focused around visiting dignitaries or business executives. One thing students find useful is the fact that classes meet in the mornings, freeing up their afternoons and evenings for group work or other commitments. Throughout your first year, you will be part of a diverse five- or six-member team, which you will work with on assignments, projects, and exams.

In the second year, instead of core courses covering every business discipline, you can choose targeted, advanced-level electives that are connected to your career aspirations. But be aware that it may be slim pickings, because there are not a great variety of subjects to choose from relative to other schools. You can major in one of four areas—accounting, finance and economics, marketing, or operations and information technology—or a combination. One major component of the second year is a required field study project, in which students earn three credits consulting in groups for a local company such as Nextel under the supervision of a faculty member.

Throughout the two years, you are frequently involved with the career management program, helping you to clarify your own personal goals. In the program, you will learn how to develop career management skills that you will be able to use throughout your career—such as self-assessment, interviewing, and resume building. "We really want to make sure that the presentation of a student when he or she speaks to a recruiter is absolutely top notch," Somers says. "We can't control whether or not he or she knows finance better than someone else, but the other things we can control."

Because the program is so small and rigorous, students get to know one another and the faculty very well. They spend a lot of time together both inside and outside the classroom,

attending most of their classes in one building, Blow Memorial Hall, on the older section of campus adjacent to the restored area of Colonial Williamsburg.

There are plenty of outdoor recreational activities in the area. In their free time, MBAs boat on the York River, hike in nearby parks, and bike along the Colonial Parkway, a 28-mile loop from Jamestown to Yorktown. Those who crave city life can drive to nearby Washington, DC. The weather is mild enough for MBAs to take in the occasional round of golf at the more than 20 PGA courses in the area or to take a day trip to Virginia Beach. Other than the townsfolk throwing back a few mugs of ale at Josiah Chowning's Tavern, the nightlife is sparse around Williamsburg. Students spend most of their time at three local hangouts a short walk from Blow Hall. Paul's Deli and the College Delly serve sandwiches, pizza, and beer, while Greenleafe is a slightly more upscale pub.

On campus, apartments are available in the Lettie Pate Whitehead Evans Graduate Housing Complex on South Henry Street. The complex, set aside specifically for graduate students, provides all of the amenities you would need and is within close proximity to the School of Business. There are two-, three-, and four-bedroom apartments. There are also a wide variety of off-campus options, and some students even choose to live in Richmond or Norfolk and make the 40-minute commute.

PLACEMENT DETAILS

As at many other B-schools, the placement numbers for the class of 2002 were down considerably compared to those for the class of 2000. Whereas in 2000, students received an average of 2.5 job offers, in 2002, those that received jobs received only one offer on average. William & Mary has traditionally had trouble in placing students by graduation, and this year was no different with only 62 percent placed, low even in the down economy. Changes are being made in the career services office to remedy this problem, but it is a bit late for students who have already received their diplomas. Though job offers decreased, starting pay packages remained exactly the same, averaging $88,000.

While few companies visit campus, there is a good deal of one-on-one interaction between students and recruiters, stemming from the personal touch that the career services office prides itself on. William & Mary is part of the MBA Consortium composed of 15 top business schools in order to get their students exposure to some of the larger corporations that do not come to campus.

TOP HIRES

KPMG (4); IBM (3); National City (3); BB&T (2); Wachovia/First Union (2); Nextel (2); Dominion (2); GE Capital (2).

OUTSTANDING FACULTY

John Strong (finance); William Geary (accounting); Deborah Hewitt (economics); Larry Ring (marketing).

APPLICANT TIPS

The application process at William & Mary is all encompassing; that is, every piece of information that a prospective student submits is carefully examined and considered, from test scores to GPA to work experience and recommendations. "A candidate really needs to have the strong quantitative skills, but they also need to have all of the soft skills that are so essential in leading a group," says Kathy Pattison, director of admissions.

The school grants about 65 research assistantships a year, but these go mostly to second-year students, due to the rigorous course load of the first year. To even this out, the majority of the scholarships go to first-year students. The school aggressively recruits women and minorities and has had a lot of success with women, in part because of the visibility of the Women in Business organization. While the percentage of women has dropped in the past few years, at 28 percent, the number still ranks near the top for all the schools mentioned.

Every student who is admitted to William & Mary is interviewed, either by phone or in person, so that the admissions board can make sure a student's focus is in the right place. Director Pattison also highly recommends visiting campus. "Because we are a small program, I think you need to have a sense about what opportunities you have here, and only if you sit in on a class, go to lunch with faculty, and talk to students, are you really going to have a sense of how special the environment is here," she says.

WILLIAM & MARY
MBAs SOUND OFF

I think that William & Mary has an outstanding MBA program. The school has a lot of work to do to be able to really compete with the larger, better-established schools. But make no mistake about this program: the level of education is second to none. I could not have asked for a better or more valuable experience.

We are a program on the move that continually strives to make the changes that meet student and business needs. We are the only program that I know of that has a "Senior Executive Resource Corps"; a group of about 75 retired and semi-retired business leaders who mentor, teach, and assist us on such a personal level that the value may be impossible to calculate.

The quality of students is tremendous and the teachers are knowledgeable, experienced, and help the students to learn from current issues in the business world. After speaking with peers from other programs, I feel that my education has far exceeded that of other students in programs that are listed as being in the top tier. I feel that the intensity and workload of this school are unsurpassed and are vital toward teaching MBAs to perform under pressure.

Despite reality, top MBA programs are looking for students who have goals of senior management in large companies (or start-ups, etc.). I did not meet this norm. I was looking for a school to prepare me for my reality, and William & Mary came through. Not only did they accept my application, but the education they provided gives me confi-

dence to begin a career that I didn't anticipate before beginning the program.

My experience was great except for the career service office, which I feel lacks empathy as well as strong contacts with many alumni. The professors are extraordinary here and the campus is beautiful. Once the career service problem is solved this school can contend with any top program.

I believe that for the investment I made in my MBA education, I received an equal or greater return. The program I attended is severely constrained with budgetary issues, but the program succeeds anyway through effective use of its quality resources.

GEORGIA
INSTITUTE OF
TECHNOLOGY

GEORGIA INSTITUTE OF TECHNOLOGY

DuPree College of Management
755 Ferst Drive
Suite 212
Atlanta, Georgia 30332-0520
E-mail address: mba@mgt.gatech.edu
Web site address: www.dupree.gatech.edu/index2.shtml

Enrollment: 210
Women: 27%
Non-U.S.: 29%
Minority: 11%
Part-time: 0
Average age: 27
Applicants accepted: 39%
Median starting pay: $64,000

Annual tuition and fees:
    resident—$5,314
    nonresident—$18,748
Estimated annual budget: $23,431
Average GMAT score: 645
Average months of work
    experience: 54
Accepted applicants enrolled: 60%

Teaching methods: case study 30%, experiential learning 10%, lecture 20%, simulations 10%, team projects 30%

Things are starting to look a bit different at the DuPree College of Management at Georgia Institute of Technology. No longer is the degree at DuPree a Master of Science in Management, but instead the traditional MBA. And, come the fall of 2003, DuPree will have a new facility to go along with the new name: a $148 million multibuilding complex at Tech Square that will house DuPree, Continuing and Executive Education, a hotel and conference center, the University Bookstore, parking, and other retail businesses. Though folks are very excited about the new digs, the most exciting aspect of the new complex is its location right in the heart of Midtown Atlanta's growing technology corridor. Explains Dean Terry Blum, "It's been an urban renaissance, of sorts, that sets up the gateway for campus."

The new complex also has given DuPree the opportunity to rethink and revamp the curriculum. Whereas in the past there were restrictions on areas such as technology due to lack of space and resources, no longer will this be an issue. "There really are no limits now," says Blum. "We have really been able to focus on our strengths and we have created an almost unfair competitive advantage in extended value training areas, financial analysis, and innovation." In terms of rankings, this couldn't have come at a better time.

In 2000, DuPree made its first appearance in the top 30 after residing in the second and third tiers since 1996. Now the school falls again into the realm of the second tier. However, with so much going on at DuPree, don't be surprised if a return to the top 30 comes sooner rather than later. "We have pushed to become the MBA for the age of technology, and I think we are getting to that point," says Blum. Nearly half of the faculty at DuPree is new to the school in the past four years, coming from all different walks of life and schools, and the number of faculty members is still rising. Class sizes at DuPree are very small—around 100 per year—something that students love. However, unlike the case for other schools, class size does not seem to greatly affect the ability to bring in recruiters, both because of the school's location in Atlanta and its grads' tech savvy. Atlanta seems an ideal home for a B-school. Says Blum, "We have no trouble getting students here; the problem is that once they are here, they don't want to leave!" Atlanta offers world-class arts and entertainment, a plethora of professional sports teams, gourmet restaurants, and a warm climate, and it is home to a good number of the world's largest companies, from Coca-Cola and CNN to Delta Air Lines and Holiday Inn Worldwide. The exposure to executives and practicing professionals through the many local industries is one of the big selling points for many prospective students.

Class size at DuPree is on the rise, with plans to get to about 150 per year. Granted, even with 150 students per class, the school still fits into the category of small, and with the new facilities and increase in number of faculty, the added students should make a difference.

The curriculum is evenly split, in terms of teaching methods, among lecture (33 percent), case study (34 percent), and other formats such as consulting and group work (33 percent). First-year students find themselves with a fairly heavy core course load and little room for electives, but most have the opportunity to take one elective during the second semester of their first year. Nevertheless, DuPree's array of core courses (which includes Financial and Managerial Accounting, Leadership and Organizational Behavior, Financial Management, and Marketing Management) tends to bypass some of the more ho-hum mathematics mainstays by requiring entering students to have a satisfactory grade in a college-level calculus course under their belts. You'll also need a familiarity with probability concepts prior to enrollment.

As a second-year student, you can concentrate in one or more areas, from Accounting and Marketing to International Business and Information Technology Management. You'll take 10 elective courses, including one international management elective, from any of the eight concentrations DuPree offers. Some of the newer course offerings are trendier or ultra-specific, with titles like Financial Reporting and Analysis of High-Tech Firms, International Accounting, Venture Creation, and Knowledge Management. Other modern classes include Business-to-Business Marketing, Global Strategic Management, and International Information Technology. But traditionalists need not fear: still prevalent are some of the more typical selections, such as Operations Strategy, Advanced Managerial Accounting, and Investments. Most students try to incorporate a variety of fields, which can also include interdisciplinary courses from other Georgia Tech master's programs. While you must complete a total of 10 electives by the end of your second year, up to 30 percent of your coursework can be taken outside of the College of Management.

DuPree reciprocates this sharing demonstrated by other programs at the university. About one out of every four students in some of the management courses are Georgia Tech grad students from outside the B-school, including the computing and architecture colleges. Grads from the class of 2002 were quick to mention the available mix of academics and how it enhanced the experience. And the school also seeks to encourage diversity in other ways. About 20 percent of the class of 2004 is composed of non-U.S. citizens, who are supported by resources like a university international office that provides legal guidance in hiring and visa issues. The fact that minorities, on the other hand, aren't equally visible (with just 9 percent in the class of 2004) is something administrators attribute to the low numbers of minorities in the engineering and science fields overall. There have been efforts made to attract minorities to the program, including expanding the school's prospective student outreach efforts among targeted groups and encouraging more of Georgia Tech's minority undergrads to enter the MBA program. These efforts have been in effect for a few years now, but to no avail. In fact, the numbers have fallen a bit since 2000. Yet, while women are also underrepresented in these fields, female students at DuPree are still able to make up a respectable 29 percent of the class.

In the past few years, DuPree has had around 500 applicants annually. Out-of-state students in the class of 2004 paid just $18,748 to attend, which places DuPree in the B-school bargain range. And though DuPree grads may not make as much money in terms of starting pay packages, the majority of students do not encounter the same steep expenses on finishing school; in fact, 60 percent remain in the South, where living is less pricey than in the heart of a big city like Washington or Los Angeles. But the school has seen a rise in the number of students heading to hot spots such as New York and the West Coast.

If the overall rankings simply reflected the comments of graduates, there is little doubt that DuPree would be in the top 30. 2002 grads seemed generally pleased with every aspect of the program, from teaching to the work of the career placement office. Grads ranked DuPree especially high in all aspects of technology—and they graduated before the new complex even opened.

A social bunch, DuPree MBAs often gather at the end of the week to venture out into some of Atlanta's more happening areas, such as Buckhead and the Virginia Highlands. Favorite food spots include Eats, Doc Chey's, Tu Tu Tango, and Vortex; and MBAs can often be found chewing the fat at popular bars and gathering spots from Park Tavern and the Prince of Whales to Neighbors and Swingers.

Students live all over the metro area, where one-bedroom apartments range from $650 to $1100 and two-bedrooms can cost anywhere from $900 to $1500 per month. Many students get a better value by opting for a multibedroom apartment and dividing the cost. Not surprisingly, prices vary mostly according to distance from the city. Single students tend to live within the perimeter, in areas such as the Virginia Highlands, Midtown, and Buckhead, while married students gravitate to outside the perimeter in the suburbs. It's best to own a car during your two years here, but if you don't, you'll be fine with an on-campus setup; Georgia Tech operates a shuttle from the Marta station.

PLACEMENT DETAILS

With the new facilities set to open in July 2003, there will be many more options for the career services office to take advantage of—from the luxury hotel on the premises for visiting recruiters and professionals to the state-of-the-art facilities for interaction between the office and students and between students and recruiters, through things like high-tech interview rooms. Currently, students are able to hone their career-building skills through a curriculum that includes videotaped mock interview sessions with critiques, one-on-one counseling, practice segments of case interviews with guest visitors from corporate America, and speaking engagements from professionals who cover such topics as dressing for success and business etiquette.

When the economy is good, DuPree has no trouble bringing in recruiters. In fact, in 2000, the school brought in more recruiters than there were students. While the economy is down, the school has still been able to attract its fair share of recruiters, but nowhere near the customary number. Now, the good majority come from the surrounding areas. With all the opportunities in the Atlanta area, it is not surprising that 60 percent of the class of 2002 stayed in the South after graduation.

For the class of 2002, 64 percent had at least one job offer by graduation, and three months out the number had risen to 77 percent. Granted, these numbers are not great, but they are respectable in comparison to other schools falling in the second tier and even the bottom of the top 30.

TOP HIRES

Delta (2); Honeywell (2); Cintas (2); McKesson (2); UPS (2).

OUTSTANDING FACULTY

Charles Mulford (accounting); Nate Bennett (organizational behavior); Shomu Banerjee (economics).

APPLICANT TIPS

While there are only about 120 spots per class at DuPree, the school does not get nearly as many applicants as some of the larger MBA programs, so nearly 50 percent of those who apply are accepted. This is not to say that the student body is sub-par: to the contrary, say students. The fact is, the program is heavily quant- and technology-based, so the students applying aren't dummies by any means.

According to Ann Scott, director of admissions, about 80 percent of students are interviewed. "Anyone can ask for an interview," she says. "Then we will interview students who we think are going to be strong candidates for the program." On top of that, if there is a student whose application does not fully explain lacking areas or raises questions with the admissions board, admissions will ask to interview the student. Scott recommends coming to campus and interviewing, if for no other reason than to see the campus and talk to students and faculty about what the program is. "They are making a decision about whether or not they are going to be happy for the rest of their lives with a Georgia Tech MBA," Scott says. "It's not a decision you can be sure of without getting a feel for what we are all about." Oddly enough, only around 40 percent of students visit campus before enrolling.

While all parts of the application are looked at evenly, Scott says that the quantitative portions of the GMAT and work experience are focused on a bit more, just because the program is more quantitatively oriented.

DuPREE MBAs SOUND OFF

I really enjoyed my time here at Tech over the last two years. I learned a tremendous amount, met many great new friends, got to know all of my professors well, and am graduating debt free. Although the economy did not help the job search process this year, I think that my timing was just bad. I think that Tech is a wonderful school with many things going for it. With the new business school building opening soon, the program should continue to improve and reputation and awareness of the school will increase. I had an excellent time here at Tech and would definitely recommend the school to anyone.

Georgia Tech's academic rigor and the quality of incoming students are superb. Our program is somewhat hindered by its small size (roughly 100 students per class), which leads to a smaller (although very dedicated) alumni network, core of campus recruiters, etc. At the same time, the small size allows excellent interaction with the other students and between students and faculty. The cost/value of Tech's program is unsurpassed.

Georgia Tech has been a phenomenal experience for me. From the strong administration to responsive faculty, and the low price tag, almost every aspect of the program was an extremely positive experience. In addition to the classes offered in the MBA program, Tech provides access to a wide variety of electives.

I was satisfied with the education and the approach of the management. Considering the tuition and the quality of the program, it is a very good value.

I had a great MBA experience though I feel that Dupree left much to be desired in the way of e-commerce which was my main interest. That was surprising considering it is a part of Georgia Tech.

OHIO STATE UNIVERSITY

OHIO STATE UNIVERSITY

Max M. Fisher College of Business
2108 Neil Avenue
100 Gerlach Hall
Columbus, Ohio 43220
E-mail address: fishergrad@cob.osu.edu
Web site address: http://fisher.osu.edu

Enrollment: 288
Women: 35%
Non-U.S.: 34%
Minority: 12%
Part-time: 287
Average age: 28
Applicants accepted: 29%
Median starting pay: $79,000

Annual tuition and fees:
  resident—$12,488
  nonresident—$22,809
Estimated annual budget: $25,500
Average GMAT score: 655
Average months of work
  experience: 60
Accepted applicants enrolled: 58%

Teaching methods: case study 30%, distance learning 5%, experiential learning 10%, lecture 25%, simulations 10%, team projects 20%

Dean Joseph Alutto has a secret. It's a secret he wants to tell, and one that his grads and current students know, and do their best to spoil, but so far haven't been able to. You see, Alutto knows his school is strong. In his 12 years as dean, he has built the Fisher College of Business at Ohio State University into a program he is very proud of, with state-of-the-art facilities and technological resources that are second to none. He believes it can compete with many of the top programs in the country. The problem, as Alutto puts it, is that no one else seems to know—yet. "Our issue here is one of trying to get the word out about what our successes are and the innovations we have had," he says. For instance, in the past few years, Fisher has set up a system that makes it possible for students to have their own personal counselor to help them find a job. This is possible because of one thing: class size. For a university with such a huge student population (over 55,000), the MBA class size is minute—only around 140 full-time students a year. "We have all of the advantages of being at a very large institution, within the context of a small, well-integrated MBA program," Alutto says.

This dynamic creates a lot of room for students to lead or at least become involved in some of the school's student organizations, from the Business Law Society and the High Tech Club to Net Impact and the Black MBA Association. Case and business plan competitions also command a large portion of students' time. Also, because they are a part of such a large university, Fisher students are able to branch out and delve into a variety of course offerings in departments around campus, from law to medicine. "A student can use the core that we have within the MBA program and augment just about any interest they have," says Alutto.

Fisher is one of the few fully integrated business campuses in the country. The campus is made up of six buildings that feature a state-of-the-art computer network, satellite uplink capabilities, video on demand, and in excess of 4000 computer ports. Students have access to private interview rooms equipped with Internet access, telephones, and fax machines, as well as the Batten Investment Management Laboratory, which gives them access to Nasdaq and Bridge terminals.

Although the small number of MBAs here helps to provide an intimate and active learning experience, it has historically hurt Ohio State in the placement area. Recently, however, the Office of Career Services has changed its approach to recruiting, and it seems to be paying off. Instead of bringing a generalized group of recruiters to campus, the office has turned to a more customer-based approach. "We are focusing on student interest and not so much on where we think the marketplace is hot and what companies are currently in recruiting mode," says Jeff Rice, director of career services. Because this approach was started before the job market turned sour, Fisher students were more successful in finding employment than those at many of the schools ranked higher. By graduation, 75 percent of the graduating class of 2002 had job offers, and three months later, over 90 percent had offers. "Our approach has paid dividends in this slower economy," Rice says. "There are jobs out there, they are just less convenient for students to find." One thing that should help attract recruiters to Columbus is the Blackwell Inn. Opened in June 2002, the Blackwell is an on-campus luxury hotel built especially to house recruiters and visiting executives.

Your two years begin in early September with a required 10-day orientation called Super September Start-Up (SSSU). During this period,

you will get a sense of what the next two years will be like for you: SSSU gives you a framework for understanding how the functional areas of business and the MBA curriculum fit together. You will take part in a number of team-building exercises, a case analysis, plant visits, a Tycoon Simulation, and social events. You will also take part in a community service activity.

In your first year of studies, Fisher gives you the business basics, providing flexibility for two electives or courses in a major area. A key feature of the program is Business Solutions Teams (BSTs), in which small groups of students spend 20 weeks working on a consulting project for a local corporation. At the project's end, each team presents its recommendations to the client firm's senior executives. In recent years, BSTs have worked with Emery Worldwide, Nationwide, Battelle, and California Fitness Centers.

During your second year, you must pick a major, and you can pick an optional minor if you so choose. Fisher offers six majors: consulting, corporate financial management, interdisciplinary studies, investment management, marketing management, and operations and logistics management. Overall, the school offers a menu of 70 elective courses; the most popular of these include Emerging Technologies and Electronic Commerce, The Stock Market, Managerial Negotiations, and Emerging Markets. You are required to take 13 core courses and 14 electives, which can all be completed in six semesters.

In addition to newer subject areas like e-commerce, operations and logistics are a key focus of the school, along with accounting and finance. Fisher puts more than $17 million of endowment money into the hands of selected MBA students so they can manage a real investment portfolio. The risk has produced big profits for the university and hands-on experience for students; in recent years, MBAs participating in the Student Investment Management Project have consistently outperformed the S&P 500 index.

The internationally oriented find plenty of global learning options at Ohio State. All MBAs have the opportunity to hear lectures by executives from around the world through the Fisher's Distinguished International Speaker Series and The Fisher Council on Global Trade and Technology, an organization established by Leslie Wexner, chairman of The Limited, Inc. (Recent guests have included former President George H. W. Bush and NAFTA expert Sidney Weintraub.) Study abroad programs for second-year MBAs are conducted with B-schools in Italy, Chile, South Korea, Germany, and Mexico. If you prefer to spend a week or so traveling, enroll in one of the quarter-long student-planned emerging markets courses that cover the business, economic, and cultural environment of countries including Egypt, Hungary, Argentina, and Brazil. The group conducts site visits during spring break at multinational companies like Accenture, IBM, and Wal-Mart in its particular country of study. Participants also write relevant case studies on their return. In addition, Ohio State offers MBAs a series of business-oriented language classes in Japanese, Chinese, Russian, Spanish, French, and more. Also, because Columbus is the capital of Ohio, there are numerous resources available for students to get more information about working abroad, and there are also many connections to be made with local politicians and business types who can aid in your pursuits.

In terms of the kind of lifestyle that MBAs lead in Columbus, there are few complaints. Granted, it is not Chicago or New York, but being the most populous area in Ohio, Columbus offers many opportunities for entertainment and excitement for a fraction of the price of what similar events would cost in the aforementioned metropolitan locales. If sports are your thing, you can check out the NHL's newest expansion franchise, the Columbus Blue Jackets, or if the World Cup got you yearning to experience a soccer match firsthand, you can go to Crew Stadium and watch the Columbus Crew defend their U.S.

Open Cup title. Then, of course, there are the Buckeyes. Ohio State Buckeye football is the real deal. Experiencing a game on a Saturday afternoon at Ohio Stadium is like nothing else. (What exactly is a buckeye? According to the university, "A small, shiny, dark brown nut with a light tan patch that comes from the official state tree of Ohio, the buckeye tree." Folklore says the buckeye resembles the eye of a deer and carrying one brings good luck.)

In addition to the sporting events Columbus has to offer, there are a number of restaurants, nightspots, galleries, and shops in Short North, the Brewery District, and German Village. There are a ton of intramural activities you can take part in, from traditional sports such as baseball and soccer to cricket and skeet shooting. Also, many students use their entrepreneurial talents to start projects within the school. In the past few years, Fisher students have started a golf association to teach beginners how to play and have organized wine tastings and trips to local plays and the opera. The school provides funding for those activities as long as students plan them.

The tuition costs at Fisher are something that students love to talk about: they can get a fine education for less than half the price of some of the top schools. In the words of many grads, Fisher is a "good bang for your buck." The return on investment is good, and the median outstanding loan debt for the class of 2002 was only $18,000, well below the average of other schools. Students also like the way that the administration responds to their needs. A complaint that some grads voice is that students have little access to alumni. There is no centralized database that students can refer to in order to network with OSU's large alumni base.

PLACEMENT DETAILS

Fisher grads tend to go into traditional fields such as finance and marketing after graduation and also tend to stay in the Midwest (59 percent of the class of 2002 accepted positions in the region). Though on-campus recruitment was down this year, Fisher was able to attract 64 companies to campus, and with the virtual conferencing technologies that are available, a good number of recruiters were able to access potential hires virtually. Also, with the new initiatives the Office of Career Services has started, students will find it easier to find positions in less traditional outlets.

Much as at other top schools, the class of 2002 had some difficulty in finding employment, with 75 percent of grads receiving one offer by graduation and 90 percent three months out. Starting pay packages also increased over the past two years, from $85,000 in 2000 to nearly $93,000 in 2002.

TOP HIRES

American Electric Power (8); Ford Motor Company (8); Ashland Chemical (4); Bank One (4); National City (4); Procter & Gamble (4); IBM (3); Nestlé (3).

OUTSTANDING FACULTY

Karen Wruck (finance); David Williams (accounting); John Persons (finance); Neeli Bendapudi (marketing); James Ginter (marketing).

APPLICANTS TIPS

There is no real formula for admittance at Fisher; each part of the application holds equal weight. Work experience is important at Fisher, with the average being around five years. "Clearly there are folks who have more, clearly there are folks who have less," says Michelle Jacobson, director of admissions. "But trust that the people who are admitted and choose to come clearly deserve to be here." In the past few years, the class size has risen at Fisher from around 140 to 150 (the class of 2004 actually has 169, but 150 is the target), but the number of applicants has also risen, so don't expect it to be any easier to be admitted.

Interviews are conducted by invitation only; however, 100 percent of the class of 2004 was interviewed, so without an interview, you don't have much of a chance of being admitted. There is no real formula for what the ideal candidate looks like, but a solid work history and background are very important. "If someone has an incredibly high GMAT, but everything else is not so strong, we are not necessarily going to accept them. It is more the whole package," says Jacobson.

FISHER MBAs SOUND OFF

Overall, I have been extremely satisfied with my experience at the Fisher College of Business at the Ohio State University. The staff is constantly in search for ways to improve the program in a relentless pursuit of satisfying all student needs. Also worth mentioning is the fact that although OSU is an extremely large university with much red tape in its administrative systems, the staff at the FCOB make this potentially negative aspect a nonfactor. It seems that all staff members will go out of their way to make sure you feel as though you are at a small, personalized school.

Overall, I believe that I have received a fantastic educational experience over the last two years. The small class size has allowed me to gain relationships with students and faculty that will last a lifetime. I believe that the curriculum has been extremely challenging and will be applicable to real, on-the-job challenges. Lastly, I believe that the career services office has done a very good job in recruiting companies in this less than optimal economic environment.

I credit much of my satisfaction at Fisher to the program's small size, which I believe lent to a favorable learning environment. The school's atmosphere was familial—help and support were always just a turn away. I will miss the daily interactions with my classmates, many of whom I now consider close friends. I was impressed with my classmates' intelligence and motivation on the whole. It was difficult for me to stand out in such an impressive group. As a result, I learned how to compete in an extremely competitive environment, especially in the face of adversity. This was an invaluable lesson for me.

Joining the Fisher MBA Program has been one of the best decisions I have ever made.

The staff, faculty, and students have all been very helpful and responsive to me. I have never felt as if I was "just a social security number." Time and time again, I have seen how the staff listens and implements our suggestions. In all, we are a strong program with a lot of substance.

The facilities in the school are just superb. The Internet connectivity in the classrooms, the equipment available in the class to make the learning experience as interactive as possible and the excellent computer labs and the resources available at the library were some things that I tended to take for granted toward the end of the program. But having come from a developing country where such facilities were unheard of I was initially in great awe. The dean was approachable at all times and the administration was always receptive to suggestions from students.

PENNSYLVANIA
STATE
UNIVERSITY

PENNSYLVANIA STATE UNIVERSITY

The Mary Jean and Frank P. Smeal College of Business
Administration
106 Business Administration Building
University Park, Pennsylvania 16802-3000
E-mail address: smealmba@psu.edu
Web site address: www.smeal.psu.edu

Enrollment: 357
Women: 26%
Non-U.S.: 36%
Minority: 8%
Part-time: 0
Average age: 27
Applicants accepted: 24%
Median starting pay: $77,300

Annual tuition and fees:
  resident—$10,304
  nonresident—$19,682
Estimated annual budget: $17,104
Average GMAT score: 645
Average months of work
  experience: 59
Accepted applicants enrolled: 48%

Teaching methods: case study 35%, experiential learning 30%, lecture 25%, team projects 10%

In 2000, Penn State's Smeal School of Business adopted a new mantra—convergence, customization, communication, and community. With these defining terms in hand, Dean Judy Olian has worked on developing a culture encompassing these four tenets. The "four C's" extended into the revamping and development of the new curriculum, which the school rolled out two years ago, and they will also play a key role in the design of a new state-of-the-art building that will house the B-school come 2005.

Olian follows the philosophy that as a dean she plays the role of the "Total CEO." "As a dean, I harvest the talent—the alumni, the corporate participation, the faculty, and students," she says. "Strategy is putting the team in place." From the dean on down, this teamwork-oriented mind-set permeates through everyone's daily activities. As a Smeal MBA, you'll encounter this team spirit on the first day of Orientation Week. You'll make your way through challenges and assignments, and by the end of the week you'll be on a first-name basis with a good number of your fellow classmates and even professors. It doesn't hurt either that the school's size is relatively small in comparison to other top MBA programs. With fewer than 200 students in the program, it's not an understatement to say you'll end up getting to know almost everyone well. The small size makes for a tightly knit community both on and off campus. The alumni network is very much in touch, says Dean Olian, adding that it's part of the reason why Smeal's ROI topped the charts on *BusinessWeek*'s rankings.

Smeal's "market facing" curriculum was redesigned with the idea of convergence in mind, explains Olian. According to Assistant Dean and Director of the MBA Program F. Robert Wheeler III, the curriculum was created with input from both recruiters and alumni. For each portfolio there is an advisory board made up of company representatives and alumni in the field. "We tailored our program so it would meet the needs of the employers," Wheeler explains. The 7-1-7 structure, with each course divided into two seven-week-long modules, is broken up by an intensive Immersion Week. Plus, the new design introduced "portfolios" or concentrations. You're required to fulfill the requirements of at least one track in your second year, although most students end up pursuing more than one. Your first year, though, you'll mainly take your core classes, which include Accounting, Economics, Finance, Marketing, Management, Communications, and Negotiations and Ethical Leadership.

During the second half of the year, you'll have the chance to take a few classes geared to your portfolio that will help you hit the ground running when you complete your summer internship. And don't discount those added Immersion Weeks. Between the first and second modules, you'll focus on global perspectives in a series of classes geared toward giving you an overview of the global business environment. After the third module, you'll partake in an information technology week to introduce you to the role of technology, and specifically the management of technology.

During your second year, you'll home in on your portfolios, which encompass eight areas—corporate financial analysis and planning, e-business, entrepreneurship, information technology for management, investment management and portfolio analysis, product and market development, strategic consulting, and supply chain management—each of which has its own mix of required courses and electives. Supply chain management is the most popular, though marketing seems to be nipping at its heels. "These portfolios aid students in creating a horizontal skill set that enables them to learn the way the market has emerged," explains Dean Olian. This time around, Immersion Weeks are more hands-on and interactive and tailored to custom-fit your portfolio. For example, students following the supply chain management track in 2002 worked on a consulting project for Sears, while students on the finance path completed a simulation and then visited New York.

Smeal also allows opportunities to explore other interests and pursue a joint degree in one of four programs—law, health services management, quality and manufacturing management, or an industry-specific program aimed at the hotel, restaurant, and recreation industry. And if you want to explore a global experience, you can take advantage of one of Smeal's exchange partnerships with B-schools in Europe, Asia, Mexico, and New Zealand.

A unique part of the Smeal MBA is the Executive Panel Competition. Besides sweating it out through the core, first-year MBAs train hard to get ready for the friendly competition. Every April, the first-year class is divided into teams of five and then presented with a complex business case, which they have 48 hours to analyze. In 2001, students took a crack at Starbucks. Each team must come up with its recommendations in the case and also prepare a concise written report and a polished oral presentation, complete with high-tech visual aids. After two grueling days and a sleepless night, students have to deliver the presentation to a mock management board made up of faculty and alumni. The top three teams then make their presentations to a panel of visiting executives and their classmates. The competition wraps up the year-long Managerial Communications course, one of the country's oldest and strongest B-school communications programs. Students have only good things to say about the program that teaches them how to write polished business memos, letters, and reports and make individual and group proposals, while integrating the skills in strategy, finance, marketing, and other business basics learned in the first year.

Tuition is a bit lower than at a number of the public schools in the top 50. Students at most of the public schools paid more in 2002–2003 than Smeal's in-state fee of $10,308 a year. There's even tuition relief through graduate assistantships and a number of scholarships. On the upside, you'll see the tuition money go to great new buildings and programs that make it worth your while. Some new additions to the school include an electronic lab providing an "eBay-like" laboratory environment. And, in 1999, Smeal opened up the William & John Schreyer Business Library, on the third floor of the Paterno Wing of the university's main Pattee Library. But perhaps the most exciting bit of news creating a buzz on campus is talk of the new B-school. Designed by Robert A. M. Stern, dean of the Yale School of Architecture, it will be the largest academic facility on Penn State's campus at 210,000 square feet. And, for the first time in over 30 years, all faculty departments, research centers, program offices, advisors, and staff will be colocated. With 22 classrooms, 14 study rooms, 10 interview rooms, an accommodating auditorium, and a welcoming atrium, the B-school will be students' "home away from home" as Olian puts it.

Though Penn State may not exactly fit your definition of an intimate setting, with over 79,000 students in 24 locations across Pennsylvania, Smeal offers a small program, which makes up for the often disjointed feel of a large campus. Furthermore, within each class, students are divided into cohorts of 60 for core courses and 25 to 40 for electives. "It's the best of both worlds," says Olian. The small size contributes to the high-touch aspect of the program, she adds. It's one of the reasons Assistant Dean Wheeler came to work for the school last July. It's a culture where people work hand in hand, Wheeler adds, and students are extremely

supportive and collaborative. He further defines his relationship with students as a "joint venture." It's just easier to change and customize the program to fit students' needs when the program is kept small, he notes.

Perhaps the one drawback could be what draws a number of students here—the location. A 2002 grad, Michele Catino was one of them. "I loved the small town and college atmosphere," she says. But she also recognized that the hidden jewel's size and location would make it more difficult when it came time to job hunt. The campus is 120 miles east of Pittsburgh and 150 miles west of Philadelphia, in the midst of mountains, which provide great terrain for the biking and hiking enthusiasts. Despite the sprawling, serene setting, the location makes things a bit more difficult in terms of recruiting, pushing students to more actively pursue independent job searches. Most MBAs live within five miles of the school, which is a plus when you need to stay late to work on a project or want to partake in the extracurriculars. And being affiliated with the larger undergraduate campus has its pluses. For one, a popular activity is attending tailgate parties and football games to cheer for Penn State's Big Ten team, the Nittany Lions. Plus, the MBA Association organizes events like a Halloween Party and a Casino Night. Off campus, there are plenty of bars downtown, of which Café 210 West ranks among the most popular for MBAs to hang out. It's the student community that makes this B-school stand out, though. There's an overall great energy and atmosphere, says Catino. "They don't call it 'Happy Valley' for nothing!"

PLACEMENT DETAILS

The career services office introduced new programming in 2002. For starters, the staff made use of the strong alumni network and had alumni meet with students to offer advice on interviewing techniques and various career paths, says Director of Marketing Kathleen

Welch, who also handles the recruitment side of placement. The office also enhanced its Career Management Workshops, which include lessons on cover letters, resumes, and interviewing. Smeal also reached out to international students, says Welch. They started a new ESL course specifically to help international students with their job search.

Welch adds that she especially worked on reaching out to a more diverse selection of alumni and recruiters in terms of industry. "We're targeting more in terms of functional areas," she notes. Her goal is to have a sufficient number of recruiters for each of the program's eight portfolios.

According to Welch, she witnessed a trend in students looking for companies that can offer career paths, rotation programs, and stability, as companies are getting more selective in finding a perfect fit. That's why she says she strives to emphasize the importance of career strategy. She adds: "You can ultimately get where you want, but it may not be the first job out the door."

That said, 86 percent of grads had job offers by three months after commencement—on par with many top 30 schools. Those offers came with starting pay packages of about $93,000.

TOP HIRES

IBM (5); ExxonMobil (3); Johnson & Johnson (3); SC Johnson (2); The Hartford (2); General Electric (2).

OUTSTANDING FACULTY

Chris Muscarella (finance); Paul Fischer (accounting); Ralph Oliva (marketing).

APPLICANT TIPS

Admissions director Michele Kirsch says she's looking for driven and motivated, hard-working students who want to experience being a part of a small community and an intimate environment, which is one of the B-school's unique aspects. At only a little over 100 slots per class, how do you make your application stand out from the crowd? First and foremost, explains Kirsch, have a sense of focus, a defined career direction, and an understanding of how a Smeal MBA will help you get there.

A strong academic record is important. But if, for instance, you're lacking experience in finance, or your GPA just isn't up to par, Kirsch recommends you take additional coursework if necessary. Though the average work experience is five years, there's no minimum requirement. Kirsch points out that she's looking for quality rather than quantity in this area.

All admitted students are interviewed, and it's here that Kirsch says she'll home in on your communication skills, especially since the B-school is well known for its strong communications program. In terms of your recommendations, seek someone who can specifically speak to your performance, work ethic, motivation, time management, and other intangible skills, Kirsch adds. Essays are the one area she says applicants need to improve on the most. "You need to pay attention to that, focus on writing well and concisely, and worry about the details," she points out. Essays are also a good place to highlight some of your strengths in teamwork and leadership skills.

SMEAL MBAs SOUND OFF

Smeal's greatest challenge is to evolve during a period of tremendous change. During my time there, we had a new dean, a new curriculum, and an economic climate that caused all B-schools to shudder. The program's emphasis on communications and networking was critical for my professional success. Smeal involves students a great deal in the running of extracurricular events and, if given more attention from recruiters, would provide a "product" that exceeds expectations—MBAs ready to roll up their sleeves and get things done, communicators with a depth and breadth of marketing, financial, analytical and strategic management skills to adapt and lead in any industry.

It was nice to be in a program that allowed ongoing interaction with the professors. Due to the smaller class size I had the opportunity to not only build relationships but ensure that I can call on any of my professors at a moment's notice if stuck on an issue in the workplace.

I found that the first-year program was a bit excessive in workload and focused heavily on GPA. Pushing the envelope can have benefits, but there are diminishing returns if pushed too far. In the end, excessive workload and the threat of harsh grading inhibited many from venturing too far beyond the prescribed learning. Much of what we learned was placed in short-term memory because information overload prohibited absorption in the minimal amount of time allotted, if one expected to do well on the exam. I would have pre-

ferred less information and more freedom to extend what was presented in a guided fashion. There was much more critical thinking in the second year, but I would have preferred a bit more throughout.

Overall, Smeal offers a good program at a great price. The biggest opportunity for improvement is with how the administration handles corporate recruiting relationships. PSU has an impressive alumni network that is vastly underutilized by the administration.

The best students, the ones who have added to my experience, have come for the education, the life enhancement, the investment in themselves. Smeal does a pretty good job of finding those people. The community is rich with diverse, interesting, accomplished, intelligent people. Many are driven to not only be the best, but to also help one another. Though it is competitive and there are a lot of type As, the overall culture is one of goodwill and ambition. Smeal is a positive place that has tons of alumni who love coming back, lending a hand and giving. If you want to enjoy the two years you are investing, and get more than you pay for—this is the place.

RICE UNIVERSITY

Jesse H. Jones Graduate School of Management
P.O. Box 2932
Houston, Texas 77252-2932
E-mail address: ricemba@rice.edu
Web site address: www.jonesgsm.rice.edu

Enrollment: 353
Women: 36%
Non-U.S.: 24%
Minority: 11%
Part-time: 0
Average age: 28
Applicants accepted: 39%

Median starting pay: $78,000
Annual tuition and fees: $28,000
Estimated annual budget: $50,000
Average GMAT score: 630
Average months of work
  experience: 60
Accepted applicants enrolled: 63%

Teaching methods: case study 25%, experiential learning 20%, lecture 25%, simulations 10%, team projects 20%

The Jesse H. Jones Graduate School of Management has a new home—a 167,000-square-foot, $60 million state-of-the-art building, which students and administrators alike say has been a long time coming. The facilities are more than three times the size of the previous building, which was beginning to feel more than a little cramped. And the new building is fully equipped with the latest technology. The posh digs are just one of the things on Dean Gilbert R. Whitaker's list of things to do that he can confidently check off as complete.

When Whitaker came back to campus in 1997 as dean (he got his BA in economics from Rice in 1953), there were a few things he wanted to see improve. Since then, he's not only physically changed the school, he's also revamped the curriculum, added a hands-on learning program, increased minority enrollment, and increased the number of faculty members, to name a few of his efforts and accomplishments.

He was also able to lure a strong team to help run the school. The main reason MBA program director Carrie Chamberlain, a 1997 MBA grad, returned to the Jones School was Whitaker. When he came on board, the changes were palpable, she says. Whitaker's efforts are clearly visible. Take one look at the class of 2004 and you'll see that black and Hispanic students make up 15 percent of the population, a huge leap forward—when Whitaker arrived in 1997 there was only one minority student. The number of faculty on the school's roster is up, too. There are now 38 faculty members, with plans to add 15 to 20 more in the next two years.

One of Whitaker's biggest initiatives came to fruition in the fall of 2002 with the opening of the new building. Creating the biggest buzz, though, is the El Paso trading room. B-school officials describe it as a flight simulator for the future fighter pilots of Wall Street, which virtually duplicates the latest technology available in major trading firms and investment houses. The new building also includes tiered classrooms to enhance case study method instruction, behavioral research and observation rooms for focus group research and interviews; 24 comfortable breakout rooms for group study and discussion; 28 terminals to access databases; and a 425-seat auditorium. There's also a 14,000-square-foot Business Information Center that provides students with everything from periodicals and annual reports to online retrieval of the latest financial information. There's even a "cyber-commons" where students and faculty can meet with coffee and ports for computer and network connectivity. You can plug in the fully loaded laptop that's included in your tuition and finish up your homework with your morning mocha. "We're really trying to capture a building to keep an intimate atmosphere yet be almost four times as large spacewise," Whitaker adds.

The Jones School's MBA program combines a challenging core with a unique opportunity for hands-on learning (the Action Learning Project) and an impressive menu of specialized electives that allow you to personalize your degree to achieve your career objectives. The curriculum follows a modular model, which Dean Whitaker says exposes students to a greater variety of areas. You've got a lot to choose from, too. Each semester is divided into three 5-week modules, with courses varying from 5 to 15 weeks in length. When you arrive for orientation, you jump right into things with a two-week long orientation that includes a communications skills assessment; quantitative and computer skills courses; workshops on time management, leadership, and team building;

and an introduction to case study methodology. In the fall, you'll take accounting, data analysis, strategy, managerial economics, organizational behavior, ethics, information technology, marketing, and finance. "We're putting our efforts and resources into having students better prepared as communicators and team players," Whitaker says. Sounds a bit overwhelming at first, but though the program may move fast—you're looking at an exam period every five weeks—the feedback from the students so far has been very positive.

In the spring, you'll hit the books in classes like World Economy, Globalization, Cost Management, Operations, Business, Government Relations, and Change Management; you'll also take a three-module Leadership and Managerial Skills sequence, which addresses issues such as effective negotiation and corporate politics; take 10-week or 5-week electives; and get hands-on experience with the Action Learning Project. The core rolls into your second year, when you'll take Business Ethics, Business and Government Relations, Globalization of Business, and Entrepreneurship.

However, the cornerstone of the curriculum is the Action Learning Project, which was launched in 1999. In January, you'll bid on a project submitted by potential host companies. Midsemester, you'll meet the members of your four- to six-person team, find out what company you'll be working with, and begin the background work on a real-time, real-world consulting project. You'll spend the last five weeks of the year on-site at your sponsoring firm, with no other class work to distract you. Project tasks span the spectrum. Most companies are Houston based, and those offered are a good mix, from banking to airlines to health care and nonprofits. The likes of Continental Airlines, ExxonMobil, Reliant Energy, and PricewaterhouseCoopers provide the training grounds for Jones MBAs.

Your second year, you'll be able to take advantage of the 11 areas of electives including accounting, organizational behavior and human resource management, entrepreneurship, information technology, finance, international business, strategy, operations, legal, marketing, and health care, but there's no concentration requirement. A few courses, such as Power Politics and Influence and a few on business law, investor relations, and strategy have been added to address more of the personal communications aspects of business. You can also look into pursuing a dual degree in engineering or medicine or a PhD focused on biotech, pharmaceuticals, and health care industries. Additionally, you have the option of heading overseas to a program at a business school in Costa Rica.

Expect to be a part of a very intimate culture if you attend. Everyone knows each other, faculty get to know students, and there's always an open-door policy, administrators say. Duly noted: students give the faculty high marks for their ability to integrate the curriculum and for their responsiveness to students' needs. These close working relationships are cultivated by the low student-to-faculty ratio of nine to one. This is one reason why students consistently recognize their professors as highly attentive and available. "They get our full attention," says Whitaker. The dean himself is available, wandering the halls, interacting with students, and hosting biweekly coffee hours. Think of Jones as a place where you'll get a rigorous education, a healthy dose of personal skills, and where you'll find a "warm, welcoming, friendly, nice blend of folks."

Though the school's small size (180 students per class) and limited alumni network (2149 living alums) may hold the school back at times, Jones uses other factors—like its prime location—to its advantage. Houston houses the second largest concentration of Fortune 500 headquarters, which attracts diverse students and draws a wide range of speakers. Plus, MBA grads now have three years' worth of executive MBA graduates helping them out, too—a resource they aptly tapped in 2002 when it came to helping students find permanent positions. One of the routes the school took this year was to write personal letters to alums for help with the job search.

The B-school sits in the middle of Rice's 300-acre campus and is surrounded by a tranquil setting—one that lets you forget that just a few miles away is Houston's bustling business district. Right across the street is the massive Texas Medical Center, which has received lots of attention from students as of late because of its innovations. Within walking distance you'll find some entertainment in the museums, the Houston Zoo, Hermann Park, and Rice Village, peppered with shops and restaurants. You're bound to find students hanging out in nearby Montrose neighborhood, home to art film houses, ethnic restaurants, boutiques, and coffeehouses, perfect for crunch time studying. Most students live in off-campus houses and apartments near the university, though new university housing for graduate students—the Rice Graduate Apartments—opened in the fall of 1999. Ranging from efficiencies to four-bedroom units, the graduate apartments are within easy walking distance of campus and also are served by shuttle bus.

PLACEMENT DETAILS

Executive director of admissions and career placement Peter Veruki says the Jones School believes it has a responsibility to help its students out in any way when it comes time to launch their career. That's why the career planning office worked closely with the admissions office.

Especially in light of the recent Houston-based issues, such as Enron and the merger of Compaq and Hewlett-Packard, Associate Director of Career Planning John Miller and his team make a concerted effort to broaden the list of recruiting companies. One tactic they used in 2002 was sending a letter from the dean to all alums for leads on contacts and open positions.

The dean also hosted several luncheons with CEOs of smaller companies that haven't historically been aggressive MBA recruiters to establish some common ground.

Another outlet Miller turned to was the Rice Alliance—a collaborative effort between the B-school and engineering and science departments to incubate, identify, and help fund ideas generated on campus. With the medical complex across the street, Miller says he tried to identify students with an interest in health care and biotech because of the tremendous number of opportunities there in an otherwise down market.

Additionally, Miller says he and his team made some inroads in marketing and consumer goods and brands such as Kraft, 3M, and P&G. The extra work paid off for the first-years especially, as 100 percent of the class secured summer internships.

The team also beefed up the workshops available. There's a new Career Planning course being added this year that will cover all material related to an effective job search. The required, noncredit course meets twice a week during the first semester and hits areas such as resume writing, interviewing skills, networking, and how to research companies. "These are life long career skills," Miller adds. "It's not just about getting you the first job."

TOP HIRES

Duke Energy (11); ExxonMobil (4); Merrill Lynch (3); JPMorgan Chase (3); Credit Suisse First Boston (2); BP (2); Shell (2); Conoco (2); Phillips (2); Pantellos (2).

OUTSTANDING FACULTY

David Ikenberry (finance); James Weston (finance); Jeff Fleming (finance); Edward Williams (entrepreneurship); Karen Schnietz (strategy); Barbara Ostdeik (finance).

APPLICANT TIPS

With applications on the rise, how do you make your application stand out? Admissions Director Staci Easterling takes a look at several key factors. Though there's no work experience requirement, the average is five years, and the practical minimum, she says, is two years. However, more important is the quality of work experience. "We want to see demonstration that students can apply their potential, ability, and education," Easterling says.

Easterling also focuses on the courses students have taken, especially the quant-based classes like economics and math. Leadership activities within the community, in college, or through volunteer work also come into play as evidence of teamwork. "Our environment is heavily dependent on teamwork," she says. "So we want to see examples of experience in teams." She also looks to see that the student has a clear sense as to why he or she wants to come to business school. "Know your career plan," she advises. This helps the admissions staff assess the student's ultimate marketability post graduation. These are areas, Easterling says, that you can highlight in the essay part of the application especially.

Interviews are by invitation only, but all those accepted were interviewed, so if invited take the offer. And foremost, since the school relies on a rolling admissions process, apply early in the season, Easterling advises. This is especially important, she notes, for those who aren't completely comfortable with a particular area in their application. If there's one piece that doesn't add up, she says, then she has time to contact the applicant and get to know him or her on an individual basis. Those who apply by the October or December deadlines can expect a response in six weeks; if you wait until February or April, you'll be waiting to hear for about two months.

Finally, Easterling advises prospective students to take a big-picture approach. When doing your research, don't be afraid to contact schools and schedule a visit, and ask lots of questions. It's important to get acquainted with the environment you might be getting into, she notes.

JONES MBAs SOUND OFF

I am extremely pleased with my MBA education at Rice University. I chose the program because of its small size and because I felt that I would have the chance to get to closely work with both faculty and other students. I found this to be very true. The faculty is approachable, and the students work well together on teams. The curriculum is strong in both finance and marketing, but in addition, it includes a wide range of topics that will help me tremendously as I advance in my career. The quality of the teaching was generally outstanding.

Overall, I am glad I went to business school. The foundations in finance, marketing and accounting have been tremendous. The career placement center needs to be revamped.

Rice's program is very intense. It wasn't enough to simply work hard on a project—you sometimes had to think about the most efficient way to tackle it or else you wouldn't have time to finish your other projects. I think that this is a valuable skill to learn.

The Rice MBA program is a challenging and difficult program. Do not come here looking for a country club education. Students work extremely hard at the Jones School to manage the heavy workload, but the program is also very rewarding. I have learned a lot, met several interesting and wonderful people, and personally grown a great deal these past two years.

The greatest strength of the Rice program is the faculty. The professors are very knowledgeable and willing to spend as much time with students as necessary. Until now, our facilities have held us back. I believe that the new facilities will continue to attract outstanding faculty and Rice will continue to fill a niche in this region and for the energy industry in particular.

The placement office needs to branch out from Houston and the Texas area. If there were more students admitted from outside Texas, this would be a better learning environment, and the Rice MBA name would be known throughout the U.S.

Rice definitely exceeded my expectations. The school really cares about the students—from professors to faculty to administration to the dean.

SOUTHERN
METHODIST
UNIVERSITY

SOUTHERN METHODIST UNIVERSITY

Edwin L. Cox School of Business
6212 Bishop Boulevard, Fincher 125
Dallas, Texas 75275-0333
E-mail address: arrion@mail.cox.smu.edu
Web site address: www.cox.smu.edu

Enrollment: 230	Median starting pay: $75,000
Women: 28%	Annual tuition and fees: $27,648
Non-U.S.: 22%	Estimated annual budget: $41,066
Minority: 10%	Average GMAT score: 660
Part-time: 0	Average months of work
Average age: 28	experience: 56
Applicants accepted: 30%	Accepted applicants enrolled: 50%

Teaching methods: lecture 20%, case study 40%, simulations 10%,
team projects 30%

Although Southern Methodist University's Edwin L. Cox School of
Business may be small—about 120 students per class—the Dallas
school's vision is not. In the last two years the Cox School has undergone a multitude of changes spearheaded by Dean Albert W. Niemi Jr.,
who came from the University of Georgia in 1997. Niemi is working on
extending the B-school's reputation beyond the borders of Dallas and
the Longhorn state. To accomplish his goals, Niemi has overhauled the
curriculum, expanded the career services office, and cultivated a more
global program. So far he's stuck to his word and has paved the way for
changes to come, such as the implementation of a new plan to recruit
Native Americans.

The curriculum first witnessed a dramatic overhaul in 2000. The
new modular system consists of eight-week short courses and focuses
on team building in the first year while offering an impressive array of
electives in the second year. In the fall of your first year, you'll take a
course load consisting of Managerial Statistics and Forecasting, Financial Accounting, Financial Management, Economics for Business Decisions, Marketing Management, Managerial Accounting, Decision
Modeling, Managing Your Career, and Communication Skills. Come
spring, you'll face Organizational Behavior, Operations Management,
Strategic Analysis in the Global Era, Global Leadership Program, and
two electives. In your second year, you'll take electives from an extensive
selection that is always changing and expanding—more than 90 percent were new in 2000. A new venture capitalist course, introduced in
the fall of 2002, gives students the opportunity to spend a part of every
week working at a venture capital firm.

Associate Dean Marci Armstrong says employers' expectations are changing and they're looking for greater depth in specialized areas. That's why, beginning in the fall of 2002, she added concentrations to the curriculum. Now you can develop expertise in an academic concentration or take a stab at a broader selection for a general management perspective. Concentrations you can choose from include accounting, finance, financial consulting, general management, management consulting and strategy, marketing (with optional specializations in marketing consulting and product and brand management), strategy and entrepreneurship, and telecommunications and electronic commerce (with further specializations in e-business and information technologies and operations management). The B-school also launched its first online course over the summer of 2002. Before stepping foot on campus, you'll take several prep courses online, including classes in statistics, marketing, and operations, to better prepare for the core courses you'll be taking your first year. The effort is designed to put everyone on the same page from day one.

According to Dean Niemi, what differentiates his program from those of other schools is its enrichment programs. It's really outside the classroom that you note the difference, he says. Niemi is dedicated to globalizing the MBA program. "I'm a big believer in the idea that you can read all about it, but until you experience it, it's not real," he says. And Cox doesn't just take you outside the classroom; the B-school has added to its international programming as of late. Cox partnered with the Chinese European International Business School for a three-week summer program, a new addition to the already established programs in Germany and France.

Moreover, the American Airlines Global Leadership Program, launched in 2000, is gaining momentum on its way to becoming a cornerstone of the curriculum. The program is required for all first-year students during the final two weeks before they take off for their summer internships. The class is divided into three groups, each focused on a different region—Latin America, Europe, or Asia. In the fall, you'll begin your preparation in a series of orientations and conduct comprehensive research on the region you'll be visiting. Then, come May, the faculty-led groups will head overseas to meet with business and government leaders and visit manufacturing facilities. In 2002, students traveling to Europe met with representatives from 16 companies and government ministries located in London, Munich, and Stockholm; the Asia contingent visited 18 companies located in Beijing, Shanghai, Taipei, and Tokyo; and the Latin America group visited 19 companies and government ministries in Buenos Aires, Monterrey, Rio de Janeiro, and São Paulo. Once back on campus, you'll take part in a three-day symposium to share your research and observations with the school and members of the Dallas business community. The best part about this program is that it doesn't cost anything extra. Unlike the international components of other MBA programs, the Global Leadership Program is entirely covered by the regular MBA tuition, thanks to a three-year gift from Dallas-based American Airlines.

Another unique feature at Cox is a mentorship program for all MBAs. The Associated Board MBA Mentoring Program matches up students with 200 local managers and executives, who provide plenty of individual attention to students. Soon after you arrive on campus, you'll be matched with mentors by occupational interests. The mentors are pulled from a pool of execs from Dallas-based companies such as American Airlines, EDS, Frito-Lay, and JCPenney. During your two years, you'll meet with your mentors on a regular basis. Mentors also invite their students to their organizations for tours and share advice on business and careers. The program might enable you to witness a meeting among senior executives and expand your networking community, and could even help you land an internship.

Cox requires that you take two leadership-oriented courses—Managing Your Career and Communication Skills. Topics run the gamut from stress management to presentation skills and negotiating tactics. Some sessions take you outdoors to complete a series of team exercises, and some are computer simulations. You'll also take a series of skill and personality tests to assess your individual strengths and weaknesses to help gauge how effective the training has been. In addition, the Career Management Center, which experienced a dramatic turnaround in the last two years, requires you to participate in a series of workshops. The sessions, led by alums and second-years, cover field-specific opportunities. Other workshops include all the trimmings—resume writing, job search strategy, and interviewing—to help ensure you've got the necessary tools to face the job search.

Alum Edwin L. Cox is still involved with the school that bears his name. Ten students are named Cox Distinguished Scholars, receiving full scholarships based on leadership ability, work experience, and academic record, thanks to a donation from the venture capitalist and investor. The scholars will also get a chance to visit Wall Street during their spring break. Dean Niemi is hoping to expand this program even further and also include a week in Washington, DC, to focus on public policy.

The small, personal environment leads to a customer-oriented feel, administrators say. Students add that the small size allows them to work closely with faculty. "The easy access to faculty members and the willingness of the administration to solve the problems of the students were the best things," says 2002 grad Rina Ray. Director of Student Services Steve Denson adds that his door is always open, just as for the rest of the faculty. He notes: "It's not unusual for my phone to ring at midnight." Besides the close-knit feel between students and teachers, students themselves say their own community is very close. "We developed close relationships with people we can count on," Rina Ray adds.

Denson's favorite thing about the students is that every year the new class has a collective personality. "Usually, they're full of life and adventure, and willing to take chances," he notes. Students are also very actively involved in the school. When they see a void, they fill it. In the last two years, students have spearheaded new groups like the Diversity Club, the International Student Club, a spouses' group, and an Ethics Club. For students who want to give back to the community, there's also the Cox for Community Club. "We want students to feel like they've had a great experience," he adds. "It's all about empowering the students."

The lush campus that houses the B-school is very inviting, and lends itself to the type of community Cox tries to be. The school lies near the middle of the university's tree-lined 160-acre campus, which is set in University Park, an affluent residential neighborhood five miles from downtown Dallas. And don't discount the Dallas business community as a tribute only to oil men or the ten-gallon-hat set. "Dallas is a wonderful laboratory for business students," says Dean Niemi.

The B-school comprises three attached, classically styled, red brick buildings arranged in a horseshoe shape around a courtyard. MBAs have their own academic building, library, and lounge. All MBA classes are held in the Trammel Crow building, and, with the completion of the James Collins Executive Education Center, a state-of-the-art teaching and conference facility, MBA students will also have access to 16 additional breakout rooms. All classrooms are Internet ready and upgraded to handle wireless capabilities and multimedia equipment.

Cox Students form a tightly knit community that is very involved both on and off campus. Campus extracurriculars cover the spectrum, from the more typically popular finance, consulting, and marketing clubs to the increasingly popular information technology, entrepreneurship, and health care clubs. In addition, for the civic-minded, the school has an active Non-Profit Club and Cox for Community Club. And if you're looking to get active on the field, the soccer and rugby clubs top the list as campus favorites.

For housing, most students head off campus and live in "the village," a maze of apartment complexes about a half mile from campus. The university's affiliation with the Methodist Church means that virtually all drinking must be done off campus, so on Thursday nights (there are no Friday classes), MBAs gather at the Old Monk, a fish-and-chips place and brewery just a few minutes south of campus in the Henderson/Knox area. You'll also find MBAs hanging out at the Green Elephant, Milo's, Stan's Blue Note, Cuba Libre, The Barley House, and the Fishbowl, to name a few. Second-year students plan out orientation for first-year students, and one thing they do is visit Deep Ellum—an artsy part of town peppered with live music venues, bars, and junk stores.

PLACEMENT DETAILS

Dennis Grindle, director of the Career Management Center, has been working with MBAs for 20 years. He's worked at several big-name B-schools and says his main mantra has always been "quality placement over quantity placement." The quality aspect emphasizes career planning, he notes, whereas the quantity technique tends to put graduates back into their former fields.

Cox's small size also helps the career center's staff keep tabs on students, allowing for more personal attention, mentoring, and advising. It's not rare to see the administration, staff, faculty, and even the dean fully involved in students' job search process. "Even sometimes when students begin to give up on themselves, we don't, we stay on top of them," Grindle adds.

Starting with the fall of 2002, the Career Management Center will be offering things like MBA coffee breaks, where students can stop by and meet with recruiters set up in the atrium. Two alumni have been hired to refine the network system database by contacting alumni, mentors, and boards of directors. Networking is key to getting hired, Grindle adds, especially now when the job market is tighter. In 2002, only 47 percent of grads had job offers by graduation, and 69 percent had found work three months later.

TOP HIRES

Sabre (6); Safety-Kleen (4); Wells Fargo (3); Celanese (3); American Airlines (3); ExxonMobil (2); Merrill Lynch (2); Wachovia Securities (1).

OUTSTANDING FACULTY

Susan Riffe (accounting); David Mauer (finance); Roger Kerin (marketing); Jame Smith (finance).

APPLICANT TIPS

Admissions Director Arrion Rathsack is not only looking for a demonstration of your academic capabilities, she's also interested in your professional and life experiences, leadership, communication, and interpersonal skills. Rathsack also wants to see those extra qualities like maturity and self-confidence, which she says you can illustrate in your invitation-based interviews.

The minimum work experience for admittance to Cox is two years, though the average is five years. As of late, applications are on the rise, allowing the school to get a bit more selective. The average GMAT shot up 50 points in the last five years. If your GMAT score isn't what you'd like it to be, Rathsack suggests taking the test multiple times as a way to show that you're committed to pursuing your MBA, a plus in her eyes. With such a small class to fill (120 slots), Rathsack says the focus is on bringing in a quality group of students. If you want to stand out from the bunch, take the opportunity to write the optional essay. "It's a great opportunity to tell us something that is unique," Rathsack adds. For example, she says, "if you've had extensive international experience, let us know about it."

Cox students are an interactive, experience- and team-oriented bunch, Rathsack says. So she's looking for applicants who are willing to be involved as part of a team. Most important, Rathsack points out, do your research. It's important, she notes, not only to research the school, but to research the location as well. She adds: "We want to see someone who wants to be here and in Dallas, in the Southwest."

COX MBAs SOUND OFF

Overall the experience was great. Those professors that were below par are currently being weeded out and replaced. The core will improve next year and should be more uniform in material covered. E-business and marketing offerings are great and the finance department is currently being overhauled to meet demands.

Cox does a great job of recruiting high-caliber people who are both intelligent and caring. My classmates definitely made the difference in my satisfaction with the school. I look forward to being friends with many of these people for years to come.

Cox is truly a program that puts student needs first. Classes and curriculums are designed to give students flexibility and vast choices when structuring their education. The Global Leadership Program provides an intensive, in-depth study of a region outside of the U.S., followed by a field study of companies within that region. This experience, which happens at the end of the first year, is amazing and incredibly educational.

I believe that the value of an institution's MBA is a combination of the academic knowledge base and leadership experiences it provides. SMU excels in both areas, but it is a leader in providing outstanding opportunities to apply the book knowledge and interact with local business leaders. SMU delivered everything it promised and more. I would strongly recommend the program to anyone.

I think there are few other business schools that deliver the extent of preparation for a business career that you find at Cox. The mix of entrepreneurialism, international business exposure, and soft skills emphasis provide Cox students with a powerful foundation from which to launch their careers. I know wherever I end up I will succeed and that Cox prepared me to pursue any avenue I choose, not just one narrow path into a designated field.

I feel that our school is somewhat shy in making its name known outside of Texas, but if it did, many people in the U.S. and the world would be surprised to find this "hidden gem." The school truthfully has an outstanding program that emphasizes personal attention and one-on-one coaching. The school could also still greatly improve its career office, and the interface between administration and students, which is often inefficient. Overall, however, this is the place where I have had the best teachers and met some of the most intelligent people in my life. The skills and experiences that I have gained are superior, and have been worth every penny and the time that I have spent on my education through these past two years.

THUNDERBIRD
(THE AMERICAN
GRADUATE
SCHOOL OF
INTERNATIONAL
MANAGEMENT)

THUNDERBIRD (THE AMERICAN GRADUATE SCHOOL OF INTERNATIONAL MANAGEMENT)

15249 N. 59th Avenue
Glendale, Arizona 85306
E-mail address: admissions@t-bird.edu
Web site address: www.thunderbird.edu

Enrollment: 1100
Women: 29%
Non-U.S.: 64%
Minority: 4%
Part-time: 0
Average age: 29
Applicants accepted: 80%

Median starting pay: $65,500
Annual tuition and fees: $27,000
Estimated annual budget: $40,900
Average GMAT score: 600
Average months of work
  experience: 64
Accepted applicants enrolled: 51%

Teaching methods: case study 40%, distance learning 5%, experiential learning 5%, lecture 20%, simulations 10%, team projects 20%

Ask any Thunderbird graduate what degree he or she received, and you'll probably hear, "an international MBA." Technically, this would be fudging the truth. But all that has changed. Starting with the class of 2002, Thunderbird graduates no longer receive a master's degree in international management (MIM). They, too, can now use the coveted three-letter acronym and unequivocally respond, "an MBA in international management." After 55-plus years in business, the school decided to get with the times and give the students what they really wanted all along: an MBA. Of course, there is a handful of naysayers who want to keep things as they were and continue having to explain to the uninitiated what the MIM is. But they are definitely the minority, according to Dean of Faculty and Programs David Bowen. "We said to ourselves, 'Really it's an MBA, so let's make it an MBA,'" says Bowen. "No longer do our graduates have to explain, apologize, work through, or disguise their degree."

Despite the degree name change, Thunderbird still prides itself on being the only B-school solely dedicated to the pursuit of international business. "Everything we do is international management. That's just something you're not going to see at other schools," says Thunderbird's president, Roy A. Herberger Jr., who is also quick to point out that the name change is really just that. "The content is fundamentally the same. We just changed the name." Finance professor Anant Sundaram agrees. "In most B-schools, 'global' is just a marketing buzzword. At Thunderbird, it is a way of life in the entire educational process from start to finish."

Once on the Thunderbird campus, it's easy to forget that you're in the American Southwest. Each day, a new "flag of the day" is hoisted up at the school's entrance, representing one of the 70 different home countries of students, and a wall welcomes you to the school in 10 different languages. Outside the administration building, a United Nations flag flutters in the occasional Arizona breeze. Even the student newspaper has a foreign name: *Das Tor* ("The Gate" in German). Sit down in the campus pub or cafeteria, and you probably won't hear much English being spoken, with 65 percent of students coming from outside the United States.

Over the past several years, the Thunderbird administration has been refining the school's curriculum. Gone is the universal requirement for a second language. Now, students have two tracks from which they can choose. Track one is very similar to that of the former MIM and lasts four trimesters. It includes second language mastery and certification. The newly implemented track two lasts only three trimesters (designed to be completed within one year) and does not require second language proficiency. The reasons for the change are manifold, says Bowen. Chief among them is the fact that the overwhelming majority of students who come to Thunderbird already speak a second or third language. Also, the job market for expatriates has softened, so language is no longer as much of an issue. "You no longer have to pay as heavy dues in cost and time to get your degree," says Bowen.

All students are still required to go through what Thunderbird calls its Flexi-Core. In either track, you can choose from a number of different modules to reach the required 33 units. After that, you'll choose a 12-unit focus area. Your options are global marketing, global finance, international development, or a customized focus area selected from electives.

Thunderbird has never been lauded for its placement record. Students constantly complain that the school's placement office doesn't do enough in helping the approximately 750 students who graduate each year find jobs either in the United States or abroad. President

Herberger is the first to admit difficulties in placing such a large and diverse student body. "It's a very complicated placement," he says, referring to the visa problems many foreign students face. "All of us in this business are going to have a tough time."

Thunderbird makes up for its dismal placement record with flexibility. Don't want to start your MBA in the fall? No problem. You can enter the program at any of three points during the year. Whichever one you choose, your education will start with a two-week orientation called Foundations of International Management. A heavy emphasis is placed on cross-cultural communication, as your classmates could come from as many as 70 countries.

One option available only to students in track one is participation in the school's extensive exchange program. Take your pick from 16 schools in Latin America, Europe, Asia, and Africa. Students in both tracks participate in Winterim, which takes place for two weeks every January. You are given two options for Winterim: you can stay on campus and hear from prominent global experts and international business leaders who lend their expertise and share their perspectives on a specific topic, or you may go abroad. Past destinations have included China, Europe, South Africa, the Middle East, and South America. While there, you can experience the culture, practice your language skills, and gain firsthand insight into a country's business practices. Students who chose Business, Politics and Culture in Emerging Markets during a past Winterim traveled to Dubai (United Arab Emirates) and Turkey. Daily seminars consisted of field trips to industrial and business enterprises and presentations by international managers in the two countries. Each year, Winterim is made up of different courses and destinations, depending on student interest and faculty availability and expertise.

"It's L.A. without the ocean," is how a lot of non–Arizona natives would describe Phoenix.

Of course, this is only partially true. While there is no ocean, there also is much less traffic than L.A., a lot fewer people, and much hotter summers. A 30-minute drive will get you to the middle of nowhere, with cacti and desert brush as far as the eye can see. (Just try that in L.A.) Half a day's drive north and you're at the Grand Canyon; head in the other direction and you're in Mexico. Glendale, where the school is actually located, is little more than suburban sprawl with lots of retired folks and RVs. But Phoenix (home to the Arizona Diamondbacks) and Tempe (home to Arizona State University) each have their own flavor and entertainment. Downtown Tempe is packed with bars and restaurants, all frequented by students and especially popular on Friday and Saturday nights. A lot of Thunderbird students choose to live in one of the approximately 500 rooms on campus. (Those overlooking the school's swimming pool are in highest demand.) Other options include a number of reasonably priced apartment complexes literally across the street from the school. Tempe, a 20-minute drive away, is especially popular with students pursuing dual degrees with Arizona State University.

PLACEMENT DETAILS

In the past, many of the Career Management Center (CMC) services available to Thunderbird students were on an "if you want it" basis. The problem with that approach was that a lot of students weren't taking advantage of all of the resources available to them through the CMC, according to Kay Keck, career services director. "We want every student to develop a relationship with the CMC while at the school," she says. Now, students are introduced to the CMC through a required career management seminar in their first trimester at the school.

As a new strategy to combat the lackluster international job market, Keck is trying to reach out more to employers outside the United States. There are more than 100 Korean students currently on campus; three of them recently accompanied a CRC staff member on a trip to Korea. Similar trips to Japan and Latin America are also being held.

For those international students who want to remain in the United States, Keck and her staff face an uphill battle. Only 15 percent have authorization to work in the United States. "We're constantly looking for companies willing to sponsor them," she says. Many Thunderbird graduates choose to stay in the United States until their student visas expire or they get a one-year practical training visa. This, along with a number of other factors, contributes to Thunderbird's low placement rates and student complaints, says Keck. Other factors include many of Thunderbird's international students returning home and then finding jobs and American students who choose to go abroad also taking longer to find positions. Often, the CRC never hears about these placements.

Keck wishes that students would concentrate less on particular countries and more on companies. "Be flexible and open to looking at the company more than the actual location," she says. And don't shy away from international positions in your own country. International employment research has shown that those people who start in their home country are inevitably the most successful.

Keck says she was relieved when the school decided to move from the MIM to the MBA. "Employers didn't necessarily know what an MIM was," she says. "Now, we've taken that hurdle away."

TOP HIRES

Johnson & Johnson (11); IBM (6); Samsung (5); Citigroup (5); Ford Motor Company (4); Merck (4); UBS Warburg (3); L'Oreal (3); KPMG (3); Hilti (3); Fisher-Scientific (3); Eli Lilly (3).

OUTSTANDING FACULTY

Ken Ferris (accounting); Sundaresan Ram (marketing); Anant Sundaram (finance); Paul Kinsinger (world business); Winter Nie (operations); Toshi Shibano (world business); Michael Moffet (finance).

APPLICANT TIPS

The exceptionally high acceptance rate at Thunderbird—80 percent—can be both deceiving and misleading, according to Director of Admissions Judy Johnson. "There's a lot of preselection that goes on," she explains. Some 60 percent of applicants choose to apply only to Thunderbird and nowhere else. Only if you have the international experience and academic background to back it up would you even want to start considering Thunderbird a safety school.

Johnson looks for the equivalent of a B or better in undergraduate studies. Work experience needs to demonstrate increasing responsibilities and significant signs of leadership. Preference is definitely given to candidates who have international work experience. "We're looking for someone who lived outside their culture and had to buy bread at the local store," says Johnson.

Thunderbird accepts new students every semester and on a rolling basis, so you can apply year round. But, if you want to apply for financial aid, then your application needs to be in by February 15. Even if aid isn't a consideration, Johnson recommends not waiting too long to get your application in the running. "Apply as early as possible. Once you're accepted, there's a lot to do before coming here and lots of loose ends that have to be tied up."

Interviews are not required at Thunderbird, but can be arranged with either the admissions department or alums around the world. "An interview doesn't hold a great deal of weight in the admissions process unless there has been an absolute no somewhere along the line," says Johnson. Still, she encourages applicants to visit the campus. "You can get a good sense of what Thunderbird is all about." Call first to find out what days walking tours of the 87-acre campus are being offered. You'll also get a free lunch in the school's dining hall and can attend an information session with the admissions office.

Fraudulent documents recently have become more of a problem in applications. The admissions department does do random checks. On occasion, when Johnson sends a thank-you note to a recommender, she will get a call from the person saying that he or she never wrote such a letter. Overseas school records can also be a problem. "We'll make a call and learn that the school doesn't even exist," says Johnson. "So, we just want to make sure that everything matches." Johnson suggests asking your recommenders to enclose a business card and to remind them to write their letters on letterhead.

THUNDERBIRD MBAs SOUND OFF

Thunderbird stands out from other MBA programs/schools because of its unique international environment. The students, faculty, staff and alumni represent hundreds of countries, languages and cultures. This international aspect of the program and of the school truly enhances the learning experience, and sets Thunderbird apart from all other schools.

I feel that the school's tuition fees are excessive and have not been commensurate to the value added received by the students, both relating to the school's reputation and the available campus facilities.

Fall 2000 through spring 2002 have been years of big change for Thunderbird. The school introduced a new curriculum, tweaked it, tweaked it again, and finally settled for creating a new degree. The change process has had an extremely negative impact on my impression of the school and my experience at Thunderbird. Quite frankly, I never knew where I stood in terms of academic requirements that I would need to meet in order to graduate. I can tell, however, that the new incoming class of students views the curriculum in a much more positive light. I also believe that the new, more rigid, lock-step program will improve the general quality of the graduating students. Like it or not, every student will be well grounded.

Thunderbird has done an excellent job of staying on the cutting edge of international management studies, and it continues to set the standard in this field. The tripartite curriculum of international business, international studies, and language and the focus on "international" are the "life blood" of the school. People who are serious about an international career should definitely look at Thunderbird.

Thunderbird has the pieces in place to have an outstanding program, but the administration lacks vision and customer orientation. The admission rates must come down in order to provide students a better in-class experience.

UNIVERSITY
OF
CALIFORNIA
AT IRVINE

UNIVERSITY OF CALIFORNIA AT IRVINE

Graduate School of Management
Irvine, California 92697
E-mail address: gsm-mba@uci.edu
Web site address: www.gsm.uci.edu

Enrollment: 232
Women: 29%
Non-U.S.: 24%
Minority: 3%
Part-time: 0
Average age: 29
Applicants accepted: 31%
Median starting pay: $72,000

Annual tuition and fees:
 resident—$11,648
 nonresident—$22,780
Estimated annual budget: $30,890
Average GMAT score: 682
Average months of work
 experience: 62
Accepted applicants enrolled: 51%

Teaching methods: case study 40%, experiential learning 2%, lecture 33%, simulations 5%, team projects 20%

If you listen closely on the campus of the University of California at Irvine, there is an unmistakable roar coming from inside the walls of the school's Graduate School of Management. Why, you ask? Because when Interim Dean Jone Pearce took office in June of 2002, she named Professor Mary Gilley vice dean for academic affairs and Professor Joanna Ho vice dean for educational programs, thus appointing women to each of the top administrative posts. "This could be the first time a coed business school was headed by a triumvirate of women," Pearce says.

Pearce was named interim dean after David Blake left the position after the 2001–2002 session. A member of the human resources management department at Irvine since 1979, Pearce knows a thing or two about the school, and, while she doesn't see herself in the position for long, she likes the change of scenery. "For one year it is an interesting learning experience, that's for sure," she says. "And while I'm here, I get to make all the decisions!" Though a professor by trade, Pearce has been the associate dean of the school on three separate occasions, so she is more than qualified to hold the position while Irvine is searching for a new leader.

Leadership is not the only thing that has changed at Irvine in the past few years. With the Internet bust and the demise in the wealth of Silicon Valley, the school has had to reconsider its focus on technology. Surprisingly, according to 2002 grads, the focus on e-business has become nonexistent in comparison to other MBA programs, ranking Irvine second to last. But the fact that changes are taking place does not mean that technology is not still a very important part of the program;

in actuality, the technology initiatives at Irvine are what separate the school from others. In 1996, the school introduced the Information Technology for Management (ITM) approach to the full-time program, and since then, ITM has been refined and expanded into the well-oiled machine it is today. Put simply, the ITM approach gives students the hands-on experience with current technologies that is imperative for business decision making. With this in mind, such technologies have been intertwined into the core curriculum as much as possible. "A lot of students come to Irvine because they are intrigued by the information technology piece," says Pearce. "It's a major part of our curriculum, and it is something that sets us apart and makes our program special."

To standardize the ITM approach, the school recommends that students purchase a specific laptop computer—and, to sweeten the deal, students are given a $500 tuition waiver when they purchase the laptop. Standardizing laptops throughout the student body (nearly 95 percent of the class of 2004 had the recommended computer) means students are able to utilize software licenses paid for by the university for programs including MS Office Professional and Microsoft Exchange. This makes it possible for the school's designed software image to be installed on each of the computers so that students can access coursework and other assignments via the network. All classrooms and public spaces in the school's main building are wired, and an extensive high-speed wireless network is also in place.

But even with such time-saving technological facilities, there's no escaping the rigors of the 92-unit-over-two-year workload, requiring a minimum of 12 units in ITM labs in which you must use commercially available software to solve problems. If you take the Operation Management Lab, for instance, you might design the logistical support for a business using SAP R/3 to assess the relationship of such factors as in-store sales, inventory, and distribution centers.

In the Marketing Lab, you'd be using Claritas software to determine the best locations for stores. In the Lincoln Mercury ITM Lab in Marketing, you use geographical information systems (GISs) such as MapInfo, census data, and other database applications to conduct market analyses and sales forecasts for products and services. But don't think that the ITM focus is solely on the use of technology. For instance, in the Social and Political Implications of IT elective, you are exposed to issues that are at the forefront of the industry, such as the digital divide, intellectual property, and taxation of e-commerce.

For the most part, 2002 grads feel that the IT focus is valuable and worthwhile (grads ranked the program in the top four in terms of technology), but there are some gripes from students about how it could be better integrated into the program. Says one grad, "I would like to have seen more material related to the successful and unsuccessful application of technology in a diverse array of companies, as opposed to focusing on pure technology companies for the majority of the program."

Though Silicon Valley may be a ghost town, Irvine's location in Southern California's so-called Tech Coast region makes it possible for MBAs to gain a great deal of exposure to some of the top tech companies in the world, in a wide range of fields from high-tech entertainment to telecommunications and biotech. In fact, Orange County, where Irvine is located, is home to such companies as America Online, Cisco Systems, Broadcom, Conexant Systems, and Quest Software. Orange County is also home to companies not known for their high-tech focus, such as Disney, Taco Bell, PacifiCare Health Systems, and Lincoln Mercury. Many 2002 grads say that the connections they were able to make from these companies alone make Irvine well worth the time and money invested into the program. Says one 2002 grad, "The networking opportunities in the Orange County area alone are insane!"

Entrepreneurship is still a major piece of the Irvine MBA. The Entrepreneurship Group is the largest student group in the MBA program, and a good number of students come to Irvine with plans to start a business when they graduate. According to Dean Pearce, to better reach out to these students, the school is currently planning a center for entrepreneurship innovation, which will combine the IT parts of the program with entrepreneurship elements that before were separate entities. With the center in place, the hope is that Irvine will be able to advertise itself better to students interested in such endeavors. "Because we are a University of California school, we haven't done as much in terms of marketing as private schools do," says Pearce. "Hopefully, with the center, we will be able to do a better job of letting people know what we are doing here."

Besides the ITM requirements, students are also required to take an international course so that they can get a feel for the globalization of the business world. Irvine also offers various options for study abroad through the International Exchange Program (IEP). The school has recently partnered with National University in Singapore and the Chinese European International Business School to provide students with additional exchange possibilities in Asia and to expand the school's network of contacts on that continent. Students can also travel to Latin America, Mexico, or Europe, depending on the semester they choose to go abroad. Students study abroad in the fall quarter of the second year of the program, receiving up to 16 units of elective credit toward their degree for approved coursework taken at the host institution. If studying abroad does not appeal, students can take an upper- or graduate-level international course in another school at Irvine or another UC campus, pending approval.

All MBAs are encouraged to participate in the ThinkTank/GSM-UCI Campus-Wide Business Plan Competition, supported jointly by the school as ThinkTank. Students from all schools and programs, both undergraduate and graduate, can now enter this event, which was previously open only to MBAs. In the competition, students present viable business plans and presentations to a panel of judges. The best idea wins a $50,000 business development award, and the runner-up receives a $10,000 award, both provided by a donation from ThinkTank.

During your first year at Irvine, you are assigned to a section of students with whom you will take your 12 required core courses, which range from Statistics for Management and Financial Accounting to Principles of Marketing and Organizational Analysis. In the spring quarter, you have room for one elective course (the other eight are taken in the second year). If you have completed substantial undergraduate work in a particular area, you can petition to waive a related required course, provided you replace it with another course. With the exception of two core courses, your second year at Irvine is made up of electives and one ITM lab.

If you are looking to find employment at a tech company or want to learn more about IT and how it works in business, Irvine is a good choice. If your goals are less technology oriented or you do not see yourself taking up residence in Southern California, you may want to think twice about Irvine. While the school brings in a good number of recruiters, the vast majority are from tech companies or are local corporations. According to one 2002 grad, "The school is well known on the West Coast, but its national reputation needs some work." One thing the school has done to attract a broader range of recruiters is sponsoring a golf event, teaming recruiters up with students looking for jobs. "We felt like the golf event was a good way to bring recruiters in and help our students get some face time with them in a different and more social environment then they are used to," says Dennis Grindle, career services director.

After hearing complaints from students for nearly five years about cramped facilities and classrooms overflowing with students, in 2001 the school opened the Multi-Purpose Administrative and Academic building directly across the street from the existing business school. The building is home to two classrooms for the B-school and offices for Student Services and the Center for Leadership Development, among others. Also in 2001, the Center for Leadership Development launched the Social Responsibility Initiative, which encourages MBAs to give back to the community while fostering the importance of corporate and personal responsibility by grouping teams of students with not-for-profit organizations on a project-by-project basis. The projects promote "experiential learning and cultivate leadership skills while supplementing classroom instruction."

There are a good number of housing options both on and off campus at Irvine. There are the typical dorms set aside for MBAs, as well as studios, units with one to three bedrooms, and townhouses. Amenities include child care centers, recreation rooms, a park, data connections to the Internet, free parking, and much more. Residents of campus housing represent every continent and practically every state in the United States. If you would like some escape from campus life, there are also a number of apartment complexes close to campus.

2002 grads ranked Irvine near the bottom of the pack in most areas; however, grads feel confident in the skills they have learned to start their own businesses and placed the program near the top in the computer and managerial skills they have picked up. Students applaud the accessibility of faculty and the fact that faculty members are very willing to help students who are interested in starting their own business. Also, the fact that students and faculty are familiar with each other put teamwork initiatives and the invaluable "personal touch" at the forefront of the program.

In all, the MBAs here are a tightly knit group. They meet every Thursday for happy hour, which is usually held in the Multi-Purpose Room (MPR) of the B-school or the on-campus pub. Students can participate in a wide variety of extracurricular activities, including clubs that highlight a range of interests from consulting to golf. Irvine is halfway between Los Angeles and San Diego (about 45 minutes away from each city), and there are plenty of restaurants, bars, movie theaters, and shopping malls near the school. Even though Irvine does not have the most recognized sports programs in the nation, there are the Anteater (that's right, the school's mascot is an anteater) faithful who pride themselves on supporting their beloved teams. The Steelhead Brewery, with its high ceilings and wingback chairs, is the local favorite among B-school students. When not in class, MBAs take advantage of Southern California's sunny climate to participate in a host of outdoor sports, including rollerblading, hiking, and mountain biking. The school's proximity to beaches makes it a great place for those who love surfing and diving.

PLACEMENT DETAILS

The Irvine MBA program is small, with around 120 students per class, and it is also very homogeneous, with 92 percent of the student body coming from the western United States. Nearly 72 percent of 2002 grads remained on the West Coast after graduation. The employment numbers for the class of 2002 were nothing short of dismal, with only 41 percent receiving a job offer by graduation and only 56 percent receiving an offer three months after graduating. Surprisingly, very few students complained about lack of support from career services, understanding that it was not the office's fault for the lack of jobs. However, no matter how bad the economy, percentages this low are staggering.

According to Director of Career Services Randy Williams, the office opens a lot of doors to students, but does not guarantee that MBAs are going to have a job hand-delivered to them. "It's a partnership between us and them. Those who accept that partnership are successful, those who are waiting for someone to hand them something, are going to be disappointed," he says.

For those students finding jobs, the starting pay packages increased considerably in comparison to 2000. In 2000, the median starting pay was $76,000; in 2002, the number was $96,000.

TOP HIRES

ARES Corporation (3); Deloitte & Touche Consulting (2); Conexant (2).

OUTSTANDING FACULTY

Connie Pechmann (marketing); Brad Killaly (strategy); Peter Navarro (economics); Rajeev Tyagi (marketing); James Wallace (accounting); Vijay Gurbaxani (information technology).

APPLICANT TIPS

Because the program is so small, Irvine expects its students to be full, participating members of the community. Those who are not willing to give something back to the community need not apply. "If you have a larger program, you have room for people who sort of sit in the back row and just take stuff in and don't really contribute," says Ann Scott, director of programming and admissions. "We don't really have room for those folks."

Interviews are required at Irvine, and usually come at the request of the school. In the past, interviews were laid-back and formatted, not really delving into the kind of person the interviewee was. Now, the process is more behavioral. Explains Scott, "We decided, in looking at what was important to us in candidates, that we needed to focus more on examples from past experiences that reflect leadership or problem

solving. So what had been slightly looser interviews have become more focused. We are now looking for some particular things."

Applicants at Irvine tend to have strong quantitative skills and at least some work experience (96 percent of the class of 2004 had at least one year of work experience).

UC IRVINE MBAs SOUND OFF

I feel that the quality of a small program can't be judged by the number of classes, but the experiences and stories of the students within the school. I've met people at this school that I would never have had the chance to meet elsewhere, people from all walks of life who wanted to improve their careers, try something new, or hone their existing financial, marketing, or strategic skills. By having the chance to meet everyone in my class, interact closely with a small but vibrant group of faculty, and get involved at all levels of the school's planning, I feel I've gotten a rewarding and healthy experience. I definitely don't feel like a number, or like a cog in a wheel designed only to write and review business cases.

Due to the weak earnings of the technology-related firms and sluggish economy, it has been a tough year for my fellow classmates to find a favorable job so far. However, they are all optimistic and confident that they will find their career path soon. I believe this is because many are satisfied with the quality of learning at the school, and there will be great demand in the near future for managers who can manage the companies in IT-related industry and/or lead the technology-driven changes in the traditional firms.

Overall the MBA program was worthwhile and challenging. However, the constant focus on grades rather than learning undermines the purpose of the program. The MBA experience should be about expanding the knowledge base of future executives, and not encouraging them to play the grade game. With regard to the school's IT focus, IT does not only concern technology companies, it affects all companies and their role in the twenty-first-century business environment. I would have liked to see more material related to the successful (and unsuccessful) application of technology in a diverse array of companies, as opposed to focusing on pure technology companies for the majority of the program.

I started a business during my first year in the program. UCI's professors were always enthusiastic and willing to offer their assistance and expertise on various topics. They were very encouraging and the core and elective classes equipped me with the tools to make intelligent business decisions in my daily life as an entrepreneur. Additionally, I used my business for many class projects and also received great feedback from my fellow classmates. One of the best resources at UCI has been the awesome people (professors, classmates, administration). I am very pleased with the education that I received at UCI.

UNIVERSITY
OF ILLINOIS
AT URBANA-
CHAMPAIGN

UNIVERSITY OF ILLINOIS AT URBANA-CHAMPAIGN

College of Commerce and Business Administration
415 David Kinley Hall, MC-706
1407 West Gregory Drive
Urbana, Illinois 61801
E-mail address: mba@uiuc.edu
Web site address: www.mba.uiuc.edu/

Enrollment: 387
Women: 29%
Non-U.S.: 47%
Minority: 7%
Part-time: 0
Average age: 26
Applicants accepted: 31%
Median starting pay: $66,000

Annual tuition and fees:
  resident—$15,276
  nonresident—$24,200
Estimated annual budget: $26,866
Average GMAT score: 640
Average months of work
  experience: 48
Accepted applicants enrolled: 46%

Teaching methods: case study 28%, experiential learning 10%, lecture 28%, simulations 4%, team projects 27%, other 3%

In 2001, Dean Avijit Ghosh moved halfway across the country to take up his new position as dean of the University of Illinois at Urbana-Champaign's B-school. Since arriving in the middle of the prairie from New York University's Leonard N. Stern School of Business, Ghosh has launched a series of innovative initiatives, most of which reflect his philosophy that technology management is the way of the future. "Technology, innovative management, and entrepreneurship are what industries need today," he says. For starters, the B-school established the KPMG/UIUC Business Measurement Research Program and the Office for the Study of Private Equity and Entrepreneurial Finance, both of which offer opportunities for collaboration with the MBA program. And, in the spring of 2002, the B-school started the Center for Enterprise Development (CED), fully run and staffed by MBAs who provide their consulting services to companies working in the University's Research Park and Incubator and regional start-ups. Not to mention that the programs available through the Office for Strategic Business Initiatives remain firmly planted at the core of the hands-on learning experience. On the horizon for 2003 is breaking ground for a new building.

Ghosh also makes it a point to have daily contact with the students—that's why you might even have him as a professor for either marketing strategy or entrepreneurship courses. Behind the scenes, faculty members have also taken giant strides in their efforts to become more actively involved with the students. For starters, they created a new curriculum review committee, and they're already planning and developing new electives to strengthen the B-school's commitment to technology management. Outside of the classroom, it's not rare to find the faculty and students mingling. One professor, Nick Petruzzi, even has his students and their families over every year to join his family for Thanksgiving.

With the technology thread in mind, the B-school introduced a new technology management concentration and added technology-oriented electives as well. The curriculum follows a seven-week-long modular plan with one-week interim periods. In the first seven weeks, you're introduced to the foundations of business in integrated modules. During the first module, you'll take courses in microeconomics, finance, marketing, decision making or statistics, accounting, and communications. This module is then followed by a one-week applied business perspective (ABP) seminar, a case study in which teams develop and present a strategic plan for a focal company, which is increasingly becoming more popular among the students. Students have three days to solve the problem and present their recommendations, financials, and cost-benefit analysis to a panel of faculty and community business leaders. The added bonus programs during the interim are what make this school unique, says economics professor Larry DeBrock. During the second seven-week module, you'll learn about designing and managing business processes, covering accounting, finance, statistics, processes, and organizational theory. Communication and teamwork skills are also heavily emphasized throughout this semester.

The second semester starts with the third module, which focuses on understanding how to identify and interact with a company's stakeholders. During the interim, you'll participate in Global Tycoon, a computer simulation in which teams of students compete against each other in a pseudo-marketplace. At the end of the exercise, a panel of executives and experts evaluates each team's performance and presentation. In the fourth module, you'll study the management of change in addition to selecting from a menu of electives that include risk analysis, Internet strategy, technology commercialization, marketing finance, and operations. By the time you reach your second year, you'll choose a specialization. The B-school offers three professional tracks, including finance, marketing, and information technology. All MBAs are required to concentrate in a specific area, of which finance still ranks as the most popular.

Students must have a course in calculus prior to enrolling at Illinois's B-school, so the school offers a math workshop in August, before the first semester begins. There's also an economics workshop that beefs up students' ability to perform microeconomic analysis. For a $100 fee per workshop, incoming students brush up on their quant skills before tackling the books.

Students praise the curriculum's hands-on approach to learning. The opportunities offered through the Office for Strategic Business Initiatives (OSBI) remain among students' favorites. MBAs work as consultants and focus their attention on technology commercialization, especially on campus, says Professor DeBrock. Because of the strength of the engineering program on campus, the management of intellectual property rights has become important. Through OSBI's programs, MBAs can use the tools they're getting in the classroom and solve real-life problems, he adds. The B-school also offers two weeklong seminars in applied business perspectives and the optional Internship Development Project. And it doesn't stop there. There are even more opportunities to gain experience outside the classroom, including the Kauffman Entrepreneurship Internship Program, which provides students with entrepreneurial training. MBAs are also involved in projects with a marketing aspect at the Food & Brand Lab, a nationally recognized research center focused on gaining a better understanding of consumers and how they relate to foods and packaged foods.

You can also pursue a joint degree in one of 12 areas—accounting science, architecture, civil and environmental engineering, computer science, education, human resource development, electrical engineering, industrial engineering, journalism, law, mechanical engineering, or medicine.

If the itch to travel gets to you, during your second year, you can earn credit toward your degree while spending a semester abroad at any one of 11 world-class educational institutions including the Rotterdam School of Management (Netherlands), the Asian Institute of Management (Philippines), and ESADE (Spain). Special summer programs are also available at Brazil's University of São Paulo and through the Manchester Business School in the UK.

A perk of attending a Big Ten school is that it's home to numerous varsity sports, with football and basketball getting most of the attention. The B-school sits on the 1500-acre Illinois campus. If you're looking for ways to spend your free time, there are plenty of things to see and do around town and on campus. For those into Big Ten sports, you can catch a game and root for the Fighting Illini. If music or theatre is your thing, you'll want to check out the performances at the Krannert Center. If that's still not enough, you can always take a road trip to Chicago, St. Louis, or Indianapolis to take in the sights—all three are within 180 miles of campus.

PLACEMENT DETAILS

In the face of a grim market, the career services office turned to small and medium-size companies that hadn't previously recruited. Mary Mille, associate dean of the MBA program, notes that though the career services staff members continue to focus on the big recruiters, such as Kraft, Lucent, and Procter & Gamble, they're paying extra-close attention to the smaller companies. And, she adds, they're perfectly placed because these companies tend to be in the Midwest.

A new initiative rolled out for the 2001–2002 school year is Sigma Six. Six to eight students are paired with a staff member at the B-school, and they meet once a week to focus on the job search. Though students weren't thrilled about being required to meet once a week, after graduation they said it was an overall boon to have that extra support from students and staff. Miller adds that a professional skills development course is also now required for the incoming class. The course helps stduents brush up on their skills through mock interviews conducted mostly by alumni, polishing resumes, mock career fairs, and perfecting a 10-second elevator pitch. For international students, there are special sessions that address the specific problems they face in terms of knowing how to work with regulations that may restrict their job search. Though Miller notes she wasn't as well prepared as she would have liked to have been for the down economy, she hopes to implement programs to anticipate a rough job hunt rather than just react to it.

TOP HIRES

Guidant (6); IBM (6); United Technologies (5); Whirlpool (4); Owens Corning (4); General Electric (4); Procter & Gamble (3); Air Products and Chemicals (3); Capital One (3).

OUTSTANDING FACULTY

Nick Petruzzi (operations); Brian Wansink (operations); Mike Sandretto (accounting); Don Kleinmuntz (business administration).

APPLICANT TIPS

"We want business leaders of the future," says Associate Dean Mary Miller. With this in mind, the biggest change in the admissions application is in the interviewing process. In the past, very few candidates were admitted with an interview, Miller says. According to her, one of the biggest pieces of feedback she's received from recruiters is that communication and interpersonal skills are crucial. So in 2002 she started an initiative to interview more candidates. Though it will remain on an invitation-only basis, Miller says eventually she hopes to interview all admitted students.

The emphasis on technology management makes the Illinois B-school unique, Miller says. "We're looking for people who have a lot of interest in managing technology and who understand the interplay between technology and communications," she adds. Though there is no minimum work experience, the average admitted student has four years.

Miller says the biggest mistake applicants make is on their essays and recommendations. She advises students to do their research and know how an Illinois MBA can help them reach their professional goals. Also, take your recommendations seriously and ask someone who actually knows you and your work capabilities well to be your reference, she adds. "We want targeted, specific recommendations from someone who can really speak to the strengths and weakness of the individual."

ILLINOIS MBAs SOUND OFF

I really feel this program has many very strong assets; however, it also has several problems as well, mostly on the administrative end. The new leadership within this program has made some very encouraging promises, and based upon their past experiences they have the capability to succeed. Illinois will be a good program to keep an eye on for the next few years.

I believe that the Illinois MBA Program is full of potential and should be viewed as a top-tier program. However, with all business schools, there is room for improvement (e.g., own building). Overall, I am proud to be a graduate from Illinois, and I expect to see the MBA program regain its top 30 ranking within the next four years now that Dean Miller has arrived.

The turnover in the administration has been very high in the past two years. At times, the students lack confidence in the administration's ability to effectively run the program. In addition, there is often a lack of communication between the administrators and the students. There tends to be many rumors circulating at any given time, which could be dispelled if communication was better. On a positive note, the OSBI program is unique and gives this program an advantage. The ability for a young MBA like myself to get some real-world experience while in school is a real asset.

The University of Illinois at Urbana-Champaign has a lot of academic as well as cultural resources. Students can make the most of these university experiences beyond the MBA program.

This program is a great mix of diversity, a great learning opportunity to broaden your horizon and will help you transform your personality to a level you cannot imagine.

UNIVERSITY OF IOWA

UNIVERSITY OF IOWA

Henry B. Tippie College of Business
108 John Pappajohn Business Building
Suite C140
Iowa City, Iowa 52242-1000
E-mail address: www.biz.uiowa.edu/mba
Web site address: www.biz.uiowa.edu

Enrollment: 152
Women: 22%
Non-U.S.: 44%
Minority: 3%
Part-time: 747
Average age: 27
Applicants accepted: 33%
Median starting pay: $75,000

Annual tuition and fees:
  resident—$9,899
  nonresident—$18,211
Estimated annual budget: $25,000
Average GMAT score: 638
Average months of work
  experience: 40
Accepted applicants enrolled: 41%

Teaching methods: case study 35%, experiential learning 5%, lecture 30%, simulations 5%, team projects 25%

At the University of Iowa's Tippie School of Management, saying people are committed is an understatement. Look around and you'll see faculty that have been at the school for years. Graduates tend to stay at their jobs for longer periods as well. Even Dean Gary Fethke has stuck around for the long haul. Not only has he served as the dean of the B-school for 10 years, but before that he was a member of the faculty for 17 years, and even before that he attended Iowa as an undergraduate. What makes the school so special? According to Fethke, an unsuspected answer is the reason—the location. That's right: it may not be New York City or Chicago, but Iowa City has a lot more to offer than just wide open space. Being in the cornfields virtually in the middle of nowhere pushes you to work extra hard in reaching out and making connections, Fethke says. "Because of our location, we have got to be good at relationship building," he adds.

This philosophy extends into every move Fethke makes at the B-school. According to Fethke, he strives to outwardly focus on the business community, both listening to and welcoming people and their ideas. This comes into play in every facet from curriculum changes to career services to the alumni network: everything revolves around Fethke's notion of regularly interacting with the community. This focus on communication, coupled with the small environment (just over 100 new MBAs each year; low tuition; a state-of-the-art building built in 1993; and a Big Ten college town feel) makes this B-school a hot contender for MBA hopefuls.

One way the school has homed in on focusing the curriculum is through strengthening the different areas of concentration. Finance has been the track most students tend to flock to, although marketing is gaining steam as of late. Fethke says he would also like to see the entrepreneurial program and the management information systems area further develop and flourish in years to come. In 1998, the curriculum went through a drastic overhaul. Now, you'll enjoy a more streamlined core that allows you to take electives before the end of your first year, which will come into play especially when applying for an increasingly important summer internship. You'll also have the option of selecting from nine concentration tracks. During your first year, you'll take seven required courses in the fall—Marketing Management, Managerial Economics, Corporate Financial Reporting, Data and Decisions, and Managerial Finance. Come spring, you'll take two remaining required courses (Organizational Behavior and Operations Management) along with a mix of electives. You'll have the opportunity to dive right into your concentration and take three advanced courses as well. When you return for your second year, the last requirement you'll have left is the capstone, team-taught integrative course in strategic management and business policy. As part of a student team, you'll undertake cases involving companies such as Baxter International, John Deere, and Pier One Imports, with visiting executives from the companies leading some discussions. The goal is to present you with a real-life situation giving you a hands-on opportunity to develop your own strategies and solutions.

At Tippie, you'll choose from among the list of concentration tracks that includes accounting, entrepreneurship, finance, human resources and organizational consulting, marketing, operations management, product development and management, and management information systems. If these concentrations don't satisfy your interests, you can design your own, with administrative approval. Or you can also pursue a dual degree in one of five areas—law, management information systems, hospital administration, nursing, or library and information systems. You're also encouraged to look beyond the B-school and to the university at large to pursue other electives even if you don't decide to follow the dual degree route. A plus side to the small size of the school, he adds, is that it's easier to coordinate across schedules and syllabi with professors. Students say their faculty here is top-notch. Two reasons Professor Tom Gruca gives are the stability and integration of the core faculty. "We work closely together," Gruca says. "When I'm covering things in my marketing class, I can refer to things they've just covered in accounting or are about to cover in finance. It's about the holistic side of business."

Take a look beyond the Tippie School and you'll find a broad selection of university-wide research centers that will provide you with a wealth of additional resources right at your fingertips. MBAs take full advantage of the John Pappajohn Entrepreneurial Center, the Iowa Institute of International Business, and the Iowa Electronic Markets, to name a few. The Entrepreneurial Center has been gaining more attention from students as of late, giving MBAs the opportunity to explore the process of identifying opportunities and leading high-growth companies. The center also houses two business competitions: the fledgling Pappajohn New Venture Business Plan Competition, which started in 2000 and awards three $5000 prizes to the top teams; and the Merle Volding Business Plan Competition, which awards two $5000 grant awards in seed money to put toward starting up a company.

Through the Iowa Institute of International Business, you'll be able to further broaden your knowledge and strengthen your skills in the international arena by participating in on-campus cultural events like the International Thanksgiving Dinner and Diwali or by venturing off campus to study abroad. As an MBA, you'll also have the opportunity to go abroad. Students especially take their winter intersession time to visit international business centers such as London, Paris, and Brazil. You can study in places like Austria, Germany, Hungary, The Netherlands, and Greece. But you can only do so during the first semester of your second year. The university houses one of the premier writing programs in the nation, the Iowa Writers Workshop, so you'll be surrounded by one of the country's best selections of used and new bookstores in addition to having the opportunity to attend authors' readings on campus, which are usually free.

Tippie students tend to be highly involved in the school, and not just in extracurricular activities. The small size makes for a collaborative nature that permeates all facets. For example, there's at least one student per every faculty committee. Some of the more popular student groups include the MBA Association, the Graduate Marketing Association, and Net-Impact. New on the roster in 2002 were the Women in Business Association, which has been restarted, and the Leadership Association, as leadership has piqued students' interests as of late. Student Services Director Jeff Emrich says students are tending toward joining more professionally themed clubs as well as taking up more leadership opportunities. Through their clubs, students also take the lead in organizing forums that are among the school's most successful and well attended. They also make corporate visits to nearby cities including Chicago and Minneapolis. Their involvement stretches across campus borders as well. The MBA Association regularly participates in community service activities such as serving meals at a nearby soup kitchen and raising money for the Big Brothers Big Sisters program.

The Iowa City campus sits on a bluff that overlooks the Iowa River. Housing can run up to $500 for a one-bedroom apartment—not so bad elsewhere, but a bit pricey by Iowa terms.

About 90 percent of MBAs live off campus, in apartment complexes or charming Victorian homes that have been divided into individual apartments. Fall and spring evenings are filled with music coming from talented guitarists and pianists that play along a pedestrian mall, an MBA gathering hot spot. Thursday nights you'll find MBAs at the Airliner, a local pub owned by former NBA player Brad Lohaus. And, although Iowa City may be a bit out of the way, students at Tippie tend to love the campus environment and the city, too. The locale also means students are very involved on campus, Professor Gruca says. Moreover, the small size makes it easier for the school to respond to students' needs. In 2000, for example, the school added 200 computers and upgraded computer/video in laboratories and classrooms. Gruca also adds that the university is really the only game in town. Because of this, quality market leaders like John Deere and Maytag tend to work with Tippie on a regular basis. He says the location is a definite boon for students because it facilitates professors' ability to make themselves available to students. "I live five miles away from campus, as do most professors," Gruca says. "We're in the middle of nowhere. There's nowhere for us to run and hide!"

PLACEMENT DETAILS

According to Career Services Director Kathie Decker, the Tippie School takes a rather unique approach to post-MBA placement. "What we've done is use an executive search model, or brokering model," she explains. This means Decker strives to work with students and recruiting companies to place the students on a one-on-one basis. The small size helps, she says. "We know our students well, we know our employers well, so we know the right fit."

The Tippie School requires that all first-years take a competitive prep class in their first semester. The noncredit course covers the basic job-hunting skills, such as letter and resume writing, as well as practice with case-based interviews. For international students, there's an option to take a higher-level business language course as well.

When it comes to working with corporate recruiters, Decker says she tries to make it as easy as possible for them. For example, if they can't make it to campus, the school will bring the students to them through the "Tippie Tour" program that takes students to interview on location.

The most important piece of advice Decker doles out to her students is to remember that "you're just one person looking for one job." Decker focuses on looking for the right fit. "In the end, that's what sells," she adds.

TOP HIRES

Kimberly-Clark (5); General Electric (3); NCS Pearson (2).

OUTSTANDING FACULTY

Matthew Billett (finance); Roy Suddaby (organization management); Baba Shiv (marketing); Thomas Gruca (marketing).

APPLICANT TIPS

If you're looking to get into the Tippie School of Management, it's important to have an idea of what you want to do post-MBA and how a Tippie MBA specifically can help get you there, says Director of Admissions Mary Spreen. "I like to see that people can articulate a certain vision for their career," she adds. Moreover, what she's looking for is demonstrated potential to be successful in a professional environment. What does that mean? Spreen and the admissions committee consider GMAT scores and under-

graduate transcripts as the easiest concrete indicator of a candidate's potential success in the program. She also evaluates what you've accomplished thus far and your leadership potential. So, she's keeping an eye out for demonstrated initiative, previous leadership experiences, extracurricular activities, and any community involvement after your undergraduate career.

Communication abilities also top Spreen's list of key components in a successful application. For this, she'll closely review essays to measure your ability to communicate in a professional manner. That also means following directions. "If we suggest one page, stick to it," she says. "When people give me a five-page essay, that's not necessarily positive. I'm looking for someone to answer our question in a concise, professional manner." Spreen will also use your interview as another measure of communication abilities. They're not a required component of the application; however, an interview is required before an admissions offer is made.

Though there's no experience minimum, Spreen says ideal candidates have two to three years under their belt. That's usually the amount of time needed in order for a candidate to get the level of experience necessary to demonstrate ability to succeed in a professional environment. If you're considering eventually applying to B-school, she says, take full advantage of any opportunities offered at your workplace. Spreen advises: "Take initiative, volunteer to take on projects, learn new things, and go the extra mile to get additional experience that may not be in the routine path."

TIPPIE MBAs SOUND OFF

The biggest ROI for me from the program is the fact that I am on a first-name basis with all the students in my program. The quality of students and faculty in the program is simply phenomenal and I am sure that these people will prove to be my best contacts in the business world tomorrow.

The associate dean is extremely responsive to students' concerns. The professors are extremely accessible. The team projects are extensive and effective. The atmosphere is professional and enjoyable. The finance department is especially strong. The students are extremely helpful—there is very little, if any, negative competition in this program. Overall, it has been an incredible experience. I would recommend this program to anyone.

Iowa is a great school. However, it seems not enough people know this. The career services department and our overall alumni relations are very, very poor, which leads to our less than stellar reputation with recruiters and makes it very difficult for investment-oriented students to find jobs.

Iowa's Tippie School does an absolutely outstanding job of supporting each student as an individual. The student services and career services staff in particular do an amazing, around-the-clock there-for-you job.

UNIVERSITY OF MINNESOTA, TWIN CITIES

Carlson School of Management
2-210 Carlson School of Management
321 19th Avenue South
Minneapolis, Minnesota 55455
E-mail address: full-timembrainfo@csom.umn.edu
Web site address: http://carlsonschool.umn.edu

Enrollment: 240
Women: 27%
Non-U.S.: 29%
Minority: 4%
Part-time: 0
Average age: 29
Applicants accepted: 40%
Median starting pay: $76,500

Annual tuition and fees:
   resident—$19,000
   nonresident—$26,000
Estimated annual budget: $40,800
Average GMAT score: 645
Average months of work
   experience: 66
Accepted applicants enrolled: 42%

Teaching methods: case study 25%, distance learning 5%, experiential learning 25%, lecture 25%, simulations 5%, team projects 10%, other 5%

Larry Benveniste never really planned on becoming the dean of the Carlson School of Business at the University of Minnesota. It just sort of happened, he says. A member of the school's faculty since 1996, he was on the search committee for a new dean after David S. Kidwell stepped down. During the search, Benveniste was appointed interim dean. In the summer of 2001, his title became permanent.

Despite his less than driven route to the deanship, Benveniste still has big plans for the school. It isn't good enough for Carlson to be known as a leading Midwest business school, he says. His goal is much grander than that: to grow the school into a leading national business school. Benveniste plans on doing this by distinguishing the full-time MBA program with a number of new offerings, enhancing the current faculty with nationally known professors, and strengthening the undergraduate business program. He would also like to see the school grow in size over the next few years from its current 128 students per class to about 180. "We're starting with a great base, and we're going to put that into a great program," says Benveniste.

One way Benveniste plans to distinguish the school is through its "enterprise offerings." Currently, there are three: Carlson Ventures, Carlson Consulting, and Carlson Funds. In 2004, the school plans to launch a fourth: Carlson Branding. Currently, about 60 percent of students participate in the optional enterprise programs. "They're going gangbusters," says Benveniste, a strong proponent of the hands-on experience the enterprise classes provide. Through them, students have a chance to get out of the classroom and manage school funds or work on consulting projects with outside firms.

Before getting to the enterprise program, you must first pass through a series of core courses in the fall semester of your first year. These include Financial Accounting, Statistics, Operations, Information Management, Finance, Marketing, Strategy, and Group Dynamics and Leadership. In addition, you will participate in a 12-hour career management course. This load might sound like a heavy load, but consider yourself lucky; this core is half the size it was before 1999, when it was last overhauled.

During your spring semester, you'll take Statistics and Managerial Accounting and Strategy, and participate in a three-day boot camp. You will also be encouraged to get your required economics courses out of the way: usually recommended are World Economy and International Environment of Business. The fall semester of your second year is your most flexible; there aren't any specific class requirements, and there is a lot of time for electives. During spring semester, you'll need to take Top Management Perspectives and Corporate Social Responsibility and Ethics. Electives include Corporate Finance: Analysis & Decisions; Corporate Financial Reporting; Debt Markets, Interest & Hedging; Negotiations; Buyer Behavior; and Management of Groups.

If you want to get out of the classroom and gain some real hands-on experience, you might want to consider one of the enterprise programs. No matter which enterprise field you choose, you will be working with real clients and spending and investing real money.

The oldest program, the Golden Gopher Growth Fund, recently had a name change. One of the first steps MBA Director Michael Barnes took when he arrived in the summer of 2002 was to rename it something "a little bit more respectable": the Carlson Funds Enterprise. There are two families of funds: the Carlson

Growth Fund and the Carlson Fixed Income Fund. Students learn by managing some $13 million of the school's money. "We have beaten the market every single year," says a proud Benveniste. The benchmark for the funds is the Russell 2000 Growth Index. Students apply to be in the enterprises at the beginning of the second semester of their first year. If selected, they are involved until they graduate. The time commitment is about 10 to 15 hours per week, according to Professor Tim Nantell. Each of the enterprises has its own lab, and students spend much of their day in these rooms. The labs are equipped with computers, AV equipment, televisions tuned to MSNBC, a library, and connections to real-time data, such as Bloomberg. Selection is competitive and requires an interview with a panel of academic and professional advisors.

The Carlson Ventures Enterprise (CVE) started in 2001. Just like real venture capitalists, students closely study business deals and decide which ideas are worth investing in. During the program's first year, there were more than 90 deals from which to choose, according to Doug Johnson, CVE's director. The students chose four, including ANDX, a genetic test used to determine whether cats will get cancer, and IdentityConcepts, an automatic device used by avid bird-watchers to help them identify types of birds.

The newest offering, the Carlson Consulting Enterprise, was launched in 2002 with 20 students and a partnership with PricewaterhouseCoopers. The program is run much like a medical student's internship experience, says Benveniste. "Students participate under the watchful eye of the faculty. It's the real thing. They are responsible and have accountability." One of the first projects was to help medical device giant Guidant develop its 10-year strategic plan. Another enterprise, Brand Management, has a planned launch in spring 2003. Carlson graduates rave about the enterprise offerings and highly recommend them to incoming students. "They added a very practical component to the classroom learning and were excellent networking opportunities," says 2002 graduate Angela Gaare.

One benefit of the Twin Cities location is that Carlson has ended up with a disproportionate number of Fortune 500 companies headquartered there. Among them: General Motors, Target, Best Buy, US Bank, 3M, and EcoLab. It's those students who want to leave the area that Benveniste wants to work on. "Part of the commitment to becoming a national business school is we need not just local jobs but national jobs to appeal to national students."

Despite the harsh and unforgiving climate, the Twin Cities—St. Paul and Minneapolis—are culturally rich, with more theaters, dance companies, and concert venues per person than anywhere outside New York. Students can be found in Dinkytown, a downtown neighborhood of Minneapolis full of student cafés, bookshops, and cheap places to eat. If you're looking for late-night action, the place to be is Uptown, south of downtown. Shoppers among you won't want to miss the Mall of America, the world's largest. If getting outdoors is more your bag, this is also the place to do it; Minnesota boasts 15,291 lakes, 25 ski areas, and 4,000 miles of hiking and biking trails. Carlson only has 15 clubs, but that number is optimal for the 128 students, says Verna Monson, director of student life. Most students can be found in the school's lounge on Thursday nights for TGIThursday.

Don't be fooled into thinking going to school in the Midwest means cheap housing. While you won't pay Manhattan rents, you will have to plunk down $800 to $1000 for off-campus apartments. If the thought of commuting to school in the dead of winter gets you down, there is the GrandMarc, graduate student housing built in 2000 right across from the B-school. But the convenience will set you back a minimum of $1100 for a one-bedroom apartment (utilities included).

PLACEMENT DETAILS

In the course of one academic year, Mike Agnew, assistant dean and director of the Business Career Center, had to shift strategic plans for career services at Carlson three times: from a normal MBA plan to the slow economy plan to the post-9/11 plan. Despite the down market, Agnew says he gives students the same advice as he gives them in the good times. "Go with what you know best, what you do well, and what you value."

Agnew has a strong team working on placements. Among the counselors you can talk to about your career are a former Disney vice president and a marketing manager from Toro. Before you even step on campus, Agnew will have your resume in the Carlson Automated Recruitment System (CARS). The system has been designed much like Monster.com: students can edit their resumes and search for jobs all with a simple log-in name and password.

"Our students are as well-prepared from a career perspective as they are from an academic perspective," says Agnew. He ensures this by introducing the students to his department early on; all students are required to take a career management class, the goal of which is to give students a clear understanding of the MBA marketplace and a personal portfolio to present to potential hirers. The course puts students ahead of the competition, says Agnew.

TOP HIRES

Medtronic (5); General Mills (4); Guidant (4); Honeywell (4); Northwest Airlines (4); Carlson Companies (4); Target (3).

OUTSTANDING FACULTY

J. Myles Shaver (strategy); Andrew Winton (finance); Mark Bergen (marketing); Ken Roering (marketing); Pri Shah (strategy); Arthur Hill (operations); Timothy Nantell (finance).

APPLICANT TIPS

Sandra Keltsenberg, the dean of admissions, has a simple idea of what kind of student she's looking for to join Carlson. "We want smart people with character," she says. Keltsenberg advises prospective students to research the specifics of the school and make sure it is the right fit before applying. "No one MBA program can be everything to everyone," she says.

Applicants are encouraged to come to the campus for a half-day visit. While there, you can visit a class and eat lunch with a current student, who will also conduct a peer interview with you. In addition, you will be interviewed by someone from the admissions staff. This isn't just a chance for the school to decide if you're right; it's also your chance to decide if Carlson is the right place for you, says Keltsenberg.

Some of the pitfalls: the school asks for two recommendations, so stick to that. Don't submit your application a number of different ways. And whatever you do, be sure to proofread. Every year, Keltsenberg receives several applications that include essays written for other business schools.

In order to accommodate international students, Carlson has added a second admissions deadline for them. The early deadline is December 1, and the final deadline is February 15. Domestic deadlines are January 1, March 1, and April 1. If you are applying for a scholarship, use one of the earlier deadlines.

CARLSON MBAs SOUND OFF

The Minnesota climate is the most commonly perceived drawback to the Carlson School, yet it's so irrelevant. The Carlson School's world-class, self-contained facility means no below-zero treks from building to building. On the contrary, it's easier to study during the cold months and snowball fights are a fun study break! Everything else about the program is excellent: elite faculty, most of whom also excel in the classroom; access to a robust and diverse career market and executive mentors; small class size promotes personal development and personal rapport with faculty; international diversity fosters global perspective; managerial communication center develops presentation and written communication skills; Minnesota culture values learning, ethics and teamwork. I recommend this program unconditionally.

This is a very strong program. It has a beautiful facility, great students with diverse backgrounds, well-rounded professors and tremendous support from the surrounding business community. I have been particularly impressed with its experiential learning programs. I participated in the school's recently started New Business Development Enterprise, which allowed me to work with many early stage companies and technologies in assessing business opportunities and developing strategies to exploit those opportunities.

Maybe it's due to cultural differences and my language incompetency, but I feel the way American students interact with international students is very superficial. Of course, there was an exception and I was very lucky to find a good American friend. The MBA office could encourage the American students to help international students more or to get their different perspectives. In contrast, support of the MBA office for international students is excellent. We have a noncredit class for international students every Friday to discuss various issues in addition to the issues stated above.

My MBA experience at the Carlson School has been incredible. With a new dean that encourages student initiatives, an excellent integrated core curriculum in year one and some of the nation's top faculty (based on research ranking) who actually enjoy teaching students, the program's foundation is very solid.

The Carlson School of Management has delivered the education, experience, and network that I needed to push my career to new levels. The program has enabled me to shift from a consulting career to a marketing career and change industries. I have absolutely no regrets about my decision to attend Carlson. I also feel that the school is one of the best MBA programs in the country because of its outstanding faculty, facilities, and connection to the Twin Cities business community. Additionally, since Carlson is a small program, students have the opportunity to truly make an impact and develop their leadership skills.

UNIVERSITY
OF
PITTSBURGH

UNIVERSITY OF PITTSBURGH

Joseph M. Katz Graduate School of Business
276 Mervis Hall
Pittsburgh, Pennsylvania 15260
E-mail address: mba@katz.pitt.edu
Web site address: www.katz.pitt.edu

Enrollment: 154
Women: 29%
Non-U.S.: 42%
Minority: 7%
Part-time: 0
Average age: 27
Applicants accepted: 54%
Median starting pay: $70,000

Annual tuition and fees:
   resident—$13,058
   nonresident—$20,571
Estimated annual budget: $13,900
Average GMAT score: 613
Average months of work
   experience: 46
Accepted applicants enrolled: 45%

Teaching methods: case study 25%, experiential learning 5%, lecture 50%, simulations 5%, team projects 15%

In the late 1950s, executives from western Pennsylvania's old industrial powerhouses approached the University of Pittsburgh's business school with a novel proposal: create an MBA program to train our workforce, and we'll guarantee that all your graduates are employed. But though the corporations wanted fully educated MBAs, they also wanted them produced with quality and—perhaps more important, because of the Steel City's tight labor market—with speed. If corporate managers didn't take a summer vacation, why should MBA students?

And so, in the 1960s, Katz separated itself from the semester-oriented calendar of the rest of the University of Pittsburgh and became a year-round enterprise, schooling MBAs in six seven-week modules so that they finished their degree in a mere 11 months. While many B-schools offer accelerated degrees, Katz historically has been the only first-rate school to require all students to complete their MBAs in this compact time span. And though you'd think that the school would adopt an "if it's not broke, don't fix it" attitude, times have changed. While the one-year program will still appeal to many as an efficient, affordable route to an MBA, the industrial center of Pittsburgh has given way to a more diverse and international corporate landscape, and students want the time to explore their post-MBA options. Beginning in fall 2003, Katz will offer prospective students the choice of the rigorous one-year accelerated MBA program or a newly created two-year traditional MBA schedule.

"It's a form of brand extension," says Dean Frederick W. Winter. Quite simply, the two-year option will allow Katz to serve a broader array of wannabe MBAs—specifically, those who might not yet have the professional direction or focus for a one-year program and can benefit by extra time spent on electives, career counseling, and a summer internship.

The 11-month program still has its advantages. Grads say that the heavy workload, rapid-fire deadlines, and teamwork-based curriculum force them to optimize their time and work more productively. It also makes B-school more affordable: for one thing, you're paying only one year's tuition and losing only one year's wages, so you're guaranteed a quicker payback on your investment than with a two-year program. But it has become clear to Katz's administration that this option really only works if you want to accelerate your career in a field with which you're already familiar and where an internship isn't necessary to help build your resume. This one-year option also works for foreign students who want to head back to their home countries sooner rather than later, or for people running family businesses, entrepreneurs, or legal and medical professionals for whom an intensive year spent learning business basics will boost their careers without a two-year hiatus from them.

The two-year option will be welcome to Katz students considering career switches, or without a strong business background to begin with. Perhaps most significantly, these MBA candidates will now have the opportunity for a summer internship. It's a lot easier to sell your finance-heavy resume to the corporate marketing department you have your eye on if you've spent a few months as an intern on the job at, say, a consumer products company.

In the past, Katz grads have complained of the Career Services Center's lack of individual attention and its inability to place students in jobs outside Pittsburgh's geographical reach. In November 2001, Katz alum Terri Gregos, a former marketing director at Pepsi, stepped in to take over the program, and she hopes to infuse it with her branding background. Though the arrival of a new staff in the midst of a tough

recruiting season has not produced immediate results in terms of increased student satisfaction, Gregos does have high hopes and a new vision for an office that will now be able to perhaps better divide its approach for two distinct groups of job seekers: those with a more directed and shorter search, and those who want a full range of professional development options.

Dean Winter is convinced that the school can move pretty seamlessly from its one-year platform to a two-year platform, due to an academic schedule of seven-week modules that accommodates both a compact core curriculum and a more flexible array of electives. Two-year students simply will need more credits to graduate (54 credits as opposed to 45 needed for the one-year program) and will satisfy them with more electives in their second year.

Both groups of students arrive on campus in August, and, after a two-week orientation that includes outward bound–type team-building exercises in the West Virginia wilderness, they mingle in the core classes that are scheduled for modules one and two. In all, the core comprises 27 credits, and one-year students will take 18 of these 27 in these first two modules, while two-year students will take just 15 credits. Then, in modules three and four, one-year students will continue to satisfy their remaining nine core credits while starting to sample some of Katz's 81 elective courses, most of which are one-module, 1½-credit classes. Two-year students will continue to take 12 more credits of the core and also will begin to take electives. Come late April/early May, when two-year students head off to do their internships, one-year students stay on campus to complete their 45 credits in modules five and six. When two-year students arrive back at Katz the next fall, they'll still have some 15 credits to fulfill through elective classes.

One way Katz will handle these different platforms will be by keeping the size of the classes small. In 2002–2003, there were only 140 students in the one-year program, and the number of students beginning in August 2003—

which will include both one-year and two-year students—will increase to just 170.

As part of the core curriculum, you'll have to take classes in organizational behavior, statistics, and accounting strategy. Then you'll be able to tailor your core courses somewhat with a choice of classes in the areas of finance, marketing, decision technologies, information systems, human resources, and managerial accounting. To help you through the fast-paced core, you'll be heavily dependent on your assigned management learning organizations (MLOs)—teams of up to six fellow classmates of differing backgrounds, with whom you'll complete class projects.

One way Katz further stresses business fundamentals within the compact core—essential, perhaps, for students who will be back out in the business world in less than a year—is by linking almost every class with a high-powered corporate partner, ensuring that students learn what's being practiced in the real world. Started in 1999, the Best Practice Partners program has attracted companies including Alcoa, Cisco, IBM, Intel, Heinz, Motorola, PNC Bank, and GlaxoSmithKline to "adopt a class" in key business areas in which the firms excel. As part of the program, the corporate partners send a senior executive into the classroom to teach alongside a regular Katz professor. Not only do the execs pepper a basic principles lecture with practical insight and relevant client examples, they sometimes review internal company documents with the class to show how theory is applied, or whole management teams will come to campus to give feedback to student projects.

Katz prides itself on the diversity and range of its elective courses, many of which are taught at night to accommodate the packed schedules of the accelerated program students. You'll be encouraged to use your elective courses to complete a signature program track, where you can focus in one of seven areas including accounting, international economics, valuation, engineered product marketing, process management, and two different management information systems areas. You'll also have opportunities to study abroad by spending a module in Central Europe, Latin and South America, Western Europe, or Asia at a partner school. Or you can take an international field study elective, such as Comparative Corporate Disclosure with Professor Bob Nachtman, where you'll spend 10 days in the country you've been studying.

There are no classes scheduled for Friday, when you'll have a chance to take optional professional workshops or sit in on the school's active speaker program. "I'd go to every event that sounded interesting and found that I learned more about corporate America and myself by doing this," says one 2002 grad, "things that coursework doesn't always help with." Dean Daria Kirby tries to give some of your time on the Katz campus a collegial feel by hosting weekly Wednesday morning "Coffee and Conversations" in the school's common area, where you can grab coffee, a doughnut, or a bagel while chatting with fellow students and professors during a break between classes. (Leftovers go on a table outside the MBA office to be snacked on during the day.) And when things get really tense—during exam weeks after the seven-week modules, for example—the school brings in professional airport massage therapists, who set up a chair for free head, neck, and shoulder massages.

Once classes end, Katz students come back together to socialize. In fact, many grads say the intense work experience creates fast bonds between them, emphasized by the fact that they know they may only have one year to spend together. The school has an active Student Executive Board that organizes weekly bowling nights, golf outings, cocktail hours, ski trips, and Thanksgiving dinners, as well as community volunteer efforts, such as helping out at a local senior citizens' home or a women's shelter. Katz's International Nights are popular schoolwide events where groups of international students take over the school for a party. Because there's no on-campus housing at Katz, which is located in Pittsburgh's hilly Oakland section, students live in apartments scattered throughout culturally diverse Oakland or the nearby, more upscale Shadyside and Squirrel Hill neighborhoods. Campus life has traditionally centered around the striking glass and steel Mervis Hall, and the newly completed PNC Team Technology Center offers more individual room for team projects and study. Students rave about this well-lit, comfortable facility, which also offers space for private study. "With the amount of time that we spent at Katz," says 2002 grad Stephanie Austria, "it felt as if that was our dorm. I stayed there until 6 A.M. once helping a friend with his Web page."

Pittsburgh, once a booming steel town, now is home to more than two dozen corporate headquarters, and is attracting a young, diverse population. It's still very affordable for students, who can find lots to do, roaming its hilly and ethnic neighborhoods, or taking advantage of its museums, theaters, and parks. Many students come to Katz because they want to work in Pittsburgh, and many who are introduced to the city for the first time want to stay.

PLACEMENT DETAILS

Developing business contacts on their own is something that Katz grads complain they've had to do because the career services office historically has been ineffective in helping them network otherwise.

Networking, however, is one of the first things Terri Gregos, a 1990 graduate of Katz, has tackled in her new position, setting up trips to Washington, DC, New York, and Chicago with alumni-oriented corporate meetings and receptions. Some grads have griped that these events were poorly attended, but this might be attributable in part to the fact that Gregos didn't have a lot of time to set them up, coming to Katz in the middle of a rather grim recruiting year.

Dean Winter emphasizes that the Career Services Center has a two-pronged approach for these different groups. For one-year students, there'll be less emphasis on the October recruiting season, which in the past came much too soon in the year, making it hard for students to give the proper attention to both their studies and the job hunt. "In the past we've always been trying to shoehorn one-year students to get them ready for October recruiting," says Winter. "There's only so much forming you can do in two months, but by April or May they're fully formed." In addition to creating individual marketing plans, the Career Services Center offers daily sessions on basic job search skills such as behavioral interviewing, case interviewing, and resume and cover letter writing.

Those who want a more comprehensive career placement experience should opt for the two-year program, which will allow more time for a guided experience and may alleviate some complaints along the lines of "there are some jobs out there, but people had to find them for themselves." Because her office will be able to get to know two-year students better, Gregos wants to use her background to market their Katz educations to companies, while pushing her staff to make stronger connections with recruiters. In 2002, results were mixed: 60 percent of grads who were seeking work had a job by graduation—but that number might be skewed, as only 61 percent of the class reported that they were seeking employment.

It's too soon to tell how Gregos's efforts are paying off—especially in a down economy—but the two-year MBA option should now take some pressure off of students who want an education at Katz and who want to be in Pittsburgh, but who feel they could use some more time to explore career options.

TOP HIRES

FedEx Ground Services (3); Ford Motor Company (2); Johnson & Johnson International (2); Medrad (2); Ernst & Young (2).

OUTSTANDING FACULTY

Prakash Mirchandani (operations); Kenneth Lehn (finance); Donald Moser (accounting); Kuldeep Shastri (finance).

APPLICANT TIPS

As with everything else at Katz, the shift to a two-year MBA program will shake things up a bit in the admissions office. How to choose to which program you should apply? "Ideal, successful students for the one-year program will know what they want and where they are headed. An internship is not integral to successful job placement for these students," says Kelly Wilson, director of admissions. "Our two-year program and dual degree option fit better for those applicants who feel that an internship is necessary to their success."

The admissions office won't hesitate to contact a student who has applied for one program but whom they feel might be better suited for the other. In general, however, you'll need good GMAT scores to show that you can handle the intense core curriculum—though these scores won't necessarily make or break your application if you've got solid work experience, recommendations, and essay answers. Wilson suggests that before you submit your application, read the essay as if it were the only piece of information that the admission committee will have to go on.

Interviews are not required, but almost all Katz admittees for 2002–2003 had been interviewed. In your interview, be prepared to articulate how an MBA fits into your overall career goals, both short-term and long-term. Come armed with anecdotes or examples that demonstrate your leadership and interpersonal skills.

Katz's admissions office is making a concerted effort to develop a personal relationship with its applicants, so to that end, you should think about visiting the campus for its "MBA for a Day" program. Instead of heading to campus on a weekend, you'll get a chance to pair up with a Katz student ambassador during an actual class day. Your ambassador will escort you around campus, and to classes, and introduce you to other students over lunch. Because Katz's student body is typically composed of 35 to 40 percent international students, the admissions office will go to popular home countries such as Brazil or India for recruiting events.

You're encouraged to apply online—in fact, your application fee will be waived if you do. That, combined with the new two-year option, might mean that you want to get your application in as early as possible, as the admissions staff will be examining applications even more closely to determine who will fit best in each program.

KATZ MBAs SOUND OFF

My MBA experience was invaluable, yet unique. Because it was only 11 months, it enabled me to take part, yet in some ways, I felt that it was rushed. There were many more electives that I would have enjoyed taking, yet time was short.

The one-year program is very intense and probably too much for most people. Be sure you are ready for it and to immerse your life into the B-school lifestyle.

Katz is a great school with a lot to offer. However, the administration and other services, such as career services, are severely lacking. The school does very little to foster the relationship between alumni and the school and as a result Katz has a very weak alumni base.

The program is like no other. It's fast, hard, and to the point—just like life. You have to learn to pick up things on the fly to do well. You have to be team oriented. You have to perform. These are all crucial in the workplace. Katz did an excellent job teaching these and many other key tools to their students.

Very collaborative environment. Students and faculty are here to help each other out. The school plans a lot of fun activities both at school and outside of school. All in all, my MBA experience was excellent—I just picked a difficult year to graduate (poor economic conditions).

UNIVERSITY
OF
WASHINGTON

UNIVERSITY OF WASHINGTON

University of Washington Business School
Box 353200 Mackenzie Hall Room 110
University of Washington
Seattle, Washington 98195-3200
E-mail address: mba@u.washington.edu
Web site address: http://depts.washington.edu/school

Enrollment: 258	Annual tuition and fees:
Women: 33%	resident—$8,469
Non-U.S.: 28%	nonresident—$17,569
Minority: 2%	Estimated annual budget: $16,990
Part-time: 149	Average GMAT score: 673
Average age: 29	Average months of work
Applicants accepted: 32%	experience: 64
Median starting pay: $80,000	Accepted applicants enrolled: 42%

Teaching methods: case study 40%, lecture 30%, experiential learning 10%, team projects 20%

Seattle could be the perfect place to attend business school: it's home to a legendary high-tech industry, as well as headquarters for innovative corporations such as Microsoft, Starbucks, and Amazon.com, and is well situated on the Pacific Rim as the closest major U.S. port to Asia. Indeed, the graduate school of business at the University of Washington has always attracted people who want to go to school in this environment—and to stick around afterward. A few years ago, in the midst of the dot-com boom, almost 99 percent of the school's graduates stayed in Seattle.

But the dot-com frenzy is over, and as the business climate in Seattle began to change, Washington's B-school—realizing, perhaps, that it had to become more than an MBA program that just happened to be in a desirable business location—cracked the *BusinessWeek* rankings. Small class sizes, a flexible curriculum, and a strong international focus attract a diverse, energetic, and collaborative student body as well as top-flight recruiters. And, despite the rather gloomy job prospects for newly minted MBAs in 2002, the school's dean, Yash Gupta, is committed to tapping into Seattle's business community to give students hands-on experience while at school and employment opportunities once they graduate. If you want to spend two years in what is still a vibrant, entrepreneurial city—not to mention one filled with coffee shops and microbreweries and in the shadow of the majestic Cascade Mountains—it's worth giving the MBA program at the University of Washington another look. "If you are looking for a cutthroat program, this is NOT it," says one recent graduate.

With only 140 students per class, the University of Washington is on the small side, but this allows students to be on a first-name basis not only with almost everyone in the class, but with the dean, the faculty, and the staff. Most students rave about the school's sense of community and collaboration. In your first year, you're put into smaller, five-person study teams to make the experience even more intimate as you tackle a core curriculum that's highly integrated through the fall and winter quarters but allows some elective choice by spring quarter. In the fall and winter, you'll take modules that include accounting, statistics, microeconomics, macroeconomics, finance, management, quantitative methods, and global business. While one recent grad described the pace of the first year as being like "a fire hose," those who have had jobs that require quantitative skills (i.e., accounting or banking), say that the curriculum isn't quite challenging enough until you get to the elective choices in the spring quarter.

The University of Washington's approach to first-year electives isn't entirely a free-for-all. You'll be able to select three out of seven "bridge electives," including finance, marketing, global business, entrepreneurship, e-business, project management, and the legal aspects of business. In these classes you'll get more foundation to continue in these areas in more depth during your second year. These will also help you find summer internships in these particular fields.

In your second year, you'll take 12 elective courses, but, before you choose them, you'll be asked to build your own personal study plan with input from faculty and specific prospective employers so that you'll choose electives that will give you the skills for a particular career. You can take up to four of your second-year courses in other departments on the large University of Washington campus, and many students end up taking courses in computer science, urban development, international studies, health care administration, or economics to build their personal curriculums.

Such curriculums can include certificate programs with the Center for Technology Entrepreneurship (CTE)—created as a direct result of the state's entrepreneurial fervor—where you'll be working with other graduate students from the engineering and medical schools. (The CTE also sponsors an annual business plan competition judged by Seattle area entrepreneurs, offering some $40,000 in prize money.) Another certificate option is offered in the field of e-business, where you'll benefit from the local presence of not only some established e-companies (e.g., Amazon.com) but also the many start-ups in the area.

One of the school's strengths is its international focus. With its proximity to Asia, the school is in a unique position to both recognize and realize the importance of an international focus in today's business climate. "Unless you run a local pizza parlor," says Dan Poston, the school's executive director, "there's no such thing as domestic business." In addition to a global business certificate, UW also offers a dual MBA/master of science in international studies degree. For the certificate, you'll need to spend time abroad on a summer internship, an exchange program, or on one of the international study tours that happen each spring. These tours to places such as Brazil, China, Finland, India, Indonesia, Japan, Korea, Malaysia, Russia, South Africa, Sweden, Taiwan, and Thailand are run almost entirely by students themselves. Most tours will have four student leaders, at least two of whom are citizens of the countries visited, and these leaders plan all the events.

"One of the most difficult decisions I made first year was to choose the Japan/Korea trip over the Scandinavia/Russia trip," says 2002 grad Ann Greeley. On her trip, students visited some 10 companies in each country and met with the CEO of a Japanese conglomerate who was a UW B-school alum, as well as side-tripping to cultural sites and being taken to dinner by the school's Tokyo alumni organization. These trips take some extra effort in both the application process and the extra money that you'll have to shell out for them, but students who took them said they were a highlight of their MBA experience.

While some students say that Seattle's start-up, technology-focused business atmosphere drew them to the University of Washington's MBA program to begin with, many students say that the connection the school has with local businesses was one of the biggest surprises. Most students end up working on projects for companies in the Seattle area—indeed, the school's proximity to so many businesses makes it possible to go to class in the morning and then run out to a company in the afternoon. "Every quarter I had at least one team that contacted a local or national company, for which we would analyze a current issue and make recommendations," says Greeley. "It was a great opportunity to see the real-world significance of our studies." In addition, the school takes advantage of the plethora of business leaders in the area by luring them to campus for lectures or club events. It's not unusual to have two or three speakers on campus every day.

Along with being in the midst of a casual yet innovative business climate, most students would also agree that living in Seattle is close to heaven for the outdoor enthusiast. Hiking and skiing in the Olympic or Cascade Mountains are just an hour away. (One 2002 grad spent every Friday and Saturday skiing with his three-year-old.) Don't want to leave the city? You can rent sailboats or canoes right on campus to spend a leisurely afternoon on Lake Washington. Weekends, when not spent exploring the city or the nearby coastal islands, are filled with Husky football, when students flock to pregame tailgate parties and the MBA bleacher section. Road-tripping caravans have been known to form to follow the team to bowl games.

Most students live off campus in one of the four neighborhoods that border the school (though the university offers subsidized bus passes for those who commute from farther

away). Rent in Seattle is probably on the steeper side on a national scale, but certainly nothing like New York or Los Angeles—you can find a two-bedroom apartment for about $1000 a month.

While off-campus life in Seattle is good, University of Washington students' biggest complaint about the program is the outdated and just plain "ugly" building that houses the MBA program—though they are all quick to point out that improvements are in the works.

Still, students stay on campus to participate in club activities, joining career clubs like the Finance Club, the Hi-Tech Club, and the Marketing Club. Friday nights bring "TG" happy hours in the student lounge (although students also spend a lot of time hanging out at Seattle's famous microbreweries). The annual Challenge for Charity is one of the year's big social events: almost half the school road-trips down to Palo Alto for a sports competition against other West Coast MBA programs.

PLACEMENT DETAILS

A few years ago, when Seattle was a hub of IT start-ups, the career services office didn't really need to do much more than help students figure out a career path and then map out a job search based on this plan. But the burst of the dot-com bubble hit Seattle hard, and in April 2002—perhaps a little too late, some recent grads might argue—the career services office was completely reinvented to focus more on helping students make direct connections with the business community.

"That effort starts with me," says Dean Yash Gupta. "The CEOs in this region will tell you I am bound to bring up job opportunities for our students at some point in every conversation. . . . We have tried to tap every connection of every person possible inside and outside the business school."

While some students say that the career services office is strong in the areas of interviewing skills and resume editing, the office's new vision had not caught up with students' needs by the time the class of 2002 graduated. "I think our grads tend to be scrappier, so career services are more of a guiding factor rather than a determining factor in the job search," says 2002 grad Sydney Davis, who used connections made during a second-year fellowship at an angel investor organization to network with executives and entrepreneurs in the area. Still, opportunities like Davis's fellowship are common at the University of Washington, and, in combination with the career office's new focus, students may end up weathering the depressing job market better than their counterparts at schools with less hands-on corporate and business involvement.

TOP HIRES

Capital One (5); Amazon.com (3); GE Capital (3); Phillips Medical Systems (2); Starbucks (2); Washington Mutual Bank (2); Wells Fargo Bank (2); Microsoft (2); Boeing (2); Deloitte Consulting (2); Lehman Brothers (2); Alliance of Angels (2).

OUTSTANDING FACULTY

Jennifer Koski (finance); Robert Higgins (finance); Ed Rice (finance); Mark Forehand (marketing); Karma Hadjimichalakis (economics); Ali Tarhouni (economics); Kamran Moinzadeh (management).

APPLICANT TIPS

Washington's admissions office is looking for students who have given some serious thought to why they want to pursue a graduate business degree. They want to see that you've done the self-assessment of your own strengths, interests, and skills to support your returning to school—

this is what will come out in your essays, interviews, and recommendation letters. Know the strengths of the Washington MBA program—entrepreneurship, technology, international business, and a connection with area businesses—and, if these aspects are what you want out of your MBA education, be able to articulate how you can contribute to them. The school offers three application workshops (scheduled on the Thursdays before the three official Friday Campus Visit Days), and local applicants might want to take advantage of these free seminars.

Interviews at the University of Washington aren't required, though it's strongly recommended that you request one—which you need to do before you submit you application. You'll also need to have taken your GMAT before you interview. In your interview, make sure you can articulate your career goals, your work experience, and why these are leading you specifically to the University of Washington for your MBA.

Because there's more time needed for processing international applications, students applying from abroad are encouraged to hit the first two application deadlines of December 1 or January 1. February 1 is the absolute final deadline for international applications.

WASHINGTON MBAs SOUND OFF

The UW MBA program is great. I am incredibly pleased by how challenged I was by the program. However, the biggest thing I think our program has to work on is to improve the quality of the facilities, specifically the classrooms and student lounge. There are major fund-raising efforts going on right now to do this. But until this occurs, I think UW suffers in comparison to other programs.

I can't say enough about how great my fellow students were. I've heard stories from other schools about backstabbing and aggressive behavior. That was not the case at UW; we helped each other. We all worked hard and we did compete, but we did it fairly, and when the job market tightened up all the students really got together to help one another. Faculty actively solicited opportunities for us and alumni really stepped in.

This is a great program, in a great location with smart, hardworking students that are always willing to help each other. Academics at UW are quite rigorous. The school is moving in many new directions and has strong leadership.

Although it is not ranked as a top school, the University of Washington is a great school with lots of respect from Seattle residents. It has a friendly environment where international students can pursue academic coursework with as little cultural friction as possible. Students are great, and faculty members and program staff are constantly working to improve the program.

Most people who come to the UW MBA program end up staying in Seattle because of the high quality of life in the Northwest. Students from the East Coast, Midwest, and other places just do not want to leave Seattle after graduating from the UW MBA program. They would rather accept a lower salary for working in Seattle or at least San Francisco. Consequently, many multinational companies stop recruiting at the UW MBA program.

The new dean is raising a lot of money to privatize the school, build a new building, and hire top-notch faculty. The program is listening to students and has been adaptable in the current tough economic environment. In the meantime, it still has some catching up to do to compete with the West Coast powerhouses. I wouldn't have traded it for the world, however, and Seattle is a killer town for business in the new economy. If you want to work and live in Seattle, UW is the right place to go.

UNIVERSITY OF WISCONSIN-MADISON

School of Business
Room 3150 Grainger Hall
975 University Avenue
Madison, Wisconsin 53706-1323
E-mail address: uwmadmba@bus.wisc.edu
Web site address: www.bus.wisc.edu/graduateprograms

Enrollment: 355	Annual tuition and fees:
Women: 29%	resident—$8,902
Non-U.S.: 37%	nonresident—$24,368
Minority: 11%	Estimated annual budget: $35,000
Part-time: 115	Average GMAT score: 632
Average age: 28	Average months of work
Applicants accepted: 27%	experience: 55
Median starting pay: $75,000	Accepted applicants enrolled: 55%

Teaching methods: case study 35%, experiential learning 10%, lecture 30%, team projects 25%

At some B-schools, students would be hard pressed to describe the dean. Not so at the University of Wisconsin-Madison, where on one recent day, rookie dean Michael Knetter had lunch with a small group of students, kept his door open for 90 minutes of open office hours, and held an evening town hall meeting. "It was definitely a day for the students," said Knetter, who assumed the post of dean in July of 2002.

While not all Knetter's days are that student focused, with many spent on the road, he says he wants to keep a "very open" dean's office. "At Wisconsin, students are getting a dean who really enjoys spending time with them," he says. Every Wednesday that he's on campus, he holds open office hours. Knetter, a Wisconsin native, came to the school by way of the Amos Tuck School of Business at Dartmouth College, where he was the associate dean of the MBA program and a professor of international economics. Prior to that, he served as a senior staff economist for the President's Council of Economic Advisors under former presidents George Bush and Bill Clinton.

It was no surprise when former dean Andrew J. Policano stepped down from the post; he gave ample warning. If Knetter has any questions for him, he doesn't have to travel very far; Policano is still a member of the school's finance department. Under the guidance of Policano, the curriculum at UW-Madison had become much more modular over the preceding six years. The goal is to give students more flexibility with their schedules. Of all of the B-schools, Madison is one of the most expansive in terms of the degrees students can earn: the MBA, a master of science in business, a master of accountancy, and a master of arts in business.

What the University of Wisconsin-Madison B-school is best known for is its specializations and the centers supporting them, which currently number 15. Each specialization has its own prerequisites and requirements for graduation. Despite the specializations, first-year students' schedules look a lot like those at any other B-school, featuring a curriculum heavily packed with core courses. In the first semester, your schedule likely will include Financial Accounting, Marketing Management, Leadership Effectiveness, Motivational Effectiveness, Data Analysis for Managers, and Business Strategy. During the second semester, you will be encouraged to take Financial Management, Managerial Accounting, Managerial Communication, and Managerial Economics. Both schedules leave room for at least one elective of the student's choosing.

After your summer internship, you will return to the school for two required modular courses in your remaining two semesters. The four required modules are ethics and social responsibility, managing the legal environment, corporate strategy, and strategic management of innovation and technology. Students use the remaining credits for their specializations or for electives if they haven't chosen a specialization.

Examples of the specialized programs include applied security analysis, supply chain management, real estate, and marketing research. Most specializations have a center (for example, the Grainger Center for Supply Chain Management) with faculty and staff members and guided by advisory boards of business professionals. "For this reason, our students get an edge early in their careers: they come out ready to help their companies immediately. They hit the ground running. We deliver these programs in new facilities in one of the most desirable places to live in America," says Dean Knetter. "Our parent company is one of the truly great research universities in the world. All this—and the fact that our students have great interpersonal skills and solid technical skills—make Wisconsin a great choice for a business school."

About half the MBA students at Madison choose one of the school's specializations; the other half stick with a more typical, general MBA. Knetter hopes to change those numbers and encourage more students to choose the specialization route. Starting with fall 2003, students will have yet another reason to choose product management as their specialization: The B-school recently received a gift of $6.4 million from alumnus Signe Ostby and her husband, Scott Cook (a cofounder of Intuit) to complete a Project Management Center, scheduled to open fall 2003.

Knetter is keeping his eye on expanding the number of centers even more. Within the next few years, he expects to see an Applied Corporate Finance Center. "These centers are a key part of our strategy," says Knetter. While the school aims for parity with the top schools in its core curriculum, Knetter aims to be among the best in the specializations. "The tracks are where we can really be distinctive and add market value," he says.

If you're interested in global studies, you won't be disappointed by UW-Madison, either. In conjunction with the University of Iowa, UW now offers short-term winter break programs in both Paris and London. You can earn three credits toward your degree in the three-week global finance course.

Maybe it's because of the myriad specializations students are pursuing, or maybe it has something to do with living between two lakes, but the students at UW-Madison's B-school don't seem nearly as uptight or cutthroat as their counterparts around the country. "Far and away the best attribute of the University of Wisconsin-Madison is the cooperative learning environment at work here," remarks one 2002 graduate. "As someone who came to business school without having studied business as an undergrad, I was especially appreciative of the culture of cooperation and my teammates' willingness to help one another."

Whatever your study habits or past experience, you should be able to remain on track with the many tech resources at your disposal in the school's Grainger Hall. The $40 million hub of the B-school houses a 30,000-square-foot library, computer lab, 30 classrooms, three auditoriums, and the Blue Chip Deli.

The nice thing about Madison is it isn't just a college town; it also happens to be the state capital. Located on an isthmus between two lakes, Mendota and Monona, Madison and its environs boast plenty of excellent spots for recreational activities, including rock climbing, fishing, biking, and hiking. Priorities do change slightly in the dead of winter, when sipping beer and munching on bratwurst becomes the extent of most students' extracurricular activities. No problem there; bars abound around the university, especially on State Street. For Frank Lloyd Wright fans, a day trip to Taliesin, the famed architect's main home, is a must.

Very few B-school students choose to live on UW's picturesque 933-acre brick and ivy campus; instead, they opt for one of the many inexpensive apartments around downtown. You can expect to pay in the $600 range for a one-bedroom apartment within two miles of campus. When it's not snowing, biking is a great way to get around this very cyclist-friendly town. Some students choose to commute the hour from Milwaukee or other nearby towns by train. Come Friday night, though, you will find them all gathered at the Memorial Union Terrace, considered by some to be the best pickup spot in the Midwest. As the night wears on, students tend to fan out to State Street, home to coffee shops and bars galore. Wisconsin has a very active GBA that sponsors a Thursday night TAPS at bars around town in the fall and spring, picnics, an annual ball, and winter and spring trips.

PLACEMENT DETAILS

Due to the tight job market, Karen Stauffacher, director of the Business Career Center (BCC), and her staff have taken a number of steps to reach out to potential employers, who now have free access to job postings, student resumes, and videoconferencing interviews.

Students can also see an array of changes, with a number of them focused on a "do it yourself" approach. The BCC brings in dozens of presenters. As part of the 2001–2002 roster, author and speaker Don Asher discussed the self-directed job search with students. A new service called Tech Central, which became available to students in early September 2002, provides them with the technology necessary to support their independent job searches, says Stauffacher. Tech Central provides video and audioconferencing capability, asynchronous interviewing, wireless Internet connectivity, a scanner, fax machine, cell phone chargers, a reference collection of books on the cyber job search and a series of 12 "Tech Tip" sheets covering today's high-tech job search. Students also have access to ReferenceUSA and CareerSearch through the service.

Students also now have access to a new alumni service: the Alumni Mentoring Program. Through the program, they can contact some of the school's 31,000 alumni living around the globe to discuss potential careers. All alumni also receive access to a password-protected online community, which includes job postings, messages, permanent e-mail forwarding, and personal home pages.

The BCC recently designated a specific staff member to work with international students on an individual basis. The process begins during orientation week, with two days planned just for international students. Each September, three seminars are offered: Networking for International Students, Etiquette for International Students, and Interviewing American Style. A "let's talk" four-session seminar is designed to offer international students opportunities to practice their conversation skills in business situations. An immigration attorney is also available to provide international students with information on employment visas in the United States.

TOP HIRES

Guidant (3); Kraft (3); Lands' End (3); American Family Insurance (2); ANB Enterprises (2); Clorox (2); Deloitte Consulting (2); General Mills (2); Grainger (2); Philip Morris USA (2); Samsung (2).

OUTSTANDING FACULTY

Robert Pricer (entrepreneurship); James Rappold (operations); Mason Carpenter (management); Jan Heide (marketing).

APPLICANT TIPS

If you're in a rush when it comes time to fill out your application for University of Wisconsin, don't skimp on your essays. Concise, well-written essays are considered one of the most important parts of the application, according to Philip J. Miller, assistant dean of graduate programs. "Essays probably carry more weight in the application than any other single component," says Miller. "Lack of care in the preparation of essays is a huge red flag for us, as is the inability of the applicant to get to the point of the actual question."

While there is no one perfect student for Wisconsin's B-school, certain characteristics can get you pretty darn close. Miller describes a successful applicant as "a bright, practical, career-directed individual who knows more or less where he or she wants to end up upon completion of the degree program."

UW-Madison is interested in making sure that you're the right fit for the program to which you apply. Research the specializations you are considering; make sure that they match your interests and experience. Check the requirements for the different degrees; they are not all the same. "A successful applicant must have done enough homework to demonstrate knowledge about our specialized program emphases and must make a convincing case that the applicant's background and goals fit the specific program to which they seek admission," says Miller.

Avoid any vague references to "wanting to become a leader" or "wanting to excel in business," says Miller. "Because of our degree of specialization, we want to see applicants' motivations to pursue a *particular* course of study."

While interviews are not required at Wisconsin's B-school, the school strongly recommends scheduling an informational interview before you even apply. If requested in advance, a tour of Grainger Hall, attendance in a B-school class, and meetings with current students can be arranged. Some applicants will be asked to attend interviews once their applications have been initially reviewed, but these interviews are by invitation only.

WISCONSIN MBAs SOUND OFF

Wisconsin is a unique program that is not for everyone. First, it is not historically strong in consulting or investment banking and as a result will never have the average salaries of a Harvard. Second, it draws its student body primarily from the Midwest and the companies that recruit on campus are a reflection of this. That said, Wisconsin has a number of well-regarded "niche" programs that offer excellent financial support for students, numerous chances to interact with professionals and faculty, and dedicated support for job searches beyond that offered through the career center. Therefore, if one participates in a "niche" program I feel that Wisconsin can deliver an education close to if not better than at many B-schools with higher rankings.

The lower cost of living in Madison, along with the availability of assistance (fellowships, project and teaching assistantships) make attending UW-Madison reasonable. The classes and other students make it an extremely worthwhile experience. Overall, the degree gave me exposure to multiple facets of a managerial problem, thus improving my lateral thinking abilities. The atmosphere in the classes was friendly with healthy competition and camaraderie among peers. Professors were very approachable and forthcoming in resolving our concerns. I enjoyed my core classes especially in finance, operations and economics. We have some outstanding faculty in operations and an excellent niche program in supply chain management at the Grainger Center. The home town of Madison is a great city to live in—the presence of two lakes and the capitol gives it that extra edge. UW-Madison is certainly a value added experience and is on a great trajectory.

The University of Wisconsin-Madison offers so many specialty programs that allow students to customize their degrees into exactly what they want to get from school. Since I was seeking a career in investments, I enrolled in the applied security analysis program in order to focus my efforts. This program allowed me to be surrounded by students with the same interests, during my second year, so I could garner the most knowledge before entering the working world.

The teaching, research, and curriculum are top notch. There is also a very well-organized network of alumni that will be valuable contacts down the road. Unfortunately, that's about the only part of the program at UW I would recommend to students with other options. The school displays a lack of leadership—that may change with the new dean—and has failed to deliver a program that is comprehensive and rigorous in its training. There are some wonderful faculty and courses, but not enough. There are almost no networking possibilities outside of the real estate department. The students are average, and the international students are not screened at all with regard to language ability, which leads to them being carried in any assignment that involves writing or verbal presentation.

Far and away the best attribute of the University of Wisconsin-Madison is the cooperative learning environment at work here. As someone who came to business school without having studied business as an undergrad, I was especially appreciative of the culture of cooperation and my teammates' willingness to help one another.

WAKE FOREST UNIVERSITY

Babcock Graduate School of Management
P.O. Box 7659
Winston-Salem, North Carolina 27109-7659
E-mail address: admissions@mba.wfu.edu
Web site address: www.mba.wfu.edu

Enrollment: 235	Median starting pay: $74,000
Women: 25%	Annual tuition and fees: $25,125
Non-U.S.: 31%	Estimated annual budget: $37,885
Minority: 8%	Average GMAT score: 639
Part-time: 0	Average months of work
Average age: 27	experience: 47
Applicants accepted: 47%	Accepted applicants enrolled: 44%

Teaching methods: case study 40%, distance learning 5%, experiential learning 15%, lecture 20%, simulations 5%, team projects 15%

"You almost never run into students who say about their undergraduate experience, 'My best classes were the big ones,' " says Charlie Moyer, dean of Wake Forest's Babcock Graduate School of Management. So to distinguish itself from bigger, top 30 B-school neighbors such as Duke, Chapel Hill, and UVA, Babcock relies on small class sizes—only about 114 students enter each year—and its 3/38 plan—three sections of some 38 students each—to market itself as a school capable of giving truly personalized attention to each student. Jason Lowe, a 2002 graduate, says this attention extends even to the first-class administration of the program. "You always feel like you're taken care of so that you can just focus on studying and job searching," he says.

These small sections mean that you get more time in classes where you're graded on participation and more chances to interact with faculty. They also mean you get to know your fellow students quite well in what many say is a positive, noncompetitive environment. (As one 2002 grad puts it: "If you're the type to put your graded test papers on the refrigerator for everyone to see and pat you on the back, don't go there.")

Winston-Salem and Wake Forest are laid-back places, and students at Babcock are no different. They call everyone from the dean on down by their first names, and students never find out their class rank—something that fosters a sense of collaboration. "I think formality and arrogance walk hand in hand," says Dean Moyer. "Informality and reality walk hand in hand."

That being said, small B-schools with tightly interwoven curriculums tend to work their students hard (witness Dartmouth, Virginia, or

Purdue), and Babcock is no exception, especially in your first year. For one thing, the 3/38 plan means you can't hide in the crowd if you're not prepared to carry your weight in class discussions, which often begin with cold calls. Babcock's integrated first-year curriculum—in which you're required to take all core classes (no exemptions and no electives)—doesn't follow a traditional semester-based schedule. You'll start off with a 10-week business foundation module that has you taking courses in accounting, communications, quantitative methods, team building, and microeconomics. The second module, which lasts 20 weeks, moves into the functions of business—finance, marketing, and operations. As these functional courses begin to deal with more sophisticated issues such as capital structure, marketing, and operations, you'll address broader issues of organizational development (using the quantitative methods you studied in the first module). The third and final module of the first year, which lasts around 10 weeks, focuses on the bigger-picture issues of macroeconomics, international business, and management information systems. Assigned teams of five to seven students tackle numerous group projects in all courses throughout the year.

Near the end of the first year, you'll go through an integrative exercise where you'll be presented with a real-world business scenario on a Wednesday afternoon. You'll have until Friday to analyze the situation and present your findings and recommendations to a faculty panel. This will test your knowledge of the concepts you've learned throughout the year, and your ability to work with teams in a high-pressure situation.

During the second year, you're only required to take two courses—half-semester capstones on international strategy and management control systems. If you have less than three years of work experience (as many Babcock students do), you'll also be required to do a field study project in which you'll work on a student team as a project consultant to real-world corporations or nonprofits. Many students who have more than three years' experience opt for the field study anyway. "It was quite challenging," says 2002 graduate Melissa Tuttle, who worked on a marketing research project with a major U.S. retailer, "with the workload and the need for professional communication when the project hit roadblocks."

As a second-year student, you must declare a career concentration, or major, from a menu of 16 possibilities, including consulting, entrepreneurship, information technology management, operations management, business-to-business marketing, brand management, investment banking, and financial analysis—or you can design your own concentration. Your primary career concentration requires 12 credit hours of study, and you can also choose a secondary concentration with 9 credit hours of study. Babcock also offers joint degrees in law or medicine.

One of Dean Moyer's stated priorities is to enhance the small school's international reputation. And indeed, with some 30 percent of the student body hailing from more than 25 countries, you'll have ample opportunity to work closely with international students in your small sections. The school's Flow Institute for International Studies brings international business leaders and scholars to campus to lead classes and give lectures. Through the Flow Institute, you can also travel abroad during the summer either as part of the East Asia Management program in China or Japan, or through the European Business Studies Program in Great Britain, France, or Central Europe. These trips can be taken in May, June, or July and last about two weeks. You can come back to the United States to do a summer internship, or you can stay on in your chosen country to do internships at places like Oji Paper in Japan or British Steel. Babcock's relationships with companies such as American Express in Brazil also offer opportunities for summer internships in São Paulo.

Second-year students have the option to take part in one of Babcock's six exchange programs at business schools in Moscow, Bordeaux, Austria, or at three different schools in Germany. The school is also working on creating exchanges with schools in Brazil, Chile, and Mexico.

In addition to the Flow Institute, Babcock is home to several other academic and research centers, including the Angell Center for Entrepreneurship, which sponsors the annual Babcock Elevator Competition. During the course of a weekend in March, more than 30 teams from top B-schools around the country take a two-minute elevator ride to the top of the Wachovia Bank headquarters building in downtown Winston-Salem to pitch their business plans to venture capitalists. If you reach the final round, you'll be competing for real start-up cash from North Carolina–based VC firms.

The beautiful Wake Forest campus in the affordable city of Winston-Salem makes Babcock a comfortable—if less than exciting—place to spend two years. Much of the school's social life centers around activities at the university, and sports fans might want to note that it may be the only ACC school at which all students can easily get basketball tickets. Every Wednesday at Babcock is doughnut day—a time for students and faculty to get together over Krispy Kremes and coffee—and every Friday there's a happy hour at the school's Worrell Center, where everyone can relax over a beer or two. The annual International Food Festival in the fall, and the Halloween party, Christmas party, and charity auction are other social highlights.

Students say that Winston-Salem's rather meager selection of bars actually induces them to spend a lot of time studying, but Winston-Salem has a surprisingly active local music scene, and students often catch bands at Ziggy's. The Blue Ridge Mountains and North Carolina's beaches are close enough for weekend hikes and trips. Winston-Salem has some gorgeous golf courses, and every spring the school hosts the Greater Babcock Open, a golf tournament for students, faculty, staff, and alumni.

There's no on-campus housing at Babcock, but students live near campus in apartments or shared houses. The admissions office hosts a house hunt every June, in which current students escort members of the incoming class around Winston-Salem to search for apartments, helping them get to know the town, the school, and each other (many students find roommates that day).

Students can also keep busy by joining a plethora of clubs, with the finance and marketing clubs among the most popular. The Operations Club shepherds students on well-attended plant tours, and in addition to the Elevator Competition, the Marketing Case Competition and the Leadership through Technology conference are big events.

PLACEMENT DETAILS

Winston-Salem is no business metropolis, and Babcock's placement record reflects both that and the fact that more than a few companies don't want to trek to North Carolina to interview just a handful of students. Students do say, however, that the career management center tries its best to get students in front of companies that aren't making the trip to campus—for example, sending them on trips up to Duke or Chapel Hill, where recruiters are more likely to go. This small school also takes advantage of the MBA Consortium (a collaboration between 18 B-schools) to send students to events in large cities such as New York, Washington, DC, and Atlanta. In addition, and especially in a weak economy, Kevin Bender, executive director of the career management center, says the school has continued to focus on "one-on-one relationship building with recruiters," where the career services staff members will go to companies themselves to help them find candidates for open positions when the company may not want to come to campus.

Babcock's career development activities run the gamut from individual resume recruiting to etiquette dinners. A mentor program matches students with executives in business and career specialties they'd like to explore. The school also has asked its Board of Visitors to get more involved with helping students find jobs. In 2002, Babcock's placement rate three months after graduation was a solid 83 percent. Still, there are some students who say that number has to do as much with their own efforts in finding a job as with the effectiveness of Babcock's career management center. "Some staff members were more helpful and savvy than others," says one 2002 graduate. "But a student had to be aggressive about getting the attention of staffers."

TOP HIRES

Wachovia (5); Emerson (4); Ingersoll-Rand (3); R.J. Reynolds (3); Progress Energy (3); BB&T (3); Philip Morris (3).

OUTSTANDING FACULTY

Ajay Patel (finance); Jon Pinder (quantitative strategy); Ram Baliga (strategy); Rick Harris (marketing/strategy).

APPLICANT TIPS

To be a good fit with Babcock you have to demonstrate to the admissions staff members that you can handle the small class sizes—so they'll be looking at your interpersonal skills, your leadership experience, and your ability to be a team player. Babcock will consider candidates without work experience—indeed, some incoming students haven't had a job before applying—but these applicants still have had internships or some sort of leadership experience, and you'll have to demonstrate that you'll be willing to speak up in class to contribute.

"I don't think people apply to our business school who don't enjoy being on teams, because that is everything we market: team environment and small class size," says Assistant Dean of Admission Mary Goss. "If we do get someone like that applying, they haven't done their homework."

Your GMAT scores and undergraduate grades will demonstrate your ability to handle the intense first-year curriculum. The school's GMAT average is 643, but even if you scored a 400 you should still consider applying to Babcock. Goss recognizes that not everyone is a great test taker, and you can prove your worth with your essay and interview. "Our whole philosophy is that we want you to be successful, and we're going to work with you to be successful," Goss says.

So while interviews are not required, they are highly recommended and are perhaps one of the most important parts of the application, especially for those coming straight out of undergraduate or with less than a year of work experience. "We've got to evaluate if this is someone we can put in front of a recruiter," says Goss. You'll want to prepare for the interview as you would for a job interview—again, do your homework. Think about what in your background will help you contribute to a school whose defining characteristic is its small class size. Goss reminds potential interviewees to remember that even small things like eye contact show confidence and interest. "You're selling yourself," she says.

If you can't make it to Winston-Salem for an interview, your essay will be weighed even more heavily than it would otherwise. "You've got to be realistic in the plans you have laid out to reach your goals in an essay," Goss says. "Don't regurgitate everything that's in our marketing material." The school's open-door policy extends to the admissions office—"Let us know who you are and what your concerns are," Goss says, adding that she always finds it strange when people don't address weaknesses in their applications. "Even if it's an admission of 'I partied a lot at first in school, but got much more focused the last two years.'"

Babcock has initiated an international alumni interviewing program for international applicants. The application deadline for international students is March 1. You can submit your applications online through *The Princeton Review* or download them from the school's Web site. If you submit your application by the early decision deadline of December 1, you'll have an answer by Christmas; those seeking financial aid should have paperwork in by March 1. The deadline for applying for 10 full-tuition Dean's Scholars Program scholarships is February 15.

BABCOCK MBAs SOUND OFF

Wake Forest University School of Management is an excellent institution that is doing its best with its limited resources. If they were able to admit more students to their program, I think they would be able to generate a greater incentive for companies to come to the school. The students are well trained and for the most part are extremely hardworking. It has been a great learning experience for me.

I think Babcock is a wonderful business school. It has over the years hired exceptional faculty and the quality of the class has been rising. My transition as an international student could not have been better at any other school. The admissions committee and my peers went out of their way to help us.

Babcock really goes a long way to try and give its students the best. I certainly appreciate the effort they make on ensuring the best education for the students.

Babcock is a wonderful experience. It has faculty who are GREAT teachers as well as wonderful scholars. My main complaints about Babcock are that the scope of electives is small (a necessary trade-off for a small program) and that the caliber of students in the bottom 20 percent of the class is not yet up to the caliber of a top program.

The youth of the student population leads to professionalism issues in class and interviews. Students are extremely bright, but some don't have the job experience that engenders the necessary poise to wow an interviewer. Some class discussions can falter as well because of this problem, and it generally is not addressed by faculty and staff. Students aren't individually addressed about personal presentation challenges, and as a result have problems during the interview process. While grad school is not the place for baby-sitting, a bit of frank constructive feedback now and then is necessary. I rarely saw evidence of this except when it was reflected in grades.

THE BEST BUSINESS SCHOOLS OUTSIDE THE UNITED STATES

Non-U.S. B-schools are a good option for many students.

MBA programs are a dime a dozen in the United States. You'll find B-schools in just about every U.S. state; and in cities such as Chicago, New York, and San Francisco, top-rated programs are sometimes located around the corner, across a river, or just a few subway stops from one another. With so many programs in the United States, how do hopeful business students set themselves apart from the pack? The answer isn't always found in the United States. These days, you'll find plenty of attractive options abroad. In fact, European and Canadian B-schools are enjoying rising popularity among applicants and corporate recruiters in search of a U.S.-modeled MBA program that explores business puzzles from all over the globe, not just American issues. Recruiters are looking for MBAs with a tested patience for cultural nuances, the ability to converse in languages other than English, and a global outlook. Students in such international programs often study with classmates from every corner of the globe, while most U.S. programs fill 70 percent of their classes with U.S. students.

Earning an MBA outside of the United States has grown so popular that *BusinessWeek* began ranking programs outside of the United States in 2000. The special rating is set apart from *BusinessWeek*'s top U.S. list mainly because the students these schools attract, the intercultural experiences offered, and the companies hiring these grads are distinct from what's happening in U.S. schools. B-schools in Europe especially have offered exclusive, high-quality programs for decades. They fill their programs with experienced professionals from various countries, with no one nationality dominating the class. When you compare *BusinessWeek*'s number 1 global B-school (INSEAD, in France and Singapore) to its number 1 rival in the U.S. ranking (Northwestern University's Kellogg School of Management), the differences become clear. Ninety-three percent of INSEAD MBAs aren't French, and at the Fontainbleau campus, MBAs hail from 74 countries. At graduation, about three-quarters of INSEAD grads found jobs in Western Europe. On the other hand, 67 percent of Kellogg's MBAs are U.S. citizens, and 83 percent of 2002 graduates found jobs in the United States. Kellogg students need to be fluent in English to start the course, while INSEAD students need to be comfortable with at least three languages by the time they graduate. Recruiters from global firms happily snatch up grads from rigorous European programs requiring such honed linguistic skills. Recruiters in 2002 told *BusinessWeek* that such graduates bring more to the table than their U.S. counterparts.

You'll find the European schools in *BusinessWeek*'s global list to be more diverse than the Canadian schools. Canadian Jen Weitzel, 29, chose to study at number 4–ranked London Business School to take advantage of the school's diverse culture. In her first-year group at LBS, she studied with a lawyer from Ireland, an Indian accountant, a female consultant from Moscow, and an economist from Uruguay. "What a phenomenal pocket of experience," she says. Students at Switzerland's IMD (number 3) average seven years of varied work experience, making class discussions real, not abstract and imaginative. On the other hand, of the four Canadian schools rated by *BusinessWeek,* only York University's Schulich School of Business (number 10) fills more than 50 percent of its full-time MBA class with students from abroad. Even then, the majority of non-Canadian Schulich MBAs come from Asia.

MBAs studying in Europe and Canada stand to benefit from shorter MBA programs, too. IMD, INSEAD, and Canada's Queen's School of Business (number 2) each offer yearlong programs, while HEC (number 9) program lasts 15 months. Rotterdam School of Management (number 7) shortened its MBA program to 15 months in 2002. Spending less time away from work means that these grads have less of a debt load than U.S. MBAs shoulder from two-year programs.

If you're studying in Europe or Canada, you're likely to enjoy a social life that's distinct from what U.S. MBAs experience. For starters, at most of *BusinessWeek*'s top global schools, integrating the local students with foreigners isn't an issue, since no one nationality commands a majority in class. So you're just as likely to be invited over to a classmate's flat for an Indian curry as you may be for an asado with the Argentine students or a pasta and wine bash with the Italians. If you're in Europe, you can escape each campus in *BusinessWeek*'s top rating within hours for a taste of another country and culture.

MBA grads say that most of their grad school enlightenment didn't come from long lectures on corporate finance or ethics. Instead, it was sharp class discussions, group meetings, and access to professors and top professionals that made their experience what it was. Your satisfaction as an MBA will be determined mostly by which school you study at, but the region of the world you choose to study in can be the icing on the cake.

INSEAD

Boulevard de Constance, 77305 Fontainebleau, France
1 Ayer Rajah Avenue, Singapore 138676
E-mail: mba.info@insead.edu
Web site: www.insead.edu/MBA

1.
INSEAD

Enrollment: 836
Women: 25%
International: 93%
Average age: 29
Applicants accepted: 27%

Total tuition: $42,200
Average GMAT score: 700
Corporate ranking: 2
Graduate ranking: 2
Intellectual capital rank: 1

Drive through French villages such as Moret-sur-Loing, Recloses, or Bourron-Marlotte, and you may pass an abundance of gray Peugeot 206 cars with red license plates. Peer into the windows of homes such as Chateau de Montmelian, Chateau de Recloses, Moulin de Moret, or Chateau de Fleury and you're likely to see lights burning into the wee hours of the morning. Come across a car or a house like that, and you've probably found an MBA from *BusinessWeek*'s 2002 number 1 B-school outside of the United States: INSEAD. (Non-Europeans studying in France get tax discounts on such vehicles, and many such chateaus have housed INSEAD MBAs for generations.)

By 8:30 A.M., the Peugeots are parked in the lovely town of Fontaine-bleau, and the drivers are in class. Across the world—a 13-hour flight from Paris—another batch of MBAs is finishing a day of classes at INSEAD's second campus in Singapore's Bouna Vista neighborhood, about 15 minutes from the city center.

But these MBAs aren't your stereotypical white males with banking or consulting backgrounds. MBAs studying at both of INSEAD's campuses average 4.8 years of work experience and come from a variety of industries. Women make up 25 percent of the student body—up from 18 percent in 1998—and more than half of the students hail from non-Western countries. The school attracts top students from nations that other B-schools can't manage to snag, such as El Salvador, Cambodia, Kenya, and Moldova. Singapore students come from 50 different countries, those at Fontainebleau from 74 nations. "No one feels a barrier to bringing up examples from their home country in class," says the dean of the MBA program, Pekka Hietala.

The 43-year-old MBA program locks MBAs into a frantic pace from day one until they receive their diplomas 10½ months later. MBAs can begin classes in September, graduating the following June, or begin in January, take a seven-week summer break to complete an internship, and finish in December. The program is divided into five eight-week periods, the first two of which are made up almost entirely of

INSEAD's 15 required core courses. All classes are taught in English. "The workload is incredible," says Kirstine Villaume, 29, a member of the class graduating in June 2003. "One of the hardest things you have to learn here is to learn what not to learn. You don't have time to learn everything." The school assigns incoming students to diverse study groups of five to seven people for most of the first four months. "With those teams, you spend long hours, and sometimes sleepless nights, writing up papers or doing group exercises," says Bob De Man, who graduated in December 2002 and split his class time between the Asian and European campuses. Be ready for as many as seven hours of extra prep work, and group work daily, he warns.

In the third period, MBAs begin taking electives in classes of about 35 students each. New electives include Culture and Management in Asia, Intellectual Property and Technology Strategy, and Venture Opportunities and Business Models. MBAs can also travel between the Singapore and Fontainebleau campuses during this period. (About 200 did just that in 2002, and the school expects more to do so in 2003.) Hietala insists that by the third period, "it's just one big program" between the campuses.

A challenging program and a global perspective aren't the only reasons INSEAD received a top ranking in 2002. The school benefits from the energy of its dean of three years, former finance professor Gabriel Hawawini. It also benefits from a growing and increasingly strong faculty. The school currently has 142 faculty members, a 6 percent increase since 2000. The administration plans to add another 14 professors to the Singapore campus, and will construct a new building behind its current space in the next few years. The Fontainebleau campus is making gains, too. By 2004, it will have an additional 25 percent of space with new amphitheaters, breakout rooms, and more. The school's entrepreneurship department has seen growth, too. (As many as 40 percent of alums work for themselves 10 years after graduating from INSEAD, so the administration now wants its grads to understand the basics of building a business before they leave.) Cushioning such growth is an endowment that has swelled to $46 million, from very little in 1994.

By 2005, the Singapore campus will accept 300 MBAs. This year more students enrolled than was expected when INSEAD Singapore opened its doors, taking 244 students, up from 115 in 2001. "We were fortunate to receive 40 to 50 percent more applications last year, so it was easy to increase the numbers," Hietala says. Singapore students don't live in chateaus, but rather in fully equipped condominiums near campus, with swimming pools, fitness clubs, and barbeque pits. "We spent great evenings there," says De Man. Having a Singapore campus helps to attract students as well. One of the reasons that Eunjin Kim, a 33-year-old 2002 graduate of INSEAD's Fontainebleau campus, now a consultant for McKinsey in Seoul, chose INSEAD was for its emphasis on Asian businesses. "With its new campus in Singapore, there's great upside potential of name value for INSEAD in the near future in Asia, where I want to build my career," Kim says.

No matter the amount of coursework, there's always time for fun. Kirstine Villaume says that there's time to taste wines after class, join a salsa dance club, go horseback riding, or, in her case, play on the school's touch rugby team. The school sends teams to compete in the MBA Olympics each year in Paris, as well as to other events around the world to compete in soccer and rugby matches or ski races. With so many international students on campus, rarely does a week pass that isn't devoted to a nation and all of the culture, food, and dance that comes with it. "There are too many things to enjoy; sometimes it's really difficult to prioritize your time," Eunjin Kim says. Students on both campuses agree that the starting point to any evening is usually a bar.

Despite its locations in France and Singapore, the B-school is anything but a French or

Asian school. An alliance formed in March 2001 with the University of Pennsylvania's Wharton School makes that clear. In 2002, about 70 INSEAD MBAs spent eight weeks studying on Wharton's campus in the United States, and Wharton MBAs got to hit the books in Asia and Europe. The schools are also working to offer executive education programs together.

INSEAD isn't an easy school to gain acceptance to. In 2002, the admissions group received 3062 applications and ultimately accepted 27 percent. The newest cohorts of students averaged a 700 score on the GMAT, and all of the admittees were interviewed at least twice, as the school worked to evaluate their emotional intelligence. MBA hopefuls with their sights set on INSEAD should listen to what Hietala says before submitting an application: "Anyone who hasn't left their home country should not apply." Along those lines, applicants without two languages down pat before applying—one of which must be English—should wait. MBAs need to be fluent in three languages before INSEAD will award them a degree.

Attending a one-year program saves INSEAD MBAs some money on tuition bills. INSEAD's tuition in 2002 was $42,200, compared to $69,892 for a two-year degree at Wharton. But, since few people have about $60,000 of disposable money to cover all of their B-school costs, INSEAD offers a loan to accepted students. Once an applicant is accepted to the Asia or Europe campus, he or she is eligible for an ABN Amro Bank loan—on passing a basic credit check, and regardless of nationality or needing a co-signer.

INSEAD's short program allows MBAs to save money and rejoin the workforce earlier, but unless they start in January and intern during the seven-week summer break, there is no time allotted for internships. As at other schools in 2001–2002, there were fewer jobs to go around. "We were down like all other schools," says Mary Boss, director of INSEAD's career management

service. About 110 companies trekked to the school's campuses in 2001 to interview MBAs graduating that year, and in June 2002, just 65 came to interview graduates in Singapore and France.

Technology is helping to fill in the gaps, however. Students who want to interview with companies that only visit the other INSEAD campus may do so via videoconferencing. Boss's office hosts five or six such interviews daily. The students can also tap into a Web-based system to help manage the job search. Since 2000, INSEAD has also participated in the Virtual Career Fair, which links MBAs to employers who don't have the wherewithal to trek to campus for presentations.

Boss insists that INSEAD's role isn't to hand students jobs at graduation. So, while these MBAs know how to interview for a job and negotiate for a good salary before they leave campus, they also know how to conduct interviews as a hiring manager and how to negotiate a salary with a candidate.

With about a year's worth of demanding classes, informal networking in class with a diverse group of classmates, and alumni, INSEAD MBAs are prepared for just about any business scenario. And with the option of studying on two continents, it's easy to see why INSEAD appeals to so many people.

INSEAD MBAs SOUND OFF

INSEAD is really quite unique in that it combines the usual search for excellence with, how should I say it, the continental charm of Europeans. My impression was that, for better or worse, MBAs here may not be as aggressive or competitive as American MBAs, but they are certainly at least as smart, hardworking, and nice toward their fellow classmates. Having previously worked only in Asia and North America, this was a fresh, eye-opening experience. I heartily recommend this program to anyone who is contemplating an MBA.

INSEAD is an outstanding school, with a truly top-notch student body. But it tries to pack too much into one year, at the expense of quality in the learning experience. There is simply no way one person can read all that is assigned—no physical way.

The jewel of INSEAD is in the strength of its faculty and depth and diversity of the student body, which contribute to the learning and growing, but the administration and placement offices are out of touch with the needs and detached from current issues of the students and job market.

I am happy about my choice of INSEAD; I believe it is the clear leader in Europe and at the same level as the best U.S. business schools.

After having spent a year at INSEAD, I'm glad that I came here. It has been a wonderful experience and has helped me to understand what I want to do in my life. The school provided me with skills I will use to achieve my professional goals and gave me lifetime friends. This experience vastly exceeded my best expectations!

QUEEN'S UNIVERSITY

Queen's School of Business—MBA for Science & Technology
143 Union Street, Goodes Hall
Queen's School of Business
Kingston, Ontario K7L 3N6, Canada
E-mail: admin@mbast.queensu.ca
Web site address: http://www.business.queensu.ca

Enrollment: 602 (66 full-time)	Total tuition: $30,000
Women: 24%	Average GMAT score: 676
International: 24%	Corporate ranking: 1
Average age: 30	Graduate ranking: 3
Applicants accepted: 33%	Intellectual capital rank: 6

Queen's business school founded its MBA program in 1960, but only in 1996 did the school decide to refocus the program on science and technology professionals. In doing so, Queen's created a leading MBA program in a short time. Queen's MBA for Science & Technology lasts 12 months, tightly packing best practices in general management into the minds of experienced professionals from the science and engineering fields. But don't let the name of the program fool you: Queen's graduates don't automatically return to their laboratories or drawing tables. The program gets its name from the type of students it admits, not the kind it graduates. Many graduates are snatched up for jobs in investment banks, marketing firms, and consulting practices by corporate recruiters who appreciate their highly specialized backgrounds and newfound management skills.

The students' popularity among recruiters, and their satisfaction with the education they received at Queen's, vaulted the program to *BusinessWeek*'s number 2 rank—Queen's first ranking ever by *BusinessWeek*.

It's a small program, with just 66 students enrolled in the class of 2003. In 2002, Queen's filled 76 percent of the class seats with Canadians, and many of the rest with Asian students. "The percentage of Canadian students is somewhat misleading," says 2003 class president S. Craig West. "We come from really diverse backgrounds," and students speak about 25 languages. A lack of English language skills is usually the reason more international students aren't accepted to Queen's. Gloria Saccon, associate director of the MBA for Science & Technology and director of admissions says, "it is imperative that international students meet the minimum criteria as set out, as well as provide evidence of fluency in conversational English and strong written communication skills." The quality of Queen's applicants stands to improve as the school's reputation becomes known abroad.

Regardless of nationality, these MBAs wield lots of professional experience. The average age of a Queen's MBA is 30, with five years of professional experience, and one-fifth of students already have a graduate degree. That's by design, because the school wants each student to add insight to class discussions and to bolster group work. Few women apply to the Queen's, and just 24 percent enrolled in 2002. Queen's wants to receive more applications from women, but having a focus on science and technology has hurt that percentage. And, until recently, fewer science professionals, such as biologists and chemists, applied to the program than engineers. With few women in engineering, the school wasn't making strides in attracting female students.

Queen's attempt to recruit more women isn't aided by the fact that the school's first female dean, Margot Northey, left campus in February 2001 abruptly and for uncertain reasons. In July, she was replaced by Lewis Johnson, a finance professor who has worked at the B-school since 1981. Johnson has taken up the reins at an opportune time. In September 2002, the school opened the doors to a new $25.5 million (Canadian) building called Goodes Hall. The B-school center was built to incorporate a Victorian schoolhouse that has sat on the property since 1892. With the modern addition, Goodes Hall has more than 110,000 square feet of classrooms, offices, lounges, and reception space. And it's wired to the ceiling with technology.

These MBAs can use all the comfortable space they can get. The intensity of the Queen's MBA is impressive, and the source of the few complaints Queen's graduates expressed in the *BusinessWeek* survey. "There was no downtime during the whole year," says graduate Zafar Bhatti. Most grads feel that they're gasping for air by the time they collect their diplomas. Plan on working on campus from 8 A.M. until 7 P.M., and another four hours of work at home. Bhatti adds, "other B-schools are rough for the first

two semesters, but the second year eases up." At Queen's, however, "I was busy from beginning until end."

Classes begin in May each year and finish 12 months later. The program is divided into four stages, the first three of which, each lasting for about three months, focus on core courses. Each stage begins with a weeklong seminar on the post-MBA job search and long-term career goals called the career advantage module. Throughout the program, MBAs work in small teams that have a trained facilitator students can call 24 hours a day if any sticky issues arise. The school chooses the teams, leaning on results from two personal assessment tests, the Myers-Briggs Type Indicator (MBTI) and the Hermann Brain Dominance Indicator (HBDI).

Students focus their studies during the fourth stage, called management concentrations. The MBAs choose one of four concentrations: strategy and management consulting, finance and investment banking, marketing management, and management of operations and information technology. Students sign on to the program understanding that they won't have many concentrations to choose from, but, in town hall meetings in 2002 (such meetings between students and administrators are held once per stage), more students voiced their ideas for new concentrations, says Craig West. During the fourth stage, students are required to complete either a management consulting project, so that they may apply course concepts to real business issues, or the New Ventures Project, which allows MBAs to develop a business plan of their own and to flesh out their business idea with a faculty mentor.

The work schedule at Queen's leaves little time for day-to-day life, such as family parties, conversation with friends, or even elective surgeries. Maria Luckevich, who graduated in 2002, put off surgery until she finished the MBA. During the program, she only saw her husband on weekends, since he lived six hours away. And when they did see each other, "he'd drive six hours just to watch me work all weekend," she says.

Still, students are students, and blowing off steam is key. "We worked hard, but we also partied hard," says Zafar Bhatti. Every Thursday, students meet for drinks at a pub, a gathering known fondly as "point-four" because MBAs figure their grade point averages drop that much from swapping their books for pint glasses. If it's not a point-four night, Queen's MBAs tend to relax with group members over dinner. The MBAs also compete in the Canadian MBA games every year.

There's plenty of housing in the Kingston area, but Kingston is a college town, and local property owners charge steep rents and don't offer much apartment for the money, grads say. For the best values, students suggest living in neighborhoods that aren't within walking distance of the school.

During the school's three career weeks, the MBAs spend a lot of time focusing on personal development, goals, and professional objectives. And while the career advice they receive is top notch, Queen's grads earn far less than graduates from their number 1 program, INSEAD in France and Singapore. In 2002, Queen's graduates reported earning a median $54,500 at graduation, while INSEAD graduates reported median starting salaries of $84,000. The career manager at Queen's, Sandra McCance, says that Queen's MBA graduates who land jobs in the United States or in other parts of the world "are consistently paid competitive salaries for those countries." And no matter their pay at graduation, the money they spend on the degree is far less than in the United States or abroad—just $48,000 (Canadian) for their 12 months of classes, including books, case materials, and all supplies. Three months after graduation in 2002, just over half of the class had found full-time jobs. And while Queen's tries to diversify its student base, it's got even more work to do on its recruiter base: every graduate who reported landing a job found that job in North America.

Getting into Queen's takes more than meeting the basic requirements, says Admissions Director Saccon. In addition to having an undergraduate degree in the sciences, or in engineering, a strong GMAT score (Queen's MBAs average 676) and serious work experience, Saccon is looking for evidence of leadership and the team skills. "Not only do [admittees] have a strong academic background and relevant work experience, they also have exceptional interpersonal skills, the ability to work as part of a productive team, and demonstrated leadership potential," she says. And Saccon wants to see that incoming students have personality. For that reason, MBA hopefuls who meet the basic requirements have to complete an interview. In a small program such as Queen's, there's no room for sour apples. In 2002, the school received 202 complete applications and accepted 33 percent. Be sure to submit your application early in the admissions process, because Saccon's office admits applications as they come through the door, and once the class is full, it's full, she says.

With a number 2 ranking, and a new building to celebrate in, Queen's is in a good position as it aims to increase the number of students it accepts in 2003 to 78.

QUEEN'S MBAs SOUND OFF

A unique aspect of the program is the emphasis on teamwork. Before entering the program we are subjected to four different social/personality tests. We were then put into teams that maximized our diversity. The six members of my team were totally different. Working together is a requirement of the program. If we could not do this we would not graduate. In order to help us in this area, we were given training on how to be an effective team, and we had the services of a facilitator to help with conflicts as they happened.

Queen's is underrated at an international level, and the administration has promised to improve the school's reputation abroad. I feel that Queen's has left me well positioned in the long term, and this is what is most important.

This program required an overwhelming amount of work and great personal sacrifice in almost all other aspects of the participants' lives. At times during its course, the program did not seem like it would ever be worth what we had to endure to get through it; it does now.

Overall Queen's is a fantastic program. I am more than satisfied with the program, and I would do it over again if I had to make the choices again. Finally, the people I met in the program were top notch and will surely be close, longtime business and personal contacts.

Queen's MBA program only offers one international business course. Queen's needs to hire more faculty to meet the needs of students who wish to pursue a focus in international business.

3.
IMD

IMD (INTERNATIONAL INSTITUTE FOR MANAGEMENT DEVELOPMENT)

Ch de Bellerive 23
P.O. Box 915
CH-1001 Lausanne, Switzerland
E-mail address: mbainfo@imd.ch
Web site address: www.imd.ch/mba

Enrollment: 160 (90 full-time)   Total tuition: $50,000
Women: 23%   Average GMAT score: 670
International: 95%   Corporate ranking: 5
Average age: 30   Graduate ranking: 4
Applicants accepted: 17%   Intellectual capital rank: 5

Ask residents of Lausanne, Switzerland what they know about the MBA program in their town, and a first response could be that the students are "monks." The International Institute for Management Development (IMD) may be set in a pristine Swiss landscape along the shores of Lake Geneva, but the students don't see much of the lake or town during their 42-week (10½-month) program. "IMD isn't about having an opportunity to see Switzerland," says Duncan Coombe, a member of the class of 2002. "You're here to have an intense, personal development process." Such a work ethic keeps IMD ranked among *BusinessWeek*'s top 10 non-U.S. B-schools and makes it one of the recruiters' favorite places to shop for MBA talent. In 2002, IMD ranked number 3, an improvement from its number 4 rank in 2000.

The school has a reputation around the world for offering an exclusive MBA program for over 30 years. With just 90 seats for MBAs from 37 nations, only 17 percent of those who apply make the cut. The result: IMD is one of the most selective schools internationally. (In 2002, number 1–ranking INSEAD accepted 27 percent of its applicants.) IMD also has one of the higher yield rates among B-schools, with 73 percent of admitted applicants opting to attend the school.

Because it's a small program that demands focus and energy, IMD is considered best suited for a professional with more work experience. IMD students have an average of seven years of top-notch experience, compared to the average of five or more years that U.S. B-schoolers wield. That keeps the crowd elite and lets the school feel at ease mixing its executive MBAs with full-time MBAs in elective courses toward the end of the program. When the students discuss a company they're reading about in a case, "it's a less abstract discussion, because someone in class has usually had experience with that company through work," explains class of 2002 member Pim Van Wesel. Fifty-four percent of MBAs come from industries such as manufacturing, oil, gas, and consumer goods; another 18 percent come from entrepreneurial jobs; and 17 percent are from consulting.

Classes begin in January and end in November of the same year. In that time, the school says that you'll be transformed from a fast-track employee to a CEO-bound star. From day one, students have access to 45 full-time faculty members—that's a student-to-teacher ratio that is tough to beat. The profs don't go easy on these rising stars: "It's not for the faint of heart," says Katty Ooms Suter, director of MBA admissions.

As an IMD MBA, you'll spend more than 1700 hours in classes that begin at 8:30 A.M. on Monday mornings and run through 1:00 P.M. on Saturdays for the first five months of the program. Because the school focuses on teamwork, you'll end up putting in 16-hour school days, between classes and group meetings that run late into the evening. "The first five months at IMD are all about intensity," says Duncan Coombe. "I never anticipated that it would be anything like this. There was a sense of relentlessness to it that never went away."

Despite the fact that IMD is an international program, English is the only language spoken in class. From January until May, students are in a fixed schedule of classes during the Building Blocks section of the program. Taking courses such as Economics, Accounting, Political Economy, and Industry Analysis, you'll read three cases per night, or about 100 pages. After the core courses end, you'll prepare for a weeklong trip to Bosnia. "They're a very privileged group of people," says Ooms Suter. "On this trip, we want them to rethink what life is like for real people."

Your international consulting projects begin in July, as does your participation in IMD's Dynamic Learning Networks. The networks link MBAs with grads and corporate partners of the school, and via the Net the teams tackle new business issues such as intrapreneurship (being an entrepreneur within a large corporation) and crisis management. Then it's on to three more weeks of classes in August.

While students are managing their own schedules by June, "they're working from 8 A.M. until midnight," says Julianne Jammers, director of MBA career services and marketing. The set schedule leaves just three weeks in October and early November for four to five electives such as Ethics & Globalization: Business Dilemmas & Challenges; Managing International Business Government Relations; Advanced Corporate Finance; and Business History: Lessons from the Past. You will get to choose from a list of 10 to 15 and study alongside executive MBAs. "Some students say that they'd prefer to choose from more electives, but that that's what you get for going to a small, intimate school," explains Pim Van Wesel.

The busy schedule is something to consider for the 50 percent of students who bring partners or families to school. Although the school doesn't offer residences, it says that finding housing is easy. The cost is about $700 per month.

When students do have a chance to catch their breath, most find their calm among the comforts of a good meal, a bottle of wine, and good conversation with classmates. In fact, many IMD students say that their best memories are of long dinner parties. Toward the beginning of the program, there's time to sneak away from campus to the ski slopes on Saturday afternoons. And every May, IMD does send a group of tired but energetic MBAs to compete in the European MBA games in Paris.

U.S. applicants beware: this is no easy school to get accepted into. In fact, Ooms Suter says that while U.S. applicants make up the fourth largest group submitting applications to IMD, the majority of U.S. applicants don't have what the school's looking for. "It's more difficult to get people with international experience from the States," she says. It's also a good idea to submit an application to IMD as close to the first deadline (February 1) as possible. "I've said no to some extremely strong candidates because I already had someone like them," Ooms Suter notes. So, if you're applying to IMD from a consulting firm, and three of your colleagues are also submitting applications, "you better be the best."

IMD graduates usually fare well at graduation. Indeed, often it's the recruiters that the school has to turn away, says Director Jammers. She can tell them whether or not she's got a student who fits what the recruiter is looking for. "In some senses, it's easier for our MBAs because they're not part of the entry-level MBA group," she says. They attract higher than average salaries, too. Reporting median salaries of $95,500, they top rivals INSEAD and London Business School, where students report starting base salaries of $84,000 and 86,000, respectively. That's not surprising, given the amount of work experience that IMD students bring to the program.

The only apparent drawback of IMD could be its relatively small alumni community of just 2253 living MBA alumni. But the small alumni community can also benefit MBAs in extraordinary ways—the groups are quite chummy. About 72 percent of the class of 2001 returned to campus in the summer of 2002 for an event with current MBAs. Thirty-nine alumni clubs can be found in 30 countries worldwide. And the campus isn't limited to just MBA participants and alumni. The school hosts about 4000 executives on campus every year in its nondegree executive education programs. From such interaction, 15 to 20 percent of the class of 2001 found jobs, says Jammers.

Compare your other B-school options to studying at a university next to a lake that harbors inspiration, and you'll probably be better off while you face the grind of one of the most demanding B-schools. And in the case of IMD, beauty comes with a strong network of program graduates, so you may work harder than ever, but you'll be in good hands when you're done.

IMD MBAs SOUND OFF

IMD's MBA is a very unique experience. I am only just realizing how much I have learned now, after the course has ended. The course is so intense it's hard to realize what and how much you are learning when in the midst of the program. But now, I and others can tell I've been to a top business school. I could only highly recommend it, but it is clearly not suited to everyone.

I don't think there is any better environment to learn this or enhance these skills than at IMD, where the class is small and intimate and the nationalities represented span the globe. No one culture or language dominates and there are different opinions on everything. This is a challenging and stimulating place to be.

IMD has a unique MBA program which may be difficult to compare to offerings of other institutions. The exceptional value of this program is the development of students as individuals as well as successful business persons.

I have never worked so hard in my entire life as I did during the MBA experience, but I have not enjoyed any other time of my life as much as I did at IMD. One of the keys to the success of this program is to enter a cohesive group of people that enjoy working in teams, look for cooperation, but also know when to challenge and how to do it. This is very much related to the maturity of the students in the school. The fact that the size of the class is smaller than at other schools to me has a disadvantage when it comes to the overall network size, but it has a huge advantage in terms of the quality of that network. Finally, the location was also very important. When you're so busy and have so little free time, it helps to be in a position to choose between skiing, hiking, or playing sports in one of the most beautiful locations in the world: on the shores of a lake with the Alps in the background.

4.
LONDON BUSINESS SCHOOL

LONDON BUSINESS SCHOOL

Regent's Park
MBA Programme Office
London, England
NW1 4SA
E-mail address: mbainfo@london.edu
Web site address: www.london.edu

Enrollment: 1515 (624 full-time)   Total tuition: $58,500
Women: 26%   Average GMAT score: 687
International: 83%   Corporate ranking: 7
Average age: 28   Graduate ranking: 1
Applicants accepted: 19%   Intellectual capital rank: 2

If you ever have the chance to stand in a crowded room of MBAs representing various business schools from around the world, the MBAs from London Business School crowd will be easy for you to find. If you're in a ski lodge, some of the students may be wearing kilts, heralding the fact that there's little on but the kilt. Stand in a bar, and they may approach you to paste a tattoo of LBS on your arm or hip. Go to a party, and the band on stage may be The LBS Band. Even if you aren't at an MBA event, you may bump into the LBS crowd around Christmas time in London: they'll be the 130 people dressed in Santa Claus suits, reindeer hats, and elf stockings singing carols on the Tube and wandering from pub to pub in the annual Santa Claus Pub Crawl.

They're a rowdy, fun bunch to associate with. And, believe it or not, they also hail from a business school that's increasingly serious about management education. There's a buzz in the air, because this B-school's 620 full-time MBAs have been attracting attention as the school continues to rank among the world's best. LBS earned *BusinessWeek*'s rating of number 4 outside of the United States in 2002, a fall from number 2 in 2000.

That fall is somewhat attributable to the recent changes at the 37-year-old B-school. The school's last dean, John Quelch, left in July 2001. Quelch was known for creating 37 alumni associations in 31 countries (the school had none before), increasing the school's revenues 50 percent, and expanding the faculty roster to 90 (the school currently has 93 full-time research and teaching faculty members).

In January 2002, the school welcomed a new dean, Laura D'Andrea Tyson, former national economic advisor to Bill Clinton and dean at the Haas School of Business at the University of California's Berkeley campus. "Tyson stops and listens to what is happening," says Teresa Pabst, an LBS graduate from 2002. "She lent support to the things we were doing." In June, Dean Tyson led a master class for second-year

MBAs entitled Redefining Business Challenges in the Global Economy. In October, Tyson delivered the school's first state of the school speech to MBAs, alumni, and faculty. In that same month, she also met Queen Elizabeth to accept The Queen's Award for Enterprise on the school's behalf. Tyson is expected to continue building the LBS brand abroad and to secure a strong internal role at the school.

The school's flagship offering is its full-time 21-month MBA. (It also offers an executive MBA, the Sloan master's degree, and a seven-year-old Master of Finance program.) The MBA program mirrors a North American approach, but it's anything but a vanguard of U.S.—or British—culture. LBS classrooms are seated with people and practices from other countries, cultures, and creeds: 83 percent of the class of 2004 hails from outside of the United Kingdom, from more than 60 countries. Although native English speakers don't face a language barrier on this campus, all LBS students must show competence in at least one language other than English by the time they graduate. In fact, a handful of people don't receive their diplomas every year because their second language isn't up to snuff.

As a testament to the school's international flair, students began a daylong event in 2001 called Tatoo. Every October, students, staff, faculty, alumni, and anyone else with a stake in LBS gather to play sports and enjoy entertainment from around the world designed by international clubs at LBS. In 2002, more than 1500 people attended Tatoo.

MBAs push through 15 required courses during the program's first nine months. You'll work in an assigned team of six to eight students for the entire year. (Watch out for Understanding Financial Analysis, and Corporate Finance, students say.) Under the guidance of the associate dean for MBA programs, George Yip, the core courses include more lessons on leadership, soft skills, and entrepreneurial know-how. The school also added a required shadowing project,

which pairs MBAs with experienced managers and finishes off with the MBAs turning in a research-based paper to their mentor and another to the school for grading.

Most MBAs intern during the summer between their first and second years. In 2001, however, the school began to offer a now popular alternative to working for someone else: the Entrepreneurship Summer School. Students interested in creating their own businesses can apply to the school, which enrolled 40 students in 2002. The nine full-time MBAs are the minority in class—perhaps the greatest advantage of the program—with 23 executive MBAs and other master's students or local businesspeople filling the remaining seats. The students work on their own business plans and present the plans to venture capitalists at the end of the session.

In the second year of study, MBAs complete 12 elective courses, choosing from a catalog of 66, and can focus their studies to concentrate on subjects such as change management, finance, international business, marketing, or technology management. LBS MBAs may also spend a semester abroad in one of the largest MBA exchange programs in the world. Nearly one-third of second-year MBAs take advantage of London's partnerships with 30 other schools, many of them in the United States as well as in the rest of Europe, and some in Asia and South America. Abroad or in London, you will have to participate in the Second Year Project, for which two students work together to complete a serious consulting project for a business between October and May. (With faculty approval, MBAs may opt to flesh out their own business plans at this time.) Among the projects in 2002, student teams wrote a business plan for a Museum of Contemporary Fashion and a plan for a company's Asian operations, and explored another company's options in music news syndication. Companies pay the students as much as £3000 for their work, though some not-for-profit organizations pay a lot less or nothing at all. The MBAs, with guidance from an LBS faculty member, usually work for about 25 days each at the company, and one-third of students complete projects for companies located outside of the United Kingdom. When the projects end, the MBAs submit a report to their client, and another copy to LBS, which awards a grade.

As the creation of the Entrepreneurship Summer School would indicate, entrepreneurship is taken seriously at LBS. Any grad hoping to start his or her own company can apply to Sussex Place Investment Management Ltd. (SPIM) for funding. And, since 1993, together with INSEAD, LBS has organized the annual European business plan competition. In 2002, an LBS team won the second runner-up prize.

The 300-person class is kept to a deliberately manageable size to create a sense of intimacy in the midst of a very urban environment. Though students live scattered throughout London and get to campus by bike, bus, or the underground (subway), many stick around after classes to down a pint or enjoy Thai food at the Windsor Castle Pub, attached to the school. LBS also boasts some 30 sports- and subject-related clubs. "There are quite a few social things to do every week, so you can't hide," says Jen Weitzel, the chair of the student association and a member of the class of 2003. LBS also competes in the European MBA games in France each May, and won in 2002.

The school recently added more group study rooms and installed a campus wireless local area network. The gym in the four-year-old, $18 million Taunton Place is gaining a mezzanine level, and students can take free gym classes during the week. Perhaps more important is that the school recently doubled the size of its pub, the MBAr (pronounced M Bar), adding more room for weekly sundowners (free drinks) on Thursday nights. The MBAr is also the place where students gather for tea time—nope, no alcohol—on Wednesdays.

Landing a spot in London's MBA class is increasingly competitive, with 19 percent of applicants snagging seats in 2002. Applications for the class of 2004 were up 55 percent in 2002, and Julia Tylor, director of the MBA at the school, expects to see another healthy—though perhaps not so hefty—increase again in 2003. Like many other admissions directors, Tylor says applicants should apply early on and "be clear about the school you want." An interview is mandatory to apply, and is the time when the school focuses on the applicant's international outlook.

Diversity is ideal. The class of 2004 has more MBAs from Africa and the Middle East—areas of the world from which MBA programs would like to attract more students. While 20 percent of the class is from North America, Tylor says that the school isn't an outpost for U.S. schools: "We don't want to find that we're dominated by North American students."

As at other B-schools in 2002, MBAs had a difficult time finding employment when classes ended. At LBS, 174 companies came to campus to recruit first-year MBAs for internships, and 296 for full-time jobs. By the school's July graduation, just 64 percent of the class had a full-time job (in the boom year of 2000, 84 percent of grads had a job by the time they received their diplomas). But, for all the headaches that arrive as soon as a graduate's first loan payment slip is due, the 4,500-person alumni population pulls through for one another. "I have an immediate network of alumni, and that opens a lot more doors," says Teresa Pabst, who was still looking for a job in September 2002. Even LBS graduates of nondegree programs roll up their sleeves for MBA grads looking for work. "You're buying into longevity, not just two years (of an MBA)."

True, but at this B-school, you're sure to have a great time balancing student life with the history and sense of tradition that London offers. Heck, LBS's lawn spills onto Regent's Park, where the Queen's Calvary still parades through once a week. Who could ask for a more interesting location to study?

LBS MBAs SOUND OFF

My MBA was an extremely challenging program. The school did provide me an excellent education. I certainly believe the school is outstanding for those who wish to excel in business.

I found the MBA program to be harder than working, but would not change it for the world. I have learned so much and made wonderful friends.

The small and cozy campus and digestible class size of LBS really makes a huge difference for maximizing what you can get out of the program. We had 51 nationalities represented in our class and no one group represented over 20 percent. This level of diversity puts to shame North American schools claiming to be "international." The best parts of LBS for me comprised the student-led cultural and sporting clubs (and their tours and conferences and events) and, of course, the local pub that's attached to our little Central London campus.

I just want to say that, in spite of the debt I have incurred and the poor economic situation, I have every faith that what I have learned at LBS will help me throughout my entire career, and that the friends and contacts I have made will be valuable for the rest of my life.

The LBS MBA presents students with one of the best finance programs worldwide. If finance is one area an MBA candidate wants to focus on during his or her studies, then LBS must be seriously considered.

LBS has a high-quality network of exchange schools, which adds to the academic and international experience.

5.
UNIVERSITY OF TORONTO

UNIVERSITY OF TORONTO

Joseph L. Rotman School of Management
105 George Street
Toronto, Ontario M5S 3E6 Canada
E-mail address: mba@rotman.utoronto.ca
Web site address: www.rotman.utoronto.ca

Enrollment: 881 (430 full-time)   Total tuition: $39,630
Women: 33%   Average GMAT score: 673
International: 47%   Corporate ranking: 3
Average age: 29   Graduate ranking: 8
Applicants accepted: 32%   Intellectual capital rank: 3

Toronto, Canada is one of the most diverse cities in North America, and one of the largest by population. Its residents can enjoy the symphony, the theater, and a Wall Street of the city's own called Bay Street, where Canadian and U.S. banks have set up shop next door to one another. After work, there are plenty of sports to watch to release tension, such as hockey, basketball, and baseball. The only U.S. sport that Toronto lacks is football, though there is plenty of football Canadian style for the soccer fans.

Set into the heart of this activity, and around the corner from one of Toronto's four Chinatowns, is a B-school that reaps the benefits of its location and growing international reputation. That's the business school that *BusinessWeek* recently ranked second in Canada, and fifth outside of the U.S.—the University of Toronto's Joseph L. Rotman School of Management.

Many attribute the school's recent attention to its dean of four years, Roger L. Martin. The Harvard-reared dean—he's a 1981 Harvard Business School alum—was a director of Monitor Company, a strategy consulting firm based in Cambridge, Massachusetts. Once he settled into his campus office in 1998, Martin began insisting that the school "break down the silos" that business education revolves around, such as finance and marketing faculties. He aimed to graduate future CEOs rather than functionally specific managers—a lesson he probably learned in his HBS days.

The moved caused a bit of commotion—some professors have left the school since Martin's arrival—but overall, students are warming to the idea. "Integrative thinking is still taking hold at Rotman," says 2002 graduate Christopher Hilborn. He adds that the concept wasn't noticed much in the first year of classes, but that the dean wove it into the second year more completely. "You learn to recognize patterns in business that can make you more competitive."

Growth is front and center at the B-school. The school recruited a class of 230 students for its class of 2004, a 33 percent increase from the year before. To do that, the school added another 60-person section of students. And one of the dean's goals is to increase the school's endowment to $100 million (Canadian), from the $54 million (Canadian) the school has now. Compare that to Wharton's nearly $360 million endowment, and it's clear that Martin has his work cut out for him.

On, and even off, campus, Martin can't be avoided. First-year MBAs get their first taste of his character during a weeklong retreat held for them every August. At a camp two hours north of Toronto, near Perry Sound, the MBAs square dance, compete in mini-Olympic games, and test their luck at blackjack. The blackjack dealer? Martin himself, who is known for donning his cowboy boots for the affair. "It sets the tone for people to be able to chat with Dean Martin and the other professors who go," says second-year MBA D'Arcy Finley. Indeed, students on campus refer to the dean as Roger, not as Dean Martin.

After orientation, the real core begins with four mini-semesters. The new mini-semesters last seven weeks each and pack 21 core courses into the first year. Alongside the classic first-year courses of Finance, Accounting, Marketing and Statistics, and Organizational Behavior are courses such as Values, Judgment, and Decision Making; Global Managerial Perspectives; and Operations Management. The second year includes two compulsory courses—Advanced Strategic Management and Management Skills Development—and then opens the door for students to choose 9 elective courses from a menu of 58.

In the second year, Martin enters the fray again to teach an increasingly sold-out class called Learning How to Learn, where students learn how to absorb more information and to do so quickly. The second year is also the time that MBAs choose which streams of concentration they want to pursue. The finance streams—investment banking, funds management, and

risk management and financial engineering—are the most popular.

Between classes, life is pretty relaxed in the busy city. Despite a decidedly intense first year, the MBAs find time to gather for Thirsty Thursdays at popular hangouts including the Bedford Academy, The Bedford Ballroom, The Madison, and the Duke of York. There's also time to volunteer, an activity that many Rotman MBAs pick up after the school's annual Community Service Week. During the winter, you're likely to find a few MBAs donning skis or snowboards and hitting the slopes at Blue Mountain on the shores of Georgian Bay or Mont Tremblant, about five hours away from campus. Students compete in the annual Canadian MBA games, too. The most popular sport? Probably drinking, some quip, but Rotman does still tout that it was the overall champion in the 2000 games, though it placed fourth overall in 2002. By spring—you'll come to appreciate the word *thaw*—students are planning for talent shows and formal dances.

Most MBAs rent condos on Bay Street, or live in The Annex, a progressive neighborhood near campus packed with writers, actors, and yes, MBA students. Just north of campus, you'll also find MBAs renting places at the intersection of Young & Elington. Students pay an average of $775 (Canadian) a month in rent ($500 U.S.). There's a subway stop up the street from Rotman's main building, but many MBAs drive, thanks to a 700-car garage under the school.

In the spring, students begin the classic scramble for internships and full-time jobs. That's when the school traditionally struggles. The school's placement strengths lie in North America and in banks. Students and graduates say that they'd like more variety in the types of recruiters coming to the Career Development Center. Right now, anyone not looking for a job in finance or consulting will have to do more legwork.

Of course, in 2002, a lot of B-schools faced difficulties wooing companies to campus. Toronto had no better luck. Just 37 companies visited campus to hold receptions for second-year MBAs, and 260 posted jobs in the CDC. By graduation in June, 65 percent of graduates had jobs. Still, by graduation, many students were earning good salaries for Canada—a median of $50,000—but mediocre compared to those of grads in the United States and Europe. Most MBAs—68 percent—took jobs in banks after graduation, and 97 percent were starting jobs in North America. Non-Canadian students need to remember that finding a job in Canada won't be possible unless they have a work visa. And to get that, you need to have a job in Canada.

The good news is that tuition is paltry compared to that of U.S. B-schools. Canadians pay Rotman a tuition of $33,166 for 16 months of classes. And, while tuition across Canada is on the rise, reaching $39,633 in 2002 for a nonresident's entire Rotman MBA, it's a clear bargain compared to a $62,244 total bill at a school such as the University of Rochester's Simon Graduate School of Business Administration.

While the thought of an inexpensive MBA is a nice one, convincing foreigners to move to Canada for an MBA is easier said than done. Tuition may be cheap in Canada compared to at U.S. schools, but loans and scholarships are sparse. Unless you're Canadian, snagging money to pay for the program isn't easy. While the school offers an interest-free tuition and laptop loan program with ScotiaBank, non-Canadians aren't eligible. Rotman MBAs can apply for some scholarships based on merit, or can pursue research or teaching assistantships in their second year to help cover their expenses. Aid packages range from $100 to $11,300.

That doesn't mean that MBA Admissions Director Cheryl Millington doesn't have a sales pitch. For one thing, students at Rotman benefit from an "innovative curriculum and teaching methods," she says. And "the Rotman degree is warranted for life. Graduates can always come back to learn more." Students have the opportunity to be mentored by local business executives and to hear from business leaders such as Peter F. Drucker; George Stalk, senior vice president of The Boston Consulting Group; Judy Elder, general manager of the consumer products division of Microsoft Canada; and Lorna Borenstein, general manager of eBay.

Applicants will probably find it more difficult to be accepted by the school in coming years. Millington says that Rotman has benefited from its appearance in various rankings, noting an increase in applications since the school's first *BusinessWeek* ranking in 2000. In 2002, 32 percent of applicants made the cut. The school is beginning to market heavily in Latin America, and held receptions in cities throughout South America in October 2002. No matter where you're from, apply early, Millington warns: "We pretty much stop making offers in March."

Anyone hoping for something more than an MBA is in luck with Rotman. The school benefits from its neighboring schools in the University of Toronto system, so MBAs can complete their MBA degree while working toward advanced degrees in law or nursing, or even a Master of Arts in Russian and East European Studies.

ROTMAN MBAs SOUND OFF

Earning my MBA was something that I had aspired to achieve for quite some time and the process of doing so turned out to be everything that I had hoped (and envisioned) it to be. It was a great experience, from both an educational and a social/personal perspective.

I am very glad I chose to do my MBA at Rotman. It greatly surpassed my all my expectations.

I have a great deal of respect for the University of Toronto's Rotman School of Management.

I know for certain that the school has played an instrumental role in helping me achieve not just my career goals, but also my goals for learning within the program. The top-notch students that I met at the school (both in my year and the years ahead and behind me) were the icing on the cake.

The Rotman School of Management is an absolutely fantastic program that has yet to receive the recognition it deserves. It is a diamond in the rough waiting to be discovered on a global level!! I really enjoyed my experience there!

Rotman is the best finance school in Canada, and is still strong in areas such as strategy and consulting. Nonetheless, the program was weakened by the overloading of material at times. The caliber of students at this school is high, and this also enhanced the learning experience.

THE UNIVERSITY OF WESTERN ONTARIO

6.
THE UNIVERSITY OF WESTERN ONTARIO

Richard Ivey School of Business
1151 Richmond Street North
London, Ontario N6A 3K7
Canada
E-mail address: mba@ivey.ca
Web site: www.ivey.uwo.ca

Enrollment: 595	Total tuition: $35,840
Women: 25%	Average GMAT score: 661
International: 40%	Corporate ranking: 8
Average age: 29	Graduate ranking: 7
Applicants accepted: 34%	Intellectual capital rank: 4

If you want the kind of MBA that builds on the case study method employed at business schools such as Harvard, but don't want to pay Harvard prices, go to London, Ontario, two hours from both Detroit and Toronto. That's where you'll find the Richard Ivey School of Business, part of The University of Western Ontario. Once again in 2002, the school, known for its knack at teaching general management, entrepreneurship, and international business, has the ability to tag itself as elite, after *BusinessWeek*'s second-ever ranking of B-schools outside of the U.S. placed the Ivey School at number 6.

The case study method of teaching rules at Ivey. MBAs read and analyze approximately 600 business cases during the two-year program. And 70 percent of the classes use case studies to teach, spending the rest of the time on lectures, simulations, and group projects. The school claims it is also the second-largest writer of cases in the world, after Harvard, and boasts a world-class faculty to teach them. (Ivey has published more than 2000 cases, producing about 150 new ones per year, and also translates its cases into Spanish, French, German, and Italian.)

Many consider Ivey to be Canada's best B-school, and it now attracts 319 new MBAs to its peaceful campus every fall. In January 2002, the school's dean, Larry G. Tapp, ended a five-year campaign to boost the school's endowment, and now has $18 million resting in the 81-year-old B-school's dockets. The school has continued to make a big effort to attract non-Canadians, moving from 10 percent in the mid-1990s to 40 percent in 2002. Students have an average of 5.5 years of work experience. A small percent of the MBAs are admitted without undergraduate degrees, an allowance the school makes because such students have about 13 years of work experience. Overall, the classroom is increasingly diverse, adding substance to class discussions.

With so many MBAs from abroad, the class of 2003 began a series of preprogram trips called Ivey Adventures to showcase the best of

Canada's national parks and attractions. Before long, the program grew to include a trek to the Great Wall of China. "It lets people have a more intimate connection with other incoming students," says class of 2003 member Spencer Low. About 15 percent of incoming students participated. The school also has a four-day orientation program complete with sports, parties, and a barbeque on Port Stanley beach. After orientation, and a few class sessions, "we're a tight group," Low says.

Classes begin at the start of September, and first-years are split into 80-person sections as they plow through the school's core curriculum. They complete such basics as Marketing and Operations, The Global Environment of Business, Business Statistics, and Management Information Systems. The mandatory classes run daily from 8:00 A.M. to 1:00 P.M. "It's a very time-intensive program in the first year," says Low. In fact, that's been such a common complaint that the school has formed a faculty group to reexamine Ivey's curriculum with the goal of making it more balanced.

In the second year, students have just one requirement, the The Ivey Client Field Project (ICFP). In small teams, the MBAs work on a strategy or operations issue for a company (Charles Schwab Canada and Meridian Technologies are former clients). Since 2001, students have been able to substitute the ICFP for a New Venture Project, allowing them to develop their own entrepreneurial idea. Otherwise, students create their own schedules based on a selection of elective courses. New electives in 2002 include Managing High-Growth Companies, Business of Biotechnology, Advanced Strategy, and others. MBAs also have the option to bid to join 70-person streams such as general management, leadership, and entrepreneurship—the school's most popular.

Some students choose to take courses outside of the business school, such as languages or working toward a dual law degree. Others opt to spend a term at one of 24 partner schools abroad. Learning a second language is encouraged, but not required unless a student participates in Ivey's Global Leadership Program. That program, which began in 2001, awards certificates in global leadership to students who successfully complete three required courses and have experience working or living abroad in at least two countries.

Like other B-schools, Ivey is attempting to forge paths and relationships in Asia, where the demand is rising for MBA skills. Ivey has a dedicated campus in Hong Kong and offers an executive MBA program. Every May, six Ivey MBA students are selected to teach a monthlong business class to students at the School of Economics and Management at Tsinghua University in Beijing. Forty-four other students travel to Eastern Europe as part of the 11-year-old LEADER (Students Leading Education and Development in Eastern Europe) program. LEADER participants teach three-week classes at selected host institutions in countries such as Russia, Ukraine, Belarus, Moldova, and, more recently, Cuba.

On the home front, Ivey's MBAs spend most of their time in the school's handsome remodeled sandstone building, set on the University of Western Ontario's 102-year-old campus. Between classes, you'll find MBAs in The Enterprise Lounge checking out the latest news, in the Ivey Atrium, or sipping on Starbucks beverages in the school's Commerce Café. In 2001–2002, a speakers series attracted managers such as Hendrick von Kuenheim, president and CEO of BMW Canada; Roger Boisjoily, project manager for the space shuttle *Challenger;* and Arkadi Kuhlmann, president and CEO of ING Direct U.S.A. No matter where they are on campus, MBAs can sneak in a few e-mails on their laptops via a wireless network.

London, Ontario is a pleasant, if quiet, university town, and most students walk or bike to campus from reasonably priced apartments or houses along Richmond Street. "The London community is fairly easy to slip into," says graduate Sarah Fogler. She adds that finding day care is easy in London, and that many MBAs enjoy the fact that their kids can choose to study in French or in English when they begin elementary school. Ivey's Section V, for families and partners, offers events for MBA kids and a rotating babysitting system so that parents can enjoy an evening away from school and parenting. When Fogler was raising a newborn her second year, and had all of the team meetings at home, "people would be holding my baby with one hand and spreading out a finance sheet with another," she says. "It's doable."

One weakness shared by most Canadian B-schools is trouble in attracting top-name recruiters to campus. At Ivey, 213 recruiters came to campus to consider hiring second-year MBAs in 2002. The school also shuttles its MBAs to meet recruiters or attend job fairs in Vancouver, New York, Florida, and Silicon Valley. But remember that second-round interviews are often in Toronto, so if you attend Ivey, expect to have a cramped second semester, with a couple of two-hour sprints into the city for an interview and a race back to campus to make the next class.

By graduation, 55 percent of the class had found full-time jobs, the school says—not the best result. Graduates who found jobs reported median starting pay packages of $75,900 for 2002.

If you're used to shopping with U.S. dollars, you'll find that the exchange rate allows you a first-rate education for a lot less than most elite U.S. schools. Though tuition is on the rise, it hit just $35,840 for the full two years of study in 2002. And you'll walk away from campus with a degree that teaches you "to analyze business situations, drill in on specific problems, develop a range of options, and then look at implementation of a solution," says director of MBA Program Services and Admissions Joanne Shoveller.

The admissions office has changed how it evaluates candidates during the 2001–2002 school year, and therefore becoming part of the full-time MBA community was more difficult than usual, with 34 percent of applicants making the cut in 2002. Under new direction from Shoveller, the office now only interviews prescreened candidates—"It's a good sign if you're called for an interview," she says—and makes a point of interviewing all international applicants to ensure they can communicate well in English. While less than half of the admitted applicants completed an interview in 2002, Shoveller says that figure will increase. "We're measuring students' suitability for teamwork, leadership, and communication."

In 2003, the school will continue going after students from the United States—or those with experience working in the United States—and from western Europe. Since most case readings focus on international companies headquartered in those regions, class discussions improve with more input from students who recognize the companies, Shoveller says.

Ivey is one of the few B-schools to offer a one-year program, MBA2 Direct, to experienced graduates of its undergraduate Honors Business Administration Program. Bearing in mind how much reading there is in this program, the shortened version will be a blessing for some. But for all the others, this is a program that will prepare you to hit the ground running once you're a manager.

IVEY MBAs SOUND OFF

The MBA Program at Ivey changed my life. I increased my analytical skills and ability to solve complex problems tremendously. More importantly, Ivey provided me with an environment where I increased my self-confidence and my comfort with taking the initiative for activities. I have advanced my leadership skills and achieved great success in the extracurricular initiatives I took on. Going to Ivey was the best thing that I ever did with my life and I would and do urge all my friends to consider going there too.

I feel that the school is actively trying to improve the program for students, faculty, and companies/recruiters. While these efforts may be misdirected at times, the effort is there and I believe that it will continue to improve and offer a better experience to future MBA classes.

Despite my doubts, Ivey has been able to provide me with the additional tools needed to sucessfully start my career in the field that I wanted. In addition, having a business background, I was looking for a school that would allow me to apply my knowledge rather than simply redoing the same thing over. Ivey was great in that regard and the courses I took outside my functional specialty (finance) made me take a fresh look at business issues.

Ivey was a great experience, and despite the tough economic environment, and rising tuition fees, I feel that the experience was unbelievable. I also feel Ivey is positioned well to be a leading B-school in the future. The current dean has positioned the school as world class, making it by far the best program in Canada, and on a par with other world class schools.

In general I was pleased with Ivey and the overall MBA experience. The school seems intent on listening to student feedback and acting on it, hopefully further improving on the experience. I was fortunate to receive what I wanted from the program, and believe that many of my classmates would say the same.

Overall, Richard Ivey is an all-around B-school and a really good value for the money you spend. The campus building has gone through an expansion this year and will bring added space for new programs.

7.
ROTTERDAM
SCHOOL OF
MANAGEMENT

ROTTERDAM SCHOOL OF MANAGEMENT

Erasmus Graduate School of Business
Burgemeester Oudlaan 50
Rotterdam 3062 PA
The Netherlands
Email address: rsm@rsm.nl
Web site address: www.rsm.nl

Enrollment: 350
Women: 20%
International: 96%
Average age: 29
Applicants accepted: 39%

Total tuition: $31,500
Average GMAT score: 630
Corporate ranking: 6
Graduate ranking: 9
Intellectual capital rank: 9

Rotterdam School of Management, part of Erasmus University, only began offering an MBA program in English 1985, but has already made its way onto many prospective MBAs' and recruiters' top choice lists. This year, the B-school's full-time MBA program took the number 7 rank among non-U.S. schools in *BusinessWeek*'s biennial ranking, down one spot from number 6 in 2000.

The young school has altered its program dramatically in the past year. In October 2002, RSM trimmed the length of its MBA program to 15 months from 18 months, because students and graduates felt that some parts of the old program were repetitive. Students now begin each fall, finish classes the following December, and graduate in March. In September 2002, the school enrolled its largest class of full-time MBAs yet, with 173 students, a 20 percent increase over the prior year. The class of 2003 hails from 47 countries, with 38 percent of students from Western Europe, 26 percent from Asia, and another 24 percent from North and South America. "The world is our market," says Connie Tai, director of admissions. These MBAs average 5.3 years of work experience and come from a mix of industries. And that's the right kind of diversity in the eyes of Canadian-born Kai Peters, the school's dean since March 2000.

RSM also added a number of new programs recently. In 2002, along with four partner B-schools in Asia and the Americas, RSM began the global Executive OneMBA Program, which enrolls execs from four continents. In the fall of 2001, the school launched two new programs: a 12-month, full-time Master of Financial Management program, for those who want an even firmer grasp of finance, and an 18-month, part-time Master of Human Resources program. RSM also has a part-time executive MBA course, which enrolls about 100 students every year. Showing the school's commitment to technology, RSM also offers a full-time MBA/MBI program in general management and information technology. The MBA/MBI students spend a lot of time with RSM's full-time MBAs, but they take an additional four courses and complete a shorter internship focused on IT.

The full-time MBA is the school's hallmark program, dating back to 1985. In the first semester of the program, MBAs focus on the basics: managerial accounting, organizational behavior, management information systems, and management science. The second semester homes in on the functional areas, such as human resources management, financial management, and marketing management. Throughout, the school holds various mandatory workshops on everything from business communications to self-assessment, writing a CV, interviewing, project management, and consulting. No one will say that the program is easy, but the curriculum "is not so intensive that students spend all their time working," says class of 2003 president David Baumslag.

Rotterdam MBAs are required to snag real-world experience during the 12-week break between their first and second years. All are required to work on a project within a company, and, at the end of the summer, students have to present a structured report to RSM for grading. Most MBAs also present the report to company mentors. During the second year, Rotterdam MBAs pick 10 electives from a menu of 70 courses. New electives in 2002 included Mobilizing People, Asian Business Enterprise, and Global Business Law. This is the time, the school says, for the MBAs to develop expertise in such subject clusters as finance, information systems, marketing, or a specific grouping of electives that follow their career goals. (The school offers the same electives to its executive MBAs, so full-timers have a chance to interact with more experienced classmates.)

Between classes, MBAs participate in business clubs, and some find time to play sports once a week. The city of Rotterdam offers plenty of distractions, including an International Film Festival every winter. Rotterdam is also a gateway to most European cities. For MBAs living in continental Europe for the first time, weekends are the time to pack a duffel bag and do some light traveling. Small clusters of MBAs can be found traveling together in Paris, sailing in the Caribbean, or exploring Berlin. Rotterdam participates in The European MBA games every year at HEC School of Management, Paris, as well as a sailing regatta in England. Around the same time, MBAs don their best for the RSM gala. Students cook and drink lots together, too. "One of my favorite activities in the past year was the Russian vodka party, where a group of students got together to eat Russian food, sing Russian songs, and of course consume copious quantities of vodka," says David Baumslag.

When it comes to living options, Rotterdam has many, and the city isn't as expensive as others in Europe, awarding cash-strapped MBAs some good housing options. The school has a housing office that can link MBAs to about 240 accommodations around Rotterdam. Of the non-Dutch MBAs (96 percent of the class) using the office, all are placed, the school says. Most are single-occupancy rooms with a shared bathroom, but some also have private kitchens for anywhere from €400 to €600 per month. Students with partners or families can rent fully furnished apartments from €800 to €1100 per month, including utilities. But one thing is a must, no matter where you live; Holland's main mode of transportation is a bicycle. Bring a sturdy lock, as bike theft is a common, albeit comic, occurrence.

Most graduates felt that their time and money were well spent at RSM. But in 2002, they did earn lower salaries than graduates from top B-schools in the United States, reporting median starting base salaries of $64,000, with a median signing bonus of $15,000. As at other European B-schools, just 64 percent of Rotterdam graduates had jobs at graduation. Most MBAs landed jobs in consulting, marketing, and finance, and 72 percent took jobs in Western Europe. "Most of our students are looking for career opportunities in Western Europe," says

Hugh Lailey, director of the RSM Career Management Center. The office contacts incoming students before they reach campus to introduce them to the B-school's online tools. There's a full day of orientation devoted to the job search, and every Friday is set aside (no classes) for CMC programs. That's when companies typically come to campus, and when Lailey's staff walks MBAs through the job search, interview skills, and the art of negotiation. RSM is also a member of the MBA Career Forum @ Europe, an online database of students from 11 European B-schools that companies can tap into after paying a subscription fee.

Getting accepted to RSM isn't as difficult as at other B-schools. The school gave the thumbs-up to 39 percent of applicants in 2002. Still, the best time to apply is early, since the admissions office fills the class as applications arrive, and when the class is full, it's full. Rotterdam requires its admitted students to complete an interview. "Rotterdam has a roll-up-your-sleeves, get-to-work attitude," says Tai, and the interview helps the school assess whether or not an applicant will fit in. The more fun an applicant is, the better his or her chances of being seen as the right fit for Rotterdam: "This is a place that appreciates creativity, energy and innovation," Tai says.

Paying for RSM's MBA program is aided by the fact that RSM has an extensive list of loan programs and scholarships for its students. The programs are listed by country on its financial aid Web site. It helps to be from Argentina, Turkey, Germany, The Netherlands, or Taiwan, where RSM has set up full scholarships (€32,500) for deserving MBAs. The Netherlands government also supports about three RSM students from developing countries every year with scholarships. Students from The Netherlands are also eligible for loans from ABN-Amro Bank (though these students need someone to cosign their loan). International students need to provide collateral to support their loan applications. And RSM is "very active

in exploring and developing financial aid possibilities for our students," says Tai.

RSM grads say that the school's alumni network is one of its strongest assets. "We have a small but close alumni circle," says graduate Yue Wang, now working in Beijing as a sales director for a major carpet manufacturer. "Everyone is ready to help each other. I can always get an immediate and helpful response to my questions from the alumni." Having such a safety net is an added bonus when the economy isn't promising as many jobs to MBAs.

ROTTERDAM MBAs SOUND OFF

The student body is so diverse that social life is astounding for those who like to have a lifetime partying and European trip experience.

RSM has a great potential for becoming one of the leading MBA programs in Europe. However, the school administration definitely has to start listening to the students and become more active in helping them in their career development.

It was an excellent experience that in many respects exceeded my expectations. The RSM school has great merit in that it is constantly able to select the right mix of people, as the number of students is small, which stimulates learning from others rather than competition. The aspect that could be improved is the amount of professors that are working full-time for the school. At present the percent of visiting professors is quite high.

RSM is a good school and I am quite satisfied with my experience here. However, the school needs to work a lot on the Career Management Center (CMC). In the past three years we have had as many CMC heads and it creates problems in building relationships with companies. We definitely need a bigger and more aggressive career office. Imagine running a school of 300 students with two people at CMC.

The only downside at the RSM is the Program Office. The communication with the students is often abrasive. Nevertheless, RSM is special because the student body has a nice mix and will provide you with a lot of learning. Their MBI program is unique and I wouldn't have missed that in a million times.

8.
IESE

IESE

The University of Navarra
21 Avenida Pearson
08034 Barcelona
Spain
E-mail address: mbainfo@iese.edu
Web site address: www.iese.edu

Enrollment: 650 (420 full-time)
Women: 24%
International: 62%
Average age: 27
Applicants accepted: 23%

Total tuition: $45,000
Average GMAT score: 670
Corporate ranking: 9
Graduate ranking: 6
Intellectual capital rank: 8

It's the afternoon, and a TV set mounted above the bar is tuned to CNBC—the U.S. markets are open. Students at IESE Business School, in Spain's second-largest city, Barcelona, are nearly done with their day. Between courses, the MBAs at IESE often stop at a bar for Spanish coffee or a beer. The students come from 55 countries—many are Europeans; others are from the Americas and Asia. Peer outside, and these students also have views of the Mediterranean and nearby mountains. Students strolling through the school's neighborhood, Pedralbes, pass examples of Antonio Gaudi's renowned architecture.

IESE is a small campus, but it's certainly not what one would call a discouraging place to study. The school first opened its doors with help from Harvard Business School in 1964 and has links to Opus Dei, a Catholic organization of laymen and priests who strive for a Christian way of life. That's one reason the school has emphasized ethics in its curriculum since the days before the collapse of Enron made teaching ethics trendy. The school practices what it teaches, too. It has set up 12 B-schools on four continents, including some of Latin America's top schools. IESE also began the International Faculty Development Program, which has trained 300 professors from countries in the former Soviet bloc in business case writing and research techniques, and by doing so promotes the development of B-schools in central and eastern Europe.

IESE is ideal for those looking to hone their business know-how and practice Spanish at the same time—the language can't be avoided in the two years you'll spend in this program. Nonnative first-year MBAs take a one-month intensive Spanish course before the program begins in October, and Spanish classes during their first year. (In 2002, the school contracted with Spain's Chamber of Commerce to offer a new exam to graduating students that tests their business Spanish and awards certificates to those who have it down pat.) Though most classes are taught in English, students can elect to take their 21 core classes in an 80-person section that uses both English and Spanish (beginning in 2002, this section uses a bit more English than Spanish). The rest are placed in one of two groups using English. That creates a certain dynamic on campus among the MBAs. "The students were unfortunately a bit divided into two camps: the Spanish and the internationals," says 2002 grad Jan Ravenstijn. "Only toward the end did the integration start to flow, as the internationals started to learn more and more Spanish."

Inside these sections, students are broken down again into smaller assigned groups. No matter the language, IESE MBAs can't avoid reading cases: 75 percent of coursework is taught using the case method. "Before, I focused too much on the details of business," says 2002 graduate Vivian Chen. "After reading so many cases, I can look at the big picture. It helps you to make decisions when you don't have all the information."

The second year includes 12 elective classes chosen from a catalog of 80. (Some elective classes are taught only in Spanish.) IESE says that entrepreneurship is one of its fortes; it began its entrepreneurship classes in 1974. In 2000, the school was given approval to form its own Entrepreneurship Foundation, which awards money to student and alumni groups with business plans that appear solid. The second year is very different from the first, graduates say. In the first year, MBAs spend about six hours every night preparing cases for the next day's courses. "In the second year, you can mix some hard courses with easy courses," says Chen. No matter the difficulty, she insists that IESE students are not competitive: "People help each other."

After classes, IESE MBAs participate in any number of student-run clubs devoted to such subjects as media and communications, finance, and women in business. MBAs began the school's first women in business club in 2000.

Academics aside, IESE is a fun place to study. Living in Barcelona is cheaper than other European cities, for instance, so a night out on

the town won't set you back the way London could. Besides common gatherings at a bar of the week, or at a classmate's apartment or house for a group dinner, the school hosts a Thanksgiving Gala Dinner for the entire school in November. They serve turkey and put on a host of shows and student skits. During a long weekend in February, close to 100 students hit the slopes in the Pyrenees. Students who are living in Europe for the first time will enjoy the fact that Barcelona is a perfect launching point for long weekends away in neighboring European countries. In April, students travel to France to compete in the annual sports tournament against European rivals London Business School, INSEAD, IMD, Rotterdam, and others. Sports clubs on campus include soccer, volleyball, basketball, and rugby. And some of the simple things about IESE make the day-to-day stress of class and project work easier to stomach, such as eating a packed lunch on the school steps in the sunshine, next to the pond.

MBAs spend around $450 a month on rent, and most students settle in the neighborhoods of Sarria and Sant Gervasi. Others perch in the trendy and central Eixample neighborhood, where some of Barcelona's best examples of cutting-edge architecture can be found. Public transportation makes navigating Barcelona easy, but most MBAs come to campus via motorbike. (Bring your helmet, because Barcelona has the highest number of motorbikes per capita in Europe.)

IESE hosts the annual MBA Career Forum each October, bringing top European and North American recruiting firms to the B-school for two days of company briefings and interviews. In recent years, IESE has attempted to attract more recruiters from more varied industries, so, instead of hearing from consulting firms or investment banks, MBAs are getting more access to automotive, pharmaceutical, and smaller consulting firms. Career days on campus in November, February, and April also bring 20 to 25 companies from smaller sectors to network with students. Aside from on-campus events, IESE MBAs also participate in the MBA Career Forum-Europe, a virtual career fair, which links companies to students at IESE and other B-schools via the Net. Most of the school's career activities are online, so, instead of having to contact the career office and then a student, recruiters can have direct access to MBAs looking for internships and full-time jobs.

The school is focusing on the kinds of MBAs it produces for the job market, so the career development office has worked hand in hand with the admissions team in recent years to screen candidates. "We're trying to find the right profile for companies, and for performance as an MBA," says Director of Career Services Mireia Ruis.

These days, IESE is far more selective. Admissions Director Alberto Arribas says that in 2002 the school received 56 percent more applications than the prior year, and accepted just 23 percent. "We have eight candidates for each seat in the class," he says. And in 2003, he's optimistic that nine candidates will jockey for each place. What counts most? The GMAT, in which IESE students average scores of 670, and the interview carry the most weight in admissions these days. Not all applicants are interviewed, however. If the school likes the look of an applicant on paper, that person is invited to interview, and, ultimately, all admitted MBAs complete interviews. The interview is the time when the school judges applicants' ability "to have a positive influence on society through their job," says Arribas.

Some 40 percent of MBAs receive financial aid through the school, which charges about $45,000 for the full two years of study. Graduates in 2002 reported starting pay packages of $84,700. About 79 percent of grads had jobs by three months after commencement, and 215 companies came to campus to recruit the class of 2002, with companies like McKinsey & Company, Barclays Capital, Johnson & Johnson, and Citigroup snapping up grads.

The number 8–ranked school also has a new dean. IESE hired Jordi Canals, formerly associate dean at the school, to become the school's new dean after Carlos Cavalle, IESE's dean for 14 years, retired in July 2001. Canals' goal is to keep IESE visible as a top European B-school. Recently, the prime minister of Spain appointed Canals to a blue-ribbon commission that will advise the government on corporate responsibility (a hot topic after the scandals that upset the U.S. business community).

An MBA program is much more than its academics and politics, though. And if you're someone that hits the business books seriously, but requires time to relax, you can't do much better than Barcelona.

IESE MBAs SOUND OFF

I strongly recommend IESE. Most of the lessons are in English if you wish! You have the chance to open your mind and meet people from other cultures (60 percent international) and enjoy excellent weather. At the same time you can take advantage of the possibility of learning Spanish, which could be very useful in Latin America, Spain, or even the United States.

IESE needs to get rid of its Spanish-language section. It fosters isolationism and provincialism and impedes the school's international aspirations.

I am extremely happy with my choice of MBA at IESE. IESE is bilingual, and so I have not just gained the MBA learning experience, but also mastery of Spanish. This for me is what gives IESE an edge on top of its other good points as a great school.

To learn in this school is the best thing I ever did for my career. It has been a gradual "reset" of my way of viewing business. . . . Lots of matters new to me. Lots of interesting approaches. I'd describe it as "full learning, full enjoying."

IESE is a great school because of its great emphasis on teaching. I did not care to go to a great research school. At IESE, professors really care for both students and for the teaching profession. The relatively small class size (210), small campus and people-oriented faculty make IESE a very social and personal school. There is a lot of emphasis on ethics and on doing good for society.

Most of the students choose an international school to make a change in their careers (industry, sector, geography) and have a strong motivation to start international careers within the EU. This goal is too many times endangered by the current EU policy of protecting the internal job market, mainly because of the time-consuming processes required to obtain the permission to work in the EU. I believe that European business schools and companies in general should take a strong stand to overcome the after-MBA placement issues within the EU for managerial positions.

9.
HEC

HEC

1 rue de la Libération
Jouy-en-Josas, 78 351, France
E-mail address: admissionmba@hec.fr
Web site address: www.hec.edu

Enrollment: 222 full-time	Total tuition: $30,000
Women: 22%	Average GMAT score: 640
International: 70%	Corporate ranking: 10
Average age: 30	Graduate ranking: 5
Applicants accepted: 26%	Intellectual capital rank: 10

Travel 20 kilometers southwest of Paris to Jouy-en-Josas, and you can swap a city pace for the settled calm of the grounds around a 121-year-old business school, HEC School of Management, Paris. HEC's 250-acre wooded campus has a lake, expansive fields, a soccer and rugby stadium, tennis courts, and even a martial arts center. And these days, the school can say it has more than just a pretty campus. HEC is enjoying its new-found popularity as a leading business school, earning the number 9 rank among non-U.S. B-schools from *BusinessWeek* in 2002.

HEC has offered an MBA since 1969, but has quietly transformed its program in recent years from a commerce course for French students to a competitive global management MBA. When HEC's dean, Bernard Ramanantsoa, began leading the school in 1995, he says that HEC was a typical French school. "We were a teaching B-school, and we had to change to be research based." At that time, just 10 percent of the HEC faculty was publishing articles in top reference journals. Since then, Ramanantsoa has hired about 35 more research faculty members—he now has a total of 100—and began offering incentives, with the result that half of the faculty now publishes annually. HEC's students have changed, too. In 1995, 43 percent of the students were French. Seven years later, the school enrolls students from 40 countries, and just 25 percent are French. Even Ramanantsoa has changed his leadership style: "I went from a being a French ruler to a more American one," he says. "The French students still call me Mr. Ramanantsoa, but the Americans call me Bernard."

But HEC is anything but a U.S.-modeled B-school, and students and administrators are quick to highlight that distinction. "The business outlook for an HEC MBA participant is international, not how to do American business abroad," says Joshua Kobb, HEC's development and admissions director. Charles Daher, a December 2001 graduate from the United States, worked in Beirut before beginning the MBA program and didn't expect the school to be so globally sensitive. "I thought that the French professors and students would not be as open-minded as their international counterparts," he says. "But I was pleasantly surprised that they were the ones who were the most internationally exposed and most sensitive to such issues."

International management is the school's specialty, so it's not surprising that HEC suggests that MBAs graduate with a working knowledge of French and fluency in English. (English is required to begin the program.) Anyone who doesn't speak French (about 10 percent of the class) can pay extra to participate in a three-week French course before core classes begin. Once in the program, the students can enroll in French, Italian, Spanish, or German lessons. HEC is one of the few B-schools that allows its students to complete a double MBA degree. Students who complete half of their courses at a partner school can receive MBA degrees from both HEC and one of HEC's four partner schools in the Americas or the Chinese University of Hong Kong. The school also offers a double degree with Tufts University's Fletcher School of Law and Diplomacy, awarding an MBA from HEC and a Master of Arts in Law and Diplomacy from Fletcher.

Students may begin classes in September or in January, though most begin in September. During the first two terms, called the Core International Management Program (CIMP), students work in diverse teams assigned by the school. HEC MBAs can opt to complete the first eight months of the program in a bilingual section, taking core courses in a mix of French and English, or in the English section. After the CIMP program, students can opt to take courses in French or in English. MBAs usually work in small groups. "Everyone is pulling for the success of everyone else," says 2001 graduate Yves Bescondv. "There's a lot of communication and networking regarding classwork and career opportunities." From mid-May to July, the MBAs complete what the school calls the Personalized Program. In this section, students are able to choose as many as six electives from a menu of 80. At least three electives must be

advanced management courses, and one must be from the area of leadership and managerial efficiency.

The school breaks for a six-week vacation on July 14, when France celebrates Bastille Day. Afterwards, each MBA pursues one of four study tracks. The first option is to specialize in entrepreneurship, international finance, management consulting, or marketing. HEC doesn't offer many specialties, and the dean doesn't plan on adding more just for the sake of doing so. "When we say it's a specialty, it's a specialty," he says. "You have to be taught by people who are specialists. We don't want to cheat the students." The second option is to complete a faculty-supervised consulting project for a company. In this case, students work on an issue at the company, and benefit from having both a B-school faculty mentor and a mentor at the company. The third option—one that one-third of the class chooses—is for MBAs to pack their bags and go to study at one of HEC's 42 exchange partner schools. Otherwise, MBAs can pursue individual studies and enroll in more electives.

Students aren't at a loss when it comes to extracurricular activities. HEC's on-campus sports centers offer plenty of distractions, as does the nine-hole golf course near-by. With such grounds, HEC MBAs have hosted the European MBA games for the past 13 years. Each May, the games attract teams of MBAs from eight European B-schools for three days of tournaments, schmoozing, and parties. There are plenty of wine courses on campus, theme nights sponsored by student groups, boat trips along the Seine, ski trips to the Alps, and a farewell party held at a chateau each spring. "It was the moment when I realized how great a time we had in our MBA, and how much we'd all miss each other," says Charles Daher.

With just under 200 MBAs in the program, the classes tend to be tightly knit. Helping the class spirit along is the fact that most HEC MBAs live on campus in an HEC building called Expansiel, which has single and double bedrooms, some meeting rooms, a big-screen TV, a pool table, a bar, and plenty of parking outside. This living option costs MBAs between €460 and €640. Students bringing families to campus tend to live elsewhere.

The nine people working in the career office help the MBAs prepare for their full-time job searches. (Only about 30 MBAs complete internships during the school's short summer break.) "We're developing new services to help the students with an individual job search, because they can't rely so much on campus recruiting," says Helen Farrow, director of HEC's Career Development Office. That's partly because the MBAs have to share the career office with the entire HEC community—about 2,800 people. Farrow's office coaches MBAs on their CVs, interview skills, and negotiation savvy. Most companies present their jobs to students in the B-school's amphitheaters on weekday nights or on Friday mornings over breakfast. Companies with deeper pockets attract MBAs to presentations in museums in Paris or at the Ritz. HEC is also part of The MBA Career Forum @ Europe, an online database of students from 11 European B-schools that recruiters can tap into from their desks.

Nearly half of the graduates find full-time jobs in Western Europe. But Farrow says that recently the school has targeted more North and South American companies, as well as companies in Asia. And while other schools struggled to place their MBAs by graduation, 71 percent of HEC's grads had an average of 206 job offers by the time they graduated. Many HEC graduates snagged jobs in consulting, banking and finance, and marketing.

Anyone hoping to attend HEC should apply early. The school accepted just 26 percent of its applicants in 2002. (Number 1–ranked INSEAD accepted 27 percent of applicants in 2002, although INSEAD receives far more applications than HEC.) No one is admitted without an in-person interview, and this is no regular interview. Each interview is conducted by about three people at once, including an HEC alumnus, a human resources professional from a company with a connection to HEC, and an admissions office representative. "It's a better way to get at the applicant's fit with the program," says Director Kobb. "And the HR rep gives us a professional view on post-MBA recruiting—a good corporate perspective on the candidate's potential for senior management."

Tuition at HEC costs €30,000 for the 16-month program. The school doesn't offer many scholarships, but recently began offering the HEC CCF-HSBC loan to its students regardless of nationality. This loan only covers tuition. In the next four years, HEC's campus will grow by 8 percent to include a new $60 million building for MBAs and for students in executive education programs. Pair that with the HEC's recent ascent in the rankings, and things stand to get much prettier for this B-school.

HEC MBAs SOUND OFF

HEC offers one of the biggest campuses in Europe. The campus infrastructure, with its accommodation on campus and extensive sports facilities, grants the best premise for multicultural fusion and learning outside of the class.

The strongest points of HEC in my opinion are: diversity—the fact that it is in Europe; balanced program (business and other types of knowledge—art, gastronomy, European culture); and teamwork—allows the development of presentation skills.

One aspect worth mentioning: the teamwork and intercultural understanding stressed and imposed all through the program brings about not only useful tips and attitudes in our future professional career in an international organization but also an evolution on a personal level and an open mind toward the diversity of our world.

I would like to highlight a major advantage that the HEC MBA has. The program is truly international and dynamic. Thus "people skills" obtained at this program are superior. HEC MBA graduates have outstanding ability to fit in any culture and deal with any group no matter what cultural and educational background group members have. Moreover, HEC enhances language skills for all participants. On average every candidate graduates with communication ability in at least three languages. That, in turn, adds to candidates' ability to better understand, interact and manage people at and outside of work. In essence, HEC provides the ground for candidates to be culturally outstanding.

Personally, I was looking for an international experience that not only helped me boost my career but also an experience that enriched me in a personal way. Europe constitutes an important cultural hub, a place that thanks to its amazing cultural and historic diversity provides constant examples and illustrations of international management theory. As a Mexican student I was greatly exposed to the American way of life and thus to the American education; therefore a European experience sounded like the perfect complement to my objectives. HEC offers a great variety of nationalities, a richness of personalities and experiences, a well-known name, a top faculty, and great networking opportunities.

10.
YORK UNIVERSITY

YORK UNIVERSITY

Schulich School of Business
4700 Keele Street
Toronto, Ontario M3J 1P3
Canada
E-mail address: admissions@schulich.yorku.ca (domestic)
intladmissions@schulich.yorku.ca (international admissions)
Web site address: www.schulich.yorku.ca

Enrollment: 1366 (649 full-time)   Total tuition: $27,000
Women: 35%   Average GMAT score: 650
International: 59%   Corporate ranking: 4
Average age: 29   Graduate ranking: 10
Applicants accepted: 48%   Intellectual capital rank: 7

One of the best values to be had among *BusinessWeek*'s top-ranking MBA programs is at Canada's Schulich School of Business at York University, where a two-year degree costs just $27,000 for non-Canadian students. The school appeared in *BusinessWeek*'s rankings for the first time in 2002, placing number 10 among non-U.S. B-schools. These MBAs leave school with an MBA degree that's appreciating in value, and an average of just $8,000 in debt.

In September 2003, the school will open the doors of its brand-new $63 million Schulich School of Business and Executive Learning Centre just 35 minutes from downtown Toronto. The center will have a 300-seat auditorium, a 20,000-square-foot library (complete with a fireplace to keep things toasty on cold Canadian winter days), 14 lecture halls, plenty of seminar rooms, Internet cafés, and an "information wall" in the foyer with TVs set to news programs. The goal, administrators say, is to create a sense of community while also improving services for out-of-town corporate recruiters visiting Schulich. (Recruiters will benefit from the Executive Learning Centre, which is being built in an adjoining tower with 60 hotel-style rooms, among other things.)

Schulich offers a number of MBA programs, and it's easy for students to get lost in the shuffle. Within the full-time program, one section of students focuses on international business. Another 569 people study at the school part-time, and another 42 students are enrolled in the Joint Kellogg-Schulich Executive MBA Program, which Schulich runs in partnership with the Kellogg School of Management in Chicago. No matter what program a student opts to take, "there's one MBA program at Schulich," says David Dimick, associate dean-academic. "Most students take the program all full-time, or all part-time, but if they want to change from one program to the other, it's relatively easy to do."

The school calls itself "Canada's First International MBA," and with 59 percent of its students from countries outside of Canada, it is more global than its neighbors, Toronto's Rotman School of Business and Queen's University School of Business. But MBA hopefuls excited by that statistic should closely examine it. In 2002, 39 percent of the international students came from Asia, and just 8 percent traveled from Eastern and Western Europe for the Schulich MBA. In the future, the class profile should improve as Schulich appears in more rankings, attracting a more diverse group of MBA candidates from around the globe.

Full-time MBAs may begin the 16-month program in September or January. The program begins with a weeklong orientation known as MBA Launch Week. MBA Launch Week includes the usual MBA appetizers, such as welcome speeches from the dean, Dezso Horvath; the president of the Graduate Business Council; and school administrators. The school also organizes a day trip to an outdoors camp, where the MBAs, in groups of 100, practice their team-building skills and complete a fun seminar on delivering presentations on the fly. After orientation, a group of about 130 MBAs heads up north for a retreat weekend. Classes begin the following week, with MBAs beginning the first of 13 core courses. The core courses are meant to give MBAs a grounding in general management before they begin talking elective courses to support a professional specialization.

The first year is a challenging year of core courses—students say that the finance and accounting courses are most demanding. In the second year, Schulich MBAs must complete two required courses. The first is a two-semester Strategy Field Study, in which the MBAs get real-world experience while evaluating a nonprofit or for-profit company. The MBAs offer ideas for improvement to company managers when the project ends. Schulich MBAs complete such projects for about 75 companies each year. The second requirement is a Strategic Management course. Aside from the two required courses, MBAs can enroll in about 9 elective courses, choosing from a list of about 100 classes.

This is the time when Schulich MBAs choose a specialization from a list of 19 options. The school encourages MBAs to specialize in more than one area, and, to do so, an MBA often needs to complete four electives in the subject area. Most MBAs enroll in popular electives such as Finance, Marketing, Strategy, and International Business, but some of the niche programs include arts and media administration, real property development, financial engineering, public management, business and the environment, financial services, nonprofit management and leadership, and entrepreneurial studies. Students who begin the program after September 2003 will also be able to consider a health care and biotechnology concentration.

Classes, especially in the second year, are spaced out to accommodate part-time students' busy schedules, so a full-time MBA could have an 8 A.M. class, and then no classes until an evening lecture that ends at 10 P.M., making a full-time MBA's schedule less compact than it would be at other B-schools. No matter the work schedule, full-time MBAs are often working on five to six group projects at once, says class of 2003 MBA Sean Siddik, also president of the Schulich Graduate Business Council. "Time management is going to become your new best friend," he says.

There's a lot going on at Schulich, and a beautiful building to come, but graduates responding to the *BusinessWeek* survey warn that organizational improvements are needed soon. Graduates say that the administration didn't respond to their concerns, and that the career office needs to cast a wider net to attract recruiters looking for more than finance- and consulting-bound graduates. Some of those complaints may be resolved, since the school has dedicated more cash to its Career Center, which will employ a staff of 12 by the autumn of 2003. The new hires come from specific industries and will focus on forging relationships between

Schulich and companies in health care and biotechnology, marketing, finance, and other industries. Overall, the extra employees will spend about 80 percent of their time helping the full-time MBAs. "We've turned into a more proactive office," says Joseph Palumbo, executive director of the Career Center. "We're absolutely focusing more on full-time MBAs."

Another common complaint among graduates is that the class wasn't filled with qualified, experienced students. Rosanne Martin graduated in 2002 and landed what she calls a "great job" as assistant treasurer at the Independent Electricity Market Operator in Toronto. But she was "disappointed" with some of the professors, as well as "the lack of business experience of fellow students." Until 2002, only non-Canadian MBAs were required to have at least two years of work experience, and even that requirement comes short of those of most top B-schools, where MBAs average four to five years of professional experience. MBA admissions director Charmaine Courtis says that beginning with the class that enters in January 2003, every MBA needs to have two years of work experience. "We are not pushing to require more than two years at this time," Courtis says.

Requiring Schulich MBAs to meet a certain threshold of experience should help the Career Center in its drive to change the school's reputation among recruiters. "Five years ago, we were known as a finance school, and for having less experienced students," explains Director Palumbo. Even today, some recruiters still expect to hire Schulich MBA graduates into entry-level jobs, and "in the United States, we're still not known." But Palumbo's office approaches recruiting in a much different way now. "Instead of simply greeting recruiters and handing them a schedule of interviews, we take recruiters out to lunch, pre-screen candidates before sending resumes to recruiters, and take feedback from the recruiters," he says. When the Schulich building opens up, his office will invest more time in helping students who are starting their own companies, too. For now, the Career Center is offering four workshops per week and trying to bring its operation up to a more competitive level with what other B-schools offer.

In 2002, 61 companies came to campus to interview students for internship positions. The majority of students intern in Canada companies, where the Career Center has strong corporate relationships. Non-Canadian students will find that snagging an internship is a patience-testing process in Canada, as non-Canadians need a visa to work in Canada. Students looking for full-time positions had more luck, as 246 companies came to campus to recruit. That said, Schulich graduates didn't earn as much money as their counterparts from U.S. B-schools. These grads reported median starting salaries of $45,000 to *BusinessWeek*. Ninety percent of the graduates found jobs in North America.

Finding a seat in Schulich's classrooms isn't nearly as difficult as it is at other top B-schools. In 2002, nearly 1800 applied to the school, and about half made the cut. The school's ideal students are "leaders, innovators, and entrepreneurs," says Courtis. "We are looking for excellent communicators. People who have already differentiated themselves from the group."

For all of the improvements to come, Schulich MBAs still have a good time. There are lots of social events throughout the program put on by the student association or various clubs on campus. Some of the highlights include the Culture Crawl each October, when cultural groups serve up ethnic food and showcase typical dances and ceremonies from their countries; and end-of-midterms and Halloween pub nights. Some evenings aim to raise money for the United Way or other organizations. Says Sean Siddick, "we spend so much time on campus, we stick together."

SCHULICH MBAs SOUND OFF

I am a happy customer because I learned what I wanted to learn during he program and I feel that I will benefit from my MBA in my future career. The MBA made it possible for me to change my career path from engineering to marketing easier and faster.

My two years at Schulich were the highlight of my life so far!!

I had a fantastic experience at school ... much better than I was expecting. Probably the biggest tangible benefit to doing an MBA at Schulich was that I learned what I needed to learn to land the exact job I wanted and at a third the price of a big-name US school.

Schulich should encourage more free input in assignments, i.e., case analysis, open assignment, more help from the career office, and should provide more links with leading companies around the world.

INDEX